THE ULTIMATE
Vegan
COOKBOOK

PAGE STREET
PUBLISHING CO.

First published in 2018 by
Page Street Publishing Co.
27 Congress Street, Suite 105
Salem, MA 01970
www.pagestreetpublishing.com

Distributed by Macmillan, sales in Canada by The Canadian Manda Group.

22   21   20   19   18   1   2   3   4   5

ISBN-13: 978-1-62414-641-1
ISBN-10: 1-62414-641-4

Library of Congress Control Number: 2018937220

Cover and book design by Kylie Alexander for Page Street Publishing Co.
Photography by Emily von Euw, Kathy Hester, Linda and Alex Meyer, Marie Reginato, Celine Steen and Amber St. Peter

Printed and bound in the United States

THE ULTIMATE
Vegan
COOKBOOK

The **Must-Have Resource** for Plant-Based Eaters

Emily von Euw, Kathy Hester, Linda and Alex Meyer,
Marie Reginato, Celine Steen, Amber St. Peter

PAGE STREET
PUBLISHING CO.

contents

INTRODUCTION 19

MAIN DISHES 25

BBQ Pulled Jackfruit Sandwich with Slaw and Caramelized Onions 26
"California Burrito" Tacos 27
San Pedro–Style Fishless Market Tray 28
Black Bean Citrus Slaw Tacos 29
Vegetable Pot Pie 30
Forbidden Rice Sushi Rolls 31
Stuffed Tomatoes with Pink Rice 32
Sweet Potato Tacos with Mint-Cilantro Salsa 33
Spring Vegetable Pasta 34
Foolproof Creamy Pesto and Roasted Veggies 34
Stuffed Butternut Squash 35
Pumpkin Curry with Coconut Brown Rice 36
Homemade Thai-Style Green Curry 37
Super Easy Sesame Cucumber Noodles 38
Indian Stuffed Potato Chaat 38
Spiralized Vegan Latkes with Red Cabbage and Apple 39
Mashed Potato–Crusted Butternut Squash, Brussels Sprouts and Tofu Pie 40
Vegan Butternut Squash Okra Gumbo with Brown Rice 41
Butternut Squash and Kale Lo Mein with Crispy Tofu 42
Potato Stuffing Balls with a Cranberry Center 43
Gluten-Free Vegan Teff Stuffing with Roasted Butternut Squash and Candied Cranberries 44
Tofu Katsu 45
Tofu Ricotta White Pizza 46
Rosemary Alfredo Pasta 47

Easy Stuffed Ravioli (Using Wonton Wrappers)	47
Roasted Sheet Pan Teriyaki	48
Full of Veggies Baked Ziti	48
Autumn Quinoa Bowls with Roasted Veggies	49
Texas BBQ Tempeh Enchiladas	50
Vegan Rarebit over Toast	51
Vietnamese Tofu Bun	51
Tofu Banh Mi with Lemongrass	52
Vegan Sloppy Joe	53
Pulled Carrot BBQ	53
Edamame Rice Burgers	54
Spinach and Sweet Potato Paninis	55
Vegan Croque Monsieur	56
Lemon and Three-Herb Risotto	56
Vegan Pesto and Portobello Flatbread Pizza	57
Veggie-Loaded Black Beans and Rice	58
Smoky Southern-Style Meatless Meatloaf	59
Bacon-Flavored Roasted Brussels Sprouts Stir-Fry	60
Sofritas Tofu Lettuce Wraps	60
Vegan Cheddar and Broccoli Stuffed Baked Potatoes	61
Sushi Bowl with Ginger Soy Dressing	62
Raw Super Sprouts Pad Thai with Spicy Peanut Sauce	63
Roasted Veggie Lentil Loaf	63
Vegan Black Bean and Mushroom Enchiladas	64
Vegan Mushroom Bourguignon	66
Spaghetti and Black Bean Meatballs	67
Oil-Free Zucchini and Carrot Fritters	68
Grilled Vegan Dirty Rice Stuffed Peppers	69
Easy Meatless Monday Taco Salad	70
Beer-Battered "Fish" Tacos with Mango Salsa	71
Baked Fresh Herb Vegan Mac 'n' Cheese	72
Penne Pasta Casserole	73
Creamy Fettuccini Alfredo	74
Chik'n and Dumplings	74
Baked Parmesan Tofu Steaks	76
Vegan Poke Bowls	76
Pumpkin Thyme-Ricotta Lasagna	77
Drop Biscuit Root Vegetable Pot Pie	78
Wild Mushroom and Ricotta Ravioli	79
Roasted Brussels Sprouts Velouté	80
Kimchi Mac and Sprouts	80

Spicy Kimchi Pizza 81

Noochy Fried Noodles 82

Crispy Corn and Bean Burritos 82

Tacos al Pastor 83

Gochujang BBQ Sauce Sandwiches 84

Sloppy Giuseppe 84

Umami Fusion Burritos 85

Indian-Spiced Chana Dal Shepherd Pie 86

Sambal Soy Curl Tacos 87

Beer-Braised Jackfruit Tacos 88

Sweet and Sour and Somewhat Spicy Tofu 88

Japanese-Inspired Sandwiches 89

Pickled Mango Curry Wraps 90

Mexican Baked Mac and Queso 90

Enchilada Roja 91

Shiitake Chickpea Crepes 92

Spanish Paprika Tofu Sandwiches 93

Savory Mushroom Galette 94

Japanese Tempeh and Sushi Rice Bowls 95

Japchae (Korean Vermicelli Stir-Fry) 96

Moroccan Pizza 96

Yogurt Drizzle for Moroccan Pizza 97

Galette Crust 97

Garlic and Herb Pizza Dough 98

Marinated Portobello Cashew Cheeseburgers with Herbs and Tomatoes 98

Jicama Onion Cakes with Cumin, Coriander, Dill and Lemon 99

Marinated Zucchini and Tomato Lasagna with Cashew Herb Cheese 100

Tacos with Tomato Corn Salsa and Spicy Nut Meat 100

Creamy Baked Butternut Squash, Broccoli and Chipotle Almond Sauce 101

Creamy Vegan Mac and Cheese with Other Good Stuff 102

Baked Yams with Sautéed Veg and Tofu 103

King Oyster Mushrooms Layered with Heirloom Tomato, Basil and Avocado 103

Beet Ravioli with Almond Thyme Pâté and Basil 104

Udon Noodle Bowl with Miso Ginger Sauce, Edamame and Green Onions 105

SLOW COOKER, INSTANT POT & AIR FRYER 106

Instant Pot Rainbow Panzanella Salad 107

Air-Fried Vegan Beignets 108

Vegan Slow Cooker Mole Mushroom Taco Filling 109

Vegan Instant Pot Teff Vegetable Soup 110

Slow Cooker Whole Wheat Spelt Potato Rolls   111
Instant Pot Vegan Black-Eyed Pea Jambalaya   112
Air-Fried Tofu Rancheros   112
Instant Pot Cranberry Sauce with a Touch of Apple Brandy   113
Vegan Instant Pot White Bean Soy Curl Chili   114
Vegan Pear and Cranberry Instant Pot Cake   115
Slow Cooker Shredded Veggies and Jackfruit BBQ   116
Air-Fried Tempeh Skewers   116
Air-Fried Vegetable Pakora with Tamarind Dipping Sauce   117
Slow Cooker Smoky Split Pea and Lentil Soup   117
Air Fryer Cheater Samosas Using Spring Roll Wrappers   118
Air-Fried Green Tomato Po' Boys   119

30 MINUTES OR LESS 120

Simple Tabbouleh   121
Mini Polenta Cakes with Mushroom Ragu   121
Spicy Aloo Gobi   122
Crunchy Brussels Sprouts Slaw with Asian Pear   122
Cauliflower Rice and Black Beans with Kale   123
Chana Masala: Quick Chickpea Curry with Rice   124
Baked Black Bean Burgers   124
Creamy Avocado Pesto Pasta   125
Taco Pie   126
One-Pot Pasta Arrabiata   126
Asian-Style Miso and Eggplant Pasta   127
Zucchini Noodle Pasta with Veggies   127
Pesto Socca Pizza   128
Quinoa and Greens Burrito with a Cheesy Spread   128
Zucchini Noodle Pasta with Pesto   129
Tempeh Reuben   130
Tomato Basil Spaghetti Squash Bake   130
Sweet Potato and Turmeric Falafels   131
Baked Sun-Dried Falafel with Tzatziki Dip   132
Veggie Rainbow Paella   133
Sage Polenta and Wild Mushrooms   133
Mushroom Fajitas   134
Arugula Pesto and Zucchini on Rye Toast   134
Roasted Tomato and Garlic Toast   135
Lean Green Portobello, Pesto and Artichoke Panini   136
Vegan Mac 'n' Cheeze   136

Mediterranean Hummus Burgers 137

Chik'n Caesar Salad Wraps 138

Pizza Grilled Cheese 139

Saucy and Sassy Cashew Noodles 140

Chickpea Salad Sandwiches 140

Zucchini Spaghetti with Sun-Dried Tomatoes and Basil 141

Steamed Sweet Potatoes with Wild Rice, Basil and Tomato Chili Sauce 142

Fresh Rice Paper Wraps with Chipotle Peanut Sauce 142

Spicy Noodle Bowl with Beet, Carrot, Zucchini and Sweet Tamarind Sauce 143

APPETIZERS, SNACKS & SIDES 144

Cheesy Baked Polenta Fries 145

Crispy Cauliflower Nuggets 146

Homemade Vegan Cheez-Its 147

Baked Jalapeño Poppers with Cilantro Lime Mayo 147

Golden Milk Chia Pudding 148

Spooky BOO Corn Baked Tortilla Chips 149

Savory Stuffed Mushrooms 150

Green Bruschetta 151

Four Layer Dip 152

Apricot and Coconut Bars 153

Maple-Roasted Carrots with Pumpkin Seed Spread 154

Roasted Winter Squash with Zesty "Ricotta" and Sage 154

Vegan Cornbread 155

Kalamata Hummus 155

Spicy Roasted Cauliflower 156

Three-Ingredient Butternut Squash Pasta 156

Muhammara (Red Pepper and Walnut) Spread 157

Edamame Bruschetta 157

Easy Vegan Black-Eyed Pea Pecan Pâté 158

Vegan Deviled Potatoes 158

Gluten-Free Vegan Teff Oat Rolls 159

Thai Red Curry Vegetables with Sweet Potato Rice 160

BBQ Jackfruit Stuffed Whole Wheat Potato Rolls 161

Aloo Jeera (Indian Cumin Potatoes) 162

Asian Tofu Vegetable Steamed Dumplings 163

Savory Pumpkin Pasties 164

Chocolate-Dipped Peanut Stuffed Dates 164

Warm Maple Pecan Brussels Sprouts 165

Oven-Fried Parmesan Zucchini Crisps 165

Lemon Curry Hummus 166

Cannellini Bean Dip 167

Peanut Sriracha Glazed Tofu Satay 167

Savory Mushroom and Ricotta Pop Tarts 168

Vegan Pretzel Bites 169

Vegan Potstickers 170

Polenta Squares with Sun-Dried Tomato Pesto and Roasted Eggplant 171

Vegan Garlic and Cashew Cheese Pull-Apart Bread 172

Honee Dough Twists 172

Rosemary Focaccia Bread 173

Yeast-Free Garlic Flatbread 174

Morisqueta 174

Morisqueta Sauce 175

Harissa Croquettes 175

Tsire Tempeh Bites 176

Citrus Chile Jackfruit 176

Citrus Chile Jackfruit Tacos 177

Harissa Fried Quinoa 177

Roasted Young Carrots with Ponzu Sauce 178

Caramelized Kimchi Hummus 178

Tsire-Spiced Hummus 179

Harissa Haricots Verts 179

Elote Grilled Corn 180

Rosemary Balsamic Roasted Potatoes 180

Wakame Ginger Kimchi 181

Spicy Chickpea Stuffers 182

Miso-Glazed Yellow Beets 182

Moroccan Marinated Vegetables 183

Tare Tofu 183

Pique (Pickled Hot Peppers) 184

Roasted Corn Pique Salsa 184

Chile Sauce Refried Beans 185

Miso-Marinated Mushrooms 185

Smoky Apple (or Pear) Pickles 186

Pickled Dried Mango 186

Caramelized Kimchi Tahini Toast 187

Nanami Togarashi Cashews 187

Summer Rolls with Garden Veggies, Basil and Tahini Chili Sauce 188

Perfect Fluffy Crispy Potatoes 188

Sweet Potato Fries with Lemon Cashew Chipotle Dip 189

Garam Masala Roasted Acorn Squash 190

Roasted Romanesco Cauliflower	190
Kung Pao Cauliflower	191
Party-Size Jackfruit Nachos	192
Loaded Vegan Nacho Fries	193
Fresh Spring Rolls	194
World's BEST Guacamole	194
Buffalo Sriracha Hummus	195
Garlicky White Bean Hummus	195
Picante Black Bean Hummus	196
Edamame Guacamole	196
Paprika Hummus	197
Homemade "Cheesy" Popcorn	197
Herby Avocado Dressing on Grilled Corn	198
Baked Churro Chips	198
Choc-Oat-Nut Granola Balls	199
Crispy Chickpea Onion Rings	200
Extra Chewy Chocolate Steel-Cut Oat Bars	200
PB and J Energy Bites	201
Midnight Balls	202
Ginger and Orange Zest Balls	202

SOUPS & SALADS 203

Chick'n Tortilla Soup	204
Creamy Tomato Soup with Homemade Cashew Cream	204
Moroccan Chickpea Soup	205
Roasted Butternut Squash and Apple Soup	206
Creamy Wild Mushroom Soup	207
Chickpea Noodle Soup	208
Lobster Mushroom Bisque	208
Fresh Herb and Watermelon Gazpacho	209
Easy Cuban Black Bean Soup	210
Roasted Carrot, Garlic and Rosemary Soup	211
Minestrone Soup with Arugula	211
Cream of Celery Soup	212
Tortilla Soup	213
Curried Pumpkin and Butternut Squash Stew	214
Homemade Yellow Curry Potato Soup	215
Smoky Vegan Corn and Potato Chowder	216
Roasted Sweet Potato Chili	217
Creamy Chik'n and Wild Rice Soup	218

Cheesy Broccoli Soup 219

Vegan Matzo Ball Soup 220

Forbidden Broth 221

Soothe-What-Ails Miso Broth 222

Moroccan Minestrone 222

Emergency Broth Powder 223

Chilled Ginger Berry Watermelon Soup with Mint 223

Tomato Avocado Mushroom Corn Soup 224

Red Kuri Squash Soup with Cumin, Coriander and Coconut ... 224

Quick Tomato Soup with Miso and Thyme 225

Thai-Style Coconut Soup (Tom Kha) 225

Warming Coconut Curry and Lentil Soup 226

Warming Vegetable and Black-Eyed Pea Soup 226

Veggie-Miso and Soba Noodle Soup 227

One-Pot Quinoa and Turmeric Stew 228

Velvety Butternut Squash Soup 228

Golden Beet Salad with Balsamic and Cashew Ricotta 229

Herbed Lemon Tahini Potato Salad 230

Pickled Cucumber Salad with Peas and Fresh Dill 230

Tangy Purple Cabbage Slaw with Dijon and Horseradish ... 231

Vegan Caesar Salad with Homemade Dill Croutons 232

Smoky Potato Salad 233

Chile-Infused Chickpea Salad 233

Huge Rainbow Salad Bowl 234

Fresh Orange and Fennel Salad 235

Warming Winter Grain Bowl 235

Perfect Summer Salad 236

Simple Winter Salad 237

Niçoise Salad 237

Grilled Fig and Peach Salad 238

Farro Salad with Basil and Tomatoes 239

Simple Grilled Zucchini Salad with Walnuts 239

Blueberry Whiskey BBQ Salad with Tempeh and Roasted Potatoes ... 240

Chik'n Salad 241

Protein Superfood Bean Salad 242

Warm Acorn Squash, Lentil and Quinoa Salad with Sage Dressing ... 243

Spicy Peanut Couscous Salad 244

Winter Citrus and Arugula Salad with Cranberry Orange Dressing ... 244

Vegan BLT Salad with Smoky Spicy Mayo 245

Jackfruit Tuna-Less Salad 246

Mediterranean Salad Wraps with Tahini Dressing 246

Southwestern Roasted Corn and Black Bean Salad   247

Sweet Potato Noodle Salad with Sriracha Lime Peanut Sauce 248

Bowl o' Salad Goodness   249

DESSERTS   250

Two-Bean Chocolate Chunk Cookies   251

Banana Oatmeal Cookies   251

Carrot Cupcakes with Orange Vanilla Cream Frosting   252

Chocolate Orange Macaroons   253

Chocolate S'mores Cookies   254

Coconut Cookie Butter Bars   255

Dark Chocolate Rosemary Cookies   256

Deep-Dish Apple Cinnamon Skillet Cake with Maple Vanilla Glaze 256

Double Chocolate Peppermint Cookies   257

Vegan Easter Creme Eggs   258

Gingersnap Buttercream Cookie Sandwiches   259

Homemade Strawberry Ice Cream   260

Mango Rosemary Sorbet   261

Orange Chocolate Cheesecake   261

Mini Key Lime Cheesecakes   262

Pecan Pie Bars   263

Pumpkin Chocolate Chip Cookies   264

Purple Sweet Potato Pie Bars   265

Strawberry Rhubarb Crumble   266

Vanilla Cashew Butter Cups   267

White Chocolate Macadamia Nut Cookies   268

Whole Wheat Cinnamon Sugar Pull-Apart Loaf   268

Salted Sweet Potato Brownies   269

Amber's Famous Peanut Butter Cookies   270

Easy Raw Snicker Slabs   270

Nectarine and Pear Crumble   271

Sweet Pear Galette   272

No-Bake Almond Butter Cookies   273

Raw Dark-Chocolate Brownies   273

Raw Blackberry Cheesecake   274

Dark Chocolate Crispies   275

Simple Maple-Nut Clusters   276

Dates Dipped in Chocolate   276

Homemade Galaxy Dark Chocolate with Raspberries   277

Five-Ingredient Peanut Butter Cups   277

Chocolate (Avocado) Mousse Pudding   278

Mango and Passion Fruit Cheesecake	278
Cinnamon-Apple Galette with Caramel Sauce	279
Vegan Chocolate Blintzes Stuffed with Vanilla Nut Cream	280
Vanilla Gluten-Free Vegan Pizzelles Made with Teff Flour	281
Gluten-Free Vegan Pumpkin Pie with a Teff Flour Pecan Crust	282
Vegan Pumpkin Gingerbread with No Added Oil	283
Vegan Blueberry Buckle—No Oil Added!	283
7-Layer Bars	284
Strawberry Shortcake	285
Lemon Berry Cashew Cheesecake Bites	285
Chocolate Chip Skillet Cookie	286
Lemon Knot Cookies	287
Cranberry Pistachio Biscotti	288
Sugar-Free Stuffed Baked Apples	288
Soft Pumpkin Spice Cookies	289
Spicy Black Bean Brownies	290
Vegan Bananas Foster	291
Chocolate Lava Cake	291
Mom's Lemon Meringue Pie	292
Frozen Hot Chocolate Cheesecake	293
Lemon Acai Cupcakes	294
Raspberry Lemon Cheesecake Bars	294
Decadent and Dangerous Peanut Butter Blondie Brownies	295
Chocolate Rosemary Cookies	296
Fudgy Tahini Cookies	297
Molasses Spice Cookies	298
Salted Caramel Panna Cotta	298
Miso Sweet Potato Galette	299
C3 Bonbons (Chocolate, Caramel and Cereal)	300
Kesar Mango Cake	301
Kesar Mango Farina	301
Fudgy Spelt Brownies	302
Chocolate Pudding Bowls with Coconut Cream and Cherries	303
Freezer Fudge Bites	303
Spicy Super-Powered Chocolate with Raspberries	304
Meyer Lemon Coconut Cream Tarts with Mint and Lavender	304
Double Chocolate Cupcakes with Buttercream Frosting	305
Strawberry Cashew Cream Cake with Carob Drizzle	306
Orange-Beetroot Tartlets with Almond-Fig Crust	306
Coffee Cream Cake with Choco Crust and Date Syrup	307
Oreo-ish Tarts: Vanilla Whipped Coco Cream with Chocolate Cookie Crust	308

Deep-Dish Caramel Apple Pie   309
Caramel Chocolate Ganache Tart with Superfood Drizzle   309
Chai Cheesecakes with Chocolate Drizzle   310
Magical Superfood Cheesecake   311
Fierce Salted Caramel Cheesecake   312
Chocolate Coconut Hazelnut Ganache Tart   313
Mini Lemon and Blueberry Jam Cheesecakes   314
Vanilla Cherry Nice Cream   315
Blueberry Blackberry Sorbet with Chia Pudding and Tahini   315
Mint Chocolate Chunk Ice Cream   316
Almond Cacao Cookies with Salted Maca Caramel   316
Almond Butter and Chia Jam Bars with Chocolate   317
Peppermint Oreos Dipped in Dark Chocolate   318
Almond Cookies with Spiced Apple Slices   319
Banana Bread Cookies with Coconut Cream and Chocolate Sauce   320
Maple Oatmeal Raisin Cookies   321
Coconut Twix Bars   321
Salted Chocolate Truffles   322
Quick 'n' Easy Chocolate Macaroons   322
Raw Vegan Bliss Balls   323
Chocolate Coconut Doughnuts   324
Blueberry Hazelnut Oat Bars   324
Three-Ingredient Vegan Fudge   325
Sexy Caramel Slice   326
Pecan Praline Bars with Salted Chocolate   326
Chocolate Mint Slice   327
Superfood Fudgy Mint Slice   328
Fudgy Chocolate Peanut Butter Slice   329
Gooey Brownies with Almond Butter Frosting   329
Strawberry Rhubarb Crumble with Almond Granola   330
Almond Bites with Maca, Vanilla and Flax   331
Nut-Free Creamy Coconut Cheesecake   331
Chocolate Molten Lava Cakes with Goji Berries   332
Blueberry Strawberry Banana Ice Cream Cake   332
Carrot Cake with Cashew Cream Cheese Frosting, Pistachios and Walnuts   333
Avocado Mint Cream Bars with Chocolate, Two Ways   334
Totally Tahini Cups with Coffee Cream Filling   334
Jewel Fruit Tart with Caramel Almond Filling   335
Maple Pecan Pie   336
Pumpkin Pie with Coconut Whipped Cream   336
Frozen Mango Lassi Pops   337

Vegan Lavender London Fog Pops   338
Superfood Double Chocolate Popsicles   338
Orange Creamsicles   339

BREAKFASTS, SMOOTHIES & DRINKS   340

Baked Pumpkin Cinnamon Sugar Doughnuts   341
Banana Cinnamon French Toast   342
Blood Orange Glazed Doughnuts   342
Blueberry Streusel Muffins   343
Coconut Bacon and Chocolate Chip Pancakes   344
Cranberry Orange Clafoutis   345
Easy Chickpeasy Breakfast Burritos   346
Healthy Homemade Granola   346
Lemon Chia Seed Loaf with Lemon Glaze   347
Mini Chocolate Chunk Scones   348
Peanut Butter and Berry Acai Bowl   349
Peanut Butter Chocolate Chip Banana Bread   350
Perfect Pancakes   350
South of the Border Scramble   351
Spiced Pumpkin Bread with Maple Vanilla Icing   352
Strawberry Phyllo Strudels   353
Sweet Cherry Coffee Cake   354
Vanilla-Glazed Matcha Scones   354
Overnight French Toast   355
Apple Cider Doughnuts   356
Stewed Cinnamon Apples in a Yogurt Parfait   357
Chia Pudding Parfait with a Dreamy Strawberry Smoothie   357
Chocolate-Gingersnap Fall Bars   358
Lemon and Poppy Seed Pancakes   358
Baked Peach and Blueberry Oatmeal   359
Cinnamon-Raisin Granola   360
Citrus and Tahini Granola   360
Macadamia Milk Porridge with Blueberry-Lemon Jam   361
Colorful Coconut Porridge   362
Simple Overnight Oats/Bircher Muesli   362
Turmeric Tofu Scramble   363
Blueberry Breakfast Doughnuts   363
Chocolate-Chip Cookie Protein Bars   364
Strawberry-Rose Morning Bars   365
Morning Greens Bowl   366

Vegan Gluten-Free Chai-Spiced Teff Waffles 367

Autumn Cinnamon Apple Biscuits 367

Vegan Baked Orange Carrot Cake Oatmeal 368

Perfect Banana Bread Belgian Waffles 369

Old-Fashioned Fluffy Pancakes with Apple Spice Compote 370

Christmas Morning Cranberry Orange Pancakes 371

Healthier Whole Wheat Strawberry Muffins 371

Chunky Monkey Chocolate Banana Muffins 372

Baked Pumpkin Spice Doughnuts with Chocolate Cinnamon Icing 373

Baked Lemon and Thyme Doughnuts 374

Vegan Cinnamon Rolls 375

Cherry Berry Quinoa Breakfast Bowl 376

Savory Vegan Mediterranean Oatmeal 376

Vegan Veggie and Herb Frittata 377

The Ultimate Veggie Tofu Scramble 378

Strawberry Cherry Pop Tarts 378

Baked Jammy Overnight Oatmeal 379

Turmeric Blueberry Muffins 380

Baked Apple and Spice Overnight Oats 381

Matcha Coconut Granola 382

Peanut Butter French Toast 382

Good Morning Miso Rice 383

Amba Breakfast Wraps 384

Kimchi Tofu Scramble 384

Corn Waffles 385

Pan con Salsa y Aguacate 386

Roasted Pecan Raisin Loaf 386

Blueberry Streusel Square 387

Good Oats with Almonds, Coconut Sugar and Vanilla 388

Fabulous Oatmeal with Berries and Seeds 388

Choco Nice Cream with Peanut Butter Oats, Chocolate Chunks and Doughnut Holes 389

Crunchy Toast with Peanut Butter and Quick Berry Jam 389

Peach Ginger Smoothie 390

Strawberry Cheesecake Smoothie 390

Roasted Strawberry Smoothie 391

Breakfast Smoothie 391

Energizing Peach-Maca Smoothie 392

Green-Vanilla Smoothie 392

A Nice Green Smoothie with Mint and Turmeric 393

Goji Apple Smoothie 393

Turmeric Smoothie (Delicious, Different and Good 4 U) 394

Blueberry Coconut Smoothie with Baobab Caramel 394

Beet and Berry Smoothie 395

Premenstrual Smoothie 395

Blackberry Walnut Smoothie 396

A Smoothie for Emotional Strength 396

Orange Crush Smoothie 396

Magical Green Smoothie with Spirulina, Ginger and Mushrooms 396

Ginger Berry Smoothie with Secret Ingredient 397

Creamy Cashew, Banana and Spirulina Smoothie 397

Golden Milk, Hot or Iced 398

Peppermint Hot Chocolate 398

The Best Hot Chocolate 399

Pumpkin Spiced Steamer 399

Sparkling Mint Lemonade 400

Cherry Chia Lemonade 400

Turmeric Milk 401

Summer Pineapple-Ginger Juice 401

Refreshing Watermelon Drink 402

Warming Apple Cider and Persimmon Juice 402

Coffee Shake 403

Vegan Hot White Chocolate 403

Vegan Warm Cinnamon Horchata with Whole Grains and Almonds 404

My Basic Green Juice Recipe for a Happy Bod 405

Glorious Dairy-Free Chocolate Milk 405

Juicy Elixir with Pineapple, Mint, Raspberry and Beet 406

Vanilla Coconut Shake with Peanut Butter Caramel 406

Coco Vanilla Shake with Chocolate Sauce 407

Vegan Hot Chocolate and Marshmallows 407

SAUCES, DRESSINGS, PASTES & SPICES 408

Zippy Chickpea Sauce 409

Scallion-Infused Oil 409

Miso Mushroom Gravy 410

Amba (Spicy, Savory and Sweet Dried Mango Spread) 410

Savory Dried Apricot Paste 411

Cashew Crema 411

Cashew Coconut Base 412

Creamy Harissa Sauce 412

Gochujang Paste 413

Enchilada Sauce 413

Ponzu Sauce 414

Yogurt Avocado Dressing   414
Peanut Butter Miso Sauce   415
Cashew Queso   415
Blackberry Balsamic Reduction   416
Tunisian Baharat   416
Tsire Spice   417
Vegan Ricotta   417
Six-Ingredient Vegan Cheddar Cheese Sauce   418
Four-Ingredient Homemade Pizza Sauce   418
Classic Vegan Walnut Pesto   419
Healthy Single-Serving Oil-Free Pesto   419
Roasted Tomato Spaghetti Sauce   420
Cashew Cheese   420
Cashew-Coconut Butter   421
Peanut Butter Caramel Sauce   421
Silky Caramel Sauce   422
Salted Caramel Sauce   422
Whipped Coconut Cream   423
Raspberry Chia Jam   423

ABOUT THE AUTHORS   424
INDEX   426

INTRODUCTION

If you were daydreaming of a massive collection of irresistible vegan recipes, today's your lucky day. You are holding in your hands *The Ultimate Vegan Cookbook*. Written by seven accomplished authors from various backgrounds, the goal of this book is to make your everyday vegan cooking life a breeze. Whether you are a seasoned vegan or entirely new to this ethical and healthy plant-based lifestyle, you will find herein all the recipes your dreams are made of, and possibly more.

With recipes ranging from weekday meals, to ethnic feasts, to raw desserts, and with gluten-free, soy-free and low-fat options, this cookbook is ideal for virtually all occasions. Whether on super-busy weekday nights when you need a quick meal with minimal preparation time, or for fancier occasions when you want to show off your vegan cooking skills to friends and family, the recipes in this book will have you and your guests walking away from the table feeling replenished and satisfied. That is, until you notice the dishes need to be washed.

We are honored to be both guides and traveling companions on your vegan journey, and we hope that this book will become a permanent fixture in your kitchen, always at the ready for delicious adventures!

—Celine Steen

WHAT IS A VEGAN LIFESTYLE AND HOW DO I FOLLOW IT?

Whether you are already a pro at all things vegan or have just taken the first steps into making the switch to a vegan lifestyle, *The Ultimate Vegan Cookbook* is here to help.

Following a vegan lifestyle means that a person chooses not to use and wear animal by-products or eat foods that come from an animal. A vegan diet, also known as a plant-based diet, focuses on eating foods made from plants. These foods have the advantage of being naturally free from cholesterol. They are also usually plentiful in dietary fiber and nutrients. But is a vegan diet going to make you lose weight automatically? Not always.

Truth be told, there is such a thing as vegan junk food. Not that there's anything wrong with that, but not all store-bought vegan foods are healthy foods. After all, it is a fact that some of us are vegan for ethical reasons first and foremost, and love diving into the occasional bag of vegan cookies or chips— *mea culpa* and all.

Indeed, there are several reasons why an individual decides to follow a vegan lifestyle. One can become vegan for ethical reasons, health reasons, environmental reasons or all of the above.

One of the go-to questions a person is asked upon going vegan is, "But what about protein?" You can tell your concerned mom or nosy coworker that they have no reason to fret over your well-being: protein doesn't solely come from eating animals. You aren't going to systematically become malnourished when ditching meat and other animal products, as long as you eat a well-thought-out, balanced plant-based diet. Beans, nuts, tofu, whole grains and so many more cruelty-free foods are amazing sources of protein, too!

Keep reading for more information on how to get acquainted with the lifestyle that is very likely to become the best decision you've ever made.

HOW TO GET STARTED

SELECT UNPROCESSED FOODS

Focus on serving raw and cooked vegetables and fruits, and in general foods that aren't overly processed. Less packaging usually implies that the food is mostly unprocessed, which allows us to reap all or most of the healthy benefits from said food.

CHOOSE ORGANIC AND FAIR TRADE FOODS IF AFFORDABLE

It's always best to purchase and serve foods that are organic in order to avoid consuming pesticides and other unwanted additions, but please don't let it worry you too much if the cost is too high for your budget. Also, Fair Trade is always a great social movement to support, as freedom from cruelty is a label that should apply to humans just as much as to animals.

PUT ON YOUR GLASSES OR CONTACT LENSES, AND READ LABELS

The vegan movement seems to constantly be getting more mainstream, which means a lot of manufacturers are making it easier to know whether a food is vegan by including a label to that effect on food items and health products. Look for the Certified Vegan label. Thoroughly scan labels for ingredient lists, and contact food manufacturers in case extra information is needed. Keep a list of the most common non-vegan ingredients handy. This will make shopping trips easier, as you can scan items for non-vegan ingredients. There are great resources online that will allow you to print out lists of the most common offenders, such as whey, lanolin and many more. Finally, try to focus on purchasing foods that have rather succinct ingredient lists. Not only does it mean your reading session won't be endless, but also foods that contain fewer ingredients are usually better for you anyway. Remember that where and what you spend your hard-earned money on speaks volumes.

DON'T SWEAT IT

Found a bit of cheese in the supposedly vegan tacos you ordered? Forgot your glasses, misread a label and belatedly noticed there was whey in the yogurt you could have sworn was plant-based? It's quite an unpleasant feeling, but that's okay—almost all of us have been there at some point. Don't waste too much time worrying about accidental ingestions of non-vegan foods. Things happen, and this doesn't make you a bad vegan at all. Just get back on the figurative horse when the next meal pops up, and move on.

TAKE YOUR TIME

There's no rush. Rome wasn't built in one day. Insert more platitudes here. But seriously, take your time to find the right way for you to do this for yourself. You don't have to tell everyone you're going vegan if you feel you won't have the proper kind of support from relatives and friends. You can also choose to only switch to one or a few vegan meals per week before going full throttle. Some people prefer going for it cold turkey, so to speak, but it doesn't mean everyone has to transition to a vegan lifestyle in a one-size-fits-all manner. Do it all at your own pace.

CHAT WITH OTHER VEGANS

With the advent of social media, it's easier than ever to have access to the wisdom of fellow vegans from all walks of life. Don't be afraid to reach out and ask questions: chances are, most of them will be more than eager to help out.

SHOP AROUND FOR NEW PLANT-BASED FAVORITES

Finding plant-based milks, cheeses and other new vegan favorites is likely to take a few taste tests. Don't be afraid to try several brands and flavors until you meet your perfect match.

SUPPLEMENTING YOUR PLANT-BASED DIET

Vegan dietitians recommend supplementing with B12 in order to avoid deficiencies, as this vitamin is harder to come by in vegan foods. Other supplements, such as vitamin D, iron and calcium, may be warranted for some vegans. The correct way to find out what's best for you is to have a blood test done to check your levels, and then talk with your doctor or dietitian.

REMEMBER WHY YOU MADE THE SWITCH

It is possible to feel burned out with pretty much anything on occasion. Focus back on what your reason was for going vegan in the first place. Visit a farm sanctuary to hang out with formerly abused animals, if you went vegan for ethical reasons. Read up on all the health benefits of veganism if your motivation was to improve your well-being.

DON'T LET YOURSELF GET BORED

There are too many fantastic vegan cuisines out there to allow yourself to get bored with what's on your plate. Experiment with new ingredients, and have lots of fun in your kitchen! A great way to keep yourself well fed with a variety of awesome foods is to make weekly meal plans, which allow you to shop in advance and get excited about the upcoming plant-based dishes you'll treat yourself with. Another fun way to keep things interesting is to make big batches of food during the weekend, or whenever you have more time to cook, and serve them throughout the workweek. This helps keep your cooking duties on the low side when you're shorter on time.

HOW TO STOCK YOUR VEGAN KITCHEN

Working in a vegan kitchen doesn't mean that you have to spend oodles on tools, bulky machines and other appliances. What follows is enough to get you started with cooking, and you probably already have most items in your kitchen already.

- Airtight glass jars and other containers for leftovers and storage
- A well-sharpened chef's knife
- A good paring knife
- Cutting boards
- Glass measuring cups and spoons for liquid ingredients
- Measuring cups and spoons for dry ingredients
- Baking sheets (including a nonstick baking mat like Silpat)
- Baking pans
- Mixing bowls
- A reliable skillet
- A small saucepan
- Heavy-bottomed Dutch oven–type pot
- Stockpot
- Zester (or microplane)
- Food processor
- Blender (high-speed models like Vitamix and Blendtec are useful; an immersion blender is also great for blending soups)
- Mixer (handheld or countertop)
- Parchment paper (for baking)
- Mandoline
- Steamer
- Fermentation crock

This book also includes recipes for the slow cooker, Instant Pot and air fryer. If those styles of cooking interest you, then you might want to invest in those appliances. Depending on what kinds of foods you want to bake, you might also need a muffin pan, cake pans, springform cake pan, tart pans, bread pans and more.

HOW TO STOCK YOUR VEGAN PANTRY AND REFRIGERATOR

Even as a seasoned vegan, you are bound to occasionally come across a new-to-you ingredient. In the meantime, here is a short list of those that are most commonly found in a well-stocked vegan pantry and refrigerator, and that will be sufficient to make most of the recipes in this book.

- Nuts and seeds (such as cashews, almonds, chia seeds and flaxseeds)
- Nut butters (such as peanut butter, almond butter or cashew butter)
- Plant-based milks (such as almond milk or cashew milk; choose unsweetened plain whenever available for a wider range of use)
- Flours (such as whole wheat or gluten-free)
- Organic cornstarch or arrowroot powder
- Coconut milk and coconut cream
- Coconut oil (refined for less flavor or unrefined for flavor)
- Neutral-flavored oils (such as grapeseed)
- Nutritional yeast (a deactivated yeast that adds a cheesy, umami-rich flavor to dishes)
- Soy sauce, tamari or coconut aminos (choose reduced-sodium whenever available to keep your sodium intake in check)
- Sea salt and coarse kosher salt

- Spices and dried herbs (such as cumin, red pepper flakes, basil, etc.)
- Specialty spices (like goshugaru, nanami togarashi, achiote or tsire spice)
- Super-firm or extra-firm tofu
- Tempeh
- Jarred or canned tomato products (such as crushed, fire-roasted, diced tomatoes, etc.)
- Canned beans (such as kidney beans and black beans)
- Canned chickpeas (the liquid in the can, known as aquafaba, can be used as an egg substitute in many of these recipes, so don't discard it!)
- Dried beans and pulses (such as chickpeas and lentils)
- Grains and seeds (such as rice and quinoa)
- Refined sugar alternatives (such as Sucanat, agave, maple syrup, dates and figs)
- Egg alternatives (such as VeganEgg or flax eggs, a combination of flaxseeds and water, see page 55)
- Dairy alternatives (Daiya brand and vegan Parmesan, for example)
- Vegan butter (such as Earth Balance)

HOW TO READ THE RECIPES

Use this handy key to select the recipes that are right for you and your family. The list below will help you identify the author of a recipe. These initials appear at the end of each recipe introduction.

KEY

GF = gluten-free
GFO = gluten-free option
SF = soy-free
SFO = soy-free option
QP = quick prep
SE = special equipment

RECIPE AUTHORS

EvE = Emily von Euw
KH = Kathy Hester
LM + AM = Linda and Alex Meyer
MR = Marie Reginato
CS = Celine Steen
AS = Amber St. Peter

one

MAIN DISHES

These recipes are for hearty, filling plates and bowls that will nourish your body, satisfy your taste buds and give you the energy you need to live your life. A stereotyped image of what vegans eat for lunch or dinner is often a sad-looking, sparse bowl of lettuce and carrots, maybe with some tofu if you're lucky. Fortunately, in reality we lettuce-lovers have a plethora of colorful, flavorful and delectable foods to choose from when we want to cook a plant-based meal. Whether you desire pasta, vegetables, protein, savory baked goods, grains or legumes, you can serve them grilled, steamed, baked, fried, roasted or sautéed, with all kinds of creamy and crunchy toppings to provide a balance of textures and tastes. Cooking vegan for your main dish absolutely doesn't have to mean missing out on delicious food. It's easy and exciting to prepare the following recipes, and they're sure to please a variety of eaters. From familiar comfort foods with big flavor, to nutrient-dense veggie bowls, to new ingredient combinations you might not have thought of, this chapter has all you need to experience the best of what (vegan) main dishes have to offer. *Bon appétit.*

BBQ PULLED JACKFRUIT SANDWICH *with* SLAW AND CARAMELIZED ONIONS

+GFO

This sandwich is spicy, garlicky, meaty, full of flavor—and amazing. The dilly slaw adds a crunchy tang and the caramelized onions round it all out . . . because caramelized onions effing rock. It is seriously incredible how pulled pork-y in texture the cooked jackfruit is. —AS

SERVES 3 TO 4

BBQ JACKFRUIT
1 (20-oz [565-g]) can (10 oz [285 g], drained) jackfruit in brine or water, NOT syrup

1 tbsp (14 g) coconut oil

1 cup (245 g) vegan BBQ sauce

¼ tsp smoked paprika (optional)

SLAW
3 cups (1 kg) thinly shredded green cabbage

1 clove garlic, minced

¼ cup (55 g) vegan mayo

1 tbsp (15 ml) apple cider vinegar

½ tsp maple syrup

½ tsp dried dill weed

⅛ tsp salt

⅛ tsp pepper

CARAMELIZED ONIONS
1 tsp coconut oil

1 small yellow onion, thinly sliced

1 tbsp (15 ml) water, as needed

3 to 4 buns (or use gluten-free buns)

FOR THE BBQ JACKFRUIT

Drain and rinse the jackfruit. Pick (discarding them. Using a fork or you the jackfruit. In a large skillet, heat over medium heat. Pour in the shre BBQ sauce and smoked paprika (if us combine. Cook for 10 to 12 minutes, st or until the sauce thickens and reduc

While the jackfruit cooks, make the

FOR THE SLAW

In a large mixing bowl, combine cabbage, garlic, mayo, vinegar, syru pepper, and toss to evenly coat the aside.

FOR THE CARAMELIZED ONIONS

In a medium skillet, melt the coconut oil over medium heat. Toss in the sliced onions, stirring regularly so they don't burn. If they begin to brown, add a tablespoon (15 ml) of water. Continue this until the onions are lightly browned, softened and caramelized, 15 to 20 minutes.

To assemble, pile the jackfruit onto a bun, and then top generously with the slaw and onions. Serve immediately. Leftovers can be refrigerated and eaten for up to a week.

*SEE PHOTO INSERT

"California Burrito" TACOS

+GF

Only in Southern California can you get authentic, traditional, spicy Mexican dishes made with love. And of course, in California, we like to mix things up. Do it our way, you know? That's probably why San Diego has become famous for putting its own twist on traditional carne asada burritos and adding french fries. Maybe it was the surfers who did it first, maybe we'll never know, but ordering a California burrito anywhere in So Cal means that you're getting a stuffed burrito—including french fries. This dish is a must-try! —AS

SERVES 4 TO 6

FRENCH FRIES
3 medium russet potatoes, cut into french fries, or about 3 cups (630 g) of your fave frozen french fries

1 tbsp (14 g) coconut oil, if making your own fries

Salt, to taste

MEATY CRUMBLES
2 cups (460 g) vegan meaty crumbles (crumbled tempeh works well here, too)

1 tbsp (14 g) coconut oil

1 tsp ground cumin

½ tsp cayenne pepper

½ tsp smoked paprika

¼ tsp chili powder

⅛ tsp salt

TOPPINGS
1 lime, quartered

1 avocado, pitted and sliced

¼ cup (38 g) sliced onion

¼ cup (10 g) chopped cilantro

Corn tortillas

Hot sauce and/or salsa, to taste

Vegan cheese, for sprinkling (optional)

FOR THE FRENCH FRIES
Preheat the oven to 400°F (204°C). If you're making fries from scratch, wash your potatoes well and slice them into fries about ¼ inch (6 mm) thick. If using your own chopped potatoes, coat a baking sheet with the coconut oil. (If using frozen fries, skip this step.) Then spread your potatoes or frozen fries onto the baking sheet and bake until golden and crispy, about 30 minutes, flipping halfway through. Season with salt and set them aside.

FOR THE MEATY CRUMBLES
Combine the meaty crumbles and coconut oil in a cast-iron pan over medium heat. Add the cumin, cayenne pepper, smoked paprika, chili powder and salt. Stir well to evenly coat the crumbles in spices, and cook over medium heat until they are heated through and smelling delicious, about 10 minutes.

FOR THE TOPPINGS
While the meaty crumbles and fries cook, prepare the toppings: slice the lime, avocado and onion, and chop the cilantro. Heat the tortillas in a separate cast-iron pan or pop in the oven for a few minutes to warm them. When they're ready, assemble the tacos starting with the corn tortillas. Then top with meaty crumbles, fries, avocado, onions, cilantro and as much lime and hot sauce or salsa (or both) as you like. If you're adding a sprinkle of cheese, toss that on, too. Leftovers can be refrigerated for up to a week, but the corn tortillas should be heated fresh for each meal.

San Pedro–Style
FISHLESS MARKET TRAY

+GF

This meal is served on a big plastic tray (like from a food court), covered in newspaper and topped with an overflowing mixture of shrimp, potatoes, onions, peppers, tomatoes and corn smothered in a spicy, delicious tomato-based sauce that you could sop up with the crusty, toasted bread served on the side. The veggies and sauce make the whole thing, and it was super easy to sub out little crustaceans with healthy plant foods. We replaced the shrimp with seasoned hearts of palm and mushrooms, which both taste and have a texture similar to the original—but you know, vegan! —AS

SERVES 4 TO 6

MARINADE
½ cup (120 ml) white cooking wine

2 tbsp (30 ml) lemon juice

1½ tsp Old Bay seasoning

¼ tsp black truffle sea salt (regular sea salt works here, too)

1 (14½-oz [410-g]) can hearts of palm, drained

1½ cups (100 g) sliced mushrooms (we used shiitake, but oyster or lobster mushrooms would be great, too!)

SAUCE
2 (6-oz [170-g]) cans tomato paste

6 oz (170 g) soyrizo (soy chorizo; optional, but worth it)

2 cloves garlic, minced

1 cube vegetable bouillon

2 tsp (4 g) chili powder

1 tsp cayenne pepper

1 tsp smoked paprika

1 tsp Old Bay seasoning

½ tsp ground cumin

¼ tsp black truffle sea salt (or regular sea salt)

¼ tsp black pepper

3 cups (710 ml) water

EVERYTHING ELSE
1 tbsp (15 ml) oil

2 large bell peppers, seeded and roughly chopped

2 medium onions, roughly chopped

2 cobs of corn, halved

4 medium red potatoes, cut into 1" to 2" (2.5- to 5-cm) cubes

1 tomato, roughly chopped

Cilantro, for garnish (optional)

FOR THE MARINADE
In a large bowl, combine the white cooking wine, lemon juice, Old Bay and salt. Drain the hearts of palm and slice them into ½-inch (1.3-cm) circles. Roughly chop the mushrooms and place the 'shrooms and hearts of palm slices into the marinade. Let marinate for at least 1 hour or as long as overnight.

FOR THE SAUCE
While the marinade comes together, make the sauce by whisking together the tomato paste, soyrizo, garlic, vegetable bouillon cube, spices and water in a large bowl. Set aside.

FOR EVERYTHING ELSE
Heat the oil over medium heat in a large cast-iron skillet. Cut the bell peppers, onions, corn, red potatoes and tomato.

Place the corn and potatoes into a medium pot and boil until fork tender. Add the bell peppers and onions to the skillet and cook until they begin to soften, about 3 to 5 minutes. Add the cooked corn coblets, potatoes and tomato, and cook them all together, stirring occasionally, for another 5 minutes. Add the sauce mixture to the pan and stir to combine. Simmer for 15 minutes.

While the veggie and sauce mixture simmers, pour the hearts of palm and mushroom marinating mixture into a medium pan and cook over medium heat until the leftover marinating liquid reduces and thickens. Remove from the heat, add to the sauce and veggie mixture and stir to combine. Cook for another minute or two, until the mixture is a bit soupy and everything is well combined. Top with cilantro, if you like, and serve with crusty bread and a squeeze of lemon.

Note: Leftovers last in a sealed container in the fridge for up to a week. It may need a little water added when reheating because the sauce will thicken as it cools.

Black Bean CITRUS SLAW TACOS

Here in Southern California, it's all about the food. We're surrounded by great local restaurants and tons of farmers' markets. We're lucky to live in a place where fresh produce, great weather and a melting pot of diversity has also attracted some amazing chefs: it's a culinary adventure living out here. That being said, there is almost no better food I've ever eaten here than a traditional Mexican street taco. So we made our own! I kicked them up a bit with my version of a tangy citrus slaw on top—it's the perfect crunchy contradiction to the smoky black beans. —AS

SERVES 2 TO 4

2 (15-oz [425-g]) cans black beans, drained (or about 2 cups [345 g] cooked black beans)

1 tbsp (14 g) coconut oil

3 tbsp (45 ml) lime juice, divided

1 tsp apple cider vinegar

1 tsp soy sauce

1 tsp ground cumin

½ tsp salt

½ tsp garlic powder

½ tsp smoked paprika

½ tsp chili powder

3 cups (1 kg) broccoli slaw (store-bought or just shredded broccoli, carrots and red cabbage)

1 tbsp (15 ml) olive oil

½ tsp salt

Tortillas, for serving

Pepitas, for garnish

Fresh chopped cilantro, for garnish

In a medium cast-iron pan or saucepan, combine the beans, coconut oil, 1 tablespoon (15 ml) of the lime juice, vinegar, soy sauce, cumin, salt, garlic powder, smoked paprika and chili powder. Stir to combine, and simmer over medium-low heat.

While the beans cook, make the broccoli slaw by tossing together the shredded broccoli, carrots and red cabbage with the remaining 2 tablespoons (30 ml) lime juice, olive oil and salt. Set aside.

Prepare the tortillas by heating them in a cast-iron skillet over medium-high heat until hot; then flip and heat them through. Keep the warm tortillas wrapped in a clean towel or a tortilla warmer until ready to serve.

Once the beans have cooked, about 10 to 15 minutes, portion them evenly into the tortillas. Then top with broccoli slaw, pepitas and cilantro. Serve immediately!

Note: Leftovers can be refrigerated separately for up to a week.

Vegetable POT PIE

Pot pies stuffed with seasonal vegetables are the best. Easy to make and even easier to eat up, they come together quickly and have plenty of room for experimentation. This easy, healthier version topped with a buttery crust has become a go-to weeknight dinner in our house! —AS

SERVES 6

CRUST

2¼ cups (270 g) all-purpose flour

1 tbsp (12 g) sugar

1 tsp salt

½ cup (120 g) cold vegan butter or coconut oil

⅓–½ cup (90–120 ml) ice water

1 tbsp (15 ml) vegan butter, melted

FILLING

1 tbsp (15 ml) olive oil

2 cloves garlic, minced

1 cup (160 g) chopped yellow onion

3 cups (475 g) frozen mixed green beans, carrots, corn and peas (or sub fresh!)

1 cup (150 g) cubed red potatoes (cut into ½" [1.3-cm] cubes)

½ cup (60 g) all-purpose flour

2 cups (480 ml) vegetable broth

2 bay leaves

1 tsp salt

½ tsp pepper

Preheat the oven to 400°F (204°C). Grease an 8 x 8-inch (20 x 20-cm) square baking dish.

FOR THE CRUST

Combine the flour, sugar and salt in a large mixing bowl. Cut in the cold butter with a pastry cutter or fork until small crumbs form and then add to the mixing bowl. Drizzle in the ice water, using a wooden spoon to stir the mixture together until a dough forms. Wrap the dough in plastic wrap and stick it in the fridge to chill.

FOR THE FILLING

Heat the olive oil in a large saucepan over medium heat. Add the garlic and onion and sauté until soft, about 5 to 7 minutes. Add the frozen (or fresh, if using) mixed vegetables and the potatoes, and stir to combine. Next, whisk in the flour and cook, stirring it into the vegetables for about 1 minute. Then whisk in the vegetable broth. Finally, add the bay leaves, salt and pepper, and simmer the mixture until thickened, about 10 minutes.

While the mixture thickens, remove the pie dough from the fridge and turn it out onto a lightly floured surface. Split the dough into two halves. Roll them out to about ¼ inch (6 mm) thickness and press half of the dough into the greased baking dish, being sure to cover the dish completely. Set the other rolled-out dough aside for the top layer of the pie.

Once the sauce has thickened, remove the bay leaves and toss them into the compost. Pour the thickened vegetable filling into the crust-lined baking dish. Carefully place the second crust over the top, using a fork or your fingers to press together the edges. Poke a few small holes in the top for steam to escape, using a fork or a toothpick. Brush the top generously with the melted vegan butter.

Bake the pie for 30 to 40 minutes, or until the crust is golden. Let it cool for 5 minutes before cutting and serving.

Leftovers last in the fridge for up to 1 week and can be frozen indefinitely.

Note: You can make the filling and crust ahead of time and just keep them separately in the fridge until you're ready to cook.

*SEE PHOTO INSERT

Forbidden Rice
SUSHI ROLLS

+QP +SF +GF

Sushi rolls are the perfect blank slate for those days where all you have lingering about your fridge are leftover veggies and rice. Toss everything into a nori sheet (the seaweed that folds to make sushi rolls), wrap and enjoy. Below is a favorite flavor combination of mine. Use what you have and I'm sure you'll construct a sushi roll equally as delicious. —MR

SERVES 2

1 sweet potato

1 eggplant

1 tbsp (15 ml) olive oil

Sprinkle of sea salt

1 cup (210 g) forbidden black rice or brown rice

1 cucumber

1 carrot

1 avocado

4 nori wraps

Tamari

Sesame seeds (optional)

Preheat the oven to 420°F (215°C). Peel and thinly slice the sweet potato into long wedges, the same length as your nori wrap. Then dice the eggplant into bite-size cubes. Drizzle the sweet potatoes and eggplant with the olive oil, sprinkle with salt and mix well. Then line a baking pan with parchment paper. Toss the vegetables on top; place in the oven for 15 to 20 minutes and cook until the edges are crispy. Check to see if they need an extra drizzle of olive oil or salt halfway through.

While the vegetables roast, cook the rice as the package instructs.

In the meantime, slice the rest of the veggies and avocado into very thin, lengthwise pieces. Once the rice has cooked, lay down 1 nori sheet and add enough rice on top to spread a thin, even layer, meeting each corner. The easiest way to make the roll is by adding a small amount of each ingredient to the left-hand side, taking up no more than a third of the entire nori roll. Then tightly roll the veggies to the opposite side. With a sharp knife, slice the roll into small pieces and enjoy your delicious veggie sushi with a dipping sauce of tamari and sesame seeds!

*SEE PHOTO INSERT

Stuffed TOMATOES WITH PINK RICE

+SF +GF

A few modest ingredients go a long way when presented beautifully. Stuffed veggies have an air of elegance— perfectly blistered tomatoes stuffed with savory rice and veggies, neatly packed and served. Yet, this dish is much easier than looks would suggest. —MR

SERVES 8

1⅓ cups (315 ml) water

1 cup (210 g) pink rice or any rice, rinsed

½ tsp salt, for rice

1 tsp coconut oil

⅔ red bell pepper

1 zucchini

⅓ small red onion

2 handfuls of macadamia nuts

8 large red tomatoes

2 tbsp (30 ml) olive oil

1½ cups (200 g) frozen peas, thawed

Salt, to taste

Preheat the oven to 350°F (177°C). Now prepare the rice by boiling the water, add in the rinsed rice (check instructions if not using pink rice), salt and coconut oil in a saucepan. Reduce the heat to a simmer, cover and let the rice cook for 20 minutes, or until all the water is absorbed.

As the rice cooks, thinly chop the red bell pepper, zucchini and red onion into bite-size pieces. Crush the macadamia nuts. Set this aside as you prepare the tomatoes.

Start by cutting the tops evenly off the tomatoes. Then take a spoon and carefully scoop out all of the pulp and juice from within the tomatoes, being careful not to poke a hole into the bottom or sides. Mash the pulp into a purée and set aside for later use.

Now warm the olive oil and the onion in a saucepan for 5 minutes over medium heat, until the onion becomes tender. Add two-thirds of the tomato purée, the chopped vegetables, the peas and the salt to the same saucepan, and sauté over medium heat for about 10 minutes.

Once the rice has finished cooking, pour it into a large bowl and add the sautéed vegetables and macadamia nuts. Stir well, and then spoon the rice mixture into each tomato. Line a baking pan with parchment paper and place each stuffed tomato on the pan. Bake the tomatoes for 30 to 35 minutes. The skin of the tomatoes should be tender and blistered when finished. Let them cool for 10 minutes, and then enjoy with a salad!

Sweet Potato TACOS WITH MINT-CILANTRO SALSA

+SF +GF

Sweet potatoes wrapped tightly in a taco might seem unusual. But it is in fact a delicious main when served with a refreshing mint-cilantro salsa, puréed black beans and avocado. Each complementary topping provides the satiating feeling that so often comes from classic tacos.—MR

SERVES 5

2 small sweet potatoes, cubed and skin attached
½ tsp ground cumin
Sea salt, to taste
½ tsp red pepper flakes
3 tbsp (45 ml) olive oil
1 (14-oz [397-g]) can black beans
1 small clove garlic
2 tbsp (30 ml) water

MINT-CILANTRO SALSA
2 ripe tomatoes
2 tbsp (5 g) chopped fresh mint leaves
2 tbsp (5 g) chopped fresh cilantro
¼ red onion
Juice of ½ lemon
Sea salt, to taste

5 corn tortillas
1 avocado, pitted and sliced

Preheat the oven to 400°F (204°C). Place the sweet potatoes on a nonstick baking sheet and toss with the cumin, sea salt, red pepper flakes and olive oil; massage the seasoning into the sweet potatoes. Place in the oven and cook for 30 minutes, turning halfway through.

In the meantime, make the black bean purée. Simply drain and rinse the black beans and blend in the food processor, with the garlic clove and water, until it becomes smooth and creamy. Sprinkle with sea salt.

FOR THE SALSA
As the sweet potatoes finish baking, make your salsa. Add all of the ingredients to the food processor. Then pulse until the salsa is chopped and broken down.

When the sweet potatoes are crispy, take them out of the oven and make the tacos. Start by smearing 2 tablespoons (25 g) of the black bean purée onto a warmed tortilla, and then add the sweet potatoes, slices of avocado and mint-cilantro salsa.

Spring ✳ VEGETABLE PASTA

+SF +GF

This pasta brings color to the table with an abundance of spring veggies wrapped in a light red sauce. —MR

SERVES 3

½ lb (227 g) brown rice pasta

Sea salt

4 tbsp (60 ml) olive oil, plus more for serving

4 cloves garlic, roughly chopped

1 cup (160 g) canned tomatoes, drained with juice reserved

1 bunch of asparagus, cut into ⅓" (1-cm) pieces

3 zucchini or yellow squash, cut into quarters

Red pepper flakes

2 cups (150 g) thinly sliced cremini mushrooms, or any variety

¾ cup (100 g) frozen peas, thawed

Start by boiling the water for the pasta. Follow the instructions on the pasta box and add 1 tablespoon (15 g) of sea salt to the water.

Now, in a large saucepan on the lowest heat, warm the olive oil. After 1 minute, add the garlic.

With the heat on medium-high, add the canned tomatoes, asparagus and zucchini to the pan, with a generous sprinkling of sea salt and a pinch of red pepper flakes. Add a few extra tablespoons (45 ml) of the tomato juice from the can to keep the sauce moist. If the sauce becomes dry as the veggies cook, add a splash of water. I like to keep the cover ajar as the veggies cook. Cook for about 15 minutes and then stir in the mushrooms and peas. Cook for another 5 minutes. Once it's ready, pour the sautéed veggies on top of the cooked pasta with a drizzle of extra olive oil and sea salt. Mix well and serve in bowls.

Foolproof CREAMY PESTO AND ROASTED VEGGIES

+SF +GF

Pesto is the five-minute condiment that has the magic to completely reshape a meal. Add a dollop of pesto to your veggies and smother it into fluffy quinoa for a rich and satisfying grain bowl. —MR

SERVES 3 TO 4

VEGGIES

4 carrots, cut into circles

2 red bell peppers, top and seeds removed, cut into thin strips and then cut crosswise

½ small red cabbage, roughly chopped

1 small red onion, cut into quarters

1 eggplant, cubed

1 sweet potato, cubed with skin attached

3 tbsp (45 ml) olive oil

Sea salt and black pepper

QUINOA

2 cups (473 ml) water

1 cup (170 g) quinoa, rinsed

1 tsp coconut oil

1 tsp salt

PESTO

2 cups (60 g) spinach

2 cups (50 g) basil

½ cup (60 g) unsalted walnuts

¼ cup (30 g) unsalted pine nuts

2½ tbsp (12 g) nutritional yeast

3 tbsp (45 ml) olive oil

2–3 cloves garlic

Sea salt, to taste

Squeeze of lemon juice

FOR THE VEGGIES

Preheat the oven to 420°F (215°C). Add all the veggies to a large bowl and mix with the olive oil, salt and pepper. Then line a baking pan with parchment paper and evenly pour all the vegetables onto the pan. Cook for 30 to 35 minutes, or until the veggies are crispy and caramelized. Turn and mix halfway through, and add a drizzle of olive oil if needed.

FOR THE QUINOA

In the meantime, boil the water and add in the rinsed quinoa, coconut oil and salt. Let the quinoa cook for 15 to 20 minutes, or until all the water is absorbed.

FOR THE PESTO

Simply add all the ingredients into a food processor and blend until creamy. Taste the pesto to see if you would like to add more salt or garlic.

Finally, remove the roasted vegetables from the oven. Serve the quinoa in a bowl and top it with a generous helping of the pesto and roasted veggies.

Stuffed BUTTERNUT SQUASH

+SF +GF

Stuffed butternut squash is brimming—better yet, overflowing—with nutrient-dense vegetables. These beautiful golden boats are stuffed with soft millet and crispy, roasted broccolini, and sealed in an avocado and pea cream: an unexpected main that would be perfect served alongside a holiday dinner. —MR

SERVES 2

STUFFED BUTTERNUT SQUASH

1 butternut squash, cut lengthwise

1 tbsp (15 ml) olive oil

Pinch of sea salt

MILLET OR BROWN RICE

1 cup (235 ml) water

½ cup (105 g) millet or brown rice

1 tsp salt

BROCCOLINI

1 head of broccolini, chopped

Drizzle of olive oil

Salt, to taste

1 clove garlic, roughly chopped

AVOCADO AND PEA CREAM

½ avocado

2 cups (270 g) frozen peas, thawed

Few squeezes of lemon juice

1 small tbsp (15 g) tahini

1 clove garlic

Pinch of sea salt

(continued)

FOR THE BUTTERNUT SQUASH

Preheat the oven to 420°F (215°C). Take the cut butternut squash and remove the seeds and flesh from the center. Rub the olive oil and sea salt on the squash, place on a baking sheet and bake for 1 hour, until the center is perfectly tender.

FOR THE MILLET OR BROWN RICE

At 30 minutes, start preparing the millet or brown rice by boiling the water in a saucepan, then add the millet and salt. Reduce the heat to a simmer and let the millet cook for 20 to 30 minutes, or until all of the liquid is absorbed.

FOR THE BROCCOLINI

When there is 20 minutes left for the butternut squash to bake, add the chopped broccolini (rubbed with a drizzle of olive oil and salt) and garlic to the baking dish.

FOR THE AVOCADO AND PEA CREAM

Now make the avocado and pea cream by simply placing all the ingredients into a food processor or blender and mixing until thick and creamy.

Once the squash is tender, fill the center with the millet, roasted broccolini and a dollop of the delicious cream.

PUMPKIN CURRY **with** COCONUT BROWN RICE

+SF +GF

Don't be turned off by the long list of ingredients, because what you get is a truly aromatic dish that uses spices to perfume a curry. Rich in coconut milk and tender pumpkin cubes, this curry can be served with a generous helping of homemade coconut brown rice. —MR

SERVES 4 TO 5

COCONUT RICE

1 cup (235 ml) water
¾ cup (177 ml) full-fat coconut milk
1 cup (210 g) brown rice, rinsed
Pinch of sea salt

PUMPKIN CURRY

1 tbsp (14 g) coconut oil
1¼ cups (295 ml) water, divided
½ cup (80 g) diced onion
3 cloves garlic, minced
½ thumb fresh ginger or 1 tsp ground ginger
1 tsp ground turmeric
Sea salt
1 tsp ground coriander
1½ tbsp (11 g) curry powder
½ tsp mustard seeds (optional)
1 kabocha squash
1 cup (110 g) green beans, cut in half
2 large carrots, cut into thin circles
1¼ cups (295 ml) full-fat coconut milk
½ cup (20 g) chopped fresh cilantro
3 bay leaves (optional)

FOR THE RICE

Start preparing the rice by boiling the water, coconut milk, brown rice and salt in a saucepan. Reduce the heat to a simmer and let the rice cook for 20 to 30 minutes (with the lid ajar), or until all the liquid is absorbed.

FOR THE PUMPKIN CURRY

Now melt the coconut oil in a deep Dutch oven (or a deep, large pot) on medium heat. Then add ¼ cup (60 ml) of water, onions, garlic, ginger, turmeric, salt, coriander, curry powder and mustard seeds (if using) to the Dutch oven and cook on medium to high heat for 5 minutes. As this cooks, cut the top off the squash and cut the squash in half. Scoop out the insides and cut the squash into large bite-size pieces (no need to peel the skin—it is edible if using kabocha). Add the squash, green beans and carrots, remaining 1 cup (235 ml) water and coconut milk to the pot, and cook for 10 minutes.

Now add the cilantro and bay leaves (if using) and season with salt to taste. Cook for another 15 to 20 minutes, or until the squash is tender. Serve in a bowl over coconut rice and enjoy!

Homemade THAI-STYLE GREEN CURRY

+GF

If you've ever wanted to make a restaurant-style curry, here is your guide. The aroma of homemade green curry—sweet yet spicy, citrusy yet earthy—is reason enough to make this dish. If you're in a pinch for time, you can always purchase premade green curry paste for a quick dinner. Enjoy over a bed of fluffy quinoa for a lighter take on Thai curry. —MR

SERVES 4 TO 6

HOMEMADE GREEN CURRY PASTE
2 tbsp (5 g) chopped fresh cilantro stems
2 small handfuls fresh cilantro leaves
6 cloves garlic
1 tbsp (7 g) ground coriander
½ tbsp (4 g) ground cumin
1" (2.5-cm) piece ginger, peeled
Juice of 1 lime

1 lemongrass stalk or zest of 1 lemon
½ cup (80 g) chopped shallots or white onion
1 tsp red pepper flakes
Sea salt

GREEN CURRY
1 tbsp (14 g) coconut oil
1 small onion, diced
1 cup (110 g) green beans, cut in half
1 large bell pepper, cut into thin strips
1 Japanese eggplant or ½ very large eggplant, cut into bite-size cubes
2 carrots, cut into thin circles
1 cup (66 g) thinly sliced mushrooms
2 tbsp (24 g) coconut sugar
Sea salt, to taste
2–3 tbsp (30–45 g) green curry paste
1¼ cups (295 ml) water, divided
1 (13½-oz [400-ml]) can full-fat coconut milk
Juice of 1 lime
A few extra cilantro leaves
Brown rice or quinoa, for serving (optional)

FOR THE CURRY PASTE

Make the curry paste by simply blending everything in the food processor until it's well mixed and ground down into a paste.

FOR THE GREEN CURRY

Over medium heat, warm the coconut oil and onion for 5 minutes in a Dutch oven (or a deep pot). Then add all the vegetables, coconut sugar, salt, curry paste and ¼ cup (60 ml) of the water, and let this simmer with the lid on for about 5 to 10 minutes. Add more water gradually so that the veggies don't burn. Once the veggies have cooked down, add the coconut milk and remaining 1 cup (235 ml) water, and cook for another 10 minutes until the veggies are fully cooked. Stir in the fresh lime juice and extra cilantro leaves. Serve over brown rice or quinoa!

*SEE PHOTO INSERT

Super Easy SESAME CUCUMBER NOODLES

+GFO +SFO

This is a great summer lunch or dinner. I've been eating it almost every day with some baked tofu straight from the fridge on the side. You can make this a day or two ahead of time to make it even a bit easier. —KH

SERVES 1

1 large English cucumber (280 g) or about 2 regular ones

2 tbsp (30 ml) soy sauce or tamari (use coconut aminos to make it soy-free and gluten-free)

1 tbsp (15 ml) rice vinegar

1 tsp toasted sesame oil (or use tahini to make oil-free)

2 tsp (8 g) toasted sesame seeds

Spiralize the cucumber. Break the noodles into soba-size lengths.

Mix the soy sauce, vinegar and oil in a medium mixing bowl. Toss the noodles in and mix. Plate up and sprinkle with sesame seeds.

Indian STUFFED POTATO CHAAT

+GF +SFO

You know what a stuffed potato is, but you might be wondering just what a chaat is. Chaat is a delicious layered dish, a type of Indian street food that can be eaten as a meal too. This dish takes a split baked potato stuffed with vegan yogurt and turmeric, then ladles on a chickpea curry and a mint chutney. —KH

SERVES 4

CILANTRO AND MINT BLENDER CHUTNEY

1 packed cup (37 g) fresh cilantro

½ packed cup (20 g) fresh mint

½ cup (120 ml) water

1 tsp minced green chile (or use more if you want it hotter)

1 tsp lemon juice

1½ tbsp (10 g) chopped fresh ginger

Salt, to taste

EASY CHICKPEA CURRY

1 (14½-oz [410-g]) can diced tomatoes

½ cup (120 ml) water

1½ tbsp (10 g) chopped fresh ginger

2 cloves garlic, minced

1½ tsp (5 g) garam masala

½ tsp ground cumin

½ tsp ground turmeric

½–1 tsp (1–2 g) chili powder, to taste

1 tsp lemon juice

Salt, to taste

1½ cups (150 g) chickpeas (1 can, drained and rinsed)

POTATOES

2 large Idaho potatoes

½ cup (123 g) unsweetened vegan yogurt, plus more for topping

½ tsp ground turmeric

½ tsp salt, or to taste

Chopped fresh cilantro, for garnish

FOR THE CHUTNEY

Add all the ingredients to your blender and blend until smooth. You can add extra water if you need it, but try to scrape down the pitcher and blend again a few times before you do. I've added too much too soon, and it makes a runny chutney.

FOR THE CHICKPEA CURRY

Add everything except for the chickpeas to your blender and process until smooth. Add the blender mixture and the chickpeas to a saucepan and heat over medium heat until warm, about 10 minutes. It's best to let the curry simmer while you're working on the potatoes.

FOR THE POTATOES

Bake the potato using any method you'd like: in the oven, slow cooker or even the microwave if you're in a pinch.

Cut them in half lengthwise and scoop the flesh out into a mixing bowl, leaving a thin layer on the skin to hold them together.

Mash the potatoes with the yogurt, turmeric and salt. Divide the mixture evenly between the 4 potato bottoms.

Put them on a serving plate and top with the chickpea curry, chutney and more unsweetened vegan yogurt. You can get fancy and garnish with some cilantro.

*SEE PHOTO INSERT

Spiralized Vegan
LATKES WITH RED CABBAGE AND APPLE

+GF +SF

There's nothing quite like a comforting potato latke, but this recipe will have your family and friends dazzled by the colors and extra flavor. Instead of serving with applesauce, we've added spiralized apple right in with the potato. The red cabbage adds nutrition, flavor and beauty. Please note that you are using the small noodle blade on your spiralizer to prepare the vegetables. —KH

MAKES 15 LATKES

About ¼ cup (60 ml) olive oil, divided

¼ cup (28 g) ground flaxseed mixed with ½ cup (120 ml) warm water

1 tsp salt

½ tsp ground black pepper

4 cups (225 g) spiralized peeled potato (about 1 large baking potato)

2 cups (397 g) spiralized red cabbage (about ½ small cabbage)

1 cup (150 g) spiralized onion (about ½ small onion)

1 cup (120 g) spiralized apple (about 1 large apple)

Unsweetened nondairy yogurt or sour cream, for garnish

Preheat the oven to 425°F (218°C). Prepare 2 baking sheets by greasing heavily with olive oil. You will use 2 tablespoons (30 ml) per baking sheet.

Mix the flaxseed mixture, salt and pepper in a bowl. This is our egg substitute.

In a large mixing bowl, combine the potato, cabbage, onion and apple. I suggest getting in there and mixing with your hands. You want to make sure you get a bite of each one in your latkes.

Add the seasoned flax mixture and mix with a spoon until the flax coats everything. This will take a little longer than you think it should, but don't give up.

Place the greased sheet pans in the oven for 6 minutes to heat up the oil.

Carefully remove from the oven and remember they are hot while you are adding the latkes!

Scoop ¼ cup (60 g) of the latke mixture onto the hot baking pan (it may sizzle) and press down or shape using a wooden spoon. Repeat until all of the mixture is used. Using a potholder, put the baking sheets back in the oven.

Cook on one side for 15 minutes, then carefully take the baking sheets out and flip the latkes using a spatula. Bake again for 12 to 18 minutes. Serve with unsweetened nondairy yogurt or sour cream and enjoy!

*SEE PHOTO INSERT

Mashed Potato–Crusted BUTTERNUT SQUASH, BRUSSELS SPROUTS AND TOFU PIE

+GF

This fun pie is the perfect dish to bring along to a Thanksgiving gathering. Nestled on a crust of mashed potatoes is a creamy tofu filling studded with pieces of butternut squash and Brussels sprouts. It's a show stealer! —KH

SERVES 6

SQUASH

1½ cups (210 g) diced butternut squash

2 tsp (10 ml) olive oil (omit to make oil-free)

¼ tsp rubbed sage

⅛ tsp salt

⅛ tsp pepper

CRUST

2 cups (450 g) diced cooked Idaho potatoes, drained

2 tbsp (10 g) nutritional yeast

½ tsp salt

¼ tsp ground black pepper

A few tbsp (45 ml) water, if needed

BRUSSELS SPROUTS

1 tbsp (15 ml) olive oil (or dry sauté to make oil-free)

½ small onion, minced (about 35 g)

1½ cups (150 g) quartered and sliced Brussels sprouts

¼ tsp rubbed sage

TOFU FILLING

1 (12-oz [340-g]) package firm silken tofu

3 tbsp (25 g) chickpea flour

2 tbsp (30 ml) olive oil (or use water to make oil-free)

2 tbsp (10 g) nutritional yeast

1 tbsp (15 ml) water

FOR THE SQUASH

Preheat the oven to 350°F (177°C), line a small baking sheet with parchment paper and oil a 9-inch (23-cm) pie pan.

Toss the butternut squash with the olive oil (if using), sage, salt and pepper. Spread it onto the prepared baking sheet and cook 15 to 20 minutes or until soft. Stir at least once while cooking.

FOR THE CRUST

Mash the cooked potatoes, nutritional yeast, salt and pepper with a potato masher. If the potatoes are too dry, add water 1 tablespoon (15 ml) at a time until the mixture is creamy. Spread the mixture into your pie pan. Make the side walls of the crust fairly thick and bring them up to the top of the pan. Then use a spatula to even out the bottom of the crust.

Bake the crust for 30 to 35 minutes, until it just begins to brown. If the crust puffs up, you can just press it down with a spatula.

FOR THE BRUSSELS SPROUTS

Heat the olive oil in a medium skillet and sauté the onion until translucent. Then add the Brussels sprouts and sage and sauté for another 5 minutes, until the sprouts begin to soften. Set aside.

FOR THE TOFU FILLING

Add all of the tofu filling ingredients to your blender and blend until smooth. Spread the filling over the baked mashed potato crust.

Carefully mix the roasted butternut squash with the sautéed Brussels sprouts. Using a large spoon, evenly distribute the veggies on top of the tofu filling. Press the veggies into the filling just enough to keep them anchored. Bake for 35 to 40 minutes or until the tofu filling is set.

*SEE PHOTO INSERT

Vegan BUTTERNUT SQUASH OKRA GUMBO WITH BROWN RICE

This is a Cajun gumbo, so it does not contain any tomatoes. The roux is what thickens the gumbo and gives it a deeper flavor. Butternut squash isn't a traditional ingredient, but I think it works well. I used my homemade vegan andouille sausage recipe from my book, The Ultimate Vegan Cookbook for Your Instant Pot, *but you can sub your favorite store-bought sausage. —KH*

SERVES 8

ROUX
¼ cup (60 ml) avocado oil (or other mild oil)

1 cup (120 g) unbleached white flour (or you can use white whole wheat)

SAUTÉ
¾ cup (113 g) minced onion

¾ cup (131 g) minced bell pepper

2 tsp (6 g) minced garlic

1 tbsp (7 g) smoked paprika

1 tbsp (5 g) dried oregano

2 tsp (4 g) regular paprika

1½ tsp (2 g) dried thyme

1½ tsp (9 g) salt (or to taste)

1 tsp ground black pepper (or to taste)

½ tsp–1 tbsp (3–5 g) ground cayenne pepper, to taste

SIMMER
8 cups (1.9 L) water

3 cups (300 g) sliced okra

2 cups (280 g) cubed butternut squash

2 cups (460 g) chopped vegan andouille sausage or your favorite cooked beans

SERVING
About 4 cups (644 g) cooked brown rice (½ cup [80 g] per serving)

Tabasco, or other vinegar-based hot sauce

FOR THE ROUX
In a large soup pot over low heat, add the oil and flour; mix well. You will slowly toast this mixture. It will start out a pale white, and then after about 15 minutes, it will be a light brown. After 15 more, it will be more maple colored.

The most important thing is to not let this burn, so stir often throughout the roux cooking process. If you burn it, you must throw it out and start again. So go low and slow. Since this process takes about 30 minutes, I like to prep my veggies while this is cooking. Cut a little, stir the roux, cut some more, etc.

FOR THE SAUTÉ
Once the roux is a medium brown and begins to smell almost like toasted nuts, add the onion, bell pepper and garlic. Turn up the heat to medium-low; stir and sauté until the veggies begin to soften, about 10 minutes.

Add the herbs and spices. You can leave the salt, pepper and cayenne to add before serving if you want. Or start small and add more at the end if you're not sure how you like it yet.

FOR THE SIMMER
Add the water, okra, butternut squash and andouille (or beans). Cover and let it cook over medium-low heat until the okra and squash are soft, about 20 minutes.

Taste and reseason with salt, pepper and cayenne as needed. I make ours very mild since I'm the only one in my household who likes spicy food. I just add lots of hot sauce to my bowl.

FOR SERVING
Serve topped with rice and hot sauce on the side.

*SEE PHOTO INSERT

Butternut Squash
AND KALE LO MEIN
WITH CRISPY TOFU

This lo mein is easy to make and a perfect healthy recipe to welcome in fall. I love how the flavors of the ginger and soy sauce really elevate the butternut squash. —KH

SERVES 4

½ (13¼-oz [375-g]) box spaghetti

1 (16-oz [455-g]) block organic extra-firm tofu, cut into small rectangles

2 tbsp (20 g) plus 2 tsp (6 g) organic cornstarch or all-purpose flour, divided

2 tbsp (30 ml) avocado oil or other vegetable oil

1 cup (235 ml) vegetable broth or water, plus 1 vegetable bouillon cube

½ cup (120 ml) orange juice

¼ cup (60 ml) low-sodium soy sauce

2 tbsp (30 ml) rice wine vinegar

2 tbsp (12 g) grated fresh ginger

2 tsp (6 g) minced fresh garlic

¼ cup (38 g) minced onion

1 (8-oz [225-g]) package mushrooms, sliced

1 (10-oz [285-g]) package butternut squash, fresh or frozen, cut into cubes (about 2 cups [280 g])

2 cups (130 g) packed chopped kale, fresh or frozen

Preheat the oven 250°F (121°C). You will use this to keep the tofu warm later in the recipe.

Cook the pasta according to package directions.

Place the tofu and 2 tablespoons (20 g) of the cornstarch in a large bowl; toss to coat well. Set aside.

Heat the oil in a medium skillet over medium-high heat until hot. Add the tofu in a single layer. Cook for 5 to 8 minutes or until one side is golden brown; turn the tofu. Reduce the heat to medium and cook for 5 minutes or until the other side is golden brown. Drain the tofu on a paper towel–lined plate. Transfer to a baking sheet; place in the oven to keep warm.

Meanwhile, in a large bowl or large measuring cup, whisk together the broth, orange juice, soy sauce, vinegar, ginger and garlic; set aside.

Add the onion to the skillet that was used for the tofu. Cook for 3 to 4 minutes or until golden brown, stirring occasionally. Add your mushrooms, cooking 5 to 7 minutes more, or until they cook down and release their juices. Stir occasionally. Reserve ¼ cup (60 ml) of the sauce mixture. Add the remaining sauce mixture to the skillet, and then stir in the squash. Cook for 10 minutes, stirring occasionally.

Whisk the remaining 2 teaspoons (6 g) cornstarch into the reserved ¼ cup (60 ml) sauce. Add to the skillet along with the kale. (Other greens such as collards or spinach can be substituted for the kale.) Stir thoroughly to mix in the cornstarch. Increase the heat to medium-high and cook 3 to 5 minutes, or until the sauce thickens. Then remove it from the heat.

Add the pasta and toss to coat. Divide the pasta-vegetable mixture among 4 bowls. Top with crispy tofu.

*SEE PHOTO INSERT

Potato STUFFING BALLS WITH A CRANBERRY CENTER

+SF

These are great in a large size as a main course or a side. Make them small and you have a very interesting appetizer! Either way, serve with some vegan gravy. —KH

MAKES 10 LARGE PLUS 24 MINIS

1 (20-oz [567-g]) package gold potatoes
1 (10-oz [283-g]) package vegan stuffing (be sure to check ingredients!)
Water or vegetable broth for stuffing
¼ cup (60 ml) olive oil (optional)
½ cup (120 ml) unsweetened nondairy milk
1 tsp salt
1 tsp rubbed sage
½ tsp celery seeds
½ tsp dried rosemary
¼ tsp black pepper
1 cup (280 g) thick cranberry sauce
1–1½ cups (120–180 g) breadcrumbs
Vegan gravy, for serving

First put the potatoes in a soup pot and cover with water. Bring to a boil; lower the heat to medium and cook for 12 to 15 minutes, or until they are easily pierced with a fork. Drain and set aside to cool.

Follow the directions on your stuffing by boiling the amount of water or vegetable broth called for. Then remove it from the heat, stir in the dry stuffing and let it sit, covered, for about 10 minutes, or until it has absorbed all the liquid.

In a large mixing bowl, mash the potatoes as is, with the peels on. Mash with a potato masher, leaving only small pieces of potato. Note: You can add up to ¼ cup (60 ml) olive oil if you want. I decided the fat in the gravy was enough to carry the dish.

Stir in the milk, salt, sage, celery seeds, rosemary and pepper. Then stir the stuffing into the potato mixture. Preheat the oven to 350°F (177°C) and cover 2 large baking sheets with parchment paper.

Now we need to get some cranberry sauce inside the mixture piece by piece. For the large ones, I used ½ cup (105 g) potato stuffing mixture and 2 teaspoons (12 g) cranberry sauce. For the small ones, I used 1 tablespoon (13 g) potato stuffing mixture and ¼ teaspoon cranberry sauce.

First, I recommend that you use a scoop to get each one about the same size. Scoop all of the stuffing mixture piece by piece and sit them on parchment paper.

Next, flatten out one of the portions of stuffing you scooped out, make an indention with your thumb, and then fill the indention with cranberry sauce. Roll everything into a ball, roll it in the breadcrumbs and set it on the baking sheet.

Repeat until both sheets are full of ready-to-bake balls. Bake the large ones for about 20 minutes or until hot in the center; bake the small ones for about 12 minutes.

Serve large ones as a main over a bed of gravy with extra drizzled on top. Serve small ones as an appetizer with a bowl of gravy to dip in or on appetizer spoons in a pool of gravy.

Gluten-Free Vegan
TEFF STUFFING WITH ROASTED BUTTERNUT SQUASH AND CANDIED CRANBERRIES

+GF +SF

Whole teff cooks up close to a porridge, so you should be aware of that before you start this one. First, you cook it up, and then you add it to the sauté to dry it out a bit. This takes about 10 minutes, so don't be surprised. It's worth the effort. —KH

SERVES 4 TO 6

TEFF
1 cup (200 g) whole teff
3 cups (710 ml) water

ROASTED BUTTERNUT SQUASH
2 cups (280 g) cubed butternut squash
2 tsp (10 ml) mild oil, such as avocado or olive
¼ tsp powdered rosemary or 1 sprig fresh
Pinch of salt and pepper

CANDIED CRANBERRY
1 cup (100 g) fresh cranberries
1 cup (235 ml) water
2 tbsp (24 g) vegan sugar

SAUTÉ
1 tbsp (15 ml) olive oil (or water sauté to make oil-free)
1 small onion, minced (about 1 cup [200 g])
1 tsp salt
1 tsp minced garlic
2 cups (150 g) chopped mushrooms
2½ tsp (6 g) poultry seasoning
½ tsp celery seeds

Preheat the oven to 350°F (177°C) and oil a baking sheet.

FOR THE TEFF

Add the teff and water to a small saucepan. Cover it and bring to a boil over high heat. Once the boil begins, turn the heat to low and cook for 15 minutes. Stir the teff and remove from the heat. Note: This can be made a day or two in advance.

FOR THE SQUASH

Toss the butternut squash, oil, rosemary, salt and pepper all together in a mixing bowl. Spread everything out on your prepared baking sheet. Bake for 15 minutes. Stir the pieces around so they won't get burned and cook 10 minutes more, or until tender. Set aside for later. Note: This can be made a day or two in advance.

FOR THE CRANBERRIES

Place the cranberries, water and sugar into an uncovered small saucepan and bring just to a boil. Then turn it down to medium heat. Stir every few minutes until the cranberries begin to burst and most of the water has cooked off. Note: This can be made a day or two in advance.

FOR THE SAUTÉ

Heat the oil over medium-high heat in a large skillet (large enough to add all of the cooked teff in a later step). Once the oil is hot, add the onion and salt, and sauté until translucent. Next, add the garlic, mushrooms, poultry seasoning and celery seeds. Sauté until the mushrooms cook down, about 10 minutes.

To prepare your stuffing, turn the heat to medium and add the cooked teff in large spoonfuls to the sauté pan. Repeat until all of the teff is mixed in. It will be sticky, but as you cook it this time, it will dry out a little bit. Chop the mixture up continuously with a large spatula.

If your teff seems like it's not drying at all, you can spread the mixture in a thin layer and flip pieces as they cook on one side. Be careful not to burn anything; you only want it just dry enough to mix with the sauté ingredients.

Once the sauté is well mixed and looks like dressing, chop it up with your spatula one last time and put it into a large serving bowl. Level off the top with the back of your spatula.

Place the roasted squash on the flattened top you just made and put the cranberries on top of the squash.

*SEE PHOTO INSERT

Tofu KATSU ✱

+GFO

This simple Japanese dish satisfies those crunchy cravings. Firm tofu coated in panko breadcrumbs and cooked until crispy is drizzled with a sweet and savory sauce. You could also add some steamed veggies to round out the meal. —KH

SERVES 4

TOFU
½ cup (60 g) whole wheat flour

½ cup (60 g) panko breadcrumbs (or use gluten-free baking blend)

½ cup (120 ml) warm water

2 tbsp (13 g) ground flaxseed

1 (16-oz [454-g]) block super-firm tofu (or regular firm tofu, pressed)

SAUCE
¼ cup (65 g) tomato paste

¼ cup (60 ml) maple syrup or agave nectar

¼ cup (60 ml) soy sauce

¼ cup (60 ml) rice vinegar

1 tsp molasses

1 tsp grated ginger

¼ tsp garlic powder

⅛ tsp onion powder

4 cups (645 g) steamed brown rice, for serving

Preheat the oven to 350°F (177°C) and prepare a baking sheet with parchment paper.

FOR THE TOFU
Place the wheat flour in one shallow bowl and the panko in another; then mix the warm water and ground flaxseed in a third shallow bowl.

Cut the tofu into 4 pieces lengthwise, and then in half to make 8 pieces. Take one slice of tofu, dip it in the flour on all sides, and then quickly dunk it into the flax mixture. Finally, coat the tofu in the panko. Place on the prepared baking sheet and repeat for all the tofu pieces.

Bake for 15 minutes; then flip and bake 15 more minutes until crispy.

FOR THE SAUCE
In the meantime, mix all of the sauce ingredients together in a 2-cup (473-ml) measuring cup or small bowl and whisk until well combined.

Serve the baked tofu over steamed rice and drizzle with the sauce.

Tofu RICOTTA WHITE PIZZA

Before I went vegan, I loved white pizza. A rich garlic sauce dotted with creamy ricotta cheese. For this vegan version, we make a ricotta from cashews and tofu. The sauce is full of garlic, and I like it best with roasted garlic. There's a recipe for pizza dough, but you can use store-bought dough if you want to save some time. —KH

MAKES 2 PIZZAS

DOUGH
1 cup (237 ml) warm water

½ tbsp (6 g) sugar, agave or maple syrup

½ tbsp (4 g) baking yeast

1 tbsp (15 ml) aquafaba (liquid from a can of chickpeas)

1½ cups (180 g) whole wheat flour

1 cup (125 g) white whole wheat flour, or use more regular whole wheat flour

1 tsp salt

TOFU RICOTTA
¾ cup (180 ml) unsweetened plain nondairy milk

⅓ cup (35 g) soaked cashews, drained

1 tbsp (5 g) nutritional yeast

1 tbsp (18 g) yellow miso

½ (16-oz [454-g]) block firm tofu

Salt, to taste

GARLIC SAUCE
2 tbsp (30 ml) olive oil

3 cloves roasted garlic or 1 tsp fresh minced garlic

¼ tsp salt

OPTIONAL PIZZA TOPPINGS
Artichoke hearts

Spinach or kale

Fresh basil

Sun-dried tomatoes

Red pizza sauce

FOR THE DOUGH

To the bowl of your mixer, add the warm water, sugar and yeast. Let it sit for 10 minutes, or until it begins to foam. If your yeast doesn't foam at all, it may be out of date and won't cause your dough to rise.

Once foamy, add the aquafaba (or use oil if you don't have any) and mix.

In a mixing bowl, combine the flours and salt; mix well. Add the flour 1 cup (125 g) at a time to the yeast mixture in the mixer. Mix using the paddle attachment until the dough begins to get too thick, and then change to the dough hook.

Finish adding the flour mixture until the dough is no longer sticky but not too dry. Knead for 10 minutes. Shape your dough into 2 pizza-shaped pieces as thin or thick as you like your pizza base. Just know you will cook it for less time if it's very thin or extra time if it's thick.

FOR THE TOFU RICOTTA

To your blender, add the nondairy milk, soaked cashews, nutritional yeast and yellow miso, and blend until creamy smooth. Crumble the tofu and add it to the blender. You don't want to blend it completely smooth, but kind of pulse until it looks like small lumps that are reminiscent of regular ricotta. Add salt to taste.

FOR THE GARLIC SAUCE

Mix all of the sauce ingredients in a small bowl. If you are using roasted garlic, mash the cloves so they incorporate into the sauce well.

Preheat the oven to 425°F (218°C). Place the shaped pizza dough on an oiled sheet pan or pizza stone. Spread the sauce over the top of the dough and drop spoonfuls of the ricotta onto the dough. Add any optional toppings and drizzle with red sauce if you like.

Bake for 8 to 15 minutes, depending on the thickness of the dough. I recommend checking at 8 minutes and cooking more if needed.

Rosemary ALFREDO PASTA ✳

+GFO +SF

This rich, creamy sauce is so easy that you could have Alfredo every night if you wanted to. It's the mixture of cauliflower and cashews that makes it thick and silky. —KH

SERVES 4

2 cups (214 g) small cauliflower florets
¼ cup (28 g) cashews
¾ cup (177 ml) water
2 tbsp (10 g) nutritional yeast
½ tsp granulated garlic
½ tsp salt
¼–½ tsp ground dried rosemary, to taste
4 servings cooked pasta (or use gluten-free pasta)
Fresh rosemary, for garnish (optional)

Steam the cauliflower and cashews on the stove until the cauliflower is just fork tender. You can also use your Instant Pot, cooking on high pressure for 5 minutes in a steamer over 1 cup (237 ml) water and releasing the pressure manually.

Transfer the cooked cauliflower and cashews to your blender and add the water, nutritional yeast, garlic, salt and dried rosemary. Blend until smooth.

Toss the sauce with warm pasta and serve. Garnish with fresh rosemary if you like.

Easy STUFFED RAVIOLI (USING WONTON WRAPPERS) ✳

+SF

Once you find vegan wonton wrappers, a whole world of shortcuts opens up to you. Most store-bought ravioli have egg in the dough. Using wonton wrappers makes short work of this. —KH

MAKES 18 RAVIOLIS

RAVIOLI FILLING
¾ cup (135 g) pumpkin purée
½ cup (60 g) breadcrumbs
2 tsp (9 g or 10 ml) brown sugar or maple syrup
¼ tsp ground cinnamon
¼ tsp salt
⅛ tsp ground nutmeg
⅛ tsp ground rosemary

1 (12-oz [340-g]) package square vegan wonton wrappers

SERVING
¼ cup (60 ml) olive oil or melted vegan butter
Chopped fresh rosemary or poultry seasoning

Mix all of the filling ingredients together in a medium mixing bowl.

Set up a cutting board for making the raviolis. Keep a small bowl of warm water to the side. Lay out 4 to 6 of the wontons on the cutting board and place a tablespoon (15 g) of the filling in the middle.

(continued)

MAIN DISHES

Dip your finger into the water and wet all the areas around the filling. Place a new wonton on top of that and press the edges together to seal them. I like to pick up the half with the filling in one hand and set the other wonton on top of it. The edges will not be even at this point, so don't worry about it. Repeat until all of the filling is used.

Use a ravioli cutter or knife and cut the uneven parts off, leaving as much wonton on as you can.

Bring a pot of water to a boil and cook 4 to 6 ravioli at a time for 3 to 4 minutes. Remove them from the water with a slotted spoon.

Drizzle the ravioli with olive oil or melted vegan butter, and garnish with a sprinkle of chopped fresh rosemary or poultry seasoning mix.

Roasted SHEET PAN TERIYAKI

+GF +SFO

Stir-fries are an easy weeknight meal, but making this teriyaki in the oven on a sheet pan means you can relax while it's cooking. Plus you'll still have dinner on the table in under an hour! —KH

SERVES 4

HOMEMADE TERIYAKI SAUCE

1 cup (200 g) brown sugar

1 cup (240 ml) water

½ cup (120 ml) soy sauce (or use gluten-free soy sauce or coconut aminos)

¼ cup (60 ml) rice vinegar

3 tbsp (19 g) grated ginger

1 tbsp (10 g) minced garlic

2 tbsp (16 g) cornstarch mixed with ½ cup (120 ml) water

VEGGIES

2 cups (250 g) carrot coins

1 (16-oz [454-g]) package extra-firm tofu (or firm tofu, pressed), or use hemp tempeh

2 cups (144 g) broccoli florets

2 cups (480 ml) teriyaki sauce, store-bought or homemade

4 cups (644 g) cooked brown rice, for serving

FOR THE HOMEMADE TERIYAKI SAUCE (OPTIONAL IF YOU USE STORE-BOUGHT SAUCE)

Place all of the ingredients in a medium saucepan and bring to a boil over high heat. Then turn the heat to medium-low and simmer until the sauce begins to thicken and reduces by about a third.

FOR THE VEGGIES

Preheat the oven to 400°F (204°C) and oil a full sheet pan. Arrange the carrots and tofu on either end in a single layer with the broccoli in between the two.

Drizzle the teriyaki sauce over the veggies and tofu on the sheet pan. Place in the oven and cook for 15 minutes. Take the sheet pan out of the oven; flip the tofu and mix the veggies. Cook for 10 to 15 minutes more, until the veggies are tender. Serve atop steamed brown rice.

Full of Veggies BAKED ZITI

+GFO +SF

I love making this ziti in the fall when there's a chill in the air. You can even cook the pasta and prepare the veggies ahead of time. Just throw it all together and let it cook while you enjoy a book by the fire. —KH

SERVES 6

1 (16-oz [454-g]) box whole wheat ziti (or use gluten-free pasta)

3 cups (720 ml) pasta sauce (store-bought or homemade)

2 cups (214 g) grated cauliflower

1 cup (75 g) minced mushrooms

1 cup (100 g) minced or grated carrot

¼ cup (20 g) nutritional yeast

Preheat the oven to 350°F (177°C). Cook the pasta according to package directions. Drain it and set aside.

In a large bowl, mix the cooked pasta, sauce, cauliflower, mushrooms, carrots and nutritional yeast. Transfer the mixture to a large oven-safe casserole dish and cover with foil.

Bake for 1 hour and 15 minutes, or until the veggies are tender.

Note: In your food processor, use the grating blade to process the cauliflower. Use the S-blade for the coarsely chopped mushrooms and carrots, pulsing until they are minced.

Autumn QUINOA BOWLS with ROASTED VEGGIES

+GF +SFO

Cook up some quinoa while the veggies roast in the oven to make this simple but delicious meal that is full of flavor. To make it even faster, prep the veggies the day before. —KH

SERVES 2

2 cups (280 g) cubed butternut squash

6 tsp (30 ml) olive oil, divided

½ tsp ground rosemary

½ tsp salt, divided

2 cups (200 g) halved Brussels sprouts

½ tsp dried thyme

2 cups (150 g) sliced mushrooms

2 tsp (10 ml) vegan Worcestershire sauce

2 tsp (10 ml) soy sauce (or use coconut aminos for soy-free or gluten-free)

½ tsp minced garlic

2 cups (370 g) cooked quinoa

Preheat the oven to 400°F (204°C). Prepare a baking sheet by spraying it with oil or using parchment paper.

Toss the butternut squash with a third of the olive oil, rosemary and ¼ teaspoon of the salt. Then spread the squash on one-third of the baking sheet toward one end.

Toss the Brussels sprouts with another third of the olive oil, dried thyme and the remaining ¼ teaspoon salt. Then spread the sprouts on one-third of the baking sheet toward the other end.

Toss the mushrooms with the remaining olive oil, vegan Worcestershire sauce, soy sauce and garlic. Spread them on the middle part of the baking sheet.

Bake for 20 to 30 minutes or until the veggies are tender. Serve over cooked quinoa.

Texas BBQ TEMPEH ENCHILADAS ✗

+GF

With layers of sauce, corn tortillas, crumbled spiced tempeh and a surprise middle of mashed green chile potatoes, this casserole is a fusion of enchilada and BBQ flavors. —KH

SERVES 6

TEMPEH

1 (8-oz [227-g]) package tempeh, cut into cubes and steamed for 10 minutes

1 tbsp (15 ml) olive oil

1 cup (150 g) minced onion

½ cup (90 g) minced green pepper

1 tsp minced garlic

1½ tsp (3 g) smoked paprika

1½ tsp (4 g) chile powder (or guajillo powder if you can find it)

1 tsp ground cumin

Salt, to taste

MASHED POTATO

3 medium (519 g) potatoes, peeled and cut into small cubes

¼ cup (60 ml) potato cooking water, or more as needed

2 tbsp (5 g) green chiles

Salt, to taste

SAUCE

2 cups (450 g) tomato purée

½ cup (120 ml) vegan BBQ sauce

1 package corn tortillas (you will not use the whole pack)

Preheat the oven to 350°F (177°C).

FOR THE TEMPEH

While the tempeh is steaming, heat the oil in a large sauté pan over medium-high heat. Once hot, add the onion and cook until translucent, about 10 minutes. Add the green pepper and garlic, and cook until the pepper begins to soften, about 5 minutes. Add the smoked paprika, chile powder and cumin, and sauté for a minute until they become more fragrant.

By now, the tempeh is finished steaming. Add it to the sauté pan, break it up into tiny pieces with your spatula and cook until the tempeh is browned. Add salt to taste.

FOR THE MASHED POTATO

Cook the potatoes in boiling water until tender, about 10 minutes. Remove them with a slotted spoon and mash in a bowl with the water and green chiles. If the potatoes are still dry, you can use more cooking water. Add salt to taste.

FOR THE SAUCE

Mix all of the sauce ingredients together in a bowl.

Oil a 9 x 13-inch (23 x 33-cm) casserole dish. Spread ½ cup (120 ml) sauce over the bottom and top with corn tortillas. You can cut them in half if that makes them fit more easily. Add half the tempeh mixture, another layer of tortillas, ½ cup (120 ml) of sauce, all of the mashed potatoes and another layer of tortillas. Finish up with the last of the tempeh mixture, another layer of tortillas and the rest of the sauce.

Cover the dish with foil and place on a baking sheet. Bake for 45 minutes.

Vegan RAREBIT OVER TOAST

+GFO +SF

If you haven't heard of rarebit, it's a cheese sauce that has hints of mustard and Worcestershire sauce. We get the thickness in this vegan version from a purée of soaked cashews and lightly steamed cauliflower. It gets its tang from dry mustard powder and vegan Worcestershire sauce. Serve over toast for a comforting meal. —KH

SERVES 4

1 cup (110 g) cauliflower florets
⅓ cup (35 g) cashews
¾ cup (180 ml) water
3 tbsp (15 g) nutritional yeast
2 tsp (10 ml) vegan Worcestershire sauce
Salt, to taste
8 pieces of toast (or use gluten-free bread)

Steam the cauliflower and cashews on the stove until the cauliflower is just fork tender. Or use your Instant Pot: cook on high pressure for 5 minutes in a steamer over 1 cup (235 ml) of water and release the pressure manually.

Transfer the cooked cauliflower and cashews to your blender and add the water, nutritional yeast and Worcestershire sauce, blending until smooth. Then add salt to taste and blend again.

You can either warm up the sauce on the stove, or if you have a high-speed blender, you can blend until warm. Then serve over toast.

Vietnamese TOFU BUN

+GFO

I've always found that this bun doesn't come on a roll but instead is a rice noodle base. Traditionally the dressing is fish sauce, but this vegan version will hit the spot just as well. This is my favorite summer lunch. I make everything in the days before and eat it straight from the fridge! —KH

SERVES 4

MARINADE
¼ cup (60 ml) water
2 tbsp (30 ml) soy sauce (use gluten-free or coconut aminos to make gluten-free)
2 tbsp (25 g) brown or coconut sugar
2 tbsp (30 ml) lime juice
½ tsp minced garlic

1 (16-oz [454-g]) block super-firm tofu (or regular firm tofu, pressed), cut into 16 pieces

BOWL BASE
1 (8-oz [227-g]) package thin brown rice (mai fun) noodles (can use white also)
1 cup (80 g) shredded lettuce
1 cup (125 g) shredded carrot
1 cup (104 g) chopped cucumber
1 cup (100 g) bean sprouts

SAUCE
¼ cup (60 ml) water
¼ cup (60 ml) soy sauce (use gluten-free or coconut aminos to make gluten-free)
3 tbsp (38 g) brown or coconut sugar
2 tbsp (30 ml) rice vinegar
2 tbsp (30 ml) lime juice
½ tsp sriracha (optional)

(continued)

MAIN DISHES

FOR THE MARINADE

Combine the marinade ingredients in a sealable container and mix well. Add the tofu and marinate for 2 to 24 hours.

FOR THE BOWL BASE

Cook the rice noodles according to the package directions and prep the veggies. You can do this up to a day in advance to make it easy the day you're serving it.

FOR THE SAUCE

Mix all the sauce ingredients together and store in the fridge until ready to use.

Right before serving, heat a large sauté pan over medium-high heat, and once hot, add the marinated tofu. Cook on one side until it browns, about 5 to 10 minutes, then flip and brown the other side.

Assemble by putting a quarter of the lettuce into each bowl, a quarter of the cold noodles, and topping with the carrots and cucumbers. Then place the warm, cooked tofu with bean sprouts on top. Serve the sauce on the side, and let each person put as much or as little on as they want.

Tofu BANH MI WITH LEMONGRASS

Right down the street from Alex's apartment there is the most amazing little banh mi shop. The week after she moved in, we began indulging in these tofu banh mi sandwiches. However, eating these sandwiches too often can leave a dent in your wallet and cause your waistband to grow! But seriously, we've made a healthier version of this amazing sandwich that you can enjoy any day of the week. —LM + AM

SERVES 2

1 baguette, cut in half and sliced down the middle

1 tsp avocado oil

1 (14-oz [397-g]) package extra-firm tofu, pressed to remove excess water

Soy sauce, to taste

1 cucumber, thinly sliced into vertical strips

1 carrot, cut into thin matchsticks

1 jalapeño, seeded and cut into circles

1 piece lemongrass, smash and remove outer peels and 1" (2.5 cm) off the end, finely diced

Drizzle of balsamic vinegar

Juice of 1 lime, or to taste

1 cup (40 g) fresh cilantro

Preheat the oven to 350°F (177°C). Warm the baguette in the oven for 10 minutes.

Heat the oil in a medium skillet over medium-high heat. Lightly brown the tofu on both sides. This should take about 1 minute per side. Once browned, remove the tofu from the pan and cool on a plate.

Drizzle some soy sauce on the bread. Layer the cucumber, carrot, jalapeño and lemongrass in the baguette. Add the tofu. Drizzle with balsamic vinegar and lime juice. Top the sandwich with cilantro sprigs.

*SEE PHOTO INSERT

Vegan SLOPPY JOE

+GFO +SFO

Both of us remember growing up with sloppy joes on the dinner menu pretty often. However, looking back, these definitely weren't the healthiest options. We've turned these meat-driven sandwiches into plant-based bites of heaven. With a combination of cauliflower and Beyond Meat beefy crumbles, this sandwich is both filling and healthy. —LM + AM

SERVES 6

1 head cauliflower

2 tsp (10 ml) avocado oil

1 onion, minced

2 cloves garlic, minced

26 oz (900 ml) strained tomatoes

1 tbsp (16 g) tomato paste

2½ tsp (2 g) Italian seasoning

¼ tsp chili powder

1 tsp liquid smoke

¾ tsp celery salt

3 tbsp (45 ml) maple syrup

1 (11-oz [312-g]) package beef substitute, such as Beyond Meat beefy crumbles (gluten and soy-free)

6 hamburger buns (or gluten-free buns)

Place a steamer basket in a pot. Fill the pot with water until it just touches the basket. Bring the water to a boil. Put the cauliflower in and cover with a lid. Steam the cauliflower for 15 minutes, or until the cauliflower is easily pierced with a fork. Let the cauliflower cool. When the cauliflower is cool enough to handle, finely chop it.

In a large skillet, heat the oil over medium heat and spread evenly throughout the pan. Add the onion and cook until soft and transparent, about 5 minutes. Stir often. Add the garlic and cook for 2 minutes.

Add the strained tomatoes, tomato paste, seasonings and maple syrup to the pan and bring to a boil. Reduce the heat to medium-low, add the cauliflower and stir frequently until the mixture is reduced and thick. Add the beef substitute and stir to combine well. Cook for 3 minutes.

Serve on toasted buns.

Pulled CARROT BBQ

+GFO +SF

Our Pulled Carrot BBQ is definitely one of the most popular recipes on our site and among our friends and family. Every time there's a potluck or dinner party, we inevitably get a request to bring our pulled carrots. We can't blame them for craving these either. Who wouldn't love roasted carrots, onion and garlic smothered in BBQ sauce? —LM + AM

SERVES 4

5 large carrots

1 large red onion

½ tsp olive oil

Sea salt and black pepper, to taste

SAUCE

1 cup (236 ml) tomato sauce

3 cloves garlic

¼ cup (60 ml) apple cider vinegar

1 tbsp (22 g) dark molasses (or gluten-free molasses)

¼ cup (50 g) brown sugar

1 tsp salt

1 tsp paprika

1 tsp onion powder

¼ tsp ground cumin

¼ tsp cayenne pepper

¼ tsp white pepper

(continued)

1 tbsp (15 ml) lime juice

1 chipotle pepper (from can of peppers in adobo sauce)

1 tsp olive oil

1 tbsp (3 g) cilantro

4 hamburger buns, to serve (or gluten-free buns)

Shredded cabbage, for topping

Preheat the oven to 375°F (190°C) and line a baking sheet with parchment paper. If you don't have parchment paper, you can line the baking sheet with lightly oiled aluminum foil or lightly grease the bottom of the pan to avoid sticking.

Shred the carrots with the shredder attachment of your food processor or with a box grater.

Thinly slice the onion. Put the carrots and onion in the baking pan and drizzle the olive oil over them. Toss well to coat and then spread the carrots and onions evenly in the pan. Sprinkle fine sea salt and pepper evenly over the top. Cover the pan with aluminum foil and roast for 20 minutes. Shake the pan every 10 minutes to ensure even roasting. After the 20 minutes, remove the aluminum foil and roast for 10 more minutes. The carrots and onions should be soft and lightly caramelized.

FOR THE SAUCE

While the carrots and onions are roasting, make the sauce. Add all of the sauce ingredients to a blender, and blend until fully combined and smooth. Pour it into a medium saucepan and bring it to a boil. Reduce to a low simmer and cook for 20 minutes, stirring occasionally to avoid scorching the sauce.

Add the roasted carrots and onions to the sauce and stir well to coat. Simmer for 15 minutes.

Pile the pulled carrots on a bun and top with the shredded cabbage to serve.

*SEE PHOTO INSERT

Edamame RICE BURGERS

+GFO +SFO

What do you do when you have a couple of cups of leftover edamame? You make the most beautiful green burger ever!

This burger is a great way to get your veggie haters to eat their greens. There's spinach hidden in every patty, and it's flavored with warm and earthy cumin and turmeric. There's also a little paprika and oregano to round out the flavor profile, as well as a slight bit of heat from the cayenne pepper. Try it—you'll love it! —LM + AM

SERVES 4

1 cup (213 g) uncooked jasmine rice

2 tbsp (14 g) ground flaxseed

6 tbsp (90 ml) water

2 cups (300 g) edamame

2 cups (60 g) chopped spinach

1 clove garlic, minced

1 tsp ground cumin

1 tsp smoked paprika

1 tsp ground turmeric

½ tsp dried oregano

¼ tsp cayenne pepper (optional, add only if you like spicy food)

Fine sea salt and ground black pepper, to taste

1 tsp avocado oil (optional)

4 hamburger buns (or gluten-free buns)

TOPPINGS

Lettuce

Tomato slices

Spinach

Sriracha

Soy sauce (or use liquid aminos for gluten-free)

Cook the rice according to the instructions on the package. Set aside.

In a small bowl, mix the flaxseed and water and stir until the mixture becomes thick and sticky. Let sit for 10 minutes. This is an egg substitute known as a "flax egg."

Bring a medium pot of water to a boil and add the edamame. Boil for 5 minutes, drain the water and rinse with cold water. When the edamame is cool enough to touch, remove the beans from the pods and place them in a bowl.

Add the edamame beans to a food processor and process until it looks like tiny pebbles. Add the spinach, rice, flax egg, garlic, cumin, paprika, turmeric, oregano, cayenne (if using), sea salt and pepper to a food processor, and process until the mixture starts to form a ball.

Divide into 4 portions and roll each piece into a ball to form into patties.

Heat a large skillet over medium heat and drizzle with the avocado oil (optional if you have a nonstick pan). When the oil is hot, add the edamame burgers and cook for 8 minutes, or until firm and browned. Flip and cook the other side for 8 minutes. You can also bake in a 375°F (190°C) oven for 15 to 20 minutes, or until they begin to brown on top.

Serve on a bun with lettuce and tomato and your favorite condiments. Or serve the patty on a bed of spinach with a drizzle of sriracha, or serve as a patty and dip in soy sauce.

Spinach and Sweet Potato PANINIS ✗

+SF +SE +GFO

Paninis are generally not the healthiest sandwiches. Ours is the exception. We filled these with antioxidant-rich spinach and sweet potato, fresh basil, red onion and a sprinkle of curry and cumin. We like to use our Rosemary Focaccia Bread (page 173), but you can use any type of bread you like. —LM + AM

SERVES 3

2 tsp (10 ml) extra-virgin olive oil, divided

1 red onion, thinly sliced

2 cups (120 g) baby spinach

1 large sweet potato, baked

1 tsp curry powder

1 tsp ground cumin

¼ tsp ground cinnamon

Salt and pepper, to taste

6 slices Rosemary Focaccia Bread (page 173) or your bread of choice (or gluten-free bread)

1 cup (25 g) basil leaves

In a medium skillet, heat 1 teaspoon of the olive oil over medium-high heat. Add the onion and cook for about 15 minutes, or until it begins to caramelize. Stir frequently. Add the spinach and cook until it wilts, about 2 minutes.

In a small bowl, scrape the baked sweet potato from its peel and add the curry, cumin, cinnamon and salt and pepper. Stir until completely combined.

(continued)

MAIN DISHES

Brush the remaining 1 teaspoon oil on the crust side of the bread and spread a third of the potato mixture on the bottom piece of bread. Add a third of the spinach mixture, and sprinkle with one-third of the basil. Top with the second piece of bread and press in a panini maker according to the instructions.

If you don't have a panini maker, cook on a grill pan and press with a heavy pan to make the marks. You can also cook it in a covered skillet for about 5 minutes per side.

Vegan CROQUE MONSIEUR

For those of you who've had the pleasure of traveling to France, you might know that the croque monsieur is a staple of French cafe cuisine. From the description of this ham and cheese, you might not give this decadent sandwich a shot. That would be a huge mistake. Our veggie version of the croque monsieur keeps the classic recipe but veganizes the béchamel sauce and assorted cheeses while topping it off with some vegan ham. —LM + AM

SERVES 2

1 cup (236 ml) plain unsweetened almond milk

2 tbsp (30 g) vegan butter

2 tbsp (16 g) flour

Salt and pepper, to taste

4 pieces of French peasant bread

2 slices vegan ham

2 slices vegan cheese

2 tbsp (10 g) vegan Parmesan

Preheat the oven to 425°F (218°C) and line a baking sheet with parchment paper.

Heat the almond milk in the microwave for 1 minute.

Begin your béchamel sauce by melting butter in a small saucepan over medium-low heat. Once the butter is completely melted, whisk in the flour. Allow the flour and butter mixture to bubble for 2 minutes. When the 2 minutes are up, immediately whisk in the heated almond milk, salt and pepper. Bring the sauce to a boil and constantly stir for 3 minutes. After the 3 minutes, remove the sauce from the heat and set aside.

To assemble the sandwiches, put 4 slices of bread on the parchment-lined baking sheet. Pour half of the béchamel sauce over 2 of the pieces of bread, allowing it to flow over the sides. On top of the sauce, layer a piece of vegan ham, a piece of cheese and a sprinkle of Parmesan. Place the last 2 pieces of bread on top and pour over the rest of the béchamel sauce. Top each sandwich with one more piece of cheese and sprinkle more Parmesan on top.

Bake the croque monsieurs for 6 to 8 minutes; then remove from the oven and serve.

LEMON and THREE-HERB RISOTTO

+GF +SF

We can't even tell you the amount of times we've made this for friends and family where it has been met with rave reviews. This creamy risotto is the perfect way to impress a large party. Bonus: it doesn't dirty up that many dishes, so you'll get to spend more time with your guests than your dishwasher! —LM + AM

SERVES 4

1 cup (112 g) raw cashews

1 tbsp (3 g) coarsely chopped fresh sage

2 tbsp (5 g) coarsely chopped fresh basil

1 tbsp (5 g) nutritional yeast (not to be confused with brewer's or active dry yeast)

¼ cup (60 ml) fresh squeezed lemon juice

⅓ cup (80 ml) unsweetened cashew or almond milk

1 tsp fine sea salt

Black pepper, to taste

4 cups (960 ml) vegetable broth

1 tbsp (15 ml) extra-virgin olive oil

2 cloves garlic, minced

1 cup (200 g) uncooked Arborio rice

1 cup (240 ml) white wine

Soak the cashews in boiling water to cover for at least 4 hours, or until they turn puffy and soft.

Drain and rinse the cashews. Put the cashews in a high-speed blender. Add the fresh herbs, nutritional yeast, lemon juice, plant milk, salt and pepper. Blend the mixture on high for about 2 minutes, or until you get a smooth and creamy sauce.

In a medium saucepan, bring the vegetable broth to a boil and then reduce to a low simmer.

In a large risotto pan or saucepan, heat the oil over medium heat. Add the garlic and cook for 1 minute. Then add the rice and stir to coat it in the oil, cooking for 1 minute more while stirring constantly. Add 1 cup (240 ml) of broth and reduce the heat to low, stirring constantly. Continue to add ½ cup (120 ml) of the broth at a time as the previous broth is absorbed. Stir constantly to avoid scorching. By the time you've added all of the broth, the rice shou have tripled in size. Add the wine and stir cons until it soaks into the rice. After the wine is absc into the rice, add the cream sauce.

Stir the risotto until the cream sauce is spre throughout the rice. Cook for a few more minutes allow the sauce to warm through. Serve immediately

Vegan PESTO AND PORTOBELLO FLATBREAD PIZZA

+SF

Take a bite into this pesto and portobello flatbread and you're instantly transported to Italy. The combination of the freshness of the pesto and the earthiness of the mushrooms perfectly complement each other in this savory dish. —LM + AM

SERVES 4

1 tbsp (15 ml) extra-virgin olive oil

24 oz (680 g) sliced portobello mushrooms

3 cloves garlic, minced

Salt and pepper, to taste

1 recipe Yeast-Free Garlic Flatbread, homemade (page 174) or store-bought

1 cup (220 g) pesto, homemade (page 419) or store-bought

½ cup (21 g) fresh basil, minced

Heat the olive oil in a large skill heat. Once the oi the sl

½ tsp
2 tsp (10
1 tsp avoca
1 medium onio
1 red bell pepper,
1½ cups (354 ml) v
1 cup (210 g) quick-coo
3 cups (90 g) baby spina

TOPPINGS
Lime wedges
Cilantro

Assemble the flatbread while the oven is heating up. Take your flatbread and place it on a baking sheet. Spread a thin layer of the pesto on top of the flatbread. Layer the mushrooms over the pesto. Once the oven is heated, put the flatbread in the oven and bake for 10 minutes.

Remove the flatbread from the oven and sprinkle with the basil.

Veggie-Loaded
BLACK BEANS AND RICE

+GF +SF

Something we love about beans and rice is that it can be such a versatile base. You can pretty much add any spice blend to beans and rice and you get to transport your taste buds to a completely different part of the world. So, take your cuisine to the south of the border with this beans and rice dish. —LM + AM

SERVES 4

1 (15-oz [425-g]) can black beans, drained and rinsed

1 tbsp (8 g) plus 1 tsp chili powder, divided

1½ tsp (3 g) ground cumin, divided

sp ground turmeric

ground black pepper

g) sea salt

do oil

n, chopped

seeded and chopped

getable broth

king brown rice

h

Drain and rinse the black beans. Place them in a medium saucepan and add water until the beans are just submerged. Bring the pot to a boil over high heat. Once the water is boiling, reduce the heat to a simmer.

Add 1 tablespoon (8 g) of the chili powder, 1 teaspoon of the cumin, turmeric and ground pepper to the beans. Stir the spices into the beans until well incorporated. Simmer the beans for another 20 minutes, stirring occasionally to prevent the beans from sticking to the bottom of the pan. Stir in the sea salt at the end of the cooking time.

In a large skillet with a lid, heat the oil over medium heat. Once the oil is hot, add the onion and bell pepper. Sauté the onions and peppers until they are tender, approximately 5 minutes, then pour the vegetable broth over them and bring to a boil.

When the broth begins to boil, stir in the rice and cover the pan. Reduce the heat to a simmer and cook for 20 minutes or according to instructions on the package.

When the time is up, remove the lid and add the spinach. Put the lid back on and allow the spinach to wilt for 5 minutes.

Transfer the beans to the vegetables and rice using a slotted spoon. Sprinkle on the remaining 1 teaspoon chili powder and ½ teaspoon cumin. Fold the beans and spices into the rice and veggies until the mixture is well combined.

Serve this dish with lime wedges and a sprinkle of cilantro.

Smoky SOUTHERN-STYLE MEATLESS MEATLOAF

+GF

For those of you who don't know, my grandmother, Linda's mom, is from the south. Because of that, my mom grew up with a lot of southern cooking, as did I. So, we can't help but introduce you all to our smoky southern-style meat loaf. It's tangy, slightly spicy and has the best hint of smoke in the aftertaste. —LM + AM

MAKES 1 (9-INCH [23-CM]) LOAF

1 (15-oz [425-g]) can chickpeas, liquid reserved, drained and rinsed

2 (15-oz [425-g]) cans black beans, drained and rinsed

1 cup (82 g) rolled oats

1 cup (160 g) cornmeal

3 tbsp (45 ml) liquid smoke

½ cup (118 ml) aquafaba (reserved chickpea liquid)

2 tsp (10 ml) olive oil

1 large yellow onion, chopped

1 tbsp (3 g) dried Italian seasoning

2 tsp (10 g) fine sea salt

1 tsp ground black pepper

2 tbsp (30 ml) vegan Worcestershire sauce

½ cup (118 ml) vegetable broth

⅓ cup (83 g) ketchup

1 cup (245 g) BBQ sauce

Preheat the oven to 350°F (177°C) and line a 9 x 5 x 3-inch (23 x 13 x 8-cm) loaf pan with parchment paper.

Blend the chickpeas in the food processor until smooth and creamy. Remove the chickpeas from the food processor and place in a large bowl.

Place 1 can (half) of the black beans in the food processor and blend until creamy. Put those black beans in the same bowl as the chickpeas.

Put the second can of beans in the food processor and pulse until the black beans turn into small pieces. Don't over-pulse. These beans should be broken down into small bits, not creamy. Toss those beans in the large bowl with the other beans.

One last time, take your food processor and add the oats. Grind the oats in the food processor until the oats turn into a coarse flour. Add the oats to the bowl with the beans.

Add the cornmeal, liquid smoke and aquafaba to the beans and mix with your hands until the ingredients are well combined.

Heat the oil in a large skillet over medium heat. Once the oil is hot, add the onion and reduce the heat to medium-low. Add the Italian seasoning, salt and pepper. Keep stirring the onions until they become soft and translucent, about 5 minutes. The onions should not brown.

Add the Worcestershire sauce, vegetable broth and ketchup to the onions. Stir the mixture until the ketchup dissolves.

Remove the onions from the pan and add them to the bean mixture. Gently fold in the onions until they are well combined with the bean mixture.

Spoon the mixture into the loaf pan and press the mixture until it is evenly distributed throughout the pan.

Evenly spread the BBQ sauce on top of the loaf and bake for 1 hour and 20 minutes, or until a wooden toothpick is inserted and comes out clean.

Cool the loaf for 10 to 15 minutes to allow it to set before cutting.

Bacon-Flavored
ROASTED BRUSSELS SPROUTS STIR-FRY

+GF

Remember when Brussels sprouts were the most hated dish at the dinner table? I distinctly remember going to someone's home for Thanksgiving where a bowl of boiled, yes boiled, Brussels sprouts sat alone on the table, completely untouched. Well, gone are the days of the past. Our Brussels sprouts are savory, salty and oh so delicious. —LM + AM

SERVES 4

2 tbsp (28 ml) extra-virgin olive oil, divided

1 small red onion, thinly sliced

1 lb (453 g) Brussels sprouts, ends trimmed and cut in half

2 tbsp (28 ml) liquid smoke

2 tbsp (28 ml) pure maple syrup

Sea salt and black pepper, to taste

1 (14-oz [397-g]) block extra-firm tofu, pressed, cut into cubes

1 cup (150 g) cherry tomatoes, cut in half

Heat 1 tablespoon (15 ml) of the olive oil in a medium cast-iron skillet over medium heat. When the oil is heated, add the onion and Brussels sprouts. Quickly stir the vegetables to coat them evenly in the oil. Cook the onion and Brussels sprouts for 10 minutes while stirring frequently, or until you can easily pierce the sprouts with a fork.

Mix the liquid smoke and maple syrup together in a small bowl until fully incorporated. Add the mixture to the pan with the sprouts and onions. Stir the mixture immediately to fully coat the veggies in the sauce. Add salt and pepper, to taste. Turn off the heat and remove the veggies from the pan.

Using the same skillet, turn the heat back to medium and add the remaining 1 tablespoon (15 ml) olive oil. Spread the oil evenly throughout the pan. Add the tofu cubes to the skillet once the oil is hot. Sear each side until golden brown, about 2 to 3 minutes per side. When the tofu is browned, add the tomatoes to the skillet and cook for about 2 minutes. Add salt and pepper, to taste.

Sofritas TOFU
LETTUCE WRAPS

+GF

We love the sofritas that you find at vegan-friendly Mexican restaurants. However, a lot of the dishes they come in aren't the healthiest. So, we've taken this tasty component and made a healthy version to recreate for as many days of the week as you want, without feeling the guilt! —LM + AM

SERVES 6

1 (14-oz [397-g]) block extra-firm tofu

1 tbsp (14 ml) avocado oil

2 large carrots, finely diced

½ red bell pepper, finely diced

½ large red onion, finely diced

2 cloves garlic, minced

1 tsp ground turmeric

2 tsp (4 g) ground cumin

1 tsp ground coriander

1 tsp ground ginger

2 tsp (5 g) chili powder

1 tbsp (8 g) red pepper flakes

2 tbsp (28 ml) teriyaki sauce

Juice of 1 lime, plus more for topping if desired

10 large romaine leaves

½ cucumber, finely diced

Chili sauce and soy sauce (optional)

Salt, to taste

Put the tofu on a plate lined with paper towels. Place a layer of paper towels on top of the tofu. Lay a heavy pan or bowl on top of the tofu and leave it for 10 minutes to allow the water to drain.

Heat the oil in a large cast-iron skillet over medium heat. When the oil is hot, add the carrots, bell pepper and red onion. Stir well to combine and cook for 10 to 15 minutes, or until the veggies are soft. Add the garlic and tofu to the mixture. Use a potato masher or fork to break the tofu down into crumbles.

To the skillet, add the turmeric, cumin, coriander, ginger, chili powder, red pepper flakes, teriyaki sauce and lime juice. Stir well until the sauce and spices are well incorporated into the tofu and veggies.

Cook the sofritas mixture for 15 minutes or until the water has cooked out of the tofu.

Let the sofritas cool slightly, then spoon the mixture into lettuce leaves and top with fresh cucumber. Squeeze more lime on top if desired, and add the sauces and salt to your liking.

*SEE PHOTO INSERT

Vegan CHEDDAR AND BROCCOLI STUFFED BAKED POTATOES

+GF +SF

This soft potato, dripping in vegan cheese and loaded with broccoli, is so delicious even kids will devour this dish! —LM + AM

SERVES 2

2 large baking potatoes, washed and pierced multiple times

1 small head broccoli florets

1 recipe Six-Ingredient Vegan Cheddar Cheese Sauce (page 418)

Salt and pepper, to taste

Fried onions, for topping (optional)

Preheat the oven to 350°F (177°C).

Bake the potatoes for about 1 hour, or until they are fork tender.

Put a steamer basket in a large pot and fill it with water until it's just touching the basket. Bring the water to a boil. Once the water is boiling, add the broccoli and cover the pot. Immediately reduce the heat to medium-low and steam the broccoli for about 10 minutes. You want the broccoli to be easily pierced with a fork but not mushy.

While the broccoli is steaming, make the cheese sauce.

In a large bowl, mix the broccoli and cheese together. Slice the potatoes down the center and squeeze the ends of the potato toward the center to open it up. Spoon the cheesy broccoli in and on top of the potato. Add salt and pepper to taste and the onions if you like.

Sushi Bowl WITH GINGER SOY DRESSING

+GF

This has to be one of our top five go-to lunches—probably because the rice, potatoes, mushrooms and sauce combine to create this completely delicious umami flavor. Make this ahead for meal prepping or serve it fresh. Either way, this bowl won't leave you disappointed. —LM + AM

SERVES 4

1 cup (210 g) uncooked jasmine rice

2 cups (473 ml) water

1 tsp avocado oil

2 medium sweet potatoes, peeled and cubed

3½ oz (100 g) shiitake mushrooms

5 cups (300 g) baby spinach leaves

1 cup (236 ml) soy sauce

3 tbsp (42 ml) rice vinegar

1½ tsp (8 g) coconut sugar

2 tsp (5 g) fresh ground ginger

2 sheets nori, sliced in half

1 medium cucumber, cut into ½" (1.3-cm) thick slices

In a medium saucepan, stir the rice and water together. Bring to a boil. Once the water is boiling, immediately reduce the heat to a simmer and cover with a tight-fitting lid. Cook the rice according to the package instructions. When the time is up, remove the rice from the heat and keep the lid on until ready to serve.

In a large cast-iron skillet or nonstick pan, heat the oil over medium-high heat. Once the oil is heated, add the potatoes and stir evenly into the pan. Cover the pan with a lid and cook for 2 minutes. When the 2 minutes are up, uncover the pan, stir the potatoes and cover again. Continue stirring the potatoes every 2 minutes until the potatoes are crispy on the outside and soft on the inside. This process should take about 10 to 15 minutes total. When they are done cooking, transfer the potatoes to a bowl and set aside.

Add the mushrooms to the same pan you used for the potatoes. Cook the mushrooms until they are just browned and tender. This should take 6 minutes. When the mushrooms are done cooking, transfer them to the bowl with the potatoes.

Turn off the heat and add the spinach to the pan. Stir the spinach until the leaves are wilted. This should take 3 to 5 minutes.

Prepare the dressing by combining the soy sauce, rice vinegar, sugar and ginger in a bowl until fully combined. Once the ingredients are fully combined, pour the mixture into a saucepan. Bring the mixture to a boil over medium heat, and then reduce to a simmer. Stir frequently until the sauce reduces and becomes thicker. This will take 5 minutes.

Line the bowls with the nori and divide the rice between the bowls. Arrange the sweet potatoes, mushrooms, spinach and cucumber over the rice and pour the dressing over each bowl.

*SEE PHOTO INSERT

Raw SUPER SPROUTS PAD THAI WITH SPICY PEANUT SAUCE

+QP +GF

Raw, spiralized yellow squash and carrot noodles with crunchy, chopped red cabbage and bean sprouts, dripping in a spicy peanut chili sauce dressing is the cleanest and healthiest way to eat one of our favorite Thai dishes. Our fresh and colorful spin on this classic high-carb dish is perfect when you're craving a lighter dish that's satisfying. —LM + AM

SERVES 2 TO 4

PEANUT SAUCE

3 tbsp (34 g) natural peanut butter

1 tbsp (15 g) chile paste

3 tbsp (45 ml) low-sodium soy sauce (choose a gluten-free soy sauce)

3–4 tbsp (45–60 ml) water

PAD THAI

½ cup (50 g) bean sprouts

½ cup (50 g) micro green sprouts

3 medium yellow squash, peeled and spiralized

3 medium carrots, peeled and spiralized

1 cup (110 g) coarsely chopped red cabbage

½ cup (20 g) coarsely chopped cilantro

FOR THE PEANUT SAUCE

Whisk the peanut butter, chile paste, soy sauce and water in a small bowl with a fork until smooth and creamy.

FOR THE PAD THAI

Blanch the sprouts in boiling water for 2 minutes, and then put them in ice-cold water. Pat them dry with a paper towel.

Put the squash, carrots, cabbage, cilantro and sprouts in a large bowl and toss with the chile peanut sauce to coat.

Roasted Veggie LENTIL LOAF

+GF +SF

This flavorful and nutritious lentil loaf is filled with savory sautéed vegetables, protein-rich green lentils, and spices and flavors that will appeal to everyone at your dinner table. We love it for the holidays and for a Sunday dinner with all of the fixings. —LM + AM

SERVES 6 TO 8

2 tbsp (13 g) ground flaxseed

5 tbsp (75 ml) water

2 cups (408 g) green lentils, rinsed and sorted

1 cup (82 g) rolled oats (use gluten-free)

1 tbsp (15 ml) extra-virgin olive oil

2 medium carrots, finely chopped

2 celery stalks, finely chopped

1 large red onion, finely chopped

6–7 large portobello mushroom caps, stems and gills removed, finely chopped

2 cloves garlic, minced

2 tbsp (6 g) Italian seasoning

1½ cups (183 g) gluten-free breadcrumbs

1 tbsp (15 ml) liquid smoke

2 cups (326 g) fire-roasted tomatoes, divided

Salt and pepper, to taste

(continued)

Preheat the oven to 375°F (190°C) and line a 9 x 5 x 3-inch (23 x 13 x 8-cm) loaf pan with parchment paper.

Combine the flaxseed and the water in a small bowl until creamy. Let it sit for at least 15 minutes. This is a "flax egg."

In a medium saucepan, cover the lentils with water and bring to a boil. Reduce the heat to a simmer and cook for about 20 minutes, or until soft. Add more water if needed. Drain the excess water in a fine-mesh colander, pushing down on the lentils to get all of the water out. Put the lentils and oats in a food processor and pulse until they're mostly creamy (you should see bits and pieces of the lentils). Put them in a large mixing bowl.

While the lentils are cooking, in a large skillet, heat the olive oil over medium-high heat. When the oil is hot, add the carrots, celery and onion. Sauté for 5 minutes, stirring once or twice to avoid scorching. Add the mushrooms and stir to combine. Cook for 5 minutes and then add the garlic and Italian seasoning. Stir and cook for 2 minutes. Remove the skillet from the heat and let it cool.

Put the vegetables in the mixing bowl with the lentils. Add the breadcrumbs, flax egg, liquid smoke, 1 cup (163 g) of the fire-roasted tomatoes and salt and pepper to taste. Stir until well combined or use your hands to mix it. Taste the mixture, and add more salt and pepper if needed.

Put the lentil loaf mixture into the pan, firmly pressing to make sure it reaches all four corners.

Bake the loaf for 1 hour. Remove it from the oven, cut 3 slashes into the top surface and evenly pour the remaining 1 cup (163 g) tomatoes on top. Don't drench it; it should just cover the loaf. Bake for 10 minutes more or until the tomato firms up.

Remove the loaf from the oven and let it set for 10 minutes.

Vegan BLACK BEAN AND MUSHROOM ENCHILADAS

+SF

Don't let the long list of ingredients in this recipe scare you. The enchilada sauce is quick and so is the cashew cream sauce. Make them ahead of time and it only takes a little effort to put these together. You'll be so happy that you did, because they're ridiculously delicious. —LM + AM

SERVES 6 TO 8

ENCHILADA SAUCE
2 tbsp (16 g) all-purpose flour
¼ cup (60 ml) water
3 cups (710 ml) vegetable broth
2 tbsp (14 g) plus 1 tsp chili powder
2 tsp (5 g) ground cumin
¾ tsp cocoa powder
Dash of ground cinnamom
1 tbsp (14 g) tomato paste
Salt, to taste
Chipotle chile powder (optional)

CASHEW CREAM
2 cups (225 g) raw cashews, soaked in boiling water overnight
1 tbsp (5 g) nutritional yeast
1 large clove garlic
2 tsp (10 ml) lemon juice
2 tsp (7 g) tapioca starch
¼ tsp fine sea salt
1–1½ cups (240–360 ml) water

BLACK BEANS
1 (15-oz [425-g]) can black beans, drained and rinsed
1 tbsp (7 g) chili powder
1 tsp ground cumin
¼ tsp garlic powder

Black pepper, to taste

1 tsp fine sea salt

MUSHROOM MIXTURE

2 tsp (10 ml) avocado oil, divided

24 oz (680 g) mushroom caps (I used portobello), stems removed and finely chopped

1 small red onion, finely chopped

1 small orange or yellow bell pepper, seeded and finely chopped

1 poblano chile pepper, seeded and finely diced

1 cup (40 g) coarsely chopped cilantro leaves

½ cup (120 ml) water

1 tsp chile powder

½ tsp smoked paprika

½ tsp fine sea salt

½ tsp ground cumin

Black pepper, to taste

ADDITIONAL INGREDIENTS

6 to 8 flour tortillas

5 cups (150 g) coarsely chopped spinach

TOPPINGS

Chopped cilantro leaves

Chopped tomato

Sliced avocado

FOR THE ENCHILADA SAUCE

In a small bowl, mix the flour with the water until it's completely dissolved and smooth. Set aside.

Heat the vegetable broth in a medium saucepan over medium heat. When it begins to boil, add the chili powder, cumin, cocoa powder, cinnamon, tomato paste and flour water; whisk together until fully combined. Add the salt. You won't need much, if any, so be careful not to oversalt. Reduce the heat to a simmer and stir occasionally until it thickens, about 10 minutes. Season with chipotle, if desired.

FOR THE CASHEW CREAM

Soak the cashews in boiling water overnight or for at least 4 hours. They should be nice and plump, and soft to the touch.

Drain and rinse the cashews, and put in a high-powered blender. Add the nutritional yeast, garlic, lemon juice, tapioca starch, sea salt and water as needed; blend for about 2 minutes or until smooth, thick and creamy. Scrape the sides down to ensure that you don't have pieces of nut in the sauce.

FOR THE BLACK BEANS

Cover the beans in water (just to the top of the beans) and bring to a boil. Reduce the heat to a simmer and stir in the chili powder, cumin, garlic powder and black pepper. Simmer until the water is almost evaporated, stirring frequently, approximately 20 minutes. Add the salt and stir well. Set aside.

FOR THE MUSHROOM MIXTURE

Heat 1 teaspoon of the oil in a cast-iron skillet over medium heat. When the oil is hot, add the mushrooms and cook until the water is released and they are nicely browned. Push them to the side and add the remaining 1 teaspoon oil to the pan. Then add the onions and bell pepper. Cook until they are soft and lightly browned. Add the poblano pepper and cilantro, and stir to combine. Deglaze the pan with the water and scrape the bottom of the pan with a spatula to remove the pieces of vegetable that are stuck to the pan. Add the spices and stir to coat well. Turn the heat down to a low simmer and cook for 10 minutes. Stir frequently.

Preheat the oven to 350°F (177°C).

Lightly grease a 13 x 9-inch (33 x 23-cm) pan and spread 3 tablespoons (45 ml) of the enchilada sauce in the pan.

Fill the center of each tortilla with the beans, mushroom filling, spinach and 3 tablespoons (45 ml) of cashew cream. Fold and lay flat in the pan. Continue with the rest of the tortillas. When the pan is full, evenly pour the enchilada sauce over the enchiladas (leave a little extra in the pan for later). Pour most of the cashew cream over the center of the enchiladas (leave a little extra for later).

(continued)

Bake for 20 minutes or until the sauce and cheese have turned a golden brown. Pour the remaining sauce and cream over the top, and bake for 2 to 3 more minutes.

Garnish with cilantro, tomato and avocado.

Keep covered in the refrigerator for up to 3 days, or freeze in a freezer-safe dish for up to a month.

*SEE PHOTO INSERT

Vegan MUSHROOM BOURGUIGNON

+GFO +SF

Remember Julia Child's famous boeuf bourguignon? Well, we've taken that cozy winter dish and made it vegan—and it's fabulous, if we do say so ourselves. Portobello mushrooms take the place of the beef, because they're thick and chewy with just the right umami flavor. Then there's the rich red wine sauce that turns this simple recipe into magic. It takes a bit of time to simmer the vegetables and sauce, but it's not difficult. Pour yourself a glass of wine and enjoy the aroma wafting up from the pan as you stir. —LM + AM

SERVES 4

2 tbsp (30 ml) olive oil, divided

2 lbs (907 g) mushroom caps (we prefer baby portobellos), stemmed and thickly sliced

Pinch of salt

6 large carrots, peeled and sliced into 1" (2.5-cm) coins

1 large yellow onion, diced

1 large shallot, thinly sliced

2 cloves garlic, minced

2 cups (480 ml) vegetable broth

1½ cups (360 ml) red wine

1 tbsp (15 g) tomato paste

2 tsp (5 g) fine sea salt, or to taste

2 tbsp (5 g) fresh thyme leaves, plus extra for garnish

2 tsp (2 g) dried Italian seasoning

Black pepper, to taste

1 tbsp (8 g) plus 1 tsp all-purpose flour (or use cornstarch for gluten-free)

⅓ cup (80 ml) water

1 (1-lb [454-g]) package fettucine (use gluten-free)

Fill a pasta pot with water and heat over medium heat to warm the water.

Heat a large skillet over medium heat and add 1 tablespoon (15 ml) of the olive oil. When the oil is hot, add the mushrooms and a pinch of salt; sauté for about 10 minutes or until browned. Remove the mushrooms from the pan and set aside.

To the same pan, add the remaining 1 tablespoon (15 ml) olive oil and the carrots. Sauté until they begin to brown, approximately 8 minutes, then add the onion. Cook the onion until it becomes translucent, approximately 5 minutes, and then add the shallot. Cook until they are browned and caramelized, about 5 to 7 minutes. Add the garlic and cook for 1 minute.

Add the vegetable broth and wine to deglaze the pan. Stir and loosen the pieces of onion and shallot that may have stuck to the pan. Add the tomato paste and stir until it liquefies. Add the salt, thyme, Italian seasoning and pepper. Stir to combine and reduce the heat to a low simmer. Cover and cook for 20 minutes. Add more seasoning if you prefer a stronger flavor.

In a small bowl, mix the flour (or cornstarch if you want to make it gluten-free) and water together until the flour breaks down and the mixture resembles a thick, milky substance. There shouldn't be any dry flour or lumps in the mixture. Add it to the wine sauce and stir well to combine. Add the mushrooms and stir to incorporate within the sauce. Cover the sauce and simmer on the lowest temperature for 20 minutes. The sauce will thicken into a stew. Be sure to lift the lid and check to make sure it's not sticking to the pan or evaporating. That shouldn't happen if the temperature is low enough, but if it does, add a small amount of broth or water and stir.

Turn the heat for the pasta water to high and bring to a boil.

Twelve minutes before the sauce is done, salt the pasta water (about 1 tablespoon [15 g]) and add the fettucine to the water. Cook according to the directions on the package.

Divide the fettucine into 4 portions and make a nest in the center of each plate. Spoon the mushroom bourguignon on top of the fettucine. Garnish with a sprinkle of fresh thyme leaves.

Spaghetti and Black Bean MEATBALLS ✖

+GFO +SF

This is classic comfort food, yet it's fancy enough to make for a dinner party or a romantic weekend dinner. Our bean ball recipe is delicious—and the balls don't fall apart. Simmer them in our flavorful marinara and pile them on top of a plate of spaghetti. It's the ultimate vegan Italian food! —LM + AM

SERVES 4

MARINARA

1 tbsp (15 ml) extra-virgin olive oil

1 medium red onion, finely diced

3 cloves garlic, minced

26 oz (737 g) crushed tomatoes (I use Pomi brand)

⅓ cup (80 ml) red wine (or 3 tbsp [45 ml] balsamic vinegar)

1 tbsp (3 g) dried Italian seasoning

2 tsp (1 g) red pepper flakes (optional)

3 tsp (15 g) fine sea salt, or to taste

Ground black pepper, to taste

½ cup (20 g) fresh chopped basil leaves

¼ cup (10 g) chopped flat-leaf parsley

BEAN BALLS

1 (15-oz [425-g]) can black beans, drained (reserve ¼ cup [60 ml] of the liquid) and rinsed well

1 tbsp (15 ml) plus 1 tsp extra-virgin olive oil, divided

1 large portobello mushroom cap, gills removed and thinly sliced

1 shallot, thinly sliced

2 cloves garlic, minced

¼ cup (10 g) flat-leaf parsley, chopped

1 tbsp (3 g) dried Italian seasoning

½ cup (61 g) breadcrumbs (use gluten-free if desired)

½ cup (86 g) cornmeal

2 tsp (6 g) tapioca starch

1 tsp fine sea salt

Black pepper, to taste

SPAGHETTI

1 tbsp (15 g) sea salt

1 (1-lb [454-g]) box spaghetti

FOR THE MARINARA

Heat the oil in a large sauté pan over medium heat. When the oil is hot, add the onion and sauté until soft and translucent, approximately 8 minutes. Add the garlic and cook for 1 minute. Add the tomatoes, wine, Italian seasoning, pepper flakes, salt and pepper; stir well to combine. Bring to a boil, then reduce the heat to a simmer and cook for 30 minutes, stirring occasionally.

FOR THE BEAN BALLS

Place the beans in the food processor.

Heat 1 teaspoon of the oil in a large skillet over medium heat. When the oil is hot, add the mushroom slices and cook until browned and soft, about 10 minutes. Flip occasionally. When the mushrooms are soft, add the shallots and cook until they begin to soften and brown, about 7 minutes. Add the garlic and cook for 1 minute. Transfer the mushrooms, shallots and garlic to the food processor with the beans.

(continued)

Add the reserved bean liquid, parsley, Italian seasoning, breadcrumbs, cornmeal, tapioca starch, salt and pepper to the food processor and process until it begins to turn into a ball. It should be smooth and sticky.

Carefully remove the blade from the food processor and scoop out ¼ cup (60 ml) of batter and form into a ball. Repeat until you've used all of the bean batter (10 to 12 balls).

Heat the remaining 1 tablespoon (15 ml) oil in a large skillet over medium-high heat. Spread the oil evenly throughout the pan. When the oil is hot, add the bean balls and cook until the side facing down in the pan is browned. Turn and brown each side. This will take about 5 minutes per side. When the bean balls are browned on each side, add them to the marinara, along with the basil and parsley (from the marinara ingredients) and roll them in the sauce to coat. Simmer for 15 minutes.

FOR THE SPAGHETTI

Bring a large pot of water to a boil. When the water is boiling, add 1 tablespoon (15 g) of salt to the boiling pasta water and cook the spaghetti according to the instructions.

Divide the pasta into 4 portions and plate. Spoon the marinara and bean balls on top of the pasta.

Oil-Free ZUCCHINI ✗ AND CARROT FRITTERS

+SF

These healthy, delicious, crispy fritters are so good for you. They're filled with zucchini, carrots, onion and fresh sage, and the flax eggs give them another nutritional boost. They're guilt-free fritters because they're baked, not fried, but you'd never know it. Go ahead and indulge. —LM + AM

SERVES 4

1 large zucchini, finely shredded (about 3 cups [372 g])

3 large carrots, peeled and finely shredded (about 3 cups [330 g])

2 tbsp (30 g) plus 1 tsp fine sea salt, divided

2 tbsp (15 g) ground flaxseed

6 tbsp (90 ml) water

1 large red onion, finely chopped

¼ cup (10 g) fresh sage, packed in the cup and then minced

1 cup (120 g) stone-ground flour or all-purpose flour

1 tsp ground black pepper

Juice from 1 lemon

Preheat the oven to 375°F (190°C) and line a baking sheet with parchment paper to prevent the fritters from sticking.

Place the shredded zucchini and carrots on a bed of paper towels. Sprinkle the 2 tablespoons (30 g) of salt evenly over the top; rub the salt throughout. Let it sit for 20 minutes until the zucchini and carrots release their water. Squeeze with paper towels to absorb the water.

In a small bowl, mix the flaxseed and water; let sit for 10 minutes. This is a "flax egg."

In a large mixing bowl, combine the zucchini, carrots, onion, sage, flax egg, flour and remaining 1 teaspoon sea salt and pepper. Stir until it turns into a sticky ball. Scoop ¼ cup (25 g) of batter and use your hands to form patties. Place on the baking sheet and squeeze the lemon juice evenly over the top of each patty. Bake for about 20 to 25 minutes, checking every 10 minutes, until they're golden brown. Flip the patties, squeeze lemon juice on top of each and bake for another 20 minutes, or until golden brown. Remove them from the oven and let them sit for 5 minutes.

Grilled Vegan
DIRTY RICE STUFFED PEPPERS

+GF +SF

I took my mom's (Alex's grandma's) stuffed pepper recipe and dirtied it up in the best possible way. The new version is filled with chewy brown basmati rice, black beans, corn, onion, jalapeño pepper and warm and zesty spices. They have so much flavor and texture—and you can heat them on the grill or in the oven, so they're perfect for any time of the year. —LM + AM

SERVES 8

1 cup (210 g) uncooked brown basmati rice

1½ cups (350 ml) vegetable broth (you can use water, but it won't be as flavorful)

1 (15-oz [425-g]) can black beans, drained and rinsed well

2 tbsp (16 g) chili powder, divided

2 tsp (5 g) ground cumin, divided

½ tsp sea salt and ground black pepper, to taste

4 large bell peppers, cut in half and seeded

2 ears of corn

1–2 jalapeño peppers (1 if you don't like a lot of heat, 2 if you do)

3 large green onions (trim the ends of the greens, but leave the greens attached to the bulb of the onion) or 1 large white onion, chopped

2 tbsp (30 ml) extra-virgin olive oil

½ cup (20 g) chopped cilantro

1 tsp chipotle chile powder

TOPPINGS
Vegan cheese (optional)

1 lime (optional)

Combine the rice and vegetable broth in a medium saucepan and bring to a boil. Once the broth is boiling, cover the pan and reduce the heat to a simmer. Cook for 40 minutes or until the broth is completely absorbed and the rice is tender. Remove it from the heat, keep covered and let it sit for 10 minutes. Note: Check the cooking instructions on the package of rice that you use and follow those directions if they're different from ours.

In a medium saucepan, cover the beans with water and add 1 tablespoon (8 g) of the chili powder, 1 teaspoon of the cumin and ½ teaspoon of fine sea salt and pepper and stir to combine the spices. Bring to a boil, then reduce the heat to a low boil and cook for 20 minutes, or until the water evaporates. Stir frequently.

While the rice and beans are cooking, rub the bell peppers, corn, jalapeños and green onions with the olive oil (this prevents them from sticking to the grill) and grill them over medium heat until you can easily pierce them with a fork, approximately 10 minutes per side. The green onions will cook faster, so take them off once they begin to brown, about 10 minutes. Make sure you turn them every few minutes to avoid burning. You'll want to see grill marks on the corn and onions. The jalapeño peppers' skin will begin to blacken and bubble, which is totally fine.

Note: If you don't have a grill, you can roast the vegetables in a 400°F (204°C) oven until they begin to brown and are easily pierced with a fork.

(continued)

MAIN DISHES

Let the vegetables cool until you can safely handle them; then cut the corn off the cob. Cut the jalapeños in half, remove the seeds and chop. Chop the onions and place all the chopped vegetables in a large bowl; add the rice, beans and cilantro. Add the remaining 1 tablespoon (8 g) chili powder, remaining 1 teaspoon cumin, chipotle and more sea salt and black pepper, if desired. Gently fold the ingredients together until combined.

Stuff the bell peppers with the filling and wrap them in foil; grill for 15 minutes.

Sprinkle some vegan cheese on top during the last few minutes of cooking, if you like. Squeeze some lime juice on top before eating, if desired. Remove the foil and plate.

Note: If you don't have a grill, you can roast the peppers in a 375°F (190°C) oven until they begin to blacken and blister. Then fill them with the beans and rice filling, cover with foil and bake for 30 to 45 minutes.

You may have extra filling left over—don't be afraid to add more of it to your plate and eat it on the side.

Easy MEATLESS MONDAY TACO SALAD

+GF +SF

This is our go-to Meatless Monday recipe. It's easy, it's healthy and it's delicious! If you love Mexican food and you love salads, then you're going to adore this recipe. It's so easy to put together, and since it's your salad, feel free to add or subtract any of the ingredients. —LM + AM

SERVES 2

BEANS
1 (15-oz [425-g]) can black beans, drained and rinsed well

1 tbsp (8 g) chili powder

2 tsp (5 g) ground cumin

1 tsp ground coriander

1 tsp smoked paprika

Salt and pepper, to taste

PEPPERS AND ONION
2 tsp (10 ml) avocado or olive oil

1 large yellow onion, thinly sliced

1 yellow bell pepper, seeded and thinly sliced

1 orange bell pepper, seeded and thinly sliced

1 poblano pepper, seeded and diced

1 tsp chili powder

1 tsp ground cumin

½ tsp ground coriander

Salt and pepper, to taste

Juice from ½ lime

1 cup (110 g) beef substitute like Beyond Meat crumbles (optional)

SALAD
6 cups (420 g) chopped lettuce of your choice

Juice from ½ lime

1 large tomato, cut into wedges

1 avocado, peeled, pitted and cubed

2 cups (52 g) crushed corn chips, more or less depending on your taste

1 cup (40 g) chopped fresh cilantro, plus more for garnish

Salsa (optional)

FOR THE BEANS

In a medium saucepan, add the beans and cover in water. Stir in the spices and bring to a boil. Reduce the heat to a simmer and cook for 20 minutes, stirring occasionally.

FOR THE PEPPERS AND ONION

Heat the oil in a large skillet over medium-high heat. When the oil is hot, add the onion and peppers and stir. Add the seasonings and stir well to coat the onions and peppers. Cook for 15 minutes or until the peppers are fork tender. Add the lime juice and stir. Add the meat substitute, if using, and cook until warm.

FOR THE SALAD

Divide the lettuce between 2 large bowls. Add the lime juice and toss. Use a slotted spoon and sprinkle the beans on the lettuce.

Add the pepper and onion mixture and the tomato, avocado, chips, cilantro and salsa, if using.

Beer-Battered "FISH" TACOS WITH MANGO SALSA ✳

We created this shortly after we went vegan. The guys in our family were making fish tacos (they no longer eat fish), and not wanting to be left out, we made these. Funny enough, once the guys tasted our "fish," they didn't want the real thing. Once you try them, you'll understand why. —LM + AM

SERVES 8

"FISH"
3 (14-oz [397-g]) packages extra-firm tofu (not silken)
1 cup (240 ml) vegan ale
1 cup (126 g) all-purpose flour
1 cup (120 g) panko breadcrumbs
1 tbsp (8 g) Old Bay seasoning
1½ tsp (7 g) fine sea salt
Pepper, to taste
1–2 cups (240–480 ml) canola oil

SALSA
2 fresh corn cobs
2 mangoes
1 small red onion, finely diced
1 jalapeño pepper, seeded and finely chopped
½ cup (20 g) cilantro, coarsely chopped
1 large tomato or 20 cherry tomatoes, finely diced
Juice from 1 large lime or 2 small limes
Fine sea salt, to taste

8 corn or flour tortillas

FOR THE "FISH"

Press the tofu between two heavy plates lined with paper towels for 20 minutes, and then slice it into thick pieces, about 3 inches (8 cm) long and 1 inch (2.5 cm) wide. Make the salsa while you press the tofu.

FOR THE SALSA

Grill the corn until you see grill marks on each side, about 20 minutes. Remove the kernels from the cob. Keep the grill hot if you want to grill the tortillas.

Peel and cut the flesh of the mango from the core and finely dice. Put in a medium bowl. Add the onion, jalapeño, cilantro, tomatoes, lime juice and salt; stir well.

Put the ale, flour and panko in three separate bowls. Whisk the Old Bay seasoning, salt and pepper into the flour until well combined. Dip the tofu in the flour and then the beer. Then dredge it in the panko until evenly covered. Place it on a plate until all of the tofu is ready to fry.

Prepare a paper bag or cookie sheet lined with paper towels to drain the excess oil from the tofu.

Pour the canola oil into a medium skillet until it is about 1 inch (2.5 cm) deep, and heat over medium-high heat. When the oil is hot (test with a small piece of tofu; if it bubbles, it's ready), use tongs to place each piece of tofu in the oil. Be careful not to burn yourself. Fry until it's golden brown, about 3 to 5 minutes, and then use the tongs to flip. Fry another 3 to 5 minutes, or until golden brown. Place the fried tofu on the paper towels to drain excess oil.

Fill a tortilla with 2 or 3 pieces of tofu and top with the salsa.

Baked Fresh Herb
VEGAN MAC 'N' CHEESE ✗

+SF +GFO

Cheese is the one food that most people say they couldn't give up if they were to go vegan, and then they try our mac 'n' cheese and realize that they don't have to. They just have to switch up the kind of cheese that they eat.

This creamy and delicious baked version of macaroni and cheese has fresh herbs and a crunchy breadcrumb topping that takes the all-American favorite to another level. —LM + AM

SERVES 6

1 tbsp (15 g) salt

1 (1-lb [454-g]) package pasta shells (use gluten-free if you like)

CHEESE SAUCE

½ cup (56 g) raw cashews, soaked in boiling water for 20 minutes or more, drained

1 (15-oz [425-g]) can cannellini beans, drained and rinsed well

⅓ cup (27 g) nutritional yeast

1 clove garlic, minced

Juice from ½ lemon or 1 tbsp (15 ml) lemon juice

¼ tsp cayenne pepper

1 tsp fine sea salt

1 cup (240 ml) pasta water

1 tbsp (3 g) minced fresh basil

1 tbsp (3 g) minced purple basil

1 tbsp (3 g) minced Greek oregano

1 tsp minced spicy oregano

BREADCRUMB TOPPING

¼ cup (30 g) breadcrumbs (use gluten-free if you like)

½ tsp extra-virgin olive oil

¼ tsp fine sea salt

1 tsp dried Italian seasoning

Black pepper, to taste

Preheat the oven to 375°F (190°C).

Fill a pot with water and bring it to a boil. Add about 1 tablespoon (15 g) of salt to the water, add the pasta shells and cook according to the instructions on the package, or until it's al dente.

FOR THE CHEESE SAUCE

Put the cashews, beans, nutritional yeast, garlic, lemon juice, cayenne and salt in a blender and blend on high speed until it's thick and creamy like melted cheese, about 2 minutes.

Add water from the pasta water, if possible. The starch in the water makes for a better sauce. Add the herbs and pulse until just combined.

When the pasta is done, drain it in a colander and then put it in a large baking pan.

Stir the cheese sauce in until the pasta is evenly coated.

FOR THE BREADCRUMB TOPPING

In a small bowl, mix the breadcrumbs, oil, salt, Italian seasoning and black pepper until combined. Evenly spread it on top of the macaroni and cheese mixture.

Bake for 10 to 15 minutes, until the breadcrumbs are lightly browned. Place under the broiler for a minute or two if you want the breadcrumbs to get extra crispy. Be sure to watch it carefully so it doesn't burn.

Penne PASTA CASSEROLE

+GFO

When we're in the mood for pasta and we want to make it a little fancier yet easy, this is what we make. It's packed with tomatoes, spinach, basil and savory spices, and a crispy breadcrumb topping to add to the texture. This is a great dish to serve those who won't eat spinach because it blends so nicely with the tomato sauce and noodles. —LM + AM

SERVES 6

1 lb (454 g) whole-grain penne pasta (use gluten-free if you like)

1 tbsp (15 ml) extra-virgin olive oil

1 red onion, chopped

2 cloves garlic, minced

1 (15-oz [425-g]) can fire-roasted tomatoes, chopped

½ cup (120 ml) water

2 tsp (2 g) Italian seasoning

1 tsp fine sea salt

Ground black pepper, to taste

3 packed cups (100 g) baby spinach

1 packed cup (30 g) fresh basil

¼ cup (30 g) breadcrumbs (or gluten-free)

CASHEW CREAM

1 cup (112 g) cashews, soaked in boiling water for at least 1 hour, drained

¾ cup (180 ml) water

1 tsp extra-virgin olive oil

1 tbsp (15 ml) fresh lemon juice

½ tsp garlic powder

½ tsp fine sea salt

Ground black pepper, to taste

Preheat the oven to 350°F (177°C).

Bring a large pot of water to a boil. Salt the water and cook the pasta according to the instructions. For best results, cook the pasta until just al dente.

In a large skillet, heat the oil over medium-high heat. Add the onion and cook until it begins to caramelize, about 10 to 15 minutes. Add the garlic and cook for 1 minute. Add the tomatoes, water and seasonings. Stir well. Bring the mixture to a boil, and then reduce the heat to a simmer and cook for 15 minutes.

FOR THE CASHEW CREAM

In a high-powered blender, add the cashews, water, olive oil, lemon juice, garlic powder, salt and pepper, and blend until the liquid is smooth and creamy, about 2 minutes. There shouldn't be any pieces of nuts in the mix.

In a large bowl or the pasta pot, add the pasta, spinach, basil, tomato sauce and cashew cream, and stir until completely combined. Spread it all into a large baking pan, cover with foil and bake for 20 minutes. Uncover the pan and evenly spread the breadcrumbs on top. Bake for 10 minutes or until the crumbs begin to turn brown.

Creamy FETTUCCINI ALFREDO ✳

+GFO +SF

Plant-based eating doesn't mean that you can't indulge in the good things, like creamy, rich, divine Alfredo sauce. In fact, you can enjoy this velvety sauce without feeling guilty, because it's made with cashews, lemon, garlic and nutritional yeast. It's cholesterol free and so delicious. —LM + AM

SERVES 4

1½ cups (169 g) raw cashews, soaked in boiling water for at least 4 hours, drained

Juice from 1 large lemon

2 cloves garlic

2 tbsp (30 ml) extra-virgin olive oil, divided

1 tbsp (5 g) nutritional yeast

½ tsp dried oregano flakes

1 tbsp (15 g) plus 1 tsp fine sea salt, divided

Black pepper, to taste

1 cup (240 ml) water

1 lb (454 g) fettuccine (or use gluten-free)

4 large portobello mushroom caps, gills removed and sliced

1 cup (40 g) chopped fresh basil, for topping

Bring a large pot of water to a boil for the pasta.

Once the cashews have soaked and are soft and puffy, drain and rinse them well. Put them in the blender along with the lemon juice, garlic, 1 tablespoon (15 ml) of the olive oil, nutritional yeast, oregano, 1 teaspoon of the sea salt, black pepper to taste and water. Blend for 2 minutes, or until smooth and creamy. If you have a Blendtec blender, select the "whole foods" setting, and the "soup" setting within that setting, for the creamiest sauce.

When the water is boiling, add the remaining 1 tablespoon (15 g) salt and place the pasta in the water. Make sure it's completely covered in the water, and cook according to the instructions on the package.

While the pasta is cooking, in a large skillet, heat the remaining 1 tablespoon (15 ml) olive oil over medium-high heat. Cook the mushrooms until they release their water and are nicely browned on both sides, about 10 minutes. Add salt and pepper, to taste.

Drain the pasta water when done and put the pasta back in the pot. Add the cashew sauce and stir to coat the pasta.

Divide the pasta Alfredo among 4 plates. Top with the mushrooms, chopped basil and black pepper, to taste.

CHIK'N and DUMPLINGS

+GFO +SFO

My mom (Alex's grandma) made the best chicken and dumplings. The dumplings and the gravy-like sauce that she cooked them in made the dish. It took us four years to master this vegan recipe, and now that we have, we're so excited to share it with you. We used jackfruit as a substitution for the chicken, and instead of re-inventing the dumplings, we used vegan butter and unsweetened almond milk. Other than that, the perfectly tender dumplings are exactly the same as we remember. —LM + AM

SERVES 4 TO 6

CHIK'N

1 (20-oz [565-g]) can young jackfruit in brine

1 tbsp (15 ml) extra-virgin olive oil

1 medium white onion, finely chopped

3 celery stalks, chopped

3 carrots, chopped

2 cups (154 g) chopped mushrooms, stems removed

2 cloves garlic, minced

2 tsp (2 g) dried Italian seasoning

¼ cup (60 ml) white wine

32 oz (907 ml) no-chicken broth or vegetable broth (we use Pacific brand)

Salt and pepper, to taste

1½ cups (200 g) frozen peas

DUMPLINGS

2 cups (253 g) all-purpose flour (or use gluten-free)

1 tsp baking powder

½ tsp baking soda

1 tsp fine sea salt

1 tsp dried parsley

¼ tsp dried thyme

Black pepper, to taste

½ cup (116 g) vegan butter, melted (use soy-free)

½ cup (120 ml) unsweetened almond milk plus 1 tbsp (15 ml) lemon juice, whisked to combine

ROUX

¼ cup (58 g) vegan butter (use soy-free)

¼ cup (32 g) all-purpose flour (use gluten-free)

⅓ cup (80 ml) plus 1 tbsp (15 ml) unsweetened almond milk

FOR THE CHIK'N

Preheat the oven to 375°F (190°C).

Drain and rinse the jackfruit really well, and then squeeze the excess water out. Rinse it one more time and squeeze the excess water out of the fruit. Spread the fruit out evenly on a parchment paper–lined baking sheet and bake for 15 minutes, or until the edges are slightly dried out. Allow the fruit to cool and then shred it with two forks or in a food processor.

In a large cast-iron skillet or Dutch oven, heat the olive oil over medium-high heat.

When the oil is hot, add the onion, celery and carrots, and cook for about 7 minutes or until the onion becomes translucent. Add the mushrooms and cook for another 7 minutes, or until they release their water and begin to brown. Add the garlic and Italian seasoning, and cook for 2 minutes, stirring frequently. Deglaze the pan with the wine, making sure to scrape up all stuck-on pieces. Add the broth, salt and pepper, shredded jackfruit and peas, and bring to a boil. Reduce the heat to a simmer and cook for 20 minutes.

FOR THE DUMPLINGS

In a large mixing bowl, whisk the flour, baking powder, baking soda, salt, parsley, thyme and pepper until fully combined. Make a well in the center of the flour, and pour the melted butter and almond milk in the well. Stir the mixture together until combined and you don't see any dry flour. The dough will be firm yet slightly sticky. Set aside.

FOR THE ROUX

In a small saucepan over medium heat, melt the butter. When the butter is completely melted, whisk in the flour until it forms a thick paste. Whisk in the milk and continue mixing until thick and creamy. Whisk it into the broth mixture until completely combined. It will thicken as it cooks.

Drop golf ball–size pieces of the dumpling dough into the broth. Drop them evenly to cover the top. Cover the pan and cook for about 20 minutes, or until they're firm to the touch.

Baked PARMESAN TOFU STEAKS ✳

+GF

We love a good crunchy and flavorful tofu steak, especially if it has a salty Parmesan flavor. Our homemade parm is so cheesy, salty and delicious, and when you add it to the panko breadcrumb coating that hugs the tofu steaks, it's another level of deliciousness.

This is an easy recipe that you can make in less than 30 minutes. Pair it with our Winter Citrus and Arugula Salad with Cranberry Orange Dressing (page 244) for a healthy and tasty meal. —LM + AM

SERVES 4

14 oz (397 g) firm tofu, pressed

VEGAN PARMESAN
1 cup (113 g) roasted and shelled pistachios
¼ cup (20 g) nutritional yeast
1½ tsp (7 g) fine sea salt

PANKO COATING
1 cup (120 g) panko breadcrumbs (use gluten-free)
½ cup (90 g) vegan Parmesan (see above)
1 cup (126 g) all-purpose flour (use gluten-free)
1 cup (240 ml) unsweetened plant-based milk (don't use coconut milk)

Preheat the oven to 400°F (204°C) and line a baking sheet with parchment paper.

Press the tofu with something heavy between several layers of paper towels until the excess water is released, about 20 minutes. Slice the tofu into 4 steaks.

FOR THE PARMESAN

In a food processor, grind the pistachios, nutritional yeast and sea salt until it resembles coarse sand, about 1 minute. This is your Parmesan.

FOR THE PANKO COATING

In a small bowl, whisk the panko breadcrumbs and the ½ cup (90 g) Parmesan until combined. Put the flour and milk into two separate small bowls.

Dip a piece of tofu into the flour and coat every side. Dip it into the milk and then coat it with the panko mixture. Put the tofu on the baking sheet and repeat with the remaining pieces of tofu.

Bake for 15 minutes, or until brown and crispy. Then flip them and bake for another 15 minutes, or until both sides are golden brown.

Vegan POKE BOWLS

+GF

Have you all noticed that poke bowls are all the rave? We have, and to be honest we wish we had gotten on board with this trend a lot earlier. These savory Hawaiian bowls are so amazing! Typically, they're topped with some sort of fish, but we've recreated the look, taste and texture with just a little bit of tomato. See for yourself, our poke bowls are the real deal. —LM + AM

SERVES 4

1 cup (210 g) uncooked jasmine rice
2 large tomatoes
1 tbsp (14 ml) soy sauce (choose a gluten-free soy sauce)
1 tbsp (14 ml) teriyaki sauce
½ tsp sesame oil
¼ tsp chile paste
1 avocado
1 cucumber
¼ head purple cabbage
½ cup (56 g) shelled edamame
1 tbsp (10 g) sesame seeds

Cook the rice according to package instructions. Once the rice is done cooking, set it aside to cool.

While the rice is cooling, bring a medium pot of water to a rolling boil. Drop the whole tomatoes into the water and cook for about 2 minutes, or until the skin begins to peel away. Remove the tomatoes with a slotted spoon.

Set the tomatoes aside and allow them to cool.

While the tomatoes are cooling, combine the soy sauce, teriyaki sauce, sesame oil and chile paste in a small bowl.

Once the tomatoes are cool to the touch, peel the skin off, remove the seeds and cut them into ½-inch (1.3-cm) cubes. Place the tomatoes in the sauce you just made, then toss and allow the tomatoes to marinate in the sauce for 10 minutes.

Prepare your vegetables by thinly slicing the avocado, cucumber and cabbage.

Assemble the bowls by scooping rice into the bottom of the bowl. Add the vegetables to the top along with the tomatoes and some of their sauce. Finish off the bowls by sprinkling the top with the edamame and sesame seeds.

Pumpkin THYME-RICOTTA LASAGNA

I think everyone has tried a classic lasagna at least once. The layers of tomato, pasta and cheese are amazing, right? Well, wait until you try our pumpkin thyme-ricotta lasagna. We think it just might be better than the original. The pumpkin sauce paired with the thyme, vegan ricotta, vegan mozzarella and noodles is the perfect fall version of this classic dish. —LM + AM

MAKES 1 (11 X 7-INCH [28 X 18-CM])
PAN OF LASAGNA

1 tbsp (15 ml) extra-virgin olive oil

1 medium yellow onion, diced

2 cloves garlic, minced

¼ cup (60 ml) red wine

15 oz (425 g) pumpkin purée

2 cups (473 ml) plain unsweetened almond milk

1 tbsp (3 g) Italian seasoning

1 tsp salt

¼ tsp black pepper

1 tbsp (8 g) minced fresh thyme

3 cups (374 g) Vegan Ricotta, homemade (page 417) or store-bought

1 (9-oz [255-g]) box no-boil lasagna noodles

2 cups (226 g) shredded vegan mozzarella

2 cups (80 g) torn fresh basil

Preheat the oven to 425°F (218°C).

In a large skillet, heat the olive oil over medium heat. Once the oil is heated, add the onions and garlic to the skillet. Sauté them until translucent. This should take about 5 minutes. When the onions are done cooking, deglaze the pan with the wine.

Add the pumpkin, almond milk, Italian seasoning, salt and black pepper to the skillet with the onions. Stir the mixture until well incorporated.

Mix the thyme and vegan ricotta together.

Assemble the lasagna by starting with a layer of the pumpkin sauce, then noodles, more sauce, ricotta, mozzarella and basil, and then start the next layer of noodles. Continue layering and top with the sauce and mozzarella. You should have enough to make 3 to 4 layers.

Bake for about 30 minutes or until the top is nicely browned.

Drop Biscuit ROOT VEGETABLE POT PIE

+GFO +SFO

This recipe is adapted from a recipe that I found in Food & Wine *magazine in 1997. Alex was only five years old the first time I made it for Christmas Day dinner, and it's been a holiday tradition ever since. Over the years I've changed bits and pieces of the recipe to suit our tastes and lifestyle, and to make it my own. It's even better now than it was the first time I made it.*

Seasonal root vegetables are sautéed in vegan butter and olive oil, then roasted in a delicious seasoned broth and finally topped with the most incredible cheddar biscuit crust that's baked to a golden brown. The crust of the biscuits are crispy and the centers are tender. Paired with the savory vegetables and reduced broth, it's a heavenly winter meal that will make you want to cozy up with your family and friends and make a toast to winter. —LM + AM

SERVES 6 TO 8

2 tbsp (30 g) vegan butter, divided (use soy-free)

2 tbsp (30 ml) extra-virgin olive oil, divided

4 large carrots, peeled and chopped

4 cups (560 g) cubed butternut squash

2 large parsnips, peeled and chopped

1 medium celery root, peeled and chopped

1 large yellow onion, chopped

16 oz (454 g) white mushroom caps, stems removed and cut in half

3 cloves garlic, minced

¼ cup (60 ml) red wine

4 cups (960 ml) mushroom broth

2 tsp (2 g) dried Italian seasoning

Salt and pepper, to taste

1 sprig of rosemary

CHEDDAR CRUST BISCUITS

2 cups (253 g) all-purpose flour (use gluten-free)

3 tsp (11 g) aluminum-free baking powder

2 cloves garlic, minced

1 tsp dried parsley

½ tsp fine sea salt

½ tsp ground black pepper

½ cup (116 g) chilled vegan butter, cut into small cubes (use soy-free)

1 cup (122 g) shredded vegan cheddar cheese (use soy-free)

1 cup (240 ml) unsweetened almond or soy milk coffee creamer (do not use coconut milk creamer)

Preheat the oven to 375°F (190°C).

In a large cast-iron skillet or frying pan, heat 1 tablespoon (15 g) of the vegan butter and 1 tablespoon (15 ml) of the olive oil over medium-high heat. When the butter is melted and beginning to sizzle, add the carrots, squash, parsnips and celery root, and stir to cover everything in the butter and oil. Cook for 10 to 12 minutes, or until the vegetables begin to brown. Stir frequently.

Put the vegetables in a large casserole dish, or, if your skillet is large enough to hold all of the vegetables, push them to the side. Add the remaining 1 tablespoon (15 g) butter and remaining 1 tablespoon (15 ml) olive oil to the skillet, and add the onion. Cook for about 5 minutes, or until the onion becomes translucent and softens. Stir often.

Add the mushrooms and cook until they release their water and are nicely browned, about 5 to 7 minutes. Add the garlic and cook for 2 minutes. Put the onion and mushrooms in the casserole dish and mix in with the carrots and squash. If you pushed the carrots and squash to the side in your skillet, stir them to combine with the mushrooms.

Add the wine to the skillet to deglaze the pan. Stir well and scrape up any stuck-on veggies. Add the mushroom broth, Italian seasoning, salt and pepper, and stir to combine (if making in the skillet, stir the vegetables and broth to combine). Bring it to a boil.

Once the broth is boiling, pour it over the vegetables in the casserole dish (or turn off the heat if you're making it in the skillet) and tuck the rosemary sprig into the center.

Cover the pan with foil and roast in the oven for 30 minutes.

FOR THE CHEDDAR CRUST BISCUITS

In a large mixing bowl, whisk the flour, baking powder, garlic, parsley, salt and pepper together until combined. Add the butter and use a pastry cutter or two butter knives to cut the butter into the flour, until the cubes are the size of peas. Stir in the shredded cheddar cheese and the milk until the dough is firm.

Remove the foil from the pan of vegetables and drop the biscuit crust evenly over the top. Roast for 25 minutes, or until the biscuits are golden brown.

Wild MUSHROOM AND RICOTTA RAVIOLI

Making homemade isn't as scary as you may think. It's actually easy and a lot of fun. The dough is just a combination of flour, vegan egg substitute, olive oil, salt and water. Mix it up and roll it out. That's it. And the filling is pretty easy to make as well. Invite your family and friends over and make a party of it. —LM + AM

SERVES 4

PASTA DOUGH

2 cups (253 g) all-purpose flour, plus more for rolling out the dough

4 tbsp (38 g) vegan egg substitute (I like Vegan Egg), plus ¾ cup (180 ml) water, whisked until blended

1 tbsp (15 ml) extra-virgin olive oil

1 tsp plus 2 tbsp (30 g) salt, divided

3–4 tbsp (45–60 ml) water

MUSHROOM FILLING

1 cup (124 g) Vegan Ricotta, homemade (page 417) or store-bought

1 tbsp (15 ml) extra-virgin olive oil

8 oz (226 g) wild mushrooms, sliced

1½ tsp (1 g) dried Italian seasoning

Salt and pepper, to taste

2 cloves garlic, minced

1 tbsp (15 ml) white wine (optional)

TOPPINGS

Roasted Tomato Spaghetti Sauce, homemade (page 420) or store-bought

Fresh chopped basil

FOR THE PASTA DOUGH

Put the flour on a clean, flat surface and make a well in the center. Put the "egg," olive oil and 1 teaspoon of the salt in the center of the well, and fold the flour into it. Add the water 1 tablespoon (15 ml) at a time as the mixture forms a solid ball of dough. Stop adding water when you can knead the dough. It shouldn't be sticky. Knead for 2 minutes and pat into a ball. Place in a bowl and cover with a towel for 30 minutes.

While the dough is resting, make the mushroom filling.

FOR THE MUSHROOM FILLING

Make the ricotta cheese.

Heat the oil in a large skillet over medium-high heat.

When the oil is hot, add the mushrooms and cook for about 5 minutes, or until they release their water. Add the seasoning, salt, pepper and garlic, and cook for 2 minutes. Deglaze the pan with the wine, if using, making sure to scrape off the pieces that are stuck to the pan. Remove from the heat.

(continued)

Start assembling your ravioli by dividing the dough in half. On a floured surface, roll half of the dough until thin, about 1⁄16 inch (1.5 mm) thick. Cut the dough into squares or use a round cookie cutter to cut out circles. Fill the center of the square/circle with the mushroom mixture and a dollop of ricotta. Put a piece of dough on top of the mixture and use the tines of a fork to press the edges together. Don't be afraid to press hard. Continue with the rest of the dough. If the dough doesn't stick together, you can brush the edges with a bit of water and they should stick together well.

Bring a pot of water to a boil. Add the remaining 2 tablespoons (30 g) sea salt. Add the ravioli and cook for 2 to 3 minutes, or until the ravioli floats to the top. Carefully drain the water and cover the ravioli in spaghetti sauce and fresh basil.

Roasted BRUSSELS SPROUTS VELOUTÉ ✗

+SF +GF

While the green, creamy-smooth velouté is perfect enough on its own, I couldn't resist making it more-ish by adding a spoonful of crema to it. —CS

SERVES 6

2 lbs (908 g) small fresh Brussels sprouts, trimmed and halved (quartered if the sprouts are larger)

2 shallots, quartered

2 large cloves garlic

Coarse kosher salt

Olive oil or grapeseed oil

6 cups (1.4 L) vegetable broth, divided (use soy-free)

½ cup (120 g) Cashew Crema (page 411)

Fresh herbs of choice, for garnish

Preheat the oven to 425°F (220°C). Place the Brussels sprouts, shallots, garlic, a generous pinch of salt and a drizzle of oil into a large baking pan. Toss to coat. Roast until the sprouts are fork tender and golden brown, stirring every 10 minutes. This should take about 30 minutes. Be sure not to char the sprouts or the soup will have a bitter taste.

You can reserve a few roasted sprouts and slice them to garnish the soup.

Transfer the sprouts to a blender in two batches, adding 3 cups (705 ml) of the broth per batch. Blend it together until smooth. Repeat with the second batch and remaining broth.

Place the blended mixture in a large pot and bring to a low boil. Lower the heat and simmer until heated through, about 8 minutes. Swirl 1 heaping table-spoon (15 g) of crema into each bowl upon serving. Garnish with your choice of fresh herbs.

Kimchi MAC AND SPROUTS

Quick notes before you dig in: the pasta dish yields four to six servings for us two, depending on the day. As for the veggies, two servings is more like it. If you're going to eat the whole pan in one shot, be sure to at least double the section for the veggie ingredients. In that case, you need to use a larger dish so that they can caramelize and not just steam.

If you are soy-reluctant and don't want to use tofu, you could replace it with a cashew mixture of similar con-sistency. Soak 1½ cups (165 g) raw cashews overnight. Drain and then add them with enough filtered water to a blender to obtain a silken tofu-like texture. Use 1 pound (454 g) of the resulting preparation.—CS

SERVES 6

1 (1-lb [454-g]) package whole wheat elbow-shaped pasta

1 lb (454 g) trimmed fresh Brussels sprouts, quartered or halved for similar size

6 oz (170 g) fresh button mushrooms, halved

2 small shallots, trimmed and quartered

2 tbsp (30 ml) toasted sesame oil, divided

1½ tsp (4 g) coarse kosher salt, divided

1 lb (454 g) silken tofu

1 (14-oz [414-ml]) can full-fat coconut milk

½ cup (120 ml) kimchi brine

¼ cup (20 g) nutritional yeast

¼ cup (80 g) Gochujang Paste (page 413)

1 tbsp (5 g) dried shiitake powder

1½ tbsp (23 ml) lemon juice

1 tbsp (15 ml) reduced-sodium tamari

4 cloves black garlic or roasted garlic

1½ cups (288 g) drained vegan kimchi, chopped if large

Smoky Apple (or Pear) Pickles (page 186)

Thinly sliced scallions

Cook the pasta in a pot of boiling salted water according to package directions. Drain and set aside.

Preheat the oven to 425°F (220°C). Combine the sprouts, mushrooms, shallots, 1 tablespoon (15 ml) of the sesame oil and 1 teaspoon of the salt in a 9-inch (23-cm) square baking pan. Roast for 30 minutes, stirring occasionally. Remove it from the oven and set aside. Lower the oven heat to 400°F (204°C).

Place the tofu, coconut milk, kimchi brine, nutritional yeast, gochujang paste, shiitake powder, lemon juice, remaining 1 tablespoon (15 ml) sesame oil, tamari, garlic and remaining ½ teaspoon salt in a blender. Blend until perfectly smooth. Fold two-thirds of the sauce and the kimchi into the cooled pasta until well combined. Place evenly in a 9 x 13-inch (23 x 33-cm) baking dish and drizzle the remaining sauce evenly on top. Bake for 20 minutes or until golden brown. During the last 5 minutes of cooking, place the veggies back into the oven to reheat slightly. Serve with fruit pickles and scallions.

*SEE PHOTO INSERT

Spicy KIMCHI PIZZA

I cannot help but make this pizza at least once a week. We're hooked. I'm aware that the pairing of harissa, kimchi and cream cheese might sound a wee bit out there, but for the love of pizza pie, trust me: I've had hardcore, nonvegan pizza lovers tell me this one truly is a pizza-force to be reckoned with. —CS

SERVES 2 TO 4, DEPENDING ON APPETITE

2 generous tbsp (50 g) harissa paste, or to taste

1 recipe Garlic and Herb Pizza Dough (page 98), after refrigeration and ready for toppings

½–¾ cup (120–180 g) vegan cream cheese

1 cup (192 g) drained, thinly chopped vegan kimchi

Optional garnishes to be added prebaking: cherry tomatoes, thinly sliced red onion or shallot rings

Optional garnishes to be added post-baking: thinly sliced scallion, chopped fresh chives, drizzle of toasted sesame oil or sesame seeds

Preheat the oven to 475°F (246°C).

Spread a thin layer of harissa all over the dough, all the way to the edges. Don't be too generous thickness-wise unless your mouth likes it that way: it's not marinara you're working with.

Spread the cream cheese on top, again, all over the dough. Sprinkle the kimchi all over the dough. Don't be too heavy-handed, as you want the dough to cook well and not be soggy. Add your prebaking garnishes, if using.

Bake for 16 to 18 minutes or until golden brown, and let it stand a couple of minutes before serving. Add your post-baking garnishes, if using.

*SEE PHOTO INSERT

Noochy FRIED NOODLES ✳

+SF

When I was a kid, my mom used to reheat leftover pasta in a little bit of oil until it got deliciously crispy, and I added a "healthy" sprinkle of a sadly MSG-laden flavoring called Fondor on top of it. This healthier version of that dish is a dead ringer for it. I see it as my ultimate indulgence, and the fact that it also happens to be ready fairly quickly is an added bonus. I love it paired with loads of roasted veggies (Brussels sprouts are my go-to), a big salad or a generous ladleful of Zippy Chickpea Sauce (page 409). —CS

SERVES 4 TO 6

1½ tbsp (23 ml) melted coconut oil

1 shallot, chopped

12 oz (340 g) dry eggless noodles, cooked according to package directions, drained and cooled slightly

3 tbsp (15 g) nutritional yeast

Scant 1 tsp smoked paprika

Scant 1 tsp smoked sea salt

Heat the oil over medium heat in a large frying pan. Add the shallot and fry until fragrant and translucent, about 3 minutes. Be sure to adjust the heat as needed. Add the pasta, nutritional yeast, paprika and salt. Fold it together to thoroughly combine, and fry until lightly browned and heated through. Do not stir too frequently; allow the pasta to brown up a bit.

Crispy CORN AND BEAN BURRITOS ✳

If I had to choose one single food to eat until th die, burritos would probably be it. Or maybe pi. let's pretend for this awesome recipe's sake the with burritos.

A note for the really hungry among us: you coul these even more substantial by adding a co tablespoons (24 g) of cooked rice to each burrit get about eight burritos out of the mix, lowe corn and bean filling to about ¼ cup (60 g) and with Cashew Crema (page 411). —CS

MAKES 6 BURRITOS

4 fresh ears of corn, trimmed, husk and silk removed

Olive oil or coconut oil (for a slightly cheesier flavor)

1 recipe Chile Sauce Refried Beans (page 185)

4 tsp (11 g) Spice and Pine Mix (page 180)

6 (10" [25-cm]) vegan flour tortillas, warmed

Favorite hot sauce (mine is Tapatío), to taste

Lightly brush the corn ears with oil. Place them on a hot grill and cook until golden brown. This should take about 10 minutes. Be sure to flip the corn around so that each side has a chance to brown. Once they're cool enough to handle, use a knife to shuck the corn into a medium bowl.

To the same medium bowl, add the refried beans and spice and pine mix, and fold to combine with the shucked corn.

In the bottom center of a gently heated tortilla, place a generous ⅓ cup (80 g) of the filling. Do not overfill. Fold the edges of the tortilla until they almost touch. Then fold the bottom of the tortilla over the filling and start rolling upward, making sure the filling is tightly wrapped. Repeat with the remaining tortillas.

Slowly heat in a lightly oiled pan over medium-low heat until they're light golden brown, crispy and heated through. This will take about 8 minutes. Be sure to flip the burritos occasionally, and adjust the heat as needed. Serve with a drizzle of hot sauce to taste.

TACOS **al Pastor**

+SF

Give me all the tacos, and particularly those that contain jackfruit. I cooked the latter in a spicy and slightly sweet concoction here, to be served with cashew crema and avocado for ultimate balance. You should be able to find achiote paste (a red paste made from annatto seeds, various spices and tomatoes) in Mexican or international food markets. My favorite tester, aka my mom, managed to purchase some where she lives in Switzerland. —CS

MAKES 12 TACOS

2 dried guajillo peppers, stemmed, seeded, rinsed and crumbled

3 cloves garlic, chopped

½ tsp dried oregano (not powder)

½ tsp ground cumin

½ tsp smoked sea salt

1½ tbsp (23 g) achiote paste

½ cup (120 ml) pure pineapple juice

¼ cup (60 ml) distilled white vinegar

1 tbsp (15 ml) olive oil

2 (20-oz [567-g]) cans young green jackfruit in brine, drained, rinsed and cut lengthwise into ¼" (6-mm) thick strips

1¼ cups (206 g) chopped fresh pineapple

¼ large red onion, sliced

Shredded green cabbage

12 (6" [15-cm]) corn tortillas, warmed

Chopped fresh cilantro

Thinly sliced scallion

Cashew Crema (page 411)

Sliced avocado

Place the peppers, garlic, oregano, cumin, salt, achiote paste, pineapple juice and vinegar in a medium saucepan. Bring to a low boil. Then lower the heat immediately and simmer for 10 minutes, until the peppers soften. Use an immersion blender or transfer to a small blender along with the oil, and blend until smooth.

In the meantime, preheat the oven to 425°F (220°C). Line a large rimmed baking sheet with parchment paper.

Place the jackfruit, pineapple, onion and marinade in a large bowl. Use a rubber spatula to thoroughly combine everything.

Transfer the mixture to the prepared sheet and spread evenly. Bake for 20 minutes; stir well. Bake for another 15 minutes, and stir again. The marinade should have been absorbed and look dry.

Place a handful of cabbage on a tortilla. Top it with jackfruit to taste, cilantro, scallion, crema and avocado. Repeat with the remaining tortillas and serve immediately.

Gochujang BBQ SAUCE SANDWICHES

I'm a newbie when it comes to cooking with soy curls, and it was love at first ravenous bite. But if soy curls cannot be found where you live, or if you prefer avoiding soy, try replacing them with 18 ounces (510 g) of prepared, plain seitan strips.

Feel free to play around with the amounts of gochujang paste and ketchup: for spicier results, increase the paste by the number of tablespoons desired, while simultaneously decreasing the amount of ketchup by the same number of tablespoons. Do the exact opposite for milder results. —CS

MAKES 8 SANDWICHES

8 oz (227 g) dry soy curls

¼ cup (60 ml) filtered water for sauce, plus more for soaking the curls, divided

½ cup (122 g) organic ketchup

¼ cup (80 g) Gochujang Paste (page 413)

1 tbsp (20 g) agave nectar

3 tbsp (45 ml) fresh lime juice

2 tbsp (30 ml) tamari

1 tbsp (5 g) dried mushroom powder

1 bag Lapsang Souchong tea (1½ tsp [4.5 g])

½ tsp ground ginger

1 tbsp (15 ml) toasted sesame oil

Vegan mayo, for spreading on bread

16 slices vegan sourdough bread, toasted

Shredded carrots and green cabbage mix

Thinly sliced scallion (white and green parts)

Smoky Apple (or Pear) Pickles (optional, page 186)

Place the soy curls in a large bowl. Add enough filtered water to generously cover the curls and allow to rehydrate for 10 minutes. Drain well, gently squeezing out the extra moisture. Leave them in the colander to further release extra moisture while preparing the sauce.

In a medium bowl, whisk to combine the ketchup, gochujang paste, remaining ¼ cup (60 ml) water, agave, lime juice, tamari, mushroom powder, the contents of the tea bag and ground ginger. Set aside.

In a large wok, heat the sesame oil over medium-high heat. Add the rehydrated soy curls and cook until browned. Adjust the heat as needed and stir occasionally. This should take about 8 minutes. Once browned, lower the heat to medium and add the sauce. Simmer uncovered for 10 minutes, stirring occasionally. I like to prepare these ahead of time and reheat gently in a pan; I find the flavors are even greater.

Once you're ready to make sandwiches, slather a fair amount of mayo on each slice of toasted bread. Top with a handful of cabbage mix, soy curls to taste, scallion and fruit pickles, if desired. Press down gently and serve immediately.

Sloppy GIUSEPPE

+SFO

The very first time I ate a sloppy Joe was when the cookbook Veganomicon came out, if memory serves right. What a blast it was to find out it was socially acceptable to eat like a mess, like I usually do in a more covert manner. This one is my own homage to Italian food, loaded with Italian herbs, pesto, olives and everything you'd expect to find in something Italian. Buonissimo! —CS

SERVES 6

1½ tsp (8 ml) olive oil

4 oz (113 g) fresh cremini mushrooms, stems removed, gently brushed clean and minced

1 shallot, minced

3 cloves garlic, minced

2 cups (400 g) cooked brown or green lentils

4 quarters marinated artichoke hearts, chopped

1 tbsp (17 g) double-concentrated tomato paste

1½ tsp (3 g) maca powder

1½ tsp (2 g) dried porcini powder

1½ tsp (2 g) dried Italian herbs

2½ tsp (13 ml) sherry vinegar or apple cider vinegar

1½ cups (360 g) fire-roasted crushed tomatoes

½ tsp coarse kosher salt, to taste

Freshly cracked rainbow peppercorn, to taste

Aleppo-style pepper flakes, to taste

Favorite vegan pesto, homemade (page 419) or store-bought

6 vegan burger buns or Kaiser rolls, well toasted (use soy-free)

Pitted and sliced olives of choice (optional)

In a large pot, heat the oil over medium-high heat. Add the mushrooms, shallot and garlic. Sauté until the mushrooms have released their moisture and are browning, about 5 minutes. Stir occasionally and adjust the heat as needed. Add the lentils, artichokes, tomato paste, maca powder, porcini powder and Italian herbs. Cook for another 2 minutes. Add the vinegar to deglaze the pan, stirring well. Add the crushed tomatoes, salt, cracked pepper and pepper flakes. Bring to a low boil, turn down the heat and simmer, partially covered, for 15 minutes, until thickened and not overly moist. Stir occasionally.

Apply a thin layer of pesto on both sides of the toasted buns. Top with a generous ½ cup (150 g) of sloppy filling, or however much will fit well without falling out too much (for there is only so much sloppiness a person can take).

Add as many olives as desired and top with the other side of the bun or slice of bread. *Mangia!*

*SEE PHOTO INSERT

Umami Fusion
BURRITOS

Loads of fermented foods star in these awesome burritos! I tried a store-bought frozen vegan burrito recently that had similar ingredients. The idea sounded fantastic but as loathe as I am to admit it, the execution was seriously lacking. They were way too dry and the flavor was pretty sad. That's where the inspiration for these came from: they don't take much time to prepare, are much cheaper and, honestly, taste a million times better. —CS

MAKES 12 BURRITOS

Toasted sesame oil

1 lb (454 g) super-firm tofu, cut into small cubes

Shoyu, to taste

3½ oz (100 g) fresh shiitake mushrooms, gently cleaned and chopped

1 shallot, minced

2 cups (384 g) vegan kimchi (not drained), chopped, with brine reserved

1 cup (168 g) dry sushi rice, cooked according to directions on package with 1 tsp toasted sesame oil added to the water before cooking, cooled

1 cup (134 g) frozen green peas or (155 g) fresh shelled edamame

12 (10" [25-cm]) vegan tortillas, heated in a pan for 10 seconds on each side to make more pliable

Gochujang Paste (page 413), to taste

Add a healthy drizzle of sesame oil to a wok or large pan. Heat the oil over medium-high heat. Add the tofu and cook until golden brown, about 6 minutes. Stir occasionally and adjust the heat as needed. Add a healthy drizzle of shoyu and cook just until evaporated, about 2 minutes. Transfer to a large plate.

(continued)

Add another drizzle of sesame oil, and cook the mushrooms and shallot until the mushrooms start to release their moisture, about 5 minutes. Add a drizzle of shoyu and cook another 2 minutes. Add the kimchi brine and cook just until evaporated, about 2 minutes. Transfer to the tofu plate.

Add the kimchi, cooked and cooled rice and peas to the wok. Cook over medium heat until the peas are thawed and the kimchi and rice are heated through. Add the tofu and mushrooms back to the wok. Heat for another 2 minutes.

In the bottom center of a gently heated tortilla, place about ¾ cup (110 g) of the filling. Do not overfill. Fold the edges of the tortilla until they almost touch. Then fold the bottom of the tortilla over the filling and start rolling upward, making sure the filling is tightly wrapped. Repeat with the remaining tortillas.

Slowly heat in a dry or lightly oiled pan over medium-low heat until light golden brown, crispy and heated through. This will take about 8 minutes. Be sure to flip the burritos occasionally. Serve with the gochujang paste as desired.

Indian-Spiced CHANA DAL SHEPHERD PIE

+GF

Behold, some healthy and quite filling comfort food. For tastiest results, serve with a generous spoonful of Amba (page 410), Savory Dried Apricot Paste (page 411) or your favorite vegan chutney.

I highly recommend not peeling the yams to retain the spuds' nutritional benefits, electing to scrub them clean instead. —CS

SERVES 6

2 lbs (908 g) raw white yams or russet potatoes (about 2 large), trimmed and cubed

1½ cups (306 g) dry chana dal, picked through and rinsed

1 cup (235 ml) canned full-fat coconut milk

Generous 1¼ tsp (7 g) smoked sea salt, divided

Scant ¼ tsp freshly grated nutmeg

1 tbsp (15 ml) toasted sesame oil

2 shallots, minced, or ½ large red onion, diced

4 cloves garlic, minced

1 medium yellow squash, trimmed and diced

2 tbsp (34 g) double-concentrated tomato paste

1 tbsp (10 g) garam masala

1½ tsp (2 g) dried shiitake or porcini mushroom powder

1½ tsp (4 g) Emergency Broth Powder (page 223)

½ tsp ground coriander

2 cups (268 g) frozen green peas

2 cups (480 g) fire-roasted crushed tomatoes

Amba (page 410), Savory Dried Apricot Paste (page 411) or favorite vegan chutney, to serve

Cook the yams and chana dal (the latter according to package directions) in separate pots to cut down on preparation time. Drain them both once fork tender (for the former) and al dente (for the latter). Add the yams back to the cooking pot once drained, and place them back on the stove for the residual heat to further remove excess moisture. Add the coconut milk, a generous ½ teaspoon of the salt and nutmeg to the pot of yams. Thoroughly mash and set aside.

Preheat the oven to 350°F (177°C).

In a large pot, combine the oil, shallots, garlic and squash. Cook over medium-high heat until the vegetables start to brown, about 4 minutes. Stir occasionally and adjust the heat as needed.

Add the tomato paste, garam masala, remaining ¾ teaspoon salt, mushroom powder, broth powder and coriander. Cook to toast the spices for another minute. Add the cooked chana dal and green peas, and cook for another minute. Add the crushed tomatoes and cook until the peas are thawed, another 4 minutes.

Transfer to a deep, 11 x 8-inch (28 x 20-cm) baking dish. Top with the mashed yams, using a slanted spatula to make waves on top. Bake for 20 minutes. Then broil for 2 minutes, or until golden brown on top. Serve with Amba, Savory Dried Apricot Paste or your favorite chutney. Reheated leftovers taste even better!

Sambal SOY CURL TACOS ✶

Every time I'm set to make this recipe, I find myself snacking on the prepared soy curls alone. And then I'm left with too little to make tacos. So I make more again. Lather, rinse, repeat. But you get the gist: these are really, really, really good.

If soy curls cannot be found or if you generally avoid soy, try replacing them with 18 ounces (510 g) of prepared, plain seitan strips. —CS

MAKES 10 TACOS

6 oz (170 g) dry soy curls

Filtered water

½ cup (96 g) Sucanat

¼ cup (60 ml) brown rice vinegar

¼ cup (60 ml) mirin

¼ cup (60 g) Asian hot chile paste or sambal oelek (quantity to taste)

¼ cup (60 ml) shoyu

2 tsp (3 g) dried shiitake powder

½ tsp ground ginger

1 tbsp (15 ml) toasted sesame oil

½ medium red onion, diced

4 cloves garlic, minced

Coarse kosher salt

Shredded Napa cabbage

Shredded carrot

10 (6" [15-cm]) corn tortillas, warmed

Thinly sliced scallion

Chopped fresh cilantro

Place the soy curls in a large bowl. Cover them with filtered water and allow them to rehydrate for 10 minutes. Drain well, gently squeezing out the extra moisture. Leave the curls in the colander to further release extra moisture while preparing the sauce.

In a small saucepan, whisk to combine the Sucanat, vinegar, mirin, sambal, shoyu, shiitake powder and ginger. Bring the mixture to a low boil, reduce the heat to medium and cook until thickened to about half the original amount. This should take about 15 minutes. Stir occasionally and adjust the heat as needed. Set the sambal sauce aside.

In a large wok or skillet, heat the oil over medium-high heat. Add the onion, garlic and rehydrated soy curls. Top with a generous pinch of salt. Fry the mixture until golden brown, about 8 minutes, stirring occasionally. Adjust the heat as needed. Pour half of the sambal sauce onto the soy curls, and cook until absorbed and glazed.

Place a small handful of cabbage and carrot on a tortilla. Top with a generous portion of soy curls and a drizzle of the remaining sambal sauce (about 1 teaspoon per taco). Top with scallion and cilantro. Repeat with the remaining tortillas.

Leftover soy curls can be stored in an airtight container in the refrigerator for up to 3 days and reheated over medium-low heat in a skillet.

✶SEE PHOTO INSERT

Beer-Braised
JACKFRUIT TACOS

I think I've already chatted your ear off about how great jackfruit is as a meat alternative, especially in tacos. So I'm going to do it again for the message to really get across. You're welcome. Here, it's braised and slow-cooked in beer (oh yeah, and other stuff), then paired with some kickass salsa and finally a touch of crema. I know Taco Tuesday is popular on the internet, but with all the awesome taco recipes in this book, you might want to make it Every-Day-is-Taco Day instead. —CS

MAKES 12 TACOS

1 tbsp (15 ml) toasted sesame oil

2 (20-oz [567-g]) cans young green jackfruit, in brine, drained, rinsed and cut into ¼" (6-mm) thick strips, lengthwise

2 shallots, minced

4 large cloves garlic, minced

2 dried shiitake mushrooms, rehydrated and minced

2 chipotle peppers from can in adobo sauce, minced

1 (12-oz [350-ml]) can vegan lager beer

1 tbsp (8 g) Emergency Broth Powder (page 223)

1 tbsp (15 ml) tamari

1 tbsp (15 ml) adobo sauce from can of chipotle peppers

1 tsp smoked sea salt

12 (6" [15-cm]) vegan corn tortillas, warmed

Roasted Corn Pique Salsa (page 184) or other favorite salsa

Cashew Crema (page 411)

Heat the oil in a large pot over medium-high heat. Add the jackfruit, shallots, garlic, minced shiitake and chipotle peppers, and brown for 8 minutes, stirring occasionally. Adjust the heat as needed.

Add the beer, broth powder, tamari, adobo sauce and salt. Stir to combine everything and simmer over medium-low heat, covered, for 1 hour. Remove the lid, and cook for 10 minutes to eliminate excess liquid.

Reheat in a 325°F (163°C) oven until golden brown, about 10 to 15 minutes.

Serve in a slightly charred tortilla with a pile of salsa and a scoop of crema on top.

Sweet and Sour
AND SOMEWHAT SPICY TOFU

My favorite way to enjoy this dish is to serve it with loads of steamed broccoli and brown rice. It makes for a well-balanced, protein-rich and flavorful meal that hits just the right spot. —CS

MAKES 1 CUP (235 ML) MARINADE, SERVES 3 TO 4

SAMBAL MARINADE

¼ cup (48 g) Sucanat

¼ cup (60 ml) brown rice vinegar

¼ cup (60 ml) mirin

¼ cup (60 g) Asian hot chile paste or sambal oelek (quantity to taste)

¼ cup (60 ml) shoyu

2 tsp (3 g) dried shiitake powder

½ tsp ground ginger

TOFU

½ cup (120 ml) sambal marinade (see above)

¼ cup (60 ml) pure pineapple juice

1 lb (454 g) super-firm tofu, cut into bite-size cubes

1 tbsp (15 ml) plus 2 tsp (10 ml) toasted sesame oil or peanut oil, divided

½ medium red onion, diced

3 cloves garlic, minced

2 bell peppers (any color), cored and chopped

1 tbsp (8 g) organic cornstarch

1¼ cups (263 g) diced fresh pineapple or chunks

Coarse kosher salt, to taste

FOR THE SAMBAL MARINADE

In a small saucepan, whisk to combine the Sucanat, vinegar, mirin, sambal, shoyu, shiitake powder and ginger. Bring to a low boil, reduce the heat to medium and cook the mixture until thickened to about half the original amount. This should take about 15 minutes. Stir occasionally and adjust the heat as needed. Set aside.

FOR THE TOFU

In a small bowl, whisk to combine the marinade and pineapple juice. Place the tofu in a shallow dish, and add a scant ¼ cup (55 ml) of the marinade mixture to it. Gently fold the tofu cubes to coat. Let it marinate for 30 minutes.

In a large wok or skillet, heat 1 tablespoon (15 ml) of the oil over medium-high heat. Remove the tofu from the marinade (do not discard it, just add the leftover marinade to the rest of the marinade mixture), and add the cubes to the heated oil. Cook until golden brown, stirring occasionally. Adjust the heat as needed. This should take about 8 minutes.

Remove the tofu from the wok and heat the remaining 2 teaspoons (10 ml) oil. Add the onion and cook until browned, about 3 minutes. Add the garlic and bell peppers, and cook until the peppers start to soften.

In the meantime, place the cornstarch in a small bowl and add 2 tablespoons (30 ml) of the marinade mixture to it. Whisk to dissolve. Pour it back into the marinade mixture and whisk to combine.

Add the tofu and pineapple to the vegetables, and pour the marinade mixture into the wok. Cook until the tofu and pineapple are heated through and the marinade mixture has thickened slightly. Adjust the seasoning and add kosher salt if desired. Serve alongside broccoli and cooked rice or noodles.

*SEE PHOTO INSERT

Japanese-Inspired
SANDWICHES

Nothing can stand in the way of a good vegan sandwich, and this version, loaded with Japanese-inspired flavors, definitely is one of the greater ones. The yield will vary upon the size of the bread used: I love a good sourdough bread with slices the size of regular sandwich bread, and it yields about 6 sandwiches with this type of bread. Any tender vegan bread roll would do the trick too. —CS

MAKES 6 SANDWICHES

Vegan bread of choice, lightly toasted

Vegan mayo for the bread

Shredded green cabbage

Thinly sliced cucumber

Thinly sliced scallion, to taste

1 recipe Tare Tofu (page 183), thinly sliced

1 recipe Miso-Marinated Mushrooms (page 185), minced

Nanami togarashi

Place your bread slices on a plate. Spread enough mayo to cover the surface of both sides of the sandwiches. Top with a handful of cabbage, a couple of slices of cucumber, scallion to taste, slices of tofu, minced mushrooms and a dash of nanami togarashi. If you have leftovers of the tare sauce used to glaze the tofu, it's brilliant to add a drizzle on top of the filling. Serve immediately.

MAIN DISHES

Pickled MANGO CURRY WRAPS

Confession time: I made these wraps so many times last summer that I might have lost count. They're healthy, fragrant, filling, refreshing and deliciously spicy. —CS

MAKES 6 WRAPS

2 tbsp (30 ml) mirin

2 tbsp (30 ml) tamari

2 tbsp (40 g) agave nectar

2 tsp (6 g) curry powder

Cayenne pepper, to taste

Pinch of coarse sea salt

1 lb (454 g) super-firm tofu, cut into ¼" (6-mm) slices

Oil spray

Vegan mayo of choice

Vegan green or red curry paste

6 vegan lavash breads or flour tortillas

6 oz (170 g) fresh baby spinach

Chopped Pickled Dried Mango (page 186)

Chopped fresh cilantro

Thinly sliced scallion

In a small bowl, whisk to combine the mirin, tamari, agave, curry powder, cayenne and salt. Pour the mixture into a shallow dish that will fit the tofu slices evenly. Add the tofu slices to the dish so that they're evenly covered in the marinade. Soak for at least 4 hours in the refrigerator, up to overnight.

Preheat the oven to 425°F (220°C). Line a baking sheet with parchment paper. Place the tofu slices evenly on top and lightly coat with spray. Bake for 20 minutes, or until golden brown and fragrant. Be sure not to overcook or the tofu will become hard to chew.

Apply a generous layer of mayo and curry paste, to taste (depending on how hot you like it), on lavash bread or a tortilla. Add a generous handful of spinach to the center of the wrap. Top with your chopped tofu slices. Add the pickled mango (with onion), cilantro and scallion to taste. Wrap tightly and repeat with the remaining wraps.

Mexican BAKED MAC AND QUESO ✳

To make this pasta dish even more decadent, and if you have some handy, you could use a generous couple of handfuls of store-bought vegan cheddar cheese instead of the one cup (235 ml) queso sauce topping. Either way, the results will be muy bueno! —CS

SERVES 6

QUESO SAUCE

1 cup (120 g) raw cashew pieces, soaked in water to cover overnight in the refrigerator, drained and rinsed

1 cup (235 ml) water

¾ cup (180 ml) canned coconut milk

1 tbsp (15 ml) lemon juice

1 medium sweet potato (about 9½ oz [270 g]), baked, peeled and chopped

¼ cup (20 g) nutritional yeast

1 tbsp (8 g) Emergency Broth Powder (page 223)

1 tsp maca powder

1 tsp adobo sauce from a can of chipotle peppers

½ tsp smoked sea salt

½ tsp chipotle powder

½ tsp ground cumin

½ tsp garlic powder

½ tsp onion powder

THE MAC

1 (1-lb [454-g]) package whole wheat penne, cooked according to package directions

1 tbsp (15 ml) grapeseed or olive oil

1 medium red onion, diced

2 large green bell peppers, cored and diced

4 cloves garlic, minced

1 tsp dried porcini powder

½ tsp ground cumin

½ tsp smoked paprika

½ tsp coarse kosher salt

½ tsp smoked salt

2 large tomatoes, diced

2 tbsp (30 ml) adobo sauce from a can of chipotle peppers

Lime wedges, sliced scallion and chopped fresh cilantro, for serving

FOR THE QUESO SAUCE

Place all of the ingredients in a blender. Blend until smooth and thoroughly combined. Set the sauce aside.

FOR THE MAC

Once the pasta is cooked, drain and set it aside. In the same pot used to cook the pasta, add the oil, onion and bell peppers. Heat over medium-high heat and cook until slightly softened, stirring occasionally, about 4 minutes. Add the garlic, porcini powder, cumin, paprika and salts, and cook until lightly browned, about 2 more minutes. Add the tomatoes and adobo sauce, and cook until reduced to a thick marinara-like consistency, about 6 more minutes.

Preheat the oven to 375°F (190°C).

Transfer the vegetables to a large and deep baking dish. Reserve 1 cup (235 ml) of the queso sauce and add the rest to the vegetables, stirring to combine. Add the cooked pasta and stir to thoroughly coat. Press down evenly, and add the reserved queso sauce evenly on top. Bake the mac for 20 minutes, or until browned. Serve immediately with a generous squeeze of lime juice. Top your mac with scallion and cilantro. Leftovers are even tastier.

ENCHILADA Roja

I like to make these red enchiladas (that's what enchilada roja means) with regular enchilada sauce for the bottom and for dipping the tortillas, and then add about 3 tablespoons (51 g) Cashew Queso (page 415) to the remaining enchilada sauce for topping before baking. It's entirely optional, but it adds some cheesiness if you want it. —CS

MAKES 8 ENCHILADAS

TOMATILLO SALSA

1 cup (120 g) frozen corn

2 large raw tomatillos (140 g), husked and halved or quartered

1 large scallion, thinly chopped

Pinch of coarse kosher salt

ENCHILADAS

1 tsp grapeseed or olive oil

2 oz (56 g) fresh cremini mushrooms, gently brushed clean and minced

1 small Mexican squash, trimmed and minced

2 cloves garlic, minced

¼ tsp ground cumin

¼ tsp smoked paprika

¼ tsp taco seasoning

¼ tsp smoked sea salt

½ lime

¾ cup (130 g) cooked black beans

Handful fresh cilantro, chopped

1 recipe Enchilada Sauce (page 413)

8 (6" [15-cm]) corn tortillas

FOR THE TOMATILLO SALSA

Preheat the oven to 425°F (220°C). Place the corn in a 9-inch (23-cm) square pan, and roast until golden brown, about 20 minutes. Set the corn aside, and keep the pan handy for baking the enchiladas.

(continued)

MAIN DISHES

Place the tomatillos in a food processor and process until saucy. Combine with the corn, scallion and salt.

FOR THE ENCHILADAS

In a pan, heat the oil over medium-high heat and cook the mushrooms, squash and garlic until lightly browned, about 4 minutes. Add the cumin, paprika, taco seasoning and salt. Toast for 2 minutes. Deglaze your pan with a squirt of lime juice from the halved lime. Then add the tomatillo salsa and the beans. Cook for another 2 minutes, stirring occasionally. Remove from the heat and add cilantro, stirring to combine.

Lower the heat of the oven to 350°F (177°C).

Place ¼ cup (60 g) of enchilada sauce in the bottom of the pan. Place the remaining sauce in a shallow dish. Dip each tortilla into the sauce, making sure all the surface is covered with sauce on both sides. Let the excess sauce drip back into the pan. Transfer the tortillas to the baking pan.

Fill each tortilla with a slightly scant ¼ cup (45 g) of filling. Arrange the filling in one line in the center and roll. Place it seam-side down in the pan. Repeat with the remaining tortillas, placing them snugly in the pan. Drizzle remaining enchilada sauce on top of the rolled tortillas and bake until bubbly, about 15 minutes.

Note: Consider roasting the corn when you're already using the oven for something else to prevent energy waste. You can also use an already-preheated oven to roast garlic or other vegetables, and even to bake potatoes. "Don't overcrowd it, but make the most out of its heat" is my oven-ly motto.

Shiitake CHICKPEA CREPES

+GF

I like to serve these super-thin pancakes alongside stir-fried vegetables and thinly sliced Tare Tofu (page 183) with a drizzle of Ponzu Sauce (page 414). Or alternatively, with a salad composed of a mix of thinly shredded green cabbage and carrot, and drizzled with a few tablespoons (45 ml) of the brine from the Miso-Marinated Mushrooms (page 185). It's a healthy, umami-filled light dinner that I make at least once a week. —CS

MAKES 4 CREPES

1 tbsp (15 ml) brown rice vinegar

1 cup minus 1 tbsp (220 ml) unsweetened plain plant-based milk of choice

1 tbsp (15 ml) toasted sesame oil

1 tbsp (15 ml) tamari

1½ tbsp (12 g) organic cornstarch

¼ cup (40 g) white rice flour (not sweet)

¼ cup (30 g) chickpea flour

1 tbsp (5 g) nutritional yeast

4 mushrooms from Miso-Marinated Mushrooms (page 185), well drained and minced

Oil spray

Thinly sliced scallion

In a large bowl, combine the vinegar with the milk. Let stand a few minutes to let the vinegar curdle the milk. Add the oil and tamari, whisking to combine. Sift the cornstarch, flours and nutritional yeast on top; whisk to combine and eliminate lumps. Stir the minced mushrooms into the batter and let it stand for 15 minutes.

Spray a large skillet with a fair amount of oil. Heat the skillet over medium-high heat.

Once hot, add ⅓ cup (80 ml) of batter to the pan, tilting it so that the batter spreads out and covers about 8 inches (20 cm) of the surface. Cook until the edges are light golden brown and the crepe slides easily, about 4 minutes. Carefully flip (using a large spatula helps) and cook for another 3 minutes or until light golden brown. Transfer the crepe to a plate and repeat with the rest of the batter. If you have a lot of trouble flipping your crepes (this can depend on the skillet used), you can skip flipping them and just cook them on one side for about 5 minutes, or until the side facing up looks set. You should get 4 crepes in all. Roll up, and serve immediately with scallion and accompaniment of choice.

*SEE PHOTO INSERT

Spanish PAPRIKA TOFU SANDWICHES ✳

Mighty delicious and certainly cheaper than a vacation to Europe, this recipe contains all the bright flavors associated with beautiful, sunny Spain packed between two slices of crusty bread!

Since all tofu blocks do not come equally shaped, feel free to cut yours however you see fit, as long as the thickness doesn't exceed ½ inch (1.3 cm). —CS

MAKES 4 SANDWICHES

2 tbsp (30 ml) sherry vinegar

1 tbsp (15 ml) olive oil

1 tbsp (15 ml) lemon juice

1 tbsp (6 g) smoked paprika

1 tsp smoked sea salt

1 tsp Aleppo-style pepper flakes

1 lb (454 g) super-firm tofu cut into square ½" (1.3-cm) thick slices

About 20 vegan buttery crackers (2 oz [56 g]), crushed into fine crumbs

1 tsp onion powder

½ cup (112 g) plain vegan mayo

8 slices vegan crusty bread of choice, toasted or 4 panini, halved and toasted

Fresh baby spinach

Thinly sliced red onion

Marinated artichoke hearts, chopped

Roasted red bell pepper, thinly sliced

Pitted Spanish olives or other favorite olives, halved

Fresh parsley

In a large, shallow dish, stir to combine the vinegar, oil, lemon juice, paprika, salt and pepper flakes. Place the tofu slices in the marinade, flipping them over to make sure each side gets coated with the marinade. Marinate in the refrigerator for at least 1 hour, flipping the slices once halfway through.

Preheat the oven to 375°F (190°C). Line a large baking sheet with parchment paper.

Place the cracker crumbs and onion powder in a shallow bowl, stirring to combine. Grab a tofu slice with one hand, letting the excess marinade drip back into the pan. With the other hand, coat the slice on both sides with cracker crumbs. Place it onto the prepared baking sheet. Repeat with the remaining slices. Do not discard the marinade!

Bake the tofu for 12 minutes on each side, or until golden brown. In the meantime, whisk the mayo with the leftover marinade in a small bowl until well combined.

Grab a couple slices of bread or a bread roll, and apply a layer of mayo. Top with a handful of spinach, a few slices of onion, 4 tofu slices, a few pieces of artichoke hearts, bell pepper, olives and a small handful of parsley. Apply the second mayo-ed slice of bread on top, press down gently and serve immediately. Repeat with the remaining sandwiches.

Savory MUSHROOM GALETTE

The fact that I'm the only mushroom-lover in my house comes in handy occasionally, because I got to eat this one all by myself. The crust is so flaky, the filling so earthy and satisfying, and the little bit of cream cheese rounds out the ultimate comfort food aspect of the galette. For best results, chill the prepared filling overnight so that the rosemary can infuse its flavor into the mushrooms, and so that the mushrooms aren't too hot to handle for the crust. —CS

SERVES 4

2 oz (56 g) mix dried mushrooms

1½ tbsp (23 ml) grapeseed oil

3½ oz (100 g) fresh shiitake mushrooms, thinly sliced

8 oz (227 g) fresh cremini mushrooms, thinly sliced

3 oz (85 g) shallots, thinly sliced

6½ oz (184 g) cooked and peeled chestnuts, coarsely chopped

1 tsp coarse kosher salt

Freshly cracked pepper, to taste

1 large sprig fresh rosemary

4 cloves garlic, minced

2 tbsp (30 ml) sherry vinegar

1 recipe Galette Crust (page 97)

4 oz (113 g) vegan cream cheese

Soak the dried mushrooms in filtered water for at least 30 minutes, or until softened. Rinse them out well to eliminate potential grit; then drain well and mince. Set aside.

In a skillet large enough to place the mushrooms in an even layer, heat the oil over medium-high heat. Add the shiitake and cremini mushrooms. Cook them until the moisture is rendered, about 4 minutes, stirring occasionally. Add the shallots and cook until lightly browned, about another 6 minutes. Add the chestnuts, salt, pepper, rosemary and garlic. Cook another 2 minutes. Deglaze with the vinegar for another 2 minutes and remove from the heat. Let it cool completely before storing covered in the refrigerator overnight. Discard the rosemary sprig.

Preheat the oven to 375°F (190°C).

Roll out the prepared dough to make a circle about 12 inches (30 cm) on a piece of parchment paper. Leaving about a 1½-inch (3.8-cm) space around the edges, add the filling evenly in the center of the dough. (There might be a little too much filling for the galette; use your judgment and keep the leftovers for stir-fries or tofu scrambles.) Tightly fold the dough onto the filling, transfer onto a baking sheet and bake for 25 minutes.

Carefully remove the galette from the oven and add spoonfuls of cream cheese on the exposed filling of the galette. Bake for another 25 minutes or until golden brown. Let it cool for 10 minutes before serving with a big salad or roasted vegetables for a balanced meal.

Japanese TEMPEH AND SUSHI RICE BOWLS

I originally served the tempeh in taco form. It was great, but then I prepared the leftovers in bowl form and it was even better! So there you have it: glazed tempeh with crisp broccoli and rice, and a great flavor boost from nanami togarashi. The latter is a Japanese spice mix composed of sesame seeds, red pepper, sansho pepper, orange peel, ginger and seaweed. It can be found at international food markets or online.

SERVES 4

TARE

¼ cup (60 ml) mirin

¼ cup (80 g) agave nectar

¼ cup (60 ml) tamari

¼ cup (60 ml) shaoxing cooking wine or sake

TEMPEH

2 tbsp (40 g) agave nectar

2 tbsp (30 ml) tamari

2 tbsp (30 ml) mirin

1 tbsp (8 g) nanami togarashi, plus extra for serving

8 oz (227 g) tempeh, cut into 4 rectangles, then each rectangle cut in half into 2 thin rectangles, then into triangles

Nonstick cooking spray or oil spray

BOWL

3 tbsp (45 ml) melted coconut oil or peanut oil, divided

24 oz (680 g) very small broccoli florets

2 tbsp (30 ml) tare (see above)

1½ cups (240 g) dry sushi rice or favorite rice, cooked according to package directions and chilled overnight

2 tbsp (30 ml) kimchi brine

1 tbsp (15 ml) shoyu or tamari

1 cup (134 g) frozen green peas

Thinly sliced scallion

Nanami Togarashi Cashews (page 187)

FOR THE TARE

Combine all the ingredients in a small, heavy-bottomed saucepan. Bring to a boil, lower the heat to a healthy simmer and cook until reduced to half, about 15 minutes. Stir occasionally. Set it aside.

FOR THE TEMPEH

In a 9-inch (23-cm) square baking dish, whisk to combine the agave, tamari, mirin and nanami togarashi. Coat all the tempeh slices on both sides and marinate in the refrigerator for 30 minutes.

Preheat the oven to 375°F (190°C).

Place the tempeh on a baking sheet lined with parchment paper. (Reserve the leftover marinade for adding to stir-fries, noodles or rice.) Lightly coat the tempeh with spray. Bake for 8 minutes on each side, until golden brown. Set aside.

FOR THE BOWL

Place 1½ tablespoons (23 ml) of the oil in a large pan or wok. Heat over medium-high heat, add the broccoli and cook for 6 minutes. Add the tare and cook for another 2 minutes, or until just tender but still crisp. Toss occasionally and adjust the heat as needed. Transfer to a large bowl.

Heat the remaining 1½ tablespoons (23 ml) oil over medium-high heat and add the rice while crumbling the larger chunks. Cook the rice for 2 minutes, tossing only occasionally and adjusting the heat as needed. Add the brine and shoyu, toss well and cook until the rice is fragrant and nutty, about 5 minutes. Add the peas and cook until just thawed, heated and still bright green.

Cut the tempeh slices into bite-size pieces. Divide the rice, broccoli and tempeh among 4 bowls. Drizzle with tare and serve with scallion, cashews and extra nanami togarashi to taste.

*SEE PHOTO INSERT

JAPCHAE (Korean Vermicelli Stir-Fry)

Japchae is a popular Korean stir-fry composed of colorful vegetables and glass noodles, with a sweet and savory note. The chewy noodles used in this dish are made from sweet potato starch and water. They can be found at international food markets or online, but if your search isn't fruitful at all, you can always use the same amount of regular glass noodles. —CS

SERVES 3 TO 4

3 tbsp (45 ml) brine from Smoky Apple (or Pear) Pickles (page 186)

3 tbsp (45 ml) shoyu or tamari

2½ tsp (17 g) Gochujang Paste (page 413), plus more for serving

8 dried shiitake mushrooms, covered with room-temperature filtered water and rehydrated for at least 1 hour

4 tsp (20 ml) toasted sesame oil, divided, plus more for serving

2 medium carrots, trimmed and peeled, cut into matchsticks

4 oz (113 g) fresh cremini mushrooms, stems removed, gently brushed clean and minced or sliced

3 cloves garlic, minced

2 packed tsp (10 g) minced fresh ginger

1 heaping cup (100 g) chopped red or green cabbage or baby bok choy

7 oz (198 g) dry Korean vermicelli glass noodles (Dang Myun), cooked according to package directions

7 oz (198 g) fresh spinach

Thinly sliced scallion, for serving

Toasted sesame seeds, for serving

In a small bowl, place the brine, shoyu and gochujang. Whisk to combine. Set aside.

When the shiitake have soaked for at least 1 hour, gently rinse them clean of any grit, squeeze them lightly, remove the stems and cut them into thin strips. Set aside. (You can keep the soaking liquid if desired: simply filter it in a fine-mesh sieve lined with a piece of clean paper towel in order to remove grit. Use it as cooking broth or to deglaze vegetables.)

In a large pan or a wok, place 2 teaspoons (10 ml) of the sesame oil, carrots, cremini mushrooms, garlic and ginger. Cook over medium-high heat, stirring occasionally, until the carrots start to become tender, about 4 minutes. Add the cabbage and cook until it just starts to become tender yet remains crisp, about 3 minutes. Set aside.

As soon as the noodles are cooked, strain the cooking liquid, rinse the pasta and toss it with the remaining 2 teaspoons (10 ml) sesame oil. Sauté with the shiitake strips over medium-high heat until lightly browned. Add the spinach, cook for another 2 minutes and stir occasionally. Add half of the shoyu mixture and cook for another 2 minutes. Add the veggies and the rest of the shoyu mixture. Toss well, cook for another minute and serve with an extra drizzle of sesame oil, extra gochujang, scallions and sesame seeds.

*SEE PHOTO INSERT

Moroccan PIZZA

+SF

It's a struggle to decide which pizza I prefer between the Spicy Kimchi Pizza (page 81) and this one. Let me have another twelve slices of each to make up my mind.

If spicy isn't nice-y to you, you can replace as much harissa paste as desired with tomato paste. Mix both pastes to combine in a small bowl, and then spread it on the pizza dough. —CS

SERVES 2 TO 4

1 recipe Garlic and Herb Pizza Dough (page 98), after refrigeration and ready for toppings

3 tbsp (63 g) harissa paste or enough to lightly cover the dough (see headnote)

½ recipe Moroccan Marinated Vegetables (page 183)

10 Kalamata olives or chalkidiki olives, halved and pitted

8 marinated artichoke heart halves

Soft sliced sun-dried tomatoes, to taste

1 recipe Yogurt Drizzle for Moroccan Pizza (page 97)

While the pizza dough rests, preheat the oven to 475°F (246°C).

Spread the harissa on the pizza dough. Top the pizza with an even layer of marinated vegetables. Top with the olives and artichoke hearts.

Bake for 18 to 20 minutes, or until golden brown.

Top the pizza with the sun-dried tomatoes and yogurt drizzle, to taste. Serve immediately.

*SEE PHOTO INSERT

Yogurt Drizzle FOR MOROCCAN PIZZA

+QP +SF +GF

This tangy drizzle is perfect to cool down the Moroccan Pizza (page 96) while bringing even more flavor to your slice of pizza pie! —CS

MAKES ½ CUP (130 G)

½ cup (120 g) plain unsweetened vegan coconut yogurt

1 tbsp (16 g) tahini paste

½ tsp lemon juice

Pinch of coarse kosher salt

Small handful fresh cilantro, mint, parsley or a combo, minced

1 clove garlic, grated

Combine all the ingredients in a small bowl. Store covered in the refrigerator until ready to use, up to 3 days.

GALETTE Crust

+SF +QP

Behold: the flakiest, easiest, least-fussy galette crust you've ever wanted. Taste its golden perfection in Miso Sweet Potato Galette (page 299) and Savory Mushroom Galette (page 94). —CS

MAKES 1 GALETTE CRUST

1¼ cups (155 g) all-purpose or whole wheat pastry flour

2 tsp (8 g) organic light brown sugar

Pinch of coarse kosher salt

Scant ¼ cup (55 ml) grapeseed oil or other neutral-flavored oil

2 tsp (10 ml) apple cider vinegar

¼ cup (60 ml) cold water, as needed

Almond, hazelnut or cashew meal, to lightly cover bottom (optional, for wet fillings mostly)

Preheat the oven to 375°F (190°C). Line a large rimmed baking sheet with parchment paper.

In a large bowl, use a fork to combine the flour, sugar and salt. Drizzle the oil and vinegar on top, and use the fork to create crumbles. Add water as needed, 1 tablespoon (15 ml) at a time, stirring with the fork until a dough forms: it should be neither too wet nor too dry. Shape into a ball and flatten it into a disk. Place it on the parchment paper.

(continued)

MAIN DISHES

Using a rolling pin, roll out the dough into about a 10-inch (25-cm) circle.

Evenly sprinkle a handful of chosen meal in the center, leaving it about 1½ inches (3.8 cm) from the edge. Follow the remaining instructions for the Miso Sweet Potato Galette (page 299) or Savory Mushroom Galette (page 94).

Garlic and Herb
PIZZA DOUGH

+SF

While I usually steer clear from declaring "this is the best ... ever" because cockiness isn't a good look, this is the best pizza dough I personally have ever eaten. It is light and flaky and crispy, and I don't think any topping could even manage to make it taste bad. See it in action with Spicy Kimchi Pizza (page 81) and Moroccan Pizza (page 96).

Note that all ingredients that go into yeast-based recipes should be at room temperature (flour, yeast and such) or lukewarm (water), never cold from the freezer or refrigerator and definitely not too hot. —CS

MAKES 1 PIZZA CRUST

2 cups (250 g) organic unbleached all-purpose flour (or an even mix white whole wheat and all-purpose, or bread flour)

¾ tsp fine sea salt

¾ tsp instant yeast

2 cloves garlic, grated

2 tsp (2 g) Italian seasoning

2 tbsp (30 ml) neutral-flavored oil

Room-temperature water (if temperature is really low, use lukewarm water)

Place the flour, salt and yeast in a large bowl, stirring to combine. Place the garlic and Italian seasoning along with the oil in a glass measuring cup. Top with just enough water to reach the 1 cup (235 ml) mark.

Pour this mixture on top of the dry ingredients, scraping the sides of the measuring cup to get it all. Use a rubber spatula to thoroughly mix all of the ingredients. Gather the dough in the center of the bowl. Cover tightly with plastic wrap and leave at room temperature for 3 hours.

Remove the plastic wrap and "punch down" the dough with a rubber spatula. Sprinkle around the dough with a handful of flour while holding it up with the spatula. Swirl the dough in the bowl. Cover the dough again with plastic wrap and place in the refrigerator for at least 18 hours.

Have a pizza sheet ready. Sprinkle evenly with a handful of flour, and transfer the rather wet dough onto the sheet using a rubber spatula. Sprinkle evenly with flour and flatten into the shape you'll want your pizza to be: thick or thin crust will depend on your preference, but I like to make mine about 12 inches (30 cm) in diameter. Make sure the surface is evenly sprinkled with a light amount of flour to keep the plastic wrap from sticking to it. Loosely cover with plastic wrap and bring it back to room temperature for 30 minutes.

Preheat the oven to 475°F (246°C). Carefully remove the plastic wrap, apply toppings and bake for 16 to 20 minutes, or until beautifully browned and crisp. Baking time will depend on thickness.

Marinated
PORTOBELLO CASHEW CHEESEBURGERS WITH HERBS AND TOMATOES

If you think these look good, they taste even better. —EvE

SERVES 2 TO 4

MARINATED MUSHROOMS

4 portobello mushrooms

1 tbsp (15 ml) extra-virgin olive oil

1 tbsp (15 ml) liquid aminos (or soy sauce)

CASHEW CHEESE

1¾ cups (195 g) cashews

½ cup (120 ml) water

⅓ cup (27 g) nutritional yeast

Juice from 1 lemon

2 cloves garlic, peeled

2 tbsp (30 g) miso

Salt and herbes de Provence, to taste

TOPPINGS

Fresh chopped chives, spinach and parsley

Sliced tomatoes

Anything else your heart desires

FOR THE MUSHROOMS

Rub the mushrooms down with the olive oil and liquid aminos. Then place them in your dehydrator or oven at its lowest temperature for about 3 hours, or until they have softened and darkened and smell amazing. While they are marinating, make the cashew cheese.

FOR THE CASHEW CHEESE

Blend all of the cheese ingredients until smooth and thick. Taste and adjust amounts accordingly. Scoop it into a bowl lined with a cheesecloth and let it sit somewhere for at least 2 hours (or, if you've got time, let it age for a few days).

When everything is ready, spread your cheese onto your mushrooms and layer with herbs and toma-toes. You can double-shroom it (that is now a term) if you want, and/or use fresh mushrooms instead of marinated.

Note: You're gonna have lots of leftover cashew cheese. Let it sit in a quiet spot overnight, and then put it in the fridge and eat it within a week.

*SEE PHOTO INSERT

Jicama ONION CAKES WITH CUMIN, CORIANDER, DILL AND LEMON

These are inspired by crab cakes and they taste freaking amazing. They taste great with avocado, just so ya know. Please don't expect this recipe to taste much like the original thing . . . the ingredients are totally different and there's no cooking involved. Enjoy the flavors and textures for what they are! Veggies are winners all by themselves! —EvE

SERVES 2 TO 4

1 cup (130 g) peeled and chopped jicama

¼ cup (38 g) chopped onion

Juice from ½ lemon

Cumin, coriander, dill, chili, salt and pepper (as desired)

1 cup (120 g) walnuts

Throw all of the ingredients except the walnuts into your food processor and pulse a few times until it's a consistency you like. Dump it into a bowl and set it aside. Now process the walnuts into a thick paste and add this to the first mixture, combining evenly so you end up with a mushy mix. It doesn't sound appetizing, but other describing words are not com-ing to mind at the moment. Shape them into cakes (I used a large cookie mold) and then dehydrate them for a few hours until they hold together (or use the oven at its lowest temperature to get the same result). Serve with herbs, avocado, veggies, spreads, crackers or whatever else you like!

*SEE PHOTO INSERT

Marinated ZUCCHINI AND TOMATO LASAGNA WITH CASHEW HERB CHEESE

I get lost in my food. By that I mean almost every time I eat, I become so raptured in the flavors, colors and textures that I forget where and who I am. When I am done with my feeding frenzy (no self-control), I usually have questions such as, "What just happened!?" "How!?" "What!?" "Where am I!?" "What is this!?" "Was that real!?" and so on and so forth. I love my food, and I think my food loves me too. I cannot imagine NOT being stoked out of my mind every time I eat! I need to a) know that the food is good for me and b) know it's gonna taste amazing—otherwise it ain't goin' down. I see myself as being in a relationship with the food I choose to eat . . . since we are going to change each other forever, right down to the molecular level. This lasagna gets me stoked. —EvE

SERVES 3 OR 4

VEGGIES

1 zucchini

5 tomatoes

Olive oil, Himalayan salt, black pepper and coriander (to your taste)

CASHEW HERB CHEESE

1 cup (110 g) cashews

1 tsp lemon juice

1 tsp dried dill

¼ cup (60 ml) water, more or less, as needed

Dash of ground turmeric, paprika and ground coriander

½ tsp Himalayan salt

1 clove garlic

1 cup (40 g) spinach

Cilantro and ground coriander, for serving

FOR THE VEGGIES

Slice the zuke into thin strips on a mandoline and chop the tomatoes. Rub them in oil and spices, and put them in the dehydrator for 1 to 3 hours, or in the oven at the lowest temperature.

FOR THE CASHEW HERB CHEESE

Blend everything until smooth and very thick.

Layer slices of the tomato, zucchini and spinach with the cheese. Sprinkle with cilantro and coriander. Chomp.

*SEE PHOTO INSERT

Tacos WITH TOMATO CORN SALSA AND SPICY NUT MEAT

+QP

This recipe requires no equipment but a knife and a hand or two. What we've got here is cabbage leaves wrapping up fresh, juicy, limey veggies with crunchy, spicy nuts and seeds. Ya can't go wrong. —EvE

SERVES 2

1 small savoy cabbage

SALSA

4 heirloom tomatoes

2 cobs of corn

1 cup (40 g) packed basil

2 limes

¼ tsp black pepper

NUT MEAT

⅓ cup (40 g) pecans

⅓ cup (53 g) sunflower seeds

1 tsp tamari

¾ tsp ground turmeric

¾ tsp ground cumin

⅛ tsp or more chili powder, if desired

Tear off the cabbage leaves gently: instant taco shells.

FOR THE SALSA

Chop the tomatoes as roughly or finely as you like. Slice the corn off the cob. Mince the basil and juice the limes. Throw everything together, including the pepper. It should taste really yummy.

FOR THE NUT MEAT

Finely chop the nuts and seeds, then toss in the tamari and spices. Nom.

Fill your "taco shells" with the salsa and nut meat.

ADAPTATIONS

Use lettuce instead of cabbage; any seeds or nuts instead of pecans and sunflower seeds; soy sauce, coconut amino or Bragg's instead of tamari; any veg you like instead of tomatoes and corn.

Creamy BAKED BUTTERNUT SQUASH, BROCCOLI AND CHIPOTLE ALMOND SAUCE

Lots of textures, colors, flavors, nutrients and mouth-gasms going on here. Along with the delicious, tender baked squash, we've got our greens in the form of steamed broccoli. Finally, the true fabulousness of this recipe is the almond sauce. Holy crap, wherever you are, I need to tell you: it's amazing. Make it. Let's eat good food now, 'kay? —EvE

SERVES 2 TO 4

BAKED BUTTERNUT SQUASH

1 small butternut squash

1 tbsp (14 g) coconut oil, melted

⅛ tsp Himalayan salt

½ tsp black pepper

1 tsp dried basil

1 tsp dried thyme

1 head broccoli

ALMOND SAUCE

2 tbsp (32 g) almond butter

1 tsp maple syrup

1 tsp tamari

1 tbsp (15 g) miso paste

1 tsp apple cider vinegar

⅛ tsp chipotle powder

1 clove garlic

3–4 tbsp (45–60 ml) water, or more as needed

¼ cup (18 g) chopped green onion, for topping

2 tsp (7 g) white sesame seeds, for topping

FOR THE SQUASH

Preheat the oven to 375°F (190°C).

Peel, deseed and cut the squash into ½-inch (1.3-cm) cubes; toss them with the melted coconut oil, salt, pepper and herbs. Spread on a baking sheet. Bake for 25 to 30 minutes, or until each piece is tender all the way through (test one with a fork).

Cut the broccoli into bite-size pieces and steam for 7 to 8 minutes, or until vibrantly green and slightly tender.

FOR THE ALMOND SAUCE

Blend all the sauce ingredients together until smooth, adding as much or as little water as you like.

Place the butternut squash and broccoli on a plate or in a bowl, drizzle with your sauce, and then sprinkle on green onion and sesame seeds.

Creamy Vegan MAC AND CHEESE WITH OTHER GOOD STUFF

The best thing about this cheese sauce is that it is made out of mainly potatoes and carrots. It gets its fat content from walnuts, which are super good for ya. I really like having it with rice and steamed kale, but you can serve it with whatever you prefer: any other whole grain, rice noodles, wheat noodles, buckwheat noodles, on veggies, on nachos . . . the list goes on. Get creative or don't. But in any case, try it out. —EvE

SERVES 2 TO 4

CHEESE SAUCE

2 yellow potatoes, peeled and chopped

1 carrot, peeled and chopped

½ onion, chopped

1 tbsp (15 g) sauerkraut

2 tbsp (30 g) miso paste

2 cloves garlic

½ tsp ground turmeric

½ tsp black pepper

½ tsp sea salt

½ cup (58 g) walnuts, ideally soaked in water for 5 hours, then rinsed

¾ tsp chipotle powder

TAHINI SAUCE

1 heaping tbsp (15 g) tahini

1 clove garlic

2–3 tbsp (30–45 ml) fresh lemon juice

1 tbsp (15 g) miso paste

¼ tsp black pepper

3–4 tbsp (45–60 ml) water, as needed

1 big bunch kale

Your fave pasta, rice, whatever (I used whole-grain kamut pasta)

1 cup (160 g) chopped tomatoes

1 tbsp (10 g) sunflower seeds, for garnish

FOR THE CHEESE SAUCE

Boil the potatoes for 3 minutes, and then add the carrots and boil for another 3 minutes. Add the onion, and keep boiling until the potatoes are tender (it'll probably take another few minutes). Then scoop out the boiled veggies—but keep the water!—and add to a blender. Add the rest of the sauce ingredients to the blender, as well as most of the water you used for boiling (maybe 1½ cups [355 ml] or so, adding as needed). Blend it all until you get a creamy cheese sauce type thing. Adjust it according to taste, adding more salt or whatever. You want it to taste very flavorful at this point and almost a little more salty than you'd normally like, because this is going to spread out on noodles/rice, so the flavor will be less strong.

FOR THE TAHINI SAUCE

Blend everything until smooth, adding more water if needed to get a creamy dressing consistency.

Rip the leaves off the kale and steam them for 5 minutes, or until vibrantly colored.

Cook your pasta, rice or whatever you're using according to directions on the package, and drain it but don't rinse. Add the cheese sauce to your pasta, rice or whatever, and mix in well. Add the kale, tahini sauce and tomatoes, along with a sprinkling of sunflower seeds. Enjoy!

Baked YAMS WITH SAUTÉED VEG AND TOFU

This recipe takes just a few minutes to whip up (not including the half hour or so for the yams to bake). It's super good for ya and tastes delicious. Obviously, I put tahini on it—because tahini is life. —EvE

SERVES 1 OR 2

1 yam

VEG
½ cup (75 g) frozen peas
¼ cup (38 g) chopped onion
1 tbsp (15 ml) tamari or soy sauce
1 tbsp (15 ml) maple syrup
2 tbsp (30 ml) apple cider vinegar or lemon juice
¼ tsp garlic powder
⅛ tsp chipotle powder
¼ package (about 3½ oz [100 g]) cubed tofu
1 cup (30 g) spinach

TOPPINGS
2 tbsp (30 g) tahini
Pinch of black pepper
Handful pumpkin seeds

Preheat the oven to 350°F (177°C). Wash the yam—no need to peel it though. Slice it in half lengthwise and bake on parchment paper for 30 minutes, or until it is tender all the way through (check with a fork) and bubbling around the edges. Leave it to cool.

FOR THE VEG

Throw all the vegetable ingredients into a pan and sauté until everything is tender and flavorful. If the pan goes dry, just add some lemon juice, soy sauce or water. I'd suggest adding the spinach last because it only needs a moment to cook. Add whatever else you like. If it needs more salt, I ain't stoppin' ya.

Plate your yam, throw on the veg and tofu mix and finish with the toppings.

King Oyster MUSHROOMS LAYERED WITH HEIRLOOM TOMATO, BASIL AND AVOCADO

King oyster mushrooms have a unique, chewy texture that reminds me, weirdly enough, of calamari. Note: you're gonna have lots of delicious basil-infused oil left over. —EvE

SERVES 1

(continued)

LAYERS

3 king oyster mushrooms

1 tbsp (15 ml) gluten-free tamari

2 large heirloom tomatoes

1 avocado

2 sprigs fresh basil

BASIL OIL

1 cup (235 ml) extra-virgin olive oil

½ cup (13 g) fresh basil

FOR THE LAYERS

Dice the mushrooms, and then toss with the tamari. Spread on a baking sheet. Leave them in the oven at its lowest temperature—or your dehydrator at 115°F (46°C)—for an hour, or until the mushrooms have softened and darkened slightly. Slice the tomatoes and avocado into thin slices. Using the inside of a large circular cookie cutter, layer the mushrooms with the avocado and tomato; top with basil.

FOR THE BASIL OIL

Blend the oil with the basil. Decorate your plate with this. You'll have lots of leftover basil oil, so try to use it up within 4 or 5 days.

Beet RAVIOLI WITH ALMOND THYME PÂTÉ AND BASIL

This is one of my favorite recipes in here—for REAL. These are decadent and beautiful, but secretly so easy to make. They're more of an appetizer than a main course, so I'd suggest serving them with a large salad (or whatever else you want, I ain't your boss). —EvE

SERVES 2 TO 4

ALMOND THYME PÂTÉ

1 cup (170 g) almonds, soaked in water to cover for 8 hours and drained

2 tbsp (30 ml) fresh lemon juice

⅛ tsp Himalayan salt

2 cloves garlic, peeled

2–3 tsp (5–8 g) fresh thyme (or more, as desired)

BEET RAVIOLI

1 beet, peeled

3 tbsp (8 g) chopped basil

1 tsp fresh thyme

FOR THE PÂTÉ

Blend everything together until smooth and thick, adjusting according to taste. Add more salt or thyme or whatever you desire. Scoop the pâté onto cheesecloth (or parchment paper) and roll up into a cylinder shape. I like to add extra thyme here to coat the outside of the pâté; it just looks pretty. Put it in the fridge overnight, or if you REALLY want ravioli, for at least a couple of hours.

FOR THE BEET RAVIOLI

Slice the beet as thin as possible on a mandoline. Scoop a teaspoon or so of the pâté onto half of a beet slice, and fold the other half over the pâté. It will hold itself in place. Taste this one and see if you want more or less pâté; assemble the rest of the raviolis accordingly. You should have leftover pâté, unless you want to make a ton of raviolis (by all means, go for it). Sprinkle with basil and thyme, and enjoy!

Udon NOODLE BOWL WITH MISO GINGER SAUCE, EDAMAME AND GREEN ONIONS

Udon noodles are slightly thicker than others, and they have a satisfying chewy texture. When I stayed with my partner in a snowy mountain town last winter, we ate something similar to this every night and always wanted more. —EvE

SERVES 2 TO 4

2½ cups (8 oz [230 g]) uncooked whole-grain, gluten-free udon noodles

2 cups (300 g) uncooked edamame

1 large carrot

¼ cup (60 ml) water, or more as needed

1 tbsp (14 g) grated ginger

1 tsp maple syrup

2 tbsp (30 g) miso paste

¾ cup (56 g) chopped green onions

¼ tsp black pepper (optional)

Cook the noodles according to the directions, but drain them a couple of minutes before the directions say, and then rinse with cold water.

Steam the edamame for 8 minutes, and then shell all the soybeans out. Peel and slice the carrot into thin strips (like noodles) on a mandoline slicer or by hand.

In a frying pan over medium-high heat, add ¼ cup (60 ml) of water and the ginger, maple syrup and miso. When the water starts steaming and bubbling slightly, stir the miso around until it combines with the water. If you want to add more water, go ahead. Lower the heat and add the noodles and carrot strips. Stir everything together so it's evenly coated in the miso sauce.

Remove it from the heat, and add the green onions. Serve in bowls with a little black pepper on top, if you like.

two

SLOW COOKER, INSTANT POT & AIR FRYER

I'm a huge believer in using appliances to make your life easier. You may have one of these or all three. No matter which, you'll find some new fun recipes that can even be made on weeknights!

A slow cooker is usually used to cook meals on low heat for a long time. It's great for things like the Vegan Slow Cooker Mole Mushroom Taco Filling on page 109 and can cook all day while you are away at work. If you're new to slow cooking, start with a soup recipe like the Vegan Instant Pot Teff Vegetable Soup on page 110. This way you'll be able to find out if your slow cooker runs a little hot without ruining your dinner. (Hint: If your slow cooker runs hot, you will need to add extra liquid to the recipe and/or cook for less time.)

An Instant Pot is actually a brand of multicooker that has a pressure cooker function. Not all things labeled multicooker do, so be sure to check that the one you want to buy does have a pressure cooker feature. The Instant Pot brand has a stainless steel insert that makes it popular, and you can sauté, steam, slow cook, pressure cook and even make soy yogurt in some models.

A question I get a ton is what's the difference between a slow cooker and an Instant Pot, so let's address that first. While the Instant Pot does have a slow cooker function, I don't recommend using it in recipes where you are baking in your slow cooker, like the Slow Cooker Whole Wheat Spelt Potato Rolls on page 111. I also think the slow cooker function on the Instant Pot doesn't do dried beans as well as its pressure cooker setting.

Okay, then, what's an air fryer? Both slow cookers and multicookers cook with wet heat. The air fryer cooks with dry heat and uses the same technology that convection ovens use. The fan blows the hot air all around the food and makes everything nice and crisp. It makes the best tofu I've ever had and heats up leftovers quickly as another bonus.

Instant Pot RAINBOW PANZANELLA SALAD

+GFO +SF

Traditional panzanella salad is full of juicy, fresh tomatoes and stale or toasted bread that soaks up all the delicious dressing. This recipe has a healthy twist that turns it into a hearty summer meal—potatoes and beets: my two favorite root veggies. —KH

SERVES 4

INSTANT POT

3 cups (435 g) chopped purple potatoes

2 cups (300 g) chopped beets, (I used a combination of golden and candy-cane beets, but red are fine)

2 cups (480 ml) water

DRESSING

¼ cup (60 ml) olive oil

3 tbsp (45 ml) balsamic vinegar

1 tsp fresh thyme

½ tsp Dijon mustard

½ tsp salt

¼ tsp pepper

¼ cup (10 g) chopped fresh basil

4 cups (800 g) chopped tomatoes (I used a combination of heirlooms to get the different colors)

4 cups (360 g) stale French or Italian bread cubes (or fresh bread cubes baked at 350°F [177°C] for 10 minutes, or until crunchy), or use gluten-free bread

FOR THE INSTANT POT

Place the potatoes, beets and water into your Instant Pot and cook on manual, high pressure for 12 minutes. (If using red beets, wrap them up in foil so the red doesn't bleed onto the potatoes.)

Manually release the pressure and remove the lid.

Pour the Instant Pot ingredients into a colander, and rinse with cold water to stop the cooking. Set it aside.

FOR THE DRESSING

Mix the dressing ingredients together in a measuring cup or small bowl.

In a large mixing bowl, add the potatoes, beets, tomatoes and dressing; mix well.

Minutes before serving, mix in the stale or toasted bread so that it can soak up some of the dressing. Top with the fresh basil right before serving.

If you are not planning on eating it all in one meal, only mix together what you will eat. Store the bread in an airtight bag separate from the tomato mixture that you will store in the fridge.

Note: If you don't have an Instant Pot, you can still make this delicious salad. Just cook the potatoes and beets in a pot on your stove over medium heat until they are easily pierced with a fork. Then proceed with the recipe.

*SEE PHOTO INSERT

Air-Fried VEGAN BEIGNETS

These beignets have a pillowy texture and are rich from the coconut milk. These have half the sugar of regular beignets because we're using Whole Earth Sweetener Baking Blend that's half raw cane sugar and half stevia. Their baking blend makes an amazing powdered sugar too! If you aren't looking to cut down on sugar, you can use regular powdered sugar in place of the powdered baking blend. —KH

MAKES 24 BEIGNETS

POWDERED BAKING BLEND

1 cup (98 g) Whole Earth Sweetener Baking Blend

1 tsp organic cornstarch

PROOFING

1 cup (240 ml) full-fat coconut milk from a can

3 tbsp (36 g) powdered baking blend (sugar)

1½ tsp (4 g) active baking yeast

DOUGH

2 tbsp (30 ml) melted coconut oil

2 tbsp (30 ml) aquafaba (the drained water from a can of chickpeas)

2 tsp (10 ml) vanilla extract

3 cups (360 g) unbleached white flour (with a little extra to sprinkle on the cutting board for later)

FOR THE BAKING BLEND

Add the Whole Earth Baking Blend and cornstarch to your blender, and blend until powdery smooth. The cornstarch will keep it from clumping, so you can store it if you don't use it all in the recipe.

FOR PROOFING

Heat the coconut milk until it's warm but cool enough that you can stick your finger in it without burning yourself. If it's too hot, you will kill the yeast. Add it to your mixer with the sugar and yeast. Let it sit for 10 minutes, until the yeast begins to foam.

FOR THE DOUGH

Using the paddle attachment, mix in the coconut oil, aquafaba and vanilla. Then add the flour a cup (125 g) at a time.

Once the flour is mixing in and the dough is coming away from the sides of the mixer, change to your dough hook if you have one. (If you don't, keep using the paddle.)

Knead the dough in your mixer for about 3 minutes. The dough will be wetter than if you were making a loaf of bread, but you should be able to scrape out the dough and form a ball without it staying on your hands.

Place the dough in a mixing bowl, cover with a clean dish towel and let it rise for 1 hour.

Sprinkle some flour over a large cutting board and pat out the dough into a rectangle that's about ⅓ inch (8 mm) thick. Cut the dough into 24 squares and let them proof for 30 minutes before you cook them.

FOR COOKING IN YOUR AIR FRYER

Preheat your air fryer to 390°F (199°C). Depending on the size of your air fryer, you can put 3 to 6 beignets in at a time.

Cook for 3 minutes on one side. Flip them, and then cook another 2 minutes. Since air fryers vary, you may need to cook yours another minute or two for them to get golden brown.

Sprinkle liberally with the powdered baking blend you made in the beginning and enjoy!

Continue cooking in batches until they are all cooked.

FOR COOKING IN THE OVEN

Preheat the oven to 350°F (177°C). Place the beignets on a baking sheet covered with parchment paper.

Bake for about 15 minutes, or until golden brown. Sprinkle liberally with the powdered baking blend.

*SEE PHOTO INSERT

Vegan Slow Cooker
MOLE MUSHROOM TACO FILLING

+GF +SF

If you've never made mole, you might think that it's hard to make. I'm here to change your mind. All you need are some dried ancho chiles, and you can get them in a large grocery or Hispanic market. You toast them, rehydrate them and then blend with a few other ingredients. Easy, right? —KH

SERVES 8

2 dried ancho chile peppers

SAUCE
½ cup (120 ml) chile cooking water (see instructions)

½ cup (120 ml) water

½ cup (120 g) crushed tomatoes or tomato purée

¼ cup (43 g) blanched almonds

½ oz (14 g) unsweetened dark chocolate

1½ tsp (3 g) oregano

1 tsp chili powder

½ tsp onion powder

½ tsp garlic powder

¼ tsp ground allspice

¼ tsp ground cinnamom

Salt, to taste

1½ lbs (680 g) mushrooms, chopped

Taco shells

Lettuce, for serving

Vegan queso fresco, for serving

Vegan sour cream, for serving

Toast the chiles in a dry skillet over medium heat. You don't want to overcook or burn them, just dry them out a bit and cook until they become fragrant, about 2 to 3 minutes.

Let them cool. Then remove the seeds, stems and ribs, and discard them. Place the flesh of the pepper in a small saucepan and cover with water. Bring to a boil. Then lower the heat and simmer for 10 minutes to reconstitute.

FOR THE SAUCE

Use tongs or a slotted spoon to carefully remove the reconstituted peppers and put them in your blender with all of the sauce ingredients *except* for the salt. Blend them until smooth, taste, add salt and taste again.

In your 3- to 4-quart (2.8- to 3.8-L) slow cooker, add the mushrooms and the sauce ingredients. Cook it on low for 7 to 9 hours. If you may be home late, add an extra ¼ cup (60 ml) water to make sure the filling doesn't burn.

Serve in soft or hard taco shells, and top with lettuce, vegan queso fresco and vegan sour cream.

Vegan Instant Pot
TEFF VEGETABLE SOUP

+GF +SF

This Vegan Instant Pot Teff Vegetable Soup is gluten-free, soy-free and has no oil added. It gets protein from teff, the world's smallest grain! —KH

SERVES 6

SAUTÉ

1 tbsp (15 ml) olive oil (or water sauté to make oil-free)

1 cup (150 g) minced onion

1 tsp minced garlic

½ cup (105 g) whole teff

FIRST COOK

6 cups (1.4 L) water or vegetable broth

1 (14.4-oz [410-g]) can diced tomatoes

1 cup (245 g) tomato purée (or 2 tbsp [28 g] tomato paste and ¾ cup [180 ml] extra water)

1 medium potato, cubed

2 tsp (2 g) Italian seasoning

SECOND COOK

1 (12-oz [340-g]) bag frozen mixed vegetables (carrot, corn, peas and green beans)

1 cup (120 g) chopped red cabbage

1 (15½-oz [440-g]) can chickpeas, drained (save liquid for baking—it's aquafaba!)

SERVING

¼–½ cup (20–40 g) nutritional yeast, to taste

1 tsp Italian seasoning, or to taste

Salt and pepper, to taste

FOR THE SAUTÉ

Use the sauté setting over normal or medium heat, and heat the oil or water. Sauté the onions until they become transparent. Then add the garlic and sauté a minute more. Add the teff and toast for about a minute.

FOR THE FIRST COOK

Add the water or broth, diced tomatoes, tomato purée, potato and Italian seasoning to your Instant Pot. Cook on high pressure for 5 minutes and carefully release the pressure manually.

FOR THE SECOND COOK

Add the frozen mixed vegetables, cabbage and chickpeas to the teff mixture. Cook on high pressure for 1 minute and let the pressure release naturally.

FOR SERVING

Stir in the nutritional yeast, Italian seasoning, salt and pepper, and then serve.

Slow Cooker WHOLE WHEAT SPELT POTATO ROLLS

+SF

When I was growing up, my aunt made these fluffy yeast rolls for every holiday dinner. I was amazed when she told me her secret was mashed potatoes and the water she cooked them in. My recipe uses whole-grain flours, and with the potatoes they are just as moist as the original. It also uses an ingredient that may be new to some of you: aquafaba. Though it sounds like a fancy name, chances are good you already have some in the pantry. It's Latin for bean water. If you have a can of chickpeas, just put a strainer over a bowl, pour out the contents and the liquid you have is aquafaba. It takes the place of eggs in baked goods. You can even make vegan meringues with it! —KH

MAKES 8 ROLLS

¾ cup (158 g) mashed Idaho potatoes

½ cup (120 ml) potato cooking water

1 tsp sugar

1 tsp active dry yeast

2 tbsp (30 ml) aquafaba

2 tbsp (30 ml) olive oil

1 tsp salt

2 cups (250 g) spelt flour (or substitute whole wheat flour)

1 cup (125 g) whole wheat flour, plus more to use on the cutting board

Make sure the potatoes and potato water have cooled to room temperature so they're not so hot that they kill the yeast.

Add the mashed potatoes, potato cooking water, sugar and yeast to the bowl of your stand mixer. Mix well with the paddle attachment and let sit for about 10 minutes, or until the yeast begins to bloom. (This may take longer on cold days.)

Add the aquafaba, olive oil, salt and spelt flour, and mix well. Remove the paddle and replace with the dough hook. Add the whole wheat flour and knead on low for 8 minutes.

If your dough is too wet and doesn't form into a ball, you may need to add extra flour. Add ¼ cup (30 g) at a time until the dough firms up and forms a ball around the dough hook.

You can use any slow cooker, though I prefer to use a round one. I made one batch in a 3-quart (2.8-L) and another in a 4-quart (3.8-L) slow cooker, and both worked fine.

Prepare your slow cooker by lining it with parchment paper so the rolls will be easy to lift out.

Sprinkle some flour on a cutting board and put the kneaded dough on it. Divide into 8 even pieces and roll into balls.

Place these in the lined slow cooker. Cover the top of the crock with a clean dish towel or a few paper towels under the lid. This keeps the condensation from dripping onto your rolls and making them soggy.

Let them rise in the slow cooker by cooking on low for 45 minutes. Then cook on high for 45 minutes to 1 hour. The tops won't brown like they would in the oven, but you can tell if they are done by looking at how brown the sides are.

*SEE PHOTO INSERT

Instant Pot Vegan
BLACK-EYED PEA JAMBALAYA

+GF +SF

This is so easy to throw together. You're going to find yourself making it every week for the next few months. There are many spices involved, but you can use your favorite Cajun spice blend in place of those to make it easier. —KH

SERVES 6

SAUTÉ

1 tbsp (15 ml) olive oil (or water sauté to make this oil-free)

½ cup (76 g) minced onion

½ cup (85 g) minced bell pepper (any color)

1 tsp minced garlic

INSTANT POT

6 cups (1.4 L) water

2 cups (420 g) long-grain brown rice

1½ cups (300 g) dried black-eyed peas

1 cup (180 g) peeled and diced sweet potato

2 tsp (4 g) smoked paprika

1 tsp dried marjoram (or use oregano)

1 tsp dried thyme

½ tsp dried cayenne pepper

¼ tsp ground allspice

Pinch of ground cloves

¼ tsp liquid smoke

SERVING

2 cups (80 g) minced kale, collards or spinach

1 (14½-oz [410-g]) can crushed tomatoes (can substitute diced tomatoes if that's all you have on hand)

2 tbsp (10 g) nutritional yeast

Salt, to taste (optional)

Hot sauce, for serving

FOR THE SAUTÉ

Use the sauté setting over normal or medium heat, and heat the oil, if using. Sauté the onion until transparent. Then add the bell pepper and garlic. Sauté a minute more.

FOR THE INSTANT POT

To the Instant Pot, add the water, rice, peas, potato, paprika, marjoram, thyme, cayenne, allspice, cloves and liquid smoke. Put the lid on and make sure that the vent is sealed. Cook on the manual setting at high pressure, and set for 24 minutes.

FOR SERVING

Let the pressure release naturally. Mix in the sautéed vegetables, greens, tomatoes and nutritional yeast. Add salt to taste, and serve with hot sauce.

*SEE PHOTO INSERT

Air-Fried TOFU RANCHEROS

+SFO

My favorite part of this recipe is the crunchy tofu that's studded with cumin and chili powder. It's so easy to make perfect tofu in your air fryer, but if you don't have one, you can make the tofu in the oven. —KH

SERVES 4

SPICE-CRUSTED TOFU

1 (20-oz [565-g]) container high-protein tofu or super-firm tofu (or firm that's been pressed for at least 1 hour), cut into cubes (omit for soy-free option)

1 tsp ground cumin

1 tsp ground chili powder (or less if you prefer mild foods)

½ tsp smoked paprika

¼ tsp salt, or to taste

SALSA BEANS

1 (15½-oz [440-g]) can organic black beans, drained (save liquid to make brownies or chocolate cookies)

¼ cup (60 ml) of your favorite mild salsa (I like Little Face Big Taste Jalapeño Cilantro Salsa), plus more for serving

⅛–¼ tsp liquid smoke, to suit your taste (or use ⅛ tsp smoked paprika)

⅛ tsp jalapeño powder (or chipotle or cayenne)

⅛ tsp ground cumin

Salt, to taste

VEGGIE TOPPING

⅓ cup (36 g) grated carrot

⅓ cup (41 g) grated zucchini

⅓ cup (41 g) grated yellow squash

⅛ tsp salt

Pinch of black pepper

BASE

4 large flour or gluten-free tortillas

1 cup (120 g) shredded vegan cheese

Chopped tomatoes, for serving

FOR THE SPICE-CRUSTED TOFU

Toss the tofu cubes with the cumin, chili powder, smoked paprika and salt.

Preheat your air fryer to 390°F (200°C) unless your model doesn't require it. Once it's hot, add the coated tofu to your air fryer basket.

Set the cooking time to 5 minutes, and when the time is up, shake or stir the tofu. Repeat for an additional 5 minutes.

No air fryer? Bake at 400°F (204°C) for 15 minutes, turn it over and cook 10 to 15 minutes more, or until crispy.

FOR THE SALSA BEANS

Add all the ingredients together in a small bowl.

FOR THE VEGGIE TOPPING

Add the grated carrot, zucchini, yellow squash, salt and a pinch of black pepper to a bowl and mix well. Set aside until you're ready to assemble the rancheros.

FOR THE BASE

Take 2 tortillas and place them on a baking sheet while preheating the oven to 350°F (177°C). Sprinkle (or spread) ¼ cup (30 g) vegan cheese on top of each tortilla. Put a quarter of the salsa beans in the middle of the tortilla and bake for 15 minutes. This will warm the beans and make the tortilla crunchy.

Once warm, add the spice-crusted tofu, the shredded veggie topping and chopped tomatoes or other veggies you'd like to pile on, like avocado or shredded lettuce.

Top it all off with a heaping spoonful of salsa!

*SEE PHOTO INSERT

Instant Pot
CRANBERRY SAUCE WITH A TOUCH OF APPLE BRANDY

+GF +SF

My Instant Pot Cranberry Sauce has some orange, cinnamon, cardamom and a touch of apple brandy. I sweetened mine with maple syrup, but you could use stevia, monk fruit or even raw or coconut sugar. —KH

MAKES 4 CUPS (500 G)

PRESSURE COOKER

3 cups (300 g) fresh cranberries (I like Hurst's Berry Farms cranberries)

2 cups (360 g) minced peeled apple

(continued)

½ cup (120 ml) orange juice (about 2 medium oranges)

½ cup (120 ml) water

1 tbsp (9 g) orange zest (about 2 medium oranges)

10 cardamom pods

2 cinnamon sticks

¼ tsp salt

SAUTÉ

2 tbsp (30 ml) apple brandy or spiced rum

Sweetener of choice, to taste (I used 2 tbsp [30 ml] of maple syrup)

¼ tsp ground cardamom

FOR THE PRESSURE COOKER

Add all the pressure cooker ingredients to your Instant Pot. Put on the lid and set the vent to sealed.

Cook on high pressure for 6 minutes. Let the pressure release naturally (wait until the pressure value drops on its own).

Once the pressure releases, you will be able to remove the lid and set aside. Press the cancel button to turn off the Instant Pot, and then press the sauté button and the adjust button until it sets to "less."

FOR THE SAUTÉ

Add the sauté ingredients. Mix well with a large spoon and mash the fruit pieces as you go.

Please note, you can use any sweetener of your choice—just add a little at a time and taste as you go.

Cook until it's at the thickness you desire. Then turn it off and remove the cardamom pods and cinnamon sticks. Store in the fridge.

Vegan Instant Pot
WHITE BEAN SOY CURL CHILI

+GF

You can make this with any white bean. The only difference is you may need to cook an extra 5 minutes if you're using old beans. If you can't get soy curls near you, you can order them online. —KH

SERVES 4

SAUTÉ

1 tbsp (15 ml) olive oil (or water sauté to make oil-free)

½ small onion, minced

1½ tsp (4 g) minced garlic

1½ tsp (3 g) ground cumin

1½ tsp (3 g) chili powder

1 cup (128 g) diced carrot

INSTANT POT

2½ cups (590 ml) water

1½ cups (about 65 g) dry soy curls, minced (or use your favorite vegan chicken sub or tempeh)

1 cup (200 g) cannellini beans (or other white bean), soaked overnight (there will be about 2¼ cups [450 g] after they are soaked)

SERVING

1 (10-oz [285-g]) can diced tomatoes with lime and cilantro

1 (4-oz [115-g]) can green chiles

¼ cup (20 g) nutritional yeast

1 tsp dried oregano

Salt and pepper, to taste

FOR THE SAUTÉ

Use the sauté setting over normal or medium heat, and heat the oil or water. Sauté the onions until they become transparent. Then add the garlic, cumin, chili powder and carrot. Sauté for a minute.

FOR THE INSTANT POT

Add the water, soy curls and soaked beans to your Instant Pot. Cook on high pressure for 15 minutes, and let the pressure release naturally. (Note: If your beans aren't completely cooked, go ahead and cook them for 5 minutes more on high pressure.)

FOR SERVING

Purée the diced tomatoes and green chiles together in your blender.

Allow the Instant Pot pressure to release naturally. Stir in the sautéed and blended mixtures, nutritional yeast, oregano, salt and pepper; serve.

*SEE PHOTO INSERT

Vegan PEAR AND CRANBERRY INSTANT POT CAKE

+GFO +SF

This cake is super moist; it's steamed and reminds me a little of an English steamed pudding. You can vary the fruits to match up with the season. —KH

SERVES 4

1¼ cups (150 g) whole wheat pastry flour (or use a gluten-free baking mix)

½ tsp ground cardamom

½ tsp baking soda

½ tsp baking powder

⅛ tsp salt

2 tbsp (14 g) ground flaxseeds

½ cup (120 ml) unsweetened nondairy milk

¼ cup (60 ml) agave syrup

2 tbsp (30 ml) mild oil (or use applesauce to make oil-free)

MIX-INS
1 cup (180 g) chopped pear
½ cup (50 g) chopped fresh cranberries

1½ cups (355 ml) water

Oil a 6- or 7-inch (15- or 18-cm) Bundt pan and set aside.

Mix all the dry ingredients—flour, cardamom, soda, powder, salt and flaxseeds—in a medium mixing bowl. Then mix all of the wet ingredients—milk, agave and oil—in a large measuring cup.

Add the wet ingredients to the dry and mix well. Fold in the mix-ins.

Spread the cake mixture into your prepared pan and cover with foil.

Put the steel insert into your Instant Pot and add the water to the bottom (along with the stainless steel steam rack with handles that came with your Instant Pot).

Place the lid on with the vent closed and cook on high pressure for 35 minutes. Let the pressure release naturally.

Once the pressure indicator goes down, remove the lid, carefully lift out the pan and remove the foil that's covering the pan.

Let cool before removing the cake from the pan and/or cutting.

*SEE PHOTO INSERT

Slow Cooker
SHREDDED VEGGIES AND JACKFRUIT BBQ

+GFO +SF

The homemade whiskey BBQ sauce plus all the veggies elevates this jackfruit into your new favorite sandwich filling. In North Carolina, they put coleslaw on a BBQ sandwich, but in this recipe we throw in some cabbage for an all-in-one meal. —KH

SERVES 8

1 (20-oz [567-g]) can young jackfruit (NOT sweetened, ripe!), drained

2 cups (250 g) shredded carrots

1 cup (91 g) shredded broccoli stems or broccoli slaw

1 cup (150 g) shredded sweet potato

1 cup (150 g) shredded cabbage

½ cup (100 g) brown sugar

¼ cup (60 ml) apple cider vinegar

¼ cup (65 g) tomato paste

2 tbsp (15 ml) bourbon or whiskey (use a gluten-free whiskey)

1 tsp minced garlic

½ tsp onion powder

½ tsp liquid smoke

½ tsp cayenne

Salt, to taste

Use your 4-quart (3.8-L) slow cooker for this. Add the jackfruit and shred as much as you can with your hands. Then add the carrots, broccoli, sweet potato, cabbage, sugar, vinegar, tomato paste, bourbon, garlic, onion powder, liquid smoke and cayenne.

Mix everything together well, and cook on low for 7 to 9 hours. Add salt to taste before serving.

Air-Fried TEMPEH
SKEWERS

+GFO +SFO

These are so simple to throw together, but it's the Asian-style marinade that makes them really special. If you don't have an air fryer, you can cook these on a grill or in the oven. —KH

MAKES 4 SKEWERS

MARINADE
¼ cup (60 ml) soy sauce (or use coconut aminos for gluten-free and soy-free)

3 tbsp (38 g) brown sugar

2 tbsp (30 ml) rice vinegar

2 tsp (4 g) grated ginger

1 tsp sriracha

SKEWERS
1 (8-oz [227-g]) package tempeh, cut into 16 cubes (or use hemp tempeh for gluten-free and soy-free)

1 bell pepper, cut into 12 pieces

8 small wedges of onion

FOR THE MARINADE
Mix the soy sauce, brown sugar, rice vinegar, grated ginger and sriracha in a container with a tight lid. Add the tempeh, secure the lid and shake. Marinate the tempeh for 2 hours to 24 hours.

FOR THE SKEWERS
Assemble the skewers, dividing the veggies and tempeh evenly between them. Set any leftover marinade to the side for later.

Cook in your air fryer at 400°F (204°C) for 5 minutes, flip the skewers, brush on the leftover marinade and cook for 5 more minutes.

Air-Fried VEGETABLE PAKORA WITH TAMARIND DIPPING SAUCE

+GF +SF

I love Indian food—especially these shredded veggies that are covered in a thick chickpea flour and spice batter. Be sure to try these with a variety of veggies. —KH

MAKES ABOUT 14 PAKORAS

1 cup (90 g) chickpea flour
1 tbsp (7 g) ground coriander
1 tsp salt
½ tsp chili powder (optional)
½ cup (120 ml) water
1 cup (150 g) thinly sliced onion
1 cup (125 g) shredded carrot
Spray oil (optional)

Mix the chickpea flour, coriander, salt and chili powder together in a large bowl. Add the water and mix. It should be a thick mixture but able to stay together. Add more water as needed.

Stir in the onion and carrot. Line your air fryer basket with perforated parchment paper. Get about 2 tablespoons (30 g) of the pakora mixture and place it on the parchment.

Repeat until you have a single layer. If you want to use the spray oil, lightly coat the tops. Cook at 400°F (204°C) for 5 minutes and turn. Then spray them with oil again, if using, and cook for 5 more minutes.

These are great with the tamarind sauce on page 118.

Slow Cooker SMOKY SPLIT PEA AND LENTIL SOUP

+GF +SF

Everyone needs an easy-to-throw-together slow cooker soup. This one is filling, flavorful and best of all, it's ready to eat when you come in the door from work. —KH

SERVES 6

4 cups (960 ml) water
¾ cup (169 g) split green peas
½ cup (100 g) autumn lentil blend (or equal parts yellow, red and brown lentils)
1 tsp liquid smoke
1 tsp marjoram
½ tsp smoked paprika
½ tsp onion powder
½ tsp garlic powder
¼ cup (20 g) nutritional yeast
Salt and pepper, to taste

In your 4-quart (3.8-L) slow cooker, add the water, split green peas, lentil blend, liquid smoke, marjoram, smoked paprika, onion powder and garlic powder. Cook on low for 7 to 9 hours.

Before serving, stir in the nutritional yeast. Then add salt and pepper, to taste.

Air Fryer CHEATER SAMOSAS USING SPRING ROLL WRAPPERS

+SF

The first time I ever had Indian food, it was samosas: little triangular pastries filled with spiced potatoes that you dip into a tart yet sweet tamarind sauce. This recipe uses vegan spring roll wrappers so you don't have to take the time to make a homemade crust. —KH

MAKES 30 SAMOSAS

FILLING

1 tbsp (15 ml) oil (or water sauté)

½ tsp coriander seeds

½ tsp cumin seeds

2 tsp (8 g) garam masala

¼ tsp ground cardamom

⅛ tsp chili powder

2 cups (450 g) cooked peeled potatoes

¾ cup (115 g) green peas

Salt, to taste

TAMARIND SAUCE

½ cup (120 ml) water

½ cup (100 g) brown sugar

1 tbsp (16 g) tamarind concentrate

1 (12-oz [340-g]) package vegan spring roll wrappers

FOR THE FILLING

Heat the oil in a large sauté pan over medium-high heat. Once warm, add the coriander seeds and cumin seeds. Cook until the seeds start to pop and their aromas are released. Then add the garam masala, cardamom and chili powder, and sauté for a minute.

Add the potatoes and peas. The mixture will look like mashed potatoes as you fold it all together. Cook until the peas are tender, about 5 minutes. Add salt to taste. Set aside and let cool.

FOR THE TAMARIND SAUCE

While you're waiting for the potato mixture to cool, make the tamarind sauce. Add the water, brown sugar and tamarind concentrate to a small saucepan. Bring it to a boil, and then lower the heat to medium. Cook until the mixture reduces and thickens, about 10 to 15 minutes.

Cut the spring roll wrappers in half lengthwise. Take one strip and place a rounded tablespoon (about 15 g) of the filling in the bottom left corner. Dip your finger in the water and wet the edges of the spring roll wrapper.

Fold the wrapper by taking the filled corner and bringing it to the top to form a rectangle. Keep wrapping until you are left with a triangle. Repeat until all the samosas are formed.

Place a single layer of samosas into your air fryer basket. Cook them on 375°F (190°C) for 5 minutes. Flip and cook them 4 to 5 minutes more or until crunchy.

Serve with the dipping sauce on the side.

Note: If you don't have an air fryer, you can cook these on a baking sheet in the oven at 350°F (177°C). Cook for about 15 minutes, and then turn and cook for 5 minutes.

Air-Fried GREEN TOMATO PO' BOYS

+GFO +SF

Green tomatoes are a treat that can usually be found either at the first or last of the season. If you leave them on your windowsill, they will eventually ripen and turn red, but there's no need for all that waiting. Just air fry them up green and enjoy them right now. —KH

SERVES 4

TOMATOES

4 medium unripe green tomatoes (*not* ripe Green Zebra or other varieties that are green once they are ripe)

½ cup (80 g) cornstarch or potato starch

½ cup (120 ml) nondairy milk

1 tsp hot sauce (like Tabasco or Texas Pete)

½ cup (75 g) fine ground cornmeal

2 tsp (8 g) no-salt Cajun spice blend

½ tsp salt

Spray oil (omit to make oil-free)

PO' BOYS

1–2 tsp (5–10 ml) hot sauce (like Tabasco or Texas Pete)

¼ cup (56 g) vegan mayo

1 French baguette (or use gluten-free bread)

FOR THE TOMATOES

Cut the tomatoes into thick slices. Add the starch to one shallow bowl or plate, and then mix the non-dairy milk in a bowl with 1 teaspoon of hot sauce. In another shallow bowl or plate, mix the cornmeal, Cajun spice and salt.

Take one slice of tomato and dip it first into the starch. Then quickly dunk it into the milk mixture, place the slice into the cornmeal mixture and cover both sides. Press the cornmeal with your hands to make sure it's adhering.

You can use a perforated parchment to line the air fryer basket and keep it cleaner. (You can find them in Asian markets.) Place as many slices as fit comfortably in your air fryer basket. You can fry these in batches.

FOR THE PO' BOYS

Mix the hot sauce in with the vegan mayo. Cut the baguette into 4 sandwich-size pieces, slather with mayo and top with the fried green tomato slices.

three

30 MINUTES OR LESS

This ultimate collection of no-fuss, straight-shooter recipes will most likely be dog-eared, highlighted and underlined more times than all the rest.

There are moments in life when soufflés and homemade croissants are fantastic, yet slightly ambitious recipe choices—we're talking when Daylight Savings rolls around or how about when your favorite show is unexpectedly pushed back and you've scored a few extra hours. But in the more likely times when all that is needed is a delectable meal, and one that's brimming with nourishment, these recipes will be your salvation. Better yet, they will be your weeknight beck and call, saving grace and all-around go-to meals simply because they only require a 30-minute timer and simple ingredients. Baked Sun-Dried Falafel with Tzatziki Dip (page 132) is a riff on a Greek classic and the perfect weeknight meal that only takes minutes to reheat. Or try your hand at the One-Pot Pasta Arrabiata (page 126) for a spicy dish that rests on only one pot to do all the heavy lifting. From a hearty Spicy Aloo Gobi (page 122) to Mini Polenta Cakes with a stunning Mushroom Ragu (page 121), these recipes let you taste the globe in less than 30 minutes.

Simple TABBOULEH

+QP +SF +GF

Swap bulgur for quinoa, add cucumbers and a tangy lemon dressing, and you've got yourself a health-forward yet modern tabbouleh: the perfect salad for on-the-go lunching. —MR

SERVES 4

1 cup (170 g) quinoa, uncooked

1 tsp tamari

2 green onions, chopped

1 medium cucumber, diced into small quarter pieces

1 cup (160 g) tomatoes, diced into small quarter pieces

2 cups (80 g) chopped cilantro and/or parsley

½ cup (55 g) macadamia nuts

2 tbsp (30 ml) olive oil

Juice of 1 lemon

Sea salt, to taste

Start by preparing the quinoa. Cook the quinoa as the package instructs. As the quinoa cooks, add the tamari. The tamari will flavor the quinoa, giving it a nice salty taste. Let the quinoa cook for 15 minutes until all the water has absorbed.

In the meantime, add the green onions, cucumber, tomatoes, cilantro and nuts to a medium bowl. Toss in the cooked quinoa, olive oil, lemon juice and salt, to taste.

Mini POLENTA CAKES WITH MUSHROOM RAGU

+QP +SF +GF

Mushroom ragu on its own is a luscious treat, but when scooped onto crispy polenta cakes, it makes for an undeniably delicious affair. —MR

MAKES 6 SLICES

3 tbsp (45 ml) olive oil, divided

½ yellow onion, thinly sliced

Pinch of sea salt

5 cups (380 g) thinly sliced wild mushrooms

1 tsp balsamic vinegar

1 tbsp (3 g) fresh thyme

½–1 tbsp (7–14 g) coconut yogurt

6 (½" [1.3-cm]) thick slices precooked polenta roll, found at most grocery stores

3 tbsp (23 g) any flour (use brown rice flour as a gluten-free option), reserved for the polenta

In a medium sauté pan over medium-high heat, warm half of the olive oil for 1 minute. Add the onion and a pinch of sea salt, and sauté for about 5 to 7 minutes, or until the onions are tender and translucent in color. Now add the mushrooms and balsamic, and cook for another 5 minutes, until the mushrooms are tender. Remove the pan from the heat and set aside for 1 to 2 minutes, letting the mushrooms cool. Then add the thyme and yogurt. Mix well. Be sure to keep this off the heat so as to keep the yogurt from curdling.

(continued)

Now add the remaining olive oil to the sauté pan. As the oil warms over medium-high heat, lightly press the polenta into the flour so that it coats each side. This will prevent the polenta from sticking when cooking in the oil. Sauté the polenta slices for 3 to 5 minutes on each side, until they're crisp and slightly golden brown. Remove from the sauté pan and pat the polenta with a paper towel to remove any excess olive oil.

Top each polenta cake with the mushroom ragu and enjoy!

Note: I would suggest using a precooked polenta roll. It saves so much time, and there are plenty of brands that offer polenta rolls with no additional flavorings.

Spicy ALOO GOBI

+QP +SF +GF

The magic of spices presents itself beautifully with Aloo Gobi: a traditional Indian dish made with cauliflower, potatoes and a slew of spices. It's a fantastic recipe for exploring the endless array of spices, their aroma and the transformative effects they have on a meal. —MR

SERVES 3 TO 5

4 tbsp (60 ml) olive oil, divided

1 head cauliflower, cut into tiny florets

1 cup (180 g) baby potatoes, whole

Sprinkle of sea salt, plus more for serving

½ tsp ground cardamom

½ tsp ground turmeric

1 tsp ground coriander

1 tsp ground ginger

½ tsp ground cinnamon

Dash of red pepper flakes

1 tbsp (15 g) tomato purée

3 cloves garlic, roughly chopped

½ cup (120 ml) water

Juice of ½–1 lemon

Rice or quinoa, for serving

Handful cilantro, for serving

Preheat the oven to 420°F (215°C). In a large mixing bowl, toss in half of the olive oil, cauliflower florets, potatoes and a generous sprinkling of sea salt. Mix well and place onto a parchment paper–lined baking dish. Cook for 25 minutes or until the cauliflower and potatoes are tender.

In the meantime, make the sauce. In a large skillet over medium heat, warm the remaining olive oil and all the spices, tomato purée and garlic. Let this simmer for a few minutes before adding the water. Add the water and let it warm for a few minutes. Now set the sauce aside until the cauliflower and potatoes have finished cooking.

Once they're done, bring the sauce back to the stove and add the roasted cauliflower, potatoes and lemon juice. Mix well, and warm over medium-high heat for about 5 minutes. Serve over a bed of rice or quinoa, and top with cilantro and sea salt.

*SEE PHOTO INSERT

Crunchy BRUSSELS SPROUTS SLAW WITH ASIAN PEAR

+QP +GF

This is a delightful salad that is as light as it is fresh. Finely shaved Brussels sprouts breathe new life into this otherwise hearty vegetable. Toss in crispy Asian pear, almond slivers and a mustard vinaigrette for a refreshing and painstakingly easy take on a traditional slaw. —MR

SERVES 2 TO 3

DRESSING

1 tbsp (15 g) whole-grain mustard

1½ tsp (8 ml) maple syrup

Zest and juice of ½ lemon

2 tbsp (30 ml) olive oil

Pinch of sea salt

SLAW

2 cups (200 g) Brussels sprouts, whole

½ large Asian pear, chopped

2 large handfuls toasted sliver almonds, unsalted

1 handful sunflower seeds, toasted

FOR THE DRESSING

Start by making the dressing. Simply add and mix all of the dressing ingredients in a small bowl. Set it aside.

FOR THE SLAW

Use a microplane to thinly shave the Brussels sprouts. If you don't have a microplane, finely chop the Brussels sprouts into very thin pieces. Add the sprouts and the remaining slaw ingredients to a large bowl. Add the salad dressing and toss to combine.

CAULIFLOWER RICE AND BLACK BEANS with Kale

+GF +SF +QP

Feeling too tired to cook dinner? This skillet comes together fast with frozen riced cauliflower and sweet potato, a can of black beans and some spices from your pantry. I used kale in mine, but any green will work wonderfully. —KH

SERVES 4

1 tbsp (15 ml) olive oil (or sauté with broth for oil-free)

½ cup (75 g) minced onion

2 cloves garlic, minced (about 14 g)

1 tsp ground cumin

½ tsp chili powder

½ tsp smoked paprika

⅛–½ tsp cayenne pepper (optional)

¼ cup (60 ml) water

1 (15½-oz [439-g]) can black beans, drained and rinsed (or 1½ cups [258 g] homemade)

1 (12-oz [340-g]) bag riced cauliflower and sweet potato (I use Green Giant)

2 cups (134 g) chopped kale

Salt and pepper, to taste

Heat the oil or broth in a large skillet over medium-high heat. Once hot, add the onions and sauté until translucent, about 5 minutes.

Add the garlic, cumin, chili powder, smoked paprika and cayenne to the skillet and turn the heat to medium. Sauté until the spices become fragrant, about 2 minutes.

Stir in the water, beans and cauliflower with sweet potato, and cook until the sweet potato becomes tender. Then add the kale and cook until it's steamed.

Before serving, add salt and pepper, to taste.

You can serve this as-is in a bowl, or fancy it up with salsa, chopped veggies and avocado. You can serve leftovers in lettuce leaves, in burritos or on salads!

Chana Masala:
QUICK CHICKPEA CURRY WITH RICE

This recipe is not exactly made traditionally, but I'm impatient and often lazy, so this is what I do when I get that chana masala craving (which is every day). —EvE

SERVES 1 OR 2

3 cloves garlic

1" (2.5-cm) chunk peeled ginger

¼ cup (60 ml) water, or more as needed

3 tbsp (45 ml) fresh lemon juice

2 tsp (3 g) garam masala powder

1 (15-oz [420-g]) can chickpeas, rinsed and drained

1 (14-oz [414-ml]) can tomato sauce

3 cups (480 g) cooked brown rice

¼ cup (10 g) chopped basil, for garnish

Finely chop the garlic and ginger. In a frying pan over medium-high heat, add the water and lemon juice, and heat until they begin to steam and lightly bubble. Add the chopped garlic and ginger and sauté for 3 minutes, adding more water if needed. Add the garam masala powder and add more water if needed, stirring everything together. Next, add the chickpeas and the tomato sauce, and stir gently for 10 to 15 minutes over medium-low heat until the mixture has thickened up.

Serve with rice and garnish with basil.

Baked BLACK BEAN BURGERS

+GF +SF +QP

We wanted to increase the goodness of these burgers as much as possible, so we added some sprouted pumpkin seeds, sweet potato, quinoa and carrots. You can just never have too much nutritional value! The addition of BBQ sauce and chili powder adds the perfect little kick to this smoky black bean burger. —AS

MAKES 12 BURGER PATTIES

3 cups (516 g) cooked black beans

1 cup (185 g) cooked quinoa

1 cup (210 g) mashed sweet potato

⅓ cup (50 g) chopped onion

½ cup (80 g) roughly chopped sprouted pumpkin seeds

1 cup (110 g) freshly grated carrot

⅓ cup (26 g) nutritional yeast

1 cup (85 g) ground flaxseed

¼ cup (28 g) chili powder

3 tbsp (45 ml) vegan barbecue sauce

1 tbsp (9 g) minced garlic

1 tsp (5 g) salt

1 tsp (3 g) pepper

½ cup (120 ml) sesame oil

¼–½ cup (60–120 ml) water

¼ cup (20 g) gluten-free oats

OPTIONAL, FOR SERVING
Tomatoes

Avocado

Grilled onions

Sprouts

Mustard

Buns

Preheat the oven to 400°F (204°C).

In a food processor, combine *all* the ingredients except the oil, water and oats. Pulse until the ingredients are all mixed but not mushy. There will still be some chunks in this burger!

Pour the contents of the food processor into a large mixing bowl. Add the oil and water, and stir well. Add the oats to the mixture, allowing them to absorb any excess moisture.

Form into hockey-puck-size patties, about 3 inches (7.5 cm) in diameter, and place onto a nonstick baking sheet. Bake for about 15 minutes on each side, or until the burgers are uniformly browned and cooked all the way through. Serve with tomatoes, avocado, grilled onions, sprouts and your favorite mustard on a delicious whole wheat or gluten-free bun.

Note: Wrap them up and they last for a week in the fridge.

Creamy AVOCADO PESTO PASTA

+GF +QP

This creamy dish is packed with flavor but comes together super easily—you can even make the pesto ahead for an easy instant meal builder. It's the perfect dish for welcoming in warm, spring weather and the recipe is easily doubled for family-size meals or lunch leftovers. Top it with a sprinkle of hemp seeds for a bit of texture, and of course serve with fresh lemon slices: they add a ton of fresh flavor when squeezed over the top! —AS

SERVES 4

1½ cups (60 g) chopped fresh basil

¼ cup (40 g) hemp seeds (shell-free), plus more for garnish

1½ tbsp (23 ml) lemon juice

2 cloves garlic

½ tsp black pepper

¼ tsp salt

¼ cup (60 ml) olive oil

1 medium avocado, halved and seed removed

16 oz (455 g) spaghetti noodles (or any pasta you prefer!)

Lemon slices, for squeezing and garnish

In a food processor or high-speed blender, combine the basil, hemp seeds, lemon juice, garlic, pepper and salt. Drizzle in the olive oil, scoop the avocado into the mixture and process until creamy. Set aside.

Bring a large pot of salted water to a boil. Cook the noodles until al dente and then drain.

Pour the avocado pesto sauce over the pasta and toss to coat evenly. Garnish with a squeeze of lemon and a sprinkle of hemp seeds. Serve and enjoy!

Note: Leftovers last in the fridge up to about a week.

*SEE PHOTO INSERT

Taco PIE

+GF +QP +SF

This taco pie is easy to throw together, takes only 30 minutes in the oven, and is even better topped with guacamole, salsa and fresh tomatoes. —AS

SERVES 4

4 (9" [23-cm]) tortillas
1 cup (160 g) cooked brown rice
1 (15-oz [425-g]) can refried beans
1 (15-oz [425-g]) can black beans, rinsed and drained
¼ cup (30 g) shredded vegan cheese

TOPPINGS
Salsa
Guacamole

Preheat the oven to 375°F (190°C).

In a 9-inch (23-cm) springform pan, layer as follows: 2 tortillas, rice, refried beans, black beans, cheese and the last 2 tortillas.

Bake for 30 minutes, or until the pie is heated, the cheese is melted and the tortillas are crispy.

Let cool for about 5 to 10 minutes before sliding it out of the springform pan and onto a flat surface for cutting.

Top with your favorite salsa and guacamole.

Note: This pie can be covered and refrigerated for 3 to 4 days.

One-Pot PASTA ARRABIATA

+QP +SF +GF

I've never seen a home cook happier than when they only have to clean one pot after a satisfying meal. And this recipe is nothing short of easy. One pot does all the work and out comes a spicy pasta, tossed with roasted tomatoes and fresh basil. Buon appetito! —MR

SERVES 4 TO 6

Drizzle olive oil
½ small red onion, thinly sliced
2 cloves garlic, thinly sliced
1 tsp red pepper flakes
1 tsp sea salt
1½ tsp (8 g) tomato paste
2¼ cups (530 ml) water
1 (14-oz [397-g]) can diced tomatoes
3–4 tbsp (15–20 g) nutritional yeast
2 cups (230 g) dry pasta (or use brown rice pasta for gluten-free)
2 cups (320 g) roasted cherry tomatoes
Handful fresh basil

In a very large saucepan or a large pot, heat the olive oil over medium-low heat. Then add the onion, garlic, red pepper flakes, salt and tomato paste. Sauté for a few minutes while you assemble the rest of the ingredients. Pour in the water, diced tomatoes, nutritional yeast and pasta. Allow it to cook over medium-high heat until the water has absorbed and the pasta is al dente, about 20 minutes. Don't forget to stir every minute or so. Top with the roasted tomatoes and basil.

Note: To make the roasted tomatoes, simply preheat the oven to 400°F (204°C) and cook the tomatoes for 20 minutes, or until the skins blister.

*SEE PHOTO INSERT

Asian-Style MISO AND EGGPLANT PASTA

+QP +GF

Asian-Style Miso and Eggplant Pasta is a great twist on a traditional Italian tomato and veggie pasta. Stretch the use of miso paste by dolloping a small amount into this pasta, creating a savory umami bomb reflected in each bite. —MR

SERVES 2 TO 4

3 tbsp (45 ml) olive oil

4 cloves garlic, thinly sliced

1½ tbsp (23 g) tomato paste

2 cups (150 g) thinly sliced cremini mushrooms

1 small eggplant, cut into bite-size cubes

4 cups (645 g) cherry tomatoes, cut in half

1 tbsp (15 g) sea salt

5¼ oz (150 g) brown rice pasta

1 tbsp (18 g) brown miso paste

½–1 tsp red pepper flakes (optional)

3–5 tbsp (45–75 ml) pasta water, as needed

½ cup (38 g) green onions, thinly sliced into rings

In a medium saucepan over medium-low heat, warm the olive oil with the garlic and tomato paste for 2 minutes. Add the mushrooms, eggplant and tomatoes to the saucepan and turn up the heat to medium. Press down on the tomatoes to release their juices. Gradually add enough water, a few tablespoons (30 ml) at a time, to the saucepan so that the vegetables don't stick to the bottom. Cook the veggies until they have softened, about 7 to 10 minutes.

As the veggies cook, add 1 tablespoon (15 g) of sea salt to a large pot of boiling water. Then add the pasta and cook according to the package instructions. Stir the pasta frequently as it cooks.

Now add the miso paste and red pepper flakes to the saucepan, and stir the miso around until it coats all the veggies and fully dissolves. If the pasta sauce starts to stick to the saucepan, add a few tablespoons (45 ml) of pasta water gradually and turn down the heat to low.

Drain the pasta and mix it together with the miso sauce. Top with extra green onions, scoop into bowls and enjoy!

*SEE PHOTO INSERT

ZUCCHINI NOODLE PASTA with Veggies

+QP +SF +GF

Zucchinis are a great substitute for modernizing pasta; their mild flavor easily adapts to most sauces and when cut with a spiralizer tool, they become long spaghettis. Alternatively, use a potato peeler to create pappardelle-like noodles. Pair it with heaps of fresh squash, peas and fennel, and simmer in a delicious tomato sauce. —MR

SERVES 2

1 carrot

3 zucchini

3 cloves garlic, roughly chopped

½ head fennel, thinly sliced crosswise

3 tbsp (45 ml) olive oil

1 (16-oz [455-g]) can whole peeled tomatoes

Handful of cherry tomatoes

Pinch of red pepper flakes

Sea salt

2 summer squash (or any), cut into thin circles

½–¾ cup (67-100 g) frozen peas, defrosted

(continued)

Start by peeling the carrot and zucchini into long ribbons with a potato peeler. Set aside as you warm the garlic, fennel and olive oil in a large saucepan over medium heat for a few minutes. Bring the heat to medium-high, add the canned tomatoes (including the sauce in the can), fresh tomatoes, red pepper flakes and a sprinkle of sea salt; cover with a lid for 5 minutes.

Once the tomato sauce has reduced, add the summer squash to cook it down. Add a few splashes of water if the sauce dries out. Cook for 10 minutes before adding the peas. Now stir in the zucchini and carrot noodles, and warm the mixture for a few minutes. Pour it into bowls and enjoy!

Pesto SOCCA PIZZA

+QP +SF +GF

You'll surprise your guests with this one: chickpea flour pizza crust. With a crispy crust keeping it light, this savory pizza is topped with creamy pesto and roasted squash. —MR

SERVES 1 TO 2

PIZZA CRUST
⅔ cup (86 g) chickpea flour (also called garbanzo bean flour)

⅓ cup (28 g) almond meal or chickpea flour

3 tbsp (45 ml) water

2 tbsp (30 ml) olive oil, divided

Sea salt

4 tbsp (56 g) pesto, homemade (page 419) or store-bought

TOPPINGS (FOR THE PIZZA PICTURED)
1 cup (140 g) roasted veggies (I enjoy winter squash)

½ radish, sliced

Sprinkle of hemp seeds

Sprinkle of fresh dill or arugula

FOR THE CRUST
Preheat the oven to 400°F (204°C). In a small bowl, combine the flour, almond meal, water, 1 tablespoon (15 ml) of the oil and salt to taste and form a ball. Then mix for about 3 minutes. It's important that you mix the dough very well. It should start to resemble Silly Putty in texture. Mix the dough for the full 3 minutes. Pop it into the fridge to set for 10 minutes.

On a clean surface, using a rolling pin, roll out the dough into a circle (dough should be about ¼ inch [6 mm] thick). Rub the top of the dough with the remaining 1 tablespoon (15 ml) olive oil.

Place it into the oven to bake for 9 to 10 minutes, or until the sides are crispy and golden brown. Remove from the oven and top with the pesto. Spread the pesto evenly onto the crust and add any topping you'd like!

*SEE PHOTO INSERT

QUINOA AND GREENS BURRITO with a Cheesy Spread

+QP +GF +SF

Chickpeas and nutritional yeast go a long way flavor-wise, when paired together. Whipped chickpeas absorb the cheesy flavor of nutritional yeast (I know, not the most attractive name). Take this spread (rename it) and smear it along the inside of a burrito that's bursting at the seams with endless greens. —MR

SERVES 2

CHEESY SPREAD
1 (14-oz [397-g]) can chickpeas, rinsed and drained

Juice of ½ lemon

1 clove garlic

1–2 tbsp (5–10 g) nutritional yeast

2 tbsp (30 ml) olive oil

2 tbsp (30 ml) water

Sea salt

BURRITO

2 large handfuls kale leaves, de-stemmed and roughly chopped

½ cup (93 g) cooked quinoa

½ avocado, sliced

Small handful Kalamata olives, roughly chopped

¼ cup (60 g) gigante beans, or any white beans

Handful almonds, toasted

Squeeze of lemon juice

Sea salt

2 burrito wraps of your choice

FOR THE CHEESY SPREAD

Start making the cheesy spread by adding everything to a food processor and blending until creamy. Check the taste and see if you'd like to add more seasoning or lemon juice. Set aside.

FOR THE BURRITO

In a large mixing bowl, toss all the ingredients for the burrito (except for the burrito wraps) and mix well with your hands. Now add in 2 to 4 tablespoons (30 to 60 g) of the cheesy spread (depending on how cheesy you like it) to the bowl and continue to mix until the kale leaves are nicely coated with the spread.

Warm the burrito wraps. Then add a thin layer of the cheesy spread to the bottom of the wrap, fill it with the kale salad, roll up and enjoy!

ZUCCHINI NOODLE PASTA with Pesto

+QP +SF +GF

Pasta is the ideal canvas for experiencing the flavors of Italian cuisine. Yet my ideal twist on this Italian staple is something a bit lighter: raw zucchini. When prepared just right, this unlikely vegetable has a pasta-like texture that can be twisted and twirled over a rich pesto sauce. Transforming zucchinis into a truly delicious pasta dish requires a sauce to complement its light al-dente texture. A creamy pesto adds a layer of substance and weight to this otherwise very delicate ingredient. Together, they create a satisfying and nourishing meal. —MR

SERVES 2

2 large zucchini

1 tbsp (15 ml) olive oil, plus more for serving

3–4 tbsp (45–60 g) pesto, homemade (page 419) or store-bought

Pinch of red pepper flakes

Pinch of sea salt

Start by making the zucchini noodles with either a spiralizer or a potato peeler. Then warm a medium saucepan with the olive oil and heat the zucchini noodles over medium heat for 3 to 5 minutes.

Scoop the pesto onto the noodles and mix until coated. Sprinkle with a pinch of red pepper flakes, sea salt and a drizzle of olive oil. Pour it into bowls and enjoy!

*SEE PHOTO INSERT

Tempeh REUBEN

+QP

This dish starts with a good, flavorful bread like rye or pumpernickel. Topped with fried tempeh, spicy vegan cheese and local sauerkraut, and you've got yourself a meal that will look as good as it tastes! —AS

SERVES 1

2 slices rye or pumpernickel bread
4 (¼" [6-mm]) slices of tempeh
1 tbsp (14 g) coconut oil or vegan butter, for frying
½ tsp liquid aminos or soy sauce
2 tbsp (30 ml) vegan Thousand Island dressing
1 slice vegan cheese
¼ cup (55 g) sauerkraut

Set aside your 2 delicious slices of rye or pumpernickel. It's good to use a darker bread here to get the caraway and espresso flavor of the bread; trust me, it adds a ton of flavor to the sandwich!

If your tempeh is in block form, slice four ¼-inch (6-mm) slices. If presliced, use 4 slices. In a frying pan, melt a little oil or butter and add the liquid aminos. Fry the tempeh strips until crispy and golden brown, about 2 to 4 minutes on each side.

Grab your bread slices and spread about 1 tablespoon (14 g) vegan Thousand Island on each side. Top them with the fried tempeh and the slice of cheese. Put the sandwich together and, using the same frying pan, grill the sandwich until the cheese melts, a few minutes on each side. Remove from the pan, separate the bread slices, top with the sauerkraut and reassemble into sandwich form. Now take a giant, gooey, cheesy bite!

Tomato Basil
SPAGHETTI SQUASH BAKE

+GF +QP +SF

The beauty of this is that you really do just throw all the ingredients into your hollowed squash halves and bake for about an hour—easy peasy! Once it's ready, just remove it from the oven, shred the squash with a fork and serve. Your guests will love the taste, and you'll love the easy cleanup. It's healthy, light and full of fresh (from our garden, in this case) veggies. So let's give three cheers for a lack of dishes and more time to eat, 'cause that's the ultimate goal. Let's do it! —AS

SERVES 4

1 medium spaghetti squash
2–3 tbsp (30–45 ml) olive oil
2 cloves garlic, minced
½ cup (120 ml) tomato sauce
½ cup (80 g) cherry tomatoes, halved
¼ cup (10 g) chopped basil, plus more for garnish
Salt and pepper, to taste
Nutritional yeast, for garnish

Preheat the oven to 375°F (190°C).

Slice the stem off the top of your squash, then turn it on its side and slice it in half lengthwise. Remove the seeds and innards, and toss in the compost. Drizzle each half with olive oil, a little over 1 tablespoon (15 ml) each, and sprinkle each side evenly with minced garlic. Pour about ¼ cup (60 ml) of sauce into each half, and then top each side evenly with sliced cherry tomatoes, basil, salt and pepper. Cover them with aluminum foil and place them on a baking sheet to catch any drippings. Bake for 50 to 60 minutes, until the mixture is bubbling and the squash is fork tender.

Once ready, remove them from the oven and use a fork to separate the squash strands. You may scoop the mixture into a bowl and stir if you like more room to work. Otherwise, use a fork to toss the squash pasta and tomato-basil mixture together right in the squash halves, and serve immediately. Sprinkle with fresh basil and nutritional yeast to garnish. This saves well in an airtight container in the fridge for up to a week.

Sweet Potato AND TURMERIC FALAFELS

+QP +SF +GF

These falafels are crisp on the outside and creamy on the inside. Sweet potato and turmeric falafels are baked in the oven for an easy and healthy weeknight meal. Enjoy them as the main accompaniment in a salad, wrapped in a pita or on their own with a drizzle of traditional tzatziki dressing. —MR

MAKES 12 TO 13 BALLS

1 sweet potato, baked or steamed (without skin)
1 (14-oz [397-g]) can chickpeas, rinsed and drained
½ cup (20 g) fresh cilantro or parsley
1 tsp ground turmeric
2 cloves garlic
1 tbsp (7 g) ground cumin
1 tbsp (7 g) ground coriander
Zest and juice of ½ lemon
1 tsp sea salt

Preheat the oven to 375°F (190°C).

Then simply place the steamed or baked sweet potato into the food processor and pulse for about 10 seconds, breaking down the sweet potato. Add the remaining ingredients to the food processor. Pulse for another 15 to 20 seconds until the chickpeas have been broken down but are not totally blended. You don't want to turn the mixture into hummus; there should be small chunks of chickpeas throughout.

On a parchment paper–lined baking sheet, scoop out the falafel mixture with an ice cream scooper and place on the sheet. Just make sure the falafels are no bigger than 1 inch (2.5 cm) thick. They should be pretty small. Bake for 15 to 20 minutes, or until the top is slightly golden brown and crispy. Remove from the oven and let cool for 10 minutes.

SERVING OPTIONS

Add 4 to 5 falafels on top of a simple salad: arugula, celery, olives, cucumber, hemp seeds and tomato salad, with a lemon and olive oil dressing.

Add the falafel to a collard green or pita wrap.

Enjoy dunked into tzatziki sauce (page 132).

Note: Since these falafels are baked, they will be more crumbly than deep-fried falafels. Use care when handling them after baking.

*SEE PHOTO INSERT

Baked SUN-DRIED FALAFEL WITH TZATZIKI DIP

+QP +SF +GF

An unexpected take on falafels, these hearty sun-dried tomato falafels have a touch of sweetness, balancing the earthier notes of cumin and paprika. Make the falafels in bulk and enjoy as a speedy weeknight meal that only takes minutes to reheat.

Since these falafels are baked, they will be more crumbly than deep-fried falafels. Be delicate when handling after they have baked. —MR

MAKES 12 TO 15 BALLS

SUN-DRIED TOMATO FALAFEL

1 (14-oz [397-g]) can chickpeas, rinsed and drained

5 sun-dried tomato pieces

Drizzle of olive oil

1 cup (40 g) fresh cilantro or parsley

3 cloves garlic

1 tbsp (7 g) ground cumin

1 tbsp (7 g) paprika

½ tsp chili powder

Juice of 1 small lemon

1 tsp sea salt

TZATZIKI SAUCE

½ cup (123 g) coconut yogurt

½ small cucumber, peeled and thinly sliced

2 cloves garlic, thinly sliced

Juice of ½ small lemon

Small handful of fresh dill, roughly chopped

Pinch of sea salt

FOR THE FALAFEL

Preheat the oven to 375°F (190°C).

Add all of the ingredients for the falafel to the food processor. Pulse for 15 to 20 seconds, until the chickpeas have broken down but are not totally blended. You don't want to turn the mixture into hummus; there should be small chunks of chickpeas and sun-dried tomatoes throughout.

On a parchment paper–lined baking sheet, scoop out the falafel mixture with an ice cream scooper and place on the sheet. Just make sure the falafel balls are no bigger than 1 inch (2.5 cm) thick. They should be pretty small. Bake for 25 to 30 minutes, or until the top is slightly golden brown and crispy and the center is creamy.

FOR THE TZATZIKI SAUCE

Simply scoop the yogurt into a bowl and mix in the cucumbers, garlic, lemon juice, dill and sea salt.

SERVING OPTIONS

Add 4 to 5 falafel balls on top of a simple salad: arugula, celery, olives, cucumber, hemp seeds and tomato with a lemon and olive oil dressing.

Or add the falafel to a collard green or pita wrap with the tzatziki dressing.

Veggie RAINBOW PAELLA

+QP +SF +GF

Paella can be a very creative affair. Keep the backbone of this classic Spanish dish alive, but take creative license by changing out any ingredient for ones you desire. Swap traditional Arborio rice for brown, and add in a medley of vegetables from bell peppers to peas. Make it in bulk and enjoy for dinner the next night. —MR

SERVES 4 TO 6

3 tbsp (45 ml) olive oil

1 small red onion, thinly sliced

3 cloves garlic, thinly sliced

2 zucchini, cut into half-moons

5 mini bell peppers (or 2 large), cut into thin strips

1 cup (134 g) frozen peas, defrosted (run under warm water for 1 minute)

2 cups (220 g) green beans

10 strands of saffron

1 tbsp (7 g) cayenne

1 tbsp (7 g) paprika

1½ cups (315 g) brown rice, uncooked

3 cups (710 ml) low-sodium vegetable broth

2 green onions, sliced

Juice of 1 lemon

Handful fresh parsley

1 cup (160 g) cherry tomatoes

Sea salt, to taste

Start by warming the olive oil in a large saucepan (or paella pan) and sauté the onion and garlic for about 5 minutes.

Add the zucchini, bell peppers, peas, green beans and all the spices, and sauté for another 10 minutes—add a splash of water occasionally so that the veggies don't stick to the pan.

To the same pan, add the uncooked rice and veggie broth. Turn the heat to high. Once this boils, bring the heat back down to a simmer and let the paella cook for about 45 to 60 minutes, stirring every 15 minutes.

Once the rice is fully cooked and the broth is completely absorbed, top with the green onions, lemon juice, parsley and cherry tomatoes. Add the sea salt to taste. Serve paella in bowls and enjoy!

Sage POLENTA AND WILD MUSHROOMS

+QP +SF +GF

The appeal of this sage polenta with wild mushrooms dish rests in knowing that fresh sage, mushrooms and polenta is all that it takes to unlock a cozy meal fit for any time of year. This is comfort food done right. —MR

SERVES 6 TO 8

SAGE POLENTA

1 cup (170 g) polenta, uncooked

1½ cups (355 ml) water

1½ cups (355 ml) almond milk

¼ cup (10 g) roughly chopped fresh sage

3 tbsp (15 g) nutritional yeast

Sea salt, to taste

MUSHROOMS

2 tbsp (30 ml) olive oil

3 cloves garlic, roughly chopped

2 cups (150 g) thinly sliced wild mushrooms

3-4 tbsp (45-60 ml) water (for the mushrooms)

Sea salt

3-4 fresh sage leaves, roughly chopped

Squeeze of lemon (optional)

(continued)

FOR THE SAGE POLENTA

Follow the recipe on your bag while using the water and almond milk as the liquid for the 1 cup (235 ml) polenta ratio. Once the polenta is nearly done cooking, stir in the sage and nutritional yeast. Add a few teaspoons (15 g) of sea salt until it's seasoned just as you like.

FOR THE MUSHROOMS

As the polenta cooks, make the sautéed mushrooms. In a medium skillet, warm the olive oil and garlic over medium-low heat. Stir in the chopped mushrooms and a splash of water, adding sea salt as desired. I like to add water so that the mushrooms never dry out or stick to the pan. Sauté for another 5 to 10 minutes, and then stir in the sage. If you like, add a small squeeze of lemon juice. Make a plate of your polenta and add the mushrooms on top.

*SEE PHOTO INSERT

Mushroom FAJITAS ✕

+QP +GF +SF

This is a classic weeknight meal that highlights the simplicity of sautéed vegetables and spices, all wrapped in a warm tortilla. Some meals need only be that simple to be delicious. —MR

SERVES 2

1 tbsp (14 g) coconut oil
1 bell pepper, sliced in thin strips lengthwise
½ yellow onion, thinly sliced
½ tsp ground cumin
½ tsp garlic powder
Sea salt
2 cups (150 g) roughly chopped wild mushrooms
¼ cup (60 g) black beans

2 tortillas
½ avocado, sliced
Handful fresh cilantro
Handful pumpkin seeds
Juice of ½ lime

In a large sauté pan, warm the coconut oil over medium heat. To the pan, add the bell pepper, onion, cumin, garlic powder and a pinch of sea salt, and sauté for about 15 to 20 minutes, caramelizing the onions. Add a splash of water if the pan ever dries out. Remove the sautéed veggies from the pan and set aside.

To the same sauté pan, add the mushrooms and sauté until tender, about 3 to 5 minutes. Set aside when cooked. Toss in the black beans to the same pan and warm for 2 minutes.

Fill the tortillas with a layer of the sautéed bell pepper and onion, followed by the mushrooms, beans, avocado slices, cilantro, pumpkin seeds, sprinkle of salt and squeeze of lime juice.

*SEE PHOTO INSERT

ARUGULA PESTO AND ZUCCHINI on Rye Toast

+QP +SF +GFO

This delicious open-face sandwich is layered in tangy lime-arugula pesto, sliced avocado and sautéed zucchini over rye toast. It's a hearty sandwich that sneaks in extra greens in the most satisfying way: over thick, warm bread. —MR

MAKES 2 SLICES

ARUGULA PESTO

2 large handfuls arugula

1 cup (125 g) pine nuts or any nut, unsalted

1 large handful spinach

Juice of 1 lime

1 tsp sea salt

3 tbsp (45 ml) olive oil

ZUCCHINI TOAST

½ large zucchini

1 tbsp (15 ml) olive oil

1 clove garlic, roughly chopped

Pinch of sea salt

Splash of water, or more as needed

2 slices rye bread or any bread

½ avocado, sliced

Handful watercress (optional)

FOR THE ARUGULA PESTO

Start making the arugula pesto by placing all the ingredients in a food processor and whipping until the pesto becomes smooth and creamy.

FOR THE ZUCCHINI TOAST

Cut the zucchini into very thin circular slices. In a small saucepan over medium heat, warm the olive oil, garlic, sea salt and a few splashes of water. Add the zucchini and sauté for about 7 minutes (turn the zucchini halfway through and cook the other side). Slowly add water if the zucchini starts to dry out as it cooks.

Toast the bread. Then spread the pesto across the toast, add the zucchini and avocado slices and top with watercress!

Roasted TOMATO AND GARLIC TOAST

+QP +SF +GFO

All that is needed for an exceptional toast is one juicy tomato. Roast it in the oven until the juices escape its blistering skin and gently place the oozing tomato on a slice of warm bread. Now you have yourself one delectable slice of toast. —MR

SERVES 2

2 large tomatoes

2 tsp (10 ml) olive oil, divided

2 slices rye bread or any bread

1 clove garlic, sliced in half

4 tbsp (61 g) vegan yogurt or cashew cheese (page 420)

Red pepper flakes

Sea salt

1 avocado (optional)

Preheat the oven to 400°F (204°C). Line a baking tray with parchment paper.

Drizzle the tomatoes with 1 teaspoon of the oil, place on the baking sheet and transfer to the oven. Once the tomatoes have softened and the skin has blistered, about 25 minutes, remove them from the oven and make your toast.

Toast your bread, and then take the sliced garlic clove and run the clove all over the toast (we are infusing the toast). Now add a layer of either yogurt or cashew cheese to the toast, and then the tomato, red pepper flakes, the remaining 1 teaspoon olive oil and sea salt. Add an avocado to make it more of a meal.

*SEE PHOTO INSERT

Lean GREEN PORTOBELLO, PESTO AND ARTICHOKE ✳ PANINI

+QP +GF +SF

I think this combo would taste great on really any bread, but I recommend splurging on a great loaf if you can enjoy it. The portobello acts as the meaty base, with a spread of basil pesto and topped with artichoke hearts, onions and creamy avocado. It's got a ton of flavor and makes a great lunch—plus it takes just a few minutes to whip up. Let's eat! —AS

MAKES 1 SANDWICH

1 medium portobello mushroom

2 tsp (10 g) coconut oil, divided

2 slices sourdough (or your favorite) bread

3-4 tbsp (40–55 g) basil pesto

2-3 artichoke hearts, roughly chopped

Onion, thinly sliced (I like a lot. Put as much as you like!)

½ avocado, thinly sliced

Gently clean the mushroom cap, remove the stem and thinly slice the cap. Lightly sauté in 1 teaspoon of the coconut oil in a medium frying pan for 3 to 4 minutes, until slightly softened. Remove from the heat.

Meanwhile, heat the remaining 1 teaspoon coconut oil on a large griddle over medium heat (or preheat your panini press and spray with nonstick spray). Spread each slice of bread with pesto on one side and assemble portobellos, artichoke hearts and sliced onion on top. Place the sandwich on the griddle and cook until golden; then flip. When finished, remove it from the heat and add the avocado slices. Slice and enjoy!

Vegan MAC 'N' ✳ CHEEZE

+QP +GF +SF

I scream, you scream, we all scream for MAC 'N' CHEEZE! Especially those of us with food allergies, dietary preferences or just a healthy appreciation for health. I decided to create a slightly spicy, flavorful, much healthier recreation of the old favorite. Loaded with secret ingredient goodies like nutritional yeast, tahini and turmeric, it's worth more than you'd expect, too. The cheezy sauce is chock full of B vitamins and anti-inflammatory power just waiting to be gobbled up! —AS

SERVES 4 TO 6

12 oz (340 g) gluten-free pasta elbows

1 cup (110 g) raw cashews

1 cup (120 ml) unsweetened nut milk substitute of choice (we've used hemp, almond and walnut: all delicious!)

2 cloves garlic

⅓ cup (25 g) nutritional yeast

2 tbsp (30 g) tahini

3 tsp (15 ml) lemon juice

1 tsp ground turmeric

⅛ tsp cayenne red pepper

⅛ tsp smoked paprika

¼ tsp salt

⅛ tsp pepper

Cook the pasta according to the directions on the package. Gluten-free pasta, especially when brown rice based, tends to absorb more water than normal, so be sure to add extra water to the pot before boiling; it usually takes a few extra minutes for GF pasta to reach the al dente stage, too. And be sure to add a little salt to the water before boiling—it flavors the pasta.

As the pasta cooks, combine the raw cashews and nut milk in a blender or food processor. I never soak mine beforehand; I prefer the slightly thicker sauce that results from not soaking them in this recipe.

Once combined, add the rest of the ingredients. Yup, all of them. (Told you this recipe was easy!) Blend until combined. Set aside.

Once the pasta is al dente—literally meaning "to the bite" (Leave a little texture in that pasta! Don't boil it into mushy submission)—strain, rinse and put it back into the pot. Pour in the cheeze sauce, using a wooden spoon to gently toss and coat the pasta.

Turn the burner back on to low and continue to cook the pasta and cheeze sauce together for about 3 to 5 minutes, stirring occasionally, until the sauce thickens and sticks to the noodles.

Serve immediately: the best grown-up vegan mac 'n' cheeze you can imagine!

To reheat it, simply warm the pasta in a pan with a little nondairy milk, stirring until creamy. Mac 'n' cheeze saves well in a refrigerated space for about a week.

Mediterranean
HUMMUS BURGERS 🗶

+QP +GFO +SF

I had my first hummus burger while visiting northern California. It was one of the best things that I ate while I was there. It was everything you'd imagine a hummus burger should be. The warm flavor of the cumin and the bright lemon complemented the nutty tahini to make the perfect burger. Topped with chopped Kalamata olives, avocado and greens, it was truly like biting into the Mediterranean. —LM + AM

SERVES 4

1 (15-oz [425-g]) can chickpeas
2 cloves garlic, chopped
Juice of 1 small lemon
⅓ cup (44 g) oat flour (use gluten-free)
⅓ cup (41 g) breadcrumbs (use gluten-free)
2 tbsp (30 g) tahini
3 tbsp (45 ml) liquid from the chickpea can
2 tsp (5 g) ground cumin
1 tsp fine sea salt
2 tbsp (30 ml) extra-virgin olive oil
4 sesame seed hamburger buns (use gluten-free)

TOPPINGS
Mashed avocado
Chopped Kalamata olives
Spinach or lettuce

Drain (reserve the liquid, it's your egg replacer) and rinse the chickpeas, and place in a food processor. Add the garlic, lemon juice, oat flour, breadcrumbs, tahini, chick pea juice, cumin and salt; process for about 30 seconds or until you get a thick and sticky mixture. Divide the mixture in four and form each into 4 large patties.

Heat the olive oil in a medium cast-iron skillet over medium-high heat. When the oil is hot, add the burgers and cover the pan. Sear for about 8 minutes per side, or until they're golden brown and heated through to the center. Cover them while heating for a better sear.

Place them on the buns and top with the avocado, olives and spinach or lettuce.

If you want super-thick burgers, double the recipe.

CHIK'N CAESAR SALAD
Wraps

+QP

If you love Caesar salad, then you're going to love this wrap. It's light yet filling, it's full of zippy flavor and it's vegan! Pack it for lunch or make them for a quick and easy dinner. —LM + AM

SERVES 4

DRESSING

1 clove garlic, minced

2 tbsp (30 ml) lemon juice

1 tsp Dijon mustard

1 tsp caper juice

1 tsp vegan Worcestershire sauce (we use Annie's brand)

1 cup (223 g) vegan mayonnaise (we use Just Mayo)

½ cup (91 g) vegan Parmesan, homemade (page 76, 150) or store-bought

Salt and pepper, to taste

FILLING

8 oz (227 g) prepared chick seitan, chopped into bite-size pieces (we use Upton's Naturals)

4 cups (300 g) chopped romaine lettuce

4 (10" [25-cm]) multigrain wraps, or wrap of choice

OPTIONAL

Diced tomato

Diced cucumber

FOR THE DRESSING

In a small bowl, whisk the garlic, lemon juice, mustard, caper juice and Worcestershire sauce until combined. Add the mayo, Parmesan, salt and pepper, and whisk until fully combined. Set it aside.

FOR THE FILLING

In a small skillet, heat the chick seitan until warmed through.

Put the lettuce, 1 cup (223 g) of the dressing and the chick seitan in a large bowl, and toss until the lettuce is coated with the dressing. Divide the filling by four and put each serving in the center of a wrap. Add a dollop or two of dressing on top of the salad filling. Fold the sides of the wrap over (about 2 inches [5 cm]) and then roll the wrap into a cylinder.

Feel free to add tomato and/or cucumber to jazz it up.

Leftover dressing should be stored in an airtight container in the refrigerator for up to a week.

Pizza GRILLED CHEESE ✸

+QP +GFO

We took everyone's favorites—pizza and grilled cheese —and combined them for one of the tastiest sandwiches we've ever had. It has it all! And best of all, they're so easy to assemble. We used our Yeast-Free Garlic Flatbread (page 174) for the bread, because it's like a pizza crust, and our Four-Ingredient Homemade Pizza Sauce (page 418). It just doesn't get much better than this. —LM + AM

SERVES 1

1 tsp extra-virgin olive oil, plus more for brushing on the bread

½ cup (33 g) sliced mushrooms

2 cups (450 g) baby spinach

2 tbsp (22 g) black olives

2 pieces Yeast-Free Garlic Flatbread (page 174) or whatever type of bread you like (see Note) (use gluten-free bread)

Vegan mozzarella or cheddar cheese, use as much as you like

¼ cup (62 g) Four-Ingredient Homemade Pizza Sauce (page 418)

In a small skillet, heat the olive oil over medium-high heat. Add the mushrooms and cook for about 10 minutes, or until they release their water and are nicely browned. Add the spinach and the olives and cook until the spinach is just wilted.

Spray or brush a thin layer of olive oil on one side of each piece of the flatbread. On one piece of flatbread, sprinkle a liberal layer (or as much as you like) of cheese on the non-oiled side. Put the mushroom and spinach mixture over the cheese and then drizzle the pizza sauce over the top. Sprinkle with a little more cheese and put the second piece of flatbread (oil-side up) on top.

Heat a griddle or the skillet you cooked the mushrooms in over medium heat.

Carefully put the sandwich in the pan and cover. Cook for about 3 to 5 minutes, or until the bread is golden brown and the cheese has melted. Gently flip the sandwich and cook for another 3 to 5 minutes, or until that side is golden brown.

Note: For the best results, use bread that will mimic pizza crust, such as focaccia or ciabatta.

Saucy and Sassy
CASHEW NOODLES

+QP +GF

Give me all the noodles! Especially those that are loaded with Asian-inspired flavors, vegetables and the most buttery of all nuts: cashews. If you want to make it even bulkier, add cubes of pan-fried tofu or tempeh to your bowl. —CS

SERVES 2 TO 3

2 tbsp (30 ml) Scallion-Infused Oil (page 409), divided

1 tbsp (15 ml) shoyu

2 tbsp (30 ml) brine from Miso-Marinated Mushrooms (page 185) or brown rice vinegar

2 tbsp (32 g) roasted cashew butter

8 oz (227 g) dry glass noodles, cooked according to package directions

1 bell pepper, any color, cored and cut with a mandoline slicer

1 medium carrot, peeled and trimmed, thickly shredded

Scallions from Scallion-Infused Oil (page 409)

TOPPINGS
Pinch of gochugaru (optional)

Chopped green parts of scallions

Chopped fresh cilantro

Toasted sesame seeds

Nanami Togarashi Cashews (page 187)

Place 1 tablespoon (15 ml) of the infused oil in a small bowl, and whisk in the shoyu, brine and cashew butter. Set aside.

Place the remaining 1 tablespoon (15 ml) infused oil in the pot used to cook the noodles. Add the bell pepper and carrot, and stir-fry until just tender but still crisp, about 4 minutes. Add the noodles and use a fork to scoop up half of the cooked scallions from the infused oil. (Let the excess oil drip into the saucepan before adding it to the noodles.) Cook over medium-low heat just to heat through. Remove the stir-fry from the heat and add the sauce. Serve immediately with an extra pinch of gochugaru (if desired), chopped scallion greens, cilantro, sesame seeds and cashews.

Chickpea SALAD
SANDWICHES ✳

+QP

When I first bit into one of these sandwiches, I couldn't quite put my finger on what they reminded me of. That is until Chaz (my husband) declared them to be just like an egg sandwich—only much better, because no egg! If you want to bring out an eggier flavor, you could add a pinch of kala namak, also known as black salt. It has a sulfur-like taste that will totally remind you of eggs. Don't overdo it as it's quite pungent. —CS

MAKES 4 SANDWICHES

1 tsp coconut oil

1 shallot, minced

1 large clove garlic, minced

½ bell pepper, trimmed and diced

2 dried shiitake mushrooms, rehydrated and minced (remove stems if tough)

1 tbsp (14 g) vegan red curry paste

1 tbsp (15 ml) tamari

Juice of ½ lemon (about 2 tbsp [30 ml])

1½ cups (256 g) cooked chickpeas

½ cup (114 g) plain vegan mayo

1½ tsp (3 g) nutritional yeast

Salt, to taste

Fresh baby spinach (about 4 handfuls)

4 vegan bread rolls of choice or 8 slices sandwich bread, toasted

Fresh cilantro, to taste

Place the oil in a large skillet. Heat it over medium-high heat and add the shallot, garlic, bell pepper and mushrooms. Cook until the bell pepper just starts to become tender, about 3 minutes. Stir occasionally.

In the meantime, whisk the curry paste, tamari and lemon juice in a small bowl. Set it aside.

Add the chickpeas to the vegetables and cook another 2 minutes. Add the sauce and cook until the liquid evaporates a little, about 2 minutes. Stir occasionally. Remove the mixture from the heat and let cool before stirring into the mayo and nutritional yeast. Mash the chickpeas to a tuna-like consistency so that the chickpeas don't roll out of the sandwiches as you eat. Adjust the seasoning as needed.

Place a generous handful of spinach on one side of the bread roll or on a slice of bread. Top with a quarter of the chickpea salad, cilantro to taste and the other side of the bread roll or another slice of bread. Repeat these steps with the remaining 3 sandwiches and serve immediately.

Zucchini SPAGHETTI WITH SUN-DRIED TOMATOES AND BASIL

+QP

I cannot get over how amazing tomatoes are when you drizzle them with some extra-virgin olive oil, salt and pepper, and allow them to dry in the sun, dehydrator or oven. They become flavor EXPLOSIONS that are the very essence of the best pizza you've ever eaten. Trust me. But wait, don't trust me. Find out for yourself by doing it. You will not be sorry. They taste so damn delicious that all you need to do to make a meal is throw them on some noodles. Bam. You just made a mind-blowingly tasty dinner that will make everyone jealous. If they aren't envious, then they are definitely missing their sense of sight or smell. The tomatoes are gonna need to taste amazing before you even add them to the noodles and stuff, because they are the star of this recipe. So try to get organic—or even better, use your own! —EvE

SERVES 1 OR 2

NOODLES
2 large zucchini

SAUCE
1 cup (150 g) sun-dried tomatoes, stored in extra-virgin olive oil

Salt, pepper, lemon juice or other spices you like

½ cup (20 g) basil (whole or chopped)

FOR THE NOODLES
Slice the zucchini into noodles on a spiral slicer, mandoline or even cheese grater. Set them aside in a large bowl.

(continued)

FOR THE SAUCE

Blend half of the tomatoes into a paste, and then mash up the rest of the tomatoes with the olive oil and the rest of the ingredients; mix everything into your noodles. Let it sit for 10 to 15 minutes and mix again. Eat. OMG.

*SEE PHOTO INSERT

FOR THE SAUCE

Blend all of the ingredients until smooth.

FOR THE BASE

In a bowl, mix the sauce into your rice and sweet potatoes. Then top with basil and enjoy!

*SEE PHOTO INSERT

Steamed SWEET POTATOES WITH WILD RICE, BASIL AND TOMATO CHILI SAUCE

+QP

I am in love with sweet potatoes. They are excellent for your brain and eye health as well as overall wellness. Basil is called the Sacred Goddess herb, tomato is great for the prostate and this whole recipe is just yummy, regardless of its health benefits! —EvE

SERVES 2 TO 4

SAUCE
1 tomato
1 tbsp (11 g) almond butter
1 tbsp (11 g) miso paste
1 tbsp (15 ml) lemon juice
1 tbsp (15 ml) maple syrup
1 tsp chili powder, to taste
1 clove garlic

BASE
2 cups (320 g) cooked wild rice
1 large sweet potato, sliced and steamed until soft and tender
¼ cup (7 g) basil

Fresh RICE PAPER WRAPS WITH CHIPOTLE PEANUT SAUCE

+QP

This recipe is a crowd pleaser for when you want to show friends (or others . . .) that eating vegan doesn't have to be weird and sad like some folks think it is. We are just throwing together some fresh, vibrant veggies in rice paper wraps and pairing them with a spicy, creamy peanut sauce. What's not to love? Dig in. —EvE

SERVES 2 OR 3

SAUCE
¼ cup (45 g) peanut butter
2 tbsp (30 ml) soy sauce
1 tbsp (15 ml) maple syrup
2 tbsp (30 ml) rice vinegar
¼ tsp chipotle powder, or more, as desired
½ tsp sesame oil

ROLLS
1 avocado
1 bell pepper
1 carrot
1 beet
1 cup (250 g) tofu
½ cup (20 g) cilantro
Rice paper sheets and warm water
1 tbsp (3 g) black sesame seeds, for garnish

FOR THE SAUCE

Stir the ingredients together until smooth. If it's too thick, add more of the liquid ingredients or even some water, lemon juice or nondairy milk. If it's too thin, add more peanut butter. Set it aside.

FOR THE ROLLS

Wash, peel and chop the veggies into strips or shred them as necessary. Dip a sheet of rice paper into a shallow bowl of warm water so it's fully submerged for 5 to 10 seconds. Lay it on a damp cloth and assemble your veggies in the middle. Wrap it up and garnish with some sesame seeds. Set it aside. Repeat these steps until you use up all your veggies! Enjoy with your dipping sauce.

Spicy NOODLE BOWL WITH BEET, CARROT, ZUCCHINI AND SWEET TAMARIND SAUCE

+QP +GF

This is inspired by Pad Thai but tastes a billion times fresher. Everyone in the house wanted a bite. —EvE

SERVES 2 TO 4

SAUCE
2 tbsp (40 g) tamarind paste
½ cup (120 ml) hot water, as needed
2" (5-cm) chunk peeled ginger
4 cloves garlic
2 tsp (10 ml) maple syrup
2 tsp (10 ml) gluten-free tamari
2 tbsp (23 g) tahini

NOODLES
2 beets
2 zucchini
2 large carrots

TOPPINGS
1 cup (160 g) chopped baby tomatoes
1 cup (40 g) cilantro
½ tsp white sesame seeds (optional)
½ tsp black sesame seeds (optional)

FOR THE SAUCE

Blend everything together until smooth, adding water as needed. Adjust the flavor as you like.

FOR THE NOODLES

Wash, peel and slice them all on a mandoline, a vegetable spiral slicer or with a vegetable peeler.

Toss the noodles with the sauce and then garnish with the toppings. YUMMAY.

four

APPETIZERS, SNACKS & SIDES

Whether you're hosting a party, bringing a snack to the neighborhood happy hour, or just in the mood for a tapas-style dinner, this chapter has got you covered.

You'll find 90 recipes for every season, every culture and every mood. There are Apricot and Coconut Bars (page 153) for summer, Spooky BOO Corn Baked Tortilla Chips (page 149) for fall and Savory Mushroom and Ricotta Pop Tarts (page 168) to warm you up in the winter.

If you're in the mood for Asian, Middle Eastern, Mexican, Italian or American, you'll find what you're looking for in this chapter. You could even host an around-the-world party and serve something from each region, such as Asian Tofu Vegetable Steamed Dumplings (page 163), Lemon Curry Hummus (page 166), Citrus Chile Jackfruit Tacos (page 177), Moroccan Marinated Vegetables (page 183) and Crispy Chickpea Onion Rings (page 200). The possibilities are endless.

Additionally, many of the recipes are gluten-free and refined sugar–free, which means that you can whip up a snack for anyone and everyone! Try Marie's Homemade "Cheesy" Popcorn (page 197), Amber's PB and J Energy Bites (page 201), Celine's Nanami Togarashi Cashews (page 187), Emily's Perfect Fluffy Crispy Potatoes (page 188), Kathy's Vegan Deviled Potatoes (page 158) and Linda and Alex's Oven-Fried Parmesan Zucchini Crisps (page 165).

Baked Pumpkin Spice Doughnuts with Chocolate Cinnamon Icing, page 373

Chickpea Noodle Soup, page 208

Bowl o' Salad Goodness, page 249

Jicama Onion Cakes with Cumin, Coriander, Dill and Lemon, page 99

Citrus Chile Jackfruit Tacos, page 177

Nut-Free Creamy Coconut Cheesecake, page 331

Summer Pineapple-Ginger Juice, page 401

Air-Fried Vegan Beignets, page 108

Chocolate Chip Skillet Cookie, page 286

Blood Orange Glazed Doughnuts, page 342

Sloppy Giuseppe, page 84

Blackberry Walnut Smoothie, page 396

One-Pot Pasta Arrabiata, page 126

Vegan Chocolate Blintzes Stuffed with Vanilla Nut Cream, page 280

Baked Lemon and Thyme Doughnuts, page 374

Vegan Caesar Salad with Homemade Dill Croutons, page 232

Kesar Mango Farina, page 301

Marinated Zucchini and Tomato Lasagna with Cashew Herb Cheese, page 100

Sage Polenta and Wild Mushrooms, page 133

Vegan Butternut Squash Okra Gumbo with Brown Rice, page 41

Tofu Banh Mi with Lemongrass, page 52

Garam Masala Roasted Acorn Squash, page 190

Forbidden Broth, page 221

Chocolate Molten Lava Cakes with Goji Berries, page 332

Turmeric Tofu Scramble, page 363

Gluten-Free Vegan Pumpkin Pie with a Teff Flour Pecan Crust, page

Amber's Famous Peanut Butter Cookies, page 270

Moroccan Minestrone, page 222

Zucchini Spaghetti with Sun-Dried Tomatoes and Basil, page 141

Edamame Bruschetta, page 157

Gluten-Free Vegan Teff Oat Rolls, page 159

Sushi Bowl with Ginger Soy Dressing, page 62

Peanut Butter and Berry Acai Bowl, page 349

Japanese Tempeh and Sushi Rice Bowls, page 95

Almond Cacao Cookies with Salted Maca Caramel, page 316

Spicy Aloo Gobi, page 122

Indian Stuffed Potato Chaat, page 38

Vegan BLT Salad with Smoky Spicy Mayo, page 245

Savory Stuffed Mushrooms, page 150

Japchae (Korean Vermicelli Stir-Fry), page 96

Double Chocolate Cupcakes with Buttercream Frosting, page 305

Mushroom Fajitas, page 134

Instant Pot Rainbow Panzanella Salad, page 107

Roasted Carrot, Garlic and Rosemary Soup, page 211

Peppermint Hot Chocolate, page 398

Kimchi Tofu Scramble, page 384

Marinated Portobello Cashew Cheeseburgers
with Herbs and Tomatoes , page 98

Thai-Style Coconut Soup, page 225

Instant Pot Vegan Black-Eyed Pea Jambalaya, page 112

Peanut Sriracha Glazed Tofu Satay, page 167

Whole Wheat Cinnamon Sugar Pull-Apart Loaf, page 268

Spicy Kimchi Pizza, page 81

ueberry Strawberry Banana Ice Cream Cake, page 332

Forbidden Rice Sushi Rolls, page 31

egan Pear and Cranberry Instant Pot Cake, page 115

Protein Superfood Bean Salad, page 242

Gingersnap Buttercream Cookie Sandwiches, page 259

Salted Caramel Panna Cotta, page 298

Tomato Avocado Mushroom Corn Soup, page 224

Lemon and Poppy Seed Pancakes, page 358

Cheesy Baked
POLENTA FRIES

+GF

Crispy, crunchy, potato-free? Yep, you betcha. And just as full of flavor as the original, but crunchier! And crunchy fries are my favorite. Polenta, a simple grain-based dish that cooks up a little like steel oats (but way creamier), is a great replacement here. The flavor is a little corn-y, the crunch is unbeatable and the cheesy flavor takes the whole dish up a notch. Plus, polenta fills you up and is a seriously cheap kitchen staple that is great to keep on hand. —AS

SERVES 2 TO 4

3 cups (710 ml) water

1 tsp salt

1½ cups (240 g) uncooked instant polenta (bramata)

½ cup (40 g) nutritional yeast

¼ cup (55 g) vegan butter

¼ tsp salt

½ tsp cracked black pepper

Coconut oil, for greasing pan

OPTIONAL
Ketchup, sriracha mayo or vegan ranch dressing

Bring the water and salt to a boil in a large pot. Once boiling, reduce the heat and pour in the polenta, stirring to combine. Cook the polenta over low heat, stirring constantly, until the mixture thickens and begins to pull away from the sides of the pot, about 5 minutes.

Remove the pot from the heat and stir in the nutritional yeast, butter, salt and pepper. Stir well, until the butter has completely melted and the mixture is smooth.

Pour the mixture onto a smooth surface like a large baking sheet (or two smaller ones), and spread it out using a rubber spatula to about a ½ inch (1.3 cm) thickness. Let it cool on the counter for at least 30 minutes, until the polenta becomes solid and cools off completely. While waiting, preheat the oven to 400°F (204°C).

Once your polenta slab has cooled, gently move it from the pan to a cutting board (best done in sections) to be cut. You can leave the mixture on the baking sheet and use a pizza cutter, if that floats your boat. Otherwise, use a large knife to cut the slab in half, and then into ¼- to ½-inch (6-mm to 1.3-cm) strips, until all the polenta has been cut. Transfer the fries to a greased (coconut oil works great in the high heat!) baking sheet, and bake for 45 to 50 minutes, flipping once, until the fries are crispy and golden.

Remove them from the oven and serve with ketchup, sriracha mayo or vegan ranch.

Note: The polenta sticks can be made ahead, wrapped in plastic and refrigerated overnight or until ready to bake.

Don't have coconut oil? That's okay. Just try to use a high-heat oil (sesame, grapeseed, avocado) to avoid burning!

Fries can be reheated in the oven at 400°F (204°C) for about 10 minutes. Overcooking them will result in uber-crunchy fries, so be careful. Cooking them just right, however, results in more deliciousness.

Crispy CAULIFLOWER NUGGETS *

+GFO

Crispy, perfectly golden, fried cauliflower nuggets will change the future of nuggets as we know it. My sweetie claimed they were better than any chicken nugget he had ever had and loved the slight crunch and the fact that he didn't feel like crap after eating them. I love all things fried (in moderation, of course), and was happy to have something to slather in ketchup—my guilty pleasure. Now I know frying is bad and we shouldn't do it, but if we're gonna splurge here, at least you're frying up a vegetable, right? —AS

SERVES 2 TO 4

FLAX WASH
¼ cup (28 g) ground flaxseed

¼ cup (25 g) almond meal

¾ cup (180 ml) water

FLOUR MIX
1½ cups (150 g) breadcrumbs (gluten-free or regular)

¼ cup (25 g) almond meal

1 tsp organic sugar

2 tbsp (10 g) nutritional yeast

½ tsp garlic salt

½ tsp sea salt

¼ tsp cracked black pepper

¼ tsp cayenne pepper

CAULIFLOWER
¼ cup (60 ml) high-heat oil, for frying (coconut, grapeseed and avocado oils are all great high-heat options)

2 cups (214 g) cauliflower florets (about ½ head of cauliflower)

FOR THE FLAX WASH
In a small bowl, make the flax wash by mixing the ground flax, almond meal and water. Set aside.

FOR THE FLOUR MIX
Next, in a medium mixing bowl, mix together the breadcrumbs, almond meal, sugar, nutritional yeast, garlic salt, sea salt, pepper and cayenne. This mixture will become your breading.

FOR THE CAULIFLOWER
Heat the oil in a large frying pan over medium heat. Dip the cauliflower florets into the flax wash mixture, coating lightly but evenly. Next, dip the cauliflower into the flour mixture and coat completely. Drop coated cauliflower nuggets into the heated oil and cook until golden and crunchy. Then flip and repeat until the nugget is evenly fried, about 2 to 3 minutes on each side. Using tongs or a spatula, move the cooked nuggets to a paper towel–lined plate to absorb excess oil, let them cool several minutes and enjoy with your favorite dipping sauce! They are best if eaten immediately. Uneaten nuggets can be reheated in the oven at 375°F (190°C) for 10 minutes, or until warm.

Not into fried foods? You can try baking these at 400°F (204°C) for about 20 to 30 minutes, flipping halfway through. They won't be nearly as crunchy and crispy, but probably much healthier. Do what you gotta do!

Homemade Vegan
CHEEZ-ITS

I decided it was about time I recreated my favorite childhood treat but knew I needed them to be totally vegan and WAY healthier. And they turned out SO GOOD! They're crispy, crunchy, cheezy, salty, savory and super snackable. Plus, there are only 9 ingredients—and you probably have them all on hand right now. These are the kind of snack you don't at all have to feel guilty about snacking on, even if you do go a bit overboard. Perfect for taking along for a lunch or snack at work and bringing on camping or road trips, so let's get snackin'! —AS

MAKES 60 TO 80 CRACKERS

¾ cup (94 g) all-purpose flour

¼ cup (43 g) cornmeal

2 tbsp (10 g) nutritional yeast

1 tsp salt

½ tsp garlic powder

¼ tsp baking powder

⅛ tsp ground turmeric

5 tbsp (72 g) vegan butter

3–4 tbsp (45–60 ml) cold water

Preheat the oven to 350°F (177°C) and line a baking sheet with parchment paper.

Add the flour, cornmeal, nutritional yeast, salt, garlic powder, baking powder and turmeric to a food processor, and process to thoroughly combine. Add the vegan butter and pulse until crumbly.

Add the cold water, 1 tablespoon (15 ml) at a time, until the dough comes together. Remove the dough from the food processor and form it into a disk. Place the disk onto a lightly floured surface. Lightly dust the top with flour and use a rolling pin to roll it to about an ⅛ inch (3 mm) thick. Use a pizza cutter or knife to cut the dough into equal-size square crackers.

Spread the crackers onto the prepared baking sheet. Bake them for 14 to 18 minutes, or until crispy and golden brown. Save leftovers in an airtight container or bag on the counter for up to a week.

*SEE PHOTO INSERT

Baked JALAPEÑO POPPERS WITH CILANTRO LIME MAYO

+GFO

This is a 'WOW' appetizer. I mean it! Your friends will be impressed. It takes a little time, but transforms a classically bad-for-you appetizer into something better for you, vegan and full of gooey, melty cheese! —AS

MAKES 10 TO 12 POPPERS

10–12 medium jalapeño peppers

¾–1 cup (90–120 g) vegan cheese

FLAX WASH

¼ cup (28 g) ground flaxseed

¼ cup (25 g) almond meal

¾ cup (180 ml) warm water

BREADCRUMB MIXTURE

1½ cups (90 g) breadcrumbs (gluten-free or regular)

¼ cup (25 g) almond meal

2 tbsp (10 g) nutritional yeast

½ tsp garlic salt

¼ tsp smoked paprika

¼ tsp ground cumin

CILANTRO LIME MAYO DIP

1 lime, squeezed (about 2 tbsp [10 ml] juice)

1–2 tbsp (3–5 g) chopped cilantro, to taste

½ cup (110 g) vegan mayo

(continued)

Preheat the oven to 350°F (177°C).

Wash the jalapeños and pat dry. Using a small sharp knife, cut off the very top of the pepper (where the stem is). Set it aside and use the knife to deseed the pepper. Try not to cut into the actual pepper as this will be holding all the melty, gooey cheese later. Repeat with all the jalapeños until each has been deseeded. Fill each pepper with about a tablespoon (15 g) of cheese, not packing them completely full. Using toothpicks, attach the stemmed cap of the pepper back onto it, pushing the toothpick into the jalapeño's flesh to hold the pieces together. Lay on their sides until breading is ready.

FOR THE FLAX WASH

Combine the ground flax, almond meal and warm water. Whisk together and set aside to thicken.

FOR THE BREADING

In a large bowl, mix the breadcrumbs, almond meal, nutritional yeast, garlic salt, smoked paprika and cumin until combined.

FOR THE DIP

Simply mix together the lime juice, chopped cilantro and mayo. Refrigerate until ready to use.

Once all the steps are ready, dip the cheese-filled jalapeños into the flax wash, using a spoon to help evenly coat the pepper. Next, dip the peppers into the breadcrumb mixture, rolling them so they are evenly coated. Be gentle, as you want the toothpick-attached tops to stay where they are. Once coated in breadcrumbs, lay the peppers onto a waxed, papered or lightly greased baking sheet. Repeat until all peppers are coated and breaded.

Bake the stuffed, coated pepper poppers for 30 minutes, until the peppers soften and the cheese melts. Remove from the oven and serve with the cilantro lime mayo to balance out the spiciness.

Golden Milk CHIA PUDDING

+QP +SF +GF

I love combining great tasting foods with meals that have great health benefits—and this one makes the perfect combo! Anti-inflammatory, good for you and it's delicious, too. —AS

SERVES 2 TO 4

1¼ cups (295 ml) nondairy milk
¾ tsp ground turmeric
½ tsp ground cinnamon
½ tsp fresh ginger
¼ tsp ground cardamom
¼ tsp black pepper
2–4 drops of vanilla stevia
4 tbsp (40 g) chia seeds

OPTIONAL
Fresh fruit
Granola

Whisk all the ingredients together in a medium bowl. Cover and refrigerate overnight. Give it a stir in the morning and enjoy! The pudding mixture will have thickened overnight.

Serve with fresh fruit or granola, or enjoy on its own!

Spooky BOO CORN BAKED TORTILLA CHIPS

+GF +SF +QP

Get into the spooky Halloween mood with these easy, baked, ghost-shaped corn tortillas! They're gluten-free and fun for kids to make, too. They look pretty spooky stacked into a guacamole graveyard, but we think they'd be super cute on a Halloween party snack table, too. —AS

MAKES ABOUT 30 CHIPS

1 cup (120 g) blue corn masa harina
1½ cups (360 ml) warm water, divided
¼ tsp salt, divided
1 cup (120 g) white corn masa harina
Coconut oil spray

In a medium mixing bowl, place the blue corn masa harina. Stir in ¾ cup (180 ml) of the warm water and ⅛ teaspoon of the salt, mixing until completely combined. Use your hands to knead the dough until it comes completely together. If the dough seems too dry, you can add a bit of water, but you want your dough to be smooth (not sticky) and be able to form a springy ball. Cover the bowl with a wet towel for 15 to 20 minutes.

In a separate bowl, repeat the process with the white corn masa harina, remaining ¾ cup (180 ml) water and remaining ⅛ teaspoon salt and set them both aside.

Fold a piece of parchment paper long enough to cover your tortilla press. If you're not using a tortilla press, spread parchment paper over the countertop and use a separate, smaller piece to separate the tortillas from the rolling pin.

Roll the blue and white corn masa dough into ¾- to 1-inch (2- to 2.5-cm) balls, leaving one ball each extra to use as eyes and mouths on the opposite color tortillas. Press each ball between the two sides of the parchment paper–lined tortilla press until they are about ⅛ inch (3 mm) thick. It may take you more than once, and if so, rotate the tortilla in between presses. If you are using a rolling pin, do the same thing—just be careful to use the same amount of pressure for an even roll. Once they are rolled out, apply 3 small balls of the opposite color as eyes and a mouth, and re-press. The ball will spread out, so start small. Continue this process until all the ghost faces are formed.

Using a knife or pizza cutter, cut the round, faced tortillas into a ghost shape and place a piece of parchment paper in between each ghost tortilla so they don't stick prior to cooking.

You can either cook the tortillas as you press them or press them all and then cook them. Your choice. Either way, when you're ready, heat a large cast-iron skillet over medium-high heat and lightly spray with coconut oil. The skillet is ready when a few beads of water dropped in the pan sizzle immediately.

Cook as many tortilla ghosts at a time as can fit in the pan (without overlapping) for 1 to 2 minutes, until the bottom is just beginning to show brown, toasted spots. Place your cooked ghosts on a paper towel–lined plate to cool while you cook the other tortillas. When you're finished, spread the heated tortillas over a wire rack to cool completely.

(continued)

While they cool, preheat the oven to 350°F (177°C). Bake the chips on a parchment-lined baking sheet for 8 to 10 minutes, flipping about halfway through, until they are browned and crisped up. Remove and place them back on the wire rack to cool, and then enjoy immediately or within a few hours of making. Leftover chips can be saved in an airtight container for up to 2 days and reheated in the oven to re-crisp as needed.

Note: You can make the chips bigger or smaller depending on how many you wanted and what you wanted to use them for. If you'd rather have just ghost tortillas instead of chips, you could skip the baking step and stuff them full of taco ingredients instead.

Masa FLOUR and masa HARINA are different in that masa HARINA is ground from corn kernels soaked in lime water and makes a much better and less brittle tortilla and chip. We have found masa harina for cheap at local Mexican markets and grocery stores, and, of course, online at Amazon.

Savory STUFFED MUSHROOMS

+GFO +SF

I know there are tons of recipes for this dish online, but I promise this one is really good. And pretty easy, too! It's packed with flavor, the filling has great texture and the homemade Parmesan cheeze on top adds some fanciness and helps keep the filling moist. The whole thing comes together in your mouth like WHOA. This is a recipe worthy of sharing at your next Holiday party—it's a serious crowd-pleaser! Let's get cookin'. —AS

SERVES 10 TO 12

STUFFED MUSHROOMS

24 oz (680 g) cremini mushrooms, stems removed

2 tbsp (28 g) coconut oil

4 cloves garlic, minced

2 shallots, chopped

4 cups (120 g) fresh spinach

1 cup (160 g) cooked wild rice

½ cup (90 g) chopped roasted red peppers

½ cup (58 g) finely chopped walnuts

½ cup (60 g) breadcrumbs

½ cup (20 g) fresh chopped parsley, plus more for garnish

1 tbsp (15 ml) plus 2 tsp (10 ml) balsamic vinegar

1 tsp salt

½ tsp pepper

PARMESAN CHEEZE

1 cup (110 g) cashews

¼ cup (20 g) nutritional yeast

¾ tsp salt

¼ tsp garlic powder

Preheat the oven to 375°F (190°C).

FOR THE MUSHROOMS

Gently wash the mushrooms and remove the stems. Place them cap-down onto a lined baking sheet and set aside.

In a large cast-iron pan, melt the coconut oil over medium heat. Sauté the garlic and shallots until soft and fragrant, about 5 minutes. Add the spinach, stirring continuously until it has wilted.

Remove the pan from the heat and pour the cooked veggies into a large mixing bowl. Stir in the wild rice, roasted red peppers, walnuts, breadcrumbs, parsley, vinegar, salt and pepper. Toss the mixture together, and set it aside to cool for a few minutes.

FOR THE PARMESAN

While the mixture cools, you can prepare the Parmesan cheeze by placing all of the ingredients into a food processor and pulsing until the mixture becomes a fine meal. Save some (about ¼ to ½ cup [45 to 90 g]) to sprinkle over the mushrooms, and save the rest in an airtight container in the fridge for up to 2 weeks.

When the mixture has cooled enough to handle, use a spoon, ice-cream scoop or your fingers to scoop the mixture into the cap of each mushroom. The amount you use will vary depending on the size of the mushroom cap. Once all the caps are filled, sprinkle the reserved Parmesan cheeze over the top.

Bake the stuffed mushrooms for 20 to 25 minutes, until tender. Remove them from the oven, let them cool slightly and serve immediately!

Note: It was hard to come up with just how many people this serves, because it really depends on how big the 'shrooms are, how many people are around and how many each person eats. *But* this recipe gave me one packed baking sheet full of stuffed mushrooms.

Leftovers can be saved in the fridge for up to 3 days. They are best reheated in a microwave or in an oven at about 350°F (177°C) for 10 to 15 minutes, though they may get slightly softer after reheating.

*SEE PHOTO INSERT

Green BRUSCHETTA

+SF +QP

Bruschetta has become one of our absolute go-to meals lately. It's simple and quick to make and is awesome as a snack or a meal. Plus, it's a great recipe to have in the case of social emergencies: when your friends just show up to hang out, before a party you forgot to make an appetizer for, or even just when you have some basics but not enough food for a really impressive spread. —AS

SERVES 4

3 cups (483 g) chopped green tomatoes

½ cup (76 g) minced onion

¼ cup (7 g) chopped fresh basil

¼ cup (10 g) chopped fresh parsley

3 tbsp (45 ml) extra-virgin olive oil

1 tbsp (15 ml) balsamic vinegar

1 clove garlic, finely chopped

½ tsp salt

¼ tsp pepper

1 sourdough baguette

In a medium bowl, toss together the tomatoes, onions, basil, parsley, olive oil, balsamic, garlic, salt and pepper. Set in the refrigerator until ready to be served.

Slice the baguette into slices about a ½ to ¾ inch (1.3 to 2 cm) thick. Place slices onto a cookie sheet and under the "broiler" setting on the oven for about 5 minutes on each side, or until both sides are golden and a little crispy. Top toasts with the bruschetta mixture and enjoy!

Four LAYER DIP

+SF +GF

Hearty black beans, silky cashew cheese, savory guaca-
mole and salsa are all layered and stacked, creating a
prolific four-layer dip. —MR

SERVES 6 TO 8

BLACK BEAN LAYER
2 cloves garlic, roughly chopped
1 tbsp (15 ml) olive oil
2 (14-oz [397-g]) cans black beans, rinsed and
drained
Salt, to taste

CASHEW CHEESE
1 cup (110 g) soaked cashews, unsalted
⅓ cup (78 ml) water
2 tbsp (30 ml) apple cider vinegar
2 cloves garlic
2 tbsp (10 g) nutritional yeast
Salt, to taste

GUACAMOLE LAYER
3 avocados, peeled and pitted
Juice of ½ lime
Pinch of sea salt
Drizzle of olive oil
Pinch of red pepper flakes (optional)

SALSA LAYER
1½ cups (240 g) roughly chopped cherry tomatoes
Pinch of sea salt
Drizzle of olive oil
Juice of ½ lime
¼ small onion, roughly chopped

FOR THE BLACK BEAN LAYER

In a small saucepan over medium heat, warm the garlic and olive oil. Once warmed, add the black beans and let them cook for 5 to 7 minutes. Add a few splashes of water and salt, to taste. Set aside.

FOR THE CASHEW CHEESE

Start by soaking the cashews in a bowl of water for at least 4 hours—this helps to soften any nut. Now drain and rinse the cashews and pour them into a high-speed blender along with the rest of the ingredients. Blend well until it turns into a creamy, silky cheese!

FOR THE GUACAMOLE LAYER

Simply mash the avocados together, forming a creamy texture. Then squeeze in the juice of half a lime, a few pinches of salt and a drizzle of olive oil. Add red pepper flakes if you would like a little heat!

FOR THE SALSA LAYER

In a small bowl, lightly smash some of the tomatoes to release the juices. Then sprinkle on a little salt, olive oil and lime juice. Toss in the onion and mix well.

ASSEMBLE

First layer the black beans, then add a few dollops of cashew cheese as the second layer, spread on the guacamole and finish off with a layer of fresh salsa.

APRICOT AND COCONUT **Bars**

+GF

This bar is so delectable and portable that it easily becomes multifaceted. Enjoy these Apricot and Coconut Bars any way you see fit, or better yet, take inspiration from the list below: crumbled as granola, mixed with nut milk as cereal, traditional granola bar, smoothie topping, post-workout snack, preworkout snack, airport bite or midday treat. —MR

MAKES 12 SQUARES

3 tbsp (30 g) chia seeds
9 tbsp (135 ml) water
1 cup (170 g) almonds
1 cup (80 g) rolled oats
1 cup (170 g) raw buckwheat
1 cup (75 g) unsweetened coconut shreds
4-5 tbsp (60-75 ml) maple syrup
3 tbsp (42 g) coconut oil
1½ bananas
1 tsp salt
1 tsp ground cinnamon
1 cup (150 g) chopped dried apricots

Preheat the oven to 320°F (160°C). Line a small baking dish (I used an 8 x 8-inch [20 x 20-cm] pan) with parchment paper.

Start by making the chia seed gel. Mix the chia seeds with the water and set aside until the chia seeds absorb all the water and expand into a gel-like mixture—this is what keeps the bars intact.

In the meantime, roughly chop the almonds and add them to a baking sheet along with the oats and buckwheat. Place them in the oven to cook for 12 minutes. Halfway through, at 6 minutes, add the coconut shreds to the same baking sheet and mix to combine all the ingredients. When ready, remove them from the oven and let them cool as you prepare the sweet maple and banana sauce.

In a small pot, heat the maple syrup and coconut oil over low heat until it has melted and combined. Now simply blend the bananas, chia gel and sweet maple mixture in the food processor until smooth (a few seconds). Add more maple syrup if you prefer it on the sweeter side.

In a large bowl, add the roasted oat mixture, the sweet maple and banana sauce, salt, cinnamon and dried apricots. Mix well. Evenly pour the mixture into the prepared baking dish, pressing down firmly with your fingertips so as to keep the oats compact and stuck together. Increase the heat to 350°F (177°C) and bake for 25 minutes.

Once it is ready, let it cool for 15 minutes or so and then slice it into large pieces.

Maple-Roasted
CARROTS WITH PUMPKIN SEED SPREAD

+GF

In this recipe, a simple drizzle of maple transforms the humble carrot. Pair it with a savory pumpkin seed spread for an easy side that elevates any weeknight meal. —MR

SERVES 2 TO 3

MAPLE-ROASTED CARROTS
8 carrots, whole
1 tbsp (15 ml) olive oil
1 tbsp (15 ml) maple syrup
Pinch of sea salt

PUMPKIN SEED SPREAD
¼ cup (10 g) chopped mint
3 tbsp (46 g) coconut yogurt
Large handful of unsalted pumpkin seeds, plus extra for topping
1 tbsp (15 ml) olive oil
1 tbsp (15 ml) water
Pinch of sea salt

FOR THE CARROTS
Preheat the oven to 425°F (218°C). Add the carrots to a parchment paper–lined baking sheet. Now drizzle the carrots with the remaining ingredients and mix well. Pop them into the oven to cook until the carrots are tender and the skin is slightly crispy, about 35 to 40 minutes.

FOR THE SPREAD
While the carrots cook, make the pumpkin seed spread. Add all the ingredients to a food processor and blend until well combined. Set this aside.

Remove the carrots from the oven and move them to a serving plate. Dollop the pumpkin seed spread over the carrots, top them with a few extra pumpkin seeds and sea salt, and enjoy!

Roasted WINTER
SQUASH WITH ZESTY "RICOTTA" AND SAGE

+SF +GF

Roasted delicata squash shines with crispy sage and a simple dollop of zesty ricotta "cheese" offers notes similar to that of lemon meringue. This is a fantastic side served with a light salad. —MR

SERVES 2 TO 3

1 delicata squash, sliced into half-moon rings
4 tbsp (60 ml) olive oil, divided
Sea salt
Zest of ½ lemon
3 tsp (15 ml) juice of the lemon, plus extra for topping
¼ cup (30 g) vegan "ricotta" cheese
10 fresh sage leaves

Preheat the oven to 410°F (210°C).

Place the delicata squash slices on a parchment paper–lined baking pan. Add 2 tablespoons (30 ml) of the olive oil and sea salt to taste and mix well. Bake for 35 to 40 minutes, or until the squash is tender and crispy around the edges.

In a bowl, mix the lemon zest, juice and ricotta together. Set aside. Heat the remaining 2 tablespoons (30 ml) olive oil in a small sauté pan over medium-high heat until hot. Fry 5 sage leaves at a time until crisp, about 3 seconds. Transfer to a paper towel to remove the excess oil, and sprinkle generously with sea salt.

Serve the roasted squash on a large serving plate with dollops of the zesty ricotta and sage leaves. Top it off with sea salt and an extra squeeze of lemon juice.

*SEE PHOTO INSERT

Vegan CORNBREAD

+SF +GF

American comfort food enthusiasts will appreciate this simple cornbread recipe. Serve with chili, soups, stews or even during breakfast smothered with jam and vegan butter. —MR

MAKES 10 TO 12 SLICES

1 tbsp (15 ml) apple cider vinegar
1½ cups (355 ml) almond milk
1 cup (120 g) almond flour
1¼ cups (213 g) cornmeal
2 tbsp (26 g) baking soda
Sea salt
6 tbsp (72 g) coconut sugar
⅓ cup (72 g) coconut oil, melted

Preheat the oven to 400°F (204°C).

As it warms, simply mix all of the ingredients in a medium bowl until combined. Pour the batter into a parchment paper–lined baking dish (about 8 x 8 inches [20 x 20 cm]) and bake for 30 to 35 minutes, or until the top is golden brown. Let it cool for 10 minutes and then slice into squares. Enjoy served alongside chili, soups or salads.

Kalamata HUMMUS

+SF +GF +QP

This is a fancied-up version of hummus. Kalamata olives whip into a silky smooth hummus while complementing the earthiness of tahini and chickpeas—a charming take on an already fantastic spread. —MR

SERVES 4 TO 6

¾ cup (135 g) Kalamata olives
1 (14-oz [397-g]) can chickpeas, rinsed and drained
Juice of 1 lemon
1 tbsp (18 g) tahini
¼ cup (60 ml) water
1 tbsp (15 ml) olive oil
½ tsp ground cumin
1 clove garlic
½ tsp salt

Simply place all the ingredients in a blender or food processor and mix until creamy. Taste to see if you would like to add more salt or water to make it a thinner, creamier hummus.

Spicy ROASTED CAULIFLOWER ✿

+GF +QP +SF

No exaggeration—this is a phenomenal side. Laced in cayenne and paprika, broiled cauliflower florets tenderize into spicy pieces. A delicious accompaniment to grain bowls, salads, pastas or even alone on toast. —MR

SERVES 4

½ large head cauliflower, cut into tiny florets

2 tbsp (30 ml) olive oil

1 tsp cayenne

1 tsp paprika

Sea salt

Preheat the oven to broil on high. Toss everything into a large mixing bowl and combine. Place the seasoned cauliflower florets on a nonstick baking sheet. Cook on broil for 10 minutes, flipping halfway through, until the florets are crispy. Serve as a side or on top of toast with avocado slices.

Note: Do not use parchment paper, since we're using the broiler method. Otherwise, the heat will burn the paper.

Three-Ingredient BUTTERNUT SQUASH PASTA ✿

+GF +QP +SF

For this recipe, the title says it all. It just goes to show what you can do with only squash, herbs and coconut milk—all blended together to make one velvety pasta sauce. —MR

SERVES 2 TO 3

½ lb (227 g) pasta (or use brown rice pasta for gluten-free)

1 cup (140 g) cubed roasted butternut squash (or any winter squash)

1 cup (235 ml) full-fat coconut milk

4 sage leaves

Pinch of sea salt

OPTIONAL
Vegan cheese

Sea salt

Drizzle of olive oil

Start by cooking your pasta as the box instructs. As the pasta is cooking, make the sauce. Add the rest of the ingredients to a high-speed blender or food processor, and mix until it turns into a very creamy sauce.

Once the pasta is done cooking, drain it and place the noodles back into the pot. Add the pasta sauce a few scoops at a time and mix well. Keep adding the sauce until your desired consistency. Serve it in bowls as is or top it off with your favorite vegan cheese, sea salt and a drizzle of olive oil!

MUHAMMARA (RED PEPPER AND WALNUT) Spread

+QP +SF +GF

Muhammara is a traditional Turkish dish where walnuts and roasted red bell peppers are at the center of the spread. Both enhance each bite, giving way to overlapping notes of earthy, sweet, savory and nutty. It's a beautiful departure from hummus and has quickly become a strong contender for the one side that will be brought to parties all year long. It's divine and truly shouldn't be missed. —MR

SERVES 4 TO 6

1 large red bell pepper, roasted until blistered, with stem, liquid and seeds removed (see Note)

2 green onion stalks, chopped

1¼ cups (150 g) unsalted walnuts, toasted

1½ tsp (3 g) ground cumin

Zest and juice of ½ lemon

3 tsp (15 ml) balsamic

2½ tsp (13 ml) maple syrup

Dash of red pepper flakes

4 tbsp (60 ml) olive or avocado oil

Sea salt

Place all of the ingredients in a food processor and blend until creamy. This spread will be on the chunkier side, so it is okay if it doesn't turn into a creamy spread similar to hummus in texture. Pour it into a bowl and serve with pita bread, crackers, on toast, in a sandwich or with raw/roasted veggies.

Note: To roast your bell pepper, simply add it whole to a baking sheet and preheat the oven to broil on high. Cook for about 10 minutes, turning halfway through, until the skin has blistered.

Traditional muhammara is made with pomegranate molasses, but to keep ingredients store-friendly, we're using a mix of balsamic and maple syrup to recreate this very distinct flavor. If you do have pomegranate molasses on hand, use 2 to 3 teaspoons (10 to 15 ml) in place of the balsamic and maple syrup.

Edamame BRUSCHETTA

+QP +SF +GF

An unusual pairing makes for a truly delightful lunch or side. A savory edamame spread is slathered onto warm toast and topped with sweet beets, microgreens and zesty lemon. I promise this is a meal you won't want to miss. —MR

SERVES 2

2 slices bread, toasted

1 tbsp (15 ml) olive oil

⅓ cup (70 g) Edamame Guacamole (page 196)

1 tomato, sliced

1 beet, cooked and thinly sliced

Handful microgreens

Squeeze of lemon juice

Sea salt

Layer the warm slices of toast with a drizzle of olive oil and a few scoops of the edamame spread. Now add the tomato and beet slices on top of the spread.

Top it off with microgreens, a squeeze of lemon juice and sea salt. Serve on a plate and enjoy!

*SEE PHOTO INSERT

Easy Vegan BLACK-EYED PEA PECAN PÂTÉ

+GF +SF

In the south, we eat black-eyed peas for luck in the New Year and I make a potful of them every year. This recipe uses up your leftover black-eyed peas and turns them into something special. —KH

MAKES 2 CUPS (416 G)

1½ cups (248 g) cooked black-eyed peas

½ cup (63 g) pecans, lightly toasted in the oven or in a sauté pan

1 tsp salt-free Cajun seasoning

½ tsp jalapeño powder

½ tsp granulated garlic

½ tsp smoked salt, or to taste

½ tsp Tabasco or other hot sauce, or to taste

¼ tsp liquid smoke, or to taste

Put all the ingredients in a food processor and purée until the ingredients are mostly smooth. I like to keep a little bit of texture.

Store leftovers in the fridge for up to a week.

Vegan DEVILED POTATOES

+GF

This recipe uses those cute, tiny red potatoes. are a perfect Halloween appetizer, though the delicious any time of year. Kala namak is a speci that is often used in Indian food and tastes remc like eggs. You can find this in Indian market stores and online. —KH

MAKES 40 HALVES

1 (24-oz [680-g]) bag small red potatoes

1 (12-oz [340-g]) package firm or extra-firm tofu

⅓ cup (80 g) vegan mayo

1 tbsp (15 ml) Dijon mustard

½ tsp black salt or kala namak (or regular kosher salt, to taste)

½ tsp ground turmeric

¼ cup (30 g) sliced olives stuffed with pimentos

Add the potatoes to a stockpot and cover with water.

Bring them to a boil, and then turn the heat to low and simmer until tender. This will take about 10 minutes, or until you are able to pierce the potato easily with a fork.

Drain and rinse the potatoes with cool water and set them aside until cool.

Combine the drained tofu, mayo, mustard, salt and turmeric in a bowl, mash the tofu and mix well.

Take the cooled potatoes and cut them in half lengthwise. Scoop out a circular hole using a melon baller or small spoon.

Spoon some tofu salad into the hole and top with a pimento-stuffed olive slice.

Gluten-Free Vegan
TEFF OAT ROLLS

+GF +SF

The best dinners have a little something for everyone. With so many people avoiding wheat and gluten, your gluten-free guests will get a warm and fuzzy feeling once they realize you made homemade rolls that they can actually eat. These are soft, moist and if you're like me, you won't be able to stop eating them. Another plus is that these rolls taste just as fresh the next day! —KH

MAKES 10 ROLLS

WET INGREDIENTS

1½ cups (375 ml) very warm water

2 tbsp (30 ml) maple syrup (or agave nectar)

2¼ tsp (7 g) active dry yeast (about 1 standard packet)

3 tbsp (45 ml) olive oil

2 tbsp (20 g) ground chia seeds

1 tbsp (15 ml) apple cider vinegar

1 tbsp (7 g) ground flaxseed

1 tbsp (7 g) ground psyllium husk

DRY INGREDIENTS

1 cup (125 g) teff flour (or brown teff flour)

1 cup (80 g) oat flour

½ cup (85 g) tapioca flour

½ cup (65 g) arrowroot flour

¼ cup (38 g) brown rice flour

1 tsp baking soda

1 tsp salt

Preheat the oven to 350°F (177°C) and prepare a baking sheet with oil or parchment paper.

FOR THE WET INGREDIENTS

Combine the warm water and maple syrup in a 4-cup (960-ml) measuring cup or small mixing bowl. Stir until the sweetener is dissolved. (The water must not be too hot or it will kill the yeast. You can test the water on the underside of your wrist. If it's too hot to touch, wait until it cools a bit. If it's winter and your house is freezing, you can put water from the tap into the microwave for about 45 seconds to warm it up.)

Sprinkle the yeast over the top of the water mixture. In a few minutes, you should notice some change as the yeast gets activated. Let it sit for 10 minutes.

FOR THE DRY INGREDIENTS

In a large mixing bowl, add the teff flour, oat flour, tapioca flour, arrowroot flour, brown rice flour, baking soda and salt. Mix well and set aside.

Go back to the wet mixture and add the olive oil, ground chia seeds, apple cider vinegar, ground flaxseed and ground psyllium husk. Mix well and allow it to sit for about 5 minutes. The mixture will thicken into a slurry.

After the 5 minutes are up, add the wet yeast mixture to the dry ingredients and stir with a wooden spoon. You can also do this in a mixer with the paddle attachment (not the dough hook).

Mix the dough until the dry ingredients are completely incorporated with the wet ones. The dough will be more sticky than a traditional wheat bread dough. Let the dough sit for about 5 minutes before making the rolls.

Form 10 rolls out of the dough, placing them on the baking sheet as you go. I also make a cut with a sharp knife down the middle for decoration. I made oval rolls, but you can make them any shape you want. If the dough is sticking to your hands, wet your hand a bit as needed.

(continued)

Cover the newly formed rolls with a clean dish towel and put them in a warm place. In the winter I put it on top of the stove because it's warmer when the oven is on. Let them rise for 20 minutes. They won't quite double in size, but they should grow a little bit bigger.

Uncover the pan and place it in the preheated oven. Cook for 20 to 30 minutes, or until the bottoms have turned a dark brown and the tops of the rolls are solid.

Store any leftover rolls in an airtight container.

*SEE PHOTO INSERT

THAI RED CURRY VEGETABLES with Sweet Potato Rice

+GF +SF

To rice the sweet potatoes, you'll start with either the shredding blade on your food processor or a spiralizer. Next, pulse the potatoes in your food processor. You could also use carrots or butternut squash in place of the sweet potatoes if that's what you have around. —KH

MAKES 1 SERVING, BUT CAN BE EASILY DOUBLED OR QUADRUPLED

1 medium sweet potato

2 cups (365 g) frozen Asian stir-fry vegetable mix (or a mix of fresh)

Oil or broth, for frying

1 tsp grated ginger

¼–½ cup (60–120 ml) light coconut milk

½–1 tsp (2–5 g) Thai red curry paste, to taste

Salt, to taste (optional)

Peel the sweet potato and either use a spiralizer or shredding blade in your food processor to break it down into long, thin strips/shreds.

Now add the strips/shreds to your food processor with the normal S-blade and pulse until the sweet potato resembles rice. (Note that if you are doubling or tripling the recipe, you may have to prepare the sweet potatoes in batches.) Set the sweet potato "rice" aside.

I separate the frozen mixed veggies, putting the onions, peppers, celery and mushrooms in one pile to sauté first. Then I put the broccoli in another and the green beans and snap peas in another. This ensures that none of the veggies gets overcooked, but you can live on the edge and throw them all in at the same time if you prefer.

Add either a little oil or some broth to the pan, and sauté the onion until it softens, about 3 to 4 minutes. Then add the sweet potato rice, ginger and medium cooking veggies like broccoli, ¼ cup (60 ml) of the coconut milk and the red curry paste.

Cook for about 5 minutes. Then add the rest of the vegetables and the remaining ¼ cup (60 ml) coconut milk (or water or broth) if needed so the mixture doesn't stick. Cook until all the veggies are heated through, about 5 more minutes. Season with salt.

Note: This recipe is for one serving, but you can quadruple it and serve it to your whole family. You can use half coconut milk and half water or broth if you want to lower the calories.

BBQ Jackfruit
STUFFED WHOLE WHEAT POTATO ROLLS

+SF

I love making bread once the weather gets chilly. This bread is made with white whole wheat flour and gets its moisture from the lovely Idaho potato. Filled with a savory and toothsome jackfruit BBQ, this will be your new go-to party food, so make a double batch and keep some in the freezer. —KH

MAKES 16 LARGE ROLLS

BBQ JACKFRUIT
1 (20-oz [565-g]) can jackfruit in brine, drained (Do not buy the one in syrup!)

2 cups (220 g) shredded carrot (or substitute sweet potato or butternut squash)

1 cup (245 g) your favorite BBQ sauce

½ cup (120 ml) water

ROLLS
¾ cup (158 g) mashed potatoes

½ cup (120 ml) potato cooking water

2 tbsp (30 ml) olive oil

2 tbsp (30 ml) aquafaba (liquid from a can of chickpeas, or use extra olive oil)

1 (¼-oz [7-g]) package fast-acting baking yeast

1 tbsp (12 g) sugar (or other sweetener)

3 cups (375 g) white whole wheat flour (plus more for shaping the rolls later)

1½ tsp (8 g) salt

Olive oil, to brush over the top of the rolls

FOR THE BBQ JACKFRUIT
I recommend that you make the BBQ the night before you plan on making the buns, because the filling should be cool when you are wrapping the dough around it.

Add the jackfruit to your slow cooker or a saucepan. Use your hands to shred it. There will be some pieces that are more solid, so just break those apart as well as you can. Then mix in the shredded carrot, BBQ sauce and water. If you are using a slow cooker, cook on low for 7 to 9 hours. Using the stove top? Add the listed ingredients to a pot and cook over medium heat, covered, for about 15 minutes. Then remove the lid and cook until the sauce is thick.

You can refrigerate the filling or let it cool while you make the dough.

FOR THE ROLLS
Add the mashed potatoes, potato cooking water, olive oil and aquafaba to a mixing bowl or your mixer. Mix well and sprinkle the yeast and sugar over the top. Let it sit for 10 to 15 minutes, or until the yeast begins to foam.

Mix in the white whole wheat flour, cup by cup (125 g), and add the salt with the final cup of flour. The dough should be soft but not stick to your hands. If it's still sticky, add more flour.

Once the dough comes together, you can either switch to the dough hook in your mixer and knead for about 10 minutes or turn out the dough onto a floured cutting board and knead until the dough begins to feel like your earlobe.

Earlobe? Yes, you read that correctly. If you squeeze your earlobe it feels about the same as well-kneaded dough, so it's a great benchmark.

Transfer the dough to an oiled mixing bowl and rub some oil on top of the dough to keep it from drying out. Cover with a clean dish towel and let it rise until it doubles in size, about 1 hour.

(continued)

Preheat the oven to 350°F (177°C), and oil two pie pans.

Roll the risen dough onto a floured cutting board and cut it into 16 equal pieces. Roll each one into a ball.

Spread a little bit of flour, pat the circle in it, turn it over and pat it again. This should give you a pretty even circle, but you can use a rolling pin if you find that easier. Do not roll thin or your filling will bust out while cooking.

Take 3 tablespoons (30 g) of cooled BBQ filling, place it in the center of the dough round and carefully pull up the edges to meet. Then pinch to seal the edges. Hint: If your hands get wet or the edges get coated with the BBQ sauce, it will not seal well.

Place the filled roll in one of the prepared pans; then repeat until all the rolls are filled and in the prepared pan. Brush the tops with olive oil.

Bake for 20 to 30 minutes, or until the tops are browned and firm to the touch.

*SEE PHOTO INSERT

Aloo Jeera (INDIAN CUMIN POTATOES)

+GF +SF

This is by far my most favorite potato meal for when the month runs longer than your paycheck. If you always have potatoes, rice and spices on hand you can make this flavorful Indian meal anytime. I serve mine with Indian mango pickles. —KH

SERVES 4

4 cups (720 g), chopped, peeled Idaho potatoes (about 4 large)

1 tbsp (15 ml) mild oil

2 tsp (5 g) cumin seeds

1½ tsp (3 g) ground coriander

½ tsp ground cumin

½ tsp ground turmeric

½ tsp chile powder, like cayenne (optional)

1 tsp grated ginger

½ tsp salt

½ cup (120 ml) water

¼ cup (10 g) chopped cilantro

Cover the potatoes with water in a medium saucepan and bring to a boil. Then turn the heat down to a simmer and cook until you can pierce a potato easily with a fork. This will take about 10 minutes. Strain the water off and set aside.

Heat the oil over medium heat in a large sauté pan.

Once the oil is hot, add the cumin seeds and toast for about 1 minute, or until they start to become fragrant.

Stir in the coriander, ground cumin, turmeric and chile powder (if using). Then cook for another minute, until the spices become more fragrant.

Mix in the ginger, salt and water. Add the potatoes and toss them in the spice paste. Serve topped with chopped cilantro.

*SEE PHOTO INSERT

Asian TOFU VEGETABLE STEAMED DUMPLINGS

Dumplings are so much fun to make. All you need are some vegan dumpling wrappers, and you can find them in Chinese markets. I've even found them in Walmart where I live. You can make the filling ahead of time and invite friends over to help you create the dumplings with it. —KH

MAKES ABOUT 50 DUMPLINGS

FILLING

1 tbsp (15 ml) oil (or water sauté to make it oil-free)

½ cup (75 g) chopped onion

4 cups (400 g) shredded cabbage

2 cups (250 g) shredded carrots

1 (8-oz [227-g]) block super-firm tofu, crumbled (or firm tofu, pressed)

¼ cup (60 ml) soy sauce

2 tbsp (30 ml) rice vinegar

1 tbsp (9 g) grated ginger

DIPPING SAUCE

¼ cup (60 ml) soy sauce

¼ cup (60 ml) rice vinegar

2 tsp (7 g) grated ginger

2 tsp (10 ml) toasted sesame oil (omit to make oil-free)

1 tsp sriracha

1 (12-oz [340-g]) package vegan wonton wrappers (see Note)

FOR THE FILLING

Heat the oil (or water) in a very large sauté pan or wok over medium-high heat. Once hot, add the onion and cook until translucent.

Add the cabbage and carrots, and reduce the heat to medium. Cook until the veggies are starting to soften. Add the crumbled tofu, soy sauce and vinegar, and cook until the veggies are tender and the tofu is warmed.

Remove from the heat and stir in the ginger. Set the mixture aside to cool before you assemble the dumplings.

FOR THE SAUCE

Mix all the sauce ingredients in a small bowl while you wait.

Get a small bowl of warm water. Place a wrapper on a cutting board and spread water around the edge of the wrapper with your fingertip. Add 1 tablespoon (about 15 g) of filling to the middle of the wrapper and fold in half, matching the edges up. Press them together. You can stop here or you can grab it by the middle of the sealed part and fold the dough in 2 places on either side. Then sit it down in the steamer with the pleated-side up.

You can cook all of these or just cook some and freeze the rest for a quick dinner another time.

Place a steamer (bamboo or metal) in a pot with about 1 cup (240 ml) water, and bring to a boil. Cover and steam for 7 to 10 minutes, or until the dumplings are cooked. You will need to do this in batches.

Serve them with dipping sauce on the side. Pack any leftovers for lunch the next day. They are good cold or warmed up.

Savory PUMPKIN PASTIES

+SF

I made these for one of my Harry Potter parties. They are little savory turnovers filled with a light curried pumpkin filling. These are great for an appetizer, meal or even breakfast. —KH

MAKES 10

CRUST
2 cups (240 g) unbleached flour
½ tsp salt
⅔ cup (76 g) vegan butter
Cold water, as needed

FILLING
¾ cup (135 g) pumpkin purée
1 tsp garam masala
½ tsp salt
¼ tsp ground cinnamon
⅛ tsp ground coriander
⅛ tsp ground turmeric

FOR THE CRUST

Preheat the oven to 350°F (177°C) and prepare a sheet pan with parchment paper.

Make the pastry by first mixing the flour and salt together. Then cut in the vegan butter with a pastry cutter or 2 knives. Add cold water 2 tablespoons (30 ml) at a time until the dough is moist enough to hold together. Roll it into a ball and put it in the fridge while you make the filling.

FOR THE FILLING

In a medium bowl, mix the filling ingredients together.

Take the dough out of the fridge and roll out on a floured cutting board to about ⅛ inch (3 mm) thick. Use a 3-inch (7.5-cm) round cookie cutter (or mug of a similar size) and cut out individual crusts for the pasties. Place 1 tablespoon (13 g) of the filling in the center of each crust and fold over to make a half circle.

Press the edges together with your fingers, and then use a fork to crimp the edges closed. Place it on the prepared baking sheet, and repeat until all the crusts have been cut out and filled.

Bake for 20 to 30 minutes, or until the crust is firm and the tops have browned.

Chocolate-Dipped PEANUT STUFFED DATES

+GF +SF

These little bitefuls taste just like Snickers, and they are so easy to make! I made these for a Halloween party and called them cockroach clusters. You wouldn't believe how fast they disappeared. —KH

MAKES ABOUT 30 DATES

¾ cup (131 g) vegan chocolate chips
1 tbsp (15 ml) coconut oil
1 (8-oz [227-g]) pack pitted dates
⅓ cup (44 g) roasted peanuts

Melt the chocolate chips with the coconut oil over a double boiler or in a small slow cooker. Mix it together a few times to help it melt faster and more evenly.

While the chocolate is melting, stuff the dates with about 3 to 4 peanuts. Once the chocolate is melted, dip each one into it and roll it around with a fork. Then place them on a sheet pan covered in parchment paper and let them dry.

Once the chocolate is hardened, you can transfer them into a storage container.

Warm MAPLE PECAN BRUSSELS SPROUTS

+GF +SF

This is my favorite way to eat Brussels sprouts—it turns sprout haters into sprout lovers. The secret is the sweet and smoky flavor. —KH

SERVES 4

4 cups (400 g) sliced or shredded Brussels sprouts

½ cup (120 ml) water

1½ tsp (7 ml) liquid smoke

2 tbsp (30 ml) maple syrup

¼ cup (27 g) pecan pieces, toasted

Salt, to taste

Add the Brussels sprouts and water to a large sauté pan and heat over medium-high heat. Once the water starts to dissipate, add the liquid smoke and maple syrup, and cook until the Brussels sprouts are tender and the pan is almost dry, about 5 to 10 minutes.

Toss in the pecans and add salt to taste. Serve as a side dish or a warm salad.

Oven-Fried PARMESAN ZUCCHINI CRISPS

+GFO +SF

When I was in high school, many decades ago, one of my favorite meals was veggie pizza with fried zucchini. It wasn't healthy, but boy was it good! Now, most of my pizza comes with extra sauce and no cheese, and I usually take a pass on anything deep fried. Thanks to these delicious crisps, I can enjoy one of my favorite appetizers again.

These crunchy and savory crisps were inspired by a blast from the past craving for deep-fried zucchini, and the good news is that oven fried is just as good as deep fried, but so much lighter. —LM + AM

SERVES 8 TO 10

1 large or 2 medium zucchini, cut into ¼" (6-mm) disks

3 tbsp (45 g) fine sea salt

1 cup (122 g) breadcrumbs (use gluten-free if you wish)

½ cup (91 g) vegan Parmesan cheese (I use Go Veggie)

½ tsp garlic powder

2 tsp Italian seasoning

Salt and pepper, to taste

1 cup (126 g) all-purpose flour (use gluten-free)

1 cup (240 ml) unsweetened almond milk

Roasted Tomato Spaghetti Sauce (page 420)

Preheat the oven to 400°F (204°C) and line a baking sheet with parchment paper.

(continued)

Wash, dry and cut off the ends of the zucchini. Then slice them into ¼-inch (6-mm) disks. Lay the disks on a sheet of paper towel and lightly sprinkle with salt. This will draw out the excess water and make your crisps crispier. Let the disks sit for about 15 minutes. Don't skip this part or the zucchini will be too watery and the breading won't stick.

In a medium bowl, whisk the breadcrumbs, vegan Parmesan, garlic powder, Italian seasoning and salt and pepper, to taste, until combined. Put the flour in a small bowl and the almond milk in another small bowl.

Take a paper towel and pat the excess water off of the zucchini disks. Don't be afraid to press into the disks; you'll probably need an extra towel if your zucchini has a lot of water.

One by one, dip the disks into the flour, and then into the almond milk to coat both sides. Now press both sides of the zucchini into the breadcrumbs. Repeat with the rest of the breaded zucchini and evenly spread them out on the baking sheet.

Bake for 15 minutes. Then flip and bake for another 10 minutes, or until golden brown and crispy. Arrange them on a pretty platter and dip them in the sauce.

Lemon CURRY HUMMUS

+GF +SF

If lemon and curry had a baby, it would be this hummus. The marriage of those two flavors is incredibly bright and delicious. It's slightly tangy from the lemon, and then earthy and warm from the curry and cumin. We suggest serving this with cucumber slices to add a crisp and fresh bite. —LM + AM

SERVES 6 TO 8

1 (15-oz [425-g]) can chickpeas

1 tsp baking soda

2 tsp (5 g) ground curry

1 tsp ground cumin

1 tsp fine sea salt

Pepper, to taste

2 tbsp (30 ml) plus 1 tsp lemon juice

1 clove garlic

3 tbsp (45 ml) extra-virgin olive oil (add more for creamier texture)

SERVING OPTIONS
Toasted pita chips

Carrot sticks

Celery sticks

Slices of sweet bell pepper

Drain and rinse the chickpeas. Then put them in a food processor with the remaining ingredients and process until smooth and creamy. Serve with pita chips, carrot sticks, celery sticks and pepper slices.

Cannellini BEAN DIP

+GF +SF

While we absolutely love hummus, having it day in and day out can get a little hum-drum. That's why we decided to mix things up. Instead of the chickpea, this dip features a much more underutilized bean: the cannellini bean. Just as delicious and versatile, it creates a creamy, flavorful and healthy dip to add to any sandwich, bowl of veggies or salad. —LM + AM

MAKES 1 CUP (246 G)

1 clove garlic
1 (15-oz [425-g]) can cannellini beans
1 cup (25 g) fresh basil
1 tbsp (15 ml) extra-virgin olive oil
½ tsp salt
¼ tsp cayenne pepper
Ground black pepper, to taste

Peel the garlic, and drain and rinse the beans. Add all of the ingredients to a food processor and blend until thick and creamy, about 2 minutes.

Peanut SRIRACHA * GLAZED TOFU SATAY

+GF

Our cooking at the Meyer household is almost always split into two categories: Mexican and Asian. Yes, Asian is a broad term for so many types of cuisine, but who can really choose between Japanese, Chinese, Indian, Thai . . . I think you get my point. So before going vegan, we used to eat a lot of satay. This dish typically consists of meat, but we've recreated this flavorful dish with a veg-friendly tofu! We think it's even better than its original version. —LM + AM

MAKES 4 SKEWERS OF SATAY

14 oz (397 g) firm tofu, pressed
2 tbsp (23 g) natural peanut butter
2 tsp (5 g) sriracha
1 tbsp (15 ml) and 1 tsp lime juice
⅓ cup (78 ml) and 1 tbsp (15 ml) water
Sea salt, to taste
1 tbsp (15 ml) vegetable oil
¼ cup (10 g) fresh cilantro, stems removed
¼ cup (40 g) crushed peanuts

Place the tofu on a paper towel–lined plate. Put more paper towels on top of the tofu and then place a heavy pan on top of the tofu. Let the tofu sit for 20 minutes, until the water is pressed out of it. Once the water is pressed out, slice it in half lengthwise. Then cut it into 8 rectangular pieces.

Whisk the peanut butter, sriracha, lime juice, water and salt together in a medium bowl. Brush a layer of the glaze on one side of the 8 sticks of tofu.

Heat the oil over medium heat in a cast-iron skillet. When the oil is hot, put the glazed sides of the tofu sticks down in the pan. Brush the glaze on the other sides of the tofu. Cook the tofu for 2 minutes; then turn them a quarter. Brush the tops of the tofu with the glaze and cook for 1 minute, repeating on all other sides. All four sides of the tofu should be nicely seared.

Insert a toothpick into the ends of the tofu steaks and drizzle with the remaining glaze. Sprinkle with fresh cilantro and crushed peanuts.

*SEE PHOTO INSERT

Savory MUSHROOM AND RICOTTA POP TARTS

+GFO

We all know of the standard sweet pop tart, but have you ever taken a bite into a savory one? Trust us, you'll want to make this weekly once you take your first bite of our mushroom and ricotta pop tarts. The flakiness of the crust along with the creamy ricotta and warm mushrooms is incredibly addicting. We challenge you not to eat at least two the first time you try these savory tarts. —LM + AM

SERVES 6

1 cup (113 g) all-purpose flour (use gluten-free)

¾ cup (177 g) vegetable shortening

2 tsp (10 g) sea salt

½ cup (75 g) cornmeal

1 tbsp (3 g) chopped thyme

¼ cup (60 ml) ice-cold water

2 tsp (10 ml) olive oil, divided

1 cup (76 g) minced baby bella mushrooms

½ medium sweet onion, minced

2 cloves garlic, minced

1 tsp black pepper

2 tbsp (16 g) lemon zest

1 cup (250 g) Vegan Ricotta, homemade (page 417) or store-bought

In a stand mixer with the paddle attachment, combine the flour, vegetable shortening and salt. Mix until well combined. At this point, add the cornmeal and thyme. While mixing, slowly pour in the water until the dough forms a tight ball. Adjust the amount of water as needed.

Remove the dough from the mixer and place it onto a well-floured surface. Roll the dough out so it is ¼ inch (6 mm) thick. Now cut 3 x 5-inch (7 x 12-cm) rectangles into the dough. When you're done, you should have about 12 individual rectangles. Lay the rectangles out on a parchment-lined baking sheet and place in the refrigerator to cool.

In a large skillet, heat 1 teaspoon of the olive oil over medium heat. Once heated, add the mushrooms. Allow the mushrooms to brown, stirring occasionally. This should take about 5 minutes. At this point, add the onions, garlic and black pepper. Continue to sauté the onion for 5 minutes, or until the onion becomes translucent.

Preheat the oven to 350°F (177°C). Whisk the lemon zest into your ricotta.

To assemble, remove your crust from the fridge. Spread a thin layer of the ricotta on all of the rectangles. Now, place a few tablespoons (45 g) of the mushroom-onion mixture on top of half of the rectangles. Take the remaining rectangles, the ones without mushrooms, and place them ricotta-side down on top of the mushroom-filled rectangles. Press the edges with a fork to seal the tarts and make 3 small slices on top of each tart. Brush the edges of the dough with a little water if they won't stick together. Brush the tops of the tarts with the remaining teaspoon of olive oil.

Bake them in the oven for 20 to 30 minutes.

Vegan PRETZEL BITES

+SF

There's this place in Chicago that has the most amazing pretzel bites with beer cheese . . . at least that's what I've heard. Unfortunately, this place is not vegan-friendly, so I've decided to make my own. And I think that ours are even better! The dough is so soft and the crunch of the salt adds just enough to keep you wanting more.
—LM + AM

MAKES ABOUT 2 DOZEN BITES

1¼ cups (295 ml) plain unsweetened almond milk

1 tbsp (16 g) vegan honey (we suggest Bee Free Honee)

2 tsp (7 g) active dry yeast

3¾ cups (450 g) all-purpose flour, plus more for dusting

1 tsp sea salt

½ cup (112 g) baking soda

1 tbsp (14 ml) olive oil

1 tbsp (15 g) coarse sea salt

Preheat the oven to 450°F (232°C) and line a baking sheet with parchment paper or a baking mat.

Heat the almond milk and "honey" together in the microwave for about 30 seconds. Once the almond milk is heated through, pour the milk into a small bowl, sprinkle the yeast over the top and stir to combine. Let the yeast activate for 5 minutes. It should appear foamy when the 5 minutes are up.

Fill a large pot with water and bring it to a rolling boil.

Pour the yeast, milk and "honey" mixture into a stand mixer. Slowly begin to add the flour ½ cup (60 g) at a time. The dough should stick to your hand, but when it is ready it should release easily when touched. Add more flour if necessary. Now add in the salt and mix until incorporated.

Lightly dust a countertop with flour and put the dough on the floured surface. Roll out the dough and cut it into 20 even-size balls of dough.

Now you're going to add the baking soda to the boiling water. Be very careful; the water should bubble up, so add the baking soda slowly.

Boil 10 of the pieces of dough at a time for about 25 seconds.

Remove the pieces of dough from the water with a slotted spoon and place them on the parchment-lined baking sheet.

Once all the pieces of dough are done boiling, brush the balls with the olive oil using a pastry brush and sprinkle with the salt.

Bake the bites for about 10 minutes, or until golden brown.

Vegan POTSTICKERS

To make these, you'll need vegan wonton wrappers, and while they are available in some stores, they can be difficult to find. When we're in the mood for pot-stickers, we have to make our own. It's a bit of work but so worth it. Our filling is made with sharp ginger and fresh cilantro, and a bit of sesame oil. It has a wonderful flavor that is just as good as anything you'll get in a restaurant. —LM + AM

MAKES ABOUT 30 POTSTICKERS

WONTON WRAPPERS
2 tbsp (21 g) vegan egg substitute

1¼ cups (300 ml) water, divided

2 cups (220 g) all-purpose flour, plus extra for rolling out the dough

½ tsp fine sea salt

FILLING
2 cups (220 g) shredded red cabbage

½ cup (20 g) minced cilantro

4 green onions, minced

2 cloves garlic, minced

2 tbsp (16 g) minced fresh ginger

Sea salt, to taste

1 tsp sesame oil

Canola oil, for frying

DIPPING SAUCES
Chili sauce

Soy sauce

FOR THE WONTON WRAPPERS

In a small bowl, whisk the vegan egg and ¾ cup (180 ml) of the water until thick and creamy.

In a large mixing bowl, whisk the flour and salt together until combined. Add the egg and fold until combined. Add 1 tablespoon (15 ml) of the remaining ½ cup (120 ml) water at a time until the dough forms a solid ball. Don't overwater or it will be sticky. Cover the bowl with a towel and let it rest for 15 minutes.

On a floured surface, knead the dough for 5 minutes and pat it into a ball. Put it in the bowl and cover it. Let it rest for 30 minutes.

While the dough is resting, make the filling.

FOR THE FILLING

In a medium bowl, mix the cabbage, cilantro, onions, garlic, ginger, salt and oil until well combined.

Divide the dough and roll out one section on a floured surface until it's paper thin. You want to roll it until it's just about to become translucent. Cut into 4-inch (10-cm) circles with a cookie cutter and fill with 1 tablespoon (15 g) of the filling. Fold the dough in half over the filling and use the tines of a fork to close the edges. Brush with a bit of water if the dough doesn't stay closed. Pinch into a crescent shape and put it on a baking sheet. Repeat with the rest of the dough and filling.

Put a thin layer of canola oil in a large skillet and heat it on medium-high. Add as many potstickers as will fit in the pan and cook for about 5 minutes, or until the bottoms are golden brown and crispy. Turn the potstickers over and add 3 tablespoons (45 ml) of water; cover with a lid for 2 minutes to steam. Repeat with the remaining potstickers. You will probably need to put more oil in the pan as you go.

Serve with chili and/or soy sauce for dipping.

Polenta SQUARES WITH SUN-DRIED TOMATO PESTO AND ROASTED EGGPLANT

+GF +SF

This is a great appetizer for your next party. Just cut it into small squares and your guests will be wowed by the gorgeous colors and the fantastic flavors. You can also make this a meal. Serve it with a simple salad, and dinner is served. —LM + AM

SERVES 6 AS AN ENTRÉE AND 24 FOR APPETIZERS

EGGPLANT
2 tbsp (30 ml) extra-virgin olive oil, divided
1 medium eggplant, peeled and chopped
1 tbsp (3 g) dried Italian seasoning
Salt and black pepper, to taste

POLENTA
3 cups (720 ml) unsweetened almond milk
¼ tsp fine sea salt
1 cup (173 g) instant polenta

PESTO
2½ cups (62 g) fresh basil
⅓ cup (42 g) pine nuts
½ cup (55 g) sun-dried tomatoes
1 clove garlic
3 tbsp (34 g) Vegan Parmesan, homemade (page 76, 232) or store-bought
1 tbsp (15 ml) lemon juice
1 cup (235 ml) extra-virgin olive oil

GARNISHES
Whole sun-dried tomatoes
Fresh basil

FOR THE EGGPLANT
In a large skillet, heat 1 tablespoon (15 ml) of the olive oil over medium-high heat. Add the eggplant, Italian seasoning and salt and pepper, and cook for about 15 minutes, or until the eggplant is fork tender.

Preheat the oven to 400°F (204°C).

FOR THE POLENTA
In a medium saucepan over medium heat, bring the almond milk and salt to a low boil, and slowly whisk in the polenta. Reduce the heat to low and whisk continuously for about 5 minutes, or until thick and creamy. Remove it from the heat and spread evenly in a 9 x 9-inch (23 x 23-cm) greased baking dish. Bake for 30 minutes or until firm to the touch. Let it cool.

FOR THE PESTO
Put all of the ingredients except the olive oil in a food processor and begin to process while slowly pouring in the olive oil. Process for about 1 minute or until it's puréed.

TO ASSEMBLE
Spread the pesto over the polenta and cover with the eggplant evenly. Cut into as many squares as you like, depending on whether they're appetizers or an entrée.

Garnish each square with a whole sun-dried tomato and a small basil leaf.

Vegan GARLIC AND CASHEW CHEESE PULL-APART BREAD

+SF

If you've been on Pinterest in the past couple of years, you've probably seen these bread loaves. They're stuffed with cheese, herbs, spices and an assortment of other food items. However, they're rarely vegan. So, we took this party pleaser and turned it into a vegan treat to please the masses. —LM + AM

MAKES 1 LOAF OF BREAD

1 loaf Italian bread

3 cloves garlic, minced

1 tsp salt

¼ cup (60 ml) olive oil

2 tbsp (6 g) Italian seasoning

1 (8-oz [227-g]) package your favorite vegan cheese, we use mozzarella shreds

Preheat the oven to 375°F (190°C).

Slice the bread three-quarters of the way through on a diagonal about 10 times. Now make the same crosses in the opposite direction to create a diamond pattern in the bread.

In a small bowl, combine the minced garlic, salt, olive oil and Italian seasoning. Mix well until all of the ingredients are thoroughly combined.

With a pastry brush, brush the olive oil mixture between each of the folds in the bread.

Stuff the folds of the bread with the cheese.

Place the bread on a baking sheet and pop it in the oven for 10 to 15 minutes.

Honee DOUGH TWISTS

These little bites of soft honee dough are the perfect pairing for literally any dish. A vegan honey substitute adds a rustic twist to a classic sweet roll, and the thyme provides the perfect savory accompaniment. Serve this knotted dough alongside anything from carrots to a spicy BBQ jackfruit. This easy petite baked good will elevate any dish. —LM + AM

MAKES 12 ROLLS

1 packet (7 g) active dry yeast

¼ cup (60 ml) warm water

1 tsp sugar

3 tbsp (45 g) vegan butter

½ cup (120 ml) and 2 tbsp (30 ml) plain unsweetened almond milk, divided

1 egg equivalent of egg replacer

2 tbsp (28 g) and 1 tsp vegan honey substitute, we prefer Bee Free Honee, divided

1 tbsp (8 g) fresh thyme

2 cups (240 g) all-purpose flour

Dissolve the yeast in the warm water with the sugar. Allow the yeast to blossom for about 2 minutes.

Melt the vegan butter with ½ cup (120 ml) of almond milk in the microwave.

Combine the butter, almond milk, egg replacer, 2 tablespoons (45 g) of the honey, thyme and yeast/water in the stand mixer, and mix until a ball of dough forms. Begin adding flour to the mixture in ½-cup (60-g) increments.

Allow the dough to sit, covered, for an hour.

After the hour is up, punch the dough down and place it on an oiled surface. Using the oil instead of flour for kneading prevents the dough from becoming too dense.

Knead the dough and roll it out into a 12 x 12-inch (30 x 30-cm) square. Cut the dough into 10 long strips of dough. Begin tying knots in each piece of dough, roughly 4 or 5 knots, and then twist the dough into a wreath-like shape. This should look almost like a mini funnel cake. Place each twist on a lined baking sheet. Allow the twists to sit covered again for another 20 minutes.

Preheat the oven to 350°F (177°C).

While the dough is rising, mix the remaining 1 teaspoon (7 g) honey with the remaining 2 tablespoons (30 ml) almond milk. Heat the mixture in the microwave to make combining easier.

Once the dough is done rising, brush the honey/almond milk mixture over each of the knots. Place the knots in the oven and bake for 18 to 20 minutes.

Rosemary FOCACCIA BREAD

+SF

Our favorite bread is this fragrant and slightly salty focaccia bread. We love the drier texture of this bread for panini sandwiches (page 55) or to eat with soup. You'll find this bread easy to make and so much better than what you find at the supermarket. —LM + AM

MAKES 1 (10-INCH [25-CM]) ROUND LOAF OF BREAD

1½ cups (360 ml) warm water

2½ tsp (8 g) active dry yeast

½ tsp vegan granulated sugar

2 tbsp (5 g) minced fresh rosemary, divided

¾ cup (180 ml) extra-virgin olive oil, divided

4 cups (506 g) all-purpose flour, plus more for kneading the bread

2 tsp (5 g) garlic powder

1 tbsp (15 g) coarse sea salt

In a small bowl, combine the water, yeast and sugar, and let it sit at room temperature for 15 minutes. It should begin to foam. If it doesn't, the yeast is no longer active and you'll need to use new yeast.

While the yeast proofs, add 1 tablespoon (2 g) of the rosemary to the olive oil and let it sit for 15 minutes.

In a large mixing bowl with a dough hook attachment, combine the flour, garlic powder, ½ cup (120 ml) of rosemary-infused olive oil and the yeast, and mix on a medium speed until it's completely combined and forms a ball. Put a thin layer of flour on a clean, flat surface and knead the dough for 3 to 4 minutes. Add more flour if the dough is too sticky. Form the dough into a ball.

Coat the mixing bowl with a thin layer of oil, place the dough back in the bowl and cover it with a towel. Put the bowl in a warm spot and let it rise for about 1 hour, or until it doubles in size.

Brush 2 tablespoons (30 ml) of the remaining oil in the bottom and sides of a 11 x 7-inch (28 x 18-cm) rectangular pan. Stretch the dough evenly in the pan, making sure to get it into the corners. Flip it over and stretch it once more. Use your fingers to poke holes evenly in the dough. Cover with the towel and let it rise for 1 hour.

Preheat the oven to 400°F (204°C).

Brush the rest of the olive oil evenly over the top of the bread and sprinkle with the sea salt. Bake for 30 minutes, or until golden brown on top. Remove the focaccia from the oven and sprinkle it with the remaining 1 tablespoon (2 g) rosemary.

Yeast-Free GARLIC FLATBREAD

We created these in a moment of desperation. We were in need of a vegan flatbread for a pizza recipe and our local grocer didn't have any. We mixed up some flour, salt, garlic and water, and this is what we got. An easy, quick and delightfully chewy flatbread that crisps up in the oven. Use them for wraps, for pizza crust or as they are. —LM + AM

MAKES 6

2 cups (250 g) white whole wheat flour, plus extra for rolling

2 tsp (7 g) baking powder

½ tsp fine sea salt

1 tsp garlic powder

Ground black pepper, to taste

2 tbsp (30 ml) extra-virgin olive oil

1 cup (240 ml) water

TOPPING

Olive oil

Sea salt

Parsley

In a large bowl, whisk the flour, baking powder, sea salt, garlic powder and black pepper together until well combined. Add the olive oil and water, and stir until it becomes a solid piece of dough. Remove the dough from the bowl and knead it on a clean, floured surface until it becomes stretchy and smooth, about 1 minute. It will start out sticky. The longer you knead, the more solid it will become.

Flour a smooth surface, tear off a golf ball-size piece of dough and form a ball with your hands. Roll the dough out into a thin disk. Repeat with the remaining dough.

Heat a large skillet over medium-high heat (the skillet should be dry, no oil necessary) and add one piece of flat bread dough. Cook for 1 minute, flip and cook for another minute. Remove it from the heat and repeat with the remaining dough.

To make them fancy, brush them with a thin layer of olive oil and sprinkle with the coarse sea salt and shredded parsley after cooking.

Morisqueta

+SF +GF

Morisqueta is a Mexican rice and bean dish topped with a deliciously spiced tomato sauce. I like to bulk mine up a little bit more by adding some green bell pepper and a spoonful of cashew crema for good measure. —CS

SERVES 3

2 tsp (10 ml) olive oil, divided, plus extra to reheat

1 cup (188 g) dry long-grain rice, thoroughly rinsed

1½–2 cups (355–470 ml) vegetable broth, depending on how firm you like your rice

1 large green bell pepper, cored and diced

1½ cups (256 g) cooked pinto beans or black beans

Morisqueta Sauce (page 175)

Thinly sliced scallion

Chopped fresh cilantro

Cashew Crema (page 411), cold (will be firm) or left out of the refrigerator for about 15 minutes (will be thinner)

Place 1 teaspoon of the oil in a large pot or use a rice cooker. Add the rinsed rice and broth. Cook the rice according to the directions on the package, and then let it stand covered for 10 minutes. Fluff. You can make the rice ahead and reheat it in a little bit of oil, fried rice–style, or you can eat it immediately. Just be sure to refrigerate it promptly once it's cool enough, and store it in an airtight container for up to 3 days.

Place the remaining 1 teaspoon oil in a large skillet. Cook the bell pepper until just tender but still crisp. Add the beans and cook to heat through, about 3 minutes. Stir occasionally. If the rice was refrigerated, reheat it in a bit of oil to heat it through, and add the bean mixture to it once heated. Otherwise, use the still-warm rice by folding it into the beans.

Serve with the sauce, scallion, cilantro and crema.

MORISQUETA **Sauce**

This tomato sauce adds more spice and flavor than it does actual heat, allowing it to elevate the humble rice and beans (page 174) and even burrito filling (page 185) to the tastiest heights. You can add a hot pepper grabbed from your Pique (page 184) jar for more heat if you are daring! —CS

MAKES 2½ CUPS (670 G)

2 dried guajillo chile peppers, stemmed, seeded and rinsed

2 dried arbol chile peppers, stemmed, seeded and rinsed

1 habanero pepper or other pepper from Pique (page 184), to taste, seeded or not (optional)

2 cups (470 ml) vegetable broth

1½ cups (360 g) fire-roasted crushed tomatoes

1 tbsp (7 g) minced soft sun-dried tomatoes (not in oil)

2 cloves garlic, chopped

1 tsp dried oregano (not powder)

1 tsp dried porcini powder

Generous ½ tsp smoked sea salt, to taste

Place the chile peppers, broth, crushed tomatoes, sun-dried tomatoes, garlic, oregano, porcini powder and salt in a medium saucepan. Bring it all to a boil, lower the heat immediately and simmer over medium-low heat until thickened, about 40 minutes. Stir occasionally and adjust the heat as needed. Transfer it to a blender and blend until completely smooth. Use immediately or store in an airtight container in the refrigerator for up to 4 days.

Harissa CROQUETTES

I love smaller batches of food, because it's just my husband and me at home most of the time, but you can easily double this recipe if you have to feed more than two people.

Also, if your harissa paste is particularly spicy or if you are a bit of a spice wuss (nothing wrong with that), you can replace 1 tablespoon (21 g) of harissa paste with 1 tablespoon (17 g) of double-concentrated tomato paste. —CS

MAKES 14 CROQUETTES

4 oz (113 g) tempeh, crumbled

2 tbsp (42 g) harissa paste

1 generous tbsp (17 ml) grapeseed oil or olive oil

2 cloves garlic, minced

¼ cup (4 g) fresh minced cilantro or scallion greens

1 tsp garam masala

½ tsp fine sea salt

Juice of ½ medium lemon (about 2 tbsp [30 ml])

¼ cup (30 g) vital wheat gluten

½ cup (32 g) panko breadcrumbs

Nonstick cooking spray or oil spray

Creamy Harissa Sauce (page 412)

Preheat the oven to 375°F (190°C). Line a baking sheet with parchment paper.

(continued)

In a large bowl, place the tempeh, harissa, oil, garlic, cilantro, garam masala, salt and lemon juice. Stir to combine. Add the gluten and breadcrumbs on top and start mixing with a spatula. Then switch to using your hand to gather the mixture together. It should be moist and stick together well when pinched. Gather 1 slightly heaping, packed tablespoon (25 g) of mixture to shape the dough into rounds. Place the croquette onto the prepared sheet. Repeat with the remaining mixture. You should get 14 croquettes in all, but the yield will vary. Wrap the parchment paper over the croquettes and fold them to close. Flip the package upside down and place them back onto the sheet. Baking the croquettes this way will allow them to remain tender.

Bake the croquettes wrapped for 20 minutes. Then remove the wrap, lightly coat with the spray and bake another 6 minutes. Let them stand 5 minutes before serving with the sauce.

*SEE PHOTO INSERT

Tsire TEMPEH BITES

This is the perfect flavor-packed, protein-rich appetizer to be dipped in a peanut-based sauce! I usually have a hard time keeping myself from snacking on these as soon as they're popped out of the oven. Don't judge. —CS

MAKES 25 BITES

8 oz (227 g) tempeh, crumbled

1 cup (170 g) cooked chickpeas

1½ tsp (4 g) berbere spice or Ras el Hanout

3 tbsp (54 g) white miso

3 tbsp (45 ml) lemon juice

½ tsp coarse kosher salt

Generous ¼ cup (25 g) chopped scallion

3 cloves garlic, minced

1 tbsp (15 ml) neutral-flavored oil

1 tbsp (8 g) light spelt flour or other flour

¼ cup (26 g) Tsire Spice (page 417)

Oil spray or cooking spray

Peanut Butter Miso Sauce (page 415)

Place the crumbled tempeh in a large bowl. Place the chickpeas, berbere, miso, lemon juice, salt, scallion, garlic and oil in a food processor, and process until a paste forms. Transfer the paste on top of the tempeh and stir to combine. Add the flour and stir just until combined. Cover the bowl and refrigerate for 1 hour.

Preheat the oven to 375°F (190°C). Line a baking sheet with parchment paper.

Place the tsire spice in a shallow bowl. Using 1 packed tablespoon (25 g) of the tempeh mixture, shape into rounds. You should get 25 bites in all, but this could vary. Roll it into the tsire spice to thoroughly coat. Repeat with all the bites. Add extra spice mixture if you run out while coating the bites. Lightly spray the bites with oil.

Bake for 20 minutes, or until golden brown and firm. Let them cool 5 minutes before enjoying with the peanut sauce.

Citrus CHILE JACKFRUIT

+GF +SF

This citrusy meat replacement can be used as a topping in Mexican-influenced bowls (with rice, beans and bell peppers), in sandwiches, or as a meat replacement in (possibly) the best tacos ever, the Citrus Chile Jackfruit Tacos (page 177). —CS

MAKES ENOUGH FOR 12 TACOS

2 (20-oz [567-g]) cans young green jackfruit in brine, drained, rinsed and cut lengthwise into ¼" (6-mm) thick strips

4 cloves garlic, minced

½ medium red onion, diced

1 green bell pepper, cored and diced

½ cup (122 g) organic ketchup

½ cup (120 ml) freshly squeezed orange juice

1 tbsp (15 ml) olive oil

1 tbsp (20 g) agave nectar

1 tbsp (15 ml) lime juice

1 tbsp (9 g) taco seasoning

1 tsp chipotle powder (halve if you aren't a fan of spicy)

1 tsp dried shiitake powder

½ tsp ground cumin

Scant 1 tsp smoked sea salt

Preheat the oven to 425°F (220°C). Line a large rimmed baking sheet with parchment paper.

Place all of the ingredients in a large bowl. Use a rubber spatula to thoroughly combine.

Transfer the jackfruit to the prepared sheet and spread evenly. Bake for 20 minutes and stir well. Bake for another 20 minutes and stir again. Turn off the oven and leave it in the oven for another 20 minutes. The jackfruit should be golden brown, not overly moist and not super dry.

It can be served warm, at room temperature or even cold.

Citrus CHILE JACKFRUIT TACOS

+GF +SFO

Having been born outside of the US, I may be considered a newbie as far as tacos go. But living in southern California gave me a crash course in their limitless awesomeness. Here, jackfruit takes center stage with its citrusy and spicy flavors. Even though jackfruit isn't exactly packed with protein, its texture makes it one of the best plant-based meat alternatives one can dream of, especially when used in tacos. —CS

MAKES 12 TACOS

12 (6" [15-cm]) vegan corn tortillas, heated

1 recipe Yogurt Avocado Dressing (page 414)

1 small head red or green cabbage, trimmed and thinly shredded

1 recipe Citrus Chile Jackfruit (page 176)

GARNISHES
Chopped fresh cilantro

Thinly sliced scallion

Roasted pepitas

Lime wedges

On a tortilla, spread enough yogurt avocado dressing to cover the center. Add a handful of shredded cabbage. Top with a healthy amount of jackfruit and your garnishes of choice. Repeat this with the remaining tortillas and serve immediately.

*SEE PHOTO INSERT

Harissa FRIED QUINOA

+GF

I absolutely love eating this side dish served with sliced fresh, super tasty summer tomatoes when they're at their peak. It adds umami to the fried quinoa and balances it out perfectly! —CS

SERVES 4

3 tbsp (45 ml) toasted sesame oil

1 tbsp (20 g) harissa paste

2 small shallots, minced

4 cloves garlic, minced

3½ packed cups (660 g) cooked and chilled quinoa

2 cups (280 g) frozen corn kernels

2 tbsp (30 ml) tamari

1 tbsp (15 ml) mirin

(continued)

Thinly sliced scallion
Chopped fresh cilantro

Place the oil and harissa in a large pan. Stir to combine. Add the shallots, garlic, quinoa and corn. On medium-high heat, start frying the quinoa. Add the tamari and stir to combine. Adjust the heat as needed. Cook until the quinoa smells nutty, about 6 to 8 minutes. Add the mirin and stir to combine. Cook for another 2 minutes and serve immediately with scallion and cilantro.

Roasted YOUNG CARROTS WITH PONZU SAUCE

This side dish is so simple, yet incredibly top notch. Note that you could also use fresh young broccoli and asparagus instead of carrots, depending on what's available and particularly good-looking at the market. The cooking times might vary, so check frequently for doneness. —CS

SERVES 2

1 lb (454 g) peeled fresh young carrots of various colors
2 large cloves garlic, peeled but left whole
Healthy drizzle toasted sesame oil
2 tbsp (30 ml) Ponzu Sauce (page 414)
Thinly sliced scallions (white and green parts)
Toasted sesame seeds

Preheat the oven to 425°F (220°C).

Place the carrots and garlic in a 9-inch (23-cm) square baking pan. Drizzle them with enough oil to coat them well. Toss with the oil and bake until fork tender, stirring occasionally. This should take about 40 minutes, but check for tenderness a bit sooner as the cooking time can vary depending on the freshness of the veggies.

Mince the garlic cloves. Serve immediately with a drizzle of the sesame oil that will have landed at the bottom of the pan, along with ponzu sauce, scallions and sesame seeds.

Caramelized KIMCHI HUMMUS

For the most efficient use of your heated oven, please combine the kimchi-caramelizing step of this recipe with that of the Caramelized Kimchi Tahini Toast (page 187) recipe. It's easy to divide the kimchi once it's done. You would have to bake 2 cups (420 g) of packed kimchi along with 1 tablespoon (15 ml) of toasted sesame oil. The baking time remains the same. The resulting weight of the caramelized kimchi is about 3.6 ounces (103 g) per recipe. Do you love me yet? I did the math for you after all. Not to mention I also come bearing this perfect hummus-y gift. —CS

MAKES ABOUT 2 CUPS (470 G)

1 packed cup (210 g) vegan kimchi, drained and gently squeezed (liquid reserved)
1½ tsp (8 ml) toasted sesame oil
1½ cups (256 g) cooked chickpeas (peeled if desired for smoothest results)
¼ cup (64 g) tahini paste
1 tbsp (15 ml) grapeseed oil or other neutral-flavored oil
6 tbsp (90 ml) vegan kimchi brine, as needed

OPTIONAL
Roasted garlic
Salt
Lemon juice

Preheat the oven to 425°F (220°C). Line a large baking sheet with a piece of parchment paper. Evenly place the kimchi on the prepared sheet. Drizzle it with oil. Bake for 15 minutes, or until lightly browned and caramelized.

In a blender (for most whipped, fluffiest results) or food processor, combine all of the ingredients except for the brine. Blend and stop occasionally to scrape the sides of the machine with a rubber spatula. Add the brine, as needed, for smooth and not too dry but not too watery results. If your kimchi is a little weak, feel free to adjust the result by adding roasted garlic, salt or lemon juice as needed. Store leftovers in an airtight container in the refrigerator.

Tsire-SPICED HUMMUS

+QP +GF +SF

Not tired of hummus yet? Good. Because this one also is a keeper. I love the slight peanutty flavor the Tsire Spice imparts here. Also, while peeling cooked chickpeas sounds like the most tedious task ever, which it kind of is, it also ensures that the hummus will be as smooth as they come. You could always ask your partner or roommate (or maybe your cat) to do this part for you, if you personally can't be bothered. —CS

MAKES 2 CUPS (510 G)

1½ cups (256 g) cooked chickpeas (peeled if desired for smoothest results)

¼ cup (27 g) Tsire Spice (page 417)

¼ cup (28 g) soft sun-dried tomatoes

¼ cup (64 g) tahini paste

2 tbsp (30 ml) olive oil or neutral-flavored oil

2 tbsp (30 ml) lime juice

1 large clove garlic, minced

½ cup (120 ml) aquafaba (cooking liquid of chickpeas), as needed

Salt, to taste (2 or 3 generous pinches of coarse kosher salt did the trick for me)

Place all the ingredients in a blender (for most whipped, fluffiest results) or food processor. Blend until perfectly smooth. Stop to scrape the sides occasionally. Add aquafaba as needed, and more if needed. Season the hummus to taste. Refrigerate your leftovers for up to 3 days. Serve with crackers, as a sandwich spread, in wraps or any dish that calls for hummus.

Harissa HARICOTS VERTS

+GF +SF

Haricots verts means green beans in French. The ones I prefer using are fine and tender, and work perfectly in this spicy side dish. Should you only find a thicker kind of green bean, you can always blanch them prior to roasting for ideal results. —CS

SERVES 4

1½ tbsp (23 ml) toasted sesame oil

1 tbsp (20 g) agave nectar

1 tbsp (20 g) harissa paste, to taste

2 lbs (908 g) fresh green beans, trimmed and washed

4 small shallots, trimmed and peeled, left whole

4 cloves garlic, peeled but left whole

½ tsp smoked sea salt, or to taste

GARNISHES
Lemon wedges or grated lemon zest

Dry-roasted pine nuts or slivered almonds

Preheat the oven to 425°F (220°C). Line two large baking sheets with parchment paper.

In a very large bowl, whisk to combine the oil, agave and harissa paste. Add the beans, shallots and garlic, and toss to thoroughly combine.

(continued)

Divide the beans between the sheets and place them evenly. Loosely cover them with pieces of foil. Bake for 20 minutes. Remove the foil and cook for another 10 to 20 minutes (this will depend on the thickness and freshness of the beans), or until the beans look shriveled and are tender.

Add salt to taste. Top with lemon and pine nuts.

*SEE PHOTO INSERT

Elote GRILLED CORN

+QP +GF +SFO

Let's face it: lightly oiled corn, grilled in the outdoors in the summertime, served with a sprinkle of salt is already great as is. But add a pine nut–based, powdery spice mix on top, a squirt of lime juice, and there you have it: heaven on the cob. —CS

SERVES 4, SCANT ½ CUP (54 G) PINE MIX

SPICE AND PINE MIX
3 tbsp (23 g) dry-roasted pine nuts
3 tbsp (15 g) nutritional yeast
Generous ½ tsp smoked sea salt
½ tsp onion powder
½ tsp smoked paprika
½ tsp ground cumin
¼ tsp chipotle powder

CORN
4 fresh ears of corn, trimmed, husk and silk removed
Olive oil, or coconut oil for a slightly cheesier flavor
4 tsp (20 g) plain vegan mayo (use soy-free)
Lime wedges

FOR THE SPICE MIX
Place all of the ingredients in a mini food processor or coffee grinder. Grind just until finely ground. Do not overprocess or the pine nuts will turn into a paste! Transfer the mix to an airtight container.

Store it at room temperature for up to 1 week or in the refrigerator for up to 1 month.

FOR THE CORN
Lightly brush the corn ears with oil. Place them on a hot grill and cook until golden brown. This should take about 10 minutes. Be sure to flip the corn around so that each side has a chance to brown

When the corn is ready, remove it from the grill and brush it with about 1 teaspoon of mayo. Sprinkle generous pinches of the spice mixture all over the surface, and drizzle with a bit of lime juice. Serve immediately.

Rosemary BALSAMIC ROASTED POTATOES

+GF +SF

A little bit of balsamic reduction brings some zing to roasted-to-perfection potatoes, with a slight rosemary flavor as an added bonus! If your garden is thriving and you grow fresh rosemary and blackberries, my anything-but-green thumb is actually green with envy. —CS

SERVES 2 TO 3

Coarse kosher salt
1 lb (454 g) small gold potatoes, quartered (choose potatoes of similar size)
1½ tbsp (23 ml) grapeseed oil or olive oil
1½ tbsp (23 ml) Blackberry Balsamic Reduction (page 416)
2 small shallots, halved
3 cloves garlic, left whole
1 large sprig fresh rosemary

Bring a pot of water to a boil. Add a generous spoonful of salt. Add the potatoes and parboil for 8 minutes. Drain and let them cool. In the meantime, preheat the oven to 425°F (220°C).

In a small bowl, whisk to combine the oil and balsamic reduction.

Place the potatoes, shallots and garlic in a 9-inch (23-cm) square baking pan. (If you're concerned the potatoes might stick to the pan, if it isn't non-stick, place a piece of parchment paper in the pan.)

Toss the potatoes with the oil and reduction mixture. Sprinkle with a couple generous pinches of salt. Add the rosemary sprig and cover the pan loosely with a piece of foil. Roast for 20 minutes. Remove the foil and roast for another 20 minutes or until the potatoes are fork tender and golden brown. Discard the rosemary, but mince the shallots and garlic, dividing them among each serving.

Wakame GINGER KIMCHI

Does it take longer to make your own kimchi than it does to purchase it from the store? Well, yes it does a little bit. Is it better though? Most definitely. I highly recommend investing in a nice ceramic fermentation crock. I tried making kimchi in glass jars, and while the results were quite good already, they're even more outstanding in a dedicated crock. —CS

MAKES ENOUGH TO FIT A 64-OUNCE (1.8-KG) JAR

1 medium head Napa cabbage (about 2 lb [908 g]), outer leaves removed and cored

¼ cup (56 g) coarse kosher salt

Filtered water

1 Asian pear, quartered, cored and thinly sliced

6 oz (170 g) shredded carrot

2–4 tbsp (16–32 g) gochugaru (Korean red pepper flakes), to taste

3 tbsp (45 ml) shoyu or tamari

1 tbsp (15 ml) lemon juice

3 tbsp (5 g) wakame (dried seaweed), soaked just to rehydrate, then drained

⅔ cup (65 g) chopped scallion (1" [2.5-cm] pieces)

4 cloves garlic, minced

1 tbsp (6 g) grated ginger

4½ oz (128 g) daikon, peeled and thinly sliced into half-moons

Cut the cabbage in half and into 1½-inch (3.8-cm) chunks. Wash thoroughly. Place it in a very large bowl and cover with salt. Put on food-safe gloves and massage the salt into the cabbage. Add enough water to generously cover the cabbage, using a plate to weigh it down in order to submerge all the leaves. Cover it with a lid or plastic wrap, and let it stand at room temperature for about 4 hours. This will soften the cabbage and start the fermentation process.

Drain the cabbage and rinse it in several runs of water, making sure to rinse between the leaves as well. Let it drain for 30 minutes.

In the meantime, place the remaining ingredients in a large bowl. Wearing food-safe gloves, massage the mixture to thoroughly combine. Add the cabbage and massage to coat all the nooks and crannies. Transfer everything to a 2-quart (2-L) fermentation crock with a water lock moat, and press down with a clean wooden spoon. Add weights to make sure the kimchi is submerged. Should there be a lack of brine preventing the kimchi from being submerged, add just enough filtered water to cover the weights. Add water to the moat and close the lid. Let the kimchi ferment at room temperature. Check once a day to see if the kimchi is ready for your taste, and use a clean wooden spoon to gently press down on the weight, ensuring that the kimchi remains submerged. Add water back to the moat as needed to make sure the kimchi is airtight.

I usually let my kimchi ferment for 2 to 3 days with great results. Then I transfer it to an airtight glass jar that I refrigerate for at least another week before partaking, for best results. The kimchi will be good for about 1 month.

Spicy CHICKPEA STUFFERS

+GF

I love to shove these little guys in a pita bread with lots of raw veggies and some dressing, or even between two slices of sourdough bread! They're a great way to boost flavor and protein intake. They don't tend to roll out as you eat, provided you squish them a bit with a potato masher or a fork before placing them in or on the bread. —CS

SERVES 3

1½ cups (256 g) cooked chickpeas

2 tsp (10 ml) toasted sesame oil

2 tsp (10 ml) tamari

1 tsp curry powder

1 tsp gochugaru (Korean red chile powder)

1 tsp tomato paste

½ tsp coarse kosher salt

¼ tsp ground ginger

½ jalapeño pepper, trimmed, cored, seeded and minced (optional)

1 small shallot, minced

Preheat the oven to 425°F (220°C). Line a 9-inch (23-cm) square pan with parchment paper. Toss all of the ingredients in a bowl, and place them evenly in the prepared pan. Bake for 20 to 25 minutes, until shrunken a bit and dry but not burnt. Serve immediately or at room temperature. They tend to have even more flavor when eaten at room temperature.

Miso-Glazed YELLOW BEETS

+GF

Fact: yellow beets are a lot less earthy-tasting than regular red beets. It's a blessing for anyone who's normally not really into beets, like my husband. These miso-coated roasted beets make for a delightful side dish! —CS

SERVES 2 TO 3

2 tbsp (36 g) white miso

2 tbsp (30 ml) lemon juice

1 tbsp (15 ml) toasted sesame oil

2 tsp (10 ml) agave nectar

3 large yellow beets (about 25 oz [709 g]), trimmed and peeled, each cut into 8 wedges

2 shallots, trimmed, halved or quartered depending on size

4 cloves garlic

OPTIONAL, TO TASTE
Gochugaru (Korean red chile powder)

Crushed pepper flakes

Cracked white peppercorn

Preheat the oven to 425°F (220°C). In an 8-inch (20-cm) square baking pan, whisk to combine the miso, lemon juice, oil and agave.

Stir the beet wedges, shallots and garlic into the mixture, making sure all are coated. Loosely cover with a piece of aluminum foil and bake for 30 minutes.

Remove the foil, stir well and bake for another 20 to 30 minutes, or until the beets are tender and the sauce has thickened. Mince the shallots and garlic and return them to the pan before serving. Season with gochugaru, pepper flakes or white peppercorn to taste.

Moroccan MARINATED VEGETABLES

+QP +GF +SF

These Moroccan-flavored vegetables aim to please in dishes such as Moroccan Pizza (page 96) and Moroccan Minestrone (page 222)! —CS

MAKES ENOUGH FOR BOTH MOROCCAN PIZZA (PAGE 96) AND MOROCCAN MINESTRONE (PAGE 222)

8 oz (227 g) cremini mushrooms, halved if small or cut into thick slices if larger

2 red bell peppers, halved, cored and thinly sliced

1 medium red onion, halved and thinly sliced

2 tsp (10 ml) olive oil

1 tsp balsamic vinegar

1 tsp Ras el Hanout

½ tsp smoked paprika

½ tsp coarse kosher salt

Cook the mushrooms in a dry pan over medium-high heat until they start to release their moisture and brown slightly, stirring occasionally. This should take about 6 minutes.

Place the mushrooms, bell peppers and onion in a large bowl. Add the oil and vinegar, Ras el Hanout, paprika and salt. Stir together to combine thoroughly. Let it marinate for 15 minutes. Use these as indicated in the Moroccan Pizza and Moroccan Minestrone recipes.

Tare TOFU

+QP

Don't you love it when things that are super easy to make yield amazing results? All the awesomeness minus the maximum amount of elbow grease. Not that we're lazy, but come on. Simple is great. —CS

SERVES 3 TO 4

1 tbsp (15 ml) toasted sesame oil

1 lb (454 g) super-firm tofu, cut into ¾" (2-cm) cubes

Scant ¼ cup (60 ml) Tare (page 95)

Place the oil in a large wok or saucepan. Heat over medium-high heat, add the tofu and fry until the tofu is golden brown on all sides, about 8 minutes. Adjust the heat as needed. Don't flip the tofu too often; allow each side to sear. Once golden brown, add the tare and cook until the tofu is glazed, about 3 minutes. Stir occasionally. Remove the pan from the heat and use in Forbidden Broth (page 221), Japanese-Inspired Sandwiches (page 89) and Shiitake Chickpea Crepes (page 92). Serve with Ponzu Sauce (page 414). Store in an airtight container in the refrigerator for up to 4 days.

Pique (PICKLED HOT PEPPERS)

+SF

Used in Roasted Corn Pique Salsa (page 184), or seeded and minced in sandwiches and salads, these pickled peppers pack a powerful punch.

Feel free to replace the peppers listed here with your own favorites. Adding a few slices of red onion would be fantastic, too. —CS

MAKES ONE 2-CUP (470-ML) JAR

3 habanero peppers, stems removed

2 Thai peppers, stems removed

1 yellow banana pepper, stem removed

2 serrano peppers, stems removed

1 jalapeño pepper, stem removed

3 cloves garlic, smashed

1 tsp dried oregano (not powder)

1 fine sprig fresh cilantro

½ tsp coarse kosher salt

⅛ fresh pineapple, cut into spears

¾ cup (180 ml) distilled vinegar

Clean the peppers well but leave them whole and drain well. Choose a jar large enough to accommodate all of the ingredients snugly. Place the peppers, garlic, oregano, cilantro, salt and pineapple in the jar. Top them off with vinegar, adding extra if the peppers aren't fully covered. Tightly seal with the lid. Shake gently to make sure everything is well combined, and then refrigerate for at least a week before using to let the flavors develop. Peppers will keep for up to 1 month.

Roasted CORN PIQUE SALSA

+SF

Not that I think anyone needs to be told how to use a really good salsa, but just in case you want to do more with this one than simply dip tortilla chips in it, have a look at Pan con Salsa y Aguacate (page 386) and Beer-Braised Jackfruit Tacos (page 88) for a couple of hints. —CS

MAKES 2 CUPS (460 G)

1½ cups (204 g) frozen corn

9½ oz (269 g) heirloom baby tomatoes, diced

1 Pique (page 184) pepper, halved, seeded and minced (quantity to taste)

2 tbsp (26 g) minced pineapple from Pique (page 184)

1 tbsp (15 ml) fresh pineapple juice

1 tbsp (15 ml) brine from Pique (page 184)

½ tsp coarse kosher salt

Preheat the oven to 425°F (220°C).

Place the corn in a 9-inch (23-cm) square baking pan. Bake the corn for 20 minutes or until lightly browned and softened. Stir the corn once halfway through. Remove it from the oven and allow it to cool.

In a medium bowl, add the corn and remaining ingredients. Gently fold to combine. Let stand for 30 minutes before using. Store in an airtight container in the refrigerator for up to 4 days.

Chile Sauce REFRIED BEANS

+SF

While I also love more traditional and slightly milder refried beans, these more tomato-y refried beans are perfect in Crispy Corn and Bean Burritos (page 82). —CS

SERVES 3 TO 4

1 tbsp (15 ml) olive oil

¼ medium red onion, diced

1¼ cups (295 ml) Morisqueta Sauce (page 175)

1½ cups (256 g) cooked pinto beans

Salt, to taste

Heat the oil in a large skillet. Add the onion and cook over medium-high heat until browned, about 8 minutes. Stir occasionally. Lower the heat and add the sauce (careful because it might spatter), stirring to combine. Add the beans. Simmer for 10 minutes, and then mash the beans. Simmer for another 5 minutes, or until thickened and not too juicy. Salt your beans as needed and serve anywhere refried beans are called for, or as a burrito filling in recipes like Crispy Corn and Bean Burritos (page 82).

Miso-Marinated MUSHROOMS

+GF

If you love umami-rich mushrooms like I do, you'll want to try these pickled wonders in Japanese-Inspired Sandwiches (page 89) and Shiitake Chickpea Crêpes (page 92).

Whatever you do, don't get rid of the brine! It's perfect to use in Saucy and Sassy Cashew Noodles (page 140) and to replace regular vinegar in Asian-inspired dishes. It's also great on its own to drizzle on shredded cabbage for a deliciously zippy and fat-free dressing. —CS

MAKES ONE 2-CUP (470-ML) JAR

2 tsp (10 ml) toasted sesame oil

3½ oz (100 g) fresh shiitake mushrooms (choose mushrooms of similar size), gently rinsed and drained

2 cloves garlic, thinly sliced

1 tsp nanami togarashi

1 tbsp (15 ml) lemon juice

1½ tbsp (27 g) white miso

½ cup (120 ml) filtered water

½ cup (120 ml) rice wine vinegar

Place the oil in a small skillet. Add the mushrooms and cook over medium-high heat until lightly browned, about 3 minutes. Stir occasionally. Do not overcook the mushrooms. Transfer them to a jar, and top with the garlic and nanami togarashi.

In a glass measuring cup, whisk to combine the lemon juice and miso. Slowly add the water and vinegar, whisking to combine. Pour this mixture into the jar on top of the mushrooms and close tightly with a lid. Refrigerate for 24 hours before using. The miso might separate from the liquid, but it isn't a problem. Feel free to occasionally stir to combine again. Use within 1 week of preparation.

Smoky APPLE (OR PEAR) PICKLES

+GF +SF

Made smoky with the use of Lapsang Souchong tea, these fruity pickles will be an awesome addition to Gochujang BBQ Sauce Sandwiches (page 84), and Kimchi Mac and Sprouts (page 80). Their brine is also put to use in Japchae (page 96). —CS

MAKES ONE 25 OUNCE (750-ML) JAR

3 tbsp (45 ml) lemon juice

1" (2.5-cm) knob fresh ginger, peeled and grated

A little over 1 lb (500 g) fresh small apples (such as Fuji) or Asian pears, quartered, cored and thinly sliced

1 tsp coarse kosher salt

½ cup (100 g) evaporated cane juice or organic granulated sugar

1 cup (235 ml) rice wine vinegar

2 tea bags (1 tbsp [6 g]) Lapsang Souchong tea

Place the lemon juice and ginger in a large bowl. As you slice the apples (using a mandoline slicer if available), gently fold them into the lemon juice to prevent browning. Set aside.

Place the salt, sugar and vinegar in a small saucepan. Bring it to a boil, lower the heat and cook until the sugar crystals are dissolved, about 1 to 2 minutes.

Remove from the heat and add the tea bags. Steep for 10 minutes. Gently squeeze the tea bags and discard them. Pour the brine on top of the apple or pear slices. The brine will fully submerge the apples or pears after softening them; just be sure to stir a few times before transferring them to a large canning jar.

Close the lid tightly, store in the refrigerator for at least 2 hours before use and keep for up to 2 weeks.

Pickled DRIED MANGO

+GF +SF

Dried mango is a great treat as it is, but have you ever thought of pickling it in a savory way? It's a really nifty addition to curries, sandwiches and Pickled Mango Curry Wraps (page 90). —CS

MAKES ONE 26½-OUNCE (784-ML) JAR

1 cup (235 ml) apple cider vinegar

¾ cup (180 ml) water

¼ cup (50 g) natural cane sugar

2 tsp (6 g) coarse kosher salt

6 oz (170 g) dried mango

1 medium red onion, cut into large pieces

1 small and short stick lemongrass, halved and lightly pounded

2 tsp (4 g) Aleppo pepper flakes or ½ tsp red pepper flakes, to taste

1 tsp toasted coriander seeds

½ tsp toasted black mustard seeds

½ tsp ground ginger

Place the vinegar, water, sugar and salt in a small saucepan. Heat over medium-high heat and cook just until the sugar crystals and salt are dissolved, about 2 minutes. Set it aside.

In an oven-safe canning jar, place the mango, onion, lemongrass, pepper flakes, coriander and mustard seeds and ginger. Pour the hot vinegar mixture on top, wipe any spills and tightly close the lid of the jar. Carefully tilt the jar back and forth to make sure all the ingredients are soaked and combined. Let it stand for 24 hours in the refrigerator before using. Use within a week, stored in the refrigerator.

Caramelized KIMCHI TAHINI TOAST

Who knew tahini would pair so nicely with caramelized kimchi? Indeed, the slightly bitter flavor of tahini works perfectly with the caramelized-therefore-slightly-sweet taste of fermented cabbage. Oh, and avocado makes a cameo of course, because it seems one cannot have toast without avocado these days. And who's complaining? —CS

MAKES 4 TOASTS

1 packed cup (210 g) vegan kimchi, drained and gently squeezed (liquid reserved)

1½ tsp (8 ml) toasted sesame oil

4 slices vegan sourdough bread, toasted

Tahini paste

2 small ripe avocados, halved, pitted and peeled

Preheat the oven to 425°F (220°C). Line a baking sheet with parchment paper. Evenly place the kimchi on the prepared sheet. Drizzle with the oil. Bake for 15 minutes or until lightly browned and carmelized.

Place the toast on plates. Spread a thin layer of tahini on each piece of toast.

Use a fork to chunkily smash the avocados. Then divide them among the toast and spread in an even layer. Top with the caramelized kimchi. Serve immediately.

Nanami TOGARASHI CASHEWS

These sweet and savory cashews are delicious as a topping to Asian-inspired salads and other dishes, such as Japanese Tempeh and Sushi Rice Bowls (page 95). They're perfect for casual snacking, too. —CS

MAKES 1¾ CUPS (230 G) CASHEWS

1¾ cups (210 g) raw cashew pieces

2 tbsp (14 g) sesame seeds

2 tsp (5 g) nanami togarashi

1 tbsp (15 ml) toasted sesame oil

1 tbsp (15 ml) shoyu

1 tbsp (20 g) agave nectar

Preheat the oven to 300°F (150°C).

Line a large rimmed baking sheet with parchment paper.

In a medium bowl, add all of the ingredients and fold to thoroughly combine. Then place the mixture evenly on the prepared sheet and bake for 10 minutes. Stir and make sure the cashews are evenly layered again. Bake for another 4 to 6 minutes, or until the nuts are fragrant, golden brown and dry. Keep a close eye on the oven to make sure the cashews don't burn. Let them cool in an even layer on the baking sheet. Store at room temperature or in the refrigerator for up to 2 weeks.

Summer Rolls WITH GARDEN VEGGIES, BASIL AND TAHINI CHILI SAUCE

YAY 4 SUMMER ROLLS! These are super cute and even more delicious to eat. —EvE

SERVES 2 TO 4

TAHINI CHILE SAUCE

2 tbsp (36 g) tahini

1 clove garlic

1 tsp grated fresh ginger

1 tbsp (18 g) miso paste

1 tbsp (15 g) sauerkraut

1 tbsp (12 g) coconut sugar

2 tbsp (30 ml) lime juice

1–2 tbsp (3–5 g) dried deseeded red chile skin, or more as desired

WRAPS

4 rice papers

1 red beet, shredded

3 carrots, shredded

3–4 tomatoes, sliced

½ cup (13 g) chopped fresh basil

¼ cup (10 g) chopped fresh mint

¼ cup (10 g) chopped fresh cilantro

Whatever else your heart desires

FOR THE TAHINI CHILE SAUCE

Blend everything together until smooth. Adjust according to your taste preferences, and add as much water as needed to get a creamy consistency.

FOR THE WRAPS

Dip a rice paper sheet in cold water for 5 seconds, and then lay it flat on a damp cloth. Let it sit for 15 seconds while you fill it up with your goodies. Fold the skin on one side over and wrap under the fillings; then wrap it up like a burrito. Repeat with the remaining rice papers.

Dip the rolls in your tahini chile sauce and enjoy.

Perfect FLUFFY CRISPY POTATOES

The method here is what makes the magic: we are gonna partially boil the potatoes so their outsides are soft, and then shake them up with a few different herbs and spices so they get coated. Then we bake them and suddenly we have potatoes that are perfectly crispy and browned on the outside, and fluffy and soft on the inside.—EvE

SERVES 3 TO 4

6 russet potatoes

1 tbsp (4 g) dried basil or other herb(s)

1 tsp nutritional yeast or asafetida powder

1 tsp garlic powder

¼ tsp cracked black pepper

¼ tsp chipotle powder

2 tbsp (28 g) vegan butter or a drizzle of olive oil (optional)

Preheat the oven to 400°F (204°C).

Peel the potatoes and chop them into large bite-size pieces. Place them all in a pot and just barely cover them with cold water; then bring it all to a boil. Once the water/potatoes are boiling, continue boiling for another 4 minutes; drain. Throw all the parboiled potatoes back in the drained pot and add in the rest of the ingredients. Put the lid on the pot and shake it up with both hands (wear oven mitts if the pot is still hot!) so the potatoes get covered in the spices and herbs and also get marred around the edges. Put all of the potatoes on a lined baking sheet and bake for 20 to 30 minutes, or until they are browned on the outside.

You can top the taters with chopped green onion and a simple tahini lemon sauce. I've also had them with ketchup, and they're too good.

Sweet Potato Fries
WITH LEMON CASHEW CHIPOTLE DIP ✗

Sweet potatoes are very good for you, but more importantly, they taste magical when you bake them with oil, spices and serve them up with a creamy, nutty, tangy sauce. Cannot. Get. Enough. Hope you like the recipe as much as I do! —EvE

SERVES 2 TO 4

FRIES
3 medium sweet potatoes
3 tbsp (41 g) coconut oil
½ tsp black pepper
½ tsp ground cumin (optional)
½ tsp ground coriander (optional)

CASHEW DIP
1 cup (110 g) cashews, preferably soaked for 4–6 hours in water, then rinsed
4 tbsp (60 ml) lemon juice
1 tbsp (18 g) miso paste
1 tbsp (15 ml) soy sauce
½ tsp chipotle powder
1 tsp maple syrup
1" (2.5-cm) chunk ginger
¼ cup (20 g) nutritional yeast
1 clove garlic (optional)

Chopped fresh herbs of choice
Flaky sea salt

FOR THE FRIES
Preheat the oven to 350°F (177°C).

Wash and scrub the sweet potatoes (no need to peel them). Slice them into fries and toss them with the oil and spices. Bake them on a parchment paper-lined baking pan for 30 to 45 minutes, or until they begin to brown. If you want them crispy, increase the oven temperature for the last 15 to 20 minutes and cut the fries thinner before baking them. Keep an eye on them so they don't burn.

FOR THE CASHEW DIP
Blend all of the ingredients together until smooth, adding water as needed. Adjust the amounts according to taste.

Serve the fries with chopped fresh herbs, flaky salt and the cashew dip.

Garam Masala
ROASTED ACORN SQUASH

+GF +SF +QP

Thanksgiving is really all about the sides for vegans. I feel like a nut loaf is okay and Tofurkey is fun, but I would be really happy with cranberry sauce, 'taters, some delicious veggies and a big ol' slice of pie instead. In an attempt to come up with creative and delicious ways to squeeze more veggies onto the table, we came up with this impressive dish. It packs so much flavor, your friends and fam won't believe you whipped it up yourself, and it looks so good you might not be able to believe it either! We love squash, but roasting it in garam masala and pairing it with tangy lemon tahini sauce, sweet pomegranate arils, crunchy pepitas and a sprinkle of fresh parsley takes it to a whole new level. Plus, it really couldn't be easier—and who really wants to spend extra time in the kitchen while everyone's catching up around the dining room table? —AS

SERVES 4

SQUASH
1 medium acorn squash
1 tbsp (14 ml) melted coconut or olive oil
¾ tsp garam masala
Salt and pepper, to taste

TAHINI SAUCE
½ cup (140 g) tahini
2 tbsp (30 ml) lemon juice
¼ tsp salt
¼–½ cup (60–120 ml) water, as needed

SERVING
¼ cup (44 g) pomegranate seeds
2 tbsp (16 g) pepitas
2 tbsp (5 g) finely chopped fresh parsley

Preheat the oven to 375°F (190°C). Line a baking sheet with parchment paper and set aside.

FOR THE SQUASH
Slice both ends off of the squash and scoop out the seed goop. Slice the squash into ½-inch (1.3-cm) slices and lay in a single layer on the lined baking sheet. Drizzle with the oil and sprinkle with the garam masala, salt and pepper. Toss it to coat. Roast for 20 to 25 minutes, until the squash is fork tender and browned.

FOR THE TAHINI SAUCE
While the squash roasts, combine your tahini, lemon juice and salt in a food processor. Add water a little at a time until you reach the desired consistency. Scoop it into a bowl.

FOR SERVING
When the squash is roasted, remove it from the oven and serve warm with the tahini sauce, pomegranate seeds, pepitas and fresh parsley.

Note: Leftovers can be saved in the fridge overnight, but it's a dish best served warm!

Don't have garam masala? Try curry! Don't have acorn squash? Try delicata! This recipe is easily customizable.

*SEE PHOTO INSERT

Roasted ROMANESCO CAULIFLOWER

+GF

This is an easy, visually pleasing dish to make, and it's super customizable. Don't have smoked paprika? Try cumin and cayenne, or curry and turmeric! Either way, run down to the farmers' market and get a head of this gorgeous cauliflower when it's in season—you won't regret it. —AS

SERVES 2 TO 4

1 large head romanesco cauliflower

¼ cup (60 ml) melted coconut or olive oil

½ cup (75 g) diced red onion

6 cloves garlic, minced

Juice of 1 lemon (about ¼ cup [60 ml]), plus more for serving

1 tsp smoked paprika

½ tsp chili powder

½ tsp salt

½ tsp pepper

½ cup (120 ml) dry sherry

Fresh chopped cilantro or parsley, for garnish

Preheat the oven to 400°F (204°C). Trim the washed cauliflower leaves and cut the stem, if necessary, so that the cauliflower stands upright in a Dutch oven or heavy cast-iron pan (with a lid). Place the cauliflower in the pan, and use a sharp knife to carve a 1-inch (2.5-cm)-deep X into the top of the cauliflower.

In a small bowl, combine the oil with diced onions, minced garlic, lemon juice, spices, salt and pepper. Pour the mixture over the cauliflower, slightly pulling the X apart so the oil can seep into the middle. Try to evenly coat the cauliflower (no need to flip it over). Pour the sherry lightly over the whole thing, and then cover the pan. Bake for 40 minutes, or until the cauliflower is fork tender. Then remove the lid and cook for another 10 to 15 minutes. Remove it from the oven, and serve with an extra squeeze of lemon juice and a sprinkle of fresh cilantro or parsley. Leftovers can be refrigerated and reheated for up to a week.

Kung Pao
CAULIFLOWER

+GF

I measure my recipe success by meal leftovers, and there were none to be found after we whipped this one up. I'm so excited about this recipe because it's healthy, crazy rich in flavor and makes a great shared meal (or leftovers!). —AS

SERVES 2

KUNG PAO SAUCE
¼ cup (60 ml) water

¼ cup (60 ml) Bragg liquid aminos or soy sauce

1 tsp apple cider vinegar

1 tsp sesame oil

1½ tbsp (18 g) sugar

1 tsp red pepper flakes

⅛ tsp wasabi powder (optional)

2 tsp (6 g) cornstarch

1 tsp coconut oil

VEGGIES
½ large head cauliflower (about 2 cups [220 g] of florets)

3 cloves garlic, minced

1 tbsp (14 g) coconut oil

1 medium onion, julienned

1 bell pepper, chopped, or about ½ cup (45 g) julienned peppers

TOPPINGS
Sprinkle sesame seeds

Chopped green onions

FOR THE KUNG PAO SAUCE
Combine all of the sauce ingredients in a bowl and whisk. Set it aside.

(continued)

FOR THE VEGGIES

In a wok or large frying pan, cook the cauliflower and garlic together with the coconut oil over medium-high heat until the cauliflower is slightly browned, about 3 minutes. Add the onion and pepper, and sauté for another 3 minutes, until your onions are just becoming glassy.

Add the sauce and cook until it thickens, another 3 to 5 minutes or so. Remove the veggies in sauce from the heat, serve it over brown rice with a sprinkle of sesame seeds and green onions, and enjoy! This saves well in the fridge for up to a week.

Party-Size
JACKFRUIT NACHOS

+GF

I've never been much of a football fan myself, but I'm always down for a party centered around eating! We're going to have some friends over before the big game this weekend and these nachos will absolutely be making an appearance. They're deceptively simple to make, big enough to share with a crowd and so good your guests might not even believe you made them yourself! No matter what team you're rooting for, you'll be glad you made these nachos to munch on . . . and so will your guests! —AS

SERVES 6 TO 10

JACKFRUIT

1 tbsp (14 g) coconut oil, for frying

2 (20-oz [565-g]) cans jackfruit in brine or water (NOT syrup), seeds removed

Juice of 1 orange (about ⅓ cup [80 ml])

Juice of 1 lime (about 2–3 tbsp [30–45 ml])

2 cloves garlic, minced

2 tbsp (28 ml) melted coconut oil

2 tsp (10 ml) soy sauce

1 tsp liquid smoke

½ tsp ground cumin

½ tsp smoked paprika

½ tsp red pepper flakes

½ tsp salt

¼ tsp cayenne pepper

1 large bag of tortilla chips

1 (15-oz [425-g]) can black beans, rinsed and drained

1–2 cups (120–240 g) vegan queso cheese, homemade (page 415) or store-bought, warmed

½ cup (75 g) finely chopped red onion

½ cup (90 g) sliced black olives

¼ cup (10 g) chopped fresh cilantro

Guacamole, for serving

Limes, for serving

Preheat the oven to 375°F (190°C). Line a baking sheet with parchment paper (or aluminum foil). Set aside.

FOR THE JACKFRUIT

Heat the coconut oil in a medium cast-iron skillet. Place the jackfruit into a mixing bowl and use two forks or your fingers to shred it. Add the orange and lime juices, garlic, melted coconut oil, soy sauce, liquid smoke, cumin, smoked paprika, pepper flakes, salt and cayenne. Mix until the jackfruit is well coated, and then pour the whole mixture into the heated skillet. Cook over medium heat for about 10 to 15 minutes, until the juices thicken and reduce and the jackfruit begins to slightly brown in the pan. Remove it from the heat and set aside.

Spread the tortilla chips evenly over the baking sheet and scatter the drained black beans over the top. Layer the seasoned, cooked jackfruit evenly over the top, and then place the baking sheet in the oven for 10 minutes. Heat the chips, beans and jackfruit together.

When finished, pull the baking sheet from the oven and immediately top with the queso cheese, chopped red onion, black olives, cilantro, guacamole and limes. Serve immediately!

Note: Save time by preparing the jackfruit and queso a day ahead. Then just reheat as necessary!

If you use a different cheese, we would recommend adding the cheese layer BEFORE baking so it melts while in the oven.

Add whatever other toppings you like! Some suggestions? Cabbage, salsa, hot sauce, green onions, jalapeños, tomatoes . . .

Loaded Vegan
NACHO FRIES

+GF +SF

I love all things NACHO, and some nights call for crazy, craving-filled dishes—like this one. I wanted fries and nachos, and couldn't decide, so I settled on BOTH! It was so, so worth it, friends. Who needs Taco Tuesday when you can have different types of nachos at every meal? —AS

SERVES 2 TO 4

FRENCH FRIES
3 medium russet potatoes, cut into french fries or about 3 cups (450 g) of your fave frozen french fries

1 tbsp (14 g) coconut oil (only if making your own fries)

Salt, to taste

EVERYTHING ELSE
1 (15-oz [425-g]) can black beans, rinsed and drained

1–2 cups (120–240 g) vegan queso cheese, homemade (page 415) or store-bought, warmed

½ cup (75 g) finely chopped red onion

½ cup (90 g) sliced black olives

¼ cup (10 g) chopped fresh cilantro

Guacamole, for serving

Lime wedges, for serving

FOR THE FRENCH FRIES
Preheat the oven to 400°F (204°C). If you're making fries from scratch, wash your potatoes well and slice into fries about ¼ inch (6 mm) thick. Coat a baking sheet in the coconut oil, then spread your potatoes or frozen fries onto a baking sheet. Bake until golden and crispy, about 30 minutes, flipping halfway through. Season with salt. Set aside.

FOR EVERYTHING ELSE
Preheat the oven to 350°F (177°C). Line a baking sheet with parchment paper (or aluminum foil). Set it aside.

Spread the french fries evenly over the baking sheet and scatter the drained black beans and queso cheese over the top. Place the baking sheet in the oven for 10 minutes, and heat the fries, beans and cheese together.

Once finished, remove the pan, move the fries to a serving plate and cover them with the red onion, black olives, cilantro, guacamole and limes. Enjoy immediately!

Fresh SPRING ROLLS

+QP +GF

These spring rolls are stuffed with buttery avocado, crunchy cucumbers and silky tofu, and then finished with a luscious almond-coconut dipping sauce. Perfect for a picnic outing or Sunday brunch. —AS

SERVES 2

SPRING ROLLS

½ large cucumber

3 carrots

6 spring roll papers

6 leaves of butter or romaine lettuce

1 avocado, peeled, pitted and sliced

¼ cup (62 g) cubed extra-firm organic tofu

Small handful cilantro

Small handful mint

Lemon juice

ALMOND-COCONUT DIPPING SAUCE

3½ tbsp (50 g) unsalted almond butter

¼ cup (60 ml) full-fat coconut milk

1 tsp tamari (or use soy sauce for gluten-free)

1 tbsp (12 g) coconut sugar

1 tsp lemon juice

Pinch of sea salt

FOR THE SPRING ROLLS

Thinly chop the cucumber and carrots into long, thin pieces. Warm the rice papers: pour hot water into a shallow dish and soak the rice paper in the water for 15 seconds. Move the soft rice paper to a damp cutting board. Lay it flat as you begin to layer on the veggies. Start by layering the butter lettuce first, then the avocado slices, tofu cubes, cucumbers and carrots. Top with a small handful of cilantro, mint and a squeeze of lemon juice. Gently fold one side of the rice paper over the veggies, tuck in the edges and continue to roll until it's sealed.

FOR THE DIPPING SAUCE

Now prepare the dipping sauce by simply mixing all of the ingredients in a bowl. Cut the spring rolls in half, dip into the sauce and enjoy!

World's BEST GUACAMOLE

+GF +QP +SF

This guacamole is our absolute favorite. We've been making this version for a few years, and it's pretty similar to Chipotle's style, if you're familiar. There are a million different ways to make this green gold, but we like ours full of fresh lime juice, red onion and cilantro. We serve it up at every taco night, take it to parties and munch it on game day, too! —AS

SERVES ABOUT 4

4 medium ripe avocados

3 tbsp (28 g) finely chopped red onion

1–2 tbsp (3–5 g) chopped fresh cilantro

1–2 tbsp (15–30 ml) freshly squeezed lime juice

¾ tsp salt

1 small jalapeño pepper, seeded and finely diced, or ¼–½ tsp cayenne pepper (optional, for spiciness)

Slice the avocados in half, lengthwise, tossing the seed and scooping the green innards into a large mixing bowl. Mash the avocado with a fork or potato masher until it reaches your desired consistency; my recommendation is to keep it a little chunky.

Add the red onion, cilantro, lime juice, salt and jalapeño, if using. Stir to combine. Serve immediately with chips or as an accompaniment to tacos or fajitas!

Note: Don't go squeezing (and ruining for everyone else) all the avocados at the store! If it has a little give and the stem doesn't just fall off, you're good. If it is overly softened or the stem falls off easily, revealing a dark or black area underneath, skip it.

The best way I've found to save leftover guac without it turning too brown is to cover it with plastic wrap, but push the plastic wrap against the guac in the bowl, so no air can stay trapped between the two. Alternatively, you can try one of the million tricks found on the internet. Again though, the plastic wrap trick works pretty well. So does scraping off the brown layer and eating the perfectly good guac underneath.

Buffalo SRIRACHA HUMMUS

+GF +QP +SF

Spicy and tangy, this hummus tastes like buffalo wings—cruelty-free style. We've been dipping with celery, cauliflower and tortilla chips . . . we'll be lucky if we have any left to serve guests! —AS

SERVES 4 TO 6

1 (15-oz [425-g]) can chickpeas, rinsed and drained

½ tsp ground cumin

¾ tsp smoked paprika

¼ tsp cayenne pepper

¾ tsp sea salt

3 cloves garlic

2 tbsp (36 g) tahini

2 tbsp (30 ml) Sriracha hot sauce

1 tbsp (15 ml) lemon juice

½ cup (80 g) roasted peppers (roasted reds are great, but a jarred mix is fine too!)

2 tbsp (30 ml) olive oil

Cayenne or fresh cilantro, for serving (optional)

Blend everything except the olive oil together in a food processor or high-speed blender. Once it's well combined, add the olive oil and mix again. Pour it into a dipping-friendly container and serve with a drizzle of olive oil and cayenne or some fresh cilantro. Hummus saves for up to 2 weeks in an airtight container in the refrigerator. Great as a dip or sandwich spread!

Garlicky WHITE BEAN HUMMUS

+GF +QP +SF

This dip is easy to throw together, full of flavor and just a ½-cup (120-g) serving will give you 23 grams of long-lasting protein, the key to fighting off snacking and making it through the day guilt free. —AS

SERVES 4 TO 6

3½ cups (700 g) white beans, rinsed and drained (about two 15-oz [425-g] cans)

2 tbsp (36 g) tahini

3 tbsp (45 ml) olive or grapeseed oil

3 cloves garlic

¼ cup (60 ml) freshly squeezed lemon juice

1 tsp salt

¾ tsp ground cumin, plus more for garnish

Chopped fresh cilantro, for garnish (optional)

Combine all the ingredients in a high-speed blender or food processor. Blend the mixture on high for about 30 seconds, until all the ingredients are combined. The resulting texture should be thick, whipped and full of garlic flavor. Serve with a dash of cumin and cilantro or on its own with chips and crackers. This garlicky hummus saves well up to a week in the fridge.

Picante BLACK BEAN HUMMUS

+GF +QP

You know what is the most frustrating thing about being a vegan? When people ask, "Well, where do you get your protein?" Like we vegans can only get it from meat. Ick. Protein can be found in all kinds of foods, and we really don't need nearly as much protein as most of us get, anyway. But that's a lame answer. Next time, just shove this recipe in their face and watch them drool. The black beans in this hummus provide you with 2.6 grams of protein for every tablespoon of them you consume. —AS

SERVES 2 TO 4

1 (15-oz [425-g]) can or about 2 cups (400 g) cooked black beans, rinsed and drained

1 tbsp (15 ml) olive oil

1 tbsp (18 g) tahini

¼ cup (10 g) fresh cilantro

1 clove garlic

2 tbsp (30 ml) freshly squeezed lime juice

½ tsp salt

½ tsp ground cumin

½ tsp cayenne

¼ tsp smoked paprika, plus extra for garnish

Green onions, for garnish (optional)

Combine all the ingredients in a high-speed blender or food processor. Blend it on high for about 30 seconds, until all the ingredients are combined.

Serve with a dash of smoked paprika and a sprinkle of green onions, or on its own with chips, veggies or on pita bread. This will save well, covered, up to a week in the fridge.

Edamame GUACAMOLE ✳

+QP +SF +GF

Keep this recipe close to your chest. It is a game changer: guacamole made without creamy avocado, and instead with chunky edamame, is an utterly delicious spread. —MR

SERVES 4 TO 6

½ cup (75 g) chopped red onion

2 cups (310 g) shelled edamame, cooked

Juice of 1 lime

Sea salt

Handful of cilantro

Diced tomatoes, optional

Red pepper flakes

Simply pulse the onion in a food processor for a few seconds. Then add the rest of the ingredients and pulse until the edamame is blended into big chunks. Enjoy this as a spread on toast, used as a dip or as pesto sauce!

For this recipe I encourage you to add more or less onion, lime and cilantro according to your preference. I like a lot of cilantro, so I'll add even more than 1 handful.

Paprika HUMMUS

+QP +SF +GF

Hummus: the ultimate snacking experience. It's quick to whip up, packed with nutrition and protein and spiced with paprika to create a near-addictive snack. It's one to make weekly and enjoy over toast, with veggies, wrapped as a spread in a burrito or stirred into a salad as dressing. —MR

SERVES 6 TO 8

2 (14-oz [397-g]) cans chickpeas, rinsed and drained

2 tsp (4 g) paprika

Juice of 2 lemons or apple cider vinegar

1 tsp ground cumin

2 tbsp (36 g) tahini

⅔ cup (155 ml) water (add more gradually if you like it thinner)

2 tbsp (30 ml) olive oil

1 clove garlic

1 tsp salt, or to taste

Simply place all of the ingredients into a blender or food processor and mix until creamy. Check to see if you would like to add more salt or water to make it a thinner, creamier hummus.

Homemade "CHEESY" POPCORN

+QP +SF +GF

Nutritional yeast may not be the prettiest sounding condiment, but definitely one to have on hand for when a taste of cheesiness is needed. It is not a yeast but a flaky golden seasoning that is a fantastic substitute for dairy cheese. Sprinkle generously on just about anything, especially fresh popcorn. Enjoy a movie night in with a new ritual: homemade "cheesy" popcorn. —MR

SERVES 3 TO 5

4 tbsp (55 g) coconut oil, divided

½ cup (105 g) organic popcorn kernels

⅓ cup (27 g) nutritional yeast

Sea salt, to taste

In a large and deep cooking pot, melt 1 tablespoon (14 g) of the coconut oil over medium-high heat. Then add 2 kernels and place a lid on top of the pot. Wait for the kernels to pop. Once they pop, add the rest of the kernels and shake the pot so that the oil coats all of the kernels.

Now, in a separate saucepan over medium heat, melt the remaining 3 tablespoons (45 ml) oil. Then add the nutritional yeast and mix well.

Once all the kernels have popped, pour the nutritional yeast seasoning over the popcorn and mix well. Sprinkle with sea salt to taste.

Herby AVOCADO DRESSING ON GRILLED CORN

+QP +GF

A dish that is as beautiful as it is scrumptious, this herby avocado dressing is folded into grilled sweet corn, creating a side that encapsulates the very best of summer. —MR

SERVES 3 TO 4

¼ cup (10 g) chopped fresh basil

¼ cup (10 g) chopped fresh cilantro

1 avocado, divided (save half for the salad)

Juice of ½ lemon or lime

1 tsp maple syrup

2 cloves garlic

¼–⅓ cup (60–78 ml) olive oil

¼–⅓ cup (60–78 ml) water

Pinch of salt

2½ cups (415 g) grilled (or boiled) corn kernels

Simply blend all of the ingredients (except for the corn) in the food processor until creamy and slightly thin in texture. We want it to be on the thinner side, as it will be used as a dressing. Then scoop a few tablespoons (45 ml) of the dressing into a mixing bowl with the grilled corn and add the remaining avocado.

Baked CHURRO CHIPS

+GF +QP +SFO

These chips bake up in minutes with very little prep needed and are a total crowd pleaser! Who doesn't love a crispy baked corn chip (or wheat, if wheat tortillas are more your thing) coated in vegan butter, cinnamon and sugar? NO ONE. Yup, double negatives. Which means EVERYONE loves them! They're crispy, crunchy, sweet and almost too easy to eat. So, let's eat! —AS

MAKES 55 TO 65 CHIPS

14–16 small corn tortillas, cut into quarters

1 cup (190 g) organic sugar

2 tsp (4 g) ground cinnamon

½ cup (120 ml) melted vegan butter or coconut oil

Preheat the oven to 350°F (177°C). Line a baking sheet with parchment paper.

Cut the tortillas into 4 to 6 equal triangles. Mix the sugar and cinnamon together in a bowl and set it aside.

Lay the chips on the baking sheet and lightly brush each chip with some of the melted butter or oil. Sprinkle about half of the cinnamon-sugar mixture over the chips so they're lightly coated. Then flip them over, lightly brush the other sides and coat them in the remaining sugar mixture.

Bake for 15 to 20 minutes. Allow the chips to cool completely before removing them from the baking sheet.

Note: You can use whatever tortillas you like: wheat or corn and any size. Just adjust accordingly!

Choc-Oat-Nut
GRANOLA BALLS

+GF +QP

I've been trying to make a truly healthy, on-the-go treat for a while now. After lots of trial and error, I finally have a really yummy, really healthy snack that tastes just like chocolate chip Quaker Chewy brand granola bars!

They aren't overly sweet, they fill you up and they're loaded with lots of good protein and fiber. Plus, they're packed with flax (full of B vitamins!) and hemp seeds (essential amino and fatty acids!) . . . with just a sprinkle of chocolate to sweeten everything up. —AS

MAKES ABOUT 20 (1-INCH [2.5-CM]) BALLS

1 cup (155 g) oats (gluten-free)

½ cup (90 g) almond butter

1 cup (75 g) shredded coconut

½ cup (55 g) ground flaxseed

¼ cup (40 g) hulled hemp seeds

1 tbsp (14 g) coconut oil, at room temperature

4 tbsp (85 g) brown rice syrup or agave

1 tsp vanilla extract

1–2 tbsp (15–30 ml) water

¼ cup (45 g) vegan chocolate chips (optional)

In a large bowl, mix together all the ingredients except the water and chocolate chips.

I've found it's easier to use a fork to mash and squish everything together, since the coconut oil can sometimes clump together.

Once everything is well combined, add the 1 to 2 tablespoons (15 to 30 ml) of water to make it all a little sticky. You want to be able to roll the finished product into balls.

Add the chocolate chips, and use your hands to mix them in.

Roll the mixture into about 1-inch (2.5-cm) balls, and place them on a flat plate or cookie sheet.

Refrigerate for an hour before eating.

To store, keep in a plastic bag or container in the refrigerator for up to a week.

Crispy CHICKPEA ONION RINGS

+GF +QP +SF

This is a favorite at our place when we need some junk food, because they're gluten-free, have plenty of batter (there's nothing I hate more than a barely coated onion ring!) and are deeeeelicious. The batter is slightly sweet and nutty with a hint of smoky flavor, which tastes great with a little sriracha mayo or even old school catsup, and even better with a beer. They're a great app for sharing at parties and Sunday sports games, but equally great all by yourself with a chick flick. No judgment here! I think you're gonna love them, so let's eat. —AS

SERVES 4

3–6 cups (710–1420 ml) vegetable or coconut oil for frying (or as needed)

1 very large red onion, sliced into rings

1 cup (130 g) chickpea (garbanzo bean) flour

1¼ tsp (3.5 g) garlic salt

½ tsp smoked paprika

¼ tsp ground pepper

¾ cup (180 ml) water

In a large deep pot or Dutch oven, pour in enough oil to completely submerge the onion rings, about 2 to 4 inches (5 to 10 cm). Heat the oil over medium-high heat to 365°F (185°C) or test the oil's readiness by dropping an onion ring and seeing how it looks. If it immediately bubbles and begins to fry and turn golden brown, you're good! If not, wait a few minutes and try again. If it burns, turn down the heat and wait for it to cool before trying again.

In a large mixing bowl, whisk together the chickpea flour, garlic salt, paprika, pepper and water. Set it aside to thicken. (It should be about as thick as pancake batter.)

Using a fork or tongs, dredge the onion slices until evenly coated in the batter. Let the excess batter drip off, but leave enough so that the onion ring is well coated. Drop it into the heated oil and let it fry about 1 to 2 minutes on each side, until golden brown and crispy. Remove the cooked rings from the oil and let them cool on a paper towel–lined plate to absorb any excess oil. Continue to cook the rings until finished, adding oil to the pan as needed to keep the depth. Be sure to bring the oil back up to temperature after adding extra oil and before adding new rings.

Extra Chewy CHOCOLATE STEEL-CUT OAT BARS

+GF +QP

I've been enjoying these chocolaty little things after a long snowshoe outside or as a sweet treat after break-fast. They're delicious! And a great way to use up all those steel-cut oats sitting in the back of the cupboard. The drizzle of chocolate adds just a bit more sweetness . . . and who doesn't love a little extra chocolate? —AS

MAKES 12 BARS

2 cups (260 g) quick-cooking steel-cut oats

½ cup (85 g) chopped almonds

¼ cup (28 g) ground flaxseed

½ cup (90 g) chocolate chips or chopped bar chocolate

¼ cup (55 g) coconut oil

½ cup (170 g) brown rice syrup, sorghum syrup or date syrup

2 tsp (10 ml) vanilla extract

1–2 oz (28–57 g) chocolate, for topping

Regular steel-cut oats are a little thicker than quick-cooking steel-cut oats. If using those, throw about half of them into a coffee grinder to get a similar consistency.

In a large mixing bowl, combine the oats, almonds, flax and chocolate chips. Set aside.

In a small saucepan, combine the oil, brown rice syrup and vanilla. Simmer on low, stirring occasionally, until the mixture melts together and comes to a uniform consistency. Pour it over the dry ingredients, using a wooden spoon to mix everything together. The chocolate will get melty at this point and turn the whole mix deliciously chocolaty . . . if you're not into that, feel free to keep the chocolate chips separate and add them to the top at the end.

Once the mixture is uniform in texture, pour the batter into a small glass baking dish (about 8 x 8-inch [20 x 20-cm]), press it to the sides and bottom and refrigerate for at least 1 hour to set. Once the bars have set, melt 1 to 2 ounces (28 to 57 g) of chocolate, and use a whisk or spoon to drizzle chocolate evenly over the bars. Let them harden, about 10 minutes in a cool place, then cut and serve. Store them in an airtight container in the fridge or freezer.

PB and J
ENERGY BITES

+GF +QP +SF

These PB and J Energy Bites are the bee's knees my friends! I made them by accident the other day when cleaning out my cabinets and trying to make a healthy, satisfying, sweet-ish treat. I didn't want to get the blender or food processor involved because they're a pain to clean, so these little cuties are stuck together using my favorite sticky ingredient: peanut butter! And because they're packed with PB, chia and flax, they're packed with protein and healthy omega-3 fatty acids, too—which makes these perfect for bringing along on a hike, picnic at the beach or on your next road trip! —AS

MAKES 16 TO 20 BALLS

1 cup (130 g) rolled oats (gluten-free)

⅔ cup (60 g) roughly chopped freeze-dried strawberries

⅓ cup (63 g) ground flaxseed

⅓ cup (53 g) chia seeds

½ cup (90 g) peanut butter

⅓ cup (80 ml) maple syrup or agave nectar

1 tsp vanilla extract

In a medium bowl, combine the oats, strawberries, flax and chia. Add the peanut butter, maple syrup and vanilla extract, and stir until thoroughly mixed. Use a spoon or cookie scoop to roll the mixture into 1-inch (2.5-cm) balls. Store them in an airtight container and keep refrigerated for up to 1 week.

Midnight BALLS

+QP +SF +GF

This recipe is nothing short of a crowd pleaser. Chocolaty energy balls are low in sugar and high in healthy fats—a kind of dream snack for the health enthusiast in your life. They're a serious contender for best dessert when you're craving something sweet but don't want to overdue it. A few midnight balls are a great choice to end the night. —MR

MAKES 12 BALLS

⅔ cup (112 g) unsalted almonds

⅔ cup (78 g) rolled oats (gluten-free)

⅓ cup (60 g) almond butter, or to your liking

2 tbsp (14 g) raw cacao powder

3 tbsp (42 g) coconut oil

3 tbsp (45 ml) nut milk

⅓ cup (57 g) Medjool dates, pitted

1 tsp vanilla extract

1 tsp ground cinnamom

Pinch of salt

Blend all the ingredients in a food processor until smooth. Then roll the mixture into small balls and enjoy! I like to store mine in the fridge or freezer for a preworkout snack and for a midnight (more like 9 p.m.) treat.

Ginger and Orange ZEST BALLS

+QP +SF +GF

Ginger and orange zest balls live on the adventurous side of the energy-ball spectrum. Unexpected pops of heat from the ginger flavor each bite, forging an irresistible take on a classic. Try them for yourself; you'll soon see why these zesty balls will become your new go-to. —MR

MAKES 12 TO 14 BALLS

1 cup (110 g) raw unsalted cashews

17 Medjool dates, pitted

1 tsp ground cinnamom

1½ tbsp (11 g) ground ginger or ½" to 1" (1.3- to 2.5-cm) piece fresh ginger, grated

Zest of 1 large orange

Pinch of sea salt

Place all of the ingredients into a food processor. Blend it up until the nuts and dates have broken down and formed a big sticky ball, about 1 minute. Roll the mixture into 1-inch (2.5-cm) balls and store in the fridge for up to a few weeks!

five

SOUPS & SALADS

Soup and salad go together like mornings and coffee, popcorn and movies, vegan cheese and wine . . . You get the picture. The wonderful thing about making a meal of the two is that you're almost always guaranteed to get an abundance of vegetables and enjoy every last bite of them.

Another wonderful thing about soup and salad is that they're always in season. Soup isn't just a cold weather food, as salads aren't just for hot and sultry days. You can enjoy them at any time of year. This chapter has 62 delicious options for you to choose from. Pick from one of 34 soups and then pair it with one of the 28 mouthwatering salad recipes. For example, on a scorching summer day, make Emily's Chilled Ginger Berry Watermelon Soup with Mint (page 223) and pair it with Marie's Perfect Summer Salad (page 236). On a cold and snowy day when all you want to do is hibernate with a blanket and a good book, make Amber's Creamy Tomato Soup with Homemade Cashew Cream (page 204) and her Vegan Caesar Salad with Homemade Dill Croutons (page 232).

Feeding a crowd? Soup and salad are the perfect duo to make entertaining easy. Make a couple of pots of soup, such as Linda and Alex's Cheesy Broccoli Soup (page 219) and Roasted Sweet Potato Chili (page 217). Add a few salad options, such as Marie's Fresh Orange and Fennel Salad (page 235) and Amber's Tangy Purple Cabbage Slaw with Dijon and Horseradish (page 231), and you've got a party.

CHICK'N TORTILLA
Soup

This soup is a step up from the stuff I was making way back when, for sure, and it takes less than an hour from start to finish. I added lots of onions, bell peppers and fresh lime juice, plus some vegan chicken—which gets more and more realistic every day. But if you're avoiding gluten, ditch the faux meat and just enjoy a delicious, veggie-loaded tortilla soup instead! —AS

SERVES 4 TO 6

1 tbsp (15 ml) oil

4 cloves garlic, minced

1 large onion, diced

1 large bell pepper, diced

2 medium tomatoes, diced

4 cups (945 ml) vegetable broth

2 limes, freshly juiced (about ⅓ cup [80 ml] juice)

1 bay leaf

1 tsp chili powder

1 tsp ground cumin

1 tsp salt

½ tsp cayenne

½ tsp smoked paprika

4 oz (113 g) vegan chick'n (Any meat-free variety that you prefer works just fine! I like Chick Seitan.)

FOR SERVING
Tortilla chips

Freshly chopped cilantro

In a large pot, heat the oil over medium heat. Sauté the garlic, onion and pepper until softened. Add your tomatoes, veggie broth, lime juice, bay leaf, spices and vegan chik'n. Simmer, stirring occasionally, for 30 to 40 minutes. When ready, serve with tortilla chips and cilantro. This soup keeps for about a week in the fridge.

Creamy
TOMATO SOUP WITH HOMEMADE CASHEW CREAM

+GF

Unlike store-bought cans, this soup is loaded with fresh vegetables, flavorful herbs and a secret ingredient: my homemade cashew cream! It adds a richness in texture and slight nutty flavor that brings this soup from average to excellent. It's simple to prepare and even easier to reheat later. Tastes best alongside a gooey grilled cheese sandwich! —AS

SERVES 6 TO 8

CASHEW CREAM
1 cup (110 g) raw cashews

1 cup (235 ml) water

TOMATO SOUP
2½ lbs (1.1 kg) tomatoes

4 tbsp (60 g) vegan butter or (60 ml) olive oil

2 medium yellow onions

6 cloves garlic

1 qt (940 ml) vegetable broth (or water)

2 bay leaves

½ cup (20 g) chopped fresh basil

1 tsp salt

½ tsp pepper

Roasted cherry tomatoes or fresh basil, for garnish

FOR THE CASHEW CREAM

Soak the cashews in warm water for 1 to 4 hours. Then drain, pour into a blender and add 1 cup (235 ml) water. Blend until the consistency is creamy and no cashew chunks remain. Set it aside.

FOR THE TOMATO SOUP

Wash, weigh and chop your tomatoes. Set them aside.

In a large soup pot, melt the butter. Add the chopped onions and garlic, and sauté for about 8 minutes, until the onions are translucent but not caramelized. Add the tomatoes and continue to cook until the onions and tomatoes are completely softened, about 15 to 20 minutes.

Add the vegetable broth, bay leaves, basil, salt and pepper, and cook over medium heat for about 30 minutes, until the smell of garlic and basil are wafting through the air. Remove the bay leaves and toss them in the compost. Pour the cashew cream into the pot, and using a regular or immersion blender, blend the soup until creamy, usually about 20 seconds in my Vitamix.

Serve this immediately while warm or simmer over low heat until ready to serve. Garnish with roasted cherry tomatoes, a drizzle of cashew cream or fresh basil leaves.

Keeps in the fridge for about a week, and makes great leftovers!

Moroccan CHICKPEA SOUP

+GF +QP

For such a simple broth, this soup is incredibly rich in flavor, blending sweet cinnamon with spicy cumin. Packed with protein from the chickpeas and vitamins A and K from the fresh spinach, this soup is a powerhouse of nutrients and good-for-you ingredients. But the best part? It'll warm you up from the inside out and keep you content all day. —AS

SERVES 6 TO 8

1 tbsp (14 g) coconut oil

1 large onion, diced

2 cloves garlic, minced

3 (15-oz [425-g]) cans chickpeas, or about 6 cups (984 g) cooked chickpeas, drained

1 (15-oz [425-g]) can diced tomatoes (about 2 cups [400 g])

4 cups (945 ml) vegetable broth

1 tsp ground cinnamon

1 tsp ground cumin

1 tsp paprika

¼ tsp cayenne pepper

1 tsp salt

½ tsp pepper

3 packed cups (150 g) fresh spinach

Drizzle of extra-virgin olive oil (optional)

In a soup pot, melt the coconut oil over medium heat. Add the onions and garlic and sauté for about 5 to 7 minutes, until the onions are softened and slightly translucent. Add the chickpeas, tomatoes, vegetable broth and spices. Stir to combine, and simmer over low heat for about 40 minutes. While simmering, wash your fresh spinach and roughly chop it into bite-size pieces. When the 40 minutes are up, taste a bite and check the tenderness of the chickpeas. They should be soft, with a slight toothiness when bitten. If they're still a little firm, throw the soup on for another 10 minutes to soften them up. Once the soup is ready to be served, add your spinach and stir, letting the heat wilt the spinach. Serve immediately with a drizzle of extra-virgin olive oil.

Note: If you throw all the spinach in and don't eat it all, don't fret. The soup can be refrigerated and the spinach will still taste great, it will just have lost its bright green color and be considerably softer. Whenever I reheat this soup, I throw in another handful of fresh spinach to give it a little more body.

Roasted BUTTERNUT SQUASH AND APPLE SOUP

+GF +SF

I love soups of all kinds, shapes, and sizes and will put just about anything into a pot with some vegetable broth. One of my favorite cozy fall soups right now is this super easy Roasted Butternut Squash and Apple Soup. It packs a ton of flavor into a ridiculously easy recipe, and is such a great way to throw some beta carotene–rich butternut squash into your diet! We like to use tart green apples, but you can use whatever apples you have on hand. We also like to blend the soup to an ultra velvety texture in our blender, but keeping some chunks in it is great if that's your style, too. It tastes great paired with naan or crusty bread and a sprinkle of toasted pepitas and nutmeg. Make a batch for dinner tonight or pour it into a thermos and take it for lunch at work all week long. —AS

SERVES 6

3 lb (1.4 kg) butternut squash, peeled, deseeded and cut into 1" (2.5-cm) cubes

1 tsp plus 1 tbsp (14 g) coconut oil, divided

1 tsp salt

½ tsp pepper

2 small yellow onions, chopped

2 cloves garlic, minced

2 medium carrots, sliced

2 celery stalks, sliced

2 tart green apples (or any apples), cored and chopped

4 cups (945 ml) vegetable broth or water

Pinch of nutmeg, plus more for garnish (optional)

Toasted pepitas, for garnish (optional)

Preheat the oven to 400°F (204°C). Place the butternut squash on a parchment paper–lined baking sheet. Drizzle with 1 teaspoon of the coconut oil and a sprinkle of salt and pepper and bake for about 30 minutes, flipping halfway through. Set it aside to cool.

While the squash roasts, heat the remaining 1 tablespoon (14 g) coconut oil over medium heat in a large pot or Dutch oven. Sauté the onions and garlic for about 5 minutes, until they become fragrant and softened. Toss in the carrots and celery, and sauté them together with the garlic and onions for another 2 to 3 minutes. Toss in the apples, vegetable broth and nutmeg, and bring it to a boil.

Reduce the heat, cover and simmer for 30 minutes.

Remove the pan from the heat, toss in the roasted squash and blend using an immersion blender or (for extra creamy soup) a high-speed blender. Blend in batches, if needed. Pour your blended soup back into the pot, and serve immediately with toasted pepitas and a sprinkle of nutmeg for garnish. This soup keeps well in the fridge for about a week and freezes indefinitely.

Note: Don't have butternut squash? Substitute any type of squash you like, or use sweet potatoes!

Creamy WILD MUSHROOM SOUP

+GF +SF

I used to vehemently despise mushrooms. The real problem was just that I had never had them prepared in a way I liked. This soup was a revelation! The earthy, umami mushroom flavor works so well when tempered with the mild cashew cream and fresh thyme. It's so rich and creamy, no one will miss the dairy. You might even convince a few fungi-haters to change their minds! —AS

SERVES 6 TO 8

CASHEW CREAM

¾ cup (130 g) raw cashews

¾ cup (180 ml) warm water

⅛ tsp salt

SOUP

2 tbsp (30 ml) olive oil

2 cloves garlic, minced

1 large yellow onion, chopped

½ lb (235 g) assorted roughly chopped mushrooms (see Note)

¼ cup (60 ml) good-quality cooking sherry

3 cups (720 ml) vegetable broth

1½ tsp (2 g) fresh chopped thyme, plus more for garnish

1 tbsp (14 g) salt

1 tsp ground pepper

FOR THE CASHEW CREAM

In a medium bowl, soak your cashews in the warm water. Set them aside to soften.

FOR THE SOUP

In a large soup pot or Dutch oven, heat the olive oil over medium heat. Sauté the garlic, onions and mushrooms until softened and fragrant, about 5 minutes. Pour in the sherry and continue cooking for about 5 more minutes, stirring occasionally, until the sherry liquid reduces by about half. Add the vegetable broth, fresh thyme, salt and pepper, and simmer for 20 to 30 minutes.

While the soup simmers, finish the cashew cream by blending the soaked cashews and the water they're soaking in, plus a pinch of salt, to create a thick cream. Pour into the simmering soup, and remove the soup from the heat. Using an immersion or high-speed blender, carefully blend the soup in batches. Garnish with fresh thyme. Serve immediately or reheat for up to a week.

Note: You can use whatever type of mushrooms you prefer. We've used wild foraged mushrooms, cremini, button or a mix! It's all delicious.

CHICKPEA NOODLE
Soup

+SF

Whether you're sick with a fever or a broken heart, this soup is the answer. We replaced the chicken in this classic comfort food with chickpeas to give you the protein you need to help recover when you're feeling sick, and the broth filled with fresh thyme and garlic will smell so good your sinuses will want to clear up all on their own! If you're still heartbroken, a little ice cream probably wouldn't hurt, either. —AS

SERVES 6

2 tbsp (30 ml) olive oil

2 medium onions, chopped

4 medium carrots, thinly sliced

4 celery stalks, thinly sliced

4 cloves garlic, minced

6–8 sprigs fresh thyme

1 bay leaf

2 qt (1892 ml) vegetable broth

8 oz (227 g) whole wheat rotini noodles (or use gluten-free noodles)

1 cup (164 g) cooked chickpeas

Salt and pepper, to taste

Chopped fresh parsley, for garnish

Crackers or bread, for garnish

In a cast-iron Dutch oven or large soup pot, heat the olive oil over medium heat until melted.

Add the onions, carrots, celery, garlic, fresh thyme and bay leaf, and sauté until your veggies are softened but not browned.

Add the vegetable broth and bring it to a boil.

Once the soup is boiling, add the noo[...] chickpeas and cook for about 8 minutes, [...] noodles are almost completely cooked (do[...] they'll continue cooking in the water). Ad[...] pepper, to taste.

Remove it from heat and serve with freshly [...] parsley and salty crackers or bread.

Leftover soup can be refrigerated for up to [...] frozen indefinitely and reheated as neede[...]

*SEE PHOTO INSERT

LOBSTER MUSHROOM
Bisque

+GF +SF

This recipe is total fancy restaurant food. Your friends will think you called in and picked up an order because how else could you have whipped up such a stunning, creamy, rich, velvety soup? I'll be surprised if there are leftovers. —AS

SERVES 6

CASHEW CREAM

2 cups (480 ml) hot water

1 cup (110 g) raw cashews

1 cup (240 ml) water

BISQUE

4 tbsp (60 g) vegan butter, divided

3 cloves garlic, minced

1 medium yellow onion, chopped

2 medium carrots, thinly sliced

2 medium celery stalks, thinly sliced

3 oz (85 g) dried lobster mushrooms or 1 lb (455 g) fresh lobster mushrooms (see Note)

½ cup (120 ml) white cooking wine

2 tbsp (20 g) all-purpose flour

6 cups (1420 ml) vegetable broth

½ tsp salt

¼ tsp pepper

Fresh parsley, for garnish

FOR THE CASHEW CREAM

Start by pouring the hot water and cashews into a bowl to soak for at least 30 minutes. Drain the water. Pour the soaked cashews and the next cup of water into a blender and blend until creamy. Pour it into a bowl and set it aside.

FOR THE BISQUE

Heat 1 tablespoon (15 g) of the vegan butter in a large soup pot or Dutch oven over medium heat. Sauté the garlic, onion, carrots, celery and mushrooms together until soft, about 5 to 6 minutes. Deglaze with the white wine and cook until the liquid reduces, about 3 to 5 minutes.

Add the remaining 3 tablespoons (45 g) vegan butter and flour, stirring to combine. Cook for about 5 minutes. Then pour in the vegetable broth, salt and pepper, and simmer for 30 minutes.

When the soup is ready, blend the soup with a high-speed or immersion blender until smooth. Pour in the cashew cream, stirring to combine. Serve with fresh parsley!

Note: Lobster mushrooms can be expensive. Buying them dried online is your best bet!

Fresh Herb AND WATERMELON GAZPACHO

+GF +SF

Gazpacho is a liquid salad that's perfect when you think you're too hot to eat. You don't have to heat up the house to make it, and you can make it ahead of time. That's my kind of hot weather dinner! —KH

SERVES 4

2 cups (320 g) chopped heirloom tomatoes, plus more for garnish

3 cups (160 g) chopped watermelon

1 small hot pepper, seeded with the ribs removed

Juice of 1 lime or lemon

½–1 cup (120–235 ml) tomato juice or water

2 tbsp (30 ml) olive oil (omit to make oil-free)

1 clove garlic, minced

½ cucumber, diced

1 small yellow bell pepper, cored and diced

2 tbsp (5 g) chopped fresh basil (lemon or lime basil works great)

Big handful of chopped fresh mint (orange or lime mint is my favorite), plus more for garnish

Salt and pepper, to taste

Purée the heirloom tomatoes, watermelon, hot pepper, lime or lemon juice, tomato juice (or water), olive oil and garlic in a blender or food processor until relatively smooth.

Pour the mixture into a large bowl or pitcher, and add the minced veggies and herbs.

Stir with a spoon to mix everything together.

Take a final taste, and decide if you need to adjust the salt and pepper or add any more herbs or lime juice.

Put it in the fridge to chill for at least an hour. Garnish with fresh mint and chopped tomatoes.

Easy CUBAN BLACK BEAN SOUP

+GF +SF

A dear friend of mine once said that soup is only for winter. While I love her, she's just plain wrong, especially regarding this soup. This Cuban Black Bean Soup is so fresh, comforting, zesty and cozy that it should be titled "throughout the seasons soup." Serve it up alongside a vegan grilled cheese in the winter to get you through those cold winter nights or top it off with some fresh guac over the summer for a refreshing dinner. —LM + AM

SERVES 6

2 (15-oz [425-g]) cans black beans, rinsed and drained

2 red bell peppers

1 large poblano pepper

1 tsp extra-virgin olive oil, plus more for brushing

1 medium red onion

1 large shallot

½ cup (120 ml) red wine

1 tbsp (7 g) smoked paprika

1 tsp ground cumin

Juice of 1 lime

1 tsp chopped fresh sage

1 cup (40 g) fresh cilantro, divided

Sea salt and black pepper, to taste

Brown sugar (optional)

TOPPINGS

Diced tomato

Vegan pepper jack cheese, for garnish

Cilantro

Place the beans in a medium pot and cover with water. Bring to a boil and simmer over low heat for about 40 minutes.

While the beans are cooking, quarter and core the peppers. Place them skin-side up on a baking sheet, brush them with a thin layer of olive oil (optional) and broil them until the skins are blackened.

Dice the onion and shallot, and sauté them in a medium skillet with the olive oil over medium heat until the onions caramelize, about 15 minutes.

Deglaze the onions with the red wine and transfer to the pot with the beans.

After the peppers have cooled a bit, scrape off the blackened skins, chop them coarsely and add them to the pot of beans.

Add enough water to the pot (about 1 to 2 cups [240 to 480 ml]) to allow an immersion blender to purée the beans and peppers.

Add the smoked paprika, cumin, lime juice, sage and half of the cilantro to the pot. Purée the mixture with the immersion blender.

Add the salt and black pepper to taste.

If the paprika gives the soup a bitter flavor, add a small quantity of brown sugar to adjust. If the soup seems a little too spicy, whisk in a bit of olive oil.

Dice the tomato and squeeze out the seeds. Add the remainder of the cilantro and a dash of salt to the tomato; toss to combine.

Garnish the soup with a sprinkle of cheese, a sprig of cilantro and a mound of chopped tomato in the center of the bowl.

*SEE PHOTO INSERT

Roasted CARROT, GARLIC AND ROSEMARY SOUP

+GF +SF

If asked to pick one word to describe this soup, it would have to be elegant. There's simply no other way to describe it. The sweetness of the carrots, the bite of the garlic and the earthiness of the rosemary all work together to create a truly elevated soup. —LM + AM

SERVES 6

12 large carrots

2 tsp (10 ml) extra-virgin olive oil

Salt and pepper

4 cloves garlic, peeled

2 tbsp (5 g) fresh rosemary

3 cups (720 ml) plain unsweetened almond milk, divided

Preheat the oven to 400°F (204°C).

Peel and slice your carrots lengthwise. Place the carrots on a lined baking sheet and drizzle the olive oil on top. Sprinkle some salt and pepper on top. Roast the carrots for 10 minutes.

Reduce the heat of the oven to 375°F (190°C) and add the garlic to the baking tray. Flip the carrots and toss the garlic cloves in the pan to make sure they're coated in olive oil. Roast for 15 minutes.

Turn the carrots one last time and roast for another 15 minutes.

Add the rosemary to the carrots and roast for 5 minutes. Remove the carrots from the oven and allow them to cool for about 5 minutes.

Place the carrots, garlic and rosemary in a high-speed blender with 1½ cups (360 ml) of the almond milk. Blend it all until smooth and uniform in consistency, about 2 minutes.

Pour the soup into a medium saucepan and add the remaining 1½ cups (360 ml) almond milk. Stir to combine. Heat the soup over medium-low heat until it reaches your desired temperature. At this point, taste and add additional salt and pepper if needed.

*SEE PHOTO INSERT

MINESTRONE SOUP **with Arugula**

+GFO +SF

This is the soup of versatility. Whether you're sick, feeling super healthy, feeding the masses or just feeding yourself, this soup is the answer. The mass quantity of vegetables and beans will leave you feeling full without having to sacrifice any of your health goals to get there. —LM + AM

SERVES 4

1 tsp olive oil

1 yellow onion, chopped

2 cloves garlic, minced

6 large tomatoes, quartered

¾ cup (83 g) green beans, sliced into bite-size pieces

1 (15-oz [425-g]) can cannellini beans, rinsed and drained

¼ cup (10 g) chopped flat-leaf parsley

6 cups (1420 ml) vegetable stock

¾ cup (75 g) orzo pasta (use gluten-free)

Salt and pepper, to taste

2 cups (80 g) arugula, plus more for garnish

Vegan Parmesan, for garnish

(continued)

Heat the olive oil over medium heat in a large stockpot. Once the olive oil is heated, add the onion and sauté until it becomes translucent. This should take about 5 minutes. Once the onion is translucent, add the garlic and tomatoes. Cook for 2 minutes.

Add the green beans, cannellini beans, parsley, stock and pasta. Bring the mixture to a boil.

Quickly reduce to a simmer and cook for 40 minutes. Stir the soup occasionally to prevent it from sticking to the bottom of the pot. When the pasta is done cooking and the soup has thickened, add the salt and pepper, to taste.

Stir in the arugula and allow it to wilt for about 1 minute.

To serve, top the soup with more arugula and the vegan Parmesan cheese.

CREAM OF CELERY
Soup

+GF +SFO

We know what you're thinking: of all the soups why a cream of celery? Are we right? Well, we were even a little surprised by the notion when we first created this vegan cream of celery. But you know what? This soup is probably one of the best we've ever tried. It's creamy and light at the same time and the flavor will leave you not wanting to share even a drop of this recipe.

—LM + AM

SERVES 4

1 head celery, bottom removed and cut in half
1 tbsp (15 ml) water
1 medium white onion, diced
¼ cup (60 ml) white wine
1 tsp vegan butter (use soy-free)
2 cups (472 ml) plain unsweetened almond milk
¼ cup (15 g) chopped basil
1 tbsp (15 ml) lemon juice
1 tsp chopped fresh celery leaf
1 tsp fine sea salt, plus more to taste
½ tsp ground white pepper

Place a steamer basket in a large pot. Fill the pot with water until the water level reaches the bottom of the basket. Bring the water to a boil. Add the celery stalks to the basket in the pot. Cover the pot and let the celery steam for about 10 minutes, or until the celery is soft.

In a medium saucepan, add the water and heat over medium heat. When the water begins to steam, add the onion and stir. Turn the heat down to medium-low and cover the pan. Let the onions sweat for about 4 minutes. When the 4 minutes are up, deglaze the pan with the wine. Turn off the heat.

Add the butter to the pan and allow it to melt into the onion.

Put the almond milk, celery, onions, basil, lemon juice, celery leaf, salt and white pepper in the blender. Blend the ingredients on the soup setting, or on high speed, until smooth and creamy.

Pour the soup back into the pan that you used to cook the onions and heat to your desired temperature.

*SEE PHOTO INSERT

TORTILLA **Soup**

+GF +SF

Taking a spoonful of this soup truly transports you to your favorite Mexican restaurants, or even Mexico! Having taken many family vacations to Mexico, living in Chicago (which has great Mexican food by the way), and just generally being obsessed with this comforting cuisine, we had to create a vegan version of our favorite tortilla soup. —LM + AM

SERVES 4

1 jalapeño pepper

1 tbsp (15 ml) avocado oil

1 large Vidalia onion, minced

1 medium carrot, peeled and finely chopped

2 bell peppers, cored, seeded and minced

3 cloves garlic

1½ tsp (3 g) ground cumin

2 tsp (5 g) smoked paprika

1 tsp dried oregano

½ cup (120 ml) white wine (feel free to replace with vegetable broth if needed)

3 cups (720 ml) vegetable broth

1 tsp lime juice

1 medium tomato, seeded and chopped

1½ tsp (8 g) sea salt

Ground black pepper, to taste

1 cup (246 ml) canola oil

3 corn tortillas

TOPPINGS

1 avocado, peeled, pitted and sliced

½ cup (20 g) fresh cilantro

Roast the jalapeño over an open flame or in a 400°F (204°C) oven until the skin is blackened and blistered. This should take about 8 minutes per side, turning halfway through, in the oven. Once you remove the jalapeño from the flame or the oven, place the pepper on a plate and cover with a bowl. Allow the jalapeño to steam. Set aside.

Heat the avocado oil in a large soup pot over medium heat. Once the oil is heated, add the onion and the carrot. Cook for 5 minutes while stirring occasionally.

Add the bell peppers and cook for another 5 minutes or until the onion begins to caramelize. Stir occasionally to avoid scorching the vegetables.

Turn the heat to medium-low and add the garlic, cumin, smoked paprika and oregano. Stir well to thoroughly combine.

At this point, add the wine to deglaze the pan and stir well. Once deglazed, add the vegetable broth and lime juice. Stir the mixture to combine.

While letting the flavors of the soup sit together, scrape the blistered skin off the jalapeño pepper and remove the seeds. We suggest tasting the pepper a bit before putting the whole thing into the pot. Jalapeño peppers can vary in heat, so add as much or as little as you want according to your heat preference.

Add the tomato, salt and pepper, and stir to combine.

Allow the soup to simmer over low heat while you prep the tortilla crisps.

Heat the canola oil in a small sauté pan over medium heat. While it is heating, slice the tortillas into small strips. Test the heat of the oil by dropping in a small piece of tortilla. When the tortilla sizzles, you can add the first third of the tortilla strips. Stir the strips to separate them. When the tortilla sticks turn golden brown and start to curl, remove them from the oil and place them on a plate lined with paper towels.

(continued)

SOUPS & SALADS

Repeat this process until all of the tortilla strips are fried.

Once the tortilla crisps are done, use an immersion blender to blend the soup until it's thick and creamy.

Garnish the soup with the fried tortilla matchsticks, avocado slices and fresh cilantro.

Curried PUMPKIN AND BUTTERNUT SQUASH STEW

+GF +SF

What is it about the word stew that makes a meal just sound cozy? Like all you want to do is wrap yourself up in your favorite blanket and eat it in front of a fireplace. Well, for this particular stew, that's exactly what you're going to want to do. Let the warmth of the spices, pumpkin, and butternut squash break through a cold winter's day. —LM + AM

SERVES 4

1 tbsp (14 g) coconut oil

1 medium yellow onion, diced

1 medium butternut squash, peeled, seeded and finely diced

2 cloves garlic, minced

4 cups (945 ml) vegetable broth

1 (15-oz [420-ml]) can coconut milk

1 (15-oz [425 g]) can pumpkin purée

1 tbsp (7 g) yellow curry powder

1 tsp ground cinnamon

1 tsp ground nutmeg

1 tbsp (15 g) fine sea salt

½ tsp ground ginger

½ tsp ground coriander

½ tsp ground turmeric

¼ tsp ground cardamom

1 head cauliflower, core removed and broken into florets

1 (15-oz [425-g]) can chickpeas, rinsed and drained

1 large tomato, seeded and finely diced

In a large stockpot, heat the oil over medium heat. When the oil is hot, add the onion and butternut squash. Stir well. Cook the onion until it is translucent and the edges of the squash are beginning to brown. This should take about 10 minutes. Make sure you're stirring the mixture frequently.

When the onion is translucent, add the garlic and stir to combine. Cook for another 2 minutes. Stir frequently to prevent the garlic from burning. If the garlic burns, the soup will taste bitter.

Add the broth, coconut milk, pumpkin purée and all of the spices. Stir well until the ingredients are well combined. Add the cauliflower and chickpeas. Bring the soup to a boil and quickly reduce to a low simmer. Stir the soup frequently.

Cook for about 40 minutes, stirring frequently. Add the tomato and stir to combine. Cook for 10 more minutes, and serve.

Homemade YELLOW CURRY POTATO SOUP

+GF +SF

We could eat curry every day all day, and this soup is one of our favorites. It has lots of savory and warm spices, a little heat from serrano peppers, creamy potatoes, red bell pepper, tomatoes, protein-rich peas and fresh cilantro. It's healthy, it's delicious and it's easy. What more could you ask for? —LM + AM

SERVES 4 TO 6

1 tsp extra-virgin olive oil or 3 tbsp (45 ml) water if you don't cook with oil

1 yellow onion, finely chopped

1 red bell pepper, seeded and cut into thin matchsticks

1 or 2 serrano peppers, seeded and cut into thin matchsticks (check the first one for heat and add according to your tastes)

4–5 small yellow potatoes, peeled and cut into small cubes

2 (14-oz [385-ml]) cans lite coconut milk

1 (14-oz [397-g]) can diced tomatoes

3 tsp (7 g) ground curry

1½ tsp (3 g) ground cumin

1 tsp ground turmeric

½ tsp nutmeg

⅛ tsp ground cloves

1 cinnamon stick or ½ tsp ground cinnamon

½ tsp ground black pepper

Sea salt, to taste

1 cup (134 g) frozen peas

1 cup (41 g) finely chopped cilantro

In a large soup pot, heat the oil or the water over medium-high heat, and add the onion and red bell pepper. Cook until they begin to soften, approximately 7 minutes.

Add the serrano pepper and stir to combine. Cook for 5 minutes.

Add the potatoes, coconut milk and tomatoes, and bring to a boil.

Reduce the heat to a low simmer, and add the spices. Stir well to combine and simmer for 20 minutes.

Add the peas and stir to combine. Simmer for 10 minutes.

Add the cilantro and stir to combine.

Smoky Vegan
CORN AND POTATO CHOWDER

+GF +SF

This soup is so hearty, so satisfying and so darn good! Inspired by our long-ago love of clam chowder, we took out the clams, added corn and a little liquid smoke to give it a wonderful smoky flavor, and added extra potatoes for the thick and creamy texture. You're going to love this soup all year round. —LM + AM

SERVES 4 TO 6

2 qt (1880 ml) low-sodium vegetable broth, divided

1 large sweet yellow onion, finely chopped

¼ cup (60 ml) white wine (optional; you can also use a little vegetable broth to deglaze the pan)

3 cups (410 g) frozen yellow corn

3 medium potatoes (we used Yukon gold), peeled and cut into bite-size cubes

2 tsp (5 g) smoked paprika

1 tsp ground white pepper

3 tsp (15 ml) liquid smoke

1½ tsp (8 g) fine sea salt, or to taste

¼ tsp cayenne pepper, or to taste

TOPPINGS (OPTIONAL)
Coconut "bacon"
Chopped baby arugula

In a large soup pot, heat 3 tablespoons (45 ml) of the vegetable broth over medium-high heat. When the broth is hot, add the onion and stir well. Cook for 5 minutes and stir occasionally. Add the wine or more vegetable broth to deglaze the pan.

Once the pot is deglazed, add the remaining vegetable broth, corn and potatoes. Stir to combine, and bring to a boil. Reduce the heat to a low simmer and add the paprika, pepper, liquid smoke, salt and cayenne, if you want the chowder to be spicy. Stir well to combine.

Cook for about 30 minutes, or until the potatoes are easily pierced with a fork.

Remove 2 cups (470 ml) of the soup from the pot and place it in a small bowl. Set it aside.

Use an immersion blender or transfer to a standing blender and blend the remaining soup in the pot until it's mostly creamy. There might be a few bits of potato and/or corn—that's fine. Now put the 2 cups (470 ml) of the soup that you removed back into the soup pot and stir to combine.

Garnish with coconut "bacon" and finely chopped baby arugula, if desired.

Roasted SWEET POTATO CHILI

+GF +SF

We love sweet potatoes and try to find as many ways as possible to use them. Putting them in chili is one of our favorite ways to eat them. The spicy heat from the chili is the perfect complement to the sweetness of the potato. They also add a gorgeous pop of color for interest—not to mention, they're so good for you.

—LM + AM

SERVES 6 TO 8

3 medium sweet potatoes, peeled and diced into bite-size cubes

2 tbsp (30 ml) extra-virgin olive oil, divided

Salt and pepper, to taste

1 poblano chile pepper

1 red onion, chopped

1 medium carrot, peeled and finely chopped

3 celery stalks, leaves on, diced

1 orange bell pepper, seeded and chopped

1 bay leaf

1 tbsp (8 g) ground cumin

¼ tsp chipotle chile powder, add slowly to taste

1 tsp paprika

1 tbsp (8 g) chili powder, add more if desired

3 cloves garlic, minced

½ cup (120 ml) white wine

4–6 cups (960–1440 ml) boiling water

2 (15-oz [425-g]) cans kidney beans, rinsed and drained

2 medium tomatoes, seeded and diced

½ cup (20 g) coarsely chopped cilantro

Preheat the oven to 400°F (204°C).

Spread the potatoes out evenly on a baking sheet and drizzle with 1 tablespoon (15 ml) of the olive oil, grinding salt and pepper over them to taste. Toss the potatoes to coat and roast for 10 minutes. Turn the potatoes and roast for another 10 minutes. Turn the potatoes and roast for 5 to 10 minutes, or until the potatoes are golden and fork tender. They shouldn't be hard and crunchy, just firm. Remove from the oven and set aside.

Roast the poblano pepper over an open flame on a gas cooktop, or in a 400°F (204°C) oven, until the skin is blistered and mostly black. Turn often while roasting. Cool on a plate with a bowl over it so it steams.

In a large stockpot, heat the remaining 1 tablespoon (15 ml) olive oil over medium heat. When the oil is hot, add the onion, carrot and celery. Stir the mixture and cook for 5 minutes, tossing frequently. Add the bell pepper, stir to combine and cook for 4 minutes.

Add the bay leaf, cumin, chipotle chile powder, paprika, chili powder and garlic; stir to combine. This will release the flavors in the spices. Cook for 2 minutes. Deglaze the pan with the wine, and then add just enough hot water to cover the vegetables. Bring it to a boil.

Scrape the blistered skin off of the poblano pepper and seed it. Dice and test the pepper to see how hot it is. Add it to the chili according to your taste.

Add the beans and cover with more water. Don't fill the pan, you just want enough water to cover the vegetables and beans. Bring it to a boil and then reduce the heat to a gentle simmer.

Add the tomatoes and simmer for 1½ hours, or until the chili thickens. Stir frequently to avoid scorching. Add salt and black pepper to taste along with the sweet potatoes. Cook for 10 minutes. Add the cilantro, stir well and serve.

Creamy CHIK'N AND WILD RICE SOUP

+GFO +SFO

Eating this creamy and hearty soup on a cold winter's night is as comforting as being wrapped up in your favorite blanket with fuzzy socks. The velvety broth is the perfect partner for the rustic and chewy wild rice, and the earthy and savory flavors are so welcoming when the temperatures start to fall.

The base of the soup is simple vegetable broth with a classic roux to give it body. The chik'n is shredded jackfruit and the rest of the ingredients are exactly what you'd expect in wild rice soup: onion, celery, shallot, carrot and of course, wild rice. Together, these whole foods come together as one body and soul–warming meal. —LM + AM

SERVES 6 TO 8

1 (20-oz [565-g]) can young green jackfruit in brine

1 tbsp (15 ml) extra-virgin olive oil or 3 tbsp (45 ml) vegetable broth

1 large white onion, finely chopped

1 shallot, finely chopped

2 celery stalks, finely chopped

2 medium carrots, peeled and finely chopped

2 cloves garlic, minced

¼ cup (60 ml) dry white wine

2 (32-oz [946-ml]) containers vegetable broth

1 cup (240 ml) water

1 cup (210 g) uncooked wild rice, rinsed

1 tbsp (3 g) dried Italian seasoning

1 bay leaf

6 tbsp (87 g) vegan butter (use soy-free)

½ cup (63 g) all-purpose flour (use gluten-

3 tbsp (45 ml) unsweetened almond or so

Salt and pepper, to taste

Preheat the oven to 375°F (190°C).

Drain the jackfruit and rinse well. Squ jackfruit to remove the excess liquid and p a rimmed baking sheet; bake for 15 minu cool and shred with two forks or in a food Set it aside.

In a large soup pot, heat the olive oil or broth over medium-high heat and add the jackfruit, onion, shal-lot, celery and carrots, and cook for 5 to 7 minutes, or until the onion becomes translucent. Stir often. Add the garlic and cook for 2 minutes. Deglaze the pan with the wine, making sure to scrape up the stuck-on bits and pieces. Add the vegetable broth, water, wild rice, Italian seasoning and bay leaf, and bring to a boil. Reduce the heat to a simmer and cook for 1 hour, or until the rice is cooked.

In a small saucepan, melt the butter over medium heat and whisk in the flour. Whisk continuously for 1 minute. Whisk in the almond milk, and keep whisking until it's smooth and creamy. Whisk it into the soup until it's well combined and simmer for 15 minutes. Remove the bay leaf before serving. Add salt and pepper to taste.

Cheesy BROCCOLI SOUP

+GF +SF

My mom's (Alex's grandma's) favorite soup is the broccoli cheese soup from Panera. Being the good daughter that I am, creating a vegan version that was just as creamy and flavorful was a duty that I took seriously. If I could convince her to love a whole food, plant-based version that would satisfy her taste buds, it would be a win for her and for me, because we could enjoy the same soup at one table. After about a half dozen tries to perfect the cheesy flavor, I finally nailed the recipe. The secret to this cheesy sauce is vegan Greek yogurt. The tanginess and the probiotics used in the yogurt mimic the same taste you'd find in cheddar cheese, and just as I expected, my mom loves my version even more than she loved the dairy version. I think you will, too. —LM + AM

SERVES 6 TO 8

CHEESE SAUCE

1 cup (112 g) raw cashews, soaked in boiling water for at least 4 hours

5 oz (142 g) plain vegan Greek yogurt (we use Kite Hill brand; see Note)

2 tbsp (10 g) nutritional yeast (not brewer's or rising yeast), add more if you want a strong cheese flavor

¼ cup (60 ml) water

½ tsp fine sea salt

SOUP

3 cups (450 g) broccoli florets

1 tbsp (15 ml) extra-virgin olive oil or 3 tbsp (45 ml) vegetable broth

3 carrots, peeled and chopped

2 celery stalks, chopped

1 large russet potato, peeled and chopped

2 cloves garlic, minced

¼ cup (60 ml) white wine or 1 tbsp (15 ml) white wine vinegar

2 (32-oz [946-ml]) containers vegetable broth

½ tsp smoked paprika

1 tbsp (5 g) nutritional yeast

Salt and pepper, to taste

TOPPINGS

Shredded vegan cheese

Toasted croutons

Green onion, chopped

FOR THE CHEESE SAUCE

Drain and rinse the soaked cashews and put them in a blender. Add the remaining cheese sauce ingredients and blend on high speed for 1 minute. Scrape the sides and blend for about 1 more minute, or until the sauce is smooth and velvety and you can't detect any small pieces of the nuts. Set it aside.

FOR THE SOUP

Put a steamer basket in a large pot and fill it with water, just to the top of the basket. Add the broccoli and bring the water to a boil. Cover and steam for about 8 to 10 minutes, or until the broccoli is just fork tender. Remove it from the pot and set it aside.

In a large soup pot, heat the oil or vegetable broth over medium-high heat. When the pan is hot, add the carrots, celery and potato, and cook, stirring often, for about 5 minutes, or until the carrot begins to brown slightly. Add the garlic and cook for 2 minutes. Deglaze the pan with the wine or vinegar. Make sure to stir the vegetables and scrape any pieces that are stuck to the pan. Add the vegetable broth, smoked paprika and nutritional yeast. Stir the mixture to combine and bring it to a boil, then reduce the heat to a simmer. Simmer for 20 minutes, or until the potato and carrots are fork tender. Add three-fourths of the broccoli and the cheese sauce, and blend with an immersion blender until thick and creamy, or blend in batches in a countertop blender. The yogurt in the cheese sauce will curdle when added to the hot soup. This is normal. As soon as you whip it up with the blender it will become smooth. Stir in the remaining broccoli and salt and pepper. Top with a sprinkle of cheese, croutons and green onion.

(continued)

SOUPS & SALADS

Note: What sets our cheese sauce apart from others we've tried is the Greek yogurt. It adds so much to the flavor of the sauce. If you can't find a vegan Greek yogurt, you can use a plain almond- or soy-milk yogurt. Just don't use coconut yogurt—that wouldn't turn out well.

Vegan MATZO BALL SOUP

If you're vegan and you love matzo ball soup, then you know how difficult it is to find a vegan version. We thought it was about time to make one that not only tasted like conventional matzo ball soup, but was also full of light and airy matzo balls—and here it is. The soup is lovely and flavorful, and the balls are absolutely perfect. They're light and tender and they float instead of sink when added to the broth. —LM + AM

SERVES 4

MATZO BALLS
4 level tbsp (38 g) vegan egg substitute (we suggest VeganEgg brand)

1 cup (240 ml) ice water

½ cup (86 g) matzo meal

½ tsp baking powder

1 tsp salt

1 tsp dried parsley

¼ tsp garlic powder

¼ tsp onion powder

Pepper, to taste

32 oz (946 ml) vegetable broth plus 32 oz (946 ml) water, or 64 oz (1.8 L) salted water

SOUP
1 tsp extra-virgin olive oil or 2 tbsp (30 ml) vegetable broth/water

1 large white or yellow onion, diced

3 carrots, diced

2 celery stalks with leaves, diced

2 cloves garlic, minced

64 oz (1.8 L) no-chicken broth or vegetable broth

3 tbsp (8 g) fresh minced dill

Salt and pepper, to taste

FOR THE MATZO BALLS
In a small bowl, whisk the vegan egg and the water until smooth and creamy.

In a medium bowl, whisk the dry ingredients until fully combined. Add the egg mixture to the dry and stir until fully combined. Cover and refrigerate for an hour so it sets.

Bring the broth and/or water to a boil.

Roll the matzo dough into 1-inch (2.5-cm) balls and add them to the boiling broth. Reduce the heat to a simmer. Cover and simmer for 30 to 40 minutes, or until the balls are floating and firm. Set it aside.

FOR THE SOUP
Heat the olive oil or broth/water in a large stockpot over medium heat and add the onion, carrots and celery. Stir and cook for 5 minutes, tossing occasionally to avoid scorching. Add the garlic and cook for 2 minutes.

Add the broth and bring to a boil, then reduce to a simmer. Cook for about 45 minutes, or until the vegetables are fork tender. Stir in the dill and salt and pepper, and serve in shallow bowls with the matzo balls.

Forbidden BROTH

Simple and healthy ingredients, rich with bold flavors and umami, make this nourishing broth a welcome reprieve from bitterly cold winter temperatures, and the most perfect supper after long days at work or school.
—CS

SERVES 3 TO 4

1 tbsp (15 ml) toasted sesame oil

1 bunch (about 11 oz [311 g]) baby bok choy, harder parts minced, leaves chopped and kept separate (all thoroughly washed and drained)

3½ oz (100 g) fresh shiitake mushrooms, trimmed and chopped (gently washed and drained)

1½ tsp (8 ml) shoyu

1 packed cup (200 g) drained vegan kimchi, chopped

1 large clove garlic, minced

2 cups (390 g) cooked Good Morning Miso Rice (page 383) or any cooked rice

3 cups (705 ml) filtered water

3 tbsp (45 ml) kimchi brine

1 tbsp (6 g) dried shiitake powder

1½ tsp (8 g) Asian hot chile paste or sambal oelek (quantity to taste)

3 tbsp (54 g) white miso

GARNISHES
Thinly sliced cubes of Tare Tofu (page 183)

Thinly sliced scallion

Chopped fresh cilantro

In a large pot, heat the oil over medium-high heat. Add the white, harder parts of the bok choy and the mushrooms. Cook until the bok choy just becomes tender yet remains crisp, and the mushrooms have rendered their moisture, about 4 minutes. Add the green parts of the bok choy, shoyu, kimchi and garlic, and cook for another 2 minutes or until the greens have wilted. Stir the rice into the vegetables and set it aside.

In a medium saucepan, bring the water, kimchi brine, shiitake powder and chile paste to a boil. Place the miso paste in a small, heat-resistant bowl. Remove ½ cup (120 ml) of the hot liquid, and whisk it into the miso paste until well combined. Pour the miso mixture back into the hot liquid and whisk to combine.

Divide the vegetables and rice among 3 or 4 bowls. Top with your desired quantity of sliced tofu and divide the broth among the bowls. Top with the scallion and cilantro. Serve immediately.

*SEE PHOTO INSERT

Soothe-What-Ails
MISO BROTH

+QP

Whenever I feel under the weather, I crave hot broth. And whenever I crave hot broth, this one is my go-to. When I'm not feeling queasy, I pour it on top of already-cooked veggies, scallion, tofu and sometimes even noodles. It's highly adaptable, so tweak it according to your needs, make it your own and sip it up. —CS

SERVES 2

2 cups (470 ml) filtered water

2 tbsp (30 ml) kimchi brine

2 tsp (4 g) dried shiitake powder

½–1 tsp Emergency Broth Powder (optional, page 223)

1 tsp brown rice vinegar

½ tsp ground turmeric

1 packed tsp freshly grated ginger

1–2 cloves garlic, grated (to taste)

2 tbsp (36 g) white miso

In a small saucepan, whisk to combine the water, kimchi brine, shiitake powder, broth powder (if using), vinegar, turmeric, ginger and garlic. Just bring it to a boil and turn off the heat.

In a small bowl, add the miso and ¼ cup (60 ml) of the broth, whisking to dissolve the miso and combine. Transfer this mixture back into the saucepan with the remaining broth and whisk to combine. Divide the broth between 2 large mugs. Serve immediately.

*SEE PHOTO INSERT

Moroccan
MINESTRONE

+GFO

Also akin to a ratatouille, this thick minestrone is loaded with flavor as well as brightness and richness, thanks to the addition of pesto. I prefer adding the couscous just before eating, otherwise it loses its brilliant al dente texture if the minestrone isn't eaten the day it is prepared. For a potentially gluten-free outcome, consider using cooked quinoa instead of the couscous. —CS

SERVES 4

1 tbsp (15 ml) olive oil

2 shallots, minced

3 cloves garlic, minced

1 large green bell pepper, cored and diced

1 large tomato, diced

1½ tsp (3 g) dried porcini powder

1 tsp Ras el Hanout

1 tsp smoked paprika

½ tsp coarse kosher salt (to taste)

1–2 tsp (7–14 g) harissa paste

1½ cups (360 g) fire-roasted crushed tomatoes

1 cup (235 ml) vegetable broth

½ recipe Moroccan Marinated Vegetables (page 183)

1 cup (200 g) cooked lentils

1 generous cup (200 g) cooked Israeli couscous (al dente), or quinoa for gluten-free

Favorite vegan pesto and Kalamata olives, for serving

In a large pot, place the oil, shallots, garlic and bell pepper. Cook over medium-high heat until lightly browned, about 3 minutes. Stir occasionally. Add the tomato and cook for 1 minute. Add the porcini powder, Ras el Hanout, paprika and salt. Cook for 1 minute.

Once the bell pepper starts to soften and the tomato is starting to become juicy, add the harissa paste and crushed tomatoes. Cook for 1 minute. Add the broth and marinated vegetables, and bring them to a boil. Simmer the mixture, covered, for 10 minutes, stirring occasionally.

Add the lentils and couscous, and simmer for another 5 minutes without the lid on. Swirl about 1 tablespoon (20 g) of pesto into each bowl, and serve with olives on the side.

*SEE PHOTO INSERT

Emergency BROTH POWDER

+QP +GF +SF

Ready in mere seconds, this deceptively simple mix is actually loaded with complex flavors that will make your dishes a million times better than they already are. No joke: I've had several absolutely nonvegan-friendly folks ask what was cooking and if they could have some when pots of foods were simmering over the stove using that broth. You'll see—it'll happen to you, too. —CS

MAKES 1⅓ CUPS (150 G)

1 cup (80 g) nutritional yeast

1 tbsp (5 g) dried tomato powder

1 tbsp (5 g) dried mushroom powder

1 tbsp (3 g) Italian seasoning or a mix of dried basil, parsley and oregano

1 tbsp (18 g) coarse kosher salt

1 tsp onion powder

1 tsp garlic powder

1 tsp Aleppo-style pepper flakes or ½ tsp red pepper flakes

1 tsp smoked paprika

Place all of the ingredients in a large mason jar. Screw the lid tightly and shake it to thoroughly combine. Store the powder at room temperature or in the refrigerator for up to 1 month.

Chilled GINGER BERRY WATERMELON SOUP WITH MINT

This "soup" is ridiculously fresh, hydrating and juicy— it's magic in the summer. If calling it a soup makes it sound less appealing, just think of it as a smoothie or juice in a bowl. —EvE

SERVES 2

3 cups (460 g) chilled chopped watermelon (keep a few cubes for garnishing)

1 cup (255 g) frozen strawberries

¾ cup (195 g) frozen cherries

1 tbsp (8 g) grated fresh ginger

1 tsp baobab powder

1 tsp acerola cherry powder (optional)

¼ cup (60 ml) coconut milk

2 tbsp (5 g) mint

Blend all ingredients together until smooth. Garnish with watermelon cubes, frozen fruit and mint if you like. YAY.

TOMATO AVOCADO MUSHROOM CORN Soup

An excellent way of eating warm, raw meals in the colder months is in soups. You can use spices, garlic, onions, other vegetables and hot water to create creamy, flavorful, healthy bowls of goodness that will have everybody asking for more! This particular recipe uses garlic to add heat and avocado for creaminess. The other ingredients are fresh and bursting with nutrition and great taste. I like adding chopped veggies to the soup so that you have another texture. Grab a spoon! —EvE

SERVES 1

MARINATED MUSHROOMS
2 mushrooms, sliced
Extra-virgin olive oil
Tamari or soy sauce

SOUP
3 white mushrooms
2 heirloom tomatoes
½ avocado
1 cup (145 g) sweet corn
2–3 cups (470–710 ml) hot water
1 tbsp (18 g) miso paste
1 clove garlic

TOPPINGS
¼ cup (36 g) sweet corn
½ avocado, cubed
Basil

FOR THE MARINATED MUSHROOMS

Toss the mushrooms in a tiny bit of extra-virgin olive oil and tamari or soy sauce. Put them in a warm spot for 30 minutes or in the oven at a very low temperature for 10 to 15 minutes. They're ready when they have darkened and softened.

FOR THE SOUP

Blend all of the ingredients until smooth and soupy. Adjust them according to taste, adding water as needed. Pour the soup into a bowl. Then drop on the marinated mushrooms and other toppings and enjoy!

*SEE PHOTO INSERT

Red Kuri SQUASH SOUP WITH CUMIN, CORIANDER AND COCONUT

This soup is delicious, thick and creamy, and it makes ya warm from the inside out. Definitely made more awesome with fresh avocado toast, plenty of snow outside and a blanket 'round your bod. —EvE

SERVES 3 OR 4

1 (2-lb [905-g]) red kuri squash
1 tbsp (8 g) cumin seeds
1 tbsp (10 g) coriander seeds
¼ tsp ground cinnamon
¼ tsp ground nutmeg
½ tsp chipotle chile powder
1 tbsp (15 ml) tamari
1 tbsp (15 ml) rice vinegar
1 (14½-oz [428-ml]) can coconut milk
2 cloves garlic
1 tbsp (8 g) grated fresh ginger
3 cups (710 ml) vegetable broth or more, depending on your preference
½ cup (55 g) walnuts (optional)

Preheat the oven to 350°F (177°C). Chop the squash into 1-inch (2.5-cm) cubes (no need to peel). Toss the cubes with the cumin, coriander, cinnamon, nutmeg, chile powder, tamari and vinegar. Spread on a baking sheet. Bake for 30 to 40 minutes, or until tender all the way through.

Transfer the baked squash to a blender, and blend with the rest of the ingredients (you might need to do it in two or three batches if your blender is smaller or less powerful). If you need to add more broth, go ahead. Mine was super thick, and that's how I like it. Also: be careful not to over-blend, or the soup will get gluey.

Once blended to a smooth, creamy consistency, serve with avocado toast, crackers, as a sauce for vegetables or pasta or however you like!

*SEE PHOTO INSERT

Quick TOMATO SOUP WITH MISO AND THYME

SO GOOD. Get your heirloom tomatoes from the farmers' market—they are magic. And if you want the tomato flavor to be stronger, let them sit in the dehydrator at 115°F (46°C) for an hour or two before blending them with everything else (or in the oven at its lowest temperature). —EvE

SERVES 3 OR 4

4 cups (645 g) chopped heirloom tomatoes
3–5 cloves garlic
2 tbsp (36 g) miso paste
2 tbsp (36 g) tahini
2 tsp (10 ml) maple syrup
½ cup (120 ml) vegetable broth or water
¼ cup (45 g) cashew butter (optional)

TOPPINGS
2 tsp (1 g) fresh thyme
¼ tsp black pepper
1½ cups (246 g) cooked chickpeas

Blend all of the soup ingredients until smooth, adding garlic as you like and cashew butter if you want it creamier. Adjust amounts according to taste and desired consistency. If you'd like hot soup, simply warm it on the stove over medium-low until it begins to steam or bubble.

Pour the soup into bowls and top with thyme, pepper and chickpeas. Nom.

Thai-Style COCONUT SOUP (TOM KHA)

+GF

Thai-style tom kha is a soup spiced with chiles, coconut milk, lime juice, eggplant and mushrooms. An impressively aromatic soup that is thrown together quickly, it can be made in batches and enjoyed throughout a busy week. —MR

SERVES 4 TO 6

½ large eggplant (or 1 Japanese eggplant)
Handful cherry tomatoes
1 cup (75 g) any mushrooms
1½ cups (355 ml) low-sodium vegetable broth
1 (14-oz [414-ml]) can full-fat coconut milk
1 red pepper or chile, chopped, or pinch of red pepper flakes (optional)
1" (2.5-cm) piece fresh ginger, peeled and thinly sliced (or galangal, if you can find it)
2 lemongrass stalks
Juice of 2 limes
1 tbsp (12 g) coconut sugar
Sea salt, to taste
2 handfuls of fresh cilantro   (continued)

Cube the eggplant into small bite-size pieces. Then slice the cherry tomatoes and mushrooms into half-size pieces. Bring the veggie broth to a boil in a large Dutch oven over high heat. Once it's boiling, turn the heat down to a simmer and add the coconut milk, eggplant, pepper and ginger slices.

Take the bottom of a cup and smash down the lemongrass stalk; this helps to release the flavors. Now cut the lemongrass into 1-inch (2.5-cm) pieces, and add it to the broth as well. Once the eggplant is almost fully cooked, about 15 minutes, toss in the mushrooms, cherry tomatoes, lime juice, sugar and a pinch of salt, and let this simmer for about 10 minutes. Once the veggies have fully cooked, stir in the cilantro. Remove the lemongrass stalks and ginger slices from the soup, serve it in bowls and enjoy!

*SEE PHOTO INSERT

Warming COCONUT CURRY AND LENTIL SOUP

+SF +GF

This is an ideal dish for a gloomy night in, as it combines two fantastic meals: curry and lentil soup. Make sure to use red lentils, as this is a crucial component to the dish. Black lentils are too stiff and won't break down the way red lentils do, which adds to the creaminess of this soup. —MR

SERVES 4

2 tbsp (28 g) coconut oil or (30 ml) olive oil
1 small red onion, roughly chopped
1 celery stalk, thinly sliced
2 large carrots, cut into thin circles
Salt, to taste
1 (13½-oz [400-ml]) can full-fat coconut milk
2½–3 cups (590-710 ml) water

1½ tbsp (10 g) curry powder
1 thumb of ginger, grated, or 1 tsp ground ginger
Juice of ½ lemon
1 sweet potato, quartered and cubed
2 cups (400 g) red lentils, uncooked
Sprinkle of raw pumpkin seeds

Start by melting the coconut oil over medium heat in a large cooking pot. Toss in the red onion, celery and carrots. Sprinkle in a few pinches of salt and let this sauté for 10 minutes. Once the vegetables have sautéed and look translucent, add the coconut milk, water, curry powder, ginger, salt, lemon juice, sweet potato cubes and lentils, and bring to a boil over high heat. Once it starts to boil, reduce the heat to a simmer and cover for 25 minutes. Stir often so that the lentils don't burn or stick to the bottom of the pot.

The soup will be ready when the lentils are soft to the bite and have absorbed much but not all of the liquid. Once it's ready, pour it into serving bowls and top with the pumpkin seeds. To reheat for later, simply add a small amount of liquid to the soup (about ¼ cup [60 ml] of water to 1 cup [235 ml] of soup).

Warming VEGETABLE AND BLACK-EYED PEA SOUP

+SF +GF

This recipe can be worked to fit the vegetables of the season. When kale makes an appearance in summer, use that. When bok choy makes its way in the winter months, choose it for its mild flavor, similar to that of cabbage. But if you can, make black-eyed peas a constant in this soup, as it's the cornerstone of the recipe, giving way to a very earthy broth. —MR

SERVES 6

2 tbsp (30 ml) olive oil

½ large red onion, diced

3 cloves garlic, roughly chopped

4 large carrots, cut into thin circles

4 celery stalks, cut into ¼" (6-mm) pieces

½ tsp ground sage or chopped fresh sage (optional)

1 tsp ground ginger

Pinch of salt

8 cups (1.9 L) vegetable stock

2 small tomatoes, halved

2 cups (400 g) dried black-eyed peas

3-4 large handfuls kale, roughly chopped

2 handfuls mushrooms, roughly chopped

2 heads bok choy, chopped

Pinch of red pepper flakes

Salt and pepper, to taste

I highly recommend using dried beans, but if you are short on time, use 3 to 4 cups (510 to 680 g) of canned beans. Add them toward the end of the cooked soup, the last 30 minutes or so—we don't want them to turn mushy.

Now warm the olive oil in a saucepan and sauté the onion and garlic until tender, about 5 minutes, over medium heat. Add the carrots, celery, sage, ginger and a pinch of salt. Sauté for 15 minutes.

In a very large cooking pot, add the vegetable stock, tomatoes, dried beans and previously sautéed vegetables; cook over medium heat for 2½ hours.

Add in the kale, mushrooms and bok choy, and cook over medium heat for the remaining 30 minutes. Add a pinch of red pepper flakes for heat, salt and pepper to taste and enjoy this nourishing soup!

VEGGIE-MISO AND SOBA NOODLE **Soup**

+SF +GF +QP

One pot chock-full of fresh vegetables and a heavy dose of miso paste is all that's needed to whip up a soup that cooks in about 15 minutes—a scrumptious soup that comes together quicker than it takes to watch an episode on Netflix. —MR

SERVES 4

8 cups (1.9 L) water

3-4 tbsp (54-72 g) white miso paste

2 zucchini, cut into thin circles

1 head broccolini or ½ head broccoli, chopped

2 cloves garlic, roughly chopped

1 tsp red pepper flakes

1 cup (75 g) thinly sliced mushrooms

3 heads bok choy, chopped

½ (10-oz [285-g]) package soba noodles (I like the buckwheat version)

1 cup (150 g) snap peas, cut in half

Handful fresh cilantro

3 green onions, roughly chopped

Sprinkle of sea salt, to taste

In a large cooking pot over high heat, mix the water and miso paste together, and bring to a boil. Stir well until the miso has dissolved. Once the water is boiling, lower the heat to medium and add the zucchini, broccolini, garlic and red pepper flakes, and cook for 10 minutes. Then toss in the remaining ingredients—mushrooms, bok choy, soba noodles and snap peas, and cook for 5 more minutes, or until the veggies are tender and the soba noodles are cooked through. Top with fresh cilantro, sliced green onions and salt. Serve in bowls and enjoy!

One-Pot QUINOA AND TURMERIC STEW

+SF +GF +QP

This is comfort food at its best—golden quinoa stew with turmeric, hearty white beans, kale and red pepper flakes. A quick weeknight meal made in only 30 minutes . . . and in one pot. —MR

SERVES 4

1 tbsp (14 g) coconut oil

4 cloves garlic, roughly chopped

1 tbsp (7 g) ground coriander

1 tbsp (7 g) ground turmeric

1 tsp chili powder

1 sweet potato, spiralized or cut into cubes

1 (14-oz [397-g]) can chopped tomatoes

1 (14-oz [414-ml]) can full-fat coconut milk

1½ cups (270 g) quinoa

1½ cups (355 ml) water

2 (14-oz [397-g]) cans cannellini beans, rinsed and drained

2 cups (280 g) frozen peas

3 big handfuls kale, roughly chopped

Juice of ½ lemon

Sea salt

Pumpkin seeds, for topping

In a large pot over medium heat, melt the coconut oil and then add the garlic, all the spices and the sweet potato to the pot. Let this warm for about 5 minutes. Then add the tomatoes, coconut milk, quinoa and water to the pot. Bring it to a boil and then lower to a simmer. Cook for about 15 minutes and then add in the beans and peas. After another 15 minutes, toss in the kale and lemon juice. Cook the kale until it wilts, then add a little sea salt and you're done! Serve in bowls with a sprinkling of pumpkin seeds.

Velvety BUTTERNUT SQUASH SOUP

+SF +GF +QP

When soup can be made in a blender, it doesn't get much better than that. Top it off with pomegranate seeds for a surprising pop of sweetness, adding to the richness of this butternut squash soup. —MR

SERVES 2

1 tbsp (14 g) coconut oil

½ yellow onion, roughly chopped

3 cloves garlic, roughly chopped

½ apple, peeled and cubed

7 oz (198 g) butternut squash, cooked and without skin (or any winter squash)

1½ cups (355 ml) low-sodium vegetable broth

1 (14-oz [414-ml]) can full-fat coconut milk

1 tsp maple syrup

½–1 tsp sea salt, to taste

TOPPINGS
Pomegranate seeds

Sliced almonds

Cilantro

In a large sauté pan, warm the coconut oil over medium-high heat. Add the onion, garlic and apple; sauté until the apples are tender, about 10 minutes. Add a splash of water if the pan ever dries out.

There are a few ways to do the next part of blending the ingredients into a puréed soup. You can either use a very powerful high-speed blender, such as a Vitamix, or use an immersion blender.

When using the high-speed blender method, simply add the sautéed mixture and the remaining ingredients to the blender. Blend until the broth turns creamy and warm. This should take at least 5 minutes on the high-speed or soup setting.

If you're using an immersion blender, transfer your sautéed veggies to a large pot, and then add the remaining ingredients. Heat the pot until the soup is warm. Then blend the soup into a purée with the immersion blender.

Serve the soup in bowls, and top with the suggested toppings!

Golden Beet Salad
WITH BALSAMIC AND CASHEW RICOTTA

+GF +QP

The golden beet is a sweet veggie that tastes great whether you pickle, bake, brine, roast or juice it. It has a mellow flavor (and color) that pairs really well with tangy, acidic flavors like balsamic vinegar, and richer textures like crunchy walnuts and creamy cashew ricotta—which is why we paired them together! Plus, yellow beets are packed with good-for-you vitamins and minerals like fiber, iron, potassium and folic acid. If you haven't tried golden beets, or have just been waiting for the right recipe to test them out in, make this salad. It comes together super easily and tastes great. Plus it somehow totally looks and sounds like a dish you'd only find at a fancy restaurant. —AS

SERVES 2

½ cup (55 g) chopped walnuts

1 cup (110 g) raw cashews

2 tbsp (30 ml) water

¼ tsp salt

4 medium golden beets

4 cups (160 g) arugula

Balsamic vinegar, for serving

Preheat the oven to 350°F (177°C). Spread the chopped walnuts on a lined baking sheet. Bake for 8 to 10 minutes, stirring once. When finished, set aside to cool.

Soak the raw cashews in warm water for at least 30 minutes. Drain the nuts and pour them into a food processor. Pour in the water and salt, and pulse until a fluffy, chunky texture is achieved (similar to ricotta cheese). Set aside.

Trim the ends of the beets, and then place them into a medium pot of water. Bring to a boil, then lower the heat and cook over medium heat until fork tender, about 20 to 30 minutes. Drain the water and let cool slightly before using your fingers to slide the skins off. Toss the skins in the compost or trash, and thinly slice the cooked beets.

Spread the arugula between two large plates and top with the toasted walnuts, a couple tablespoons of the cashew ricotta, sliced golden beets and a drizzle of balsamic vinegar. Serve immediately! (Or, just prep it and take it for lunch to work all week!)

Leftovers last up to a week in the fridge.

Herbed LEMON TAHINI POTATO SALAD

+GF

I LOVE pouring tahini on all things potato normally, and literally make a snack out of baked potatoes with tahini, lemon and dill on the regular. So how had I never poured any in my potato salad and served it up? Well, it was love at first taste. The addition of crunchy veggies and a little vegan mayo for creaminess makes it next-level good. I've been eating the leftovers all week! You and your dinner guests will love it, too, I promise. So what're we waiting for?! Let's eat! —AS

SERVES 6 TO 8

2 lbs (905 g) red potatoes, chopped

1 cup (220 g) vegan mayo

1 cup (290 g) tahini

2–4 tbsp (30–60 ml) lemon juice

3 tbsp (9 g) freshly chopped dill

1 tsp salt

½ tsp pepper

½ red onion, chopped

4 green onions, thinly sliced

3 celery stalks, thinly sliced

Place the potatoes in a large pot of water over medium heat and bring to a boil. Cook for 10 to 15 minutes, or until the potatoes are fork tender. Drain and set aside to cool.

In a large mixing bowl, whisk together the mayo, tahini, lemon juice, dill, salt and pepper. Throw in the potatoes, chopped onions and celery, and toss to combine.

Serve and enjoy immediately, or keep it in the fridge up to a week!

Note: Leftovers may need to be tossed out, as the lemon juice and tahini will separate slightly over time.

Pickled CUCUMBER SALAD WITH PEAS AND FRESH DILL

+GF +QP

We're hooked on munching this easy-to-whip-up summer salad with quick-pickled cukes, crunchy English peas, spicy shallot and a bunch of fresh dill to kick it up a notch (you know, Emeril-style). It's a great recipe for eating up garden-grown goodies and for feeling a little reset after a week of treatin' yo'self! —AS

SERVES 4

2 large cucumbers

1 large shallot

1½ tbsp (23 g) sea salt

1½ tbsp (22 ml) champagne vinegar or apple cider vinegar

1 tsp organic sugar

2 tbsp (10 g) finely chopped fresh dill, plus more for garnish

1 cup (200 g) uncooked English peas

¼ tsp ground black pepper

Wash and peel the cucumbers. Remove the ends and cut them lengthwise, using a spoon to scoop out the seeds from the middle so you have two boat-like halves. Slice the halves thinly into little crescent moon shapes. Place into a medium colander. Thinly slice the shallot and add it to the colander. Toss the shallots and cucumbers in the salt and let them sit for about 20 minutes. Once ready, squeeze the veggies to drain any excess liquid and rinse the veggies well under cool water. Place the drained and rinsed veggies into a medium mixing bowl and set aside.

In a small bowl, combine the vinegar and sugar and stir well. Toss this into the cucumber and shallot mixture, and stir in the dill, peas and pepper. Toss everything to combine, and serve immediately with an extra sprig of fresh dill. Leftovers can be refrigerated for up to 3 days.

Tangy PURPLE CABBAGE SLAW WITH DIJON AND HORSERADISH

What's an easy way to sneak more veggies into your diet? Make them taste incredible! This slaw packs a serious punch and a ton of flavor. The combination of sweet, spicy and tangy come together in the best kind of way. It's great on its own, as a sandwich or burger topper, or even in tacos! Who knew vegetables could taste so good? —AS

SERVES 4 TO 6

½ cup (110 g) vegan mayo
1 small clove garlic, minced
1 tbsp (10 g) whole-grain Dijon mustard
1½ tsp (7 ml) apple cider vinegar
1½ tsp (8 g) finely grated fresh horseradish
½ tsp sugar
¼ tsp salt
¼ tsp pepper
4 cups (400 g) shredded purple cabbage

In a large mixing bowl, whisk together the mayo, garlic, mustard, vinegar, horseradish, sugar, salt and pepper. Pour in the shredded cabbage and toss to coat evenly. Serve immediately!

Leftovers keep for about 4 days in the fridge.

Vegan CAESAR SALAD WITH HOMEMADE DILL CROUTONS

I love a good Caesar salad! It's the perfect lunch or light dinner and tastes good any time of the year. This dressing is as rich and salty as the original, but much better for you. The homemade dill croutons are tangy and crunchy, and the Parmesan cheese takes the salad to a whole new level of delicious! This salad is the perfect excuse for working more greens into your diet. —AS

SERVES 6

2 medium bunches romaine lettuce, chopped (about 8 cups [560 g])

1 medium bunch lacinato kale, stems removed, chopped (about 3 cups [210 g])

1 cup (75 g) thinly sliced green onions

DRESSING

½ cup (75 g) raw cashews

1 cup (240 ml) hot water

2 tbsp (30 ml) olive oil

1 tbsp (15 ml) lemon juice

2 tsp (8 g) Dijon mustard

3 cloves garlic

2 tbsp (10 g) nutritional yeast

½ tsp salt

½ tsp pepper

¼ cup (60 ml) water

DILL CROUTONS

6 cups (300 g) cubed stale sourdough bread (1" [2.5-cm] cubes)

3 tbsp (45 ml) olive oil

3 tbsp (9 g) chopped fresh dill

½ tsp salt

¼ tsp pepper

PARMESAN "CHEESE"

1 cup (110 g) raw cashews

¼ cup (20 g) nutritional yeast

¾ tsp salt

¼ tsp garlic powder

Preheat the oven to 375°F (177°C). Line a baking sheet with parchment paper.

Place the chopped greens and onions into a large salad bowl and set aside in the fridge to chill.

FOR THE DRESSING

Soak the raw cashews in the hot water for at least 30 minutes. Drain the water off and pour the cashews into a food processor or high-speed blender. Pour in the olive oil, lemon juice, Dijon, garlic, nutritional yeast, salt, pepper and water, and blend on high until the mixture becomes creamy. Pour the dressing into a small bowl and place it in the fridge to chill with the greens.

FOR THE DILL CROUTONS

Spread the stale bread cubes over the lined baking sheet and drizzle evenly with the olive oil. Toss the cubes to evenly coat them in the oil, then sprinkle the fresh dill, salt and pepper over the top. Bake for 8 to 10 minutes, flipping halfway through. Set aside to cool.

FOR THE "CHEESE"

While the croutons bake, prepare the Parmesan cheese by combining the cashews, nutritional yeast, salt and garlic powder in a food processor. Pulse everything until the mixture becomes a fine meal.

a set of tongs to toss the greens.
Sprinkle the croutons and Parmesan cheese generously over the top, and serve immediately!

You may have leftover dressing and cheese. The dressing and cheese will both keep for up to 2 weeks in airtight containers in the refrigerator.

*SEE PHOTO INSERT

Smoky
POTATO SALAD

I brought this to a girls night get together with my friends and it was a TOTAL HIT! And this was before we broke out the wine. It's smoky, a little spicy and super flavorful—more than you'd expect from a simple potato salad! It whips up quickly and serves plenty: the definition of perfect party food. —AS

SERVES 6 TO 8

6 cups (1.1 kg) cubed red potatoes (1" [2.5-cm] cubes)
Pinch of salt
1 cup (165 g) finely diced celery
1 cup (170 g) finely diced red onion
½ cup (80 g) finely diced radishes
1¼ cups (300 g) vegan mayo
1 tbsp (15 ml) apple cider vinegar
1 tbsp (15 ml) lemon juice
2 tbsp (6 g) chopped fresh dill, plus more for garnish
1 clove garlic, minced
1 tsp smoked paprika
½ tsp cayenne pepper
½ tsp salt
½ tsp pepper

pot, adding the
tatoes.

While the potatoes ...
them into a large bowl. Set tha...

In a smaller bowl, whisk together the m...
gar, lemon juice, dill, garlic, paprika, cayenne,
and pepper. Pour this into the veggies and toss
to combine.

When the potatoes have cooled completely, toss them into the veggie mayo mixture until completely combined. Garnish with fresh dill and serve!

Leftovers last in the fridge for up to a week.

Chile-Infused
CHICKPEA SALAD

+GF +QP

There is pure magic in spices. Even the simplest understanding of spices can elevate a meal to new heights. Take the humble chickpea for example. It doesn't have much flavor on its own, but when sautéed with just red pepper flakes, paprika and maple syrup, it dramatically comes to life in a matter of seconds. Spices help shape a dish, and this is one recipe that cements this sentiment. Enjoy this chile-infused chickpea salad, and watch it become an instant classic. —MR

SERVES 2

DRESSING
1 tbsp (15 ml) water
1½ tsp (7 ml) maple syrup
1½ tsp (7 ml) lemon juice or apple cider vinegar

(continued)

SALAD

1 tsp coconut oil

1 (14-oz [397-g]) can chickpeas, rinsed and drained

1 tbsp (7 g) paprika

Salt, to taste

½ tsp red pepper flakes (more if you like it really spicy)

Handful of spinach

FOR THE DRESSING

First, whisk together the dressing ingredients and set it aside.

FOR THE SALAD

Next, simply heat the coconut oil in a medium saucepan over low heat until melted. Then add the chickpeas, paprika, salt and red pepper flakes to the saucepan. Mixing the ingredients well, cook over medium-low heat until golden brown, about 5 to 7 minutes. Once it's cooked, pour the prepared dressing on top of the chickpeas, and let this sit for a few minutes in the pan, infusing the chickpeas. Now pour the chickpeas on top of a bed of spinach and enjoy!

Huge Rainbow
SALAD BOWL

+SF +GF +QP

A salad starring only lettuce isn't that enticing. But a salad that takes on the shades of an edible rainbow—mixing the colors and flavors of chili chickpeas, paprika hummus and a creamy lentil-rice side—now this is a salad we can all get behind. —MR

SERVES 2

1 recipe Chile-Infused Chickpea Salad (page 233)

1 recipe Paprika Hummus (page 197)

½ cup (105 g) uncooked brown rice

½ cup (100 g) uncooked red lentils

Sprinkle of sea salt

2 cups (470 ml) water

2 cloves garlic, roughly chopped

1 tbsp (15 ml) olive oil

2 large handfuls spinach

½ avocado, sliced

½ cup (87 g) pomegranate seeds

Start by making the Chile-Infused Chickpea Salad recipe (page 233), or simply warm up the leftover chickpeas. Then prepare the Paprika Hummus (page 197).

Once these are finished, start making the rice and lentil mixture by rinsing and draining both. Then in a saucepan, add the rinsed rice and lentils, a sprinkle of sea salt and the water, and bring it to a boil with the lid on top. Once this starts to boil, reduce the heat to low and cook until all of the water is absorbed. This will make more rice than needed in one sitting, so just store the rest in an airtight container in the refrigerator.

For the sautéed spinach, add the garlic and olive oil to a small saucepan. Cook over medium heat for a few minutes, and then add the spinach. Allow the spinach to wilt down to about half the size.

Finally, add a portion of all the delicious ingredients to your bowl with a side of avocado and pomegranate seeds. Mix it together and enjoy this fantastic meal!

Fresh ORANGE AND FENNEL SALAD

+GF +QP +SF

This is one salad saturated in taste, beauty and color. Navel and blood oranges are balanced by crisp fennel and mint. Finish it off with a squeeze of orange and lemon juice for a salad that evokes the freshness of the season. Enjoy this salad before or after a full meal. —MR

SERVES 2

6 oranges (I like a mix of 3 blood oranges and 3 navel), peeled

1 small fennel bulb

Juice of ½ lemon

Juice of ½ orange

2 tbsp (10 g) roughly chopped fresh mint

Thinly cut the oranges crosswise, making 5 large circular orange slices. Cut the bottom and top off the fennel. Then peel back the outer layer and discard. Thinly chop the fennel just as you did the orange but into thinner slices, creating thin rings. Add them both to a serving dish and set it aside.

Squeeze the orange and lemon juice into a small bowl and toss in the mint. Pour this over the orange and fennel slices, mix and enjoy!

Warming WINTER GRAIN BOWL

+SF +QP

Barley is no newcomer on the food scene. But recently it made its "trendy food" debut as a great addition to grain bowls, and for good reason. If you're a fan of farro, then think of barley as farro's very friendly cousin. It's nutty, packed with nutrition and quite filling, making barley a fantastic main ingredient to bulk up any salad. —MR

SERVES 2 TO 3

1 cup (185 g) uncooked barley

2 cups (150 g) cremini mushrooms

1 small onion

2 zucchini

1 head broccolini or ½ head broccoli

½ tsp paprika

½ tsp ground turmeric

1 tbsp (15 ml) plus 1 tsp olive oil, divided

Sea salt

Handful raw and unsalted pecans, chopped

Juice of ½–1 lemon

Avocado slices (optional)

Start preparing the barley by cooking it according to package instructions.

Now preheat the oven to 420°F (215°C).

Cut the mushrooms, onion and zucchinis into large bite-size pieces. Then chop the broccolini into medium pieces, keeping the stem attached; the stem is delicious and edible.

(continued)

SOUPS & SALADS

In a large mixing bowl, add the vegetables, spices, 1 tablespoon (15 ml) of the oil and salt. Mix well and place them on a prepared baking sheet to bake for 15 to 20 minutes. Five minutes before the vegetables are crispy and done, toss in the pecans to toast for the remaining time.

Finally, separate half of the barley and add all the vegetables to it. Add more barley if you like; the rest can be saved for a hearty addition to a salad later in the week. Finally, add the lemon juice, drizzle on the remaining teaspoon olive oil and add a pinch of sea salt and the avocado slices.

Perfect SUMMER SALAD

+GF +QP

There is nothing quite like the taste of a summer peach—so sweet and ripe, dripping with juice from every bite. Now take that same peach, slice it into a kale salad and wrap it in a maple-tahini dressing for a mouthwatering meal that sings the flavor of summer with every sumptuous bite. —MR

SERVES 1

DRESSING
3 tbsp (45 ml) olive oil
½ tbsp (7 ml) maple syrup
2 tbsp (30 ml) apple cider vinegar or lemon juice
1 tbsp (18 g) tahini

SALAD
3 large handfuls kale
⅓ apple, cubed
1 peach, cubed
½ avocado, cubed
1 green onion, thinly sliced
Few sprinkles of hemp seeds
Few sprinkles of pumpkin seeds
Few sprinkles of currants
Drizzle of olive oil

FOR THE DRESSING
Prepare the dressing by whisking all ingredients in a small bowl. Set it aside.

FOR THE SALAD
Start by tearing the kale into bite-size pieces, disregarding the stems. Wash the kale and pat it dry. Before you massage the kale, you want to pour the tahini dressing on top of the leaves. Then use your hands to massage the dressing into the kale. The acid from the dressing will help break down the leaves. Massage for 2 to 3 minutes. The longer you massage, the softer the kale will become.

Now add all of the remaining salad ingredients to the kale salad and mix well. Serve on plates with an extra drizzle of olive oil, and enjoy!

Simple WINTER SALAD

+GF +QP

Ever heard of massaged kale? This is a simple hack that transforms stiff kale leaves into its softer counterpart. For one minute, massage kale leaves between your fingers. This technique of rubbing the leaves in lemon juice helps to soften the leaves and makes it far easier to eat . . . and enjoy. Now adorn with an abundance of winter produce, from sweet persimmons to ruby red beets, crisp apples and juicy pomegranates. —MR

SERVES 1

TURMERIC DRESSING
½ tsp ground turmeric

1 tbsp (18 g) tahini

2 tsp (10 ml) maple syrup

1 small clove garlic, thinly chopped

1½ tbsp (27 ml) apple cider vinegar or lemon juice

2 tbsp (30 ml) water

SIMPLE WINTER SALAD
3 large handfuls kale

½ large red beet, cooked and cubed

½ persimmon, thinly sliced

⅓ red apple, thinly sliced

Small handful of raisins

Small handful of pecans or any nut

Handful of pomegranate seeds

FOR THE TURMERIC DRESSING
Make the dressing by simply whisking everything together in a small bowl.

FOR THE SALAD
Start by tearing the kale leaves into bite-size pieces, disregarding the stems. Then wash the kale leaves and pat dry. Before you massage the kale, you'll want to pour your turmeric dressing on top of the leaves. Then use your hands to massage the dressing into the kale. The acid from the dressing will help break down the leaves. Massage for 1 to 2 minutes. The longer you massage, the softer the kale will become.

Now add all of the remaining salad ingredients to the kale salad and mix well.

Serve it on plates and enjoy!

NIÇOISE Salad

+SF +GF +QP

Niçoise salad is a staple in French cuisine. It traditionally calls for greens, green beans, eggs and seafood. But here we're going to keep the greens and instead, embellish this classic with a creamy coconut yogurt–basil dressing. I must admit that this remake stretches the original, but it does hold a few constants: green beans, cucumbers and olives. —MR

SERVES 2 TO 3

SALAD
½ cup (100 g) whole baby red potatoes

2 cups (200 g) halved green beans

4 cups (160 g) arugula

⅓ cup (35 g) sliced cucumber

Small handful Kalamata olives

2 tbsp (20 g) hemp seeds, for topping

Sea salt, for topping

(continued)

DRESSING

⅓ cup (80 g) coconut yogurt

⅓ cup (8 g) chopped basil

Juice of 1 lemon

Drizzle of extra-virgin olive oil

1 tbsp (15 g) whole-grain mustard

1 tsp capers

Sea salt

FOR THE SALAD

Start by cooking the potatoes and green beans. Bring a large pot of water to boil, and add the potatoes and green beans. Cook for 10 minutes or until the vegetables are fork tender.

FOR THE DRESSING

In the meantime, make the dressing by adding all of the ingredients to a food processor or blender. Blend until smooth and creamy.

In a large bowl, toss together the remaining ingredients for the salad with the cooked potatoes and green beans, adding the dressing on top. Mix until the dressing has coated the entire salad. Serve on plates with a sprinkling of hemp seeds and a pinch of sea salt.

Grilled FIG AND PEACH SALAD

+GF +QP

If you have never grilled a peach before, then this recipe might act as your gateway to the wide world of grilling. Place the fruit on the grill, walk away, have a snack and check your phone, and minutes later you have a peach transformed. The grill has a way of deepening the sweet and smoky aroma of fruit, which now perfumes the entire salad. —MR

SERVES 2 TO 3

MAPLE PECANS

1 cup (110 g) pecans, chopped

½ tbsp (8 ml) maple syrup

Pinch of sea salt

SALAD

2 peaches, sliced in half lengthwise, pitted

5 fresh figs, quartered lengthwise

1 corn on the cob

1 tbsp (15 ml) olive oil, plus more for brushing

¼ fennel bulb, very thinly shaven

Juice of ½ orange

A few fresh mint leaves, roughly chopped

Pinch of sea salt

FOR THE MAPLE PECANS

Preheat the oven to 350°F (177°C) and add all of the ingredients to a parchment-lined baking pan. Mix well. Cook for 10 minutes, or until the nuts are caramelized but not burnt.

FOR THE SALAD

Brush each side of the peaches, figs and corn with olive oil. Cook the peaches, cut-side down, on a hot grill pan until the fruit has grill marks, about 5 minutes. Repeat this process to grill the figs and corn (the corn will take about 15 minutes). When grilling the corn, rotate so that each side will have grill marks.

When the corn is done, remove it from the heat and use a knife to remove the kernels from the cob, cutting down lengthwise from the top.

Add all of the grilled fruit and corn, fennel, orange juice, mint, olive oil and salt to a large mixing bowl and toss well. Serve the salad in bowls and top with the maple-roasted pecans.

Farro Salad WITH BASIL AND TOMATOES

+SF

This farro salad is the perfect example of what to do when you think you have nothing in your kitchen to cook with. Farro and chickpeas provide the bulk, while tomatoes and arugula lighten up the dish. Use the ingredients in this recipe as bullet points for what you can whip together with a few last minute kitchen staples, yet swap them out when needed. —MR

SERVES 3 TO 4

1 cup (200 g) uncooked farro

2 handfuls arugula

Handful Kalamata olives, halved

1 (14-oz [397-g]) can chickpeas, rinsed and drained

½ avocado, cubed

1 cup (160 g) cherry tomatoes, sliced in half

Handful fresh basil, roughly chopped

Small handful pumpkin seeds

Juice of ½ lemon

1–2 tbsp (15–30 ml) olive oil

Sea salt

Start by cooking the farro as the packet instructs. In the meantime, add all of the salad ingredients to a large mixing bowl, including the lemon juice, olive oil and sea salt. When ready, toss in the warm farro and mix well. Serve it in bowls and enjoy!

Simple GRILLED ZUCCHINI SALAD WITH WALNUTS

+SF +GF +QP

Need a flavor boost? Head straight to the grill. Looking to add a smoky aroma? Grill it up. What about transforming a modest vegetable into the main star? Grill that sucker up. Grilling is a surefire way to add flavor, texture and character to any meal. And that is exactly what we did here. Tenderized zucchinis work beautifully in a salad paired with crunchy walnuts and sweet tomatoes. —MR

SERVES 2

¼ cup (30 g) unsalted raw walnuts

1½ cups (240 g) cherry tomatoes

2 large zucchini, thinly sliced into ¼" (6-mm) strips lengthwise

1 corn on the cob

2 tbsp (30 ml) olive oil, divided

Sea salt

Juice of ½ lemon

Preheat the oven to 400°F (204°C). Add the walnuts and tomatoes to a parchment-lined baking pan. Cook for 10 minutes.

Brush each side of the zucchini slices and corn with 1 tablespoon (15 ml) of the olive oil and sprinkle with salt. Cook on a hot grill pan until the vegetables have grill marks, about 5 minutes for the zucchini and 15 for the corn. Rotate the corn so that each side has grill marks.

When the corn is done, remove it from the heat and use a knife to remove the kernels from the cob, cutting down lengthwise from the top. Add all of the grilled veggies, walnuts, tomatoes, lemon juice, the remaining 1 tablespoon (15 ml) olive oil and sea salt to a large mixing bowl. Serve.

Blueberry WHISKEY BBQ SALAD WITH TEMPEH AND ROASTED POTATOES

+GF

There are a few components you need to make for this salad, but believe me it's all worth it. Plus it's easier than it seems. You make your own Blueberry Whiskey BBQ Sauce that you use to coat the tempeh and make a dressing. You'll also roast some smoky potatoes and chop a few of your favorite veggies. You can even do all of this ahead of time—even the day before! —KH

SERVES 4, 2 CUPS (470 ML) SAUCE

BLUEBERRY WHISKEY BBQ SAUCE
1 medium dried whole ancho chile, stem and seeds removed

1 tbsp (15 ml) olive oil (or dry sauté to make oil-free)

½ cup (75 g) chopped onion

6 cloves garlic, chopped

2 cups (300 g) blueberries

½ cup (120 ml) whiskey or bourbon

½ cup (120 ml) apple cider vinegar

⅓ cup (48 g) brown or coconut sugar

¼ cup (88 g) blackstrap molasses

3 tbsp (48 g) tomato paste

½ tsp salt, or to taste

½ tsp liquid smoke

¼ tsp ground allspice

¼ tsp ground coriander

SMOKY ROASTED POTATOES AND TEMPEH
4 medium purple or Yellow Finn potatoes, cut into cubes

½ tsp smoked paprika

¼ tsp salt

¼ tsp pepper

1 tbsp (15 ml) olive oil (optional)

½ lb (227 g) tempeh, cut into small squares (or you can use extra-firm or pressed tofu)

½ cup (60 ml) Blueberry Whiskey BBQ Sauce

BLUEBERRY BALSAMIC SALAD DRESSING
¼ cup (60 ml) Blueberry Whiskey BBQ Sauce

¼ cup (60 ml) balsamic vinegar

2 tbsp (30 ml) olive oil

BLUEBERRY WHISKEY SALAD
8 cups (240 g) spring greens or lettuce leaves

2 cups (300 g) blueberries

VEGETABLE OPTIONS
1 cucumber, chopped

½ red onion, chopped

1 large ripe tomato, chopped

FOR THE BLUEBERRY WHISKEY BBQ SAUCE

Toast the ancho chile pepper in a saucepan over medium heat until it becomes brittle and fragrant. Set it aside for later.

Heat the olive oil in the saucepan over medium heat. Once hot, add the onion and sauté until it's translucent. Then add the garlic and sauté for 2 minutes.

Add the blueberries, whiskey, vinegar, sugar, molasses, tomato paste and the toasted ancho chile. Simmer over medium-low until the ancho chile is reconstituted and soft.

Carefully pour the hot mixture into your blender, and add in the salt, liquid smoke, allspice and coriander. Blend until silky smooth.

Pour the blended mixture back into the saucepan and simmer over low heat until the sauce is thick and has reduced to about 2 cups (470 ml).

FOR THE SMOKY ROASTED POTATOES AND TEMPEH

Preheat the oven to 375°F (190°C). Spread parchment paper on two sheet pans (or spray with oil).

Toss the potatoes with smoked paprika, salt, pepper and olive oil, if using. Then spread them on one of the sheet pans and place it on the bottom rack of the oven. Set the timer for 15 minutes.

Next, toss the tempeh in the Blueberry Whiskey BBQ Sauce, spread it on the second sheet pan and place it on the top rack of the oven. This probably will take about 5 minutes to prep, so you can let the tempeh cook for 10 minutes using the same timer as the potatoes.

When the timer goes off, take the potatoes out and turn them over. Then, when you open the oven to put the potatoes back in, set the timer for 15 minutes again. Then take the tempeh out, turn the pieces over and place them back in the oven.

Remove both sheet pans when the timer goes off. You can serve this on your salad immediately or wait until they cool, if you prefer not to have wilted lettuce.

FOR THE BLUEBERRY BALSAMIC SALAD DRESSING

Add all the ingredients to a salad shaker or a mason jar. Twist the lid on tight and shake until the ingredients incorporate. You could also whisk them together if you prefer.

FOR THE BLUEBERRY WHISKEY SALAD

Assemble the salads or set up a table to be your own salad bar!

First, make a base of greens, and then layer a quarter of the potatoes and tempeh on top of each salad.

Then add the vegetable extras and fresh blueberries. Serve the dressing on the side or drizzle it over the top.

CHIK'N **Salad**

+GF +SF

When the idea of chicken salad comes to mind, there's one thing that we typically think of: mayonnaise. Let us be the first to tell you that mayo was never a staple in our home. In fact, I recall one person in the Meyer household referring to it as "the devil's food" they despised it so much. So, we've taken this mayo and chicken-riddled "salad" and turned it into a healthy vegan version. —LM + AM

SERVES 4

1 qt (960 ml) no-chicken broth or vegetable broth

1 (20-oz [565-g]) can young jackfruit in water

½ cup (56 g) raw cashews, soaked in water for at least 4 hours

⅓ cup (80 ml) unsweetened almond milk

Juice from ½ lemon

1 clove garlic, sliced

½ tsp sea salt

1 large celery stalk, finely chopped

1 green onion, finely chopped

1 cup (184 g) halved red grapes

⅔ cup (88 g) dried tart cherries

1 tbsp (2 g) fresh minced thyme, stems removed

Fine sea salt and black pepper, to taste

(continued)

Bring the broth to a boil in a saucepan and reduce the heat to a simmer. Put the drained and rinsed jackfruit in the saucepan with the broth, and simmer for 1 hour. After the hour is up, drain the broth and shred the jackfruit.

Drain and rinse the cashews and put them into a high-powered blender with the almond milk, lemon juice, garlic and salt. Blend the cashew mixture until smooth and creamy, about 90 seconds. You should not see or taste any pieces of the nuts.

Put the jackfruit, cashew cream (add slowly until you get the desired amount of creaminess), celery, green onion, grapes, cherries, thyme, salt and pepper in a large bowl, and stir until well combined. Chill or eat at room temperature.

*SEE PHOTO INSERT

Protein SUPERFOOD BEAN SALAD

+GF +SF

Are you looking for a great way to kick-start a healthy lifestyle? If so, we highly recommend making a huge batch of this superfood salad. It has a great balance of carbohydrates, fats and protein. Make a big batch at the beginning of the week and have it for lunch each day. Trust us, this bean salad will transform you from a junk food queen to a healthy-eating machine. —LM + AM

SERVES 2

1 cup (170 g) uncooked black quinoa

2 cups (480 ml) water

1 (15-oz [425-g]) can black beans, rinsed and drained

1 (15-oz [425-g]) can chickpeas, rinsed and drained

3 cups (210 g) coarsely chopped kale

3 cups (180 g) baby spinach

2 green onions

⅓ cup (80 ml) white wine vinegar

1 clove garlic, finely minced

½ tsp vegan honey substitute (we suggest Bee Free Honee)

½ tsp ground ginger

Salt and pepper, to taste

1 tbsp (15 ml) extra-virgin olive oil

Rinse the quinoa thoroughly in a fine-mesh strainer. Transfer the quinoa to a saucepan and add the water. Bring the quinoa and water to a boil. Immediately after the quinoa and water have reached a boil, cover with a lid and reduce the heat to a low simmer. Cook the quinoa for about 15 minutes or until the germ has separated from the grain. Remove the quinoa from the heat and allow it to cool.

Place the beans in a large salad bowl with the kale and spinach. Add the cooled quinoa.

Finely mince the white bulb of the green onions and place in a small bowl with the vinegar. Finely slice the green stems of the onions and set them aside.

Add the garlic, vegan honey substitute, ginger, salt, pepper and olive oil to the onions and vinegar, and whisk well.

Add the dressing to the quinoa, beans and greens. Toss until everything is coated in the dressing. Sprinkle with the sliced greens from the onions.

*SEE PHOTO INSERT

1 large acorn squash

2 tsp (10 ml) olive oil, divided

Sea salt and pepper, to taste

6 cups (1410 ml) water, divided

1 cup (200 g) lentils

1 cup (60 g) coarsely chopped spinach

1 cup (180 g) quinoa

1 cup (154 g) shelled pistachios

1 cup (154 g) dried tart cherries

½ cup (118 ml) white wine vinegar

Juice from 1 large orange

3 tbsp (8 g) fresh minced sage

1 tsp fresh minced mint

1 tsp maple syrup

Preheat the oven to 400°F (204°C). Cut the acorn squash in half and remove the seeds. Then cut the acorn squash into 1-inch (2.5-cm) thick wedges and lay them on a baking sheet. Drizzle the acorn squash with 1 teaspoon of the olive oil. Sprinkle with salt and black pepper to taste.

the remaining 2 cups (470 ml) water and quinoa to a boil. When the water is boiling, cover the pan with a tight-fitting lid. Reduce the heat to a simmer. Cook the quinoa for 15 minutes or until the water is absorbed.

Add the lentils, spinach, quinoa, pistachios and dried cherries to a large salad bowl. Toss the ingredients with a bit of fine sea salt and black pepper to your liking.

In a small bowl, combine the vinegar, orange juice, sage, mint, maple syrup, remaining 1 teaspoon olive oil, salt and pepper. Whisk until the mixture is well combined. Drizzle the mixture over the salad and toss until well combined.

Top the salad with the cubed acorn squash and serve.

Spicy PEANUT COUSCOUS SALAD

+GF +SFO

In the Meyer household, the easiest way to sell any of us on a dish is using the word "spicy." But don't worry, this dish won't send your mouth hunting for the nearest jug of water. It's perfectly balanced and a great way to get a little extra kick into your day. —LM + AM

SERVES 2

1¼ cups (295 ml) water, divided

1 cup (173 g) tricolored pearl couscous

1 mango, diced into ½" (1.3-cm) cubes

1 medium cucumber, diced into ½" (1.3-cm) cubes

1 small red onion, thinly sliced

1½ cups (230 g) cooked peas

½ cup (76 g) peanuts

½ cup (38 g) coconut flakes

2 tbsp (23 g) creamy peanut butter

Juice of 1 small lime

2 tsp (10 ml) soy sauce (use liquid aminos for soy-free)

½ tsp coconut sugar

½ tsp ground turmeric

½ tsp red pepper flakes

In a medium pot, bring 1 cup (235 ml) of the water to a boil. Once the water is boiling, add the couscous. Then cover the pot with a lid and reduce the heat to a simmer. Simmer the couscous for 8 to 10 minutes, or until the water is completely absorbed.

Cool the couscous in a large bowl. Add the mango, cucumber, red onion and peas. Stir the mixture gently to combine. Top with the peanuts and coconut flakes.

Make the dressing by combining the peanut butter, lime juice, soy sauce, coconut sugar, turmeric and red pepper flakes in a small bowl. Slowly add the remaining ¼ cup (60 ml) water while stirring until the dressing is thin but still creamy. You may not need all of the water depending on how thin your peanut butter was to start. Pour over the salad and toss to coat.

Winter CITRUS AND ARUGULA SALAD WITH CRANBERRY ORANGE DRESSING

+GF +SF

Is there anything better than winter citrus? The sweetness of an orange, the tartness of a grapefruit—and how about the gorgeous color of cranberries? We've picked our favorite winter fruits and mixed them into one amazing salad. —LM + AM

SERVES 6

6 cups (240 g) baby arugula

1 large grapefruit, peeled and sliced

2 blood oranges, peeled and sliced

2 cups (174 g) shredded fennel

½ cup (85 g) coarsely chopped raw almonds

¼ cup (60 ml) cranberry juice

¼ cup (60 ml) blood orange juice

¼ cup (60 ml) champagne vinegar

Pinch of ground cloves

¼ tsp olive oil

Fine sea salt, to taste

In a large bowl, on top of the arugula, layer the grapefruit, blood orange, fennel and almonds.

In a small bowl, whisk the cranberry juice, blood orange juice, vinegar, cloves, olive oil and sea salt until well blended.

Pour the dressing on the salad and toss it to coat.

Vegan BLT SALAD WITH SMOKY SPICY MAYO

+GF +SF

We used to love a good BLT. The smoky and salty flavors, along with the fresh, crisp lettuce and the juicy tomato was such a treat, until we thought about what we were really eating. Even though we didn't miss turkey bacon when we went vegan, we did miss that salty and smoky flavor, so we came up with a way to satisfy that craving while staying true to our core belief of living cruelty-free lives. It turned out that portobello mushrooms, soaked in maple syrup, salt and liquid smoke is a great way to quench those cravings. This recipe is one of our most popular, and we think you'll understand why once you try this salad. —LM + AM

SERVES 3 TO 4

"BACON"
3 tbsp (45 ml) liquid smoke (use less if you don't like a strong smoky flavor)
¾ cup (180 ml) pure maple syrup
1 tsp fine sea salt, or to taste
Ground black pepper, to taste
3 large portobello mushrooms, washed, gills removed, patted dry
1 tbsp (15 g) coconut oil

DRESSING
¾ cup (85 g) raw cashews, soaked in water for at least 4 hours
Juice of 1 lemon
2 cloves garlic, sliced

5 tbsp (75 ml) unsweetened almond milk
1 tsp smoked paprika
¼ tsp fine sea salt
⅛ to ¼ tsp cayenne pepper (optional)

SALAD
1 large head romaine lettuce, chopped
2 cups (326 g) sliced cherry tomatoes
1 avocado, peeled, pitted and sliced (optional)

FOR THE "BACON"
In a bowl that is large enough to marinate the mushroom slices, combine the liquid smoke, maple syrup, salt and pepper.

Cut the mushroom into thin strips, no more than ¼ inch (6 mm) thick, and marinate both sides in the liquid mixture, at least 15 minutes per side.

Heat the oil in a medium skillet over medium-high heat and cook the mushrooms for 5 to 8 minutes, or until they release their water and the edges get crispy. Then flip them and cook for 8 more minutes. They should be browned and the edges should look crispy.

FOR THE DRESSING
Rinse the soaked cashews and place them in a high-powered blender. Add the lemon juice, garlic, almond milk, paprika, salt and cayenne (skip if you don't like spicy). Blend on high speed for about 2 minutes, or until the dressing is creamy. You shouldn't see or taste any solid pieces of the nuts.

FOR THE SALAD
In a large salad bowl, toss the lettuce and tomatoes with the dressing to coat. Put the "bacon" on top or cut it into small pieces and toss. Add a few slices of avocado on top, if desired.

*SEE PHOTO INSERT

JACKFRUIT TUNA-LESS **Salad**

+GF

Hail to the jackfruit! This versatile fruit has made being a vegan so easy. We make BBQ with it, crab cakes, chili and now, tuna salad without the fish. The texture and flavors are spot on. We have served this salad to friends, and they couldn't believe they weren't eating tuna. If you've been missing a good tuna salad, or if you want to avoid consuming mercury (commonly found in canned tuna), try this. You won't believe it's not tuna. —LM + AM

SERVES 4

1 (14-oz [397-g]) can young jackfruit (we order it on Amazon)

1 celery stalk, finely chopped

1 small red onion, finely chopped

1 heaping tbsp (3 g) chopped fresh parsley

3 tbsp (33 g) Dijon mustard

2 tbsp (30 g) unsweetened plain plant-based yogurt (don't use coconut yogurt)

½ tsp paprika

Fine sea salt and pepper, to taste

Drain and rinse the jackfruit well, and then press the excess liquid out of it. Pulse it in a food processor until it's shredded and resembles canned tuna. If you don't have a food processor, you can chop it with a knife.

Put the jackfruit in a medium mixing bowl and add the celery, onion, parsley, mustard, yogurt, paprika and salt and pepper. Stir until it's fully combined.

Serve as is or in a sandwich.

Mediterranean
SALAD WRAPS WITH TAHINI DRESSING

+GF +SF

Fresh, crunchy, healthy and so, so good, is how we describe these beautiful Mediterranean veggie wraps. We used giant collard greens to wrap up the vegetables so they'd be as healthy as possible. These are gluten-free, dairy-free, sugar-free and guilt-free, but don't let that fool you—they're full of flavor and lots of crunch. Go ahead, eat as much as you want. —LM + AM

SERVES 4 TO 6

DRESSING

½ cup (124 g) tahini

¼ cup (60 ml) water

¼ cup (60 ml) lemon juice

1 clove garlic, minced

1 tbsp (15 g) minced cilantro

1 tsp minced Greek oregano

¼ tsp ground cumin

Sea salt and black pepper, to taste

WRAPS

1 (15-oz [425-g]) can chickpeas, rinsed and drained

1 (12-oz [340-g]) jar quartered and marinated artichoke hearts, drained and chopped

1 cup (182 g) pitted Kalamata olives, chopped

1 large tomato, cubed

1 medium cucumber, cubed

1 large celery stalk, chopped

2 medium carrots, chopped

1 red onion, chopped

8–10 large collard leaves

FOR THE DRESSING

Whisk the tahini, water, lemon juice, garlic, cilantro, oregano, cumin and salt and pepper together until well combined.

FOR THE WRAPS

In a large bowl, combine the chickpeas, artichokes, olives, tomato, cucumber, celery, carrots, onion and dressing until well combined.

Cut the stem off and pound the tough part of the center vein of the collard green leaf until it bends easily. It may split a little; don't worry about it. Steam the collard greens in a pot of boiling water with a steamer basket for 3 minutes to soften. Fill the center of the leaf with the salad, and roll it up. Cut into 3 pieces. Repeat with the rest of the wraps.

Southwestern
ROASTED CORN AND BLACK BEAN SALAD

+GF +SF

If you love a little spice mixed in with fresh sweet corn, then this salad is for you. We eat this as a meal because it has protein and healthy carbs. We also eat it as a dip. And if you want to get really fancy, fill a tortilla with it, add some guacamole and wrap it up like a burrito.
—LM + AM

SERVES 6 TO 8

2 (15-oz [425-g]) cans black beans, rinsed and drained

1 tbsp (15 g) plus 2 tsp (10 g) sea salt, divided

1 tbsp (8 g) ground cumin

1 tbsp (15 g) ground chipotle pepper

2 ears of corn (leave in husks and soak in water for 30 minutes before grilling or remove the husks and brush with olive oil and sprinkle with salt and pepper)

1 large Vidalia or sweet white onion, sliced into ½" (1.3-cm) thick slices

Olive oil

Black pepper

2 poblano peppers

1 orange bell pepper

Juice from 2 large limes

1 cup (40 g) cilantro, coarsely chopped

2 large colorful heirloom tomatoes, seeded and diced

Note: Prepare the corn and onions before grilling so you can grill the corn, onion and poblano peppers while the beans are cooking.

In a medium saucepan, cover the beans with water and bring to a boil. Reduce the heat to low and add 1 tablespoon (15 g) of the salt, the cumin and the chipotle pepper. Cook for 15 minutes, then drain the beans in a colander and place them in a large bowl. Much of the salt and spices will drain with the water, so don't be afraid to add the full amount.

If you soaked the corn in the husks, grill for about 15 minutes. Turn frequently. If the husks are removed, brush the cobs lightly with olive oil and sprinkle with salt and pepper. Grill for about 10 minutes, turning frequently. Let them cool until you can safely remove the husks; cut the corn off of the cobs over the bowl with the beans so you don't lose any of the kernels.

Brush the onion slices with a light coat of olive oil and sprinkle them with salt and pepper. Grill for about 4 minutes per side, or until they show grill marks. You don't want to cook them until they're soft; they should maintain their crispness. Dice them and put them in the bowl with the beans.

(continued)

Grill the poblano peppers for about 4 minutes per side, or until the skins begin to blacken and blister. When they're cool enough to handle, scrape the skin off, seed and dice. Put them in the bowl with the beans.

Seed and dice the bell pepper and add it to the bowl with the beans.

Squeeze the juice of one of the limes over the bean and vegetable mixture while it's hot, and sprinkle the remaining 2 teaspoons (10 g) of salt, or to taste, and toss it to coat. Refrigerate for at least 20 minutes to cool.

Note: The acid in the lime juice will continue the cooking process of the beans and vegetables, so make sure you add the juice of the lime at this step.

Remove the salad from the refrigerator. Then add the cilantro, tomatoes and the juice of the second lime. Toss the salad to combine.

Sweet Potato NOODLE SALAD WITH SRIRACHA LIME PEANUT SAUCE

+GF +SE +SF

Fun. This salad is pure fun. It's fun to make, because you get to create sweet potato noodles with a spiralizer. It's fun to look at because it's a bright and happy orange with a sprinkling of green. And finally, it's so much fun to eat. The sweetness of the noodles paired with the spicy peanut sauce, mixed with the fresh basil and the creamy chickpeas is a big bowl of delicious happiness. We make this salad regularly and will never tire of it. Try it and you'll understand. —LM + AM

SERVES 2

SALAD
1 tbsp (15 g) coconut oil

1 large sweet potato, peeled and spiralized

1 (15-oz [425-g]) can chickpeas, rinsed and drained

Sea salt and black pepper, to taste

A handful fresh basil, coarsely chopped

SAUCE
3 tbsp (34 g) chunky or smooth peanut butter

1 tbsp (15 ml) sriracha

Juice from 1 lime

3–4 tbsp (45–60 ml) water

FOR THE SALAD

Heat the coconut oil in a large skillet over medium heat, and add the spiralized sweet potato and chickpeas. Stir to coat in the oil and cook until the potato softens to the consistency of noodles, approximately 8 minutes. They should be soft and malleable, not mushy. Add salt and pepper, to taste, and remove it from the pan. Put the mixture in a large bowl and refrigerate it while you make the sauce.

FOR THE SAUCE

Whisk the peanut butter, sriracha, lime juice and water until the ingredients are smooth and thin enough to pour over the sweet potato and chickpeas. If you prefer a thin sauce, add more water, but taste it to make sure it isn't too diluted. If it's lacking flavor, add more lime and/or sriracha.

Note: If you're sensitive to spicy food, start with a teaspoon sriracha and add more to taste.

Toss the sauce and the sweet potato and chickpeas until the sauce is completely covering the salad. Throw in the fresh basil.

BOWL O' SALAD
Goodness

+GFO +SFO

If you ask me whose salad dressing is the best in the whole wide world, I will tell you straight up it's my mom's. She was here for a few months visiting me a while back, and I bugged her every day until she whipped some up for me. We came up with the combination of ingredients in this salad and ate huge bowls of it as often as we could. Memoriiiiiiiiiiiies . . . —CS

SERVES 4

Freshly cracked peppercorn, to taste

1 tsp maca powder

1 tsp white miso (optional for soy-free)

1½ tsp (5 g) mild Dijon mustard or other favorite mustard (use gluten-free)

⅓ cup (27 g) minced scallion

2 tbsp (30 ml) white balsamic vinegar

2 tbsp (30 ml) extra-virgin olive oil

2 tbsp (30 ml) other fancy oil of choice (such as roasted hazelnut or walnut) or 2 tbsp (30 g) unsweetened plain vegan yogurt

2 cups (170 g) packed thinly chopped red or green cabbage

1 cup (150 g) diced raw golden beet (peeled)

1½ cups (105 g) sliced raw cremini or button mushrooms (gently cleaned and stemmed, if desired)

1 avocado (not too ripe), halved, pitted and chopped

In a large bowl, whisk to combine the pepper, maca, miso, mustard and scallion. Add the vinegar and whisk to emulsify. Slowly add the oils, or oil and yogurt if choosing that option, and continue whisking to emulsify. Add the cabbage, beet, mushrooms and avocado. Gently toss until perfectly coated and serve immediately. As the salad contains avocado, I cannot recommend keeping leftovers.

*SEE PHOTO INSERT

six

DESSERTS

You've made it to the best (and my personal favorite) part of the book, friends—because I've always been a sucker for a good dessert! I like to have a little something sweet every night after dinner, usually a bit of dark chocolate, but a couple of cookies if they're around. Making brownies or a birthday cake? I'll always lick the bowl after you've scooped out your batter, if you let me! And since these desserts are totally dairy- and egg-free, you can lick the spoon (save the bowl for me!) totally guilt-free, and without risk of salmonella, too. Desserts help finish off the most memorable of meals and complement the conversation with a little something extra. Whether you've come looking for the best batch of cookies ever, brownies that'll knock the socks off of your mother-in-law, or just a really great dairy-free ice cream—we've got you covered! From simple, six-ingredient desserts you can make with only what's in your pantry to decadent, rich, date-night-worthy cakes and cream pies, this chapter is guaranteed to offer something that'll satisfy your sweet tooth and keep your hot date coming back for more. Let's eat!

TWO-BEAN CHOCOLATE CHUNK Cookies

These are made from a base of garbanzo and white beans, which blend into a creamy sweet dough that you can barely resist eating before transferring it to the pan. Because they're made with beans, they are loaded with fiber and protein and fill you up pretty quickly, eliminating the need to munch on four before feeling satisfied. The best part? They only take about half an hour to prepare, start to finish. —AS

MAKES 16 COOKIES

1 (15-oz [425-g]) can chickpeas

1 (15-oz [425-g]) can white beans

½ cup (90 g) almond butter

3 tbsp (24 g) whole wheat flour

1 tbsp (15 ml) maple syrup

½ tsp vanilla extract

½ tsp salt

1 tbsp (15 ml) agave nectar

1–2 tbsp (15–30 ml) nondairy milk, such as hemp

½ cup (90 g) vegan chocolate chips (or chunks!)

Preheat the oven to 400°F (204°C).

The first step is by far the most tedious, but NOT skippable. First, open your cans. Drain each. Pour the chickpeas into a colander. Essentially, you'll want to shuck your beans. To do this, squeeze each little bean until the outer whitish film surrounding it pops off. Discard the skins and put the shucked beans back into the colander. Shucked chickpeas kind of look like tiny brains, so it becomes easier and easier to tell the peeled from the not peeled. You kind of get into a groove after a few minutes and it all goes by really quickly. You really can't skip this step or your cookies will be yucky and chunky and taste a little too much like chickpeas.

After your beans are shucked, you'll need to combine all of the ingredients except for the hemp milk and chocolate chips in a food processor. Mix on high until combined completely. While the processor is on, add the drizzle of hemp milk until it all reaches a smooth and even doughy consistency. Transfer the dough to a mixing bowl and fold in the chocolate chips. Line a cookie sheet with parchment paper.

Drop heaping spoonfuls of dough onto the cookie sheet, about 1 inch (2.5 cm) apart each. Bake for 15 minutes, or until a toothpick inserted comes out clean.

BANANA OATMEAL Cookies

Ready for THE yummiest cookies? They're moist, chewy and made with fruit! Plus, they taste like miniature servings of banana bread . . . and who can say no to that!? —AS

MAKES 12 TO 16 COOKIES

1½ cups (195 g) whole wheat flour

1 tsp baking soda

1½ tsp (4 g) ground cinnamon

½ tsp salt

1 cup (200 g) brown sugar

½ cup (100 g) granulated sugar

⅓ cup (78 ml) and 1 tsp oil

3 tbsp (45 ml) water

1 large or 2 smaller bananas

1½ tsp (8 g) vanilla extract

2¼ cups (180 g) oats

Preheat the oven to 350°F (177°C).

In a bowl, mix together the flour, baking soda, cinnamon and salt. Set it aside.

In a separate bowl, mix the sugars, oil and water until combined.

(continued)

DESSERTS

Add the bananas and vanilla to the wet mixture, and stir until completely combined, mashing up the bananas with the whisk as you go.

Add the dry ingredients to the wet ingredients about ½ cup (60 g) at a time, stirring all the while. Once completely combined, add the oats and stir again.

Spoon 1- to 2-inch (2.5- to 5-cm) balls of the dough onto a cookie sheet. Bake for 10 to 12 minutes or until the edges are golden.

Carrot Cupcakes
WITH ORANGE VANILLA CREAM FROSTING

These are easy to whip up and come out light and sweet: lots of fresh carrot to keep them moist and flavorful, and plenty of orange vanilla cream frosting to keep them sweet and kid-friendly. Perfect for sharing after a strenuous Easter egg hunt or for munching while you Netflix binge! Either way, they're the perfect carrot cupcake. —AS

MAKES 16 CUPCAKES

CARROT CUPCAKES

2 cups (250 g) unbleached wheat flour

1 tbsp (11 g) baking powder

1 tsp baking soda

1 tsp salt

½ tsp ground ginger

½ tsp ground cinnamom

½ tsp nutmeg

1 cup (235 ml) coconut milk

1 cup (190 g) organic sugar

½ cup (115 g) mashed banana

½ cup (120 ml) melted coconut oil

2 tbsp (14 g) ground flaxseed

2 tsp (10 ml) vanilla extract

2 cups (310 g) grated carrots

ORANGE VANILLA CREAM FROSTING

⅓ cup (75 g) cold vegan butter or vegetable shortening

2 tbsp (30 ml) orange juice

1 tsp orange zest

1 tsp vanilla extract

2–3 cups (260–390 g) powdered sugar

Chopped walnuts, for garnish (optional)

FOR THE CARROT CUPCAKES

Preheat the oven to 350°F (177°C).

In a medium bowl, sift together the flour, baking powder, soda, salt, ginger, cinnamon and nutmeg. In a large mixing bowl or electric mixer, combine the coconut milk, sugar, mashed banana, coconut oil, ground flaxseed and vanilla extract. Add the dry ingredients about a cup (125 g) at a time, stirring continuously. Once the batter comes together, fold in the grated carrots. Pour the batter into greased or lined cupcake pans until the cups are about three-fourths full. Bake for 25 to 30 minutes, or until an inserted toothpick comes out clean. Let them cool completely while you whip up the frosting!

FOR THE ORANGE VANILLA CREAM FROSTING

In a food processor or high-speed blender, combine the vegan butter, orange juice and zest with the vanilla extract. Add the powdered sugar 1 cup (130 g) at a time until it reaches your desired consistency. Refrigerate until the cupcakes are completely cooled. (If you use butter, your cupcakes may need to be refrigerated to keep the frosting from melting. Shortening melts less, but still be wary of leaving them out on a warm day for too long!)

When the cupcakes have cooled, generously spread each one with a layer of creamy orange vanilla frosting.

*SEE PHOTO INSERT

CHOCOLATE ORANGE
Macaroons

+GF +SF

Dipped in melted dark chocolate and topped with freshly grated orange zest, these sweet confections are a perfect dessert for sharing . . . or not! —AS

MAKES ABOUT 12 MACAROONS

2 cups (150 g) unsweetened shredded coconut

¼ cup (55 g) coconut oil, at room temperature (not melted)

¼ cup (28 g) coconut flour (whole wheat works here, too)

¼ cup (28 g) cocoa powder

⅓ cup (80 ml) maple syrup or agave nectar

½ tsp salt

1 tsp orange extract

½ tsp vanilla extract

2–4 tsp (10–20 ml) cold water

2 oz (57 g) dark chocolate

Combine the coconut, coconut oil, flour, cocoa powder, syrup, salt, orange and vanilla extracts. Coconut oil should NOT be melted. You want to have to fork the mixture together until the solid coconut oil has been completely smooshed up and combined with everything else. It takes about 2 minutes of dedicated forking.

Add the water, starting with 2 teaspoons (10 ml), and stir until the mixture comes together and becomes sticky.

Once combined, use your hands to form the mixture into (about) 1-inch (2.5-cm) balls. Or 2-inch (5-cm) balls . . . because who am I to tell you how much macaroon to enjoy? Once your macaroons are formed, set them on a paper-lined cookie sheet in a cool place. The fridge will work beautifully here.

While the macaroons are chillin', melt the chocolate. To keep the recipe raw, use the double-boiler method. To do this, fill a large saucepan with water. Bring the water to a boil, and cover with a heat safe bowl, never allowing the heat safe bowl to come into contact with the water. Gently melt the chocolate.

Once the chocolate is fully melted, remove the macaroons from their cooling area. Dip the macaroons carefully into the chocolate, being careful not to coat them, but rather add the chocolate as more of an accent, 'cause these babies are rich! (Sometimes we use a piping bag to add a little decorative chocolate to the tops.) This is most easily done using a spoon and/or your fingers.

Once a little chocolate has been added, place the completed macaroons back onto a lined cookie sheet and refrigerate for about 30 to 60 minutes, allowing the chocolate to set. This process can be sped up by placing the entire cookie sheet into the freezer until the chocolate cools completely.

Once the macaroons are hardened and the chocolate has set, pull them out of the fridge and enjoy! They're best after coming to room temperature but are equally delicious chilled!

CHOCOLATE S'MORES
Cookies

+GFO

These cookies are a spin on my favorite chocolate cookie base, but are PACKED with scrumptious s'more goodness in every bite. The ooey-gooey marshmallows, the rich dark chocolate and the crunch of buttery graham cracker . . . excuse me while I wipe the drool off my keyboard. But seriously, these are a crowd-pleasin', sweet-tooth-satisfying, chocolate-lover's dream cookie. They're perfect for sharing and giving as gifts . . . or hoarding. Plus, since I reduced the sugar by nearly half, they're a little easier to recover from when you DO eat seven of them. —AS

MAKES ABOUT 20 COOKIES

2 cups (250 g) all-purpose flour or all-purpose GF flour mix

⅔ cup (73 g) cocoa powder

1 tsp baking soda

½ tsp xanthan gum (optional and only necessary if your GF flour mix has none)

½ tsp salt

½ cup (110 g) coconut oil, softened

1 cup (235 ml) maple syrup

1 tbsp (7 g) and 1 tsp ground flaxseed

½ cup (120 ml) dairy-free milk

2 tsp (10 ml) vanilla extract

¾ cup (135 g) chocolate chips

¾ cup (67 g) crushed vegan-friendly graham crackers

¾ cup (37 g) mini vegan marshmallows or regular-size marshmallows, quartered

Preheat the oven to 350°F (177°C).

In a large mixing bowl, whisk together the flour, cocoa powder, baking soda, xanthan gum (if using) and salt until well mixed. Set it aside.

In a mixer or with hand beaters, cream together the softened coconut oil and maple syrup. Add the ground flaxseed, milk and vanilla extract, and mix until totally combined. Add the dry ingredients to the wet mixture about a cup (125 g) at a time, mixing them together until all of the dry ingredients are completely incorporated into the wet and a soft dough forms. Pour in your chocolate chips, crushed crackers and marshmallows, and use a wooden spoon or spatula to work them into the dough.

Using an ice cream scoop or a spoon, scoop 1-inch (2.5-cm) balls of dough onto a greased cookie sheet about 2 inches (5 cm) apart. Bake for 10 to 12 minutes, until the edges are crisp and the 'mallows begin to brown. Remove them from oven, move to a cooling rack and allow them to cool. Once cool, they can be moved to a plastic bag or airtight container and stored for about a week. Frozen, they'll be good for several months—then you can pull out just one at a time instead of having an entire batch at your disposal. I never get that far.

Coconut COOKIE BUTTER BARS

+GFO

This sweet treat is a celebration of independence and deliciousness, of new beginnings and late night snacking—and man, it is good. But I won't lie, it's a dessert you may want to eat in moderation. It's rich, fudgy and filled with crunchy, sweet cookie butter . . . perfect for celebrating, and even better when shared with your significant other. —AS

MAKES 12 SQUARE BARS, 2 X 2 INCHES (5 X 5 CM)

SUGAR COOKIE LAYER

2½ cups (325 g) whole wheat flour or gluten-free all-purpose flour

½ tsp xanthan gum (only if using GF flour)

1 tsp baking powder

½ tsp salt

2 cups (385 g) organic sugar (we used coconut sugar, which is why our batter is slightly browner than usual)

1 cup (218 g) coconut oil or vegan butter

2 tsp (10 ml) vanilla extract

2 ripe bananas, mashed

½ cup (38 g) shredded coconut

COOKIE BUTTER LAYER

½ cup (110 g) coconut oil or vegan butter

1 cup (230 g) cookie butter

CHOCOLATE LAYER

1 cup (180 g) chocolate chips or chopped bar chocolate

½ cup (110 g) coconut oil or vegan butter

FOR THE SUGAR COOKIE LAYER

Preheat the oven to 350°F (177°C). In a medium mixing bowl, combine the flour, xanthan (if using), baking powder and salt. Set aside. In a stand mixer, beat together the sugar and coconut oil (or butter) until whipped, about 1 full minute on high speed. Add the vanilla and bananas, and continue to mix until combined. Add the dry ingredients and mix again until a batter forms. Toss in the shredded coconut and mix one last time to distribute it throughout the batter. Pour the batter into a greased or lined 8 x 8-inch (20 x 20-cm) glass baking dish (for thinner bars, feel free to use a 9 x 13-inch [23 x 33-cm] pan), and bake for 30 minutes, or until an inserted toothpick comes out clean. When finished, let it cool on the counter for at least an hour (but up to overnight) or in the fridge for at least 30 minutes to set. While cooling, make the cookie butter mixture.

FOR THE COOKIE BUTTER LAYER

In a small saucepan, combine the coconut oil and cookie butter over low heat. Stir frequently, until the mixture melts together, and then promptly remove it from the heat and let it cool and thicken. Once thickened to the consistency of slightly thinned cookie butter, pour or spread the mixture over the cooled cookie base. To set the cookie butter layer, immediately store it in the fridge or freezer for about 30 minutes. While setting, begin the chocolate layer.

FOR THE CHOCOLATE LAYER

In a small saucepan, combine the chocolate and coconut oil over low heat, stirring frequently until the mixture melts together. Remove it from the heat, pour the chocolate mixture over the chilled cookie butter layer and immediately place the bars back into the fridge or freezer for about 30 more minutes to set completely.

Once the entire dessert has set, remove it from the fridge or freezer and cut it. If frozen, allow the dessert to warm slightly to room temperature so the chocolate doesn't crack. Cut it into 12 (or more) squares and serve. This saves well in a covered container in the fridge for about a week, or in the freezer indefinitely.

DARK CHOCOLATE ROSEMARY **Cookies**

+GF

I used a double chocolate base to really bring out the flavor of the rosemary and kept them gluten-free so I could enjoy them without getting a tummy ache. They're the ultimate chewy chocolate cookie. —AS

MAKES ABOUT 20 COOKIES

2 cups (250 g) all-purpose gluten-free flour mix (We used 1 cup [125 g] teff flour + 1 cup [95 g] almond flour, our favorite blend. Whole wheat works here, too!)

⅔ cup (74 g) cocoa powder

1 tsp baking soda

½ tsp xanthan gum (if you use GF flour)

½ tsp salt

½ cup (110 g) coconut oil, softened

1½ cups (288 g) sugar

1 tbsp (7 g) and 1 tsp ground flaxseed

½ cup (120 ml) nut milk

2 tsp (10 ml) vanilla extract

2 tsp (2 g) dried, chopped rosemary (if using fresh rosemary, substitute 2 tbsp [3.4 g])

¾ cup (135 g) dark chocolate chips or chopped bar chocolate

Preheat the oven to 350°F (177°C). In a large mixing bowl, whisk together the flours, cocoa powder, baking soda, xanthan gum and salt until well mixed. Set it aside. In a mixer or with hand beaters, cream together the softened coconut oil and sugar. Add the ground flaxseed, nut milk, vanilla and chopped rosemary, and mix until totally combined. Add the dry ingredients to the wet mixture about a cup (125 g) at a time, mixing them together until all of the dry ingredients are completely incorporated into the wet and a soft dough forms. Pour in the chocolate chips (or chunks) and use a wooden spoon or spatula to work them into the dough.

Use an ice cream scoop or a spoon to scoop 1-inch (2.5-cm) balls of dough onto a greased cookie sheet about 2 inches (5 cm) apart. Bake for 12 to 13 minutes, until the edges are crisp and the tops begin to crack. Remove them from the oven, move to a cooling rack and try not to eat them all before they cool. Once cool, they can be moved to a plastic bag or an airtight container and stored for about a week. Frozen, they'll be good for several months.

They're great next to a tall glass of almond milk and somehow get even tastier the next day.

Deep-Dish APPLE CINNAMON SKILLET CAKE WITH MAPLE VANILLA GLAZE

+GF

How much do you associate the flavors of apple and cinnamon with fall?

For me, it's a nearly impossible combination to avoid as the temperature drops and the leaves fall. Something about the warm, cozy smell of spicy cinnamon and nutmeg and crisp, sweet baked apples makes me swoon. This cake is perfect for fall-themed parties and will definitely be making an appearance on our Fall Holiday table this year! —AS

SERVES 6 TO 10

2 tbsp (14 g) ground flaxseed

6 tbsp (90 ml) warm water

1 cup (220 g) vegan butter or coconut oil

1 cup (190 g) granulated sugar

1 cup (145 g) brown sugar

½ cup (120 ml) nut milk

1 tsp vanilla extract

2 cups (250 g) GF all-purpose flour (or your favorite blend; we used 1 cup [125 g] teff and 1 cup [125 g] white rice flour)

1 tsp baking powder

1 tsp xanthan gum (if you use GF flour)

½ tsp salt

2 tsp (4 g) ground cinnamon

½ tsp ground nutmeg

3 cups (540 g) peeled and diced crisp apples

Preheat the oven to 350°F (177°C). Grease a large cast-iron skillet and set aside. We used a deep-dish, 9-inch (23-cm) cast-iron skillet for baking. This cake doesn't rise a ton, so alternatively you can bake the batter in a regular 9-inch (23-cm) baking dish—it'll work just fine. Just be sure to adjust the cooking times so it isn't undercooked or overcooked. You can check the doneness with a toothpick.

In a small mixing bowl, whisk together the flaxseed and warm water and set aside to gelatinize.

In another mixing bowl, beat together the butter (or softened coconut oil) and sugars until fluffy. Add the flax mixture and whisk until completely combined. Add the milk and vanilla, stirring until a goopy batter starts to form.

In a separate, medium bowl, combine the flour, baking powder, xanthan gum, salt, cinnamon and nutmeg. Add the dry ingredients to the wet, and combine. Then add the diced apples and mix them well.

Pour the batter into the pan and bake for 45 to 55 minutes, until a toothpick comes out clean. This cake will save, covered, for up to 5 days in the fridge.

DOUBLE CHOCOLATE PEPPERMINT **Cookies**

+GF

Between the chewy cookie, chunks of rich, dark chocolate and the refreshing addition of peppermint oil, you're going to love these cookies. And the peppermint chunks? Well those are purely optional, but certainly add to the festiveness! They're the ultimate chewy chocolate cookie, a crowd pleaser for sure! —AS

MAKES ABOUT 20 COOKIES

2 cups (250 g) all-purpose gluten-free flour mix (whole wheat works here too!)

⅔ cup (74 g) cocoa powder

1 tsp baking soda

½ tsp xanthan gum (optional, use only if NOT included in your GF flour mixture)

½ tsp salt

½ cup (110 g) coconut oil, softened

1½ cups (288 g) sugar

1 tbsp (7 g) and 1 tsp ground flaxseed

½ cup (120 ml) nut milk

2 tsp (10 ml) vanilla extract

1 tsp peppermint extract

¾ cup (135 g) dark chocolate chips or chopped bar chocolate

Crushed peppermint candy, for garnish

(continued)

Preheat the oven to 350°F (177°C).

In a large mixing bowl, whisk together the flours, cocoa powder, baking soda, xanthan gum (if using) and salt until well mixed. Set it aside. In a mixer or with hand beaters, cream together the softened coconut oil and sugar. Add the ground flax, nut milk, vanilla and peppermint extracts, and mix until totally combined. Add the dry ingredients to the wet mixture about a cup (125 g) at a time, mixing them together until all of the dry ingredients are completely incorporated into the wet and a soft dough forms. Pour in the chocolate chips and use a wooden spoon or spatula to work them into the dough.

Use an ice cream scoop or a spoon to scoop 1-inch (2.5-cm) balls of dough onto a greased cookie sheet about 2 inches (5 cm) apart. Bake for 12 to 13 minutes, until the edges are crisp and the tops begin to crack. Remove the cookies from the oven and then to a cooling rack. Top with peppermint candy. Try not to eat them all before they cool. Once cool, they can be moved to a plastic bag or an airtight container and stored for about a week. Frozen, they'll be good for several months.

Vegan EASTER CREME EGGS

+GF

I've recreated a nearly perfect Cadbury Creme Egg with this recipe, but with completely vegan ingredients! Let me stop you right here—I didn't ditch the sugar, and these are in no way "healthy." What they are is delicious and a re-creation of one of my childhood favorites. And in that sense, we nailed it. We even took the time to add dyed yellow "yolks," just to be authentic and such. But don't worry, no chickies were harmed in the making of these gems . . . just my waistline! —AS

MAKES 16 EGGS

½ cup (95 g) and 2 tbsp (24 g) sugar

2 tbsp (30 ml) hot water

¼ cup (57 g) vegan butter

1 tbsp (15 ml) unsweetened almond milk

1 tsp vanilla extract

⅛ tsp salt

3 cups (390 g) powdered sugar

A few drops of yellow food coloring (we used Color Garden brand pure natural food colors)

10 oz (285 g) chocolate chips or chopped bar chocolate

8 egg-shaped molds (or any-shaped molds, really!)

Heat a small pot over low heat. Pour in the sugar and water, stirring until the sugar is completely dissolved. Turn off the heat and pour the mixture into a large mixing bowl.

Add the butter, milk, vanilla and salt, and beat the mixture together. Pour the powdered sugar into the bowl about a cup (130 g) at a time, beating continuously until a thick fondant-like paste forms.

Scoop about three-fourths of the mixture into a small bowl and the remaining quarter into another small bowl. Into the smaller bowl, add a few drops of yellow food coloring and stir until the entire mixture is evenly dyed. Set it aside.

Using the double-boiler method, melt the chocolate. Pour the melted chocolate into the molds, gently turning the mold pan to evenly coat the inner molds. (Obviously we used an egg shape, but if you only have a heart shape, use it! You could probably also just roll the fondant-like sugar mixture into balls and dip it in chocolate, but no guarantees on how they'll look.) Tap out the excess chocolate and pop the molds into the fridge or freezer for a few minutes to harden.

Once hardened, fill the molds about two-thirds of the way full with the white fondant mixture (which for us was a little under a tablespoon [14 g]), then add a small amount of the yellow fondant mixture (a bit under a teaspoon [5 g] for us) to the middle. You want the eggs nearly full, but not so full you can't easily add the chocolate top layer. Place the molds back into the fridge to set the fondant layer, about 15 to 20 minutes.

Once set, gently pour the melted chocolate over the top of each filled egg mold, using the back of a butter knife or spatula to scrape any excess chocolate from the top of the molds. Pop the molds into the fridge or freezer to set, about 30 minutes. Once the chocolate has hardened and set, you can immediately enjoy the creme eggs! Otherwise, see the note below for saving them.

Note: This makes sixteen 2-inch (5-cm) eggs, or you can get crafty and apply a bit more melted chocolate to the backs of 2 half-eggs, connecting them to make 8 large creme eggs.

These are best kept refrigerated or in a cool place, but are fine on the counter (or in an Easter basket) for several hours. They last up to a month in the fridge or indefinitely in the freezer.

*SEE PHOTO INSERT

GINGERSNAP BUTTERCREAM
Cookie Sandwiches

Using fresh ginger and nutmeg in these cookies really makes the flavors rich and bright. And the molasses helps keep them chewy—and adds some iron and calcium so you can pretend they're a health food. That's how that works, right? Wanna cut the sugar? Skip the buttercream frosting and just eat the cookies as is; they're pretty darn delicious on their own! —AS

MAKES 20 COOKIES OR 10 COOKIE SANDWICHES

COOKIES
1¼ cups (155 g) all-purpose flour
1 tsp baking soda
½ tsp baking powder
½ tsp salt
½ tsp ground cinnamom
¼ tsp freshly grated nutmeg, plus more for garnish
¾ cup (150 g) packed brown sugar
½ cup (120 g) coconut oil or vegan butter
3 tbsp (21 g) ground flaxseed
3 tbsp (65 g) molasses
2 tbsp (29 g) grated fresh ginger
1 tsp vanilla extract

BUTTERCREAM FILLING
2 cups (260 g) powdered sugar
¼ cup (57 g) vegan butter
1 tsp vanilla extract
1–2 tbsp (15–30 ml) unsweetened nondairy milk

(continued)

FOR THE COOKIES

Preheat the oven to 350°F (177°C).

In a large mixing bowl, combine the flour, baking soda, baking powder, salt, cinnamon and nutmeg.

In a separate bowl or stand mixer, cream together the brown sugar and coconut oil. Stir in the ground flax, molasses, ginger and vanilla until completely combined.

Pour the dry ingredients into the wet mixture about a cup (125 g) at a time, stirring continuously, until the cookie dough comes together.

Scoop 1-inch (2.5-cm) balls of cookie dough onto a lined baking sheet and bake for 10 to 12 minutes, until the edges are firm. Move the cookies to a wire rack to cool.

FOR THE BUTTERCREAM FILLING

Beat together the powdered sugar, butter and vanilla. Add the milk a bit at a time, until the desired frosting texture is achieved.

Spread the buttercream onto half of the cooled cookies, and move them to the fridge or freezer for 10 minutes to firm the frosting before topping it with another cookie. Once they have been assembled, grate fresh nutmeg over the sandwiches and gobble them up!

Note: After the cookies cooled, we placed some of the frosting on top. We then placed them in the freezer for 10 minutes to set the frosting before placing the second cookie on top. Otherwise, the frosting tends to smoosh out the sides a bit. If you won't be serving them immediately, I recommend keeping them in the fridge until just before serving.

*SEE PHOTO INSERT

Homemade
STRAWBERRY ICE CREAM

+GF +QP

This recipe couldn't be easier. It is super simple, healthy and a guilt-free sweet treat you can snuggle up with after dinner! —AS

SERVES 4

2 (15-oz [444-ml]) cans full-fat organic coconut milk

2 cups (303 g) frozen strawberries

2 tbsp (30 ml) maple syrup or agave nectar

1 tsp vanilla extract

Refrigerate the cans of coconut milk overnight on a stable shelf. When ready, open the cans and scoop the full-fat, thick white layer off of the top half of the can and into a high-speed blender or food processor. Save the clear-ish liquid at the bottom to use in smoothies, oatmeal or anything else that requires a milk substitute.

Add the strawberries, syrup and vanilla to the blender, and start to blend, slowly at first, faster as the strawberries break down. Blend it all together for about 1 minute, or until all of the ingredients are completely combined in a soft-serve texture. Scoop the mixture into a medium mixing bowl or loaf pan, and toss it in the freezer for at least 3 hours, but preferably overnight. Stir the mixture about every hour or so to aerate the ice cream and make it easier to scoop later.

When ready to eat, let it sit on the counter for 5 to 10 minutes to soften up enough for serving. Scoop it out into bowls, top it with sprinkles if desired and share with your Valentine! Saves in the freezer indefinitely if stored in a sealed container.

MANGO ROSEMARY
Sorbet

+GF +QP +SF

Mango and rosemary. Oh yeah. You betcha. I dreamed up this flavor combo while explaining how something about mangoes always tastes piney to me. I know a lot of people agree with me, but (surprise!) some people just don't get it. I suppose the riper a mango is, the less piney in flavor, but it always has a hint of it to my taste buds. Combine that subtle hint of pine with the aromatic and earthy flavor of rosemary, and you've got a new favorite flavor combo. The sweetness of the mango and added maple syrup balance out any residual "woodsy" taste, and the orange juice adds just a snap of citrus to round the flavors out. —AS

SERVES 2

1 (15-oz [444-ml]) can coconut milk

1 mango, peeled, pitted and cubed

2 tbsp (5 g) chopped fresh rosemary

2 tbsp (30 ml) maple syrup or agave nectar

2 tbsp (30 ml) freshly squeezed orange juice

In a high-speed blender or food processor, combine the coconut milk, mango, rosemary, maple syrup and orange juice, and blend until combined. Pour it into a freezer-safe dish and cover. Freeze for at least 3 hours, but overnight if possible. Remove it from the freezer about 10 minutes prior to serving to allow the sorbet to soften for scooping. Serve with a sprig of fresh rosemary and a cookie. Any kind will do. This will stay fresh in the freezer, if well covered, indefinitely.

ORANGE CHOCOLATE
Cheesecake

+GF +SF +QP

On our fourth Valentine's Day together, I wanted to make my then-boyfriend something extra delicious. So I started raiding the cabinets. I came out with a half bottle of orange extract and lot of cocoa powder . . . and got right to work! And when it was done? I was so proud of myself. It was creamy, rich, decadent . . . a perfect sweet treat for my handsome valentine. —AS

SERVES 8 TO 12

CRUST

½ cup (85 g) pitted dates

1½ cups (255 g) raw almonds

3 tbsp (45 ml) melted coconut oil

CHEESECAKE

3 cups (330 g) cashews, soaked and then drained

¾ cup (180 ml) orange juice

⅔ cup (160 ml) agave

¼ cup (28 g) cocoa powder

1 tsp (5 g) salt

1 tsp orange extract

¾ cup (180 ml) melted coconut oil

¼ cup (25 g) grated dark chocolate, for garnish (optional)

FOR THE CRUST

Blend all the ingredients together in a food processor or strong blender. I use my Vitamix, and it works like a charm every time. You want the nuts and dates to the consistency of a sort of chunky, less malleable cookie dough.

(continued)

Scoop the mixture into a 9-inch (23-cm) springform pan (the easiest way) or line a cake or pie tin with parchment paper (less easy) and scoop it into that.

Press the mixture into the sides and bottom of the pan.

Freeze it to set, at least 1 hour or more.

FOR THE CHEESECAKE

After your cashews have soaked for at least an hour, throw them in your blender or food processor. Add the freshly squeezed orange juice, agave, cocoa powder, salt, orange extract and coconut oil. Blend on high for about a minute, more if your machine needs it. The consistency will be that of a thick pudding, whipped and mostly pourable.

Remove the crust from the freezer and pour the cheesecake filling on top, tapping the pan several times on the counter to level the filling completely flat.

Place the assembled cheesecake back in the freezer or in the refrigerator, at least 3 hours to set completely. Placing it in the freezer will result in a firmer, more ice-cream-like texture. Placing it in the fridge will leave it much softer and more like a custard.

Once the cheesecake has set, remove it from the fridge/freezer and top around the outer edge (or anywhere you like, really) with grated chocolate.

Slice, serve and enjoy.

Mini KEY LIME CHEESECAKE

+GF +QP +SF

These cheesecakes are so easy to whip up, they'll have you feeling like you really ARE on summer vacation already. And maybe you are! In that case, have two margaritas. This recipe is broken up into several "set it and forget it" steps, followed by a large serving of DELICIOUS. You're gonna love the creamy, zesty lime flavor accented by a sprinkle of coarse sea salt and the chewy, sweet date and nut crust. Perfect for sharing, summer-size portions and adorable snacking, this can also be made in cake-pan size if you prefer. Either way, I'll see you at the beach. —AS

MAKES 4 TO 6 SMALL RAMEKINS (OR TARTS) OR 1 (9-INCH [23-CM]) CHEESECAKE

CRUST
½ cup (85 g) pitted dates
1½ cups (255 g) nuts (I used almonds and cashews)
3 tbsp (45 ml) melted coconut oil

CHEESECAKE
3 cups (330 g) cashews, soaked and drained
¾ cup (180 ml) freshly squeezed Key lime juice
⅔ cup (160 ml) agave nectar or maple syrup
¾ cup (180 ml) melted coconut oil
1 tsp sea salt
1 tsp vanilla extract
Zest of 1 Key lime (about 1 tsp)
Sprinkle of coarse sea salt, for garnish
Lime wedge, for serving

FOR THE CRUST

Blend all the ingredients together in a food processor or high-speed blender. Grease or line 4 to 6 ramekins (or tart dishes) or one 9-inch (23-cm) springform pan. Press the date and nut mixture into the bottom of the ramekins or pan. Refrigerate or freeze to set the coconut oil, about 1 hour.

FOR THE CHEESECAKE

Soak the cashews in warm water for at least 1 hour. Blend the cashews, lime juice, agave, coconut oil, salt, vanilla and lime zest in a food processor or high-speed blender until completely combined. Remove the ramekins or cake pan from the fridge and fill to the top with the Key lime mixture. Put it in the freezer or fridge to set for at least 3 hours before serving (or just eat it—it might not keep its shape as well, but it'll still taste delicious). When ready, remove it from the fridge and plate it. Sprinkle with coarse sea salt and a lime wedge to garnish. Serve and enjoy! This is great topped with coconut whipped cream or all by itself and lasts indefinitely covered in the freezer, or at least 1 week in the fridge.

PECAN PIE **Bars**

Pecans are rich, earthy nuts that pair well with all kinds of fruit—but like most things, they taste best drowned in a sugary syrup and baked on a crust. Pecan pies are great, but things in mini-form are cuter and easier to share. Plus, at our age we're mostly celebrating Friendsgivings and less formal family dinners, and presliced goodies are easier to pack into doggy bags for your friends. These bars are super easy to whip up and are as equally delicious as their round cousin, but better because there's more crust—and that's my favorite part. —AS

MAKES 12 BARS

CRUST

1 cup (230 g) vegan butter

½ cup (110 g) packed brown sugar

2½ cups (325 g) whole wheat flour

½ tsp salt

TOPPING

½ cup (115 g) vegan butter

1 cup (220 g) packed brown sugar

1 tbsp (15 ml) coconut cream (see Note)

1 tsp vanilla extract

2 cups (220 g) chopped pecans

Whipped coconut cream, to serve

Sprinkle of ground cinnamon, for garnish

Preheat the oven to 350°F (177°C).

FOR THE CRUST

Cream together the butter and brown sugar in a stand mixer or with hand beaters. Add the flour and salt, and mix until crumbly. Press it into a parchment-lined 9 x 13-inch (23 x 33-cm) pan. Bake the crust for 20 minutes or until golden.

(continued)

DESSERTS

While the crust bakes, prep the pecan topping by whisking together the butter, brown sugar, coconut cream and vanilla in a medium saucepan over medium heat until everything melts and combines, about 5 minutes. Once the mixture comes completely together, add the chopped pecans and mix them in. Continue cooking over low heat, stirring occasionally, until the crust is finished cooking.

When the crust finishes, remove it from the oven and pour the pecan mixture on top. Return the pan to the oven and bake for an additional 20 minutes.

Remove it from the oven, let it cool completely and then slice it up into 12 (or more) equal squares.

Note: Coconut cream is the thick white cream layer from the top of a can of full-fat coconut milk. We also like using Trader Joe's brand coconut cream.

Leftover bars can be saved in an airtight container on the counter for up to a week.

PUMPKIN CHOCOLATE CHIP **Cookies**

I usually eat a very healthy diet and rarely sugar splurge, but when I'm on my period and I want chocolate and sugar, these cookies are heavenly and dreamy and amazing. You will love them. Everyone will! These are "impress your mother-in-law" cookies. These are celebrating your birthday cookies. They're follow with a glass of champagne cookies. They're decadent and rich and insanely delicious. If you're on a diet, these are not for you. If you wanna have a fall-flavored mouthgasm, then these are definitely for you. Your choice. But let's be honest, with an intro like that, don't you wanna bake up a batch? We'll do it together and share the guilt. Let's eat! —AS

MAKES 36 COOKIES

2½ cups (325 g) all-purpose flour

1 tbsp (6 g) pumpkin pie spice

1 tsp baking soda

1 tsp (5 g) sea salt

1 cup (218 g) coconut oil or vegan butter, melted

1 cup (190 g) organic sugar

½ cup (90 g) pumpkin purée

3 tbsp (14 g) ground flaxseed

1 tsp vanilla extract

¾ cup (135 g) chocolate chips

Preheat the oven to 350°F (177°C).

In a medium bowl, mix together the flour, pumpkin spice, baking soda and sea salt. Set this aside.

In a larger mixing bowl, whisk the melted coconut oil or butter, sugar, pumpkin purée, ground flaxseed and vanilla. Pour the wet ingredients into your dry ingredients and stir until completely combined, or process in a food processor with the dough blade.

Fold in the chocolate chips until they're evenly distributed in the dough. Then use a spoon or cookie dough scoop to place 1-inch (2.5-cm) balls of dough onto a greased or parchment-lined cookie sheet. Bake for 8 to 10 minutes, or until golden. Let them cool on a wire rack, and then enjoy! Cookies last in the fridge for about a week and in the freezer indefinitely.

Note: You can safely sub in half of the all-purpose flour for whole wheat flour, if you prefer, but you will get a denser cookie.

Defrost frozen cookies by placing them onto a plate and leaving on the counter for about 2 hours, or by microwaving them for a few seconds at a time.

You could definitely sub in applesauce or a healthier replacement for some of the oil if you want, but I would recommend only subbing in about half the amount to maintain the cookie texture.

Purple SWEET POTATO PIE BARS

+GF +SF

The sweet potatoes are paired with warm fall flavors like maple, cinnamon and ginger on a chewy cashew-date-macadamia crust that makes them irresistible—much like a traditional sweet potato pie, but far healthier! They are totally naturally sweetened, and you can omit the maple syrup if you prefer to keep them date-sweetened only. Eat them on their own, or top them with a bit of whipped cream and a sprinkle of fresh nutmeg for the perfect fall treat. They're an indulgence you don't have to have any guilt about, so go ahead—have two! —AS

MAKES 16 TO 20 BARS

CASHEW DATE MACADAMIA CRUST LAYER

1½ cups (165 g) cashews

1 cup (110 g) macadamia nuts (or skinless almonds [150 g])

1 cup (170 g) pitted dates

3 tbsp (42 g) coconut oil

PURPLE SWEET POTATO PIE LAYER

1½ lbs (680 g) purple sweet potatoes

¾ cup (180 ml) unsweetened almond milk

3 tbsp (45 ml) maple syrup

1 tbsp (14 g) coconut oil

1 tbsp (15 ml) lemon juice

1 tsp vanilla extract

½ tsp ground ginger

½ tsp ground cinnamon

⅛ tsp ground nutmeg

⅛ tsp salt

FOR THE CASHEW DATE MACADAMIA CRUST LAYER

Soak the cashews and macadamia nuts in warm water for at least 1 hour. Drain off the liquid and pour the soaked nuts into the food processor. Add the pitted dates and coconut oil, and process until a sticky crust forms.

Grease or line a 9 x 9-inch (23 x 23-cm) glass baking dish. Scrape the crust mixture into the baking dish and use a rubber spatula or spoon to press the mixture firmly and evenly into the pan. Refrigerate or freeze it to set the crust, about 1 hour, before topping with the sweet potato mixture. Wipe the processor bowl out with a paper towel and set it aside.

FOR THE PURPLE SWEET POTATO PIE LAYER

Place the sweet potatoes into a large pot of water and bring it to a boil. Cook until the potatoes are fork tender, about 10 to 15 minutes. Remove them from the water and let them cool completely. Once cooled, remove the skins and toss them into the compost. Place the sweet potatoes into the processor bowl with the almond milk, maple syrup, coconut oil, lemon juice, vanilla, ginger, cinnamon, nutmeg and salt. Process on high until the mixture is completely combined and smooth.

Pour the mixture over the cooled crust layer and spread it evenly around. Place the baking dish back into the freezer to firm up—they'll be much easier to slice this way. Once they're firm, about 3 or more hours later, slice the bars into even squares. Serve immediately or let them soften in the fridge until you're ready to enjoy!

Leftovers can be saved in the fridge for several days or the freezer indefinitely.

Note: Purple sweet potatoes are different than Japanese sweet potatoes, which are purple on the outside but white on the inside. Make sure you double-check, or your pie squares—while delicious!—certainly won't come out looking like ours.

STRAWBERRY RHUBARB **Crumble**

+GF +SF

This crumble is the BEST. It is yummy, sugar-free and so simple it'll blow your mind. Oh, and did I mention gluten-free? And soy-free? It ticks those boxes too, babes. It's a baked good you can feel good about eating and will feel good about eating because it tastes damn delicious. I did well, guys. And I think you're gonna be really proud of me. —AS

SERVES 6 TO 8

CRUMBLE

4 heaping cups (610 g) fresh chopped strawberries

2 cups (245 g) fresh sliced rhubarb

2 tbsp (30 ml) lemon juice

1 tbsp (10 g) chia seeds

1 cup (95 g) almond flour

2 cups (160 g) GF oats

¼ cup (60 ml) monk fruit sweetener (or sweetener of your choice—sugar works if you're into it, and the ratio is 1:1)

1 tsp baking powder

¼ tsp salt

½ cup (110 g) coconut oil, softened

COCO WHIP

2 (15-oz [425-g]) cans full-fat coconut milk

1-3 tbsp (15-45 ml) monk fruit sweetener (again, use your fave sweetener here if you prefer)

1-3 tbsp (15-45 ml) nondairy milk

1 tsp vanilla extract

Preheat the oven to 375°F (190°C). Grease a 9 x 13-inch (23 x 33-cm) glass baking dish and set it aside.

FOR THE CRUMBLE

In a large mixing bowl, toss your strawberries and rhubarb in the lemon juice and chia seeds until they're evenly coated. In a separate mixing bowl, combine the almond flour, oats, monk fruit sweetener, baking powder and salt. Add the softened coconut oil and stir until crumbs begin to form. Pour the strawberry-rhubarb mixture evenly into the greased glass baking dish. Top with the oat and almond flour crumble mixture, distributing evenly. Put the crumble into the oven and bake for 35 to 45 minutes, until the crumble topping becomes golden and the berry mixture bubbles. Remove it from the oven and let it cool completely before serving.

FOR THE COCO WHIP

To prepare the coconut whip, simply scoop the firm solids from the cans of coconut milk into a large mixing bowl and toss in the sweetener, milk and vanilla; whip it with the beaters until fluffy. Scoop it onto your crumble and enjoy!

Leftovers—both the crumble and the whip—last for up to a week wrapped separately in the fridge.

Note: To reheat, cover with the foil and reheat at 350°F (177°C) for about 20 to 30 minutes, or until warm in the middle.

Vanilla CASHEW BUTTER CUPS

+GF +QP

These sweet little treats are almost too easy to make! They're rich, creamy and decadent—and you'd never know they had no added sugar. —AS

MAKES 12 TO 14 CUPS

VANILLA CASHEW BUTTER
2 cups (220 g) raw cashews

1 vanilla bean, scraped

¼ tsp ground cinnamon

Pinch of salt

VANILLA CASHEW BUTTER CUPS
3 cups (540 g) dairy-free chocolate chips or chunks

¼ cup (55 g) coconut oil (optional)

1-3 drops vanilla stevia (optional)

FOR THE VANILLA CASHEW BUTTER

Preheat the oven to 325°F (163°C). Line a baking sheet with parchment paper. Spread the cashews onto the baking sheet and roast for 10 to 15 minutes, stirring once, until golden and fragrant.

Let the cashews cool completely, and then pour them into a food processor with the vanilla bean innards, cinnamon and salt. Process until smooth. It might take a while; it took us about 5 continuous minutes of processing to get a super smooth consistency. Of course, if you prefer it a little chunky, you do you—just stop processing while there are still some chunks left. Pour the nut butter into an airtight container and set it aside.

FOR THE VANILLA CASHEW BUTTER CUPS

Line a muffin tin with paper liners and set it aside.

Using the double-boiler method, begin to melt the chocolate chips over medium heat, stirring as they soften. Pour in the coconut oil and stevia, if using, and continue to stir until the chocolate is completely melted and smooth.

Pour about 1 tablespoon (15 ml) of melted chocolate into each lined cup. Pop the tray into the freezer for 5 to 10 minutes to set. Pull the tray out and scoop about 1 tablespoon (15 g) of the vanilla cashew butter onto the chocolate layer of each cup, centering it as best you can. Once all the cups have the cashew butter, pop the tray in the freezer for another 5 to 10 minutes to set again. While it sets, make sure your chocolate is still melty and ready to go.

When set, pull the tray from the freezer again and top each cup with 1 to 2 tablespoons (15 to 30 ml) of the remaining melted chocolate mixture, until the cashew butter is completely covered or "sealed" within each cup. Pop the tray back in the freezer to set for another 10 to 15 minutes. Once set, remove the cups from the tray and enjoy! They will soften at room temperature if coconut oil was added, so keep them in a cool place until you're ready to eat them.

Note: Leftover vanilla cashew butter doesn't need to be refrigerated, and should keep for at least 2 weeks out of the fridge. It will last indefinitely in the fridge.

Leftover cups are best saved in an airtight container in the fridge or freezer for up to 6 months.

WHITE CHOCOLATE MACADAMIA NUT
Cookies

I love cookies of all shapes and sizes—I'm not one to discriminate. That being said, there just aren't enough vegan white chocolate macadamia nut cookies around. At least not readily available for purchase...so I came up with my own recipe so I could have them whenever I got a craving. In these, I used chopped cacao butter instead of using a store-bought vegan white chocolate—which is REALLY hard to find. (I have found it online, though.) Cacao butter is the edible vegetable fat extracted from the cocoa bean, and it both smells and tastes like chocolate. It's the perfect substitute—and it's packed with antioxidants to help give you healthy hair and skin. So they're basically a health food...right?! —AS

MAKES 16 BARS

1 cup (230 g) vegan butter or vegetable shortening

⅔ cup (160 ml) maple syrup (see Note)

1½ tsp (8 ml) vanilla extract

¾ tsp salt

2 cups (250 g) all-purpose flour

½ cup (90 g) roughly chopped vegan white chocolate or cacao butter

½ cup (55 g) roughly chopped macadamia nuts

Preheat the oven to 350°F (177°C).

Using a handheld or stand mixer, cream together the butter, syrup, vanilla and salt until light and fluffy. Add the flour. When it's fully incorporated, stir in the white chocolate and nuts.

Pour the cookie dough into a greased 9 x 13-inch (23 x 33-cm) baking dish. Press the dough very firmly with plastic wrap or a spatula until the top is silky smooth and free of cracks or bubbles.

Bake for 23 to 28 minutes until slightly golden and crisp on the edges. An inserted toothpick should come out clean. Cool completely, and then cut into triangles (or squares) with a sharp knife. Scoop out the bars and enjoy!

Note: You can sub 1 cup (190 g) organic sugar for the maple syrup here. The cookie bars will be crispier if you do this.

For thicker bars, you can also try baking in an 8 x 8-inch (20 x 20-cm) pan, but the cooking time may need to be adjusted.

Leftovers last in the fridge for about a week.

Whole Wheat
CINNAMON SUGAR PULL-APART LOAF

If you're looking for a brunch main that will totally impress your guests, you've come to the right place. This pull-apart loaf is super sharable and looks like you had to go to pastry school to learn to construct it. But I swear—it's really easy! Just make the dough, cover it in cinnamon sugar, slice and bake. You're gonna be a hit at the breakfast table! —AS

SERVES 4 TO 6

LOAF
2¼ tsp (7 g) active dry yeast

1¼ cups (300 ml) warm water

2 cups (250 g) all-purpose flour

1½ cups (230 g) whole wheat pastry flour

¼ cup (50 g) sugar

⅛ tsp salt

1 tbsp (15 ml) olive oil, plus extra for the bowl and pan

FILLING
1 cup (200 g) sugar

2 tsp (6 g) ground cinnamon

½ tsp fresh ground nutmeg

4 tbsp (60 g) vegan butter

FOR THE LOAF

Preheat the oven to 350°F (177°C). Lightly grease a loaf pan and set it aside.

Mix the active dry yeast into the warm water and set it aside.

In a stand mixer fitted with a dough hook, mix together the all-purpose flour, whole wheat pastry flour, sugar, salt, olive oil and yeast mixture. Knead the mixture on medium speed until the dough formed is smooth and well incorporated. It shouldn't be too sticky, but you may add a few drops of water as needed if it seems too dry.

Form the dough into a ball and place it in a large, lightly greased mixing bowl. Cover the bowl with plastic wrap or a clean dishtowel and place it somewhere warm to double in size, about 1 to 2 hours.

FOR THE FILLING

While the dough rises, you can prepare the cinnamon-sugar filling by whisking together the sugar, cinnamon and nutmeg in a small bowl. In a separate small bowl, melt the vegan butter. Set them aside.

Once the dough has risen, turn it onto a lightly floured surface and use a rolling pin to roll the dough out to about 12 x 20 inches (30 x 50 cm).

Brush the rolled-out dough evenly with the melted butter, and spread the entirety of the cinnamon-sugar mixture over the top. Using a pizza cutter or pastry knife, cut the dough into 6 long strips, lengthwise. Stack the strips and slice them into 6 even stacks. Lay the stacks onto their sides in the greased loaf pan. Bake for 35 to 40 minutes, until golden. Then pull them from the oven and let them cool before enjoying.

*SEE PHOTO INSERT

SALTED SWEET POTATO **Brownies**

+GF +SF +QP

I love brownies more than most desserts. There's something about getting that perfect fudgy, gooey chocolaty bite that makes life seem complete. And these brownies are gluten-free and filled with good-for-you ingredients, which means you get to eat at least twice as many! —AS

MAKES 12 BROWNIES

1 lb (455 g) sweet potatoes

½–¾ cup (48–72 g) almond flour

½ cup (40 g) GF oats

½ cup (55 g) and 2 tbsp (14 g) cocoa powder

⅓ cup (63 g) coconut sugar

1 tsp (5 g) flaked sea salt

Peel, chop and steam or boil the sweet potatoes until soft (about 25 minutes). Set them aside to cool.

Preheat the oven to 350°F (177°C).

In a food processor, combine the almond flour and oats, pulsing until a fine flour begins to form. Add the cooled sweet potatoes, cocoa powder and coconut sugar, and blend until smooth.

Then spread the batter into a lined, 8 x 8-inch (20 x 20-cm) baking dish and sprinkle with the flaked sea salt. Bake for 25 to 30 minutes, or until an inserted toothpick comes nearly clean. Let the brownies cool completely before cutting.

Amber's FAMOUS PEANUT BUTTER COOKIES

This is the perfect peanut butter cookie recipe. I might be biased, but seriously—chewy on the inside, a little crunchy on the outside, sugary, rich and packed with peanut butter—they check all the boxes! This is my favorite cookie recipe to date, and I can't wait for you to try them, too. —AS

MAKES ABOUT 24 COOKIES

1 tbsp (6 g) ground flaxseed

3 tbsp (45 ml) warm water

½ cup (120 g) cold vegan butter

½ cup (100 g) granulated sugar, plus more for rolling

⅓ cup (77 g) packed brown sugar

3 tbsp (45 ml) unsweetened almond milk

1 tsp vanilla extract

¾ cup (135 g) smooth or chunky peanut butter

1¾ cups (210 g) all-purpose flour

1 tsp baking soda

½ tsp salt

⅛ tsp ground nutmeg

Combine the flaxseed and warm water in a small bowl; set it aside to thicken.

Add the butter and sugars to a large bowl or stand mixer, and beat it until fluffy. Add the flax mixture, milk, vanilla and peanut butter. Beat the mixture for another 2 to 3 minutes or so, until it is well incorporated and fluffy.

In a separate mixing bowl, sift together the flour, baking soda, salt and ground nutmeg. Pour this mixture into the wet ingredients and mix until just combined. Cover the bowl and refrigerate the dough for at least 30 minutes.

While the dough chills, preheat the oven to 350°F (177°C) and line a baking sheet with parchment paper. Pour the rolling sugar into a small bowl.

Take the dough from the fridge, and scoop out 1-inch (2.5-cm) balls. Roll them in granulated sugar and place them onto the baking sheet, using a fork to flatten them.

Bake the cookies for 10 to 12 minutes until golden. Cool them on a wire rack before serving.

Note: If your dough seems crumbly at all at the end, simply add a few drops of milk at a time until it comes together.

*SEE PHOTO INSERT

Easy Raw SNICKER SLABS

+GF

If there is one candy bar that epitomizes the American love for sweets, it's the Snickers Bar. And since giving up such a treat would be a shame, we've gone ahead and made it healthier!

These snicker slabs mimic the near-addictive taste of a Snickers Bar, yet the ingredients are a far cry from the original. First comes a nougat base made with nuts and a touch of maple. Then enter the whipped peanut butter–caramel layer, which is delicious enough to eat alone, but when sandwiched between melted chocolate and nougat, I must say you've got yourself the perfect dessert. —MR

MAKES 10 TO 12 BARS

NOUGAT BASE

1 cup (80 g) ground rolled gluten-free oats

1 cup (170 g) ground raw and unsalted almonds or cashews

¼ cup (60 ml) maple syrup

1½ tbsp (21 g) coconut oil

1 tsp vanilla powder

Pinch of sea salt

PEANUT CARAMEL LAYER

2 cups (340 g) pitted Medjool dates

¼ cup and 2 tbsp (96 g) unsalted peanut butter

1 tsp vanilla extract

1 tbsp (14 g) coconut oil

1-2 tbsp (15-30 ml) water

5 oz (142 g) dark chocolate, melted

Pinch of sea salt

Small handful of unsalted peanuts, crushed

FOR THE NOUGAT BASE

Mix all the ingredients together in a food processor and blend until smooth, about 30 seconds. Press the dough firmly into a small, lined baking dish, until the dough is evenly spread and is about ½ inch (1.3 cm) thick.

FOR THE PEANUT CARAMEL LAYER

Add all the ingredients into the food processor and blend until smooth, about 30 seconds. Spread the caramel layer on top of the nougat base.

Top with the melted chocolate, a pinch of sea salt and crushed peanuts, and store in the freezer to harden.

Slice and enjoy.

NECTARINE AND PEAR Crumble

+GF

A good fruit crumble can remedy almost any ailment. This is a dessert that brings an immediate coziness, the way only homemade crumble can do.

Nectarines and pears stew down into a sweet sauce of maple, vanilla and ginger, while a crunchy layer of granola bakes over the fruit, sealing in the spiced juices below. Top with a generous scoop of coconut whipped cream for a soul healing and belly craving weeknight dessert. —MR

SERVES 4

FILLING

4 nectarines, pitted and cubed

3 pears, cored and cubed

⅓ cup (80 ml) water

⅓ cup (80 ml) maple syrup

1 tsp vanilla powder or extract

½ tsp ground ginger

TOPPING

½ cup (55 g) raw unsalted pecans

½ cup (55 g) raw unsalted walnuts

1 cup (80 g) GF rolled oats

2 tbsp (28 g) coconut oil

Pinch of sea salt

FOR THE FILLING

Preheat the oven to 375°F (190°C). Toss the fruit into a large sauté pan along with the water, maple syrup, vanilla and ginger. Cook over medium-high heat for about 15 minutes, or until the fruit becomes tender but not mushy.

(continued)

FOR THE TOPPING

In the meantime, place the nuts into a food processor and pulse for a few seconds, until the nuts are chopped into small chunks but not fully into flour. Add the oats, coconut oil and sea salt, and pulse once more until everything is well combined. You want the topping to be a crumbly texture.

Now separate the fruit from the fruit juice in the saucepan, and set both aside in bowls (we will use the juice later). Pour the fruit into individual ramekins or into a small baking dish.

Take the leftover fruit juice that you set aside and pour it onto your crumble topping. Gently mix with your hands until small chunks start to form.

Place this on top of the fruit and bake for 15 to 20 minutes, until the tops are golden brown. Serve on a plate with a scoop of ice cream and enjoy.

Sweet PEAR GALETTE

+SF

This galette recipe has paved the way for all the galettes to come in my life—which at this point is nearing about thirty recipes, so you see it's a classic. Delicious pears caramelize in a petite galette filled with cinnamon, coconut sugar and ginger. Keep the crust a constant and switch out the fruits for those in season. This is the first and original recipe, and it happens to be a crowd favorite, especially when served at Sunday brunch or as a weeknight dessert. —MR

SERVES 4

CRUST
1¼ cups (160 g) spelt flour
1 tbsp (12 g) coconut sugar
¼ cup (55 g) coconut oil
6 tbsp (90 ml) ice water
Pinch of sea salt
Zest of 1 small lemon

FILLING
1 tbsp (8 g) spelt flour
3 tbsp (36 g) coconut sugar
1 tsp ground cinnamon
½ tsp ground ginger
Pinch of sea salt
2 red pears, cored and sliced
1 tbsp (14 g) coconut oil

Preheat the oven to 350°F (177°C).

FOR THE CRUST

Mix all the dry ingredients in a large bowl. Melt the coconut oil and let it cool. Once it has cooled, pour the oil into the bowl in fourths (pouring and mixing a total of four times). With each pour of oil, mix the dough evenly between your fingers. Then slowly add the ice water, using the same mixing method with your fingers. Be careful not to overmix. Form a small ball and let it sit in the refrigerator for 20 minutes.

Remove the dough from the refrigerator and roll it out into a flat circle (about 12 inches [30 cm] wide). Place the crust on a baking sheet covered with a sheet of parchment paper.

FOR THE FILLING

Combine the flour, sugar, cinnamon, ginger and salt in a bowl. Add the pear slices and toss to coat. Lay the pear slices into the center of the crust, overlapping each other while forming a circle. Gently fold the edges of the crust on top of the outer sides of the pears. Add small chunks of coconut oil on top of the galette and bake in the oven for 20 minutes, or until the crust is golden brown. Remove it from the oven and let it cool for 10 minutes. Slice and enjoy.

No-Bake ALMOND BUTTER COOKIES

+GF +QP

A no-bake cookie recipe doesn't come much easier than this. Put simply, this is a phenomenal tasting almond butter cookie. And if almond butter isn't your thing, set your inhibitions free and scoop in any nut butter combination that pleases your appetite. —MR

MAKES 10 COOKIES

¾ cup (72 g) almond flour or oat flour

¼ cup (63 g) unsalted almond butter

¼ cup (19 g) unsweetened coconut flakes, plus extra for topping

1 tsp ground cinnamon

2–3 tbsp (30–45 ml) maple syrup

1 tbsp (15 ml) almond milk or water

Sea salt, for topping

Simply place all of the ingredients (except the salt) in a food processor and mix them until combined and creamy, about 1 minute. Now let the dough set in the refrigerator for 30 minutes to harden.

Then scoop out a teaspoon amount of the dough and roll it into a ball with your hands. Use the back end of a fork to press the cookie ball down into a flat circle. Sprinkle it with sea salt and coconut flakes and enjoy! Store these in the refrigerator to keep them fresh and delicious.

Raw DARK-CHOCOLATE BROWNIES

+GF

When you don't have the patience to wait for baked brownies, this is the perfect alternative. Sweet dates, nuts and creamy hemp seeds blitz together in a rich chocolate sauce, crafting one decadent brownie bite.

Completely devoid of refined sugar, butter or flour, these brownies are a healthy counterpart to the traditional boxed brownie mix of the past. Enjoy the sweet satisfaction of brownies that work with your body and your taste buds. —MR

MAKES 15 BROWNIE SLICES

BROWNIE
½ cup (55 g) raw unsalted walnuts

½ cup (55 g) raw unsalted pecans

1 cup (170 g) pitted Medjool dates

½ cup (80 g) hemp seeds or any seeds

½ cup (55 g) raw cacao powder

2 tbsp (30 ml) maple syrup

Few pinches of sea salt

CHOCOLATE SAUCE
3 tbsp (42 g) coconut oil

¼ cup (27 g) raw cacao powder

2–3 tbsp (30–45 ml) maple syrup (depends on how sweet you like it)

¼ tsp vanilla extract

Pinch of sea salt

(continued)

FOR THE BROWNIE

Simply pulse the walnuts and pecans in a food processor until a crumbly flour forms. Then add the dates and hemp seeds to your food processor, and pulse until very sticky pieces start to form. If you don't have the Medjool variety of dates, soak the firmer dates in water for 1 hour before pulsing.

Now add the cacao powder, maple syrup and salt, and process until all the ingredients are combined and very sticky. At this point a large ball will start to form.

Line a small pan with parchment paper and evenly press the brownie mix into the pan. The brownies will be short, less than 1 inch (2.5 cm) tall. Place in the freezer to set while you prepare the chocolate sauce.

FOR THE CHOCOLATE SAUCE

Melt the coconut oil in a saucepan over low heat. Once it has fully melted, remove it from the heat and stir in the cacao powder, maple syrup, vanilla extract and sea salt. Taste the mixture to see if you would like to add more sweetener or cacao.

Remove the chocolate brownies from the freezer and pour the silky chocolate sauce on top, letting it overflow onto the sides of the brownie. Chill for another 30 minutes. If you enjoy extra cacao, sprinkle some on the top as well! Cut it into slices, and enjoy. Store these brownies in the freezer.

Raw BLACKBERRY CHEESECAKE

+GF

How to make a dessert without baking, one does wonder. Well the answer rests in this raw blackberry cheesecake. Soaked cashews provide a creamy base that is signature to a great cheesecake recipe. What might seem like a strange concept is actually the cornerstone when making raw dessert recipes taste delicious while amplifying a silky texture. And since cashews are mild in taste, they pair well with an array of flavors. Enjoy this nontraditional yet equally decadent cheesecake! —MR

SERVES 8

BASE
½ cup (55 g) raw unsalted hazelnuts

½ cup (55 g) raw unsalted pecans

1 tsp ground cinnamon

2 cups (340 g) pitted Medjool dates

TOP
2 cups (220 g) raw unsalted cashews, soaked in water overnight or at least 4 hours

5 pitted Medjool dates

1 banana, frozen

2 cups (290 g) blackberries

Juice of 1 lemon

1 tbsp (14 g) coconut oil

¼ cup (60 ml) water

⅓ cup (80 ml) maple syrup

Fresh berries, for topping

FOR THE BASE

To make the base, simply place all of the nuts in a food processor and blend until a crumble forms, roughly 1 minute. Then add the cinnamon and dates, and blend until a very sticky ball forms. With your fingers, evenly press the mixture into the bottom of a cake pan and place it in the freezer while you prepare the filling.

FOR THE TOP

Drain the water and rinse the cashews. Add them to the food processor along with the other set of dates, banana, blackberries, lemon juice, coconut oil, water and maple syrup. Blend for 3 minutes until you have a creamy filling. Add more maple if you would like it sweeter or add water to thin the mixture. Make sure to add the juice of 1 lemon; this is what gives it the traditional tangy cheesecake taste. Pour the filling on top of the base and place it in the freezer for 3 hours to set. Once it is time to eat, remove the cheesecake from the freezer, top it with fresh berries and let it warm up for a few minutes before slicing.

DARK CHOCOLATE
Crispies

+GF +QP

Dark chocolate quinoa crispies is a healthy take on Rice Crispy Treats. It's a quick dessert that comes together in 10 minutes. Pop them in the freezer and enjoy one when a chocolate craving comes on strong . . . there's nothing better than chocolate on-demand. —MR

MAKES 14 TO 16 CRISPIES

3 tbsp (42 g) coconut oil

½ cup (55 g) raw cacao powder

1 tbsp (18 g) tahini (or any nut butter)

1 tsp ground cinnamon

⅓ cup (80 ml) maple syrup

1 tsp vanilla powder

Sea salt

2½ cups (55 g) puffed/popped quinoa (or popped brown rice)

Start by making the chocolate sauce. In a small pan over medium-low heat, melt the coconut oil, raw cacao, tahini, cinnamon, maple syrup, vanilla and sea salt together until it becomes a thicker chocolaty mixture. Now pour the chocolate sauce over the popped quinoa and mix well. Scoop a large tablespoon of the chocolate crispies into small baking cups. Pop them in the freezer for at least 20 minutes to harden. Store them in the freezer and enjoy!

*SEE PHOTO INSERT

Simple MAPLE-NUT CLUSTERS

+GF +QP

Nuts and maple syrup are baked to create an effortless dessert that showcases the beauty of what you can dream up with only a handful of wholesome ingredients. —MR

MAKES 12 CLUSTERS

½ cup (85 g) roughly chopped raw unsalted almonds

½ cup (55 g) roughly chopped raw unsalted walnuts

½ cup (55 g) roughly chopped raw unsalted pecans

4 tbsp (60 ml) brown rice syrup or maple syrup

Sprinkle of sea salt, plus more for topping

Preheat the oven to 350°F (177°C).

Place the nuts in a mixing bowl along with the brown rice syrup and a sprinkle of sea salt. Once all the nuts have been mixed and well coated, place a small amount of the mixture into lined cupcake-baking trays. Sprinkle each cluster with a little extra sea salt and bake them for 8 minutes, until the clusters are roasted and form together. Once it's done, let the clusters cool in the fridge for 10 minutes. Don't let it cool in the freezer, as the syrup will stick to the bottom of the lined baking tray. Remove them from the fridge and enjoy!

Dates DIPPED IN CHOCOLATE

+GF

This is a treat for those nights when only a quick fix of chocolate will satisfy your sweet cravings. It doesn't get much easier than this: dates dipped in chocolate and coated in nuts. Dessert simplicity at its best. —MR

MAKES 15 DATES

CHOCOLATE DATES
1 (2- to 3-oz [55- to 85-g]) bar vegan chocolate

15 Medjool dates, pitted

Crushed nuts

Hemp seeds

Goji berries

Cacao nibs

TO SERVE
Nut butter

Raspberries or other berries

Maple syrup

FOR THE CHOCOLATE DATES

Melt the bar of chocolate over low heat in a saucepan, stirring as it melts. Then dip the dates into the chocolate sauce and immediately top with crushed nuts, hemp seeds, goji berries or cacao nibs, and place them in the freezer to harden for 15 minutes.

FOR SERVING

To stuff the dates, simply cut the date in half. Then add a dollop of almond butter into the hole of the date and top with a piece of fruit—I love it with raspberry and a drizzle of maple syrup.

Homemade GALAXY DARK CHOCOLATE WITH RASPBERRIES

+GF

If the thought of making homemade chocolate from scratch never crossed your mind, well here's a case for doing it soon . . . or tonight. Homemade dark chocolate is made simple with three ingredients: cacao butter, cacao powder and maple syrup. Top with anything your heart desires, and just like that—you're now a bonafide chocolatier. —MR

MAKES 15 SMALL BARS

1 cup (230 g) cacao butter

¾ cup (180 ml) maple syrup

1¼ cups (135 g) cacao powder

1 cup (15 g) puffed quinoa

½ cup (45 g) freeze-dried raspberries

Pinch of sea salt

Using the double-boiler method, fill a small saucepan with ⅓ cup (80 ml) of water and place a glass or metal bowl on top, covering the saucepan. Once the bowl is hot and the water below is boiling, melt the cacao butter inside the top bowl. Once it has melted, stir in the maple syrup and cacao powder for a few minutes until the chocolate thickens.

Then mix in most of the puffed quinoa and raspberries, saving a few to sprinkle on top. Pour into a lined baking pan (I use an 8 x 8-inch [20 x 20-cm] pan), add a pinch of sea salt over the top and leave it to set in the freezer for an hour or so. Slice the chocolate into bars and store in the freezer or fridge.

Five-Ingredient PEANUT BUTTER CUPS

+GF +QP

Ever unwrap peanut butter cups only to find the middle layer nearing the side of expiration, giving way to a bland, chalky filling? Is there even a situation worse than money spent on inedible chocolate? Not likely.

Like a phoenix rising from the ashes, this peanut butter cup recipe is a saving grace. A few ingredients, most importantly real peanut butter, are mixed to create the perfect creamy center. Never again will your palate suffer the fate of chalky peanut butter cups. —MR

MAKES 10 PIECES

⅔ cup (150 g) cacao butter

⅓ cup (80 ml) maple syrup

¾ cup (80 g) cacao powder

2–3 tbsp (16–24 g) gluten-free oat flour or any flour

⅓ cup (60 g) unsalted peanut butter

Sea salt

Start by making the chocolate sauce. Using the double-boiler method, fill a small saucepan with ⅓ cup (80 ml) of water and place a bowl on top, covering the saucepan. Turn on the heat, and once the bowl is hot and the water below is boiling, melt the cacao butter inside the top bowl. Once it has melted, stir in the maple syrup and cacao powder for a few minutes until the chocolate thickens.

Using a cupcake holder (I use a silicone one), fill the bottom layer with a small teaspoon of the chocolate mixture. You want to make sure that it thinly coats the bottom layer—you don't want it to be too thick either. Once you've filled the bottom of each cupcake holder, pop them into the freezer for 15 minutes to set. As it sets, mix the oat flour with the peanut butter; the flour helps keep the peanut butter intact so that it forms small balls.

(continued)

Take the frozen chocolate out of the freezer and dollop ½ teaspoon of the peanut butter mixture on top of the frozen chocolate layer. Press down so that the peanut butter is even. Once this is done, pour the remaining melted chocolate over each peanut butter dollop, so that it covers everything. Sprinkle with sea salt and let this sit in the freezer for 20 minutes, or until it hardens. You can store these in the freezer or refrigerator.

Note: If you don't have all the ingredients to make chocolate from scratch, simply use the double-boiler method to melt four 5-ounce (140-g) bars of dark chocolate. Then carry on with the rest of the instructions below.

Chocolate (AVOCADO) MOUSSE PUDDING

+GF +QP

Avocados in chocolate mousse? Let's talk about this recipe for a second. This will be my attempt to dissuade you from having an internal crisis when you hear the words chocolate and avocado in the title for dessert.

I too thought this was a pretty bizarre concept. Yet, similar to adding spinach to a smoothie, all other flavors work in a concerted effort to mask any lingering spinach, or in this case, avocado, flavor. And here comes the second bit of confusion: why is balsamic vinegar making an appearance? And this is where I tell you to forget anything you know about chocolate and to just try it out, because balsamic has a way of intensifying the cacao flavor (removing any avocado taste). And that's the kind of healthy pudding I want to have—creamy, chocolaty and without any vegetable aftertastes.—MR

SERVES 3

3 ripe avocados

¾ cup (82 g) raw cacao powder, plus more for sprinkling

5–7 tbsp (75–105 ml) maple syrup, depending on how sweet you like it

¾ cup (180 ml) almond milk

1 tsp balsamic vinegar (helps to intensify the chocolate flavor)

Pinch of sea salt

Simply blend all of the ingredients in a food processor until creamy and smooth. Make sure there are no avocado lumps! Pour the batter into ramekins or small bowls and keep them in the refrigerator to set and chill for about 15 minutes. Sprinkle them with raw cacao powder right before you eat, and enjoy!

Note: As a friendly nudge, before serving this to any friends, don't tell them that it's a healthy dessert—and for the love of god, please do not mention that there is an avocado hidden inside. No one really needs to know that . . . unless they are allergic.

*SEE PHOTO INSERT

MANGO AND PASSION FRUIT Cheesecake

+GF

The aroma of mango and fresh passion fruit is enough reason to make this beautiful dessert. If you're looking for a dessert to transport you to island life, then this is your ticket. Creamy cashews soak overnight to create a silky cheesecake, while mangos are whipped and softened into a fluffy center. Top it off with fresh passion fruit for an instant hit of island life. —MR

SERVES 6 TO 8

BASE

1½ cups (255 g) raw unsalted almonds, or any nut

1 cup (170 g) pitted dates

1 tbsp (14 g) coconut oil

MANGO FILLING

3 cups (330 g) raw unsalted cashews, soaked overnight or for 4 hours

4½ cups (1.13 kg) frozen mango

Juice of ½ lime

¼ cup (60 ml) maple syrup

1 tbsp (15 ml) vanilla extract

TOPPING

½–¾ cup (90–135 g) fresh passion fruit pulp

FOR THE BASE

Place all of the base ingredients into a food processor and blend until a fine consistency is formed. Now press it into the base of a cake tin and set it in the freezer until firm, about 15 minutes.

FOR THE MANGO FILLING

Blend all of the filling ingredients in a food processor until a creamy and thick texture forms. Now pour the filling mixture on top of the crust in the cake tin.

Then top it off with the pulp of the passion fruit. Set it in the freezer for about 2 hours, or until firm. When you're ready to eat, remove the cheesecake from the freezer and let it thaw out for about 10 to 15 minutes. Cut it into slices and enjoy!

Cinnamon-Apple
GALETTE WITH CARAMEL SAUCE

+SF

A strong contender for the Thanksgiving dessert, this galette showcases just how delicious a vegan pastry can be—sans refined sugar, flour and butter. And if you still haven't committed to baking this galette just yet, know that there is a silky caramel sauce involved that just might tempt you otherwise. —MR

SERVES 2 TO 3

CRUST

1½ cups (185 g) spelt flour

2 tbsp (24 g) coconut sugar

Sea salt

6 tbsp (85 g) coconut oil

¼ cup (60 ml) cold water

FILLING

1 apple, thinly sliced lengthwise

1 tbsp (8 g) spelt flour

3 tbsp (36 g) coconut sugar

1 tsp ground cinnamon

Pinch of sea salt

1 tbsp (14 g) coconut oil

TOPPING

Generous drizzle of the Silky Caramel Sauce (page 422)

(continued)

Preheat the oven to 350°F (177°C).

FOR THE CRUST

Make the crust by adding the flour, coconut sugar and sea salt to the food processor. Slowly add the coconut oil and water, and pulse frequently as this gently blends into the flour. Pulse the mixture only enough until the ingredients combine, 30 seconds or so. Now fold the dough into a ball and let it rest in the fridge for 30 minutes to 1 hour.

Remove the dough from the refrigerator and roll it out into a flat circle (about 10 inches [25 cm] wide and ¼ inch [6 mm] thick). Transfer the dough to a parchment-lined baking sheet.

FOR THE FILLING

Mix all of the filling ingredients (aside from the coconut oil) in a bowl with the sliced apples. Mix until the apple slices are coated in cinnamon and coconut sugar.

Now layer the apple slices in a circle evenly in the center of the dough. Leave about a 1-inch (2.5-cm) rim from the center of the galette to the edge (this will be the crust that you fold over the apples).

Gently fold the edges of the crust on top of the outer sides of the apple slices. Add small chunks of the coconut oil on top of the galette and bake in the oven for 20 minutes, or until the crust is flaky and the apples are cooked through. Top with a generous drizzle of the caramel sauce and enjoy!

*SEE PHOTO INSERT

Vegan CHOCOLATE BLINTZES STUFFED WITH VANILLA NUT CREAM

+GF +SF

These delicious little blintzes are perfect for a fancy brunch or a romantic dessert. You can use the sweetener of your choice, to taste, if you are avoiding sugar. Want to make these on a moment's notice? Cook the nuts in separate pans covered with water for about ten minutes to soften them up. That way you can use them without waiting! —KH

MAKES 12 TO 14 BLINTZES

FILLING
½ cup (56 g) raw cashews, soaked overnight and drained

½ cup (120 ml) unsweetened nondairy milk

3 tbsp (38 g) sugar

1 tsp apple cider vinegar or lemon juice

1 tsp vanilla extract

½ tsp salt

1½ cups (255 g) raw skinned slivered almonds, soaked overnight then drained

CREPE
2 tbsp (12 g) ground flaxseed mixed with ¼ cup (60 ml) warm water

2 cups (480 ml) unsweetened nondairy milk

¼ cup plus 2 tbsp (80 g) vegan sugar

1 tbsp (15 ml) mild oil

1 tsp vanilla extract

¾ cup (94 g) brown teff flour

¼ cup (40 g) tapioca starch

¼ cup (40 g) brown rice flour

¼ cup (20 g) cocoa powder

1 tsp baking powder

1 tsp salt

Spray oil to use in pan

FOR THE FILLING

Add the cashews, nondairy milk, sugar, vinegar, vanilla and salt to your blender and blend well. You will need to stop and scrape down the container a few times.

Once smooth, add the almonds and blend again until mostly smooth. You don't want any large pieces, but it will be a little bumpy like ricotta. Set this aside.

FOR THE CREPE

In a medium bowl, mix the flaxseed mixture, non-dairy milk, sugar, oil and vanilla.

In a small bowl, mix the teff flour, tapioca starch, brown rice flour, cocoa powder, baking powder and salt, and stir well.

Add the dry mixture to the wet and whisk until smooth.

Spray some oil lightly on a medium sauté pan and heat the pan over medium heat.

Once hot, measure out ¼ cup (60 ml) of batter, remove the skillet from the heat and pour the batter in, swirling the skillet to coat the bottom evenly.

Cook the first side for about 3 minutes. The edges will begin to pull away from the pan.

Carefully flip the crepe using your hands or a spatula, and cook for a minute.

Place on a plate and repeat until all the crepe batter has been used.

Fill each crepe with the vanilla nut cream filling and roll it up. Serve topped with powdered sugar, berries or chocolate sauce.

*SEE PHOTO INSERT

Vanilla Gluten-Free Vegan PIZZELLES MADE WITH TEFF FLOUR

+GF +SF

Pizzelles are beautiful thin cookies that delight your mouth with their crispness. These are made without dairy or egg, unlike most traditional recipes. I made these vanilla, but you can change out the extract to customize them or add a teaspoon of cinnamon, cardamom or even a pinch of cloves. —KH

MAKES 10 PIZZELLES

Spray oil
½ cup (63 g) teff flour
½ cup (63 g) powdered sugar
Pinch of salt
¼ cup (120 ml) unsweetened nondairy milk
1 tbsp (7 g) ground flaxseed mixed with 2 tbsp (30 ml) warm water
1 tbsp (15 ml) melted coconut oil (or other mild oil)
1 tsp vanilla extract

Plug in your pizzelle maker and lightly spray the inside with a mild spray oil.

Mix the dry ingredients together in a medium mixing bowl. Then mix the wet ingredients in a measuring cup.

Add the wet to the dry and mix well. The batter will be a little thick.

By now, your pizzelle maker should be hot. Drop a tablespoon (15 ml) of batter in the center of each cookie indention in your maker. Mine makes 2 at a time but some make 3.

(continued)

Cook for 30 seconds to 1 minute, or as your pizzelle manual recommends, or until golden brown. (I found that just over 1 minute worked for my pizzelle maker, but this will vary between makes and models.)

Carefully remove the cookie from the maker with a silicone spatula. The cookies will be pliable while warm, so you should place them on a wire rack to cool them.

Make the rest of the cookies by spraying oil, dropping tablespoons of batter and repeating until all the batter is used.

*SEE PHOTO INSERT

Gluten-Free Vegan
PUMPKIN PIE WITH A TEFF FLOUR PECAN CRUST

+GF +SF

This pie is a perfect way to end your Thanksgiving celebration. The spiced pumpkin filling is lightly sweetened with brown sugar and a hint of molasses. You can make the pie up to 2 days before your celebration. If you make it the day you plan to eat it, make sure to leave time for it to cool in the refrigerator for about 3 hours before serving. —KH

SERVES 8

CRUST
1 cup (125 g) teff flour
¼ cup (55 g) coconut oil
2 tbsp (25 g) brown sugar or coconut sugar
1 tsp ground cinnamon
¼ tsp salt
½ cup (60 g) minced pecans
¼ cup (60 ml) water

FILLING
1 (15-oz [425-g]) can puréed pumpkin, or 1½ cups (270 g) homemade
¾ cup (180 ml) unsweetened nondairy milk
½ cup (95 g) brown sugar or coconut sugar
3 tbsp (28 g) organic cornstarch
1 tbsp (22 g) molasses
1 tsp ground cinnamon
1 tsp ground allspice
½ tsp ground ginger
½ tsp ground nutmeg
½ tsp salt
¼ tsp ground cloves

Preheat the oven to 350°F (177°C) and oil a 9-inch (23-cm) pie pan.

FOR THE CRUST
Put the teff flour, coconut oil, brown sugar, cinnamon and salt into your food processor. Pulse until the mixture looks like a coarse cornmeal.

Add the pecans and water to your food processor and pulse until a dough ball forms. Place the dough, in a tight ball, into the refrigerator for 20 minutes.

Spread some flour on a cutting board and shape the dough into a disk. Then transfer it to the pie pan and press it evenly up the sides. Use a fork or your fingers to decorate the edges.

Bake for 5 minutes; then remove it from the oven and let it cool before you add the filling.

FOR THE FILLING
Put the pumpkin, milk, sugar, cornstarch, molasses, cinnamon, allspice, ginger, nutmeg, salt and cloves into your blender, and blend until smooth.

ASSEMBLY
Put the pie pan with the prepared crust on a sheet pan. This will keep the oven clean and make it easier to grab the hot pie out of the oven later.

Pour the filling into the crust and spread it evenly using a spatula. Put it in the oven and bake for 40 minutes.

After the pie pan is cool enough to touch, move the pie to your refrigerator and let it chill for 3 hours so the filling will set up.

*SEE PHOTO INSERT

Vegan PUMPKIN GINGERBREAD WITH NO ADDED OIL

+SF

These little spicy muffins are soy-free and have no added oil. You can use your favorite gluten-free blend in place of the wheat flour to make it gluten-free too! —KH

MAKES 48 MINI MUFFINS

2 cups (250 g) all-purpose flour or whole wheat flour

1½ tsp (6 g) baking soda

1½ tbsp (11 g) ground ginger

1 tsp ground cinnamon

½ tsp ground cloves

½ tsp allspice

¼ tsp nutmeg

¼ tsp salt

2 tbsp (14 g) ground flaxseed plus 4 tbsp (60 ml) water

1 cup (180 g) pumpkin purée

½ cup (120 ml) unsweetened nondairy milk

½ cup (175 g) molasses

½ cup (95 g) brown sugar or coconut sugar

1 tsp vanilla extract

Preheat the oven to 350°F (177°C). Place muffin paper liners in your mini-muffin pans. If you don't have any liners on hand, you can oil the tin, but this recipe will no longer be oil-free.

Mix the dry ingredients in a large bowl.

Mix the flax and warm water together in another bowl.

Combine the rest of the wet ingredients in a small bowl, and then add the flax mixture.

Add the dry mixture to the wet, and stir with a wooden spoon until it is just combined.

Scoop the dough into your prepared mini-muffin baking pans and bake 13 to 15 minutes, or until the top springs back after you touch it.

Vegan BLUEBERRY BUCKLE—NO OIL ADDED!

+SF +GFO

This is a cake that thinks it might be a coffeecake. A buckle is a cake that's usually studded with fresh blueberries and has a crisp-like topping. —KH

SERVES 6 TO 8

BASE

1 cup (130 g) whole wheat pastry flour (or gluten-free baking mix)

2 tsp (8 g) baking powder

¼ tsp salt

1 tbsp (7 g) ground flaxseed mixed with 3 tbsp (45 ml) warm water

½ cup (95 g) sugar

⅓ cup (80 ml) nondairy milk

¼ cup (62 g) applesauce

¼ tsp lemon oil or 1 tsp lemon extract

(continued)

DESSERTS

TOPPING

½ cup (40 g) rolled oats

¼ cup (33 g) whole wheat pastry flour

¼ cup (47 g) sugar

¼ cup (60 ml) nondairy milk

Pinch of salt

2 cups (295 g) fresh blueberries

Preheat the oven to 350°F (177°C) and prepare a 9-inch (23-cm) square baking dish or equivalent with spray oil, or line with parchment paper to keep it 100 percent oil-free.

FOR THE BASE

Mix the dry ingredients in a small bowl and set it aside. Then mix the wet ones in a medium mixing bowl and set that aside.

FOR THE TOPPING

Now mix the topping ingredients in a bowl; you will use this last.

Fold the dry ingredients into the wet and spread the mixture evenly in the bottom of the pan. Sprinkle the blueberries over the top and press them in slightly.

Crumble the topping over the base and blueberries and bake for 30 to 40 minutes, until a fork comes out clean when you test the middle of the cake.

*SEE PHOTO INSERT

7-LAYER **Bars**

+SF

As soon as I saw sweetened condensed coconut milk in the store, I was thrilled. I could finally make my favorite seven layer bars without having to make my own sweetened condensed coconut milk. This is one thing that I love eating out of the can! —KH

MAKES 12 BARS

¾ cups (68 g) rolled oats

¼ cup (31 g) pecans

¼ cup (33 g) whole wheat pastry flour

1 tbsp (12.5 g) brown sugar

¼ tsp salt

3 tbsp (45 ml) coconut oil, melted

1 tbsp (7 g) ground flaxseed mixed with 2 tbsp (30 ml) warm water

1 cup (124 g) chopped pecans

½ cup (86 g) vegan chocolate chips

½ cup (38 g) shredded coconut

1 (7.4-oz [210-g]) can sweetened condensed coconut milk

Preheat the oven to 350°F (177°C) and oil a square brownie pan.

Add the oats, pecans, flour, sugar and salt to your food processor, and pulse until it's mixed well and the mixture begins to break up some. Add the melted coconut oil and flaxseed mixture, and pulse until it forms a ball. If it's still dry, you can add extra water a tablespoon (15 ml) at a time until it's moist enough to hold together.

Press the crust into an oiled square brownie pan. Bake the crust for 8 minutes and remove it from the oven.

Evenly spread the pecans, chocolate chips and coconut across the top of the crust, and then pour the sweetened condensed coconut milk over the topping and spread as evenly as possible.

Bake for 25 to 35 minutes, until the edges begin to brown. Let it cool, and then cut and serve.

STRAWBERRY
Shortcake

+SF

These delicate little dessert stacks are such a great way to impress dinner guests. They look like they're so complicated to put together, but we'll let you in on our little secret. They're super easy to make! Just pile the cake high with strawberries and some vegan cream. —LM + AM

SERVES 6

2 cups (253 g) all-purpose flour

3 tsp (11 g) baking powder

4 tbsp (48 g) sugar, divided

½ tsp fine sea salt

¼ tsp ground cardamom

1 cup (240 ml) unsweetened almond milk

1 tbsp (15 ml) melted coconut oil

2 tsp (10 ml) pure vanilla extract, divided

1 lb (454 g) strawberries, sliced

1 (14-oz [414-ml]) can of chilled full-fat coconut milk

To prepare, preheat the oven to 350°F (177°C). Line a baking sheet with parchment paper or lightly grease the pan with vegan butter. Put your stand mixer bowl in the freezer.

In a medium bowl, whisk the flour, baking powder, 2 tablespoons (24 g) of sugar, sea salt and cardamom until combined. Add the almond milk, coconut oil and vanilla, and stir until well combined. The dough will be thick and sticky.

Divide the dough into 6 pieces and drop them onto the cookie sheet. Bake for 30 minutes, or until they are a light golden brown. Remove them from the oven and let them cool.

In a medium bowl, stir the strawberries and 1 tablespoon (12 g) of sugar together until combined. Let it stand for 30 minutes so the strawberries can macerate.

Take your mixing bowl out of the freezer and add the solid part of the coconut milk, 1 tablespoon (12 g) of sugar and the vanilla, and mix with the whisk attachment on the highest speed until the coconut milk becomes thick like whipped cream. This could take several minutes depending on your mixer. Be patient.

Slice the shortcake in half and spread some of the coconut cream on the bottom. Add a layer of strawberries, a dollop of cream on the strawberries, the top of the shortbread over the berries and cream, and add one more dollop of coconut cream.

*SEE PHOTO INSERT

LEMON BERRY CASHEW
Cheesecake Bites

+GF +SF

Creamy, zesty, and sweet—those are the three perfect words to describe these little bites of heaven. By using cashews, we've recreated a texture that exactly mirrors that of a traditional cheesecake. So serve these up to vegans and nonvegans alike! Everyone will love them. —LM + AM

MAKES 12 CHEESECAKE BITES

1 cup (122 g) pecans

3 tbsp (45 g) whole oats (not steel-cut) (use gluten-free)

1 tbsp (15 g) ground flaxseed

3 large dates, pits removed

½ tsp fine sea salt

2 cups (226 g) raw cashews, soaked in water overnight

Zest from 1½ large lemons, divided

(continued)

Juice from 1½ large lemons

2 tbsp (30 ml) pure maple syrup

1 tbsp (15 ml) melted coconut oil

1 tbsp (15 ml) unsweetened almond milk

Fresh blueberries and raspberries, for decorating

Place 12 cupcake liners in a muffin tin.

Put the pecans, oats, flaxseed, dates and salt in a food processor, and blend until it forms a solid and sticky crust. It will be slightly oily, because the pecans will release their oil. Don't worry about it. Line a muffin tin with cupcake liners and put 1 level tablespoon (15 g) of the crust in each liner. Press evenly throughout the bottom.

Drain and rinse the cashews and place them in a high-powered blender. Add the lemon zest from 1 lemon, lemon juice, maple syrup, coconut oil and almond milk, and blend on a high setting for 90 seconds. Scrape the sides and blend for another 90 seconds, or until the filling is smooth and creamy. You shouldn't be able to taste any solid pieces of the cashews. If you like your filling sweeter, add more maple syrup to taste. Spoon 1½ tablespoons (23 g) of the filling in each muffin tin, and top with the berries and lemon zest from the half lemon.

Refrigerate cheesecake bites for 3 or more hours. Remove the cupcake liners and serve them chilled.

CHOCOLATE CHIP SKILLET *Cookie*

+SFO

Ok, we're calling it. The best way to eat a chocolate chip cookie is from a skillet. Firstly, cookie skillets are just fun. There's no better way to impress someone than serving them a giant cookie in a cast-iron skillet. And secondly, the skillet allows the cookie to retain its heat, allows the chocolate to stay melted, and gives the edges that nice cookie crispiness while keeping the center just gooey enough. —LM + AM

SERVES 12

1 tbsp (7 g) ground flaxseed

3 tbsp (45 ml) water

1¾ cups (222 g) all-purpose flour

¾ tsp baking soda

¼ tsp fine sea salt

8 tbsp (116 g) vegan butter (use soy-free)

¼ cup (49 g) sugar

½ cup (80 g) light brown sugar

1 tbsp (15 ml) pure vanilla extract

3 tbsp (45 ml) pure maple syrup

10 oz (283 g) vegan semisweet chocolate chunks (we use Enjoy Life brand)

TOPPINGS

Vanilla ice cream

Melted chocolate

Preheat the oven to 350°F (177°C) and lightly grease a 10-inch (25-cm) iron skillet.

Whisk the flaxseed and water together. Allow the mixture to sit for 2 minutes.

While the flaxseed mixture is sitting, take a medium bowl and whisk together the flour, baking soda and sea salt until well incorporated.

In a large mixing bowl, beat the butter and sugars together until combined. Once the butter-sugar mixture is uniform in consistency, add the vanilla, maple syrup and flax egg. Beat the mixture again until the blend is light and fluffy.

Once you've achieved the fluffy texture, begin to pour the flour mixture in ¼ or ⅓ cup (30 or 40 g) at a time. When the flour is completely mixed into the batter, fold in the chocolate chunks.

Take the greased pan, and spread the chocolate chip mixture evenly inside the pan.

Bake on the middle rack for 15 to 18 minutes, or until golden brown and firm in the middle.

Serve with a scoop of vegan vanilla ice cream and a drizzle of melted chocolate.

*SEE PHOTO INSERT

LEMON KNOT **Cookies**

+SFO

Do any of you remember when a ubiquitous coffee chain used to sell lemon knot cookies? They were so light, sweet and perfect that we sometimes had them as a special treat. After reminiscing about the '90s, we couldn't help but want to recreate those perfect little cookies. So we did. —LM + AM

MAKES 1 DOZEN COOKIES

2 cups (253 g) all-purpose flour

2 tsp (7 g) baking powder

⅛ tsp fine sea salt

¼ cup (60 ml) melted vegan butter (use soy-free)

½ cup (112 g) granulated sugar

¼ cup (60 ml) aquafaba (liquid from a can of chickpeas)

¼ cup (60 ml) Meyer lemon juice

Zest from 1 lemon

2½ tsp (13 ml) pure lemon extract

½ cup (118 ml) almond milk

⅓ cup (36 g) powdered sugar

1 tbsp (14 ml) water

¼ tsp lemon extract

Preheat the oven to 350°F (177°C) and line a cookie sheet with parchment paper or a baking mat.

In a medium bowl, whisk the flour, baking powder and salt together until well combined.

In a large mixing bowl, whip the butter and granulated sugar together until combined. Scrape the sides to make sure that all of the sugar is blended with the butter. Add the aquafaba and blend until just combined. Add the lemon juice, zest and lemon extract; mix until well blended. Slowly add a third of the flour mixture and a third of the almond milk, one at a time. Continue until all of the flour and milk are just combined with the sugar and butter mixture. Let the dough rest in the refrigerator for 15 minutes.

Scoop out a heaping tablespoon of dough on the cookie sheet, roll it into a 6-inch (15-cm) log, take one end and wind it into a circle, and tuck the end into the center to form a knot. Continue with the rest of the dough and bake for about 15 minutes, or until the cookies are puffy and begin to turn a light golden brown. Let them cool completely on a wire rack.

Mix the powdered sugar, water and lemon extract together until it forms a thick glaze. Dollop the glaze on the cookies, and let it spread out and run down the cookies.

*SEE PHOTO INSERT

CRANBERRY PISTACHIO **Biscotti**

+SF

Every Christmas in the Meyer household, batches upon batches of these biscotti are made. While sugar cookies and gingerbread seem to dominate the cookie scene come December, we encourage you to mix it up and whip up some biscotti. This Italian treat goes perfectly with a peppermint mocha or a vegan eggnog latte. —LM + AM

MAKES 2 DOZEN BISCOTTI

2 cups (256 g) all-purpose flour

2 tsp (8 g) baking powder

½ tsp fine sea salt

¾ cup (150 g) sugar

Zest of 1 small orange

1 cup (153 g) coarsely chopped pistachios

1 cup (153 g) dried cranberries

1 cup (236 ml) aquafaba (liquid from a can of chickpeas)

1 tsp vanilla extract

Preheat the oven to 350°F (177°C) and line a large baking sheet with parchment paper or a baking mat.

In a large mixing bowl, whisk the dry ingredients together. Create a well in the dry ingredients for the wet ingredients. In a small bowl, combine the aquafaba and vanilla until uniform. Into the well, pour the aquafaba mixture. Begin kneading the dough until the flour is fully incorporated and the dough forms a ball.

Divide the dough evenly into 2 pieces and form 2 logs on the cookie sheet that are about 12 x 3 inches (30 x 8 cm). Bake the dough for 25 minutes. Remove the dough from the oven and let it cool for 15 minutes. Reduce the oven to 300°F (149°C).

Gently remove the logs from the cookie sheet, and place them on a clean, hard surface. Slice the cookies diagonally into 1-inch (2.5-cm) slices. For best results, use a sharp serrated knife and gently saw through the log. Don't press too hard or you may crack the dough. Lay the cookies flat on the cookie sheet and bake for about 20 more minutes, or until light golden brown and firm.

Sugar-Free STUFFED BAKED APPLES

+GF +SFO

Baked apples, stuffed with oats, nuts, dried fruit and spice are such a treat. The apples get soft and almost creamy, which highlights their natural sweetness, and the spicy oat mixture adds a warm, nutty flavor and texture that makes every bite a delight.

This is an easy, guilt-free dessert that's perfect for a busy week night and pretty enough to serve at a dinner party. —LM + AM

SERVES 8

8 medium to large apples

1 cup (81 g) GF rolled oats

1 cup (117 g) chopped walnuts

½ cup (76 g) dried unsweetened cranberries or raisins

2 tsp (5 g) ground cinnamon

1 tsp pure vanilla extract

⅛ tsp fine sea salt

2 tbsp (29 g) chilled vegan butter, cut into small pieces (use soy-free)

1 cup (240 ml) and 3 tbsp (45 ml) water, divided

TOPPING

Vegan vanilla ice cream

Butternut Squash and Kale Lo Mein with Crispy Tofu, page 42

Cream of Celery Soup, page 212

Strawberry Phyllo Strudels, page 353

Shiitake Chickpea Crepes, page 92

Carrot Cake with Cashew Cream Cheese Frosting, Pistachios and Walnuts, page 333

Roasted Winter Squash with Zesty "Ricotta" and Sage, page 154

Mashed Potato-Crusted Butternut Squash, Brussels Sprouts and Tofu Pie, page 40

Lemon Knot Cookies, page 287

reamy Avocado Pesto Pasta, page 125

Harissa Croquettes, page 175

Totally Tahini Cups with Coffee Cream Filling, page 334

Dark Chocolate Crispies, page 275

Vanilla Gluten-Free Vegan Pizzelles Made with Teff Flour, page 281

Savory Vegan Mediterranean Oatmeal, page 376

Soothe-What-Ails Miso Broth, page 222

Maple Pecan Pie, page 336

Asian-Style Miso and Eggplant Pasta, page 127

Aloo Jeera (Indian Cumin Potatoes), page 162

Six-Ingredient Vegan Chedder Cheese Sauce, page 418

Sambal Soy Curl Tacos, page 87

Red Kuri Squash Soup with Cumin, Coriander and Coconut, page 224

Homemade Thai-Style Green Curry, page 37

Carrot Cupcakes with Orange Vanilla Cream Frosting, page 252

Slow Cooker Whole Wheat Spelt Potato Rolls, page 111

Citrus and Tahini Granola, page 360

Spiralized Vegan Latkes with Red Cabbage and Apple, page 39

Sugar-Free Stuffed Baked Apples, page 288

Baked Pumpkin Cinnamon Sugar Doughnuts, page 341

Blueberry Streusel Square, page 387

Jewel Fruit Tart with Caramel Almond Filling, page 335

Cinnamon-Apple Galette with Caramel Sauce, page 279

Gluten-Free Vegan Teff Stuffing with Roasted Butternut Squash and Candied Cranberries, page 44

Spicy Black Bean Brownies, page 290

Sweet Cherry Coffee Cake, page 354

Corn Waffles, page 385

Almond Butter and Chia Jam Bars with Chocolate, page 317

Zucchini Noodle Pasta with Pesto, page 129

Air-Fried Tofu Rancheros, page 112

Pulled Carrot BBQ, page 53

Harissa Haricots Verts, page 179

Steamed Sweet Potatoes with Wild Rice, Basil and
Tomato Chili Sauce, page 142

Roasted Tomato and Garlic Toast, page 135

Sparkling Mint Lemonade, page 400

Vegan Blueberry Buckle—No Oil Added!, page 283

Sofritas Tofu Lettuce Wraps, page 60

Vegan Easter Creme Eggs, page 258

imchi Mac and Sprouts, page 80

Avocado Mint Cream Bars with Chocolate, Two Ways, page 334

Chocolate (Avocado) Mousse Pudding, page 278

Vegan Gluten-Free Chai-Spiced Teff Waffles, page 367

Chik'n Salad, page 241

Apple Cider Doughnuts, page 356

weet and Sour and Somewhat Spicy Tofu, page 88

Sweet Potato and Turmeric Falafels, page 131

rawberry Shortcake, page 285

Homemade Vegan Cheez-Its, page 147

Moroccan Pizza, page 96

Chocolate-Gingersnap Fall Bars, page 358

Vegan Instant Pot White Bean Soy Curl Chili, page 114

Stewed Cinnamon Apples in a Yogurt Parfait, page 357

Preheat the oven to 350°F (177°C).

Wash and carefully core the apples with a paring knife. Scrape the bottom of the core out with a spoon, making sure that you don't put a hole in the bottom of the apple.

In a large mixing bowl, combine the oats, walnuts, cranberries, cinnamon, vanilla, salt, vegan butter and 3 tablespoons (45 ml) of the water. Use your hands to mix it together, pressing the butter into the oats until it becomes sticky.

Put the apples in a deep baking dish and pour the remaining 1 cup (240 ml) water into the pan. Liberally spoon the filling into the apples to the top, and cover the pan with foil.

Bake for about 1 hour or until fork tender. Serve warm and top with vanilla ice cream if desired.

*SEE PHOTO INSERT

Soft PUMPKIN SPICE COOKIES

+SFO

Our soft and pillowy cookies are made with real pumpkin and warm and savory spices, such as cinnamon, nutmeg and cloves. They taste like a bite of autumn, and we make a batch a week from September through November.

You can eat them with or without the sweet glaze—either way, they're delicious. —LM + AM

MAKES ABOUT 16 COOKIES

COOKIES
2¾ cups (438 g) all-purpose flour
1 tsp baking powder
1 tsp baking soda
½ tsp fine sea salt
1 tsp ground cinnamon

1 tsp ground nutmeg
¼ tsp ground allspice
⅛ tsp ground black pepper
¾ cup (175 g) vegan butter, at room temperature (use soy-free)
1 cup (146 g) brown sugar
½ cup (97 g) vegan granulated sugar
½ cup (124 g) applesauce plus 1 tsp baking powder, whisked together
2 tsp (10 ml) pure vanilla extract
1 cup (182 g) pumpkin purée
2 tbsp (30 ml) almond milk, or more as needed, divided

GLAZE
1 cup (132 g) powdered sugar
1 tsp vanilla extract
½ tsp ground cinnamon
Almond milk: add by the teaspoon until you get the consistency that you like

FOR THE COOKIES
Preheat the oven to 350°F (177°C) and line a cookie sheet with parchment paper.

In a medium bowl, whisk the flour, baking powder, baking soda, sea salt, cinnamon, nutmeg, allspice and ground black pepper together until well combined and the flour looks fluffy.

In a large mixing bowl, beat the butter and sugars together until light and creamy. Add the applesauce and baking powder mixture and beat until well combined. Add the vanilla and pumpkin purée and beat until well combined. Add half of the flour mixture and 1 tablespoon (15 ml) of almond milk; mix until almost combined. Add the second half of the flour and remaining 1 tablespoon (15 ml) almond milk, mixing until almost combined. Add 1 or more tablespoons of almond milk if needed. The consistency should be thick enough to spoon onto a cookie sheet.

(continued)

Note: The consistency of the pumpkin purée will determine how much almond milk you'll need to add. If it's a thick and solid purée, you might need to add more milk. If it's a thin, soupy mixture, you probably won't need to add more than 2 tablespoons (30 ml).

Finish blending the flour into the mixture with a spoon. Drop the dough by tablespoons (15 g) onto the cookie sheet and bake for 12 minutes, or until they are firm to the touch. Cool on a wire rack.

FOR THE GLAZE

In a medium bowl, mix the powdered sugar, vanilla, cinnamon and 1 teaspoon of almond milk together. Add more almond milk by the teaspoon until you get the consistency that you desire. Some people like a thick and gooey glaze, and others like a thin glaze.

Frost the cookies with the glaze and put the cookies in the refrigerator until the glaze hardens, about 1 hour.

Store the cookies in an airtight container in the refrigerator for up to 1 week. Store them in a freezer bag for up to 1 month.

Spicy BLACK BEAN BROWNIES

+GF +SF

If you haven't made brownies with black beans, you must! You can't taste them; they're there to give the brownies a wonderful fudgy texture and lots of protein. We eat these as a post-workout snack because they're so healthy. Made with maple syrup instead of refined sugar, and oat flour, this is a dessert you can feel good about eating. Of course, the cayenne pepper takes them to another level. —LM + AM

MAKES 1 DOZEN

2 tbsp (14 g) ground flaxseed

6 tbsp (90 ml) water

1 cup (132 g) oat flour (use gluten-free)

1¼ cups (141 g) cacao or unsweetened cocoa powder

1 tsp baking powder

1 tsp fine sea salt

2 tsp (5 g) ground cinnamon

½ tsp cayenne powder (optional)

2 (15-oz [425-g]) cans black beans, rinsed and drained

1 cup (240 ml) pure maple syrup (add more if you like it sweeter)

2 tsp (10 ml) pure vanilla extract

¼ cup (60 ml) water, add more by the tsp if needed

Preheat the oven to 350°F (177°C) and grease a 11 x 7-inch (28 x 18-cm) pan.

Mix the flaxseed and water in a small bowl and let it sit for 10 minutes; this is a "flax egg." Add the oats, cacao, baking powder, salt, cinnamon and cayenne to the food processor and grind the oats into flour. Add the beans, flax egg, maple syrup, vanilla and water, and process until the batter is smooth and creamy. If it's too thick, add 1 teaspoon of water at a time until it's spreadable but not watery. It should be thicker than cake batter but not as thick as cookie dough.

Bake for 30 minutes, or until an inserted toothpick comes out clean. Cool them on a rack.

⋆SEE PHOTO INSERT

Vegan BANANAS FOSTER

+GF

This decadent and fun-to-make dessert is a New Orleans classic. We make this for special occasions, such as anniversaries and birthdays. The flavors of the banana, orange and rum are intoxicating (not literally because the alcohol burns off when it's ignited) and so unique. You'll love the caramelized brown sugar and the bananas with the melty vegan vanilla ice cream. It's an adult version of a banana split! —LM + AM

SERVES 4

½ tsp coconut oil

½ cup (120 ml) almond milk creamer

½ cup (112 g) brown sugar

2 tbsp (30 ml) Grand Marnier

Juice from ½ orange

2 bananas, cut in half lengthwise (cut them in the skin so they don't break apart) and then peeled

¼ cup (60 ml) rum

1 pt (473 g) vegan vanilla ice cream (we use So Delicious)

¼ cup (31 g) crushed pecans (optional)

Note: Read the disclaimer and safety precautions before making this recipe.

Heat a large shallow pan over medium heat. Add the oil and creamer, and then add the sugar when the oil is melted. With a metal fork, whisk the sugar with the bottom of the fork (tines flat to the pan) in a circular motion. Wear an oven mitt if the fork gets hot. Whisk until the sugar spreads out and begins to foam and bubble, about 4 minutes.

Add the Grand Marnier and the juice from the orange, and whisk for 1 minute. Put the banana slices in, cut-side down, and cook for 1 minute. Flip the bananas and cook for another minute.

Remove the pan from the heat and add the rum. Using a long match or lighter, light the alcohol by placing the flame just inside the outer edge of the pan. Stand as far back from the pan as possible, keeping your face and hands away from the pan. The flame will be a faint blue but will be very hot. It should extinguish in 5 to 10 seconds. Once the flame is out, hold the pan handle with an oven mitt, and gently shake the pan from side to side to coat the bananas with the sauce.

Place the bananas on a platter or in individual bowls, scoop the ice cream on top and spoon the sauce over the ice cream and bananas. Add crushed pecans for garnish if you like.

DISCLAIMER AND SAFETY PRECAUTIONS

When igniting alcohol, use extreme caution.

Remove the pan from the heat source before adding the alcohol, and make sure that there is plenty of space around the entire pan. Remove any towels, fabric or combustible materials.

CHOCOLATE Lava Cake

+GFO +SFO

My first lava cake was an accident. I had leftover chocolate cake batter so I put it in a small ramekin and baked it. I let my son have it when it was done, and he discovered that the center was still gooey and chocolaty. He loved it! I took that accident and created my own version of lava cake, and it's a huge hit in our family. We hope it will be one of your favorites as well. —LM + AM

SERVES 4

(continued)

½ cup (116 g) vegan butter (use soy-free)

5 oz (141 g) semisweet chocolate

⅓ cup (83 g) unsweetened applesauce plus ½ tsp baking powder, whisked together until combined

1 tsp pure vanilla extract

¾ cup (146 g) sugar

⅛ tsp fine sea salt

½ cup (63 g) all-purpose flour (use gluten-free)

TOPPINGS
Vegan vanilla ice cream

Ground cinnamon

Preheat the oven to 425°F (218°C). Grease four 6-inch (15-cm) ramekins and dust with flour.

In a large saucepan over medium-low heat, melt the butter and chocolate. Stir constantly to avoid scorching. Remove the mixture from the heat, and whisk in the applesauce and vanilla until combined. Whisk in the sugar and salt until dissolved. Fold in the flour until just combined and you don't see any flour. Fill each ramekin to the middle of the dish and bake for about 15 minutes, or until the edges are firm and the center is soft. Serve with vegan vanilla ice cream and a dusting of cinnamon.

Mom's LEMON MERINGUE PIE

My mom (Alex's grandma) made the best lemon meringue pie ever. She didn't make it often, and she did use Jello Pudding to make it, but it was incredible. When I set out to create a vegan version, I thought I had my work cut out for me. Thankfully, it wasn't that difficult. After trying to reinvent the wheel, I decided to just make a homemade lemon pudding, only vegan, and it worked. This pie is just like the one I remember, only better, because you won't find any eggs in this one. —LM + AM

MAKES 1 (9-INCH [23-CM]) PIE

1 vegan pie crust, homemade or store-bought

FILLING
4 tbsp (38 g) vegan egg substitute

2 cups (480 ml) water, divided

¾ cup (180 ml) lemon juice

1 cup (194 g) vegan granulated sugar

3 tbsp (24 g) cornstarch

¼ tsp fine sea salt

2 tbsp (30 g) lemon zest

MERINGUE
¼ tsp cream of tartar

Liquid from 1 (15-oz [425-g]) can chickpeas (aquafaba)

¾ cup (145 g) finely ground sugar (see Note)

1½ tsp (8 ml) pure vanilla extract

Preheat the oven to 350°F (177°C)

Bake the pie crust in a 9 x 1½-inch (23 x 4-cm) round pie pan for 40 minutes, or until just golden brown. Line the bottom of the crust with parchment paper and cover it with dried beans to prevent bubbling while baking. Remove it from the oven and let it cool slightly. Dispose of the parchment paper and beans after baking.

FOR THE FILLING
In a small bowl, whisk the vegan egg and 1 cup (240 ml) of the water until smooth and creamy. Set it aside.

In a large saucepan, whisk the remaining 1 cup (240 ml) water, lemon juice, sugar, cornstarch and salt together over medium heat. Keep whisking until the mixture comes to a low boil and is thick and creamy, approximately 10 minutes. Add 1 cup (240 ml) of the lemon mixture to the vegan egg and whisk until combined. This prevents the egg from curdling. Add the egg mixture to the pan of lemon mixture, and whisk continuously until it just begins to boil and is thick and creamy, approximately 5 minutes. Remove it from the heat and whisk in the lemon zest.

FOR THE MERINGUE

In a large mixing bowl, add the cream of tartar to the aquafaba and mix with a whisk attachment on high speed for 10 to 15 minutes, or until the meringue forms stiff peaks. Depending on the aquafaba, it can take 15 minutes or more for it to turn into meringue. Don't give up; it takes time. Slowly pour the sugar and the vanilla into the meringue and beat until combined. Spread evenly over the pie, trying to create peaks.

Place the pie under a broiler (for a minute or two) or use a torch to brown the peaks of the meringue. Watch it carefully so it doesn't burn. Refrigerate the pie for at least 6 hours so the lemon filling sets.

Note: If you can't find finely ground vegan sugar, you can grind it in a food processor or a clean coffee grinder.

Frozen HOT CHOCOLATE CHEESECAKE

+GF +SFO

This rich and wonderful dessert was all Alex's idea. She asked me to make it for the holidays, and of course I said yes. It's everything you'd expect from a cup of hot cocoa, only it's in cheesecake form and it's frozen.

—LM + AM

MAKES 1 (8-INCH [20-CM]) ROUND CAKE

FILLING
2 cups (225 g) raw cashews, soaked in boiling water for at least 4 hours

2½ tbsp (34 g) refined coconut oil, melted

½ cup (120 ml) plant-based milk (don't use coconut milk)

½ cup (120 ml) pure maple syrup

½ cup (56 g) cocoa powder

2 tsp (6 g) tapioca starch

1 tbsp (15 ml) lemon juice

¼ tsp fine sea salt

CRUST
2 cups (340 g) roasted almonds

3 large pitted dates

¼ tsp fine sea salt

3–4 tbsp (45–60 ml) water

½ cup (91 g) semisweet vegan chocolate chips (use soy-free)

TOPPINGS
Vegan marshmallows

Melted chocolate

Crushed peppermint candy

FOR THE FILLING

Drain and rinse the cashews and put them in the blender. Add the coconut oil, milk, maple syrup, cocoa powder, tapioca starch, lemon juice and salt. Blend the mixture on a high speed for about 2 minutes, scraping the sides when needed. It should be smooth and creamy.

FOR THE CRUST

Add the almonds, dates and salt to a food processor, and start to process. Add 1 tablespoon (15 ml) of water at a time until it turns into a ball. Remove the ball and press it evenly into the bottom of an 8-inch (20-cm) springform pan.

Melt the chocolate chips and spread it evenly on top of the crust. Pour the cheesecake filling over the crust and spread it evenly in the pan. Freeze overnight.

Remove it from the freezer and wait an hour before cutting. Top it off with vegan marshmallows, drizzle with melted chocolate and sprinkle with crushed peppermint candy.

LEMON ACAI
Cupcakes

+SFO

While we can't claim that these cupcakes are a health food, we do find the combination of the superfood acai and lemon to be a dynamic duo. Take a bite of these unique cupcakes and you'll probably wind up eating at least three of them. —LM + AM

MAKES 1 DOZEN CUPCAKES

1 cup (226 g) vegan butter, at room temperature, divided (use soy-free)

1 cup (225 g) vegan granulated sugar

1 tbsp (14 ml) pure lemon extract

¼ cup (60 ml) aquafaba (liquid from a can of chickpeas), at room temperature

1½ cups (177 g) cake flour (see Note)

1 tsp baking powder

¼ tsp fine sea salt

1 cup (240 ml) plus 1 tbsp (15 ml) cashew milk at room temperature, divided

2 cups (260 g) vegan powdered sugar

1 tsp acai powder

1 tsp vanilla extract

Preheat the oven to 375°F (190°C) and line a muffin pan with cupcake liners.

In a large mixing bowl, beat ½ cup (113 g) of the butter and granulated sugar on high until smooth and creamy, about 3 minutes. Add the lemon extract and aquafaba, and beat on high for 1 minute.

In a medium bowl, whisk the flour, baking powder and salt until combined. Add half to the butter mixture and beat on low for 30 seconds while adding ½ cup (120 ml) of the milk. Add the rest of the flour mixture and beat while adding ½ cup (120 ml) more milk. Beat until just combined, about 30 to 45 seconds. Stir.

Use a spatula to scrape the sides, and stir until you don't see any dry flour.

Spoon about ¼ cup (60 g) of the batter into each liner, and bake on the center rack for 10 minutes. Reduce the heat to 350°F (177°C) and bake for another 15 to 20 minutes, or until a wooden toothpick comes out clean when inserted into the center of a cupcake.

Cool completely before frosting.

To make the frosting, beat the remaining ½ cup (113 g) butter, powdered sugar, remaining 1 tablespoon (15 ml) cashew milk, acai and vanilla extract in a stand mixer until smooth and creamy. Top each of the cupcakes with the frosting and serve.

Note: For best results, use cake flour. All-purpose flour makes a dense cupcake that can sink in the center. Also, make sure that the butter, aquafaba and milk are room temperature or the cupcakes will fall in the center.

RASPBERRY LEMON
Cheesecake Bars

These rich and creamy cheesecake bars are neighbor tested and approved. Our nonvegan friends couldn't believe they weren't made with dairy cream cheese. If you've been craving a bright and fruity dessert with a bit of tanginess, this is for you.—LM + AM

MAKES 16 BARS

CRUST

1½ cups (136 g) or 1 packet vegan graham crackers (we use Nabisco Grahams Original)

6 tbsp (87 g) vegan butter, melted

¼ tsp fine sea salt

1 tbsp (15 ml) water

FILLING

1½ cups (169 g) raw cashews, soaked in boiling water for at least 4 hours

¾ cup (180 ml) lemon juice

2 tbsp (20 g) lemon zest

¼ cup (60 ml) pure maple syrup

1 tbsp (15 g) coconut oil, melted

¼ cup (61 g) vegan cream cheese

½ cup (61 g) fresh raspberries

Preheat the oven to 350°F (177°C).

FOR THE CRUST

Put the graham crackers in a food processor and grind the crackers into crumbs, about 30 seconds. Transfer the crumbs to a medium bowl and stir in the melted butter, salt and water. Press it firmly and evenly into the bottom of the pan. Bake for 10 minutes. Let it cool while you make the filling.

FOR THE FILLING

Drain and rinse the cashews and put them in a high-powered blender with the lemon juice, zest, maple syrup and coconut oil. Blend everything on high speed for about 2 minutes, or until the mixture is thick and creamy. Scrape the sides as necessary. Put the filling in a medium bowl.

Add the cream cheese to the bowl with the filling and stir until it's combined. You may need to really press the cream cheese into the lemon filling until it's completely absorbed. Don't put the cream cheese in the blender with the filling. It will make the filling too wet.

Put the raspberries in the blender and blend until they're ground up. Then stir them into the lemon filling until they're evenly distributed.

Spread the cheesecake filling evenly over the graham cracker crust, cover and refrigerate for at least 4 hours.

Best when served chilled.

Decadent and Dangerous PEANUT BUTTER BLONDIE BROWNIES

These are fudgy and chewy, chocolaty and buttery, half blondie and half brownie in one decadent and delicious pan of temptation. Why are they dangerous? Because Linda is one of the most disciplined people on the planet when it comes to food, and these made her toss her willpower to the curb.

If you love the combination of brownies, browned butter blondies, peanut butter and semisweet chocolate chips, you're going to dive into a pan of these. Make them for a birthday celebration, your next party or just because you deserve a little sugar in your life. —LM + AM

SERVES 12

BLONDIES

½ cup (116 g) vegan butter

1 cup (223 g) packed brown sugar

2 cups (253 g) all-purpose flour

1 tsp aluminum-free baking powder

½ tsp fine sea salt

½ cup (90 g) creamy peanut butter

½ cup (124 g) unsweetened applesauce

2 tsp (10 ml) pure vanilla extract

½ cup (91 g) semisweet chocolate chips

BROWNIES

½ cup (116 g) vegan butter

1 cup (200 g) granulated sugar (see Note)

1 cup (126 g) all-purpose flour

¾ cup (85 g) cocoa powder

1 tsp aluminum-free baking powder

1 tsp fine sea salt

½ cup (124 g) unsweetened applesauce

1 tsp pure vanilla extract

½ cup (91 g) semisweet chocolate chips

(continued)

Preheat the oven to 350°F (177°C) and grease a 9 x 9-inch (23 x 23-cm) pan.

FOR THE BLONDIES

In a saucepan, melt the butter and the brown sugar over medium-low heat until the butter is melted and the sugar is dissolved. Stir constantly to avoid scorching.

Cook for about 4 minutes. It should look glassy and creamy. Remove from the heat and let it cool.

In a medium mixing bowl, whisk the flour, baking powder and salt until combined.

Add the peanut butter, applesauce and vanilla to the butter and sugar mixture, and stir until the peanut butter melts, about 1 minute. Then pour it into the flour mixture and add the chocolate chips. Stir until just combined. Spread the blondie batter evenly in the greased pan.

FOR THE BROWNIES

In a saucepan, melt the butter and sugar over medium-low heat until the butter melts and the sugar dissolves. Stir constantly to avoid scorching. Cook for about 4 minutes. Remove from the heat and set it aside.

In a medium mixing bowl, whisk the flour, cocoa powder, baking powder and salt until they are well combined.

Add the applesauce and vanilla to the butter and sugar mixture, and stir until completely combined. Pour it into the flour mixture, add the chocolate chips and stir until just combined. Spread the batter evenly over the blondie mixture.

Gently tap the bottom of the pan on a flat surface to remove air bubbles and bake for 35 to 40 minutes, or until a wooden toothpick comes out clean, or with a few crumbs, from the center of the pan. Let it cool before cutting.

Note: Some brands of granulated sugar use bone char to filter it. You can go to the PETA website to find the brands that are vegan.

CHOCOLATE ROSEMARY **Cookies**

+SFO

Rosemary is about the only thing I manage to grow successfully in my garden, so I might as well put it to good use while simultaneously eating comfort foods such as these cookies. Ideally your ingredients should all be at room temperature so that the coconut oil doesn't seize, which would make the dough a pain in the neck to handle. —CS

MAKES 12 COOKIES

1 tbsp (8 g) ground flaxseed

3 tbsp (45 ml) water

⅓ cup (80 ml) melted coconut oil

½ cup (100 g) natural cane sugar

½ cup (120 g) packed organic light brown sugar

¾ tsp organic orange zest

1 packed tsp minced fresh rosemary

½ tsp Himalayan pink salt

1½ cups (180 g) whole wheat pastry or all-purpose flour

1 tsp baking soda

½ cup (84 g) chopped vegan dark chocolate (use soy-free)

Line a cookie sheet with parchment paper. In a large bowl (or the bowl of a stand mixer if that's what you'll use to mix), whisk to combine the flaxseed and water (this is a "flax egg"). Let it stand for 10 minutes to thicken. Add the oil and whisk to combine. Add the sugars and whisk again to combine until creamy. Add the zest, rosemary and salt, and whisk to combine.

Sift the flour and baking soda on top. Use a hand-held mixer or a stand mixer fitted with the paddle attachment to combine everything well. Fold in the chocolate, or if the weather is really cold and making the dough a little resistant, use a clean hand to mix them in. Scoop up a scant ¼ cup (50 g) of dough and place it on the prepared cookie sheet, shaped into a ball. Repeat with the remaining dough. You should get 12 cookies in all. Loosely cover them with plastic wrap and refrigerate for at least 1 hour before baking, up to overnight.

Preheat the oven to 350°F (177°C). Line a second cookie sheet with parchment paper, remove the plastic wrap from the refrigerated sheet and divide the cookies between the two sheets. There's no need to flatten the cookies, as they will spread out fine on their own while baking.

Bake for 14 minutes or until light golden brown around the edges. Let them cool on the sheet for 2 minutes before transferring to a cooling rack.

These cookies taste even better the day after baking. Store them in an airtight container at room temperature for up to 3 days.

FUDGY TAHINI
Cookies

+SFO

A rather liquid tahini paste means that no refined oil is called for in these warmly spiced, fudgy cookies. If chocolate isn't your cuppa, you could replace it with the same amount of raisins, chopped pitted dates or even dried apricots. —CS

MAKES 14 COOKIES

6 tbsp (120 g) agave nectar

6 tbsp (96 g) tahini paste (use a rather liquid tahini; dry won't do)

2 tbsp (24 g) Sucanat

1½ tsp (6 g) Tunisian Baharat (page 416)

1 tsp organic orange zest

2 pinches of coarse kosher salt

½ cup (60 g) whole wheat pastry or all-purpose flour

¼ tsp baking soda

¼ cup (44 g) vegan chocolate chips or chopped vegan dark chocolate (use soy-free)

Preheat the oven to 350°F (177°C). Line a cookie sheet with parchment paper.

In a medium bowl, whisk to combine the agave, tahini, Sucanat, baharat, zest and salt. Add the flour, baking soda and chocolate on top. Stir it to thoroughly mix. Scoop up a heaping tablespoon (20 g) of cookie dough and press it down onto the prepared sheet. The cookies won't spread while baking, so you should be able to fit them all on one sheet. Repeat with the remaining dough.

(continued)

Bake for 8 minutes, or until the cookies just start to be light brown around the edges. Do not overbake—the cookies won't be quite as fudgy and delicious if left in the oven for too long! Let them stand on the sheet for 2 minutes before transferring them to a cooling rack.

MOLASSES SPICE
Cookies

+SFO

These are the ideal wintertime cookies! Loaded with typical warm spices and rolled into a cinnamon-y sugar crunch mix, the recipe yields the type of cookie you'll want to add to Santa's plate so that he doesn't deem you to be too naughty this year. Judgmental much? —CS

MAKES 20 COOKIES

10 tbsp (120 g) evaporated cane juice, divided

¼ cup (48 g) organic light brown sugar, not packed

⅓ cup (80 ml) combination half grapeseed oil and half melted coconut oil

2 tbsp (40 g) blackstrap molasses

1 tsp pure vanilla extract

1 tsp ground cinnamon, divided

¼ tsp ground cardamom

⅛ tsp ground nutmeg

¼ tsp fine sea salt

1½ cups (180 g) whole wheat pastry flour

½ tsp baking soda

3 tbsp (45 ml) unsweetened plain plant-based milk (use soy-free)

Preheat the oven to 350°F (177°C). Line a cookie sheet with parchment paper.

Place 8 tablespoons (96 g) of the cane juice, the sugar, combination of oils, molasses, vanilla, ½ teaspoon of the cinnamon, cardamom, nutmeg and salt in a large bowl. Stir to combine. Sift the flour and baking soda on top. Stir it all to combine: the mixture will be sandy. Add the milk and stir to combine. You can use a clean hand to stir the dough.

Combine the remaining 2 tablespoons (24 g) cane juice with the remaining ½ teaspoon ground cinnamon in a small, shallow bowl. Set aside.

Scoop 1 packed tablespoon (25 g) of dough per cookie, and roll it into a ball. Repeat this with the remaining dough. You should get 20 cookies.

Roll each ball of cookie dough in the cinnamon sugar. Place it on the prepared sheet and flatten it just slightly.

Bake for 10 minutes. Remove them from the oven and leave on the cookie sheet for 2 minutes before transferring the cookies to a cooling rack.

SALTED CARAMEL
Panna Cotta

+GF

This is a simple dessert with fancy and outstanding results! If your molds are efficiently nonstick, coating them might very well be unnecessary. You be the judge. The peanut brittle-like chopped nuts on top add another textural note you're bound to love. —CS

SERVES 4

Glazed pecan topping from Miso Sweet Potato Galette (page 299), made with peanuts

Oil spray

¾ cup (180 ml) full-fat canned coconut milk (grab as much of the creamy part as you can)

8 oz (227 g) unsweetened plain or vanilla-flavored coconut yogurt

⅓ cup (88 g) Salted Caramel Sauce (page 422), plus more for serving

1½ tsp (3 g) agar powder

Prepare the glazed peanuts according to the recipe, cooking them until the glaze isn't liquid anymore, a minute or two longer than the original recipe. Place them evenly on a piece of parchment paper and refrigerate until ready to use.

Very lightly coat 4 small jelly molds with a thin layer of spray.

In a small saucepan, whisk to combine the milk, yogurt, sauce and agar. Bring to a low boil, reduce heat to low and cook for 5 minutes in order to activate the agar. Divide the mixture among the prepared molds. Let it cool to room temperature before transferring to the refrigerator to firm for at least 3 hours.

When you're almost ready to serve, thinly chop the peanuts. Wrap the leftovers and place them back in the refrigerator for up to 1 week.

Remove the desserts from the molds: using a toothpick to carefully lift the edge helps facilitate the release without damaging the desserts. Serve with a healthy drizzle of caramel sauce and a sprinkle of glazed peanuts.

*SEE PHOTO INSERT

MISO SWEET POTATO
Galette

If I have to eat only one dessert for the rest of my life, I want this one to be it. Flaky crust? Check. Salty sweet filling? Check again. Sweet and rich and crunchy pecan topping? Check, check, check. The proverbial cherry on top is a kickass dollop of whipped coconut cream here. Want to make this galette into four smaller ones? Go for it. Divide the dough into four equal pieces, roll them out to about 6 inches (15 cm), and divide the filling equally among each mini galette. The baking time remains about the same, but check occasionally to ensure proper baking to golden brown crust perfection. —CS

SERVES 6 TO 8

1 recipe Galette Crust (page 97)

FILLING
½ cup plus 2 tbsp (150 g) Cashew Crema (page 411)

2 medium sweet potatoes, peeled, boiled and mashed (about 9 oz [255 g] once peeled and mashed)

11 tbsp (132 g) organic light brown sugar, not packed

2 tbsp (16 g) organic cornstarch

Scant 2 tbsp (32 g) white miso

1½ tsp (8 ml) pure vanilla extract

½ tsp ground cinnamon

½ tsp ground ginger

Pinch of ground cloves

Pinch of ground nutmeg

TOPPING
1 tbsp (15 ml) coconut oil

2 tbsp (24 g) Sucanat

Pinch of coarse kosher salt

1 tbsp (15 ml) plain unsweetened vegan creamer of choice (I use Nutpods)

1 cup (120 g) unsalted dry-toasted pecan pieces

Whipped Coconut Cream (page 423)

(continued)

Preheat the oven to 375°F (190°C). Have the crust rolled out and ready.

FOR THE FILLING

Combine all the filling ingredients in a food processor and pulse until smooth, stopping once or twice to scrape the sides of the bowl with a rubber spatula. Scrape the filling onto the center of the crust and spread evenly. Fold the edges on top of the filling, overlapping where needed and pressing slightly to seal.

Bake for 50 minutes, or until golden brown. Let it cool on a wire rack, and refrigerate covered or wrapped in foil overnight.

FOR THE TOPPING

Place the oil, Sucanat, salt and creamer in a medium skillet. Cook over medium heat, stirring frequently until the sugar crystals are dissolved. This should take about 2 minutes. Add the pecans and cook until the caramel has thickened slightly, about 2 more minutes. Be sure to stir frequently and adjust the heat as needed. Place evenly on top of the visible filling of the galette, and refrigerate for another 2 hours before serving. Cut it into slices and top with a good scoop of Whipped Coconut Cream (page 423).

C5 Bonbons (CHOCOLATE, CARAMEL AND CEREAL)

Use the rest of the Peanut Butter Caramel Sauce (page 421) made to drizzle upon Peanut Butter French Toast (page 382) in these beautiful little treats, wrapped in a thin chocolate shell. And fear not: this recipe can easily be doubled or even tripled if you're a chocolate fiend like me. —CS

MAKES 9 BONBONS

½ cup (60 g) unsalted dry-toasted pecan pieces

½ cup (40 g, weight will vary) vegan cornflake-type cereal with granola clusters (I like Peace Vanilla Almond)

¼ cup (70 g) Peanut Butter Caramel Sauce (page 421)

Pinch of coarse kosher salt

¼ tsp pure vanilla extract

1¾ oz (50 g) vegan semisweet chocolate, chopped

1½ tsp (7 g) coconut oil

Place the pecans in a food processor, and pulse to grind them to a breadcrumb-like consistency. Add the cereal and pulse until ground to a coarse consistency as well. Add the caramel, salt and extract. Pulse until combined. The batter should hold together rather well when pinched, but might still be somewhat sticky. Refrigerate it to firm it up.

Line a small plate with wax paper. Use 1 packed tablespoon (25 g) to shape into spheres, and place the spheres on the wax paper. You should get 9 bonbons in all. Freeze them for about 30 minutes.

Prepare the chocolate coating by melting the chocolate and oil in a double boiler, stirring to combine. Let it cool just slightly. Use a fork or a toothpick to roll the frozen spheres into the chocolate. Let the excess drip back into the bowl, and place the bonbons on the wax paper. Refrigerate them for a couple of hours before serving. Keep refrigerated until ready to eat, and store any leftovers in an airtight container for up to 3 days.

Kesar MANGO CAKE

+SF

This cake is so tender and perfect—it disappears quicker than you can say "boo."

Kesar mango pulp can be found in canned form at most international food markets. It is made from the sweetest mango available and has the consistency of a smoothie. To prevent the coconut oil from seizing, it is best to work with ingredients that have been brought back to room temperature if stored in the refrigerator. —CS

SERVES 6 TO 8

Nonstick cooking spray or oil spray

1 cup (200 g) canned Kesar mango pulp, sweetened

¾ cup (144 g) evaporated cane juice or organic granulated sugar

½ cup (120 ml) unsweetened plain cashew milk or almond milk

¼ cup (56 g) coconut oil, melted

½ tsp ground ginger

¼ tsp ground cardamom

½ tsp coarse kosher salt

2 cups (240 g) whole wheat pastry or all-purpose flour

2 tsp (9 g) baking powder

Whipped Coconut Cream (page 423)

Thin slices of fresh mango

Fresh mint

Preheat the oven to 350°F (177°C). Lightly coat a 9-inch (23-cm) square or round baking pan with spray.

In a large bowl, whisk to combine the mango pulp, sugar, milk, melted oil, ginger, cardamom and salt. Sift the flour and baking powder on top, and use a handheld mixer to thoroughly combine without overmixing.

Transfer to the prepared pan in an even layer, baking until golden brown and firm on top, about 35 minutes. You can also insert a toothpick in the center of the cake to check for doneness. Remove it from the oven and place it on a cooling rack. Wait about 15 minutes before carefully removing it from the pan. Slice and serve only once it has completely cooled.

Decorate with a touch of whipped coconut cream, mango slices and a few small mint leaves.

Kesar MANGO FARINA

+GFO +SFO

I always think of farina as an updated version of the rice pudding of my youth. Which may or may not have been a million years ago. Anyway, I went with one of my favorite flavor combos here: coconut, mango, ginger and cardamom. The raisins that are cooked along with the farina take on a beautifully plump and chewy texture. It makes them the perfect surprise to come across while enjoying this breakfast, snack or dessert. A reminder about kesar mango pulp: it can be found in canned form at most international food markets. It is made from the sweetest mango available and has the consistency of a smoothie. —CS

SERVES 4 TO 6

1 cup (235 ml) canned coconut milk

2 cups (470 ml) unsweetened plain cashew milk or almond milk (use soy-free)

1 tbsp (14 g) coconut oil

⅔ cup (109 g) dry brown rice farina for gluten-free or other farina

¼ tsp ground ginger

¼ tsp ground cardamom

Pinch of coarse kosher salt

⅔ cup (133 g) Kesar mango pulp, sweetened

Generous handful golden raisins

2 tbsp (40 g) agave nectar, or to taste

(continued)

Toasted coconut flakes, for garnish

Cubed fresh mango, for garnish

Place the milks in a small saucepan and heat until really hot without boiling.

In the meantime, place the oil in a skillet and heat over medium heat. Add the farina and toast until light golden brown and fragrant, stirring frequently and adjusting the heat as needed. This should take about 5 minutes.

Add the ginger, cardamom and salt. Toast for another minute. Add the mango pulp, raisins and agave nectar, and stir to combine. Slowly add the hot milk to the farina, using a whisk to stir. Simmer uncovered and stir frequently until thickened and tender, about 10 minutes. Remove it from the heat. Cover and let it stand another 10 minutes.

This breakfast, dessert or snack can be served at room temperature or cold. Garnish each serving with coconut flakes and fresh mango. Leftovers can be stored in an airtight container in the refrigerator for up to 3 days.

*SEE PHOTO INSERT

FUDGY SPELT
Brownies

+SF

Once again, I go forth and put the bean in the brownie. Except the bean isn't quite there. Confused yet? Well, unless you live under a rock like I do 99 percent of the time, you must have heard about aquafaba, the liquid left over from cooking chickpeas, aka garbanzo beans. I use it here in blended, whipped form to add structure and binding to these beautifully chewy brownies. —CS

MAKES 16 (1-INCH [2.5-CM]) BROWNIES

¼ cup (60 g) coconut oil

7 oz (198 g) chopped vegan semisweet chocolate, divided (use soy-free)

1 cup (200 g) organic light brown sugar, not packed

2 tsp (10 ml) pure vanilla extract

2 tsp (4 g) instant coffee granules

½ tsp fine sea salt

½ cup (120 ml) aquafaba (liquid from a can of chickpeas)

1½ cups (180 g) light spelt flour

Preheat the oven to 350°F (177°C). Line an 8-inch (20-cm) square baking pan with parchment paper.

Place the oil and 4 ounces (113 g) of the chopped chocolate in a double boiler, and gently melt. (Alternatively, use a glass measuring cup in a microwave to melt the oil and chocolate, stopping to stir the chocolate after 1 minute to prevent burning and continuing in 30-second increments until melted.) Transfer to a medium bowl.

Stir the sugar, vanilla, coffee granules and salt into the chocolate mixture.

In a separate bowl, use an immersion blender to blend the aquafaba until it foams up to twice its size. It will be white after being blended. Pour it onto the chocolate mixture and stir it until thoroughly combined. Add the flour and remaining 3 ounces (85 g) chopped chocolate on top; stir until thoroughly combined. Scrape it into the prepared pan and make sure it's evenly spread. Bake for 25 minutes, and then transfer to a cooling rack. Refrigerate the pan, once cooled, for at least 3 hours. Serve the brownies cold.

Chocolate Pudding
BOWLS WITH COCONUT CREAM AND CHERRIES

This recipe is everything you want chocolate pudding to be. —EvE

SERVES 4 OR 5

COCO CREAM
1 (14-oz [414-ml]) can coconut cream or full-fat coconut milk
½ tsp vanilla extract (optional)

PUDDING
2 avocados
¼ cup (60 ml) maple syrup
¼ cup (27 g) cacao powder
Pinch of Himalayan salt
⅛ tsp ground cinnamon
¼ tsp vanilla powder
½ cup (120 ml) almond milk

TOPPINGS
Cherries
Cacao nibs

FOR THE COCO CREAM

Scrape out the cream top of either the chilled coconut cream or milk into a chilled bowl. With a mixer, beat for 30 seconds until creamy, adding vanilla if desired. Use immediately or refrigerate; it will keep for 1 to 2 weeks.

FOR THE PUDDING

Blend everything together until smooth, creamy and thick. Adjust amounts according to preference. Serve pudding in bowls with whipped coco cream, cherries and cacao nibs.

Freezer FUDGE BITES

This recipe is SUPER basic: ya just throw nut butter into dates and stick them in the freezer for a few minutes. But the result is fabulous. They are gooey, cold, creamy, salty (if you sprinkle on a li'l salt . . . do it), sweet and decadent. They're also made of foods that are good for you. These fudge bites are dual functioning: they are a rich treat/dessert but also an energy snack. Eat as many as you want, whenever you want. —EvE

SERVES 3 TO 6

6 scant tsp (65 g) walnut butter
6 pitted dates
6 walnut halves
Pinch of Himalayan salt (optional)

Scoop a little nut butter into the dates, top with a walnut half, sprinkle on the teensiest amount of salt and put it in the freezer for 10 minutes.

Note: You can use any variety of dates. Medjools work well because they are giant, but lately I've preferred Bam dates (aka Mazafati dates, according to Wikipedia). You can use any nut or seed butter you like. You can add whatever toppings you want. I threw on some sesame seeds for aesthetic reasons here. And use any nut to top the bites! I happened to have walnuts, so I used walnuts.

Spicy Super-Powered CHOCOLATE WITH RASPBERRIES

I put this recipe together on an island for friends to share. I love making up recipes in other people's kitchens because it challenges me to use new ingredients and different equipment (or sometimes no equipment). Plus, merely being in a new environment ignites my foodie creativity. Now, without further ado, here is some delicious chocolate to super-power your day and your life. The spices are anti-inflammatory, the berries are loaded with antioxidants and chocolate is good for the soul! —EvE

SERVES 8 TO 12

CHOCOLATE

1 cup (225 g) coconut oil

⅓ cup (80 ml) maple syrup

⅓ cup (40 g) cacao powder

2 tbsp (12 g) ground ginger

1 tsp ground turmeric

1 tsp ground cinnamon

½ tsp ground cumin

2 tbsp (11 g) coffee powder

TOPPINGS

¼ tsp fleur de sel

¼ cup (35 g) raspberries

1 tsp sesame seeds

2 tbsp (9 g) shredded coconut

Melt the coconut oil in a pot over low heat, and then whisk in the rest of the ingredients until the mixture becomes liquid chocolate: smooth, thick and delicious. Adjust the amounts according to taste and add whatever else you like. Top with the toppings and leave in the freezer or fridge until it has hardened up, which will only take 10 to 15 minutes.

Meyer Lemon COCONUT CREAM TARTS WITH MINT AND LAVENDER

What we've got is a gluten-free crust made with buckwheat groats and almonds. That's then filled up with a creamy, decadent cream of coconut, cashews and sweet lemon juice. It is then garnished with mint, lemon zest and dried lavender flowers—a light and satisfying, sweet treat for lemon and floral lovers. —EvE

SERVES 4 TO 6

CRUST

½ cup (85 g) buckwheat groats

½ cup (85 g) almonds

1 tsp maple syrup (optional)

LEMON COCONUT CREAM

1 cup (75 g) shredded coconut

1 cup (110 g) cashews

¼–½ cup (60–120 ml) fresh lemon juice (preferably from Meyer lemons since they're sweeter)

2 tsp (10 ml) maple syrup

GARNISH

A few mint leaves

1 tsp dried lavender flowers

1 tsp lemon zest

½ tsp maple syrup (optional)

FOR THE CRUST

Put the groats and almonds into a high-speed blender and blend until it turns into a thick, slightly crumbly paste. If needed or desired, add a little maple syrup and then press it into tartlet molds or whatever shapes/molds you like. Put them in the fridge.

FOR THE LEMON COCONUT CREAM

Put the coconut and cashews into your high-speed blender and blend until it turns into a thick paste/butter. Stir in ¼ cup (60 ml) of lemon juice and the maple syrup until evenly combined (or blend it in). If you'd like more lemon flavor, add more lemon juice! I like mine quite tart—no pun intended, seriously—so I used ½ cup (120 ml). Spread this mixture evenly into your crusts; then let them sit in the fridge overnight or for at least a couple hours so the flavors can get to know each other. Garnish them with mint, lavender, lemon zest, maple syrup or whatever else you like! Life is good!

Double Chocolate
CUPCAKES WITH BUTTERCREAM FROSTING

These are happy cupcakes. The ingredients are good for you in every way. They are healthy, wholesome, delicious and easy to make. They are lovely to look at and fun to share. They are a mini celebration of all that is good in this world! (Not to be overdramatic.) —EvE

MAKES 5 BIG CUPCAKES WITH LEFTOVER FROSTING

CUPCAKES
2 tbsp (20 g) chia seeds
¾ cup (180 ml) water, divided
½ cup (40 g) rolled oats
½ cup (38 g) dried coconut meat
½ cup (85 g) dates
3 tbsp (21 g) carob powder

BUTTERCREAM
1 cup (170 g) dates
¾ cup (180 ml) water
Juice from 1 lemon
¼ cup (27 g) cacao powder
2 tbsp (22 g) cashew butter
2 tbsp (28 g) coconut oil
2 tbsp (30 ml) maple syrup
1 tsp vanilla extract
Pinch of salt

COCONUT POWDER
½ cup (38 g) dried coconut meat

FOR THE CUPCAKES

Stir the chia seeds into ¼ cup (60 ml) of the water and let them sit for 5 to 10 minutes so they puff up. Grind the oats and coconut into a fine powder, and set that aside in a bowl. Blend the dates with the remaining ½ cup (120 ml) water and carob powder until smooth. Mix this into the oat/coconut powder by hand, and then mix in the puffed-up chia mixture as well, until it's all well combined and like a dense, slightly wet chocolate dough. If it's too crumbly, add a little more water. Press it into the cupcake papers and keep them in the fridge until set (I let them sit overnight, covered with a cloth).

FOR THE BUTTERCREAM

Blend all of the buttercream ingredients until smooth. Refrigerate it overnight so it can develop those magical flavors.

FOR THE COCONUT POWDER

Grind the coconut meat into powder in a high-speed blender. Frost the cupcakes with the buttercream, then sprinkle them with your powdered coconut and enjoy!

VARIATIONS

Use buckwheat, almond, coconut or quinoa flour instead of rolled oats and/or coconut; use cocoa or cacao instead of carob.

*SEE PHOTO INSERT

DESSERTS

Strawberry
CASHEW CREAM CAKE WITH CAROB DRIZZLE

This cake tastes like a strawberry milkshake. —EvE

SERVES 8 TO 10

CRUST
1 cup (80 g) rolled oats
1 cup (170 g) almonds
Dates, if needed

CREAM CAKE
2 cups (220 g) cashews, soaked in water for at least an hour, then rinsed
1 tsp vanilla extract
½ tsp sea salt
2 tbsp (30 ml) maple syrup
½ cup (120 ml) water
2 tbsp (30 ml) lemon juice
2 tbsp (28 g) coconut oil
2 cups (510 g) frozen strawberries

CAROB DRIZZLE
1 tbsp (14 g) coconut oil (optional)
1 tbsp (7 g) carob powder
2 tbsp (30 ml) maple syrup

GARNISH
Fresh strawberries, sliced, or fruit of choice
Toasted nuts of choice

FOR THE CRUST

Grind the oats and almonds into flour in a high-speed blender, and then continue until they become a paste. If the mixture isn't sticking together, you may need to add some dates (so it sticks together more) and do it in a food processor. You want to end up with a mixture that holds its shape when you press it together, so add as many dates as needed, or some coconut oil or water. Press it into the bottom of a lined springform pan (mine was about 6 inches [15 cm]). Put it in the fridge.

FOR THE CREAM CAKE

Blend all of the ingredients (except the strawberries) together until smooth and thick, like nondairy yogurt. Set aside about one-fourth or one-third of this mixture in a bowl. Throw the strawberries in the blender with the mixture that's still in there and blend until it's smooth and a lovely pink. You still want the texture to be like very thick yogurt, so if it's too thin, add some more coconut oil, cashews or some dates. Pour it onto your crust, and then scoop on the remaining white cream mixture, spreading it evenly. Or not. Put the cake in the fridge for at least 12 hours, but preferably 24 to 48 hours, so the flavors can get to know each other.

FOR THE CAROB DRIZZLE

Melt the coconut oil (if using) and then stir together all the ingredients until smooth. Garnish the cake with fruit and nuts, drizzle it with carob sauce and enjoy!

Orange-Beetroot
TARTLETS WITH ALMOND-FIG CRUST

I personally love the flavor of beets, and their earthiness pairs wonderfully with the light, tangy citrus of orange. The color of the filling is outstanding. —EvE

SERVES 4 TO 6

CRUST

1 cup (165 g) gooey dried figs

¾ cup (72 g) almond flour

CREAM

1 cup (110 g) cashews, soaked in water for 3 hours, then rinsed

¼ cup (34 g) peeled and chopped red beet

2 tbsp (24 g) coconut sugar

1 tsp lemon juice

1 orange, peeled and chopped

3 tbsp (22 g) chopped pistachios

FOR THE CRUST

Blend the figs and almond flour together until you get a sticky, very thick paste that's similar to heavy dough. Press it into lined tart tins. If the dough is too sticky when you're trying to press it into the tart tins, just wet your fingers a little.

FOR THE CREAM

Blend all of ingredients together until smooth and like very thick yogurt. Pour it into your tart crusts and refrigerate overnight so the flavors can develop. Garnish them with chopped pistachios and enjoy! (I had some leftover cream so I blended it with water and got pink cashew beet milk. Cool.)

VARIATIONS

Use any other gooey dried fruit instead of figs. Or if you don't have gooey dried fruit, add some water to the crust mixture to compensate. Use any other un-refined flour instead of almond flour, or grind up your own flour from oats, nuts, etc. Use young coconut meat or any other nuts instead of cashews. Use any other unrefined sweetener instead of coconut sugar.

Coffee CREAM CAKE WITH CHOCO CRUST AND DATE SYRUP

This cake is damn fine. Basically it's like vanilla cheese-cake but with coffee and chocolate infused. Yup, I know. I added goji berries and pumpkin seeds on top because A) color and B) yum. Very rich and decadent. —EvE

SERVES 8 TO 12

CHOCO CRUST

1½ cups (255 g) buckwheat flour

¼ cup (60 ml) date syrup

2 tbsp (28 g) coconut butter

2 tbsp (14 g) carob powder

COFFEE CREAM

2 cups (220 g) raw cashews, soaked for 3 hours in water, then rinsed

¼ tsp vanilla bean seeds

3 tbsp (45 ml) melted coconut oil

¼ cup (60 ml) date syrup

⅛ tsp salt

½ cup (120 ml) very strong brewed organic coffee

TOPPINGS

Pumpkin seeds

Goji berries

Date syrup

FOR THE CHOCO CRUST

Stir the flour with the syrup, coco butter and carob powder until it resembles a crumbly dough that holds its shape when pressed together between a couple fingers. If it's too crumbly, add more date syrup. If it's too moist, add more flour. Press it into the bottom of a springform pan or adjustable pan (mine was about 7 or 8 inches [18 or 20 cm]). Put it in the fridge.

(continued)

FOR THE COFFEE CREAM

Blend all the ingredients together until smooth and delicious. Add some more liquid if it's too thick or some dates or coconut oil if it's too thin. You want it to have the consistency of thick yogurt. Spread it evenly onto your crust and leave it in the fridge for 24 hours so the flavors can develop and the cake can set.

Decorate with the toppings and enjoy!

Oreo-ish Tarts:
VANILLA WHIPPED COCO CREAM WITH CHOCOLATE COOKIE CRUST

These are LUSCIOUS. Nothing is sexier than whipped coconut cream. Period. —EvE

SERVES 4 TO 6

CHOCOLATE COOKIE CRUST
1 cup (110 g) cashews

¼ cup (27 g) cacao powder

Scant ½ cup (55 g) ground flaxseed

3 tbsp (45 ml) maple syrup

1 tsp vanilla extract

Pinch of Himalayan salt

VANILLA WHIPPED COCO CREAM
1 (13½-oz [400-ml]) can full-fat coconut milk, left in the fridge overnight

¼ cup (47 g) coconut sugar, ground into powder

¼ tsp vanilla bean seeds

FOR THE COOKIE CRUST

Grind the cashews into flour, and then throw the cashew flour into a bowl and mix in the rest of the ingredients until you have a doughy mixture that holds its shape. Set aside a scant ¼ cup (30 g) of this mixture for the cookie crumble. Press the remaining dough into tart tins or whatever shape you like, and put them in the fridge for an hour or more so they harden up.

FOR THE COOKIE CRUMBLE

Roll out the dough you set aside and leave it in the oven at its lowest temperature until it gets crispy. This may take 2 to 3 hours. Or use your dehydrator. Then chop it up into cookie pieces. I only left mine in the oven for an hour so it didn't get crispy, but I used it anyway. It's all good.

FOR THE COCO CREAM

Scoop the cream from the top of the can of coconut milk into a mixer. Whip until thickened, about 5 minutes. Add the sugar and vanilla and whip to combine. Scoop the whipped coco cream into the cookie crusts. Sprinkle on the cookie pieces and enjoy!

VARIATIONS

You can use any nut instead of cashews; you can use cocoa or carob powder instead of cacao; you can use dates instead of flax seeds; you can use any other sweetener instead of maple syrup; you can use vanilla extract instead of vanilla bean seeds.

Deep-Dish CARAMEL APPLE PIE

This pie is DELICIOUS. I have ample evidence of this, thanks to the fact that it was hastily devoured by the crowd at a vegan potluck I cohosted last month. It's sweet, decadent, cinnamon-y and made with 100 percent good-for-you ingredients. I'm talkin' about nuts, oats, chai spices, fresh apples and dried fruit. I highly recommend you chow this down with some coconut vanilla ice cream. —EvE

SERVES 8 TO 12

CRUST

1½ cups (165 g) walnuts

1 cup (80 g) oats

½ cup (56 g) ground flaxseed

2 cups (340 g) pitted dates

1 tbsp (14 g) coconut oil

Pinch of Himalayan salt

CARAMEL

1 cup (170 g) pitted dates

Pinch of Himalayan salt

½ tsp vanilla powder

¾ tsp ground cinnamon

¾ tsp ground ginger

½ cup (120 ml) water

2 tbsp (30 ml) lemon juice

Scant ¼ cup (60 ml) maple syrup

Scant ¼ cup (45 g) almond butter

Scant ¼ cup (55 g) coconut oil

6 medium apples (I used a mix of Gala, Ambrosia and Spartan)

FOR THE CRUST

Grind the walnuts, oats and flaxseed into a crumbly flour in a food processor. Add the rest of the crust ingredients and process until it lumps together in a sticky mass; it should be able to hold its shape when pressed between two fingers. Press it into the bottom and sides of a lined tart tin or 9-inch (23-cm) springform pan, and put it in the fridge.

FOR THE CARAMEL

Blend all the ingredients together until smooth; it should be thick like yogurt.

Cut the apples into halves and core them, then slice thinly on a mandoline slicer. The slices should be thin enough to bend without breaking. Drizzle the caramel onto the apple slices in a big bowl and rub the caramel into them until they are all evenly coated. You may have leftover caramel. Let them sit for 30 minutes to soften. Fill your crust with the apples and let it sit in the fridge overnight.

Note: The pie might be a little messy to cut, so the sharper your knife, the better. Alternatively, you could make mini deep-dish tarts! Way less messy.

Caramel CHOCOLATE GANACHE TART WITH SUPERFOOD DRIZZLE

Very decadent and rich! But also, really good for ya! This tart is full of healthy fats, fiber and probably a decent amount of protein too. We've got a crust made from dates, oats and almonds topped off with a date-based salted caramel and smooth chocolate layer. The finale is a deliciously tart, sweet drizzle made with ingredients from whole foods like berries, maca root, lucuma and chia seeds. —EvE

SERVES 12; MAKES ONE 9-INCH (23-CM) TART

(continued)

DESSERTS

CRUST

1 cup (80 g) rolled oats

1 cup (170 g) almonds, preferably soaked for
4–8 hours, then rinsed

1½ cups (255 g) pitted dates

CARAMEL

¼ cup (55 g) coconut oil

¼ cup (60 ml) coconut milk, or more as needed

¼ tsp Himalayan salt

½ tsp vanilla powder

1 cup (110 g) cashews, preferably soaked for
4 hours, then rinsed

1½ cups (255 g) pitted dates

3 tbsp (45 ml) maple syrup

CHOCOLATE

2 tbsp (28 g) coconut oil

¼ cup (60 ml) caramel (see above)

2 tbsp (14 g) cacao powder

Slivered almonds (optional)

DRIZZLE

1 heaping tbsp (15 g) coconut oil

2 tbsp (30 ml) maple syrup

1 heaping tbsp (8 g) Oh My Glow Superfood
Beauty Blend

FOR THE CRUST

Grind the oats and almonds into flour in a food processor, then add the dates and process them until it becomes a crumbly mixture that holds its shape when pressed between two fingers. If needed, you can add some water for moisture to help it stick together better. Press it into the bottom of a lined 9-inch (23-cm) tart or cake pan and put it in the freezer.

FOR THE CARAMEL

In a blender, blend all the ingredients until smooth. If it's too thick for your blender to handle, add a little more coconut milk. Set aside ¼ cup (60 ml) of the caramel for the chocolate layer. Spread the remaining caramel over your crust and put it back in the fridge.

FOR THE CHOCOLATE

Melt the coconut oil, then stir in the rest of the ingredients until it's smooth. Spread this on top of your caramel layer and place it back in the freezer overnight. If desired, sprinkle the tart with slivered almonds.

FOR THE DRIZZLE

Melt the coconut oil. Then stir in the rest of the ingredients and drizzle it over your tart. Slice and enjoy! Store in the freezer for up to a week.

Chai CHEESECAKES WITH CHOCOLATE DRIZZLE

This recipe is the bomb. It's creamy, decadent, sweet and full of wholesome stuff my body wants (like nuts, chocolate and chai spices). I flip flop a lot on what to call vegan cheesecakes: I've gone through phases of not caring, to preferring to call them cheeZecakes, to labelling them as cream cakes, and now I've gone full circle and am back to calling them cheesecakes because while no, they don't contain any dairy cheese, they are vegan cheesecake! —EvE

SERVES 3 TO 6

CHEESECAKES

1 cup (110 g) cashews

¼ cup (43 g) dates

3 tbsp (45 ml) maple syrup

3–4 tbsp (45–60 ml) water or lemon juice

3 tbsp (42 g) coconut oil

⅛ tsp ground cinnamon

⅛ tsp nutmeg powder

⅛ tsp ground ginger

⅛ tsp vanilla powder

3–5 seeds from a cardamom pod

CRUST

⅙ cup (19 g) coconut flour

⅙ cup (16 g) almond flour

1 tbsp (15 ml) maple syrup

1 tbsp (15 ml) melted coconut oil

1 tbsp (7 g) cacao powder

2 tbsp (30 ml) water

Pinch of Himalayan salt

CHOCOLATE DRIZZLE

1 tbsp (15 ml) melted cacao butter

1 tbsp (7 g) cacao powder

2 tbsp (30 ml) maple syrup

FOR THE CHEESECAKES

Blend all of the ingredients together until smooth, thick and delicious. Set it aside.

FOR THE CRUST

Stir together all the ingredients until you get a semi-crumbly mixture that holds its shape when pressed between two fingers. If it's still too crumbly, add some more water. Press the crust into lined cupcake molds, and then fill them with the cheesecake mix. Leave them in the freezer or fridge overnight. Gently remove the cheesecakes from the molds.

FOR THE CHOCOLATE DRIZZLE

Stir together the ingredients—ya just made chocolate sauce! Drizzle it over your cheesecakes and enjoy.

Magical SUPERFOOD CHEESECAKE

This cake recipe is "magical" because it's pretty AND secretly very nutrient-dense. It is full of healthy fats from nuts and seeds, multi-source vitamin B (thanks to Pranin Organic's PureFood B), complex carbs like oats, and dried fruits. It is creamy, rich, sweet, satisfying, easy to make and let's be real, it's also gorgeous (*pats self on back*). In short: I FRICKIN' LOVE PLANTS. AGH. —EvE

SERVES 8 TO 12; MAKES ONE 9-INCH (23-CM) CHEESECAKE

CRUST

1 cup (170 g) almonds

1 cup (80 g) rolled oats

1½ cups (227 g) raisins

VANILLA CREAM

¼ cup (57 g) cacao butter, melted

1½ cups (165 g) cashews

⅛ tsp sea salt

3 tbsp (45 ml) lemon juice

¼ cup (60 ml) maple syrup

2 tsp (10 ml) vanilla extract

½ tsp vanilla bean

MINT CREAM

1 cup (170 g) dates

3 tbsp (45 ml) lemon juice

¼ cup (55 g) coconut oil, melted

⅙ cup (40 ml) maple syrup

1 cup (110 g) Brazil nuts

3 tsp (21 g) Pranin Organic PureFood B

¼ cup (10 g) chopped fresh mint

(continued)

STRAWBERRY CREAM

1 cup (150 g) dried cranberries

¾ cup (128 g) almonds

¼ cup (38 g) strawberries

2 tbsp (5 g) chopped beet

⅙ cup (40 ml) maple syrup

3 tbsp (45 ml) lime juice

¼ cup (55 g) coconut oil, melted

FOR THE CRUST

Grind the almond and oats into flour in a food processor, then add the raisins and process until you get a sticky, moist dough. Press it into the bottom of a lined springform pan. I used a 6-inch (15-cm) springform cake pan. Leave it in the fridge.

FOR EACH LAYER

Simply blend the ingredients for each layer until smooth and thick. If your blender can't handle the thickness, add more liquid in the form of maple syrup, melted cacao or coconut butter/oil or lemon/lime juice; you can also add water, but it'll make the result less creamy. You'll end up with a white vanilla mixture, a green mint layer and a pink strawberry layer. Spread each successively into the cake pan in the order you want and leave it in the freezer overnight so the cake can set and flavors can develop. Decorate it with berries, flowers, nuts, mint, seeds—whatever you like!

Fierce SALTED CARAMEL CHEESECAKE

Salted. Caramel. Cheesecake. It's vegan. It's raw. It's even more delicious than it sounds. But don't trust me: make it yourself and experience the sensual seduction firsthand. This cheesecake was inspired by a recipe from Amy Lyons. —EvE

SERVES 10 TO 12; MAKES ONE 9-INCH (23-CM) CHEESECAKE

CRUST

⅔ cup (55 g) rolled oats

⅓ cup (37 g) ground flaxseed

¾ cup (57 g) shredded coconut

⅛ tsp sea salt

1 cup (150 g) gooey dates

CARAMEL

1½ cups (225 g) gooey dates

¼ cup (60 ml) water, or more as needed

Heaping ¼ cup (50 g) almond butter

¼ tsp sea salt

1 tsp vanilla extract

2 tbsp (30 ml) melted coconut oil

CHEESECAKE BATTER

2 cups (220 g) cashews, preferably soaked for 4 hours

½ cup (120 ml) melted coconut oil

⅔ cup (100 g) gooey dates

⅛ tsp sea salt

1 tbsp (15 ml) vanilla extract

½ cup (120 ml) coconut milk or water, or more as needed

2 tbsp (30 ml) lemon juice

FOR THE CRUST

Grind the oats, flax, coconut and salt into flour in a blender or food processor. Add the dates and process into a thick dough that holds its shape when pressed between two fingers. Press it into the bottom of a lined 6-inch (15-cm) springform cake pan and leave it in the fridge.

FOR THE CARAMEL

Blend everything until smooth and thick and delish. Set it aside in a bowl.

FOR THE CHEESECAKE BATTER

Blend everything until smooth and thick and delish!

ASSEMBLY

Scoop some caramel onto your crust, and then pour over some cheesecake batter. Keep doing this until you've used everything up. Swirl it around with a chopstick and then leave it to set in the freezer overnight. I decorated my cake with almonds, frozen berries, chia seeds and baobab drizzle (see Chocolate Coconut Hazelnut Ganache Tart, page 313).

Chocolate COCONUT HAZELNUT GANACHE TART

It is 100 percent COOL to just have a recipe be mostly coconut cream, coconut sugar and some hazelnuts. Rich, alluring and elegant. So does this ganache tart secretly pack 50 percent of your RDI for iron or something? Probably not. And that is OK. It tastes damn good and certainly isn't gonna hurt your bod. At the very least, it will be good for your soul. This is still a raw vegan tart that is made with mostly whole foods. That is a big ole win in my books. Please: enjoy! Oh, and P.S. the crust recipe can be used to make some delicious cookies if you have leftovers. —EvE

SERVE 8 TO 12; MAKES ONE 9-INCH (23-CM) TART

CRUST
¾ cup (60 g) rolled oats
¾ cup (57 g) shredded coconut
½ cup (55 g) hazelnuts
½ cup (95 g) coconut sugar
1 tbsp (14 g) coconut oil

GANACHE
1 (13½-oz [400-ml]) can full-fat coconut milk
¼ cup (47 g) coconut sugar
1 tsp vanilla powder
¼ tsp sea salt
¼ cup (27 g) cacao powder
¼ cup (30 g) hazelnuts
2 tbsp (28 g) coconut oil
3 tbsp (45 ml) melted cacao butter

BAOBAB DRIZZLE (OPTIONAL)
3 tbsp (42 g) coconut oil
2 tbsp (14 g) baobab powder
2 tbsp (30 ml) maple syrup

Chopped hazelnuts, for garnish

FOR THE CRUST

Grind the oats, coconut, hazelnuts and sugar into flour in a high-powered blender or food processor. Add the coconut oil and blend until you have a crumbly dough that holds its shape when pressed between two fingers. Press it into the bottom of a lined springform pan (I used a 6-inch [15-cm]). Leave it in the fridge.

FOR THE GANACHE

Blend everything until smooth and delicious! It will be very liquidy at this point, but not to worry: it hardens up. Pour this over your crust and leave it in the fridge overnight.

FOR THE BAOBAB DRIZZLE

If you wanna make this optional drizzle, melt the coconut oil in a small pot and whisk in the other ingredients. After a moment it will become a lovely caramel mixture. Drizzle this over your cake and decorate with some chopped hazelnuts. Slice and enjoy!

Mini LEMON AND BLUEBERRY JAM CHEESECAKES

NEW FAVE RECIPE ALERT (and it doesn't even contain chocolate!?): I LOVE my blueberries. In winter, when they aren't growing fresh in my home province of British Columbia (aka Turtle Island on First Nations land)—the biggest highbush blueberry–producing region in the world—or the bushes in our front yard, I am sad and miss them. But, I know I can still grab them frozen in the grocery store. And I do. Because I crave blueberries on the daily. In desserts, smoothies, on toast . . . basically everywhere in my life. —EvE

SERVES 3 TO 6

CRUST

1 cup (75 g) shredded coconut

1 cup (110 g) walnuts

½ cup (56 g) ground flaxseed

1 cup (170 g) pitted dates

BLUEBERRY JAM

3 cups (690 g) frozen blueberries

⅓ cup (53 g) chia seeds

2 tbsp (30 ml) fresh lemon juice

¼ cup (47 g) coconut sugar

1 tsp vanilla powder

CHEESECAKE BATTER

1½ cups (165 g) cashews

¼ cup (60 ml) fresh lemon juice

¼ cup (60 ml) melted cacao butter

¼ cup (60 ml) maple syrup

½ tsp sea salt

1 (14½-oz [430-ml]) can full-fat coconut milk

FOR THE CRUST

Grind the coconut, walnuts and flax into flour in a high-speed blender. Then add the dates and continue blending until you have a thick, moist dough. It should be able to hold its shape when pressed between two fingers. Press it into the bottom of cupcake molds (or whatever mold/shape you like). Leave it in the fridge to harden up.

FOR THE BLUEBERRY JAM

Thaw the berries (or throw them in the microwave) until they're soft. Mash them into a paste with a fork (or if you want it super smooth, use a blender) and add the rest of the ingredients. Leave this to sit for 10 to 15 minutes: the chia seeds will soak up the berry juice and the mixture will thicken up like jam.

FOR THE CHEESECAKE BATTER

Open the can of coconut milk and scoop off the thick, white fat that should be on top. The rest of the can should be filled with a translucent white liquid. You want to use only the thick, white fat. Don't use the milky liquid. Blend all of the ingredients until smooth. Scoop half of this mixture onto your crust(s), followed by some (but not all) of the berry jam. Pour the rest of the cheesecake batter over the jam, and add the rest of the jam on top of that. Swirl the jam around with a spoon or finger for decoration. Leave it in the freezer overnight and store it in the fridge.

Vanilla CHERRY NICE CREAM

This dessert is simple and satisfying, especially on hotter days. Cherries and vanilla are a heavenly match. —EvE

SERVES 1 OR 2

4 peeled, frozen, chopped bananas
⅓ cup (80 g) pitted cherries
⅛ tsp whole vanilla bean (see Note)

TOPPING
⅓ cup (80 g) pitted cherries

Blend it all up until it's like soft serve. Yum. Then top with the leftover cherries and eat.

Note: If you don't have whole vanilla bean, use ⅛ teaspoon vanilla powder or ¼ teaspoon vanilla extract.

*SEE PHOTO INSERT

Blueberry BLACKBERRY SORBET WITH CHIA PUDDING AND TAHINI

In this recipe, I am combining blueberries with another food of the goddesses—the blackberry—into luscious sorbet and serving it alongside creamy chia pudding, drizzled in rich tahini. For obvious reasons, I added chunks of dark chocolate. This is a bit of an uncommon combination but it works wonderfully. So wonderfully, in fact, that I ended up eating the whole bowl myself even though I had initially planned to share with a friend. Whoops. I love the variety of textures, temperatures and colors in this dish. I hope you do too. —EvE

SERVES 1 OR 2

CHIA PUDDING
⅓ cup (27 g) rolled oats
2 tbsp (20 g) chia seeds
1 cup (235 ml) coconut milk
1 tbsp (15 ml) maple syrup
1 tbsp (9 g) sunflower seeds
½ tsp vanilla extract
1 heaping tbsp (9 g) dried cranberries
¼ cup (37 g) blueberries

BERRY SORBET
½ cup (90 g) frozen banana chunks
¼ cup (38 g) frozen blackberries
½ cup (115 g) frozen blueberries
Pinch of stevia powder
1 tsp lime juice
1 tsp lucuma powder (optional)
Splash of coconut milk, if needed or desired

TOPPINGS
2 tbsp (36 g) tahini
Dark chocolate, grated
Extra sunflower seeds and berries

FOR THE CHIA PUDDING
Stir together all of the ingredients in a bowl. Let it sit in the fridge for at least 20 minutes so the chia seeds can thicken the mixture into a consistency like rice pudding. Ideally, let it sit overnight in the fridge, covered.

FOR THE BERRY SORBET
Blend all of the ingredients together until smooth and thick (like sorbet).

ASSEMBLY
Scoop your pudding into the bottom of a bowl and top with scoops of the sorbet, a drizzle of tahini, grated chocolate and seeds or berries.

MINT CHOCOLATE CHUNK Ice Cream

This ice cream is creamy, sweet and full of chocolate chunks and mint flavor; in other words it's everything ice cream should be and MORE. The "more" is because it's also vegan and made with ingredients that my body actually likes. —EvE

SERVES 4 TO 6

CHOCOLATE CHUNKS
2 tbsp (28 g) coconut oil

4 tbsp (60 ml) maple syrup

2 tbsp (14 g) cacao powder

2 tbsp (30 ml) water, as needed

ICE CREAM
1 cup (75 g) fresh young coconut meat

¾ cup (180 ml) coconut water, as needed

2 tbsp (28 g) coconut oil

1 cup (110 g) cashews, soaked for 3 hours in water, then rinsed

¼ cup (27 g) coconut sugar

¼ cup (15 g) tightly packed mint

¼ tsp spirulina powder (optional)

FOR THE CHOCOLATE CHUNKS
Melt the coconut oil, and then stir all the ingredients together, adding water as needed to get it nice and smooth. Pour it onto a plate and place in the freezer until solid. Chop it into chunks and leave in the fridge. Go ahead and make more if you want. I did, and then drizzled it on top before scooping the finished ice cream into bowls.

FOR THE ICE CREAM
Blend everything together, adding coconut water as needed. You want it to have the consistency of thick yogurt. Stir in the chocolate chunks by hand. Pour it into an ice-cream maker and follow its instructions. Or, if you don't have an ice-cream maker (like me), pour it into a container and put it in the freezer, taking it out and stirring everything up every 30 minutes until you get ice cream.

VARIATIONS
Use coconut butter instead of coconut oil; use water instead of coconut water; use dried coconut meat instead of fresh coconut meat; use avocado instead of cashews; use 1 (13½-oz [400-ml]) can of coconut milk instead of the coconut meat, coconut water and coconut oil.

Almond CACAO COOKIES WITH SALTED MACA CARAMEL

Maca is great for improving my mood and balancing my hormones because of its adaptogenic properties. It has a unique flavor that works well with chocolate—try it out! —EvE

MAKES 8 TO 10 COOKIES

ALMOND CACAO COOKIES
1 cup (170 g) almonds

1 cup (170 g) dates

2 heaping tbsp (14 g) cacao powder

1 tsp vanilla extract

SALTED MACA CARAMEL
1 cup (170 g) dates

2 tbsp (14 g) maca powder

Himalayan pink crystal salt, to taste

¾ cup (180 ml) water, more or less as needed

TOPPINGS (OPTIONAL)

Pecan halves, walnut halves and/or almonds

FOR THE ALMOND CACAO COOKIES

Pulse the almonds into flour in a food processor, adding the rest of the ingredients and pulsing until it all sticks together. Press it into the bottom of a lined baking pan and put it in the fridge.

FOR THE SALTED MACA CARAMEL

Blend all the ingredients until smooth and thick like whipped cream. Put this in the fridge for about 2 hours.

Use a cookie cutter to make your cookies, and then scoop a spoonful of caramel on top of each one. Press a walnut, almond or pecan onto the dollop of caramel. Refrigerate overnight or at least for a few hours . . . then enjoy with fresh almond milk!

*SEE PHOTO INSERT

Almond Butter AND CHIA JAM BARS WITH CHOCOLATE

These bars are gooey, sweet and comfortable. Maybe you think comfortable is a weird adjective for food, but I think it's appropriate. Of course this recipe is reminiscent of PB&J (aka, the foodstuff of my childhood), so the flavor combo brings back memories for me of being young and not having a substantial care in the world. Comfort. I will be the first to admit these bars can get messy. So have a napkin handy . . . or #yolo it and proudly wear bits of jam and chocolate on your face for the remainder of the day, I won't judge. Isn't getting a bit dirty part of life, anyway? —EvE

MAKES 6 TO 8 BARS

ALMOND BUTTER BASE

1 cup (80 g) rolled oats

½ cup (90 g) almond butter

1 tbsp (15 ml) maple syrup

¼ cup (28 g) ground flaxseed

JAM

1 cup (150 g) berries of choice

4 tbsp (40 g) chia seeds

1 cup (180 g) raw or dark chocolate, melted

FOR THE ALMOND BUTTER BASE

Grind the rolled oats into flour in a blender. Then mix this together with the other ingredients in a bowl. Press it into the bottom of a lined bread pan (I used two small ones). Put it in the fridge.

FOR THE JAM

Mash or blend the berries until smooth, and then thoroughly stir in the chia seeds, letting it sit for 10 to 15 minutes so the chia seeds can gel with the mashed berries and thicken into jam. Spread this onto your base, drizzling the chocolate on evenly. I swirled in some more almond butter at this point because . . . why not? Stick it back in the fridge and let it sit for an hour; then slice and munch! Slice them carefully—the jam is gooey.

*SEE PHOTO INSERT

Peppermint OREOS DIPPED IN DARK CHOCOLATE

We've got chewy chocolate cookies sandwiching a peppermint vanilla coconut creme filling. Yup. Oh right—then all the cookies are dipped in chocolate, making them double chocolate. Can life get any better? Well, yeah, because these are also really good for you and easy to make. Okay, now life can't get any better. Unless you throw in a bowl of banana ice cream (but that is a constant truth). —EvE

SERVES 10 TO 12

COOKIES

⅔ cup (112 g) almonds

⅔ cup (75 g) Brazil nuts

1 cup (170 g) dates

3 tbsp (21 g) carob powder

Pinch of sea salt

1–3 tbsp (15–45 ml) water, if needed

VANILLA CREME

1 cup (80 g) coconut chips

1 cup (75 g) coconut shreds

2 tbsp (22 g) almond butter

2 tbsp (30 ml) melted coconut oil

½ tsp vanilla powder

1–3 drops of peppermint essential oil, as desired

DARK CHOCOLATE

½ cup (160 g) coconut nectar or date paste

¾ cup (82 g) cacao powder or carob powder

⅓ cup (80 g) coconut oil or cacao butter, melted

FOR THE COOKIES

Grind the nuts into flour in a high-speed blender or food processor. Add the rest of the ingredients (except the water) to the nut flour in a food processor and process until it all sticks together in a ball. If it's still too crumbly after a few minutes, add a little water. I did this, and suddenly my very dry mixture became the perfect cookie dough consistency! Roll this dough out between two pieces of parchment paper, and then cut out cookies with a cookie cutter. Put them in the freezer until they are solid and can be handled without falling apart. If you have any extra dough, make a giant "ugly" cookie and sprinkle it with some sea salt. No dough left behind.

FOR THE VANILLA CREME

Blend all the ingredients together in a high-speed blender, adding the peppermint oil to taste (it's very potent!). If your blender isn't powerful enough to blend everything into a thick, coconut butter–like mixture, then add some more coconut oil and perhaps a liquid sweetener, or some dates and water.

Sandwich the vanilla creme with cookies, making little dollops on each cookie and then gently pressing down another cookie on top. Throw them in the freezer for another 30 minutes or until they are solid and very cold.

FOR THE DARK CHOCOLATE

Whisk all the ingredients until smooth and ridiculously delicious. Then pour the chocolate into a tall, narrow bowl and dip in your frozen cookies. You will have to have 2 to 3 rounds of dipping, letting the chocolate on the cookies harden in the fridge or freezer after each time.

Note: If you want the cookies to be darker, add more carob powder; if you want the creme to be whiter, try omitting the nut butter and adding more coconut oil or maple syrup.

Use oat flour, buckwheat flour or any nuts instead of almonds or Brazil nuts; use cacao or cocoa powder instead of carob; use vanilla extract instead of powder; salt is always optional; use more coconut shreds instead of coconut chips; use any nut butter instead of almond; use date paste instead of coconut oil; use peppermint leaves instead of essential oil.

Almond Cookies
WITH SPICED APPLE SLICES

These cookies are SO FREAKIN' GOOD by themselves, and then they are topped off with warm, gooey apple slices marinated with cinnamon and nutmeg. There's no going wrong here. Make this recipe ASAP. —EvE

SERVES 4 TO 6

SPICED APPLES
1 cup (180 g) thinly sliced apples
½ tsp ground cinnamon
¼ tsp ground nutmeg
¼ tsp ground ginger
2 tbsp (30 ml) maple syrup
½ tsp vanilla extract

COOKIES
1 cup (170 g) almonds
3 tbsp (45 ml) maple syrup
3 tbsp (45 ml) melted coconut oil

FOR THE SPICED APPLES

Toss the apples with the spices, maple syrup and vanilla. Put them in the oven at a very low temperature or in a dehydrator for an hour, or until they have softened. Check often to make sure they don't dry out or burn—you want them warm, soft and gooey.

FOR THE COOKIES

Grind the almonds into flour in a food processor or blender. Throw the almond flour into a bowl, and stir in the maple syrup and coconut oil until you get a sticky, crumbly mixture. If it's not sticking together, add some more maple syrup. If it's too wet, add some ground flaxseeds or more almond flour. Spread the cookie dough evenly onto a cookie sheet, about ½ inch (1.3 cm) thick, and put it in the fridge or freezer until solid, an hour or two. Cut it into cookies.

Spoon some warm apple slices onto your cookies and dig in!

Banana Bread
COOKIES WITH COCONUT CREAM AND CHOCOLATE SAUCE

For banana bread lovers—that's all of us, right?? —EvE

MAKES 8 LARGE COOKIES

COOKIES
3 very ripe bananas, peeled
⅔ cup (64 g) almond flour
⅔ cup (112 g) buckwheat groats
2 tsp (4 g) ground cinnamon
2 tsp (6 g) chia seeds
1 tsp vanilla powder
¼ tsp nutmeg powder
¼ tsp ground ginger
⅛ tsp Himalayan salt

COCONUT CREAM
¼ cup (19 g) young coconut meat
¼ cup (60 ml) water
1 tsp maple syrup

CHOCOLATE DRIZZLE
1 tbsp (15 ml) maple syrup
1 tsp cacao powder
1 tsp water

FOR THE COOKIES
Mash the bananas with a fork (or your hands, woo) and then mix in everything else. You should end up with a gooey wet dough that holds it shape. Scoop it into cookies with an ice cream scoop (or whatever) onto a lined dehydrator tray and dehydrate for 2 to 3 hours at 115°F (46°C). Or just use the oven at its lowest temperature like I do. The cookies are done when they hold their shape and are a little chewy. Let them cool if you want.

FOR THE COCONUT CREAM
Blend it all until smooth. If your blender is big, you may have to double the amounts. But seriously—when has leftover coconut cream ever been an issue?

FOR THE CHOCOLATE DRIZZLE
Stir the ingredients together until smooth; it will take a second for the cacao to combine with the liquid.

Spread the coconut cream on the cookies and drizzle on chocolate sauce. Eaaaaat.

VARIATIONS
Use buckwheat or oat flour instead of almond flour; use rolled oats or coconut shreds instead of buckwheat; use vanilla extract instead of vanilla powder. Add some peanut butter into the cookie dough—ya really can't go wrong with PB and bananas.

MAPLE OATMEAL RAISIN **Cookies**

These cookies are delish. When I was living in Montreal, I fell back in love with maple syrup, and I fell harder than ever before. I literally drank it from the jar some days. And even now I will have spoonfuls of the golden amber stuff like it's medicine . . . (which IT. IS.) I cannot get over the different flavor notes in it. I mean, yes, it's damn sweet so that is mainly why my brain/tongue love it. But it's MORE THAN THAT. It's like butterscotch and caramel. The cookies themselves are kind of amazing, and after you've had one you're probably gonna want another. I say: go for it. I need to recommend you eat them with Whipped Coconut Cream (page 423). Somehow the whole thing reminds me of doughnuts?? —EvE

MAKES 12 COOKIES

COOKIES
1½ cups (120 g) rolled oats, divided

1 cup (120 g) walnuts

1 tsp ground ginger

1 tsp ground cinnamon

Pinch of Himalayan salt

¼ cup (28 g) ground flaxseed

¼ cup (40 g) chia seeds

¾ cup (114 g) raisins

¼ cup (60 ml) maple syrup

3 tbsp (45 ml) melted coconut oil

TOPPING
Whipped coconut cream (optional, page 423)

Grind 1 cup (80 g) of the oats and all the walnuts into a flour, then add the rest of the dry ingredients (including the remaining ½ cup [40 g] rolled oats) and mix together evenly.

Pour on the maple syrup and coconut oil, and stir together until a thick dough forms. Press it into cookies and leave them in the fridge for a few hours or overnight until they are solid. I highly suggest whipping up some coco cream with vanilla beans and maple syrup and spreading it on the cookies before you eat them. Yum.

COCONUT TWIX **Bars**

A fan favorite. —EvE

MAKES 7 TO 8 BARS

COOKIE LAYER
½ cup (56 g) coconut flour

½ cup (50 g) almond flour

¼ cup (60 ml) maple syrup

Pinch of Himalayan salt

1–2 tbsp (15–30 ml) melted coconut oil, if needed

CARAMEL LAYER
¾ cup (130 g) pitted dates

¼ cup (45 g) cashew butter (or peanut butter)

3 tbsp (45 ml) water, or more as needed

Pinch of Himalayan salt

2 tbsp (28 g) coconut oil

CHOCOLATE COATING
⅓ cup (80 ml) melted coconut oil

¼ cup (27 g) cacao powder

¼ cup (60 ml) maple syrup

1 tsp vanilla extract

(continued)

FOR THE COOKIE

Stir together the ingredients until slightly crumbly and moist. It should hold its shape when pressed between two fingers. If it's still too crumbly, add some coconut oil (or water). Press it into the bottom of a lined bread loaf pan. Place it in the freezer.

FOR THE CARAMEL

Soak the dates in warm water to cover for 10 minutes (then keep this water for the recipe). Blend all the ingredients until smooth, thick and caramel-y! It should taste amazing. Spread it evenly onto the cookie layer and place it back in the freezer until solid. It will take a couple hours to harden up.

FOR THE CHOCOLATE

Whisk the ingredients together until you have liquid chocolate. Yummm. Take your caramel-cookie concoction out of the freezer and slice it with a sharp knife into bars. Drizzle the chocolate over the bars, or dip the bars in the chocolate. It's up to you. I drizzled. Keep them in the freezer and enjoy whenever!

Salted CHOCOLATE TRUFFLES

I am callin' these truffles, but loosely. They could also be called nut- and oat-based energy balls coated in chocolate, but it's not as catchy or enticing. In my opinion. What you need to know is that they are delicious, quick to make, satisfying and good for ya bod. They're great on their own, on ice cream, as an energy pick-me-up, pre or post-workout bite, whatever you like. —EvE

MAKES ABOUT 12 TRUFFLES

TRUFFLES
¾ cup (60 g) rolled oats
¾ cup (85 g) Brazil nuts
2 tbsp (30 ml) melted coconut oil
2 tbsp (30 ml) maple syrup

CHOCOLATE COATING
⅙ cup (40 ml) melted coconut oil
⅙ cup (40 ml) maple syrup
⅙ cup (19 g) cacao powder

TOPPING
Fleur de sel or other salt

FOR THE TRUFFLES

Grind the oats and nuts into flour. Transfer it to a bowl. Stir in the coconut oil and maple syrup until you have a sticky, thick dough that holds its shape. Shape it into balls and put it in the freezer until solid.

FOR THE CHOCOLATE

Stir together the ingredients until smooth. Dip the truffles in the chocolate; the chocolate should harden pretty fast, so dip them another one or two times if you like. Sprinkle on the salt and put the truffles in the fridge or freezer to enjoy whenever you like! Leave them in the freezer if you want them more firm or the fridge if you prefer a softer texture.

Quick 'n' Easy CHOCOLATE MACAROONS

Delicious, decadent, pretty healthy and they come together in SERIOUSLY under 20 minutes. Keep them in the freezer for a chocolaty snack whenever you want one (i.e. every day). You can fancy up the recipe or make it more basic as you see fit.

MAKES 6 BIG MACAROONS

⅙ cup (40 ml) maple syrup

¼ cup (45 g) your fave nut butter

¼ cup (60 ml) melted coconut oil

2 heaping tbsp (14 g) cacao powder

⅛ tsp vanilla powder (optional)

Pinch of Himalayan salt (optional)

¾ cup (57 g) coconut shreds

¾ cup (60 g) rolled oats

Whisk together the maple syrup, nut butter and coconut oil until evenly combined. Whisk in the cacao powder, vanilla powder (if using) and salt until you have a smooth, liquid chocolate mixture. Stir in the coconut and oats until they're fully coated in the chocolate. Scoop it into balls (I used an ice-cream scoop) and throw them in the freezer for 10 to 15 minutes.

Raw Vegan
BLISS BALLS

These are pretty much anything you want them to be: dessert, snack, energy bite, whatever. Heck, eat them all for dinner if you wanna. They are dense, nutritious and chocolaty, and really quick to make. I tried to keep the ingredients simple and, as usual, there are a ton of substitution options in case you don't have all the ingredients. —EvE

MAKES ABOUT 12 BALLS

¼ cup (27 g) cacao powder

Pinch of Himalayan salt

¼ tsp vanilla powder or extract

1 tbsp (7 g) maca powder (see Note)

1 cup (120 g) walnuts, preferably soaked for 4 hours in water, then rinsed

1 cup (80 g) rolled oats

1 cup (170 g) pitted dates

2–3 tbsp (28–42 g) coconut oil, as needed

1–2 tbsp (15–30 ml) water, if needed

COATINGS

Sesame seeds

Hemp seeds

Maca powder

Cacao powder

In a food processor, grind the dry ingredients into a rough flour. Add the rest of the ingredients and keep processing until a moist dough is formed. Ideally it will form itself into a ball, or at least when you press some of the mixture between your fingers, it will hold its shape and your fingers will be slightly oily. If the mixture is too crumbly, add more water, coconut oil or dates. If it's too moist, add some more oats.

Roll the dough into balls and then coat in whatever you like! I used sesame seeds, hemp seeds, maca powder and cacao powder. Other ideas: cinnamon, berry powder, coconut flakes... it's up to you! Leave them in the fridge for a couple hours or eat them right away.

Note: If you don't have maca powder, don't sweat it—just leave it out. You can use vanilla extract instead of vanilla powder. You can use cocoa powder instead of cacao powder. You can use any other nuts or seeds instead of oats and walnuts.

CHOCOLATE COCONUT
Doughnuts

Some friends' thoughts on these doughnuts:
"I like that they're bite-size, that was cute."
"I think Oprah would love them."
"Just sweet enough." —EvE

MAKES 12 MINI DOUGHNUTS

DOUGHNUTS
1 cup (132 g) oat flour
1 cup (112 g) coconut flour
¼ cup (27 g) cacao powder
2 tbsp (14 g) carob powder
Pinch of Himalayan salt
1 cup (170 g) gooey pitted dates
¼ cup (55 g) coconut oil
¼ cup (60 ml) maple syrup
1 tsp vanilla extract
Coconut milk, as needed

ICING
¼ cup (60 ml) maple syrup
¼ cup (55 g) coconut oil
¼ cup (45 g) almond butter
¼ cup (27 g) cacao powder
¼ tsp vanilla extract
Coconut milk, as needed

TOPPINGS
Slivered almonds
Coconut flour

FOR THE DOUGHNUTS

Put all the ingredients in a food processor and process until the mixture becomes moist, fine and crumbly but will hold its shape when pressed between two fingers (add coconut milk until you get this consistency). Grease a doughnut mold with coconut oil; then press the mixture into the doughnut mold and put it in the freezer until solid. If you have extra mixture, throw it in a lined bread pan for brownies!

FOR THE ICING

Blend all the ingredients together until smooth and sooooo delicious (add coconut milk until you get this consistency). Don't over-blend or else the coconut oil will combine too much with the other ingredients and make it into one homologous mass. Dip the doughnuts into the icing or spread the icing on the doughnuts. I sprinkled my doughnuts with almond slivers and coconut flour.

BLUEBERRY
HAZELNUT **Oat Bars**

This recipe was inspired by blueberry crumble. But I made my own version, and it is more bar and less crumble. There IS a crumble topping. And a creamy blueberry filling. And a hazelnut-y crust. You cannot go wrong. In my brain I was envisioning a perfectly sliced blueberry oat bar topped with a sexy orb of melty ice cream. A friend went and bought me a pint of vanilla coco ice cream for this recipe, so all my dreams have now come true. —EvE

MAKES 9 BIG BARS

BASE
1 cup (120 g) hazelnuts

1 cup (80 g) rolled oats

2 tbsp (30 ml) melted coconut oil

2 tbsp (30 ml) maple syrup

FILLING
2 cups (295 g) blueberries

⅓ cup (50 g) raisins

½ tsp vanilla powder

1 tbsp (15 ml) lemon juice

1 tbsp (15 ml) melted coconut oil

¼ cup (40 g) chia seeds

TOPPING
½ cup (40 g) rolled oats

½ cup (48 g) almond flour

⅛ tsp Himalayan salt

½ tsp ground cinnamon

½ tsp ground ginger

1 tbsp (15 ml) melted coconut oil

1 tbsp (15 ml) maple syrup

2 tbsp (30 ml) water or lemon juice

FOR THE BASE
Grind the nuts and oats into flour. Stir in the coconut oil and maple syrup with a spoon until you have a moist dough that holds its shape. Press it into a lined pan and leave it in the fridge.

FOR THE FILLING
Blend all the ingredients, except the chia seeds, until as smooth as desired (I like mine a little chunky for texture). Stir in the chia seeds. It should soon start to thicken up thanks to the chia: you want a yogurt-like consistency. If it's too thin, add more chia seeds and/or coconut oil. Scoop it onto your crust, spreading evenly, and leave it in the fridge or freezer until solid (a couple hours).

FOR THE TOPPING
Mix together all the ingredients with a spoon, and then press this on top of your blueberry filling layer. Leave it in the fridge or freezer overnight; then slice and serve with vegan ice cream! I used vanilla coconut ice cream and it was heavenly.

Three-Ingredient
VEGAN FUDGE

Folks, I've figured it out. The secret is using brown rice syrup. It is very thick at room temperature so it gets gooey when refrigerated and makes the perfect sweetener for easy vegan fudge. The ingredients, amounts and instructions here are like my chocolate recipes, but the brown rice syrup makes the final product chewy—fudge!—instead of totally solid. —EvE

SERVES AROUND 9

BASE
½ cup (120 g) coconut oil

⅔ cup (74 g) cacao powder

⅔ cup (160 ml) brown rice syrup

OPTIONAL ADD-INS
Flaked salt

Vanilla powder

Melt the coconut oil, and then stir all the base ingredients together until you have a smooth, thick chocolate batter. If it's too sweet, add more coconut oil or cacao powder. If it's not sweet enough, add more brown syrup. Add some salt and/or vanilla if you like. Spread it evenly into a lined pan and leave it in the fridge until solid; it should take an hour or less. Slice it up into 9 bars (or as many as you desire) and serve. The fudge will keep for a week in the fridge.

Sexy CARAMEL SLICE

I wanted something decadent and sweet, so I made this pan of caramel slices. The base is mostly oats and almonds, the caramel is a mix of dates and cashews, and the layer on top is simply raw dark chocolate sprinkled with some flaked salt. The result of all these glorious whole foods coming together is a luscious, rich treat that is at once nourishing and food-orgasmic. —EvE

SERVES 9 TO 12

BASE
1 cup (170 g) almonds
1 cup (80 g) rolled oats
1½ cups (255 g) pitted dates

CARAMEL
1 tbsp (15 ml) lemon juice
¼ cup (55 g) coconut oil
2 cups (340 g) pitted dates
1 cup (110 g) cashews
¼ tsp sea salt
½ tsp vanilla extract

CHOCOLATE
¼ cup (55 g) coconut oil
⅙ cup (40 ml) maple syrup
3 heaping tbsp (25 g) cacao powder

FOR THE BASE
Grind the almonds and oats into flour in a food processor. Add the dates and process until you form a sticky dough. Press it into a lined baking pan and put it in the fridge.

FOR THE CARAMEL
Blend all the ingredients together in a blender until smooth and thick. Spread it evenly over your base and put it back in the fridge.

FOR THE CHOCOLATE
Melt the coconut oil and stir in the rest of the ingredients until smooth. Pour it over your caramel and leave it in the fridge or freezer until solid, at least a couple hours (but preferably overnight) so the flavors can develop.

Pecan PRALINE BARS WITH SALTED CHOCOLATE

This recipe is inspired by an absolutely magnificent creation I have had many times from Chau Veggie Express, a veggie restaurant with killer desserts on Victoria Drive in Vancouver, BC. —EvE

SERVES 9 TO 12

COOKIE BASE
1 cup (75 g) shredded coconut
¾ cup (90 g) rice flour
¼ cup (27 g) cacao powder
Pinch of sea salt
¼ cup (60 ml) melted coconut oil
¼ cup (48 g) coconut sugar
⅓ cup (57 g) gooey pitted dates

PRALINE CREAM
1 cup (235 ml) full-fat coconut cream
⅓ cup (63 g) coconut sugar
1 tsp vanilla extract
⅓ cup (60 g) pecan butter
¼ cup (60 ml) melted coconut oil
1 tbsp (15 ml) melted cacao butter
Pinch of sea salt

SALTED CHOCOLATE

2 tbsp (14 g) cacao powder

3 tbsp (45 ml) melted coconut oil

3 tbsp (45 ml) maple syrup

1 tbsp (15 ml) coconut milk

¼ tsp fleur de sel

FOR THE COOKIE BASE

Grind the coconut into rough flour. Then process all of the ingredients together in a food processor, until they form a moist dough that holds its shape when pressed between two fingers. Press it into the bottom of a lined baking pan. I used a 6-inch (15-cm) square pan lined with parchment paper. Leave it in the fridge.

FOR THE PRALINE CREAM

Blend all of the ingredients until smooth and thick like cream. Adjust according to taste. Pour it over your cookie base and leave in the fridge until it has solidified, preferably overnight.

FOR THE SALTED CHOCOLATE

Whisk all the ingredients (except the fleur de sel) together until you have formed liquid chocolate. Pour it over your praline cream layer, sprinkle on the fleur de sel and leave it in the fridge until solid. Slice into bars and enjoy!

CHOCOLATE MINT
Slice

A nostalgic pairing, this dessert was inspired by a recipe from Jean-Christian Jury and Jörg Lehmann. —EvE

SERVES 9 TO 12

CHOCOLATE LAYER

Scant ¼ cup (55 g) coconut oil

¼ cup (45 g) cacao butter

1¼ cups (137 g) cacao powder

½ tsp sea salt

¼ cup (60 ml) maple syrup

MINT LAYER

1¾ cups (133 g) shredded coconut

Scant ¼ cup (60 ml) melted coconut oil

3 tbsp (45 ml) maple syrup

2–4 drops peppermint essential oil

FOR THE CHOCOLATE LAYER

Melt the coconut oil and cacao butter in a heavy-bottomed pot over low heat, and then whisk in the rest of the ingredients until you have a lusciously smooth chocolate mixture. Spread half of this mixture evenly into the bottom of a lined pan and put it in the fridge. Set aside the remaining half to use in a moment.

FOR THE MINT LAYER

Blend everything until smooth. Spread it evenly over your chocolate layer in the pan and finish by spreading the remaining chocolate over this. Leave it in the fridge for at least a few hours and slice. If they stick around longer than a day and you keep them refrigerated overnight, I'd recommend letting them sit at room temperature for around 10 to 15 minutes before eating so they soften.

Superfood FUDGY MINT SLICE

This is a delicious, luscious, creamy, sweet recipe. Made up of mostly vanilla cashew cream and topped with a layer of fudge, it has a subtle mint flavor. Basically, heaven in your mouth. All the ingredients have health benefits, but there's one in particular that is exceptionally nutritious: chlorella! It's dried green algae. Sounds gross and weird, yes. But once you get to know it, ya might love it like I do. —EvE

SERVES 8 TO 10

BASE

1 cup (80 g) rolled oats

1 tbsp (7 g) cacao powder

½ cup (85 g) pitted dates

2 tbsp (30 ml) melted coconut oil

Pinch of sea salt

MIDDLE

1 cup (110 g) cashews (preferably soaked for 6 hours in water, then rinsed)

¼ cup (48 g) coconut sugar

2 tbsp (30 ml) melted coconut oil

2 tbsp (30 ml) melted cacao butter

¼ tsp vanilla powder

2 tbsp (30 ml) fresh lemon juice

Water, as needed (I used about 2 tbsp [30 ml])

1 tsp Sun Chlorella pure powder

1 drop peppermint essential oil

TOP

1 recipe Three-Ingredient Vegan Fudge (page 325)

FOR THE BASE

Process the oats into flour in a food processor or blender, and then add the rest of the ingredients and process until a thick, moist dough forms. It should hold its shape when pressed between two fingers. If it's too moist, add some more oats. If it's too crumbly, add some more dates or coconut oil. Press this into the bottom of a lined baking pan and leave it in the fridge.

FOR THE MIDDLE

Blend all ingredients together—except the chlorella and mint oil—until smooth, like yogurt in consistency but slightly thicker. Adjust according to taste. Scoop half of this onto your base. Now add the chlorella and mint oil to the remaining mix in the blender and blend. Pour over your first layer.

Put it in the fridge so it can thicken up, and then pour the fudge over the top. Leave it in the fridge overnight and slice the next day.

Note: I had fudge in the fridge already before I started this recipe, so I sliced some pieces of it and put them in between my white and green layers, and then melted the rest and added it to the top. Do this if you wanna! It makes it cute. And we like it cute.

Fudgy CHOCOLATE PEANUT BUTTER SLICE

These bars are sweet, chocolaty, fudgy, chewy, rich and perfect for any time. Eat as many as you want, because it's your life and it should be delicious and fulfilling. I just ate one for breakfast and it's probably the best decision I've ever made. —EvE

SERVES 4 TO 8

¼ cup (45 g) cacao butter

¼ cup (55 g) coconut oil

¼ cup (27 g) cacao powder

1 tbsp (12 g) coconut sugar

1 cup (170 g) pitted dates

⅛ tsp sea salt, plus more for sprinkling

½ tsp vanilla powder

1 tsp ashwagandha powder (optional)

1 tsp reishi mushroom powder (optional)

¼ cup (60 ml) coconut milk, or more as needed

⅓ cup (60 g) unsalted peanut butter or your fave nut/seed butter

Melt the cacao butter and coconut oil over low heat in a small, heavy pot. Blend this together with the rest of the ingredients (except the peanut butter), adding coconut milk as needed to get a very thick, creamy mixture. Spread half of this evenly into a small lined baking pan. Spread on the peanut butter. Finally spread on the remaining fudge. Sprinkle with more salt if you like. Leave it in the fridge overnight, slice and enjoy!

Gooey BROWNIES WITH ALMOND BUTTER FROSTING

In place of ingredients like white flour, white sugar, butter and eggs; we can use almonds and other nuts, dates and other dried fruits, coconut, sesame and other seeds, fresh fruits, wholesome sweeteners and flours—and sometimes even sneak in some veggies. In this recipe, you would NEVER know, but we've got applesauce, sweet potato, black beans, no gluten and no refined sugar or refined flour. These plants are stealthy.

The best thing about this recipe is how gooey it is. This is because several of the ingredients have a lot of natural moisture. It's hard to overbake for the same reason, which might be welcome news for ya new cooks out there. After I let the brownies cool and I sliced them, I found the middle to be practically raw batter even though the edges were perfect. At first I thought I had failed, but over the course of the next week I realized this was ideal. The brownies around the outside were eaten first, and then the more gooey ones in the center later in the week. I would microwave them for just a sec and it would leave the middle like a molten lava cake. HEAVEN. If you like a firm or even crumbly brownie, this is not the one for you. But if you like your brownies super moist and almost half-baked, look no further. —EvE

MAKES 16 BROWNIES

BROWNIES

1 medium-small cooked sweet potato, roughly chopped

1½ cups (258 g) cooked black beans

⅓ cup (57 g) pitted Medjool dates

½ cup (55 g) cacao powder

¾ cup (90 g) tigernut flour (or your fave wholesome flour)

1 tbsp (7 g) ground flaxseed

1 tbsp (11 g) baking powder

⅙ cup (36 g) coconut oil

(continued)

⅙ cup (40 ml) almond milk

1 tsp vanilla extract

½ tsp sea salt

¼ cup (62 g) applesauce

SALTED ALMOND BUTTER FROSTING

2 tbsp (30 ml) melted coconut oil

3 tbsp (45 ml) maple syrup

¼ cup (45 g) almond butter

¼ tsp sea salt, or more if desired

GARNISHES (OPTIONAL)

Sliced nuts of choice

Vegan chocolate chips

FOR THE BROWNIES

Preheat the oven to 350°F (177°C). Throw everything in a food processor and process until you have a thick, wet batter. If you want the brownies to be a bit firmer once baked, add a li'l more flour at this point. Pour the batter into a lined baking pan. Bake for 30 to 35 minutes, or until they smell ready and a fork or toothpick comes out clean. They will still be very moist, but that's why I'm callin' this a GOOEY brownie recipe.

FOR THE FROSTING

Stir all the ingredients together until smooth and delicious. Spread it over your brownies once they've cooled. Garnish with some sliced nuts, sea salt or chocolate chips. Slice and enjoy!

Strawberry
RHUBARB CRUMBLE WITH ALMOND GRANOLA

Rhubarb is my new best friend. Its magic is elevated when paired with vanilla and coconut. —EvE

SERVES 6 TO 8

FILLING

3 cups (360 g) roughly chopped rhubarb

2 cups (300 g) roughly chopped strawberries

¼ cup (48 g) coconut sugar

4 tbsp (24 g) almond flour

2 tbsp (30 ml) melted coconut oil

1 tsp ground cinnamon

TOPPING

¾ cup (60 g) rolled oats

½ cup (48 g) almond flour

Scant ¼ cup (60 ml) maple syrup

¼ cup (60 ml) fresh orange juice, or more as needed

1 tsp vanilla extract

1 tbsp (15 ml) melted coconut oil

Pinch of sea salt

1 cup (73 g) of your favorite almond granola (I use Hippie Snacks Vanilla Almond Granola)

Preheat the oven to 350°F (177°C).

FOR THE FILLING

Toss all of the filling ingredients together until the rhubarb and strawberries are evenly coated. Scoop it into a baking pan or ceramic dish (it will cook down, so you can overfill a little here).

FOR THE TOPPING

Toss all the topping ingredients together until evenly mixed. It should be moist enough that parts are clumping together and if you press it together, it mostly holds its shape. If it's too crumbly, add more orange juice. If it's too moist, add more granola. Press firmly and evenly on top of your filling. Put a pan on the bottom rack of the oven and your crumble on the rack above this. It will get bubbly and might bubble over the sides of the dish, so you want a pan to catch the juices. Bake your crumble for 30 to 40 minutes, or until the topping is golden brown and the filling is bubbling over. If it's still quite juicy and you don't want that, cover the top with foil and bake for an additional 15 minutes at 375°F (190°C).

Highly recommended: serve hot with vanilla coconut ice cream and extra granola!

Almond Bites
WITH MACA, VANILLA AND FLAX

Unusual ingredients and flavors are used here . . . but it's fun to try new stuff, right? I like to switch things up every now and then. —EvE

MAKES 20 SMALL BITES

1 cup (85 g) almond pulp (left over from making almond milk)

1 cup (120 g) walnuts

½ tsp vanilla powder

2 tbsp (14 g) maca powder

1 tbsp (7 g) ground flaxseed

1 tbsp (7 g) camu camu powder

¼ cup (60 ml) maple syrup

3 tbsp (45 ml) melted coconut oil

Throw all the ingredients in a food processor and process until you have a moist, slightly crumbly dough. When you press some together between your fingers, it should hold its shape. If it's too crumbly, add 1 tablespoon (14 g) more of coconut oil or fresh lemon juice (15 ml). If it's too moist, add 1 to 2 tablespoons (7 to 14 g) more of ground flax or other flour or powder.

Roll it into balls, or press it into cookies and coat with whatever you like. I used black sesame seeds; other options would be chia seeds, shredded coconut, ground cinnamon or cacao powder. Another excellent idea: cover them in melted dark chocolate. Yes. Do that.

Nut-Free
CREAMY COCONUT CHEESECAKE

You're gonna love my LACK of nut . . . in this recipe (I really hope you got that reference). To be honest I prefer this recipe to some nut-based cheesecake recipes. It's exceptionally silky smooth and I frankly cannot resist coconut. This cheesecake leaves nothing to be desired . . . except maybe a second slice. Serve with fruit if you like and double or triple the recipe for a larger cake. —EvE

SERVES 5 TO 7

CRUST

½ cup (40 g) oats or buckwheat groats

½ cup (90 g) pitted dates

CHEESECAKE

¾ cup (60 g) fresh young coconut meat

¼ cup (60 ml) melted coconut oil

2 tbsp plus 2 tsp (40 ml) preferred liquid sweetener (more or less, to taste)

⅓ cup (30 g) coconut flakes

Juice of 1 lemon

FOR THE CRUST

Process the oats into flour and then add the dates. Process until it all begins to stick together in crumbs. Press it into the bottom of a small springform pan (mine is 4½ inches [11.5 cm]).

FOR THE CHEESECAKE

Blend all of the cake ingredients until smooth. Pour everything onto your crust and refrigerate overnight so it can set and develop flavor. The next day it should be solid and ready to chow down on!

*SEE PHOTO INSERT

DESSERTS

351

Chocolate MOLTEN LAVA CAKES WITH GOJI BERRIES

This is still an all-time favorite on my blog, and I can't say I'm surprised. Just look at the gooey chocolate goodness. Can YOU resist? —EvE

SERVES 4 TO 8

CAKES
⅓ cup (30 g) raw oats
⅓ cup (40 g) walnuts
¼ cup (30 g) cacao powder
⅓ cup (60 g) pitted dates
⅓ cup (50 g) raisins

MOLTEN LAVA MIDDLE
⅓ cup (80 ml) melted cacao butter
⅓ cup (80 ml) maple syrup
⅓ cup (60 g) pitted dates
⅓ cup (40 g) cacao powder
¼ tsp ground cinnamon
¼ tsp Himalayan sea salt
¼ tsp chili powder
Vegan milk, as needed

GARNISH
Cacao nibs
Goji berries

FOR THE CAKES
Pulse the oats, walnuts and cacao powder in your food processor until they become a rough flour. Add the dates and raisins and process until it all starts to stick together. Using about two-thirds of the mix (you have to save some for the tops), press it into the bottom and sides of lined cupcake tins and put them in the fridge. Use the rest of the mix to make the tops by pressing it into cookie molds the same diameter of your cupcake tins. Put those in the fridge as well.

FOR THE MOLTEN LAVA MIDDLE
Blend all the middle ingredients until smooth, adding the milk as needed to make it creamy and a "molten" consistency (whatever that means . . . hopefully you know). Take the cakes out of the cupcake molds and pour the molten mixture into each one, filling up almost to the top. Now carefully press the tops onto the cakes, gently pressing together the edges. Flip them over and decorate with cacao nibs and goji berries. Eat da lava, mohn.

VARIATIONS
To make these gluten-free, use buckwheat groats instead of oats. If you don't want to use cacao, use coconut oil instead of cacao butter and carob instead of cacao powder.

*SEE PHOTO INSERT

BLUEBERRY STRAWBERRY BANANA Ice Cream Cake

This cake was so delicious I couldn't wait for it to completely freeze before I started eating it . . . #YOLO —EvE

SERVES 8 TO 12

10 strawberries, cut in half

VANILLA ICE CREAM CAKE LAYER
2 cups (220 g) cashews
2 bananas
1 cup (170 g) pitted dates
¼ cup (60 ml) melted coconut oil
Seeds from 1 vanilla pod
Vegan milk or coconut water, as needed

BERRY LAYER
1 cup (225 g) frozen blueberries
1 cup (225 g) frozen strawberries

1 cup (236 ml) vegan milk or coconut water, as needed

1 cup (170 g) pitted dates, walnuts or another banana

Place the halved strawberries around the edge of a springform pan. Set it aside.

FOR THE CAKE LAYER

Blend all the vanilla ice cream cake ingredients together until smooth, adding as little vegan milk or coconut water as possible (I used about ¼ cup [60 ml]). Spread this into the bottom of the pan; it should press the berries to the outer edge. Put it in the freezer.

FOR THE BERRY LAYER

Blend all the berry ingredients until smooth. Carefully spread it on top of the vanilla ice cream cake layer and put it in the freezer for about 2 or 3 hours, until it's set. Then cut it and serve with other berries! Let it soften a little before eating—it makes it creamier.

*SEE PHOTO INSERT

Carrot Cake WITH CASHEW CREAM CHEESE FROSTING, PISTACHIOS AND WALNUTS

One of my most popular recipes of all time. —EvE

SERVES 8 TO 12

CASHEW FROSTING

2 cups (220 g) cashews, preferably soaked for a couple hours

1-2 tbsp (15-30 ml) lemon juice

2 tbsp (30 ml) melted coconut oil

⅓ cup (80 ml) maple syrup

Water, as needed

CAKE

2 large carrots, peeled

1½ cups (120 g) oat flour or buckwheat flour

1 cup (170 g) dates

1 cup (150 g) dried pineapple (or more dates)

½ cup (38 g) dried coconut

½ tsp ground cinnamon

FOR THE CASHEW FROSTING

Blend all the frosting ingredients in your high-speed blender until smooth, adding as little water as possible. Taste it—mmmm. Put in a bowl and set aside.

FOR THE CAKE

Cut the carrots into small chunks. Then throw all the ingredients (including the carrots) in your food processor and pulse until it's all in really small pieces and sticks together.

Press half the cake mix into the bottom of an adjustable springform pan; mine was about 6 inches (15 cm). Then spread on about one-third of the frosting. Put it in the freezer until the layer of frosting is hard. Then press on the rest of the cake mix. I let it set in the fridge overnight and then frosted the whole thing, but you can do it right away if you want. Take it out of the pan and use the remaining frosting. Cover with whatever garnishes you like.

*SEE PHOTO INSERT

AVOCADO MINT CREAM BARS WITH CHOCOLATE, Two Ways

These were surprisingly delicious. I was, of course, expecting them to taste good, but I was seriously excited when I took my first bite of the finished product. They are creamy, sweet, minty and chocolaty all at once. I was originally going to call them Nanaimo bars but after tasting them, I felt they deserved a name unto themselves. Think of mint chocolate chip ice cream, in square form—that's what these are. You can use a banana in the filling and freeze the recipe to make ice-cream sandwich bars (smart move), or use coconut meat and keep them in the fridge (also an intelligent choice). No wrong moves here, folks. —EvE

MAKES 12 TO 14 BARS

BASE
1 cup (170 g) almonds
1 cup (170 g) pitted dates
1 heaping tbsp (10 g) cacao powder

MIDDLE
1 avocado, peeled and pitted
3 tbsp (45 ml) melted coconut oil
3–4 tbsp (45–60 ml) maple syrup, to taste
1 banana or 1 cup (80 g) young coconut meat
½ tsp vanilla extract
Pinch of salt (optional)

TOP
3 tbsp (24 g) cacao powder
3 tbsp (45 ml) melted coconut oil
2 tbsp (30 ml) maple syrup

FOR THE BASE
Pulse all of the ingredients in your food processor until they stick together. Press evenly into the bottom of a lined 9 x 9-inch (23 x 23-cm) baking pan. Put it in the fridge.

FOR THE MIDDLE
Blend all of the ingredients until smooth and thick; then spread it over your base layer and put it back in the fridge.

FOR THE TOP
Mix all of the ingredients together until smooth. Pour it evenly on top of your middle layer and put it in the fridge or freezer, depending on what ingredient you used in the middle. Let set until firm, then slice into bars.

*SEE PHOTO INSERT

Totally TAHINI CUPS WITH COFFEE CREAM FILLING

Simple, sublime, stylish . . . sassy? Okay, enough with the alliteration. These are just plain yummy. I know not everyone has a major sweet tooth like me, so this recipe is for those folks. Tahini is delicious, but it is also quite bitter. It has a strong nutty flavor (from the sesame seeds it's made of) that goes perfectly with savory meals. However, its nutty bitterness can still work wonderfully in desserts as well. Here, it's combined with salt and coconut oil to make a shell encompassing sweet coffee-date cream. Can you say yum!? Probably not, because your mouth will be too full of these terrifically tasty tahini cups. —EvE

SERVES 6

TAHINI SHELL

⅓ cup (80 g) tahini

⅓ cup (80 ml) melted coconut oil

Salt, to taste

COFFEE CREAM

1 cup (170 g) pitted dates

½ cup (118 ml) strong brewed coffee (more or less as needed)

Sea salt, for topping

FOR THE TAHINI SHELL

Combine the ingredients by hand or in a food processor until smooth. It will be a bit watery, but the coconut oil will harden up in the fridge. Pour this into the bottom of 6 cupcake papers and put them in the fridge until solid. Set aside the remaining tahini mixture.

FOR THE COFFEE CREAM

Put the dates in your food processor, and process until smooth and very thick, adding the coffee as needed. This could take a few minutes, and you may have to stop the food processor to scrape down the sides a few times so that everything continues to combine evenly.

ASSEMBLY

Scoop a dollop of the filling into each of the hardened bottoms in your cupcake papers. Pour enough of the remaining tahini mixture on each to cover the dollop. Put it back in the fridge until solid, then sprinkle with salt and enjoy!

*SEE PHOTO INSERT

Jewel Fruit TART WITH CARAMEL ALMOND FILLING

I love how frozen berries look just like gems, and that is showcased in this recipe. Here's a challenge: try not to eat all of the almond caramel before putting it in your crust. —EvE

SERVES 8 TO 12

CRUST

2 cups (240 g) walnuts

2 cups (300 g) raisins

ALMOND CARAMEL FILLING

¼ cup (45 g) almond butter

¼ cup (60 ml) melted coconut oil

¼ cup (60 ml) maple syrup

½ tsp ground cinnamon

TOPPINGS

3 cups (750 g) frozen berries (or however much you want)

½ cup (75 g) goji berries

FOR THE CRUST

Pulse the walnuts in your food processor until they become a rough flour. Add the raisins and process until it sticks together, forming a dough. Press it into a tart tin. Put it in the fridge and let it set for about 2 hours.

FOR THE ALMOND CARAMEL FILLING

Blend all the filling ingredients until smooth, adding water if needed. Spread it gently into the bottom of your tart crust and then let it harden in the fridge for 30 to 60 minutes. Now top the tart off with all the berries, slice and serve!

*SEE PHOTO INSERT

Maple PECAN PIE

Ooooh, baby. My dad loves pecan pie, so I decided I may as well try my hand at making a raw version for him. Success! This is a very rich recipe, so you won't need a big slice. Try it out for Thanksgiving or Christmas. Or, you know . . . any occasion. This pie deserves a celebration all on its own. —EvE

SERVES 8 TO 10

CRUST
1 cup (110 g) pecans
1 cup (170 g) pitted dates

FILLING
½ cup (120 g) cashew butter
½ cup (118 g) coconut oil
1 cup (170 g) pitted dates
½ tsp vanilla extract
1 tbsp (15 ml) maple syrup
½ cup (40 g) coconut flakes
Pinch of salt

TOPPING
Whole pecans

FOR THE CRUST

Blend the nuts into powder in a food processor, then add the dates and keep processing until everything sticks together. Press it into a pie dish and put it in the fridge.

FOR THE FILLING

Blend all of the ingredients until smooth. Spread this onto your crust and arrange the whole pecans on top. Put it back in the fridge for 2 hours or overnight. Slice. Chomp.

*SEE PHOTO INSERT

Pumpkin Pie WITH COCONUT WHIPPED CREAM

One of my favorite pies, this was inspired by a recipe from Emma Knight with Hana James, Deeva Green and Lee Reitelman. —EvE

SERVES 8 TO 12

CRUST
¾ cup (128 g) almonds
⅓ cup (50 g) raisins
1 tsp vanilla extract
¼ cup (19 g) shredded coconut

FILLING
1¾ cups (315 g) pumpkin purée
¼ cup (60 ml) melted coconut oil (or cacao butter, if you want it to be firmer)
¼ cup (60 ml) almond milk
1 tsp vanilla extract
Pinch of sea salt
¼ cup (30 g) dried cranberries
¼ cup (30 g) dried goji berries
¼ cup (60 ml) maple syrup
1 heaping tbsp (7 g) pumpkin pie spice

COCONUT WHIPPED CREAM
1 (13½-oz [400-ml]) can full-fat coconut cream
½ tsp vanilla powder
1 tsp maple syrup

SALTED CARAMEL
2 tbsp (30 ml) melted coconut oil
2 tbsp (30 ml) brown rice syrup
1 tbsp (15 ml) maple syrup
½ tsp sea salt
¼ tsp ground cinnamon

FOR THE CRUST

Grind the almonds into flour in a food processor, then add the raisins and process until the raisins are broken down. Add the rest of the ingredients and process until the dough is slightly sticky, crumbly and can hold its shape when pressed between two fingers. Press it evenly into the bottom of a pie dish or springform pan (I used a 6-inch [15-cm] springform cake pan lined with parchment) and leave it in the fridge.

FOR THE FILLING

Blend all of the ingredients until smooth and DE-LICIOUS. Pour it evenly over your crust and let it set in the fridge overnight or for at least 5 hours; otherwise, it'll be more like pudding (which isn't necessarily a bad thing).

FOR THE COCONUT WHIPPED CREAM

Open the can of coconut cream and scoop the solid white fat off the top. Whip this with the vanilla and maple syrup in a chilled mixer or with an electric whisk until it's the consistency of whipped cream! Spread it over your pie.

FOR THE SALTED CARAMEL

Stir together the ingredients until you have a sweet, salty, drizzly mixture. Drizzle it over your pie, slice and enjoy!

Frozen MANGO LASSI POPS

+GF, +SFO

It's pretty awesome to sip a mango lassi, a traditional Indian yogurt drink, to cool down. This frozen pop recipe makes it even cooler, and you can freeze it in your favorite icy pop molds. —KH

MAKES 6 TO 8 FROZEN POPS

1½ cups (225 g) chopped mango (about 2 small mangos)

1 cup (245 g) plain vegan soy or coconut yogurt

2 tbsp (30 ml) agave nectar (or sweetener of your choice, to taste)

1 tsp rosewater

¼ tsp ground cardamom

Add all of the ingredients to your blender and purée until smooth.

Fill up the freezer pop molds and freeze for at least 8 hours. Run cold water over the molds to release the frozen treats.

Vegan LAVENDER LONDON FOG POPS

+GF +SF

When it's too hot to have hot tea in the morning, I put all the flavors of a London Fog—vanilla, Earl Grey tea and nondairy milk with the extra special addition of lavender—into a refreshing frozen ice pop. —KH

MAKES 6 MEDIUM POPS

2 cups (480 ml) nondairy unsweetened vanilla milk

1 tsp dried culinary lavender

1½ tsp (6 g) Earl Grey tea

½ tsp vanilla extract (use 1 tsp if you use plain nondairy milk)

¼ cup (56 g) vegan sugar (or sweetener of choice, to taste)

Put the nondairy milk and lavender into a saucepan over medium-high heat. Heat until the milk starts to rise and almost comes to a boil.

Take it off the heat and stir in the tea, vanilla and sugar. Set a timer for 4 minutes. Stir until the sugar dissolves.

When the timer goes off, pour the mixture through a strainer into a bowl or large measuring cup with a pour spout.

Pour into freezer pop molds. Freeze for at least 5 hours to overnight to make them hard enough to unmold. These will keep for at least a month.

Superfood DOUBLE CHOCOLATE POPSICLES

These are DELISH; packed with powerful foods like turmeric and mushrooms—sounds gross and weird, I know, but trust me—they taste like chai-y chocolate ice-cream pops. This recipe was originally gonna be some simple chocolate milk, but then I started adding a bunch of ingredients to it and it became super rich and thick, so I figured . . . it's hot out, may as well make these into ice cream!!? And I did. Then I dipped them in more chocolate for good measure, and here we are. —EvE

SERVES 9 TO 12

POPS

2 heaping tbsp (15 g) cacao powder

2 heaping tbsp (24 g) coconut sugar

2 tbsp (28 g) coconut oil

2 tbsp (30 ml) maple syrup

1 tsp ground cinnamon

1 tsp ground ginger

½ tsp ground coriander

½ tsp ground turmeric

½ tsp ground cumin

½ tsp ashwagandha powder

½ tsp your fave edible mushroom powder

⅛ tsp black pepper

⅛ tsp sea salt

2 cups (480 ml) coconut cream

½ cup (55 g) cashews, preferably soaked for 4 hours in water, then rinsed

½ cup (120 ml) water

CHOCOLATE COATING

¼ cup (55 g) coconut oil

3 heaping tbsp (21 g) cacao powder

3 tbsp (45 ml) maple syrup

Pinch of sea salt

½ tsp vanilla extract

GARNISH

Seeds and/or chopped nuts of choice

FOR THE POPS

Blend everything together until smooth, thick and creamy. Adjust according to taste. Pour it into the freezer pop molds and freeze until solid.

FOR THE CHOCOLATE COATING

Melt the coconut oil and stir all the ingredients together. Unmold the pops. Dip the frozen pops in your liquid chocolate and decorate them with seeds and nuts (I used sesame seeds, pumpkin seeds and chia seeds)!

Orange
CREAMSICLES

+GF +QP

These creamsicles are refreshing, light and the perfect amount of sweet. They taste like a frozen, portable Orange Julius. Mmmm. Plus, they cool ya' down and give you a hearty dose of vitamin C. Oh yeah, did we mention this recipe has FOUR ingredients? Get out your popsicle molds folks—your afternoon is about to get really delicious, really quick. —AS

SERVES 6 TO 8

1 (13½-oz [400-ml]) can coconut milk

1½ cups (355 ml) freshly squeezed orange juice

¼ cup (60 ml) agave nectar

1 tsp vanilla extract

Blend or stir all the ingredients together until combined. Pour it into the freezer pop molds (6 to 8, depending on size) and freeze for at least 3 hours but preferably overnight, until the pops are completely frozen. To remove the pops from their molds, gently rinse the mold under warm water for several seconds. Pull on the stick or base and the pop should slide right out! If it's still stuck, run under water for a few more seconds. These pops last indefinitely in the freezer.

seven

BREAKFASTS, SMOOTHIES & DRINKS

The best part of waking up is waking up to a healthy, hearty plant-based breakfast! The second-best part of waking up is knowing that you have a full day of delicious, healthy meal opportunities ahead of you beyond breakfast! No matter which part you're more excited for, we've got a recipe that'll get you up, get you moving and keep you fueled all day long. Friends, we've come together and rounded up our best breakfast recipes: from pancakes, waffles and egg-free French toast to muffins, doughnuts and strudels, there's a crowd-pleasing dish for every kind of morning! Some are healthier, some more splurge-worthy—all perfect for a simple breakfast at home with your family or a brunch-themed baby shower for twelve hungry mamas. We've thrown in our favorite thirst quenchers and hydrating, nutrient-packed sippers so you can plan for a full day of energy, hydration and a happy tummy! We've even got cozy morning mugs, creative cocktails and sparkling mocktails perfect for a holiday or special occasion. Grab your waffle iron, blender—maybe the shaker too—and let's drink up!

Baked PUMPKIN CINNAMON SUGAR DOUGHNUTS

These baked pumpkin doughnuts are rolled in cinnamon sugar and are SO EASY to make that I thought I must be doing it wrong. From start to finish this was maybe a half-hour project, and I was so happy with how they came out. These are the kind of doughnuts that give you street cred for being such a great cook. And you'll be like "Oh these easy things? I whipped these up lickety split!" So grab a doughnut pan, and let's bake! —AS

MAKES 6 DOUGHNUTS

DOUGHNUTS

1¼ cups (155 g) all-purpose flour

2 tsp (6 g) pumpkin pie spice (see Note)

1 tsp baking powder

½ tsp salt

½ cup (110 g) packed brown sugar

½ cup (120 ml) unsweetened almond milk

⅓ cup (60 g) pumpkin pureé (see Note)

2 tbsp (28 g) coconut oil, melted

1 tsp vanilla

TOPPING

¼ cup (60 ml) melted coconut oil or vegan butter

1 cup (190 g) organic granulated sugar

1 tbsp (9 g) ground cinnamon

FOR THE DOUGHNUTS

Preheat the oven to 350°F (177°C) and grease a doughnut pan.

In a large mixing bowl, combine the flour, pumpkin pie spice, baking powder and salt. In a separate mixing bowl, whisk together the brown sugar, almond milk, pumpkin purée, coconut oil and vanilla.

Mix the dry ingredients into the wet ingredients about ½ cup (63 g) at a time, stirring to combine. The batter should be a little thick, not pourable.

Once mixed, use a spoon to place the batter into the doughnut pan, distributing the batter evenly between each doughnut mold. Bake for 10 to 12 minutes, until an inserted toothpick comes out clean and the doughnuts spring back lightly when pressed. Cool them on a wire rack.

FOR THE TOPPING

While the doughnuts cool, pour the ¼ cup (60 ml) of melted coconut oil or butter into a shallow bowl. In a separate shallow bowl, mix together the granulated sugar and cinnamon. When the doughnuts have cooled, dip one side lightly into the oil or butter; then dip it into the cinnamon-sugar mixture, shaking off the excess. Flip the doughnut over and repeat the process, trying to coat the edges as well so that when you coat the other side with cinnamon-sugar, the whole doughnut becomes covered in the mixture. Repeat this process with all the doughnuts before moving them to a wire rack or stuffing them in your mouth.

Doughnuts are best served fresh, but if you have leftovers you'd like to save, my best recommendation is to line a ziplock bag with paper towels, place the doughnuts (not touching) into the bag and put them in the fridge overnight. If left on the counter, the oil could make them soggy overnight.

Note: If you don't have a doughnut pan, you can try to arrange the dough into doughnut shapes on a parchment-lined baking sheet. They won't look exactly the same and might be a little wonky, but still delicious!

If you don't have any pumpkin pie spice on hand (available at most grocery stores in the spices section), you can substitute with a mixture of cinnamon, ginger, nutmeg, allspice and cloves.

If you have some freshly roasted pumpkin, go ahead and use that. If not, canned pumpkin purée works great, too!

*SEE PHOTO INSERT

Banana CINNAMON FRENCH TOAST

+QP +GFO

After mixing my batter, I always like to pour it into a wider, shallower dish for dipping. A pie pan or casserole dish works great and makes dipping, flipping and coating your French toast slices super easy. The bread is really the secret to a great French toast, though. Thin, soft bread makes for soggy French toast; bread too thickly sliced will be too dry in the middle.

Thick, crusty bread cut into ½-inch (1.3-cm) slices is best. Having air pockets in the bread allows trapped batter to get gooey and gives you pockets of warm, melty cinnamon goodness. Mmmm! —AS

SERVES 3 TO 4

2 ripe bananas
¾ cup (180 ml) hemp milk
1½ tsp (5 g) ground cinnamon
1½ tsp (8 ml) vanilla extract
6–8 slices crusty vegan bread (gluten-free)

TOPPINGS
Maple syrup
Agave nectar
Fresh fruit

Mash the bananas in a medium mixing bowl with a fork. Whisk in the milk, cinnamon and vanilla until combined.

Pour the mixture into a shallow dish—a pie plate works great. Dip your bread into the wet mixture, flipping to coat the whole slice evenly.

Place dipped slices onto a preheated and greased skillet, and let them cook about 3 to 5 minutes on each side, until the edges no longer bubble and both sides are golden brown and crispy.

Enjoy these while warm with maple syrup, agave nectar or fresh fruit!

BLOOD ORANGE GLAZED Doughnuts

+SF

I love whipping up batches of healthier baked dough-nuts! These ones are covered in sweet, seasonal blood orange glaze, which gives them a really lovely pink color and a light citrus taste. They're perfectly fluffy, and the added flax means you can have two (or three . . .) instead of just one, because flax makes everything healthier, right? —AS

MAKES 6

DOUGHNUTS
1 cup (125 g) all-purpose flour
1 tbsp (12 g) baking powder
½ tsp ground ginger
¼ tsp salt
2 tbsp (14 g) ground flaxseed
6 tbsp (90 ml) warm water
½ cup (95 g) sugar
1 tsp blood orange zest
¼ cup (60 ml) unsweetened almond milk
2 tbsp (28 g) coconut oil, melted
1 tbsp (15 ml) apple cider vinegar

BLOOD ORANGE GLAZE
1 cup (130 g) powdered sugar
2 tbsp (30 ml) blood orange juice
1 tsp blood orange zest
1 tsp vanilla extract

Preheat the oven to 375°F (190°C).

FOR THE DOUGHNUTS
In a large mixing bowl, combine the flour, baking powder, ground ginger and salt. Set it aside.

Whisk together the ground flax and warm water in a small dish to gelatinize, about 5 minutes.

In a separate large bowl, mix together the sugar and orange zest until fragrant. Pour in the flax mixture, milk, oil and vinegar. Mix the dry ingredients into the wet ingredients about a cup (125 g) at a time, stirring until a batter forms. Let the batter set while you grease a 6-mold doughnut pan.

Pour the batter equally between the 6 doughnut molds and bake for 15 minutes, or until an inserted toothpick comes clean.

FOR THE BLOOD ORANGE GLAZE

While the doughnuts bake, whisk together the powdered sugar, blood orange juice, zest and vanilla in a shallow bowl to make the glaze. When the doughnuts finish cooking, move them to a rack to cool slightly; then dip them generously in the glaze. Serve immediately!

*SEE PHOTO INSERT

Blueberry STREUSEL MUFFINS

+GF

Even without any applesauce or bananas, these muffins are incredibly moist and flavorful—especially since they're gluten-free. And if you're still watching your sugar intake or aren't ready for a little splurge, skip the streusel topping. You'll still be left with a delicious, hearty muffin! —AS

MAKES 12 MUFFINS

MUFFINS
2¼ cups (250 g) GF flour (we used 1 cup [96 g] almond flour and 1¼ cups [155 g] teff flour)

2 tsp (8 g) baking powder

1 tsp baking soda

1½ tsp (6 g) xanthan gum

1 tsp (5 g) salt

½ cup (110 g) coconut oil, melted

1 cup (235 ml) nondairy milk

½ cup (95 g) organic sugar

2 tsp (10 ml) vanilla extract

1 cup (160 g) fresh or frozen blueberries (not thawed)

STREUSEL
½ cup (48 g) almond flour

⅓ cup (63 g) organic sugar

¼ cup (55 g) coconut oil (not melted)

¼ tsp ground nutmeg

¼ tsp ground cinnamon

Preheat the oven to 350°F (177°C). Grease a 12-cup muffin tin and set aside.

FOR THE MUFFINS

In a large mixing bowl, combine the flour, baking powder, baking soda, xanthan gum and salt. In a separate mixing bowl, whisk together coconut oil, nondairy milk, sugar and vanilla. Slowly add the dry ingredients to the wet, mixing together to combine. Be careful not to overmix! A little air left in the batter is best. Once combined, add the blueberries and use a rubber spatula to distribute them through the batter. Pour the batter into greased muffin tins, filling about three-fourths full. Set aside.

FOR THE STREUSEL

In a small dish, fork together all of the streusel ingredients until completely combined. Sprinkle a little streusel on top of each filled muffin tin, right on top of the batter. We put about a tablespoon (15 g) of streusel on each muffin.

Put the muffins in the oven and bake for 30 minutes, rotating the pan halfway through to ensure even cooking. Once finished, remove them from the oven and let them cool for at least 30 minutes before eating. Save them in an airtight container for several days.

Coconut BACON AND CHOCOLATE CHIP PANCAKES

+GFO +SF +QP

Rich, smoky, chocolaty pancakes . . . and that was before we added maple syrup to the equation! As they were cooking, we were drooling. Perfectly golden pancakes with melty chocolate and sprinkled with salty coconut bacon? Yeah, I'll take 10. —AS

SERVES 2

COCONUT BACON

2 tbsp (30 ml) liquid smoke

1 tbsp (15 ml) Bragg liquid aminos or soy sauce

1 tbsp (15 ml) pure maple syrup

1 tbsp (15 ml) water

3½ cups (265 g) flaked unsweetened coconut

1 tsp smoked paprika (optional)

PANCAKES

1¼ cups (155 g) gluten-free all-purpose flour or whole wheat flour

2 tbsp (24 g) organic sugar

2 tsp (8 g) baking powder

½ tsp salt

¼ tsp xanthan gum (only if using GF flour)

1¼ cups (295 ml) water

1 tbsp (14 g) coconut oil, melted

¼ cup (45 g) chocolate chips or chopped bar chocolate

¼–½ cup (20–40 g) coconut bacon (see above)

FOR THE COCONUT BACON

First, if necessary, prepare a recipe (or a half recipe) of coconut bacon. (You can buy it online, but you save TONS of money making it yourself—and you'll have leftovers!)

Preheat the oven to 325°F (163°C).

In a large mixing bowl, combine your liquid smoke, aminos, maple syrup and water. Pour in the flaked coconut, using a wooden spoon to gently toss the coconut in the liquid mixture. If adding smoked paprika, add and toss to coat evenly. Once the coconut is evenly coated, pour it onto a nonstick baking sheet and slide it into the oven. Bake for 20 to 25 minutes, using a spatula to flip the "bacon" about every 5 minutes so it cooks evenly. This stuff WILL burn if you're not keeping an eye on it and regularly flipping it, so please do. Coconut bacon can be stored in a sealed bag or container for up to a month, refrigerator optional. Set it aside.

FOR THE PANCAKES

In a large mixing bowl, combine the flour, sugar, baking powder, salt and xanthan, if using. Stir together; then use the spoon or whisk to form a well in the center of the dry ingredients, pushing the flour mixture to the outsides of the bowl. Pour in the water and oil, and whisk together completely. (If the batter seems a bit thin, add a little flour. If the batter seems a bit thick, add a little more water.) Once your batter is ready, mix in the chocolate chips.

Heat a greased skillet over medium heat. Pour ¼ cup (60 ml) of batter onto the skillet and sprinkle with coconut bacon. Gently pour a little bit more batter (about a tablespoon [15 ml]) over the coconut bacon layer, and let it cook until bubbles form and the edges begin to crisp. Flip the pancakes once, allowing the bottom side to cook until golden before removing from the skillet and serving. Serve with maple syrup (the real stuff!) and a little vegan butter, and enjoy!

Cranberry ORANGE CLAFOUTIS

+GF

Clafoutis, pronounced KLA-FOO-TEE, is a French dessert that is custard-y in texture and studded with fruit. Cherries seem to be the traditionally paired flavor, but since cranberries are in season and have such a great tart flavor, we used them instead. They work nicely to balance out the sweet, eggy flavor and texture of the cake, and they taste all kinds of seasonal with a bit of added orange zest. It works as a breakfast dish or dessert, and is an impressive-looking one at that! This recipe is deceptively simple and makes you seem like a real chef, especially when you start throwing around words like "clafoutis" and "aquafaba." —AS

SERVES 4 TO 6

1 cup (235 ml) unsweetened almond milk

½ cup (120 ml) and 1 tbsp (15 ml) aquafaba (liquid from a can of chickpeas)

½ cup (95 g) granulated sugar

2 tbsp (30 ml) melted vegan butter

2 tsp (10 ml) vanilla

1 tsp orange zest

½ cup (60 g) all-purpose flour

1 cup (100 g) fresh cranberries

Powdered sugar, for garnish

Preheat the oven to 325°F (163°C).

In a large mixing bowl, combine the almond milk, aquafaba, granulated sugar, melted butter, vanilla and orange zest. Add the flour, whisking until smooth. Pour the batter into a greased 8-inch (20-cm) cast-iron pan or baking dish. Scatter the cranberries over the top and place the whole pan into the oven.

Bake for 50 to 60 minutes, until the dough is puffed and golden along the edges. Remove it from the oven and let it sit at least 2 hours to set. The result should be very custard-like, a thick "pancake" similar to flan. Sprinkle with powdered sugar and serve!

Note: Texture is key in this dish. Don't dig in too early or the base won't set properly. It might seem undercooked or a little jiggly when you first pull it out of the oven, but I promise, that's what you want. However, if the sides haven't browned up, you'll want to keep it in a few extra minutes.

Cranberries not your jam? Use your favorite berries or stone fruit here instead!

Easy CHICKPEASY BREAKFAST BURRITOS

+GF +QP +SF

The aquafaba keeps the texture of the chickpeas "egg like" and you cook them up just like you would a pan of scrambled eggs. You can toss in any chopped veggies you like, but we liked them slathered in avocado, hot sauce and cilantro. They have a slightly hummus-y flavor and are packed with protein. And even though we've been enjoying them in the mornings, they're great ANY time of the day. They whip up in under 15 minutes, so let's eat! —AS

MAKES 2 BURRITOS

1 tsp coconut oil
1 (15-oz [425-g]) can chickpeas, *not* drained
1 clove garlic
1 tsp ground cumin
1 tsp smoked paprika
½ tsp salt
½ tsp pepper
2 tortillas
Avocado, halved, pitted and sliced
Hot sauce, to taste (optional)
Cilantro, roughly chopped (optional)
1 lime, quartered

Heat the coconut oil in a medium skillet over medium heat.

Pour an entire can of chickpeas *including* the brine, or aquafaba, into a blender or food processor. Toss in the garlic and spices, and blend until the mixture becomes mostly smooth but pourable.

Pour the mixture into the heated pan, using a spatula to move it around as it begins to cook, letting it get slightly browned before flipping the mixture onto itself (like scrambled eggs). Continue cooking the mixture until it has thickened and browned slightly, becoming almost mashed potato–like in texture. Lay a tortilla flat, scooping about half of the chickpea mixture on top. Top with slices of avocado, hot sauce, cilantro and a squeeze of fresh lime. Fold the tortilla around your mixture and enjoy!

To make freezer burritos, simply fold the tortilla around the chickpea mixture and wrap the whole burrito tightly in tin foil. Freeze indefinitely. When you're ready to reheat, remove it from the freezer and bake at 350°F (177°C) until the inner mixture is heated through and the tortilla begins to brown. Add the avocado and condiments, and eat them up.

Healthy HOMEMADE GRANOLA

+GF +QP

The cashews and almonds keep you full, and the light smattering of agave will help curb that sweet tooth. It's the kind of snack you can feel pretty good about snackin' on. And if you like dried fruit (raisins, craisins, etc.) feel free to toss in a handful when it's cool. —AS

SERVES 6 TO 8

3 cups (240 g) GF rolled oats
1 cup (170 g) roughly chopped almonds
1 cup (110 g) roughly chopped cashews
½ cup (38 g) shredded coconut
¼ cup (40 g) hemp seeds
¼ cup (28 g) flaxseeds
½ tsp salt
¼ cup (55 g) coconut oil, melted
¼ cup (60 ml) agave nectar or maple syrup

½ cup (90 g) chocolate chips or cacao nibs

1 cup (150 g) raisins or craisins

½ cup (75 g) goji berries

Handful of sunflower seeds

Preheat the oven to 350°F (177°C).

In a large mixing bowl, combine everything but the oil and agave (or maple syrup). Mix well to combine. Add in the liquid oil and sweetener and mix very well, so everything gets coated evenly. Spread it onto a large, ungreased baking sheet and bake for 20 to 30 minutes, stirring about every 5 to 10 minutes as needed. Granola cooks quickly and even crisps up a bit after being removed from the oven and sitting on the pan cooling. So remember to pull it from the oven before it gets too dark. Once you have removed the pan from the oven, let it cool for at least 20 minutes.

Once cool, add in any additional little bits (i.e., the cacao nibs, dried fruit or whatever) and move it to a sealed storage container, like a glass jar or large plastic bag. Stays fresh for up to 2 weeks.

Lemon CHIA SEED LOAF WITH LEMON GLAZE

+GF

It's moist, sweet, full of flavor and a perfect spring treat—perfect for breakfast, dessert or for a graduation party or baby shower. Keeping it gluten-free means sharing with everyone at the party, which makes you an instant success. Yep, this recipe = success. Making you a winner. Go you! Not a loaf kinda gal? Bake them up as muffins! Watching your sugar intake? Cut out two-thirds of the sugar by ditching the glaze. —AS

MAKES 1 LOAF

LEMON CHIA SEED LOAF
2¼ cups (245 g) gluten-free flour (we used 1¼ cups [120 g] almond flour and 1 cup [125 g] teff flour)

2 tsp (8 g) baking soda

1 tsp baking powder

1½ tsp (6 g) xanthan gum

1 tsp (5 g) salt

½ cup (110 g) coconut oil, melted

1 cup (235 ml) dairy-free milk

¼ cup (48 g) organic granulated sugar

1 tsp vanilla extract

1 heaping tbsp (10 g) freshly grated lemon zest, plus more for garnish

⅓ cup (80 ml) freshly squeezed lemon juice

2 tbsp (20 g) chia seeds, plus more for garnish

LEMON GLAZE
½ cup (65 g) powdered sugar

1–2 tsp (5–10 ml) lemon juice

(continued)

FOR THE LEMON CHIA SEED LOAF

Preheat the oven to 350°F (177°C).

In a large mixing bowl, combine the flour, baking soda, baking powder, xanthan gum and salt. In a separate mixing bowl, whisk together the coconut oil, milk, granulated sugar, vanilla, lemon zest and lemon juice. Pour the wet mixture into the dry, stirring to combine. Once well mixed, pour in the chia seeds and stir again to distribute them evenly through the batter. Pour the batter into a greased or lined loaf pan (or into a 12-muffin tin) and toss it in the oven. Bake for 50 to 60 minutes (less time for muffins), until an inserted toothpick comes out clean. When finished, remove it from the oven and move to a cooling rack. Let it cool completely before removing it from the loaf pan.

FOR THE LEMON GLAZE

While the loaf cools, make the lemon glaze by simply mixing the powdered sugar and lemon juice together until a thick, runny glaze is achieved. Add as much or as little liquid as you like, but the more liquid, the thinner the glaze. I recommend starting slow.

When the loaf cools, drizzle it with glaze and garnish with a sprinkle of chia seeds and some lemon zest. This lasts 3 days covered on the counter, 5-ish sealed in the fridge.

Note: The glaze is optional but delicious.

Whole wheat flour *should* be interchangeable here, though I haven't tried it. If you do use whole wheat, omit the xanthan.

Sub poppy seeds if you like!

This recipe can be used to make 12 muffins instead of a loaf, if you prefer. They will take less time to cook, however, so keep an eye on them.

Mini CHOCOLATE CHUNK SCONES

+GF

From start to finish, this recipe takes less than an hour and has options for both gluten-free and wheat-eatin' readers. The chunks of rich, dark chocolate in the scones make breakfast feel just a little more fancy than usual and totally acceptable as an after-dinner treat, too. —AS

MAKES 14 MINI SCONES OR 6 LARGE ONES

2 cups (250 g) gluten-free all-purpose flour (or 2 cups [260 g] whole wheat flour)

⅛ tsp salt

1 tbsp (12 g) baking powder

1 tsp xanthan gum (omit if using whole wheat flour)

3 tbsp (36 g) organic sugar

½ cup (115 g) cold vegan butter or shortening

⅔–¾ cup (160–180 ml) cold nondairy milk

½ cup (90 g) chocolate chips or chopped bar chocolate

Preheat the oven to 425°F (218°C).

In a large mixing bowl, whisk together the flour, salt, baking powder, xanthan (if using) and sugar. Using a pastry cutter or two knives, cut the butter into the flour mixture until uniform crumbs form (sometimes it helps to fork the butter into the flour if you're having trouble with your knives). Pour in the cold nondairy milk a little at a time, mixing until a soft, slightly sticky dough forms. Fold in the chocolate chips with a wooden spoon until they are evenly distributed.

Roll the dough onto a clean, floured surface and, using a rolling pin, roll out to about a 1 inch (2.5 cm) thickness. Cut out scone shapes using a cookie cutter or the top of a round, glass cup. We used a glass cup with about a 2-inch (5-cm) opening. It's important when cutting shapes that you push the cutter straight down into the dough and not turn or wiggle the cutter too much, or the dough will lose some of its air and be much denser.

Once your shapes are cut, place them onto a greased cookie sheet and bake them for 15 to 18 minutes, until they turn golden on the bottom and an inserted toothpick comes out clean. Let them cool for several minutes and enjoy!

We got 14 mini scones from this recipe, but if you prefer larger, normal-size scones, you should get about 6. Scones save well in an airtight container for several days.

Peanut Butter AND BERRY ACAI BOWL

+GF +QP

There's just something magical and so right about eating ripe, juicy fruit when the weather is warm! Whipped into smoothies, pressed into juice, sliced on top of my oatmeal—I'll eat it all, friends. Sometimes though, you realize that something you've been buying all along can be made in your own kitchen more cheaply and easily than running to the juice bar to get it! Combine my love for fresh summer fruit with my sheer laziness about driving across town to the juice bar, and you get this sweet gem. I like to top it with lots of extra berries, granola, nuts and chia seeds, but we'll offer some other fun ideas below. —AS

SERVES 2 OR MAKES 1 LARGE SMOOTHIE BOWL

1 acai smoothie pack (we use 3½-oz [100-g] frozen packs found in most grocery store freezer sections)

1 cup (235 ml) coconut water or dairy-free milk

1 cup (150 g) fresh or frozen strawberries

1 cup (150 g) fresh or frozen mixed berries (or you can sub 1 banana for ½ cup [75 g] berries here if you like)

2 tbsp (23 g) peanut butter

Fresh fruit and granola, for toppings

OPTIONAL ADD-INS (ABOUT 1–2 TBSP [10–30 G] EACH)
Ground flaxseed

Chia seeds

Hemp seeds

Protein powder

Goji berries

Maca

Lucuma

Nuts

Coconut

Cacao nibs

Agave

Blend up all your ingredients in a high-speed blender until thick and well combined. Scoop the mixture into a bowl and top it with fresh fruit, granola and any other delicious toppings you'd like! Enjoy immediately and freeze the leftovers.

*SEE PHOTO INSERT

Peanut Butter
CHOCOLATE CHIP BANANA BREAD

+GFO

I like bananas just as much as the next girl, but they're not my favorite, and sometimes they get a little too brown before we have a chance to gobble them up. Turning mushy, overripe bananas into banana bread is probably my real favorite way to enjoy my bananas, so I never really mind letting them get to that point. And this combo: mashed with peanut butter and sweet chocolate chunks? IT'S AMAZING. —AS

MAKES 1 LOAF

2-3 ripe bananas

⅓ cup (80 ml) oil

¼ cup (48 g) sugar

¾ cup (180 ml) nondairy milk

¼ cup (45 g) peanut butter

1 tsp vanilla extract

1 tsp vinegar

2 cups (260 g) whole wheat flour (we have also used a GF flour blend here, but used about 1¾ cups [219 g])

½ tsp baking soda

½ tsp baking powder

½ tsp salt

¾ cup (135 g) chocolate chunks (or chips)

Preheat the oven to 350°F (177°C). In a large bowl, mash your bananas. Set them aside.

In a large mixing bowl or in an electric mixer, whisk together the oil, sugar, milk, peanut butter, vanilla and vinegar. Let it sit for 3 to 5 minutes while you grab a third bowl and combine the flour, baking soda, baking powder and salt. Once the wet ingredients are ready, slowly add the dry ingredients, and stir it to combine. Once the two are completely combined and a batter has formed, add the mashed bananas. Stir again.

Finally, add in the chocolate chunks and mix once to combine. Pour it into a greased, lined or nonstick loaf pan. We used a nonstick pan with a little parchment paper for easy removal. Bake for 45 to 60 minutes, depending on the oven. The bread is finished when a toothpick comes out clean. Remove it from the oven and let it cool for at least 30 minutes before enjoying a piece. Cover and save for up to a week, or freeze indefinitely!

*SEE PHOTO INSERT

Perfect PANCAKES

+QP +SF

Seriously, guys. This pancake recipe is by far THE BEST one I've ever made. Light, fluffy and sweet, these pancakes completely changed my mind about vegan pancakes. When I went vegan, pancakes were one of the first things we made on our own. We love pancakes and eat them entirely more often than we should. Sadly, it seemed like every recipe produced super dense pancakes! Too much flour was involved or too much soy milk. And they were always flavorless! But these pancakes are delicious and consistently a hit at the breakfast table . . . enjoy! —AS

SERVES 2 TO 4

1¼ cups (163 g) whole wheat flour

2 tbsp (24 g) vegan granulated sugar

2 tsp (8 g) baking powder

½ tsp salt

1¼ cups (295 ml) water

1 tbsp (15 ml) vegetable oil

Sift the flour, sugar, baking powder and salt together in a mixing bowl. In a separate bowl, whisk together the water and oil. Make a well in the center of the dry ingredients and pour in the oil and water mixture. Stir until just blended. The mixture should be just a little lumpy.

Spoon heaping ¼ cup (60 ml) amounts of batter onto an oiled and heated griddle. Cook until bubbles form and the edges brown, then flip and cook until golden brown, about 3 minutes per side.

Serve with fresh maple syrup and some vegan butter, like Earth Balance. (Or some almond butter and agave nectar! Or fruit!)

South OF THE BORDER SCRAMBLE

+GF +QP

I've been toying with the idea of a tofu scramble for a while, but was hesitant. Would it be delicious? I never even liked scrambled eggs . . . do I even want to try to replicate them? Trust me, you do. These taste absolutely nothing like eggs. They taste like HEAVEN! The texture and look is reminiscent of eggs for sure—light, fluffy tofu, turned a bright golden yellow thanks to a little turmeric. Yum! —AS

SERVES 2

8 oz (225 g) extra-firm tofu

¼ cup (38 g) chopped onion

¼ cup (40 g) chopped tomato

1 tsp plus 1 tbsp (15 ml) olive oil, divided

½ tsp ground turmeric

½ tsp onion powder

½ tsp garlic powder

¼ tsp ground cumin

1 tsp red pepper flakes

Salt and pepper, to taste

Salsa

Sliced avocado

First, drain your tofu and press it between paper towels. Put the tofu into a bowl and use a fork to mash it to the consistency of scrambled eggs.

Add the onion and tomato to a saucepan with 1 teaspoon of the olive oil. Cook until the onions are slightly softened and translucent, about 5 minutes.

In a separate saucepan, add the mashed tofu, remaining 1 tablespoon (15 ml) olive oil and the spices, and cook over medium heat for about 5 to 8 minutes, or until the tofu is heated and beginning to brown. Add the veggies to the tofu scramble and stir. Season with salt and pepper.

Serve with salsa and avocado.

Spiced PUMPKIN BREAD WITH MAPLE VANILLA ICING

+SF

Prepare yourselves: the weather's getting cooler and it's about to get all kinds of pumpkin up in here. After walking the aisles of Trader Joe's last week and seeing pumpkin-themed snacks EVERYWHERE, I was inspired to make this drool-worthy, frosted Spiced Pumpkin Bread! —AS

MAKES 1 LOAF

SPICED PUMPKIN BREAD
⅓ cup (73 g) coconut oil, softened

½ cup (96 g) organic sugar

½ cup (120 ml) nondairy milk

1 tsp vanilla extract

1 tsp apple cider vinegar

2 cups (260 g) whole wheat or gluten-free flour blend

½ tsp baking soda

½ tsp baking powder

½ tsp salt

¼ tsp ground cinnamon

⅛ tsp ground ginger

1 (15-oz [425-g]) can pumpkin purée (about 1½ cups [270 g])

MAPLE VANILLA ICING
1½ cups (165 g) raw cashews, soaked in water to cover, drained

3 tbsp (45 ml) maple syrup

1½ tsp (8 ml) vanilla extract

¼–⅓ cup (60–80 ml) water

FOR THE SPICED PUMPKIN BREAD
Preheat the oven to 350°F (177°C).

In a large mixing bowl, combine the coconut oil, sugar, milk, vanilla and vinegar. Let it sit for 3 to 5 minutes. While you wait, grab a second mixing bowl and combine the flour, baking soda, baking powder, salt, cinnamon and ginger.

Once the wet ingredients are ready (slightly bubbly), slowly add the dry ingredients and stir to combine. Once the two are completely combined and a batter has formed, add the pumpkin purée. Stir to combine.

Pour the batter into a greased, lined or nonstick loaf pan. (We used a nonstick pan with a little parchment paper, for easy removal.) Bake for 45 to 60 minutes, until an inserted toothpick comes out clean. Remove the bread from the oven and let it cool for at least 30 minutes before transferring to a wire cooling rack.

FOR THE MAPLE VANILLA ICING
While the bread cools, whip up the icing by combining the soaked cashews, maple syrup, vanilla and water in a food processor or high-speed blender. Fill a piping bag or zip-top bag (with one corner cut off) with the icing mixture, and pipe icing over the cooled loaf.

This pumpkin loaf lasts well on the counter or in the fridge for about a week or can be frozen indefinitely.

Strawberry PHYLLO STRUDELS

+QP

I'm officially dubbing these "lazy girl pop tarts." They are SO simple to make, don't require you to whip up any dough, are ready in less than half an hour and are made of just six simple ingredients. Plus, they're actually pretty healthy! We didn't add any sugar, just fruit, to the filling and brushed the stacked layers of phyllo with melted coconut oil. The cream cheese glaze, while optional, is rich, perfectly sweet and really takes these to the next level. These flaky strudels are portable, too, making them perfect for on-the-go munching. Stuffed with fresh strawberries, they're perfect for summer— but you can sub in whatever fruit you have on hand. I think a mixed berry version would be delicious! —AS

MAKES 8

12 large phyllo sheets (mine were 13" x 18" [33 x 45 cm]), divided and folded in half

¼ cup (55 g) coconut oil, melted

2 cups (300 g) washed, hulled and chopped fresh strawberries

½ cup (120 g) plain vegan cream cheese

3 tbsp (45 ml) maple syrup

1 tsp vanilla extract

Preheat the oven to 400°F (204°C). Line a baking sheet with parchment paper.

Layer the folded phyllo sheets on the prepared baking sheet, brushing each sheet with the melted coconut oil before adding the next. Brush the sixth sheet with coconut oil and spread the strawberries, leaving about a 1-inch (2.5-cm) border around the edges.

Layer the remaining 6 phyllo sheets, continuing to brush with coconut oil. Once the top layer has been brushed, use a large sharp knife or pizza cutter to slice the pastry into 8 equal rectangles. (You do this because once the pastry has baked, the phyllo will become slightly crisp and brittle and if cut *after* baking, it will crumble quite a bit.)

Place the baking sheet into the oven and bake for 12 to 16 minutes, or until golden brown.

While the pastries bake, prepare the cream cheese glaze by whisking together the cream cheese, maple syrup and vanilla until smooth. When the pastries are finished, let them cool for at least 10 minutes before drizzling with the cream cheese glaze.

Note: Leftovers last without glaze, on the counter, for up to 3 days. With glaze, they'll be good for 1 to 2 days in the fridge. So go ahead and have a second or third . . .

The easiest way to get that drizzle evenly over the whole thing (IMO) is to scoop the cream cheese glaze into a small zip-top sandwich baggie, cut the corner off with scissors and—*voilà!*—you have yourself a DIY icing bag.

*SEE PHOTO INSERT

Sweet CHERRY COFFEE CAKE

This cake comes out moist, lightly sweet and stuffed full of delicious summer cherries. It's my favorite cake of any kind that I've had in a while. We tried to keep the sugar low in the cake mixture because of the super sweet crumb topping, but it's still a splurgy breakfast for sure. And even though coffee cake sounds like a morning thing, it definitely tasted just as good at ten o'clock at night. You could probably sub in any summer berries here for a tasty seasonal treat; we will definitely be making versions of this recipe year-round. —AS

SERVES 6 TO 8

1 heaping cup (160 g) sweet cherries

CRUMBLE TOPPING
1½ cups (185 g) all-purpose flour

½ cup (72 g) brown sugar

1 tsp ground cinnamon

Pinch of salt

½ cup (55 g) coconut oil or vegan butter, softened

COFFEE CAKE
6 tbsp (85 g) vegan butter or coconut oil

6 tbsp (85 g) coconut butter

½ cup (96 g) granulated sugar

1 cup (235 ml) nondairy milk

1 tbsp (7 g) ground flaxseed

1 tbsp (9 g) cornstarch

1 tsp apple cider vinegar

1½ cups (185 g) all-purpose flour

2 tsp (8 g) baking powder

½ tsp baking soda

½ tsp salt

Preheat the oven to 350°F (177°C). Grease a 9 x 9-inch (23 x 23-cm) glass baking dish and set aside.

Wash, pit and halve the sweet cherries.

FOR THE CRUMBLE TOPPING

Mix together the flour, brown sugar, cinnamon and salt in a medium mixing bowl. Pour in the softened coconut oil or butter and use a fork to combine the mixture until small crumbs form. Set it aside.

FOR THE COFFEE CAKE

In a separate mixing bowl, cream together the butter (or oil), coconut butter and granulated sugar. Add the milk, ground flaxseed, cornstarch and vinegar, stirring until completely combined.

In a third mixing bowl, combine the flour, baking powder, baking soda and salt. Pour the milk mixture into the flour mixture and stir until just combined. Don't overmix! Fold in the sweet cherries.

Pour the prepared batter into your greased baking dish and spread the crumble mixture evenly over the top. Bake for 25 to 30 minutes, until an inserted toothpick comes out clean of cake and the crumble mixture has turned a nice golden brown. Let it cool for at least 20 minutes before serving.

Note: Leftovers can be saved in an airtight container on the counter for 3 days and in the fridge for about a week

*SEE PHOTO INSERT

Vanilla-Glazed MATCHA SCONES

They're sweet, fluffy and moist inside—the PERFECT scone, especially if you like matcha! It's important to use a high-quality matcha powder to get a vibrant green color in your scones, too. The light drizzle of vanilla glaze sweetens them up just enough: they're perfect for breakfast and dessert! —AS

MAKES 8 SCONES

MATCHA SCONES

2 cups (260 g) whole wheat pastry flour

2 tbsp (14 g) matcha powder

1 tbsp (12 g) baking powder

½ tsp ginger

½ tsp salt

6 tbsp (85 g) cold vegan butter

¾ cup (135 g) mashed banana

¼ cup (60 ml) almond milk

2 tbsp (30 ml) maple syrup

1 tsp vanilla extract

VANILLA GLAZE

½ cup (65 g) powdered sugar

1 tbsp (15 ml) nondairy milk

¼ tsp vanilla extract

Preheat the oven to 425°F (218°C). Line a baking sheet with parchment paper.

FOR THE MATCHA SCONES

In a large mixing bowl, whisk together the flour, matcha powder, baking powder, ginger and salt. Using a pastry cutter or fork, cut in the cold vegan butter until small crumbs form. Pour in the mashed banana, almond milk, maple syrup and vanilla, and stir it together with a wooden spoon until a sticky dough forms.

Turn the dough onto a lightly floured surface and form a 1-inch (2.5-cm) thick disk. Cut the disk into 8 equal scone wedges, like a pizza. Place the scones on the prepared baking sheet and bake for 15 to 17 minutes, until golden. Place the scones on a wire rack to cool.

FOR THE VANILLA GLAZE

Whisk together the powdered sugar, nondairy milk and vanilla in a small bowl. Drizzle the glaze over the completely cooled scones and enjoy!

Note: Leftovers save well sealed in an airtight container on the counter for up to 3 days.

Overnight
FRENCH TOAST

This is a dish I always LOVED at the holidays and begged my mom to make year-round . . . veganized! This is the perfect set-it and forget-it until baking time kind of recipe! —AS

SERVES 4 TO 6

1 loaf fresh bread, sliced into about 1" (2.5-cm) slices

½ cup (65 g) whole wheat flour

1¾–2 cups (415–470 ml) nondairy milk

½ cup (120 ml) pure maple syrup

2 tsp (10 ml) vanilla extract

2 tsp (6 g) ground cinnamon

½ tsp ground nutmeg

¼ tsp ground cardamom

¼ tsp sea salt

TOPPINGS
Fresh fruit

Maple syrup

Whipped Coconut Cream (page 423)

Grease an 8 x 8-inch (20 x 20-cm) glass baking dish. Layer the sliced bread into the dish, piling it in until the dish is nearly full. Set it aside.

In a small bowl, whisk together the flour, milk, maple syrup, vanilla, cinnamon, nutmeg, cardamom and sea salt. Pour the mixture evenly over the sliced bread, covering it completely. Wrap the entire dish with plastic and chill for several hours, or overnight.

In the morning, preheat the oven to 375°F (190°C) and bake, uncovered, for about 30 to 40 minutes, or until they're golden brown on top and cooked through in the middle. Serve with fresh fruit, syrup and whipped coconut cream.

Apple Cider
DOUGHNUTS

+SF +QP

Growing up in Maine, I would often visit orchards in the fall with my elementary school classes to pick apples, press cider and munch as many apple cider doughnuts as we could get our tiny hands on. Of course, the doughnuts were always the highlight of the trip for me. Luckily I'm an adult now, so I can pick apples more than once a year and make these delicious homemade doughnuts anytime I want. This recipe is almost too easy—you'll have fresh, sweet doughnuts in half an hour or less! —AS

MAKES 6

1 cup (125 g) all-purpose flour

1 tsp baking powder

1 tsp baking soda

2 tsp (6 g) ground cinnamon, divided

¼ tsp ground nutmeg

¼ tsp ground ginger

⅛ tsp salt

½ cup (124 g) applesauce

½ cup (100 g) granulated sugar

¼ cup (60 ml) apple cider

2 tbsp (30 ml) apple cider vinegar

2 tbsp (30 ml) melted coconut oil

¾ cup (98 g) powdered sugar, for coating

Preheat the oven to 375°F (190°C).

In a large mixing bowl, combine the flour, baking powder, baking soda, 1 teaspoon of the cinnamon, nutmeg, ginger and salt.

In a separate mixing bowl, whisk together the applesauce, granulated sugar, apple cider and vinegar. Mix the dry ingredients into the wet ingredients about a cup (120 g) at a time, stirring to combine. Pour in the melted coconut oil and whisk to incorporate. Let the mixture set while you grease a 6-mold doughnut pan.

Once the pan is greased and the oven is preheated, pour the mixture equally between the 6 doughnut molds and bake for 15 minutes. While the doughnuts bake, whisk together the powdered sugar and remaining 1 teaspoon cinnamon in a wide dish.

When the doughnuts finish cooking, move them to a cooling rack to cool slightly and then roll them in the powdered sugar mixture until they're completely coated. Enjoy immediately!

Leftover doughnuts last for 1 to 2 days in an airtight container on the counter but are best enjoyed fresh.

*SEE PHOTO INSERT

Stewed CINNAMON APPLES IN A YOGURT PARFAIT

+QP +SF +GF

You'll surprise your friends with this stewed parfait. With winter comes crisp apples and juicy oranges. Luckily not much is needed to coax the flavors of seasonal fruit. Let the fruit simmer in a bath of cinnamon-ginger and generously pour it over a bowl of creamy coconut yogurt.

If you're pressed for time, an easy trick for an even quicker breakfast parfait is to make the stewed fruit the night before. It only takes 10 minutes, and what you are left with is far better than what you could have missed out on—a yogurt bowl filled with the best that winter has to offer. —MR

SERVES 2

1 apple, cored and cubed

1 tbsp (14 g) coconut oil

1 tsp ground cinnamon

½ tsp ground ginger

Juice of 1 orange

1 pear, cored and cubed

Handful raisins or currants

2 cups (490 g) coconut yogurt

Toss the apple into a small saucepan along with the coconut oil, spices and orange juice. Then warm everything over medium-high heat for 10 minutes—with the lid halfway on. Toss the pear and raisins into the same saucepan to warm for another 5 minutes. The stewed fruit will be done cooking when the pieces have softened and can easily be pierced with a fork. Add a splash of water if the pot ever dries out. Stir the stewed fruit into a bowl of yogurt and enjoy!

*SEE PHOTO INSERT

Chia Pudding PARFAIT WITH A DREAMY STRAWBERRY SMOOTHIE

+GF

This is the ultimate breakfast for the days when indecision strikes and not just a smoothie or chia pudding curbs your appetite, but a little of both. With this meal two pillars of healthy living collide—chia pudding topped off with a smoothie. Need I say more? —MR

SERVES 2

COCONUT CHIA SEED PUDDING

¾–1 cup (180–235 ml) full-fat, unsweetened coconut milk or any nut milk

3 tbsp (30 g) chia seeds

1 tbsp (15 ml) maple syrup

SMOOTHIE LAYER

¾ cup (115 g) frozen strawberries

⅓ cup (35 g) frozen pomegranate seeds (optional)

½–1 frozen peeled banana, cubed

½ cup (120 ml) any nut milk

2 pitted dates (optional)

Small handful unsweetened coconut shreds (optional)

FOR THE PUDDING

Combine the coconut milk, chia seeds and maple syrup in a small bowl and mix well. Place in the refrigerator to expand and settle overnight, or for at least 3 hours.

FOR THE SMOOTHIE

When the chia pudding has set, prepare your smoothie. Place all of the ingredients in a blender and blend until creamy. Then layer half the pudding in the bottom of a jar and pour half the smoothie on top. Do the same for the other cup and enjoy!

CHOCOLATE-GINGERSNAP
Fall Bars

+SF +GF

These chocolate-gingersnap fall bars are a love letter to the holidays. Chunks of hazelnuts, pumpkin seeds and pecans come together with a delicious holiday spice blend, helping to capture the best of the season. They also make for quite the perfect homemade gift. —MR

MAKES 10 TO 12 BARS

GINGERSNAP SPICE MIX
¾ tsp ground cinnamon
½ tsp ground ginger
½ tsp ground allspice
¼ tsp ground nutmeg
Sea salt

CHOCOLATE-GINGERSNAP BARS
½ cup and 2 tbsp (148 g) coconut oil, melted
½ cup and 1 tbsp (62 g) cacao powder
1¼ cups (190 g) Medjool dates, pitted
1 cup (120 g) hazelnuts
1 cup (120 g) pecans
1 cup (65 g) pumpkin seeds
Extra nuts and seeds, for garnish

FOR THE SPICE MIX
In a small bowl, mix together the cinnamon, ginger, allspice, nutmeg and salt. Set it aside.

FOR THE BARS
First add the coconut oil, cacao and dates to the food processor and blend until well combined, about 1 minute. Then add the nuts, seeds and spice mix, and pulse until they are mixed into the batter but still remain crunchy.

Pour the batter onto a lined 8 x 8-inch (20 x 20-cm) pan. Press the batter into the pan, to ¾ inch (2 cm) thick, and sprinkle the top with extra nuts and seeds. Store the bars in the freezer for an hour. Cut them into squares and enjoy! I like to store mine in the freezer or fridge to stay cool.

*SEE PHOTO INSERT

Lemon AND POPPY SEED PANCAKES

+QP +GFO

I can't think of a more elegant way to serve and enjoy pancakes. Speckled with poppy seeds and a touch of citrus, these pancakes are a welcomed adaptation to an American classic. —MR

MAKES 7 TO 10 SMALL PANCAKES

1½ cups (185 g) spelt flour, or buckwheat if gluten-free
1 tbsp (12 g) baking powder
1½ tbsp (15 g) poppy seeds
1 tsp vanilla powder or extract
2 tbsp (14 g) ground flaxseed
5 tbsp (75 ml) warm water
1 cup (235 ml) almond milk
Zest of 1 lemon
3 tbsp (45 ml) lemon juice
2–3 tbsp (30–45 ml) maple syrup
1 tbsp (15 ml) melted coconut oil, plus more for the pan
Coconut yogurt, for topping

Mix the flour, baking powder, poppy seeds and vanilla powder (if using extract, add it with the wet ingredients) in a large bowl. Combine the flaxseed and water in a small bowl and let sit for 10 minutes to thicken. This is your "flax egg." Slowly whisk the flax egg, almond milk, lemon zest and juice, maple syrup and coconut oil into the dry ingredients until you get the right consistency. We're looking for a thicker batter, but if you prefer it runnier, add more almond milk.

Over medium heat, warm your frying pan with coconut oil. Ladle about ¼ cup (60 ml) batter per pancake into the pan. Cook the pancake on one side until the batter starts to bubble slightly in the center. Then flip the pancake over and cook until golden brown on the other side. Add more coconut oil to the pan once you have a new batch to cook. Top with anything you'd like! I love coconut yogurt, maple syrup and slices of fruit.

*SEE PHOTO INSERT

Baked PEACH AND BLUEBERRY OATMEAL

+GF

There is not a dish I've made that has gotten more mileage than this one right here. For many reasons, baked oatmeal is an essential breakfast in my home. For one, it tastes absolutely divine: warmed fruit bursting across oatmeal makes for a delicious scene. For seconds, you can make this oatmeal on Sunday and have enough to last you for five days of breakfast, snacking or what have you. And lastly, it's a godsend for the busy life—fitting in a nutrient-dense breakfast for the entire workweek in a near 20 minutes. —MR

SERVES 5

2 cups (160 g) GF rolled oats

1 tbsp (10 g) chia seeds

1½ cups (355 ml) hot water

2 bananas, chopped, divided

1½ peaches, pitted and chopped, divided

½ cup (60 g) chopped pecans

½ cup (75 g) blueberries

½ cup (75 g) raspberries or strawberries

¼ cup (38 g) raisins

½ cup (75 g) currants

4 tsp (12 g) ground cinnamon

2 tsp (14 g) maca powder (optional)

¾ cup (180 ml) almond milk

Preheat the oven to 350°F (177°C).

In a medium bowl, add the oats and chia seeds, and pour the hot water on top. Let this sit until the oats have absorbed all the water. Be sure not to add more chia seeds, as they will expand and turn the oatmeal too gooey and it will be hard to mix.

In the meantime, add 1½ of the bananas, 1 of the peaches and your pecans to a large mixing bowl. Add the remaining fruit, raisins, currants, cinnamon and maca powder to this bowl. Now also add the oats and almond milk and mix very well, so that all the fruit is coated in the delicious cinnamon almond milk.

Pour the batch evenly into a baking dish (I used an 8 x 8-inch [20 x 20-cm] pan) and top with thin slices of the remaining peach and banana; bake for 20 minutes.

Feel free to reheat this the next morning until warmed. I have done this many times and it tastes absolutely delicious! Enjoy this any time of day!

CINNAMON-RAISIN
Granola

+GF +QP

If you were a fan of the 1990s cereal phenomenon that is Raisin Bran, then I have a feeling you're going to love this granola. Speckled with juicy raisins and a touch of cinnamon, this granola hints at the classic but with a few appreciated additions. Sweet apricots and chunks of creamy macadamia nuts are added to the mix, bringing a heartier breakfast granola to the table. Top it off with a splash of almond milk and you have yourself an updated Raisin Bran cereal fit for the healthy home cook. —MR

SERVES 6

2½ cups (200 g) GF rolled oats

2 tbsp (30 ml) almond milk or water

½ cup (75 g) dried apricots or any dried fruit

⅓ cup (40 g) flaxseeds

1 cup (170 g) chopped almonds

½ cup (55 g) chopped macadamia nuts

1 cup (150 g) raisins

3 tbsp (42 g) coconut oil

4 tsp (12 g) ground cinnamon

3 tbsp (45 ml) maple syrup

Sprinkle of sea salt

Preheat the oven to 350°F (177°C).

In a large bowl, mix the oats, almond milk, dried apricots, flaxseeds, nuts and raisins. Now, in a small saucepan, heat the coconut oil, cinnamon and maple syrup over low heat until dissolved. Pour this sauce onto the oat mixture and mix until well coated.

Line a baking pan with parchment paper and evenly pour the sweet granola on top. Firmly press with your fingers to keep the batch compact, and then sprinkle with sea salt.

Bake for 17 to 20 minutes, turning the granola at 10 minutes. Be careful to make sure the edges are crisp but not burnt. When crispy, remove it from the oven and let it cool for 10 minutes.

Store the granola in an airtight container for a few weeks. Enjoy on top of yogurt, in smoothies, with ice cream or on its own with almond milk.

CITRUS AND TAHINI
Granola

+GF +QP

The combination of orange, vanilla and tahini alone is utterly divine. For starters, it is the most delicious melding of unexpected flavors. It can also be used in many other sweet recipes. In this recipe, it perfumes the granola in a heavenly scent of citrus and warming spices. It is the heart and soul of this recipe that shouldn't be missed. —MR

SERVES 6

1 cup (80 g) GF rolled oats

1 cup (132 g) GF oat flour (or pulse rolled oats in the food processor until ground into a flour-like consistency)

½ cup (75 g) dried apricots or any dried fruit

1 cup (150 g) dried cherries (optional)

1 cup (110–170 g) any nuts (I used almonds)

2-3 tsp (6-9 g) ground cinnamon

3 tbsp (42 g) coconut oil

3 tbsp (45 ml) maple syrup

3 tbsp (36 g) coconut sugar

1 huge tbsp (18 g) tahini

1 tbsp (7 g) vanilla powder or extract (15 ml)

Zest and juice of 1 orange

Sprinkle of sea salt

Preheat the oven to 350°F (177°C).

In a large bowl, mix the oats, oat flour, dried fruit, nuts and cinnamon. Set aside. Now, in a small saucepan over low heat, combine the coconut oil, maple syrup, coconut sugar, tahini, vanilla, orange zest and juice. Warm the mixture for 1 minute until the coconut oil has dissolved and everything is well mixed. Pour this sauce onto the oat mixture and blend until it's evenly coated.

Line a baking sheet with parchment paper and evenly pour the granola on top. Firmly press the granola with your fingers to keep the batch compact; sprinkle with sea salt. Bake for 17 to 20 minutes while turning the granola once halfway through. Be careful to make sure the edges are crisp but not burnt. Then remove it from the oven and let cool for 10 minutes.

Store in an airtight container (like a mason jar) for a few weeks. Enjoy this granola on top of yogurt, in smoothies, with ice cream or on its own with almond milk.

*SEE PHOTO INSERT

Macadamia MILK PORRIDGE WITH BLUEBERRY-LEMON JAM

+GF

Macadamia nut milk is creamy and luxurious—the perfect counterpart to hearty buckwheat with zesty blueberry-lemon jam. If macadamia nut milk is not an option, cashew milk is a close second, or even almond. Nonetheless, both will make a great porridge. —MR

SERVES 2

PORRIDGE

1 cup (170 g) raw buckwheat groats or GF rolled oats

2 cups (470 ml) macadamia milk or almond milk

1 tbsp (15 ml) maple syrup

Sprinkle of sea salt

BLUEBERRY LEMON SYRUP

2 cups (300 g) frozen blueberries, rinsed under warm water

Zest of 1 small lemon

1 tbsp (10 g) chia seeds

FOR THE PORRIDGE

Mix all the porridge ingredients in a bowl and let this sit overnight to soften. When you're ready, add the porridge to a saucepan and cook it over low heat for 7 to 10 minutes, or until all the liquid has been absorbed.

FOR THE BLUEBERRY LEMON SYRUP

As the buckwheat is cooking, warm the blueberries and lemon zest in a small saucepan over medium heat until it starts to bubble, about 5 minutes. Then stir in the chia seeds and let it sit for about 5 minutes. Top your porridge with the warm jam and enjoy!

Colorful COCONUT PORRIDGE

+QP +GF

This is a when-in-doubt-make-porridge kind of a recipe. The ingredients here are kitchen staples, and with the assistance of creamy coconut milk, a few slices of bananas and berries, you have yourself a downright delicious breakfast in a matter of minutes. Let the blueberries stew as you cook down the oats. Now sit back and wait for an explosion of colors from the simmering blueberries—this is the best part. —MR

SERVES 1

⅓ cup (27 g) GF rolled oats

¾ cup (180 ml) full-fat coconut milk

¼ cup (60 ml) water

1 handful blueberries

½ ripe banana, sliced

1 tsp ground cinnamon

1 tsp maca powder (optional)

1 tsp maple syrup if you prefer it sweeter (optional)

Add the oats, coconut milk, water, blueberries and banana to a saucepan, and cook over medium-low heat for about 7 minutes, until all the liquid has been absorbed and you are left with a creamy porridge. Now stir in the cinnamon, maca powder and maple syrup; mix well. Pour it into a bowl and enjoy with your favorite toppings!

Simple OVERNIGHT OATS/BIRCHER MUESLI

+GF +QP

When pressed for time, bircher muesli is the dream breakfast companion. Leave the oats to soak in nut milk, and come morning, the oats will have plumped, softened and absorbed the delicious milk.

Keep in mind that oats and milk alone don't offer an array of flavors. Add your favorite berries, dried fruit and nuts for a bircher muesli that is equally packed with nutrition and flavor. —MR

SERVES 1

1 cup (235 ml) cashew milk or any nut milk

1 tbsp (15 ml) maple syrup

¾ cup (92 g) raspberries or any berry

½ ripe banana

¾ cup (60 g) GF rolled oats or instant oats

Small handful of raw cacao nibs (optional)

Fill a bowl with the cashew milk and maple syrup, add the raspberries and banana and mash with the back end of a fork, releasing all their juices into the same bowl. Then add the oats and raw cacao nibs (if using); mix well. Place a cover over the muesli and store in the refrigerator overnight or for at least 3 hours.

Enjoy this hearty breakfast with fresh fruit or nuts.

Turmeric TOFU SCRAMBLE

+SF +GF +QP

The fate of a great tofu scramble rests in its spice blend. Tofu on its own doesn't bring much flavor to a meal; rather it beautifully absorbs all the favors that are mixed with it. Try not to be put off by the list of spices and veggies used here. Most are kitchen staples and can be substituted for what you have on hand. A few spices, greens and a generous pinch of sea salt will turn out a delightful tofu scramble every time. —MR

SERVES 2 TO 3

2 tbsp (30 ml) olive oil

1 clove garlic, thinly chopped

½ small yellow onion, roughly chopped

Sea salt

1½ cups (240 g) cherry tomatoes

3–4 big handfuls spinach or kale

½ cup (73 g) frozen peas, defrosted

3–4 tsp (5–7 g) nutritional yeast

1 tsp ground turmeric

1 (12-oz [340-g]) block organic, extra-firm tofu

Red pepper flakes

Squeeze of lemon juice

2–3 pieces of toast (optional)

½ avocado, sliced

Small handful chives, minced

In a medium sauté pan, warm the olive oil, garlic, onion and a pinch of sea salt over medium heat for 5 minutes. Toss in the cherry tomatoes and cook until the skins of the tomatoes blister, about 7 minutes. Add the spinach, peas, nutritional yeast and turmeric, and cook until the spinach wilts down.

Now, using your fingers, crumble the tofu into the sauté pan and add the red pepper flakes, lemon juice and another pinch of salt. Mix until the tofu is well combined and fully coated, turning lightly yellow in color (from the turmeric). Taste the scramble and see if you'd like to add more salt, lemon juice or red pepper flakes.

Serve the scramble over toast, if desired, with slices of avocado and minced chives.

*SEE PHOTO INSERT

Blueberry BREAKFAST DOUGHNUTS

+GF +QP

If you're the kind of person who's looking for a good excuse to eat a doughnut for breakfast, well I've just gifted you permission. Bursting with pockets of juicy blueberries and Medjool dates, these doughnuts are hearty enough to be considered a healthier breakfast. You only live once, so here is a brilliant breakfast doughnut to reflect this sentiment. —MR

MAKES 6 DOUGHNUTS

(continued)

1 cup (132 g) GF oat flour (or rolled oats ground into a flour in the food processor)

1 cup (96 g) almond flour

½ tsp baking soda

½ tsp baking powder

½ tsp ground cinnamon

Pinch of sea salt

2 tbsp (14 g) ground flaxseed

5 tbsp (75 ml) warm water

¼ cup (55 g) coconut oil, plus more for the pan

¾ cup (180 ml) almond milk

1 tsp vanilla extract or powder

¾ cup (134 g) pitted Medjool dates

1 cup (150 g) frozen blueberries (you can use fresh but the juice spreads across the doughnut more)

Preheat the oven to 350°F (177°C).

In a large mixing bowl, combine the flours, baking soda, baking powder, cinnamon and salt.

Combine the flaxseed and warm water in a small bowl and let sit for 10 minutes to thicken. This is a "flax egg."

Now using a food processor, add the flax eggs and all the wet ingredients, except for the blueberries, and mix until the dates break down and are well combined.

Add the wet ingredients to the bowl with the dry and mix well. Then gently fold the blueberries into the mixture.

Grease the doughnut pan with coconut oil. Fill the doughnut pan holes with the batter and pop it into the oven to cook for 17 to 20 minutes. Let the doughnuts cool for a few minutes, and then enjoy!

Store them in an airtight container on the counter or in the fridge, and enjoy as your breakfast, snack or even dessert throughout the week.

Chocolate-Chip
COOKIE PROTEIN BARS

+GF +QP

This recipe came about after a love affair with a similar bar from a charming vegan café in San Francisco. When I moved, I knew this would be the bar I needed to recreate. And here it is. With a plant-based protein layer sealed in melted chocolate, this bar tastes like dessert and doubles as breakfast. As an added bonus: it's far less expensive than fancy café protein bars. —MR

MAKES 10 TO 12 SQUARES

BARS

1 cup (96 g) almond flour

¾ cup (96 g) GF oat flour

⅔ cup (73 g) plant-based vanilla protein powder

2 tbsp (14 g) ground flaxseed

¼ cup (60 ml) maple syrup

½ cup (90 g) cashew butter

6 tbsp (90 ml) almond milk

1 tsp ground cinnamon

2 handfuls chocolate chips

CHOCOLATE TOPPING

1 tsp coconut oil

⅓ cup (60 g) vegan chocolate chips

Pinch of sea salt (optional)

FOR THE BARS

Combine all the ingredients (except the chocolate chips) in a food processor and pulse until the batter is mixed well. Add the chocolate chips and pulse until combined but not completely chopped. Remove the dough and press it firmly into a small baking dish lined with parchment paper, until the dough is evenly spread and is about ⅓ inch (8 mm) thick. Set it aside while you prepare the melted chocolate using the double-boiler method.

FOR THE CHOCOLATE TOPPING

Fill a small saucepan with ¼ cup (60 ml) of water, and place a separate glass or metal bowl on top, covering the saucepan below. Once the top bowl is hot and the water below is boiling, add the coconut oil to the bowl and let it melt. Add the chocolate chips and mix slowly, sprinkling a pinch of salt if desired. Remove the chocolate sauce from the heat right after it has melted. Pour it evenly over the dough and pop it in the freezer to set for 20 minutes.

Once it has set, cut it into small bars. Enjoy it as a pre- or post-workout snack or as a quick breakfast.

Strawberry-Rose
MORNING BARS

+GF

This is an adaption from my beloved morning bar recipe in my first cookbook Alternative Vegan. *A splash of rose water extract perfumes the bars in a subtle floral aroma. Matched perfectly with strawberries, this sweet combination is an unexpected, yet outright delicious breakfast bar. —MR*

MAKES 10 TO 12 SQUARES

BASE
1½ cups (120 g) GF rolled oats
¾ cup (84 g) cashews or almonds
2 tbsp (30 ml) date or maple syrup
1 tsp ground cinnamon
1 tbsp (15 ml) melted coconut oil
¼ cup (60 ml) water
Pinch of sea salt

FILLING
½ cup (80 g) dried figs (cut off the hard stem on top if attached)
½ cup (85 g) pitted Medjool dates
1 cup (150 g) fresh strawberries
1 tbsp (15 ml) date or maple syrup
¼ cup (60 ml) water
⅛ tsp rose water/extract (optional, but adds a lovely floral aroma)
1 tbsp (8 g) arrowroot powder

TOPPING
¾ cup (60 g) GF rolled oats
1 tbsp (15 ml) date or maple syrup
½ tsp ground cinnamon
1½ tbsp (22 ml) melted coconut oil
Pinch of sea salt

FOR THE BASE

Preheat the oven to 350°F (177°C) and line a small baking dish with parchment paper.

Add all the base ingredients to the food processor and blend for about 20 seconds, until part of the cashews have broken down and a solid batter has formed, sticking together. Press the batter into the lined baking dish, about ½ inch (1.3 cm) thick. Keep pressing it into the dish until a solid, tight base forms. Bake for 7 minutes. In the meantime, make the filling.

FOR THE FILLING

Add the figs and dates to a food processor and pulse for about 20 seconds to break them down into smaller pieces. Toss the strawberries into the processor as well and pulse for 10 seconds; we want to roughly chop the strawberries into smaller pieces.

Now add all the filling ingredients, except the arrowroot powder, to a small saucepan and cook over medium-high heat for 5 minutes. Turn off the heat. Then stir in the arrowroot and let it rest for a few minutes.

(continued)

While that's resting, mix all the topping ingredients together in a small bowl.

Assemble the bars by layering the strawberry filling evenly on top of the cooked base. Then add the topping over the filling, gently pressing down, covering the strawberry mixture below.

Bake for 25 to 28 minutes, or until the top is golden brown. Let it cool for 10 minutes and then slice it into bars.

Note: For the filling, you can also use only dried figs if you don't have dates on hand. But do not use only dates—this will make the bars overly sweet.

Morning GREENS BOWL

+SF +GF +QP

When a cozy breakfast is in order, this will be waiting for you: a morning bowl that's overflowing with greens, creamy avocado and fresh dill. Sauté the greens until tender, add a slew of seasonings and enjoy over warm toast or served straight up in a big, beautiful bowl. —MR

SERVES 3 TO 4

1 tbsp (15 ml) olive oil, plus more for serving

½ small red onion, quartered and thinly sliced

½ fennel bulb, thinly sliced

2 cloves garlic, roughly chopped

1½ tsp (5 g) ground cumin

Pinch of red pepper flakes

Pinch of sea salt

3 cups (210 g) roughly chopped kale (or Swiss chard), stems removed

1½ cups (112 g) thinly sliced mushrooms

1 cup (30 g) spinach

¾ cup (120 g) halved cherry tomatoes

1 avocado, peeled, pitted and cut into fourths

1½ tbsp (5 g) chopped fresh dill

2 tbsp (20 g) unsalted pumpkin seeds, toasted

Squeeze of lemon juice

Vegan ricotta cheese (optional, page 46)

3-4 slices bread (optional)

In a medium saucepan, melt the olive oil over medium-high heat. Add the onion, fennel, garlic, cumin, red pepper flakes and a pinch of sea salt. Sauté for 7 to 10 minutes, or until the onions are slightly translucent and have softened. If the bottom of the pan starts to dry out, add a splash of water and mix all the ingredients together.

Now toss in the kale and mushrooms, and sauté for another 7 to 10 minutes, or until the kale and mushrooms wilt down and soften. Now toss in the spinach and cherry tomatoes and warm until the spinach wilts. Remove it from the heat and mix in the avocado slices, dill, pumpkin seeds, squeeze of lemon and vegan ricotta cheese (if using). Toast your bread, if using, and top it with a drizzle of olive oil before adding the sautéed veggies. Or serve in a bowl.

Vegan Gluten-Free
CHAI-SPICED TEFF WAFFLES

+GF +SF

Teff is a tiny whole grain that originates from Ethiopia. If you've ever had Ethiopian food, you've eaten teff in the spongy sourdough flatbread called injera. I made these waffles in my Belgian waffle iron because to me a thick waffle is the best kind of waffle. I'm sure you can use this batter in a regular waffle maker or even make pancakes out of it, but you'll end up with more than the four Belgian waffles I got out of it. —KH

MAKES 4 WAFFLES

1 cup (125 g) brown teff flour

¼ cup (40 g) brown rice flour

2 tsp (8 g) baking powder

2 tsp (8 g) ground cinnamon

1 tsp ground cardamom

¾ tsp ground ginger

⅛ tsp ground cloves

1¼ cups (300 ml) unsweetened nondairy milk

¼ cup (60 ml) avocado oil or other mild oil

¼ cup (50 g) brown sugar or coconut sugar

Heat your waffle iron. Mix the dry ingredients (flour and spices) together in a small mixing bowl. Then mix the wet ingredients (milk, oil, sugar) in a medium mixing bowl.

Pour the dry ingredients into the wet and mix well.

Spray both of the cooking sides of the waffle iron with spray oil. Pour a heaping ⅓ cup (80 ml) of batter in the center. Close the waffle iron and cook as directed.

Cook the waffle until crispy, remove it carefully with tongs and put it on a cooling rack to keep it crisp as you finish cooking the others.

Do not forgo the oil, because these waffles tend to stick more than others I have made.

*SEE PHOTO INSERT

Autumn CINNAMON APPLE BISCUITS

+SFO

These biscuits are flavored with the essence of autumn and packed full of juicy apples. Slightly sweet, these make a great grab-and-go breakfast. —KH

MAKES 10 BISCUITS

2¼ cups (280 g) whole wheat pastry flour (or mix of all-purpose and whole wheat pastry flour)

¼ cup (50 g) brown sugar or coconut sugar

1 tbsp (11 g) baking powder

½ tsp salt

1 tsp ground cinnamon

⅛ tsp allspice

⅓ cup (80 g) coconut oil

2 medium apples, peeled, cored and chopped (about 1½ cups [180 g])

½ cup (120 ml) unsweetened nondairy milk

½ cup (122 g) plain coconut or soy yogurt

(continued)

Preheat the oven to 375°F (190°C) and oil two baking sheets.

Combine the flour, sugar, baking powder, salt, cinnamon and allspice in a large mixing bowl. Mix well.

Cut the coconut oil in with a pastry blender or with two forks, until the mixture resembles a coarse cornmeal.

Stir in the apples, milk and yogurt until just combined. Pour the mixture out onto a floured cutting board, patting the dough to about ½ inch (1.3 cm) thick.

Using a round biscuit cutter or seasonal cookie cutter, cut out the biscuits and place them on the greased baking sheet.

Re-form your dough and pat it down again to ½ inch (1.3 cm); cut out more biscuits. Repeat until all the dough is used.

Bake for 20 to 25 minutes, or until the bottoms are browned and the middle of the biscuit is firm.

Vegan Baked
ORANGE CARROT CAKE OATMEAL

+GF +SF

This just may be the best oatmeal I have ever made! It's just like eating carrot cake for breakfast, but without any of the guilt. —KH

SERVES 6

2 cups (160 g) GF rolled oats

1 tsp baking powder

1 tsp ground cinnamon

½ tsp salt

1½ cups (355 ml) nondairy milk

1 cup (145 g) finely shredded carrot

½ cup (120 ml) agave nectar or maple syrup

2 tbsp (14 g) ground flaxseed mixed with 4 tbsp (60 ml) warm water

1 tsp vanilla extract

1 tsp orange zest

3 (6-oz [170-g]) containers nondairy yogurt

OPTIONAL TOPPINGS
Sprinkle of chopped walnuts

Drizzle of maple syrup

Preheat the oven to 350°F (177°C). Oil a medium casserole dish or line with parchment paper to make it oil-free.

Mix the dry ingredients in a large mixing bowl. Next, add the wet ingredients to a small mixing bowl and combine well. Finally, add the wet ingredients to the dry, and mix well.

Pour the mixture into the prepared casserole pan and smooth it out with a spatula. Bake uncovered for 45 minutes. It will be wetter than a regular cake, but as long as it's as thick as bread pudding, it's good to go.

Top each serving with half a small container of nondairy yogurt to serve as your icing.

You can also sprinkle chopped walnuts and drizzle on a little maple syrup to make the most impressive breakfast you've ever served your family!

Perfect BANANA BREAD BELGIAN WAFFLES

+SF

What do you do when one person wants banana bread for breakfast and another wants waffles? You compromise and make these big and hearty banana bread waffles. These delicious giants are filled with bananas, cinnamon, walnuts and a little cornmeal for a crispier texture. If you want to make them even more decadent, top them with sliced bananas, toasted walnuts, a sprinkle of ground cinnamon and lots of warm and buttery maple syrup. This is what weekend mornings are all about. —LM + AM

SERVES 4

2 tbsp (14 g) ground flaxseed

4 tbsp (60 ml) water

½ cup (59 g) chopped walnuts

2 very ripe bananas

1½ cups (185 g) all-purpose flour

½ cup (89 g) cornmeal

1 tbsp (12 g) sugar

3 tsp (11 g) baking powder

½ tsp ground cinnamon

⅛ tsp fine sea salt

1½ cups (360 ml) almond milk

3 tbsp (44 g) vegan butter, melted (use soy-free)

1 tbsp (15 ml) lemon juice

1 tsp pure vanilla extract

2 tbsp (30 ml) melted coconut oil (to brush the waffle iron with so the waffles don't stick)

TOPPINGS

Sliced bananas

Toasted walnuts

Ground cinnamon

Pure maple syrup

Heat your waffle iron.

Mix the flaxseed and water together in a small bowl until it's thick and sticky. Set it aside. This is your "flax egg."

Toast the walnuts in a cast-iron skillet or nonstick pan over medium heat (shake the pan frequently to avoid burning) until they're golden brown and fragrant, about 3 to 4 minutes.

Purée the bananas until they're smooth and creamy.

In a large mixing bowl, whisk the dry ingredients until they're fully combined. In a medium bowl, whisk the almond milk, melted butter, lemon juice and vanilla extract until combined; pour the liquid into the dry mixture. Add the flax mixture and the puréed bananas; stir until the wet and dry mixtures, and the bananas, are combined. Fold in the walnuts.

Brush a thin layer of coconut oil on the waffle iron. Make sure the pockets of the grid are well oiled or the waffle will stick. Fill the grid with batter until it's three-fourths full. Close the iron and cook for 6 to 7 minutes, or until it stops steaming and the waffle is firm and golden brown.

Note: Because there is a lot of banana in the batter, you will have to cook the waffle a lot longer than you'd cook a plain waffle.

Old-Fashioned
FLUFFY PANCAKES WITH APPLE SPICE COMPOTE

+SF

My husband, Alex's dad, is fondly known as the Breakfast King in our family. He makes the best breakfast foods, like these stunning hot cakes. They're thick and fluffy, exactly what pancakes are supposed to be—and then some. They puff up like pillows and have the perfect texture.

The apple spice compote takes those old-fashioned pancakes to another level. The apples are cooked in cinnamon, allspice and ginger, with a splash of Grand Marnier until they're tender and oh so delicious. They're savory and slightly sweet all at the same time. Smother your pancakes with them and dig into a little slice of heaven. —LM + AM

MAKES 6 LARGE OR 12 SMALL
PANCAKES AND ABOUT 2 CUPS
(364 G) COMPOTE

COMPOTE
1 tsp coconut oil
2 green apples, peeled, cored, and finely diced
1 tsp ground cinnamon
¼ tsp ground cloves
¼ tsp ground allspice
¼ tsp ground ginger
2 tbsp (28 g) brown sugar
Pinch of sea salt
3 tbsp (45 ml) Grand Marnier or orange juice

PANCAKES
2 cups (253 g) all-purpose flour
1 tsp granulated sugar (optional)

2 tsp (7 g) baking powder
¾ tsp baking soda
½ tsp fine sea salt
½ cup (124 g) unsweetened applesauce
½ tsp pure vanilla extract
2 tbsp (30 ml) canola oil, plus more for the griddle
Juice from ¼ lemon
1½ cups (360 ml) almond milk

FOR THE COMPOTE

In a saucepan, heat the oil over medium heat. When the oil is hot, add the apples and toss them to coat. Add the spices, brown sugar and salt, and stir to combine. Cook for about 5 minutes, or until the apples begin to release their juices and begin to stick to the pan. Deglaze your pan with the Grand Marnier and reduce the heat to a gentle simmer. Add a little water, if necessary, to avoid scorching the apples. Simmer until the apples are soft and the sauce is thick, approximately 15 minutes.

FOR THE PANCAKES

Lightly oil and heat a pancake griddle over medium heat.

In a medium mixing bowl, whisk the flour, granulated sugar (if using), baking powder, baking soda and salt until well combined.

In a small bowl, whisk the applesauce, vanilla, oil, lemon juice and milk together.

Pour the wet ingredients into the dry and stir until just blended. Don't overmix or the batter will get tough and won't rise well.

Use a ladle or a large spoon to pour the batter onto the hot griddle. Cook for about 4 minutes, or until the tops are bubbling, the sides are firm and the bottom is golden brown. Gently flip the pancakes over and cook for another 4 minutes, or until the bottom is golden brown and the sides are fully cooked and firm.

Christmas Morning
CRANBERRY ORANGE PANCAKES

+SF

These are the ultimate Christmas morning pancakes. The cranberry and orange make them so festive, they taste like the holidays. Prepare the cranberries the night before and then just whip up the batter in the morning. —LM + AM

MAKES 6 LARGE OR 12 SMALL PANCAKES

1½ cups (190 g) all-purpose flour

½ cup (85 g) finely ground cornmeal

2 tsp (7 g) baking powder

1 tsp sugar

½ tsp ground cinnamon

⅛ tsp fine sea salt

1¾ cups (420 ml) unsweetened almond milk

1 cup (250 g) applesauce

Juice from ½ large orange (about ½ cup [120 ml])

1 tsp pure vanilla extract

2 tbsp (30 ml) melted coconut oil, plus more for the griddle

1 heaping cup (100 g) fresh cranberries, halved, and ¼ cup (25 g), whole, for the syrup, divided

2 cups (480 ml) pure maple syrup

Whisk the dry ingredients together in a large mixing bowl until well combined, and make a well in the center.

Whisk the almond milk and applesauce together, then add the orange juice, vanilla and melted coconut oil and pour it into the center of the well in the dry ingredients. Fold until just combined. The batter should be thick but pourable. Add more almond milk if it's too thick. Fold in 1 cup (100 g) of halved cranberries until evenly distributed.

Put the maple syrup and remaining ¼ cup (25 g) whole cranberries in a small saucepan over medium-low heat. Stir occasionally until the cranberries pop. Remove it from the heat.

Heat a cast-iron griddle or a large pan over medium-high heat, and evenly spread a thin layer of coconut oil over the surface. If you're cooking with a nonstick pan, you may not need to add the oil. When the griddle is hot, use a ladle or a measuring cup (the size depends on how large you want your pancakes) and pour batter onto the griddle. Cook until the center begins to bubble and the edges are dry, about 3 minutes, then flip it over. Cook until the pancake is golden brown and firm to the touch, about 3 minutes.

If you're making breakfast for a large crowd, heat the oven at a low temperature. Keep the pancakes warm until they're all cooked so you can serve them at once.

Healthier WHOLE WHEAT STRAWBERRY MUFFINS

+SF

Who doesn't love a good muffin? We certainly do, especially when they have a slightly crisp exterior and a tender strawberry-filled center. These muffins have both! The secret to the crisp crust is the canola oil and the cinnamon sugar—they create an outstanding texture, both inside and out.

What makes them healthier than the average muffin? They're made with whole wheat flour, almond milk, a banana and fresh strawberries. Oh, and lots of love. XO —LM + AM

MAKES 12 MUFFINS

(continued)

1 banana

2 tbsp (30 ml) canola oil

1 tsp pure vanilla extract

Juice of ½ lemon

1½ cups (360 ml) almond milk

2 cups (264 g) whole wheat flour

2 tsp (7 g) baking powder

¼ tsp fine sea salt

¼ tsp ground cinnamon

⅓ cup (65 g) vegan granulated sugar

1 cup (154 g) fresh diced strawberries

Cinnamon-sugar, for sprinkling

Preheat the oven to 385°F (196°C) and lightly grease your favorite muffin tin with cooking spray.

In a medium mixing bowl, mash the banana until there are no lumps. Add the canola oil, vanilla, lemon juice and milk, whisking to mix.

In a separate mixing bowl, whisk the whole wheat flour, baking powder, sea salt, cinnamon and sugar until fully combined.

OK, it's show time! Add the dry ingredients to the wet and stir until just moistened. Add the strawberries. Fold them into the mixture, minimizing the amount of mixing so that the muffins don't turn out tough.

Use an ice-cream scoop or a measuring cup to fill each muffin tin three-fourths full. Sprinkle a bit of cinnamon-sugar evenly over the tops and place the tin in the oven on the center rack.

Bake them for about 20 minutes, or until a toothpick inserted into the center of the largest one comes out clean.

Place the tin on a wire rack for 5 minutes to cool, and then invert the muffins onto the rack, allowing them to sit upside down for a few minutes. This will allow any extra moisture in the bottoms to move back toward the tops for better consistency.

Chunky Monkey
CHOCOLATE BANANA MUFFINS

+SF

When my kids were little, they discovered the Chunky Monkey while vacationing in Mexico. It's a thick and creamy frozen drink that combines chocolate and bananas. It's pretty awesome. This muffin recipe was inspired by that drink. My kids are all grown up now, and they still love a good chunky monkey, especially in muffin form. You're going to love it, too. It's made with cacao powder, chocolate chips and banana. Every bite consists of gooey melted chocolate and perfectly ripe bananas. The best part: they're really easy to make. —LM + AM

MAKES 12 MUFFINS

2½ cups (330 g) stone-ground flour

¼ cup (28 g) cacao powder

½ cup (97 g) sugar

2 tsp (7 g) aluminum-free baking powder

1 tsp salt

1 cup (240 ml) nondairy milk (I used cashew milk, but unsweetened almond milk will work too)

½ cup (124 g) unsweetened applesauce

1 tbsp (15 ml) melted coconut oil

1 tsp pure vanilla extract

1 large banana, diced

½ cup (91 g) vegan chocolate chunks or chips (we use Enjoy Life brand)

Preheat the oven to 350°F (177°C). Grease and flour or line a muffin tin with liners.

In a large mixing bowl, whisk the flour, cacao powder, sugar, baking powder and salt together until well blended and the cacao is evenly distributed.

Add the milk, applesauce, coconut oil and vanilla, stirring until just combined. Don't overdo it or the batter will get tough. Gently fold in the banana and chocolate chips until evenly combined.

Spoon the batter into the muffin tins until three-fourths full. Bake for about 20 minutes, or until the tops are puffy and cracked and a toothpick inserted in the center comes out clean. Cool them on a wire rack for 15 minutes before removing from the muffin tin.

Baked PUMPKIN SPICE DOUGHNUTS WITH CHOCOLATE CINNAMON ICING

+SF

The minute the calendar switches to September, we're all about pumpkin spice. There are few things that smell and taste like our favorite season of the year. The earthy aromas of the cinnamon, nutmeg, ginger and cloves remind us of walking through a pile of leaves on a crisp day. When you top that with chocolate and cinnamon, well, there are no words to describe how satisfying that flavor profile tastes.

Our baked doughnuts are so much healthier than fried, yet they're just as delicious. The texture is tender and chewy, just like it's supposed to be. Make a batch and see for yourself. —LM + AM

MAKES 6 DOUGHNUTS

DOUGHNUTS
1¼ cups (158 g) all-purpose flour

1 tsp aluminum-free baking powder

1 tsp ground cinnamon

½ tsp ground nutmeg

½ tsp fine sea salt

¼ tsp ground ginger

¼ tsp ground cloves

¼ cup (62 g) unsweetened applesauce and 1 tsp baking powder, combined

⅓ cup (64 g) coconut sugar or light brown sugar

½ cup (91 g) pumpkin purée

1 tbsp (15 ml) maple syrup

1 tsp pure vanilla extract

¼ cup (60 ml) unsweetened almond milk

CHOCOLATE CINNAMON ICING
1 cup (132 g) powdered sugar

3 tbsp (21 g) cocoa powder

3 tbsp (45 ml) unsweetened almond milk, more or less to get the desired consistency

1 tsp ground cinnamon

Preheat the oven to 350°F (177°C) and grease the doughnut pan if it's not nonstick.

FOR THE DOUGHNUTS
In a medium bowl, whisk the dry ingredients until well combined and set it aside.

In a large mixing bowl, add the applesauce mixture and the coconut sugar and mix until well combined. Add the pumpkin purée, maple syrup and vanilla, mixing until well combined. Add half of the flour mixture and half of the almond milk, and mix until just combined. Add the second half of the flour mixture and milk, and mix until combined. Add more milk if the batter is too stiff. It should be firm, not wet like cake batter. Scrape into the prepared pan.

Bake for about 25 minutes, or until a toothpick inserted in the center comes out clean. Cool the doughnuts on a wire rack for 10 minutes. Then remove them from the pan and place them on the rack until completely cool.

(continued)

FOR THE CHOCOLATE CINNAMON ICING

In a medium bowl, stir the powdered sugar, cocoa, milk and cinnamon until it's smooth and creamy. The texture should be between a frosting and a glaze. Add more milk if needed. When the doughnuts are completely cool, frost them and enjoy!

*SEE PHOTO INSERT

Baked LEMON AND THYME DOUGHNUTS

+SF

These bright and sunny doughnuts are a taste of summer. There's a hint of fresh thyme and a bold taste of zippy lemon that will light up your morning even on the cloudiest of days.

Made with fresh-squeezed lemon juice, grated lemon zest and beautiful green thyme, they're as pretty as they are delicious. —LM + AM

MAKES 6 DOUGHNUTS

DOUGHNUTS
2½ cups (228 g) cake flour
2 tsp (7 g) aluminum-free baking powder
½ tsp fine sea salt
¼ cup (60 ml) extra-virgin olive oil
½ cup (100 g) granulated sugar
½ cup (111 g) brown sugar
¼ cup (60 ml) aquafaba (liquid from a can of chickpeas)
½ cup (120 ml) lemon juice
3 tbsp (18 g) lemon zest, divided
1 tsp pure vanilla extract
3 tbsp (6 g) minced thyme, plus 1 sprig for garnish

GLAZE
⅓ cup (44 g) powdered sugar
2 tbsp (30 ml) lemon juice

Preheat the oven to 350°F (177°C) and lightly grease your doughnut pan if it's not a nonstick pan.

FOR THE DOUGHNUTS

In a medium bowl, whisk the flour, baking powder and salt until completely combined.

In a large mixing bowl, beat the olive oil, sugars, aquafaba, lemon juice, 2 tablespoons (12 g) of the lemon zest and vanilla until the sugar is mostly dissolved. Add the flour mixture and thyme to the sugar mixture, and stir until just combined. Spoon the batter into the doughnut pans, about three-fourths of the way full.

Bake for 15 minutes, or until a toothpick comes out clean when inserted into the center of the doughnuts. Let them cool for 5 minutes, then invert them onto a wire cooling rack until completely cool.

FOR THE GLAZE

Mix the powdered sugar and lemon juice until it's smooth and creamy. Dip the tops of the cooled doughnuts into the glaze. Sprinkle with the remaining 1 tablespoon (6 g) lemon zest and a sprig of thyme.

*SEE PHOTO INSERT

Vegan CINNAMON ROLLS

+SFO

How to describe cinnamon rolls? Cozy, luscious and distinctive are three words that come to mind. They're a special morning surprise that will brighten any day. So whether you're popping them in the oven for a family gathering, dessert for friends or just because you deserve it, take the time to enjoy a breakfast roll that is fit for a king. —LM + AM

MAKES 8 CINNAMON ROLLS

3 tbsp (45 g) vegan butter or coconut oil, divided

1⅓ cups (315 ml) plain unsweetened almond milk, divided

1 packet (7 g) active dry yeast

½ cup (100 g) granulated sugar

¼ tsp fine sea salt

2 cups (250 g) and 1 tbsp (8 g) all-purpose flour, divided

2 tsp (10 ml) vegetable oil

1 tbsp (8 g) ground cinnamon

2 tbsp (24 g) coconut sugar

1 cup (120 g) powdered sugar

Preheat the oven to 375°F (190°C) and prepare a round cake pan by greasing it with 1 tablespoon (15 g) of the vegan butter.

Warm 1 cup (235 ml) of the almond milk in a small saucepan over medium-low heat. When the milk is heated, about 3 minutes later, add the remaining 2 tablespoons (30 g) vegan butter to the almond milk and stir until the butter is melted into the milk. Remove the mixture from the stove.

Next, add the yeast to the milk and butter mixture. Make sure the milk is warm to the touch but not hot enough to kill the yeast. Pour the milk and butter mixture into a stand mixer with a whisk attachment. Whisk in the sugar and salt until all the ingredients are well incorporated and the mixture begins to foam. This process should take about 10 minutes.

Remove the bowl from the stand mixture and fold 2 cups (250 g) of the flour into the mixture using your hands. The dough will be slightly sticky.

Cover a clean surface with the remaining 1 tablespoon (8 g) flour. Take the dough from the bowl, pour the vegetable oil into your hands and coat the dough. Knead the dough for 1 minute on the floured surface and roll it back into a ball. Place the dough in the cake pan and cover with a clean towel. Allow the dough to rise in a warm place for 30 minutes.

After 30 minutes, place the dough back onto the floured surface and roll it out into a long rectangle.

In a small bowl, combine the cinnamon and coconut sugar. Sprinkle the top of the dough with the cinnamon-sugar.

Roll the dough long-side up. Using a serrated knife, gently slice the roll into 2-inch (5-cm) pieces. Arrange the pieces sliced-side up in the cake pan and bake for 25 minutes, or until golden brown.

While the rolls are baking, create the glaze by mixing the powdered sugar and remaining ⅓ cup (80 ml) almond milk until the mixture is well combined.

When the rolls are done baking, drizzle the glaze over the rolls and serve them warm.

Cherry BERRY QUINOA BREAKFAST BOWL

+GF +SF

Want to feel like a health queen after breakfast? Then this is the bowl for you. Stuffed with cherries, blueberries, hemp seeds and quinoa, you'll leave breakfast feeling satisfied—yet like you're walking on a cloud. Plus, the nutty flavors from the seeds, the tartness of the berries and the sweetness of the maple syrup is a crowd pleaser. So, no need to make a healthy breakfast for yourself and something different for everyone else in your life! This will make everyone happy. —LM + AM

SERVES 4

1½ cups (360 ml) water

1 cup (180 g) uncooked quinoa, rinsed

1 cup (240 ml) almond milk

1 tbsp (15 ml) pure maple syrup

1 tsp ground cinnamon

Pinch of salt

1 cup (170 g) almonds, soaked in water to cover, drained

2 tbsp (20 g) hulled hemp seeds

1½ cups (300 g) fresh pitted and diced cherries

1 cup (150 g) blueberries

½ cup (40 g) unsweetened coconut flakes

In a medium saucepan, bring the water and quinoa to a boil. Once boiling, cover the pan and reduce the heat to a simmer. Cook the quinoa for 15 minutes, or until the water is completely absorbed.

Remove the pan from the heat and allow it to sit, covered, for 10 minutes.

Take off the lid and fluff the quinoa.

Place the quinoa in a medium bowl to cool. In a separate bowl, mix the almond milk, maple syrup, cinnamon and salt until combined. Pour the mixture into the bowl of quinoa. Fold in the almonds, hemp seeds, cherries, blueberries and coconut.

Savory VEGAN MEDITERRANEAN OATMEAL

+GF +SFO

While images of breakfast usually contain sugary cereals, sweetened yogurt (nondairy of course) and candied breakfast pastries, we tend to prefer something a little different. In the Meyer household, a savory breakfast is always welcomed with open arms. So, take a step into our kitchen and try out this salty, savory umami breakfast bowl. —LM + AM

SERVES 4

2 cups (474 ml) water

½ tsp sea salt

¾ cup (60 g) GF steel-cut oats

1 cup (30 g) spinach

1 cup (160 g) cherry tomatoes

¾ cup (135 g) Kalamata olives

¼ cup (7 g) basil leaves

1 tsp vegan butter (use soy-free)

In a medium saucepan, bring the water and salt to a boil. Stir in the steel-cut oats and reduce the heat to a simmer. Stir occasionally until the oats begin to thicken. This will take about 5 minutes.

While the oats are thickening, take this time to roughly chop your spinach, slice the tomatoes into ¼-inch (6-mm) thin slices, coarsely chop the Kalamata olives and chop up your basil leaves.

After the oats thicken, add the spinach and stir it into the oats. Cook until the spinach is wilted, about 2 minutes.

At this point, add the tomatoes and olives. Stir them to combine and cook until all the ingredients are warmed through. This should take another 2 to 3 minutes.

To finish the oats, add the basil and butter. Stir to combine, and serve.

*SEE PHOTO INSERT

Vegan VEGGIE AND HERB FRITTATA

Ask anyone who's tried this dish and they'll tell you that everyone leaves feeling full, content and not missing eggs. Thanks to the Vegan Egg and the rest of these delicious ingredients, we've created the most convincing vegan frittata ever. You'll definitely be coming back for seconds . . . and maybe even thirds! —LM + AM

SERVES 4

2 slices bread

3 tsp (15 ml) extra-virgin olive oil, divided

Dash of sea salt

6 egg equivalent (60 g) of vegan egg substitute (we use Follow Your Heart VeganEgg)

½ cup (118 ml) plain unsweetened almond milk

½ tsp sea salt, plus extra to taste

2 tbsp (5 g) chopped fresh basil

1 tsp chopped fresh thyme

1 tsp chopped fresh oregano

1 tsp chopped fresh rosemary

Black pepper, to taste

1 tbsp (4 g) red pepper flakes (optional)

1 cup (67 g) sliced baby portobello mushrooms

1 medium sweet onion

1 cup (40 g) chopped baby spinach

½ cup (56 g) vegan mozzarella shreds

½ cup (56 g) vegan cheddar shreds, divided

¾ cup (135 g) drained and halved Kalamata olives

1 medium tomato, thinly sliced

Preheat the oven to 375°F (190°C).

Cut the bread into ½-inch (1.3-cm) cubes and toss with 1 teaspoon of the olive oil and a dash of sea salt. Place the cubes of bread onto a baking sheet and pop them in the oven; bake, shaking the pan occasionally, until crisp. This should take about 5 to 7 minutes.

While the bread is toasting, prepare 6 vegan eggs according to the instructions listed on the package. Whisk the almond milk into the eggs along with the sea salt, basil, thyme, oregano, rosemary, a dash of black pepper and optional red pepper flakes.

Sauté the mushroom slices and onion in a skillet over medium heat in 1 teaspoon of olive oil. Once the mushrooms begin to look browned and the onions are slightly translucent, about 4 minutes, add the spinach and toss it until wilted.

Fold the mushrooms, onion and spinach into the egg mixture. Then add the mozzarella and ¼ cup (28 g) of the cheddar to the egg mixture. Now fold in the bread cubes and olives.

Coat the inside of two 9-inch (23-cm) pie plates with the remaining 1 teaspoon olive oil and fill them with the egg and vegetable mixture. Top the frittata with the olives and 5 thin slices of tomato, and sprinkle the top with the remaining ¼ cup (28 g) vegan cheddar.

Bake for 20 minutes, until firm and slightly browned on top. Allow the frittata to rest for 5 to 10 minutes prior to serving.

*SEE PHOTO INSERT

The Ultimate VEGGIE TOFU SCRAMBLE

+GF

You know that feeling you get after drinking a green juice for the first time in a couple weeks? The feeling like "I'm a healthy glowing goddess who's going to take over the world" only to have that feeling tumble down a rocky cliff once the hunger sets in? Well, this scramble has all the health benefits, all the glowing goddess-producing qualities, with no sharp hunger pains about 30 minutes later, and a plethora of decadent Mediterranean flavors.
—LM + AM

SERVES 4

1 (12-oz [340-g]) package extra-firm tofu

1 tbsp (15 ml) extra-virgin olive oil

1 small red onion, finely diced

1 small red bell pepper, seeded and finely diced

1 tomato, seeded and finely diced

1 clove garlic, minced

½ cup (91 g) pitted and chopped Kalamata olives

2 cups (80 g) fresh baby spinach

½ cup (20 g) chopped fresh basil

2 tbsp (3 g) chopped fresh oregano

Salt and pepper, to taste

Drain the tofu and then press it by placing the tofu between dry sheets of paper towels and placing a heavy object, such as a pan filled with cans, on top of the tofu. Allow the tofu to sit like this for 15 minutes.

While your tofu is draining, take this opportunity to chop and mince the vegetables and herbs, if you have not done so already. Now, take your drained tofu and crumble it so that it has the appearance of pieces of cooked scrambled eggs.

In a large cast-iron skillet or sauté pan, heat the olive oil over medium heat. Once the oil is hot, add the onion and bell pepper. Stir occasionally during the 3 to 5 minutes it takes for the onion to soften and become translucent.

Add the tofu, tomato, garlic and olives to the onion–bell pepper mixture. Cook for 5 more minutes, stirring occasionally. Finish by adding the spinach and herbs, allowing them to wilt for about 2 to 3 minutes. Top the scramble with your desired level of salt and pepper.

STRAWBERRY CHERRY Pop Tarts

+GF

Looking back, most of us can remember this overly sugary, sticky and somewhat chemical-smelling breakfast food. You guys know what we're talking about. We've taken this kid-breakfast-staple and turned it on its head. Our pop tarts are fresh, sweet, slightly tart and way healthier than your typical boxed version.

—LM + AM

MAKES 8 POP TARTS

1¾ cups (268 g) frozen cherries

1¾ cups (268 g) frozen whole strawberries

Juice and zest of 1 clementine

1 tbsp (14 g) vegan granulated sugar

1 tbsp (8 g) all-purpose flour

1 (16-oz [453-g]) package premade pie dough

1 cup (125 g) vegan powdered sugar

3 tbsp (45 ml) almond milk

In a large pot, add the cherries and strawberries, and heat over medium heat. Add the clementine juice, zest and granulated sugar to the pot. Stir the mixture well enough to see the sugar dissolve, about 3 minutes. Once the sugar is dissolved, cover the pot with a lid and let the fruit, sugar and clementine juice cook for 10 minutes.

While the fruit is cooking, dust your clean countertop with the flour. Take your vegan pie crust and roll it out over the flour. Cut the pie crust into 3 x 5-inch (7 x 12-cm) rectangles until you're completely out of dough. You should have at least 6 pairs of rectangles. Place the rectangles on a parchment-lined baking sheet. Cut about three 1-inch (2.5-cm) slits into half of the rectangles.

Remove the lid from the pot and stir the fruit. Keep the lid off of the pot and allow the fruit to reduce until all of the liquid is gone. This should take about 25 minutes.

Once the liquid is gone, remove the pot from the heat and allow the fruit to cool. At this point, pre-heat the oven to the temperature instructed on the pie dough container.

Assemble the tarts by piling about 2 tablespoons (30 g) of fruit onto the half of the rectangles that don't have the cuts in them. Layer the other rectangles on top of the fruit. Press the edges of the tarts together with a fork.

Put the tarts in the oven for the amount of time instructed on the pie crust packaging.

Remove the pop tarts from the oven and allow them to cool for at least 5 minutes before serving.

To make the frosting, whisk the powdered sugar and almond milk in a small bowl until thick and creamy. If the frosting is too thick, add a bit more milk. If the frosting is too thin, add a bit more sugar until you get the consistency you're looking for. Drizzle on the cooled pop tarts.

Baked JAMMY OVERNIGHT OATMEAL

+SFO +GFO

I'm still not a fan of regular porridge—it's a texture thing. But baked oatmeal sure has won me over, especially when paired with jam and fresh fruit.

Feel free to choose a different nut butter than cashew and a jam other than berry. Switch the fresh fruit garnish accordingly to match that of the jam, and the nut garnish to match that of the nut butter as well. —CS

SERVES 4

3 cups (710 ml) and 3 tbsp (45 ml) unsweetened plain or vanilla cashew milk (or other favorite plant-based milk), divided

1 tbsp (12 g) plus 2 tsp (8 g) chia seeds, divided

¼ cup (64 g) natural creamy cashew butter

2½ tbsp (50 g) agave nectar

1½ tsp (8 ml) pure vanilla extract

Pinch of coarse kosher salt

½ tsp ground ginger

¼ tsp grated nutmeg

1 tsp dried or fresh orange zest

2 cups (160 g) old-fashioned rolled oats (use gluten-free oats)

¾ cup (180 g) favorite vegan berry jam, preferably fruit-sweetened

1 tsp baking powder

TOPPINGS
Fresh berries
Unsalted dry-roasted cashew pieces

(continued)

In an 8 x 10-inch (20 x 25-cm) or 9-inch (23-cm) square baking dish, combine 3 tablespoons (45 ml) of the milk with 1 tablespoon (12 g) of the chia seeds. In the meantime, blend the remaining 3 cups (710 ml) milk with the cashew butter, agave nectar, vanilla, salt, ginger, nutmeg and orange zest. Add the oats to the chia and milk mixture. Pour the liquid ingredients on top of the oats and fold to thoroughly combine. Cover and refrigerate overnight, for about 8 hours.

Preheat the oven to 350°F (177°C). In a small bowl, combine the jam with the remaining 2 teaspoons (8 g) chia seeds. Set it aside.

Stir the baking powder into the overnight oats, making sure to thoroughly combine. Drop the jam by spoonfuls on top of the oats, then swirl it with the tip of a butter knife. Bake the oatmeal for 1 hour, or until golden brown and set in the center. Serve with fresh berries and cashew pieces.

Turmeric BLUEBERRY MUFFINS

+SFO

This is a small batch of yellow-hued muffins for smaller households! You can definitely double the recipe for a more generous outcome. Otherwise, these will also bake really well in a countertop oven if you happen to have one of those. I love the yellow hue the turmeric gives these, and do I even need to sing the praises of the awesome blue-colored berry? You already know how great they are in pretty much anything. —CS

MAKES 6 MUFFINS

STREUSEL
1 tbsp (5 g) old-fashioned oats
2 tbsp (15 g) light spelt flour
2 tbsp (30 g) packed organic light brown sugar

½ tsp ground cinnamon
1 tbsp (15 ml) neutral-flavored oil

MUFFINS
5 tbsp (75 g) organic light brown sugar
5 tbsp (75 ml) unsweetened vegan milk (use soy-free)
3 tbsp (45 g) vanilla-flavored vegan yogurt (use soy-free)
2 tbsp (30 ml) neutral-flavored oil
1 tsp pure vanilla extract
1 tsp ground turmeric
¼ tsp pink sea salt
1 cup (120 g) light spelt flour
1 tsp baking powder
½ cup (74 g) fresh blueberries

Preheat the oven to 350°F (177°C). Line 6 cups of a muffin tin with liners.

FOR THE STREUSEL
Place the oats, flour, sugar and cinnamon in a small bowl. Stir to combine. Add the oil and use your fingers to thoroughly mix and create the streusel. Set it aside.

FOR THE MUFFINS
In a medium bowl, whisk to combine the sugar, milk, yogurt, oil, vanilla, turmeric and salt. Sift the flour and baking powder on top, and stir until just combined. Gently fold the blueberries into the batter. Divide the batter among your prepared liners and divide the streusel among the muffins, lightly pressing down.

Bake for 26 minutes, or until a toothpick inserted in the center of a muffin comes out clean. Carefully remove muffins from the tin and place them on a cooling rack. Let them cool before eating.

*SEE PHOTO INSERT

Baked APPLE AND SPICE OVERNIGHT OATS

+GFO +SFO

While I'm not the biggest fan of warm oats, there's nothing I wouldn't do for a bowl of overnight cereal such as this one. With a nice mix of rich spices and tender apples to boost its flavor, it's the ideal warmer weather breakfast item. You can peel the apples if you prefer, but I never do. Leaving the peel on also makes for pretty results with red apples such as Gala. —CS

SERVES 2 TO 4

OATS

1 cup (80 g) old-fashioned oats (use gluten-free)

1 cup (235 ml) unsweetened plain or vanilla cashew milk, or other plant-based milk (use soy-free)

1 cup (240 g) unsweetened plain or vanilla coconut yogurt (soy-free, optional)

Pinch coarse kosher salt

GARNISHES

6 small apples, quartered and cored, each quarter cut into 2 wedges

2 tbsp (30 ml) lemon juice, divided

1 tsp ground cinnamon

¼ cup (80 g) agave nectar

¼ tsp ground ginger

¼ tsp ground turmeric

2 tbsp (32 g) roasted cashew butter

¾ cup (90 g) toasted cashew pieces

Roasted black and white sesame seeds

FOR THE OATS

In a medium bowl, stir to combine the oats, milk, yogurt (if using) and salt. Cover tightly and refrigerate overnight, or for about 8 hours. Bring the oats back to room temperature before serving, about 1 hour.

FOR THE GARNISHES

In the meantime, preheat the oven to 400°F (204°C). Line a baking sheet with parchment paper.

In a large bowl, toss the apples with 1 tablespoon (15 ml) of the lemon juice and the cinnamon until well coated. Place them evenly on the prepared sheet, and bake until just tender, about 30 minutes. Set it aside. You can chop the apples before adding them to the oats if desired.

In a small bowl, whisk to combine the agave, remaining 1 tablespoon (15 ml) lemon juice, ginger and turmeric.

Stir the cashew butter into the oats. Divide it among 2 or 4 bowls, depending on your appetite. Top with the agave mixture, baked apples, cashew pieces and sesame seeds to taste. Serve immediately.

Matcha COCONUT GRANOLA

+SF +GFO

With its earthy flavor, matcha is the perfect match-ah for the richness of coconut and almond or cashew butter. You can also rejoice because this granola yields large clusters! It's perfect to enjoy with a big splash of any plant-based milk or a super-large spoonful of plain coconut yogurt. —CS

MAKES 6 CUPS (520 G)

½ cup (160 g) agave nectar

¼ cup (56 g) solid coconut oil

3 tbsp (48 g) natural almond or cashew butter (roasted or not)

½ tsp coarse kosher salt

2 generous cups (200 g) old-fashioned rolled oats (use gluten-free)

1 cup (75 g) unsweetened coconut flakes

½ cup (85 g) blanched raw whole almonds or cashews

2 tsp (4 g) matcha green tea powder

Preheat the oven to 275°F (135°C). Line a large rimmed baking sheet with parchment paper.

Place the agave, oil, almond butter and salt in a small saucepan. Warm over low heat until the ingredients are smooth and melted. Set it aside to cool for a couple of minutes.

In a large bowl, stir to combine the oats, coconut, almonds and green tea. Pour the liquid ingredients onto the dry and fold to thoroughly combine.

Evenly place the mixture on the prepared sheet and bake for 40 minutes, or until golden brown. Flip with a large spatula once after 20 minutes, and then every 10 minutes. Keep a close eye on the granola so as not to let it burn. Once ready, let the granola cool on the sheet in an even layer. It will crisp up as it cools. Once completely cooled, break into clusters and store in an airtight container at room temperature for up to 1 week.

Peanut Butter FRENCH TOAST

+SFO +GFO

Decadent breakfast, ahoy. Not only is there nut butter in the French toast batter itself, but it can also be found in the caramel to be drizzled on top! Now you'll know a real nut butter lover when you see one. —CS

MAKES 10 SLICES (WILL VARY DEPENDING ON THE SIZE OF SLICES USED)

1 cup (235 ml) unsweetened plain plant-based milk of choice (use soy-free)

½ cup (90 g) natural creamy peanut butter or any nut butter

1½ tbsp (12 g) organic cornstarch

1 tbsp (8 g) chickpea flour

1 tsp pure vanilla extract (use gluten-free)

½ tsp ground cinnamon

Pinch of coarse kosher salt

Oil spray

10 slices stale vegan bread (sourdough or pretzel breads are both great) (use gluten-free)

Peanut Butter Caramel Sauce (page 421)

Whipped Coconut Cream (optional, page 423)

In a blender, combine the milk, nut butter, cornstarch, chickpea flour, vanilla, cinnamon and salt; blend until smooth. Transfer the mixture to a large, shallow dish.

Spray a large skillet with a fair amount of oil. Heat on medium-high. Dip 1 slice of bread at a time in the batter, letting the excess drip back into the dish. Be sure to add extra milk as needed if the batter is too thick. You want to work in batches of 2 to 3 slices to avoid overcrowding the pan. Cook on each side for about 4 to 5 minutes, or until golden brown. Adjust the heat as needed. Repeat with the remaining slices, adding an extra coat of oil spray if needed. Serve immediately with a healthy drizzle of caramel and a little dollop of whipped cream, if desired.

Good Morning
MISO RICE

Occasionally, sweet breakfasts just won't do and I go craving something healthy, filling and savory. This would make for a beautiful lunch or supper as well!

I love the nutty and earthy flavor of forbidden rice (also known as black rice), but you can use whatever rice or grain you prefer here. Just be sure to adjust the amount of cooking liquid and time needed accordingly.

Sunchokes are also known as Jerusalem artichokes. They are a root vegetable with a flavor reminiscent of artichokes, hence the name. Word to the wise: sunchokes are delicious but they contain inulin, a carbohydrate that can cause digestive issues in sensitive individuals. It's best to slowly ease into your love-affair-to-be with the, um, tooty rooty. —CS

SERVES 4

8 dried shiitake mushrooms

MISO RICE
1 tsp toasted sesame oil

1 cup (210 g) dry forbidden rice, thoroughly rinsed and drained

1¾ cups (415 ml) water (including the reserved mushroom liquid above)

1 tbsp (18 g) white miso

1 tsp Emergency Broth Powder (page 223)

¼ cup (60 ml) water (or use vegetable broth and nix the broth powder)

VEGETABLE TOPPING
1 lb (454 g) fresh sunchokes, brushed clean and cut into bite-size pieces, steamed until fork-tender

1 tbsp (15 ml) toasted sesame oil

¾ cup (144 g) drained vegan kimchi, minced

Minced scallion greens

Soak the mushrooms in filtered water for at least 30 minutes. Once rehydrated, drain in a fine-mesh sieve lined with a paper towel on top of a bowl large enough to catch the soaking liquid. Set the liquid aside. Give a quick rinse to the mushrooms to remove any grit, and gently squeeze out any extra moisture. Mince the mushrooms and discard the stems if they are tough.

FOR THE MISO RICE
In a large pot, combine the oil, rinsed rice and water (don't forget to include the mushroom-soaking liquid in the water, too). Cover with a lid, bring to a boil, lower the heat and cook until the water is absorbed, about 25 minutes. Let it stand, covered, for 10 minutes, and then fluff. Refrigerate in an airtight container for up to 3 days.

Once ready to reheat, combine the miso with the broth powder and plain water, whisking to combine. Pour this mixture onto the rice and simmer just until the rice is heated through and the liquid has evaporated slightly, about 5 minutes.

FOR THE VEGETABLE TOPPING
Gently and partially smash the steamed sunchokes and add to the saucepan with the sesame oil. Cook until golden brown, about 6 minutes, stirring occasionally. Adjust the heat as needed. Add the minced mushrooms and kimchi. Cook until heated through and fragrant, about 4 minutes. Divide the rice among the bowls, and top with the vegetables and scallions.

Amba BREAKFAST WRAPS

These fun, portable and nutrition-packed wraps are kept just mild enough to be a knockout come breakfast time. —CS

SERVES 4

1 tbsp (15 ml) melted coconut oil

1 lb (454 g) super-firm tofu, crumbled into bite-size pieces

3 scallions, trimmed, white and green parts separated, chopped

1 tsp Emergency Broth Powder (page 223)

1 tbsp (15 ml) shoyu

1 tbsp (15 ml) mirin

1½–3 tsp (7–14 g) vegan green or red curry paste (quantity to taste)

1 large clove garlic, minced

1 cup (134 g) frozen green peas

Vegan mayo or roasted cashew butter

Amba (page 410)

4 (10-inch [25-cm]) vegan flour tortillas, lavash bread or pita bread

Fresh baby spinach

1 avocado, halved, pitted, peeled and sliced (optional)

Chopped fresh cilantro (optional)

Place the oil in a large wok or skillet over medium-high heat and add the tofu and white parts of the scallion. Fry for 2 minutes and add the broth powder, stirring to combine. Fry until golden brown, about another 4 minutes. Adjust the heat as needed and stir occasionally.

In the meantime, whisk the shoyu, mirin, curry paste and garlic in a small bowl. Pour it onto the tofu and stir to combine. Add the green peas and cook until thawed, about 4 minutes.

Spread the mayo or cashew butter and amba (to taste) on a flour tortilla. Add a handful of baby spinach, curried tofu, avocado (if using), chopped green parts of the scallion and cilantro (if using). Wrap it up tightly, repeat with the remaining tortillas and eat.

Kimchi TOFU SCRAMBLE

I love to eat this umami-rich tofu scramble on its own, but if you need an especially energy-packed meal, serve it on top of your favorite noodles or rice. —CS

SERVES 3 TO 4

1 tbsp (15 ml) toasted sesame oil

1 lb (454 g) super-firm tofu, crumbled or cut into ½-inch (1.3-cm) pieces

3 tbsp (45 ml) kimchi brine

1–2 tbsp (20–40 g) Gochujang Paste (page 413), to taste

3 tbsp (45 ml) tamari

1 cup (192 g) drained and chopped vegan kimchi

6 dried shiitake mushrooms, rehydrated, rinsed and minced

1 lb (454 g) small fresh broccoli florets, steamed or roasted until just tender and still crisp

Cooked Asian noodles or rice of choice, enough to serve 3 to 4 (optional)

Sliced scallion, for topping

Roasted black or white sesame seeds, for topping

Heat the oil in a large skillet and add the tofu. Cook over medium-high heat until the tofu is browned, about 8 minutes. Stir occasionally. In the meantime, in a small bowl, whisk to combine the kimchi brine, gochujang paste and tamari. Set aside. Add the kimchi and mushrooms to the pan, and cook for 2 minutes. Add half of the kimchi brine mixture and cook until evaporated, about 4 minutes. Stir frequently. Add the broccoli and cook just until heated through.

Serve on top of noodles or rice, if desired, with drizzles of remaining kimchi brine mixture. Top with scallion and sesame seeds.

*SEE PHOTO INSERT

Corn WAFFLES

A little insider tip: you can make these into breakfast-friendly waffles by nixing the pepper and scallion, using fine sea salt instead of smoked sea salt and switching from cornmeal to 1 cup (120 g) whole wheat pastry or all-purpose flour instead. They're so crispy and great with fruit and maple syrup! Otherwise, I serve this as is with homemade chili, fresh salsa or even hummus. If you'd like, you could use a pepper and some pineapple from the Pique (page 184) instead of the jalapeño pepper, if using. —CS

SERVES 6

1 tbsp (8 g) organic cornstarch

½ cup (120 ml) water

1 cup (235 ml) unsweetened plain plant-based milk of choice

1 tbsp (15 ml) apple cider vinegar

½ cup (120 ml) vegan lager beer

¼ cup (60 ml) grapeseed oil or olive oil

1 generous tsp smoked sea salt or fine sea salt

2 tbsp (24 g) organic light brown sugar

1 jalapeño pepper, trimmed, cored and minced

1 large scallion, trimmed and minced

1 cup (120 g) whole wheat pastry or all-purpose flour

1 cup (160 g) organic medium-grind cornmeal

2 tbsp (10 g) nutritional yeast

2 tsp (7 g) baking powder

½ tsp baking soda

Nonstick cooking spray or oil spray

In a small bowl, combine the cornstarch and water and whisk to dissolve. Cook in the microwave for 30 seconds, or until cloudy and thickened to a jelly-like consistency. Don't overcook or the mixture will get clumpy. Use ¼ cup (60 ml) of the mixture. Discard the rest. (Alternatively, do this in a small saucepan over medium heat for about 2 minutes, stirring occasionally.)

In a large bowl, combine the milk with the vinegar. Let it stand 5 minutes so that it curdles.

Whisk the cornstarch mixture, beer, oil, salt, sugar, pepper and scallion into the curdled milk. Add the flour, cornmeal, nutritional yeast, baking powder and baking soda on top of the wet ingredients, and briefly whisk to combine. It's fine if a few lumps remain, but do not overmix.

Let it stand for 15 minutes, and then preheat the waffle iron to give extra time to the batter. Once the iron is hot, give a quick stir to the batter, generously coat the waffle iron with spray and cover the entire heating plate with batter (or follow the manufacturer's specific instructions). I get a total of 12 deep-pocketed, ¾-inch (2-cm) thick Belgian waffles on my iron, cooking those 4 at a time. Cook until golden brown and crisp: it usually takes 8 to 10 full minutes on my waffle iron heated to 400°F (204°C).

Transfer the waffles to a cooling rack and repeat with the remaining batter, making sure to gently stir the batter before making each waffle.

Reheat in a 325°F (163°C) oven until crisp again, about 10 minutes. These can also be toasted to reheat.

*SEE PHOTO INSERT

PAN CON SALSA Y Aguacate

+SF

Food always sounds fancier in another language, doesn't it? Pan = bread, con = with, salsa = salsa, y = and, aguacate = avocado. Get it? Avocado toast with salsa. Nothing could possibly be wrong with this concept. —CS

SERVES 4

4 slices vegan sourdough bread, toasted
2 small ripe avocados, halved, pitted and peeled
Roasted Corn Pique Salsa (page 184)
Minced fresh cilantro

Place the toast on plates. Use a fork to chunkily smash the avocados. Divide it among the toast and arrange in an even layer. Top with a fair amount of salsa, without overloading to avoid making for messy eats. Top with cilantro and serve immediately.

Roasted PECAN RAISIN LOAF

+SFO

Such a comforting and beautifully textured loaf usually doesn't last too long in my household! Serve with a cup of tea or coffee, or a glass of plant-based milk and kick your shoes off while you're at it. Life (and loaf) is suddenly good again. Once cooled, add a glaze if desired by whisking together until smooth: half a cup (60 g) of organic powdered sugar with 1 to 1½ tablespoons (15 to 23 ml) of orange juice. Make sure it's just liquid enough to spread without being too runny, plus add an extra handful of dry roasted pecan pieces on top for extra crunch. —CS

MAKES ONE 8-INCH (20-CM) LOAF

1 cup plus 2 tbsp (265 ml) fresh orange juice
¾ cup plus 2 tbsp (168 g) organic light brown sugar or Sucanat
½ cup (120 g) unsweetened plain coconut yogurt or other plant-based yogurt (use soy-free)
¼ cup (60 ml) grapeseed oil or other mild-flavored oil
2 tbsp (30 ml) Barbados rum or other rum
2 tsp (10 ml) pure vanilla extract
Generous 1 tsp dried or fresh orange zest
½ tsp Himalayan pink salt
½ tsp ground cinnamon
½ cup (60 g) golden raisins
2½ cups (300 g) whole wheat pastry or all-purpose flour
2½ tsp (10 g) baking powder
½ cup (60 g) chopped toasted pecans

Preheat the oven to 350°F (177°C). Line an 8 x 4-inch (20 x 10-cm) loaf pan with parchment paper, or lightly coat with nonstick cooking spray (use soy-free).

In a large bowl, whisk to combine the orange juice, sugar, yogurt, oil, rum, vanilla, zest, salt and cinnamon. Add the raisins and stir to combine. Sift the flour and baking powder on top. Then add pecans and stir until just combined. Use a rubber spatula to scrape the batter into the prepared pan.

Bake for 1 hour, or until a toothpick inserted in the center of the cake comes out clean. Place it on a wire rack for 15 minutes before carefully removing from the pan. Let it cool completely before slicing.

Store the loaf wrapped in foil at room temperature or in the refrigerator for up to 4 days.

Blueberry STREUSEL SQUARE

+SFO

While I'm on the subject of gardening disasters, we tried to grow our very own blueberry bushes this year, and needless to say, it didn't take long for them to go out in flames. Not literally. But still, sigh. Rest assured that blueberries bought from the market will work just beautifully in these sweet and tart slices, if you're anything of a gardening drama queen like I am. And if you manage to grow your own, you big show-off? All the better. —CS

SERVES 6

FILLING
12 oz (340 g) fresh blueberries

¼ cup (50 g) natural cane sugar

1½ tsp (8 ml) lime or lemon juice

1 tbsp (8 g) organic cornstarch

CRUST
1¾ cups (210 g) light spelt flour

⅓ cup (40 g) plus ¼ cup (30 g) hazelnut meal, divided

¼ cup plus 2 tbsp (72 g) organic light brown sugar, not packed

¼ cup plus 2 tbsp (72 g) natural cane sugar

½ tsp fine sea salt

⅓ cup plus 2 tbsp (110 ml) neutral-flavored oil

⅓ cup (80 ml) cold water, as needed

Vegan vanilla ice cream, for serving (use soy-free)

Preheat the oven to 375°F (190°C). Line a 9-inch (23-cm) pan with parchment paper. Set it aside.

FOR THE FILLING
In a small bowl, combine the blueberries, sugar and lime juice. Sprinkle the cornstarch on top and fold to combine. Set it aside.

FOR THE CRUST
In a large bowl, combine the flour, ⅓ cup (40 g) of hazelnut meal, sugars and salt. Drizzle the oil on top, stirring with a fork to combine. Add the water, still stirring with a fork, until moist enough to stick together when pinched. Reserve a generous ½ cup (120 g) of the dough. Press the rest down evenly in the prepared pan, with raised edges of about ½ inch (1.3 cm). Cover the bottom evenly with the remaining ¼ cup (30 g) hazelnut meal.

Top evenly with the blueberry mixture. Break the reserved dough into crumbs, and sprinkle it over the blueberry mixture, pressing down just slightly.

Bake for 26 minutes, or until the crust is golden brown and the blueberries are juicy. Let it cool slightly before slicing and serve with a generous scoop of vegan ice cream. Leftovers will keep well at room temperature until the next day, tightly wrapped in foil.

*SEE PHOTO INSERT

Good Oats WITH ALMONDS, COCONUT SUGAR AND VANILLA

This oatmeal! It's my fave way to make oats and it never gets old. I make it almost every day, and it gives me fuel for bike rides, the gym and life. It's great for breakfast, lunch or dinner. The recipe takes a few minutes to make and tastes like cake. The best part is that you can dress it up or down as you see fit. Sometimes I'll add a whack load of stuff like cinnamon, ginger, chia seeds and goji berries, and other days I'll just do coconut sugar with some nut butter. IT'S UP TO YOU. Since this recipe is more on the decadent side, it's perfect for folks who are trying to get into eating oatmeal everyday. —EvE

SERVES 1

½ cup (40 g) rolled oats

1 cup (235 ml) cold water

Pinch of Himalayan salt

1–3 tbsp (15-45 ml) nondairy milk (optional)

TOPPINGS
2–3 tbsp (24-36 g) coconut sugar

1–2 tbsp (14-28 g) almond butter

¼ tsp vanilla powder

2 tbsp (21 g) chopped almonds (optional)

In a small pot, combine the oats and the cold water with a pinch of salt. Bring it to a boil, stirring occasionally with a spurtle or wooden spoon. Once boiling, lower the heat to low (still stirring occasionally) until the oats are the consistency you like. I like mine thick. Then I add nondairy milk to thin it out *and* cool it down so I can eat it right away.

Top it off with all the goodies you want, adjusting the amounts according to your own preferences.

Fabulous OATMEAL WITH BERRIES AND SEEDS

I eat oatmeal every morning, and if I don't get the chance at the start of my day, I often end up making it for dinner. I guess my body just needs its daily dose. I make my oatmeal in a particular way that gets it nice and creamy, and I LOVE sweet things (big surprise, look at my blog and my first cookbook, Rawsome Vegan Baking) so my oats are regularly smothered in nut butter and coconut sugar. I am essentially eating a giant bowl of warm cookie dough each time I sit down with my oatmeal. I am not mad about it. This recipe is extra nutritious though, thanks to the berries and seeds. —EvE

SERVES 3

3 cups (710 ml) cold water

⅛ tsp sea salt

1½ cups (120 g) rolled oats

1 tsp ground cinnamon

1 tsp vanilla extract

1 tsp ground ginger

¼ cup (48 g) coconut sugar or your fave sweetener

3–4 tbsp (42-56 g) almond butter or your fave nut butter

½ cup (120 ml) cold nondairy milk

TOPPINGS
1 cup (150 g) raspberries

1 cup (150 g) blackberries

3–4 tbsp (24-32 g) pumpkin seeds

3 tbsp (30 g) chia seeds

3 tbsp (30 g) hemp seeds

In a small saucepan, combine the water, salt and rolled oats and bring to a boil. Then reduce the heat to low and add the rest of the ingredients except the milk. Once the oats are the consistency you like, remove them from the heat and pour in the milk. It will cool it down so you can eat it right away and it makes the oatmeal even creamier! Add more of anything you want.

Top with . . . the toppings. And enjoy! I sprinkle a li'l more coconut sugar on mine, because I live for sugar.

Choco NICE CREAM WITH PEANUT BUTTER OATS, CHOCOLATE CHUNKS AND DOUGHNUT HOLES

JUST WOW. #DessertForBreakfast —EvE

SERVES 1 OR 2

OATS
1 cup (235 ml) cold water
½ cup (40 g) rolled oats
Pinch of Himalayan salt

NICE CREAM
3 frozen bananas
2 tbsp (14 g) cacao powder
½ tsp vanilla powder
¼ cup (60 ml) almond milk

TOPPINGS
Peanut butter
Raw vegan doughnut holes
Chocolate chunks
Coconut sugar

FOR THE OATS

In a small saucepan, combine the water, oats and salt. Bring it to a boil, stirring occasionally with a spurtle or wooden spoon. Once boiling, reduce the heat to low and cook (still stirring occasionally) until the oats are the consistency you like. I like mine thick, and then I add nondairy milk to thin it out. (As the oats cook, make your nice cream).

FOR THE NICE CREAM

Blend all of the ingredients until smooth. Scoop it into a bowl, and then pour your oats around it. Top with peanut butter, raw doughnut holes, chocolate chunks, coconut sugar and whatever else you like!

Crunchy TOAST WITH PEANUT BUTTER AND QUICK BERRY JAM

This jam is about as basic as you can get: it's just berries mashed up and mixed with chia seeds. The chia seeds make the texture like jam. It's awesome, very good for you and takes like 10 minutes to whip up. I do recommend eating the jam ASAP, though; it's too fresh to keep in the fridge in large amounts for a week. As expected, PB&J is a classic fave for a reason: it's freaking delicious. The textures of crunchy toast with creamy, salty peanut butter and finally sweet, gooey jam . . . WHAT'S NOT TO WORSHIP!? I topped mine off with more seeds and berries because it looks pretty, and drizzled on some maple syrup because "add maple syrup" is my one consistent life rule.

SERVES 1 OR 2

BERRY CHIA JAM
⅓ cup (50 g) fresh or frozen berries
2 tbsp (20 g) chia seeds
1 tsp acerola cherry powder (optional)

(continued)

PEANUT BUTTER TOAST

2–4 tbsp (22–45 g) peanut butter or almond butter

2 slices your fave bread, toasted to crunchy perfection

TOPPINGS

Handful of fresh or frozen berries

2 tbsp (16 g) pumpkin seeds

1 tbsp (10 g) hemp seeds

2 tbsp (30 ml) maple syrup

FOR THE BERRY CHIA JAM

Thaw the berries if frozen (I just threw mine in a microwave for a minute). Mash the berries into a chunky paste. Stir in the chia seeds and let the seeds and berries sit together for 15 minutes or so: the chia seeds will thicken up the mixture into delicious, fresh jam. Add the cherry powder if you want.

FOR THE PEANUT BUTTER TOAST

Spread the peanut butter on your toast, followed by the jam. Then garnish with your toppings and enjoy!

Peach GINGER SMOOTHIE

+GF +QP

I've made three of these smoothies in three days . . . and yes, all for myself. There's no sharing when you find a drink that is this delicious. There just can't be! Trust me, one sip and you're sucked into the world of peachy spring goodness, with just a hint of ginger for snap. —AS

SERVES 1 TO 2

1 cup (235 ml) hemp milk

1 large banana

1 cup (150 g) frozen peaches

1" (2.5-cm) piece fresh ginger, finely chopped or grated (about 1 tbsp [8 g])

1 tbsp (14 g) ground flaxseed

1 cup (235 g) ice

Add everything to a blender or food processor, giving a quick blend between the addition of each two ingredients to ensure perfect mixing. Mix the entirety of ingredients for 1 to 2 minutes. Pour the smoothie into a large glass and enjoy!

Strawberry CHEESECAKE SMOOTHIE

Vanilla protein powder gives this smoothie a rich, creamy taste—hence the cheesecake part of the title. The addition of more cashews adds a bit of fullness and more protein to the smoothie, while the strawberry and granola "crust" keep it light and sweet . . . like having dessert for breakfast! —AS

SERVES 1 TO 2

1 scoop (7 g) vegan vanilla protein powder

1 cup (150 g) fresh strawberries

½ cup (55 g) raw cashews

3 pitted Medjool dates

1½ cups (355 ml) nondairy milk (we like coconut!)

1 cup (235 g) ice

Granola, for garnish (optional)

Blend all the ingredients except the granola in a high-speed blender until smooth. Top with a bit of granola (it's like the "crust" of the cheesecake!) and serve in two small glasses—or one big one.

Roasted STRAWBERRY SMOOTHIE

The only thing better than fresh summer strawberries? Rich, sweet, roasted strawberries—any time of the year! If you want a decadent-tasting smoothie without a ton of work, try this beauty on for size. —AS

SERVES 1 TO 2

2 cups (300 g) fresh strawberries

1 large frozen banana

3 pitted Medjool dates

1½ cups (355 ml) nondairy milk

1 cup (235 g) ice

1 scoop (about 7 g) vegan protein powder (optional)

Preheat the oven to 450°F (232°C). Then spread the strawberries onto a lined baking sheet and roast in the oven for 15 to 20 minutes, until the berries are caramelized and smelling sticky sweet. Remove from the oven and let cool.

Once cooled, place the strawberries, frozen banana, dates, milk, ice and protein powder into a high-speed blender and blend until smooth. Serve in two small glasses or one large one.

Breakfast SMOOTHIE

+SF +GF +QP

Let this recipe be a blueprint for all your breakfast smoothies to come. The beauty of smoothies is that with the flip of a switch you have all you need for a filling breakfast in a matter of minutes. This recipe is easily adaptable to suit your preferred fruit, greens and nut butter. —MR

SERVES 1

1 cup (150 g) frozen berries

½ frozen banana, cubed

1 tsp chia seeds

1 small handful rolled oats

1 tbsp (11 g) almond butter or any nut butter

¾ cup (180 ml) almond milk or water

1 large handful spinach

1 tsp maca powder (optional)

Simply blend all of the ingredients in a blender until smooth and creamy. Place it in a mason jar or cup, and take it with you on your way out the door!

Note: If you're new to breakfast smoothies, consider sticking with spinach (as opposed to kale) for your greens of choice. It is mild in flavor and completely masked by the taste of the fruit.

Energizing
PEACH-MACA SMOOTHIE

+SF +GF +QP

If there were ever a superfood to invest in, it would be maca powder. Maca's flavor profile veers towards caramel (which is never a bad thing). It supplies the body with a natural energy boost—and therein lies its value as a superfood. Cheers to a great morning smoothie that is spiked with just the right amount of maca! —MR

SERVES 1

½ cup (75 g) frozen chopped peaches
½ cup (75 g) frozen strawberries
½–1 frozen banana
¾–1 cup (180–235 ml) almond milk
2 pitted Medjool dates
1 tbsp (7 g) maca powder

TOPPINGS
Cacao nibs
Any fruit (I love pomegranate seeds)
Unsweetened coconut flakes
Dried goji or mulberries (optional)

Simply add all of the ingredients to a blender, and mix until smooth and creamy. Pour it into a bowl and add as many toppings as you would like!

GREEN-VANILLA
Smoothie

+GF +QP

This is the ideal breakfast for when you don't have time for one. The nutty aroma of ground almonds mingles with maple and vanilla, creating a delicious smoothie that leans on the side of indulgence. Pause the morning rush for a well-crafted smoothie that is as functional as it is satisfying. —MR

SERVES 2

3 big handfuls spinach or kale
2 ripe bananas, cubed
2 small handfuls rolled oats
2 tbsp (23 g) almond butter or cashew butter
2 cups (470 ml) almond milk
1 tbsp (15 ml) maple syrup (optional)
1 tsp pure vanilla powder or extract

Simply place everything in a blender, and blend until the spinach or kale has been fully broken down and incorporated. Pour it into a mason jar or cup and enjoy on the go!

A Nice GREEN SMOOTHIE WITH MINT AND TURMERIC

I was gonna call this a "healing" green smoothie blah blah blah, but then I thought, "Hmm, don't wanna buy into that pseudoscience stuff, so I'll keep it simple." Honestly, I don't know if this smoothie will heal anything for you, but in my opinion it's at least certainly nice and yummy and green. I'll leave it at that. I am not a doctor. —EvE

SERVES 2

3 frozen bananas

2 tbsp (5 g) chopped fresh mint

½ tsp ground turmeric

½ tsp ground ginger

¼ tsp vanilla bean powder

1 tbsp (15 ml) date syrup

2 cups (470 ml) water

¼ cup (32 g) pumpkin seeds

1-2 cups (40-80 g) spinach

Blend everything up, adjust according to taste and drink!

Goji APPLE SMOOTHIE

This recipe came together randomly and ended up blowing my mind. It's nice and sweet but also super nutritious. It contains nearly 20 percent of your recommended daily intake for protein, 58 percent for riboflavin (B2), 79 percent for pyridoxine (B6), 499 percent for vitamin C (!!!), 107 percent for copper, 28 percent for vitamin K, 37 percent for magnesium, 64 percent for manganese, 36 percent for potassium, 30 percent for selenium, and I could just keep going. —EvE

SERVES 1 OR 2

1 frozen, chopped apple

2 frozen, peeled bananas

2 cups (184 g) green grapes

¼ cup (38 g) dried goji berries

1-2 cups (235-470 ml) water, as desired

Blend it all up and drink it all down.

Turmeric SMOOTHIE (DELICIOUS, DIFFERENT AND GOOD 4 U)

I highly suggest making this or something like this every day. Everyone agrees turmeric is suuuuper good for you; there are pretty legit claims it helps prevent cancer development and other diseases no one wants. Adding black pepper to turmeric allows it to be better absorbed by your body—by literally 200 to 2000 percent! —EvE

SERVES 1

1 red bell pepper, cored and roughly chopped

1 cup (150 g) frozen strawberries

¼ tsp ground turmeric

⅛ tsp ground black pepper

½ cup (120 ml) coconut milk

1 tsp maple syrup, or whatever sweetener you like

1 cup (235 ml) fresh orange juice

Blend it all up and drink it down.

Blueberry COCONUT SMOOTHIE WITH BAOBAB CARAMEL

The recipe is simple: basically just a bunch of frozen fruit blended together with coconut meat. Instead of plain maple syrup, I make a baobab caramel type thing; it's actually kinda freaky how it resembles caramel once you stir together the ingredients. Finally, we top it all off with fresh mango and chia seeds, because why not. I hope you thoroughly enjoy it. I definitely recommend pouring extra maple syrup on it. —EvE

SERVES 1 OR 2

SMOOTHIE

1 cup (150 g) frozen blueberries

1 cup (200 g) frozen pineapple

½ cup (38 g) coconut meat

1–2 cups (235–470 ml) coconut milk, or more as needed

BAOBAB CARAMEL

1 tbsp (15 ml) melted coconut oil

1 heaping tsp baobab powder

1 tbsp (15 ml) maple syrup

ADD-ONS

Fresh mango or other fruit

Chia seeds

Whatever your heart desires

FOR THE SMOOTHIE

Blend together the smoothie ingredients until smooth and thick like melty soft serve, adding coconut milk or other liquid as you go. Scoop it into a bowl.

FOR THE BAOBAB CARAMEL

Stir together the ingredients until it looks like caramel; it only takes a few seconds. Magic.

Scoop the fresh mango, caramel and chia seeds onto your smoothie and dig in with a spoon.

BEET AND BERRY
Smoothie

What can I say about this recipe? It's very bright, yummy and good for my bod. It takes 5 minutes to make and tastes like earthy sweet sunshine. If you don't like beets, you will not like this smoothie. If you do like beets, you will love this smoothie. —EvE

SERVES 1

1 peeled, chopped beet

1 cup (150 g) frozen raspberries

2 bananas

⅛ tsp vanilla powder

2 cups (470 ml) almond milk

Blend it all up until smooth and delicious. If you wanna add other ingredients, go right ahead.

PREMENSTRUAL
Smoothie

According to studies, there are certain foods that can help to decrease the discomforts of menstruation. Two of these are ginger and fennel. Consuming ⅛ teaspoon of ground ginger three times a day during your period can reduce menstrual bleeding by 50 percent, and eating fennel seeds can be as effective at alleviating cramps as pain-relief drugs like ibuprofen (probably because of fennel's ability to relax muscles). —EvE

SERVES 1

1 banana

1 orange

1 cup (150 g) frozen strawberries

¼ tsp fennel seeds

¼ tsp ground ginger

¼ tsp ground cinnamon

¼ tsp ground turmeric

⅛ tsp black pepper

1–2 cups (235–470 ml) nondairy milk, fresh juice or water

Blend everything together until smooth and delicious.

BLACKBERRY WALNUT
Smoothie

Creamy, sweet, rich and packed with nutrients: this one's a keeper. It reminds me of blueberry milkshakes, to be honest. —EvE

SERVES 1 OR 2

2 bananas

Heaping ¼ cup (38 g) frozen blackberries

1 tbsp (10 g) baobab powder

1 cup (235 ml) almond milk

Scant ¼ cup (30 g) walnuts

2 Brazil nuts

Blend it all up. Drink it down. Yum.

*SEE PHOTO INSERT

A Smoothie FOR EMOTIONAL STRENGTH

Keep yourself hydrated and in a positive mindset with this drink. And hey . . . you CAN do it! (Whatever it is.) —EvE

SERVES 1

1 cup (255 g) frozen mango

2 cups (470 ml) chilled coconut water

½ tsp ground turmeric

1 cup (195 g) pineapple chunks

1 yellow bell pepper, cored and chopped

1 banana

Blend it all up. LIVE YOUR LIFE.

ORANGE CRUSH
Smoothie

This smoothie has some veggies snuck in but you can't even tell: it's sweet, frosty and delicious. It reminded me of a slushie. Get your vitamin A and vitamin C right here, folks! —EvE

SERVES 1 OR 2

1 cup (255 g) frozen mango or banana

1 cup (195 g) pineapple chunks

1 orange bell pepper, cored and chopped

1 carrot, chopped

1 tbsp (10 g) baobab powder (optional)

2 cups (470 ml) chilled coconut water

Blend it all up and enjoy!

Magical GREEN SMOOTHIE WITH SPIRULINA, GINGER AND MUSHROOMS

I am very appreciative of the mushrooms in my life— how they help me to get into more positive thinking patterns and not obsess over negative ideas or irrational beliefs. You probably won't even taste the mushrooms in this drink, but they'll do ya good! Chaga and reishi are some of the original superfoods. —EvE

SERVES 1 OR 2

2 frozen bananas

¼ cup (10 g) chopped fresh mint

1 tsp spirulina powder

1½ cups (355 ml) chilled coconut milk

½ tsp grated fresh ginger

½ tsp reishi mushroom powder

½ tsp chaga mushroom powder

Pinch of stevia powder

1 tsp lemon juice

2 Brazil nuts

Handful of ice cubes (optional)

Blend all of the ingredients together until smooth. If you'd like it lighter and colder, add some ice cubes.

Ginger Berry
SMOOTHIE WITH SECRET INGREDIENT

I try to get vegetables into my diet whenever I can: they are incredibly good for you. The secret ingredient here is broccoli! Zucchini and cauliflower are other solid options for sneaking into fruity smoothies, thanks to their subtle flavors and colors. —EvE

SERVES 1 OR 2

1 frozen banana

½ cup (75 g) frozen blueberries

2 tbsp (20 g) hemp seeds

1 cup (70 g) chopped broccoli

2 cups (470 ml) grape juice

1 tsp ground ginger

½ tsp ground cinnamon

½ cup (98 g) pineapple chunks

Blend it all up and drink it all down. I topped mine with more bloobs and some chopped pistachios, 'cuz why not.

Creamy CASHEW, BANANA AND SPIRULINA SMOOTHIE

Spirulina is an excellent food: it's nutritious and full of protein and iron. In this recipe I combine it with sweet banana, mango, orange, creamy cashew milk and some vanilla. Spirulina has been consumed globally for centuries, with good reason. It's considered a dietary supplement because it's so nutritionally-dense. I try to get some in every day. —EvE

SERVES 1

¼ cup (27 g) cashews (preferably soaked in water for 6 hours, then rinsed)

1½ cups (355 ml) water

1 frozen banana

¼ cup (64 g) frozen mango

1 orange

¼ tsp vanilla

Pinch of sea salt

1 tsp spirulina powder

1 tbsp (10 g) chia seeds

⅓ cup (80 g) chia pudding (optional)

Blend the cashews and water together until smooth. You just made cashew milk. Add the rest of the ingredients except the pudding and blend until smooth. Adjust ingredients according to taste. Pour the chia pudding into the bottom of a glass; then pour your smoothie over top.

VARIATIONS

You can use chlorella powder instead of spirulina; you can use vanilla extract instead of vanilla powder; you can use any nondairy milk instead of using cashews and water.

GOLDEN MILK, **Hot or Iced**

+GF +QP

Golden Milk is made from steaming milk and blending in spices, sweetener and vanilla. It's like a steamer that tastes similar to a chai or spiced tea but is much creamier due to the milk, and a little warmer thanks to the addition of the turmeric. Golden Milk recipes have kind of exploded online lately, and I was lucky enough to try some at a friend's a few months ago, where I totally fell in love with it. So I've started making it myself at home! It's way cheaper, and it feels good knowing I can make an equally delicious version at home for about a tenth of the price. —AS

SERVES 1 TO 2

2 cups (470 ml) almond or coconut milk

2–3 tbsp (30–45 ml) maple syrup

1 tsp vanilla extract

1 tsp ground turmeric

½ tsp ground ginger

¼ tsp ground cinnamon

⅛ tsp ground cardamom

⅛ tsp nutmeg

Pinch of black pepper

Heat your almond or coconut milk in a small saucepan over medium heat (do NOT bring to a boil). Add the maple syrup, vanilla and spices, whisking until the spices are completely dissolved. Simmer for 4 to 5 minutes, until the milk is hot and everything is well combined. Taste and adjust the flavors to your preference.

Serve immediately or let the milk cool to room temperature, and then serve over ice. Refrigerated leftovers can either be reheated or served chilled over ice as well.

Note: Turmeric STAINS. Badly. Avoid using white dishes to cook or serve in unless you can wash them right after, and if you do get some turmeric stains on your countertop, I've read that vegetable oil and regular cleanser will usually get it off.

Peppermint HOT CHOCOLATE

+GF +QP

Ever since I first whipped this recipe up a few weeks ago, I've been coming back to this seasonal sipper on the regular because it's rich, chocolaty and envelops you in a sweet, decadent, Holiday-charged hug. Top it with a few marshmallows and DAMN GINA! You're gonna get just as addicted as I am, I just know it. —AS

SERVES 1 TO 2

1 (15-oz [444-ml]) can full-fat coconut milk

¼ cup (48 g) sugar

Pinch of salt

1 oz (28 g) chocolate chips or chopped bar chocolate

2 tbsp (14 g) cocoa powder

1 tsp vanilla extract

¾ tsp peppermint extract

Vegan marshmallows, if you like them

Mint, for garnish

In a medium saucepan, whisk together the milk, sugar and salt over low heat until the sugar dissolves. Whisk in the chocolate, cocoa powder, vanilla and peppermint extracts and cook until hot, NOT boiling. Pour it into a large mug, top with marshmallows and a fresh sprig of mint, and enjoy!

Note: For a lighter cup of hot chocolate, sub your favorite nondairy milk in place of the coconut milk.

For a plain mug of cocoa, you can omit the peppermint—or get creative and sub a different flavor like orange or lavender!

*SEE PHOTO INSERT

The Best
HOT CHOCOLATE

+GF +QP

This is a drink to tap into your childhood desires. With a pinch of cinnamon and rich almond milk, this hot chocolate is velvety smooth and utterly delicious, warming the body and the spirit. —MR

SERVES 2

2 cups (470 ml) almond milk
2 tbsp (14 g) raw cacao powder
3 tsp (15 ml) maple syrup
Dash of ground cinnamon

Warm the almond milk in a saucepan over low heat. Stir in the raw cacao powder, maple syrup and cinnamon, and heat until a low simmer starts. Then remove it from the heat and pour this delicious goodness into a mug to enjoy.

PUMPKIN SPICED
Steamer

+GF +QP

Why must coffee chains put dairy in their pumpkin spice mixture?! We vegans love our pumpkin.

So this is how we get our fix! A frothy, foamy, sweet, pumpkin-y cup of steamed dairy-free milk blended with cinnamon, nutmeg and ginger. It's fall, all wrapped up in a mug. Topped with a spoonful of coconut whip would be lovely, but this drink stands just fine on its own. It's the perfect fall drink for those avoiding caffeine or who just want a kid-friendly version. —AS

SERVES 1 TO 2

2 cups (470 ml) cold, dairy-free milk (we prefer coconut!)
3 tbsp (34 g) pumpkin purée
2 tbsp (30 ml) maple syrup
½ tsp vanilla extract
⅛ tsp ground ginger
⅛ tsp ground cinnamon
⅛ tsp ground nutmeg
⅛ tsp pumpkin pie spice (optional, just enhances the pumpkin flavor!)

In a saucepan, heat your milk on low to medium heat. Whisk in the pumpkin purée, maple syrup, vanilla and spices. Heat to your desired temperature, stirring occasionally.

If you have a milk frother (we have an attachment on our hand mixer), pour the milk into a large mug, or two smaller ones, and froth milk on high to create a thick foam. If you don't have a milk frother, pour the hot mixture into a high-speed blender and blend for 20 to 30 seconds, until a thick foam is created. Pour it into mugs and enjoy!

Leftovers can be refrigerated and reheated later.

Sparkling
MINT LEMONADE

This lemonade packs a ton of fresh flavor. And the addition of ginger beer gives it an extra kick! It's perfect for poolside sipping and is a great nonalcoholic fancy drink to serve at parties or with friends! —AS

SERVES 2

1 cup (240 ml) freshly squeezed lemon juice

½ cup (120 ml) nonalcoholic ginger beer

½ cup (12 g) packed fresh mint

4 tbsp (50 g) sugar

2 cups (480 ml) sparkling mineral water

2–3 cups (480-720 g) ice

Lemon slices, for garnish

Fresh mint sprigs, for garnish

Combine all of the ingredients except the lemon and mint in a high-speed blender until smooth, cracking the top just slightly while blending to release the air pressure inside. Serve with lemon slices and fresh mint sprigs!

Note: If your blender doesn't allow for air to be released while blending, blend everything BUT the sparkling water together and just stir that in afterwards to avoid a blender-splosion!

*SEE PHOTO INSERT

Cherry Chia
LEMONADE

If you're looking for the ultimate refreshing summer drink—you've found it! Full of fresh fruit and healthy chia seeds, this drink will taste as good as it makes you feel. —AS

SERVES 2 OR 3

8 cups (1.9 L) water

¼ cup (36 g) lemon zest

1 cup (235 ml) lemon juice

½ cup (120 ml) maple syrup or (100 g) sugar

1 cup (150 g) fresh cherries, pitted and halved

2 tbsp (20 g) chia seeds

In a pot, combine the water, lemon zest, lemon juice and maple syrup or sugar. Bring it to a boil.

Turn off the heat, toss in the cherries and chia seeds, and allow the mixture to cool. Refrigerate and serve over ice. Garnish with extra fresh cherry pieces if you like.

Note: You can always strain out the cherry chunks and lemon zest if you prefer, but do so before you add the chia seeds!

Turmeric MILK

+GF +QP

If coffee isn't your thing and neither is tea, well consider golden milk a happy medium. As pretty as it sounds, golden milk is also brimming with wellness. Nutrient-dense turmeric powder aids in anti-inflammatory properties while providing an earthy aroma. Top it off with a splash of maple and a pinch of cinnamon to balance the savory notes. Prepare for a delicious morning drink that will soon be added to your early morning ritual. —MR

SERVES 2

2 cups (470 ml) almond milk
1 tsp ground turmeric
1 tsp ground cinnamon
Pinch of ground ginger
1 tbsp (15 ml) maple syrup
Splash of vanilla extract (optional, but I love it)

Simply add all of the ingredients to a small saucepan and warm for a few minutes over low heat, until the sides start to simmer. Use a handheld milk frother to froth the golden milk for about 30 seconds. Remove it from the heat, pour the milk into a mug and enjoy this delicious drink!

Summer PINEAPPLE-GINGER JUICE

+SF +GF +QP

Think of this pineapple-ginger juice as the perfect Goldilocks drink—it's not too green and not too sweet but finds just the right balance between heat from the ginger and lightness from the pineapple. Juice novice or not, this is a beautiful drink to enjoy when a taste for a classic green juice arises. —MR

SERVES 3 TO 4

2 medium cucumbers
½ pineapple, peeled and cored
5 celery stalks
½" to 1" (1.3- to 2.5-cm) piece fresh ginger

Simply add all of the ingredients to your juicer and juice slowly. Store the juice in an airtight container and keep in the fridge for up to 3 days. Also, if you like your juice on the sweeter side, just add more pineapple; and if you like it spicier, add more ginger.

*SEE PHOTO INSERT

Refreshing
WATERMELON DRINK

+SF +GF +QP

There are a million and one recipes for watermelon juice on the Internet, but this is the one I turn to time and time again. It only asks of a few humble ingredients—watermelon, cucumber, mint and fennel—and from there you have a refreshing midday drink or the perfect accompaniment to a Sunday brunch. —MR

SERVES 2

½ small watermelon, rind and seeds removed

1 small cucumber, peeled

1 handful fresh mint

¼ fennel head, cored

Place all of the ingredients into a juicer and juice slowly until all the liquid is pulled through. Add the juice to a pitcher with ice and enjoy! Store the juice in an airtight container and keep it in the fridge for up to 3 days.

Warming APPLE
CIDER AND
PERSIMMON JUICE

+SF +GF +QP

The combination of freshly juiced apples and persimmons, warmed with cinnamon sticks, is breathtakingly delicious. It is a simple drink that has brought on many compliments over the years. Enjoy it during the winter months as a wonderful nightcap to end a long day. —MR

SERVES 1

2 apples, chopped

3 persimmons, chopped

1 cinnamon stick or ½ tsp ground cinnamon

Add the apples and persimmons to your juicer and juice slowly. Then, with the cinnamon stick, warm the freshly pressed juice in a saucepan over low heat for a few minutes. Discard the cinnamon stick, pour into a mug and enjoy!

Coffee SHAKE

+SF +GF +QP

Anyone living in the US in the last decade knows the deliciousness of a Frappuccino. Well this coffee shake is a welcomed alternative—and one that can be made in the comfort of your own kitchen, sans the long coffee line. Just a few staple ingredients blend together and out comes a healthier, and very frothy, new age Frappuccino. Bottoms up! —MR

SERVES 1

1 small ripe banana, frozen or unfrozen

⅔ cup (160 ml) almond milk

1 shot of espresso

2 pitted Medjool dates

1 tsp ground cinnamon

Handful of ice cubes

Blend all of the ingredients in a blender until combined and frothy. Pour it into a glass and enjoy!

Vegan HOT WHITE CHOCOLATE

+GFO +SF

This drink is thick, rich and pretty much unforgettable. It does have simple flavors, so the vanilla is important to zing it up. You can add coffee to make a vegan white mocha. This is the opposite of fat free, but if you are on a fat-free eating plan, try adding extra vanilla and maybe some cacao or cocoa powder to make an oil-free hot chocolate. —KH

SERVES 2

MILK

2 cups (470 ml) water

2 tbsp (14 g) raw cashews

2 tbsp (21 g) raw almonds

1 tbsp (5 g) oats (steel-cut, Scottish or rolled will work)

4 pitted dates (optional)

THE REST

4 tbsp (57 g) cacao butter, chopped

½ vanilla bean, split, or 1 tsp vanilla extract

Sweetener of choice, to taste if not using dates

FOR THE MILK

Combine the water, cashews, almonds, oats and dates in a large bowl and soak for at least 8 hours. I like to toss everything in my Vitamix before I leave the house for work.

After it's soaked, blend well. Put a fine-mesh strainer over a saucepan and strain the milk mixture to remove the sediment. You should have pulp left over. You can use this in a baked good or your morning bowl of oatmeal.

(continued)

FOR THE REST

Add the milk, cacao butter and vanilla (either scraped or extract) to a saucepan. If you didn't use dates earlier, now is the time to add your sweetener. I used 2 tablespoons (24 g) of sugar in one batch, dates in another and monk fruit in the last. They all worked well, and you will be able to add more later if it's not sweet enough for you.

Heat over medium heat, whisking all the time. First the cocoa butter will melt and cover the top of the mixture like an oil slick. Don't panic—this is supposed to happen.

Keep whisking. The oil will incorporate and the oats in the milk will begin to thicken ever so slightly.

It's a fine line between making it just right and cooking it too long until it looks like gravy. It is tasty gravy, so if that happens just whisk in some nondairy milk you have hiding in the fridge.

I like to take it off the heat as soon as the oil droplets disappear—this takes between 5 to 10 minutes—but still whisk a minute more. If it doesn't thicken up enough, put it back on the heat for another minute or so.

I've made this thick like a liquid truffle or French hot chocolate and I like it that way. It will continue to thicken, so err on the side of thinness.

Vegan WARM CINNAMON HORCHATA WITH WHOLE GRAINS AND ALMONDS

+GF +SF

Wow your friends with this unusual hot drink. You make a plant-based milk with oats, rice and almonds, and flavor it with cinnamon and vanilla. Then heat it up and warm yourself up! —KH

SERVES 4

3 cups (710 ml) water

¼ cup (42 g) raw almonds

¼ cup (53 g) long-grain brown rice

¼ cup (20 g) steel-cut oats (or an additional ¼ cup [53 g] brown rice)

3 cinnamon sticks

Sweetener of choice, to taste (I used ¼ cup [48 g] raw sugar)

1 tsp vanilla extract

Pinch of salt (optional)

Add the water, almonds, brown rice, oats and cinnamon sticks to your blender and soak overnight or for up to 12 hours.

Transfer the cinnamon sticks to a medium saucepan, and then blend the rest of the ingredients until smooth. Strain through a fine-mesh strainer or nut-milk bag into the saucepan.

Add the sweetener, vanilla and a pinch of salt, if using. Then heat over low heat, stirring constantly to keep the oat milk from forming small lumps, until it's just hot.

If there are some lumps, just pop it back into the blender and it will come out creamy.

My Basic GREEN JUICE RECIPE FOR A HAPPY BOD

Okay, here's the thing: smoothies are great, salads are great, rice bowls are great, but juice gives me something I can't get anywhere else. When I get into the rhythm of having a glass of green juice or carrot juice or beet juice a few times a week, I notice I feel cleaner and clearer. I feel lighter. My skin glows a little bit. I think I might have more energy, but that could be wishful thinking. —EvE

SERVES 1 OR 2

4 celery stalks

2 cups (60 g) chopped fresh parsley or cilantro

3 cups (120 g) spinach

¼ cup (41 g) pineapple chunks

1" (2.5-cm) chunk ginger

1 lemon

Wash everything; then juice it all and drink. WOO! If it's too tart, add an apple or more pineapple, but eventually I guarantee you're gonna grow to love the flavor without any extra sweetness.

Glorious DAIRY-FREE CHOCOLATE MILK

When I was a kid, I loved chocolate milk. At my elementary school there would be special lunches once a month when we'd get to choose between pizza and sushi for food, and plain milk or chocolate milk for a drink. I always chose chocolate milk. It came in a plastic cup with a sealed tin foil lid. So you'd break the tin foil with a straw and then drink up the sweet nectar inside, and all was well because life was simple back then. Now life is overwhelmingly complicated but chocolate milk is still amazing. I just make it myself and don't use dairy (leave cow milk to the baby cows). Everything I remember about chocolate milk, everything I loved about it—it's all in this vegan recipe. —EvE

SERVES 4

4 cups (945 ml) water

1 heaping tbsp (8 g) cacao powder

1 heaping tbsp (7 g) carob powder

¼ tsp ground cinnamon

¼ tsp ground ginger

½ tsp vanilla powder

¼ cup (45 g) pitted dates

¼ cup (42 g) raw almonds (preferably soaked in water overnight, then rinsed)

½ tsp reishi mushroom powder (optional)

Pinch of Himalayan salt

Blend everything together until very smooth. Adjust it according to taste: add more dates, nuts, cacao, etc. Strain through a cheesecloth or nut milk bag. Then I like to let mine sit in the fridge to chill (in a covered jar).

Note: If you don't have a cheesecloth or a nut milk bag, use 3 tablespoons (34 g) almond butter (or any nut or seed butter) instead of almonds. You can use vanilla extract instead of vanilla powder. You can use any sweetener instead of dates (e.g., maple syrup, agave nectar or coconut sugar).

Juicy Elixir WITH PINEAPPLE, MINT, RASPBERRY AND BEET

I am always trying to figure out ways to incorporate apple cider vinegar into my diet because it's so damn good for me. It makes my skin gloooow and improves my digestion. This drink is SO TASTY and refreshing and good for ya. It's perfect for summer and gives you energy and mouth-watering vibes. I savor every sip. —EvE

SERVES 2 OR 3

¼ cup (45 g) frozen raspberries

¼ cup (10 g) packed fresh mint

3 cups (710 ml) chilled coconut water

2 tbsp (30 ml) apple cider vinegar

2 tbsp (30 ml) maple syrup

¼ cup (60 ml) beet juice

¼ cup (60 ml) pineapple juice

Ice cubes

Gently smash the raspberries in the bottom of one or two glasses. Throw in some mint, too. Pour in the coconut water, apple cider vinegar and maple syrup. Pour in the beet and pineapple juices until you like the color of the drink (or just pour it all in, it's gonna taste great no matter the color). Stick a straw in, add some ice cubes and enjoy!

Vanilla COCONUT SHAKE WITH PEANUT BUTTER CARAMEL

WHAT IS EVEN HAPPENING!? This recipe is too good to be true, yet here it is. In all its luscious glory: the vegan shake. —EvE

SERVES 1 OR 2

SHAKE

1 (13½-oz [400-ml]) can full-fat coconut milk, preferably left in the fridge overnight

3 frozen bananas, chopped

½ tsp chopped vanilla bean or vanilla extract

1 tbsp (15 ml) maple syrup

PEANUT BUTTER CARAMEL

2 tbsp (23 g) peanut butter

1 tbsp (15 ml) maple syrup

2 tbsp (30 ml) nondairy milk

FOR THE SHAKE

Scoop out the thick, creamy white coconut cream that should have set in the top of the can: this is what you want to use (if this doesn't happen, don't worry about it—your shake just won't be as thick . . . but if you want it to be thick, add another banana). Blend all of the ingredients together until smooth, thick and sexy.

FOR THE PEANUT BUTTER CARAMEL

Whisk all of the caramel ingredients together until smooth.

Pour some caramel into a glass or two, then scoop in some shake, and keep doing this until you've used everything up.

Coco VANILLA SHAKE WITH CHOCOLATE SAUCE

There are not actually words in the English dictionary that I know of to accurately describe how delicious this shake is. And I only speak English, so I can't look to other languages here. Basically, you need it in your life immediately. Whether you're vegan or not, it's gonna blow your mind and take your taste buds to new heights. Please make it ASAP. —EvE

SERVES 1 OR 2

SHAKE
4 frozen bananas
½ (13½-oz [400-ml]) can full-fat coconut milk
2 tbsp (30 ml) maple syrup
½ tsp vanilla powder

CHOCOLATE SAUCE
1 tbsp (15 ml) melted coconut oil
2 tbsp (14 g) cacao powder
3 tbsp (45 ml) full-fat coconut milk
2 tbsp (30 ml) maple syrup

FOR THE SHAKE

Blend all the ingredients together until smooth, creamy and DELICIOUS. If it's too thin, add more banana; if it's too thick, add more coconut milk.

FOR THE CHOCOLATE SAUCE

Whisk together the ingredients until you have chocolate. If it's too thick, add more coconut milk or maple syrup; if it's too thin, add more coconut oil.

Scoop the shake into glasses along with drizzles of the chocolate sauce, until your glasses are full. Decorate with sliced banana and cacao nibs if you like. ENJOY!

Vegan HOT CHOCOLATE AND MARSHMALLOWS

The marshmallows in this recipe really make it special, so do yourself a favor and buy some. YOU DESERVE IT. They are sugary clouds of joy and they make me feel like everything is okay, especially on those cold winter days. —EvE

SERVES 1 OR 2

2 cups (470 ml) plain unsweetened almond milk
3 tbsp (21 g) cocoa powder
½ tsp vanilla extract
Pinch of sea salt
¼ cup (43 g) pitted Medjool dates
¼ tsp ground ginger
¼ tsp ground cinnamon

TOPPINGS (OPTIONAL, BUT VERY RECOMMENDED)
Vegan marshmallows
Chocolate shavings

Blend all the hot chocolate ingredients until smooth, luscious and sweet. Adjust according to taste and texture preferences. Add to a saucepan and warm over low heat. Pour into mugs. Add marshmallows and chocolate shavings if desired!

eight

SAUCES, DRESSINGS, PASTES & SPICES

I believe that sauce makes the meal. Think of some plain steamed quinoa with veggies on top, and you'll have a nutritious dinner. But drizzle some Miso Mushroom Gravy (page 410), Cashew Queso (page 415) or even some Scallion-Infused Oil (page 409) over the top, and it becomes a main event!

I love to make my own staples, and this chapter shows you how to make your own pizza sauce, enchilada sauce, vegan pestos, blackberry balsamic vinegar and so much more. Every recipe is a delight to the senses, and you'll save money by making it yourself.

Recipes full of cashew magic will delight and amaze your friends. No one will miss the dairy with Six-Ingredient Vegan Cheddar Cheese Sauce (page 418), Cashew Crema (page 411), Cashew Coconut Base (page 412), Vegan Ricotta (page 417) or Cashew Cheese (page 420).

Making spice blends from scratch means you can temper them to your own tastes. It is also much cheaper when you source spices at the Indian or other international market. You have to try the Tsire Spice on page 417 and the Tunisian Baharat on page 416. They are my new favorite blends.

Zippy CHICKPEA SAUCE

+GF +SF

Can anyone dislike chickpeas, really? It seems there is nothing they (or their brine, aka aquafaba) cannot do. I whipped them up as a sassy protein- and fiber-rich sauce here, most often to be served with my favorite noodles ever, aka Noochy Fried Noodles (page 82). —CS

SERVES 4

1½ tsp (8 ml) olive oil

3 bell peppers, cored and chopped (any color)

2 medium shallots, chopped

3 large cloves garlic, minced

2½ cups (410 g) cooked chickpeas

1 tbsp (5 g) dried porcini powder

1 tbsp (3 g) Italian seasoning

1–2 tsp (1–2 g) Aleppo-style pepper, or use half the amount of crushed pepper flakes

1 tsp coarse kosher salt

2 tbsp (30 ml) sherry vinegar or apple cider vinegar

1 (28-oz [794-g]) can fire-roasted diced or crushed tomatoes

Place the oil, peppers, shallots and garlic in a large pot. Cook over medium-high heat until the peppers just start becoming tender, about 6 minutes depending on freshness. Stir occasionally. Add the chickpeas, porcini powder, Italian seasoning, pepper flakes and salt. Cook for another 2 minutes, stirring well. Add the vinegar to deglaze. Add the tomatoes, stirring to combine. Lower the heat to medium and cover partially with a lid. Simmer for 20 minutes, until the sauce has thickened and the peppers are completely tender but not mushy.

SCALLION-INFUSED Oil

+GF +SF

Quick and easy to make, this infused oil will add an extra layer of flavored awesomeness to pan-fried vegetables, tofu, noodles, rice . . . and the list goes on. Be sure to reserve the scallion greens for your Saucy and Sassy Cashew Noodles (page 140)! —CS

MAKES ¼ CUP (60 ML) OIL

¼ cup (60 ml) peanut oil or grapeseed oil

3 scallions, trimmed: use white parts only, cut with a mandoline slicer

1 tsp gochugaru (Korean red chile powder) or red pepper flakes, quantity to taste, plus extra to serve

1 large clove garlic, thinly sliced

1 small knob fresh ginger, peeled and minced (knob should be the same size as clove of garlic)

1 tbsp (15 ml) toasted sesame oil

Place the peanut oil, cut scallions and gochugaru in a small saucepan. Heat over low heat, and cook until the scallions soften and turn light golden brown, about 10 minutes. Be sure to stir occasionally and adjust the heat as needed. Do not burn the scallions. Add the garlic and ginger, cooking another 2 minutes. Remove from the heat and add the sesame oil.

This oil can be used to stir-fry vegetables or added to other noodle or rice recipes. Store the infused oil in an airtight container in the refrigerator for up to 1 week.

Miso MUSHROOM GRAVY

This gravy is so smooth, creamy and rich in umami flavors! Serve with vegan holiday roasts, mashed potatoes, eggless noodles or anywhere gravy is a great fit. —CS

MAKES 2 CUPS (490 G)

¾ oz (20 g) dried shiitake mushrooms

Filtered water

2 tbsp (36 g) white miso

3 tbsp (45 ml) unsweetened plain plant-based creamer or milk

1½ tsp (8 ml) Ponzu Sauce (page 414)

2 tbsp (30 ml) grapeseed oil or peanut oil

1 shallot, minced

1 clove garlic, minced

2 tbsp (15 g) all-purpose flour

Coarse kosher salt, to taste

In a large glass measuring cup, add the mushrooms and cover them with enough filtered water to reach the 2-cup (470-ml) mark. Let them stand for at least 30 minutes, or until softened.

Once ready, line a fine-mesh sieve with a paper towel. Remove the mushrooms, squeezing the excess liquid back into the measuring cup, and place in another fine-mesh sieve. Filter the soaking water through the sieve lined with paper towel in order to remove potential grit. Reserve the soaking water. Gently rinse the mushrooms to remove grit, squeezing out the excess liquid. Discard the stems and mince the mushrooms. Place the miso in a small bowl. Take 3 tablespoons (45 ml) out of the reserved soaking water and whisk to combine. Set it aside.

Stir the creamer and ponzu sauce into the remaining reserved soaking water, and whisk to combine. Set this aside.

In the meantime, heat the oil over medium heat in a medium saucepan. Add the minced mushrooms, shallot and garlic. Cook until fragrant and lightly browned, about 4 minutes. Stir occasionally and adjust the heat as needed. Add the flour and cook until toasted, about 2 minutes, stirring frequently and adjusting the heat as needed. Using a whisk, slowly add the reserved soaking water (not the one containing miso!). Be sure not to add the liquid too quickly in order to prevent lumps. Continue cooking over medium heat and whisking occasionally until the gravy thickens, about 8 minutes. Add the miso-containing reserved liquid and whisk to combine. Continue cooking for about 2 minutes, or until the gravy is thickened to taste. Serve immediately or refrigerate in an airtight container for up to 4 days. Reheat slowly.

Amba (SPICY, SAVORY AND SWEET DRIED MANGO SPREAD)

+GF +SF

I absolutely love to serve this spread as one would any chutney—for example, served with Indian-Spiced Chana Dal Shepherd Pie (page 86) or in Amba Breakfast Wraps (page 384), but it's also great as an addition to roasted nut butter on toast instead of jam. —CS

MAKES 1¼ CUPS (400 G)

½ tsp toasted sesame oil

1 small shallot, minced

6 oz (170 g) soft, sweetened dried mango, minced

1 tsp coarse kosher salt

1 tsp ground sumac

1 tsp Aleppo-style pepper flakes

½ tsp ground coriander

½ tsp smoked paprika

2 tbsp (30 ml) apple cider vinegar

½ cup (120 ml) freshly squeezed orange juice (about 1 orange)

¼ cup (80 g) agave nectar

Place the oil and shallot in a medium pot. Cook over medium heat until the shallots are translucent and fragrant, about 4 minutes. Stir occasionally and adjust the heat as needed. Add the mango, salt, sumac, pepper flakes, coriander and paprika, and cook for another minute, making sure to stir frequently. This will toast the spices and develop their flavor. Add the vinegar (careful not to inhale the fumes; it's unpleasant but not dangerous), and stir well. Add the orange juice and agave. Bring to a low boil, reduce the heat and cook for 6 minutes.

Transfer to a heat-safe jar that can accommodate the size of an immersion blender, or transfer to a small blender or food processor. Pulse to blend it into a thick spread: it's lovely to leave small pieces of mango, so don't make it smooth. Let it cool completely and store in the refrigerator for up to 1 week.

Savory DRIED APRICOT PASTE

This super simple chutney-like paste is good to enjoy alongside Indian or Asian dishes that require a slightly sweet and savory sidekick. I love it paired with Indian-Spiced Chana Dal Shepherd Pie (page 86). —CS

MAKES 1 CUP (310 G)

6 oz (170 g) dried Turkish apricots, minced

3 tbsp (60 g) agave nectar

3 tbsp (45 ml) brown rice vinegar

3 tbsp (45 ml) lemon juice

2 tbsp (30 ml) shoyu

1 tsp gochugaru (Korean red chile powder)

Place all the ingredients in a small saucepan. Bring to a low boil, lower the heat to a simmer and cook, stirring occasionally, until thickened and paste-like.

The apricots should be completely soft and fall apart, 10 to 15 minutes. Let cool, transfer to an airtight container and store in the refrigerator for up to 2 weeks.

Cashew CREMA

+SF

This cashew crema takes a little bit of time to prepare, but the hands-on work is pretty minimal. Lusciously velvety, rich and creamy, it's a must on tacos, chili or anywhere regular crema is usually called for. Although crema is supposed to be a bit thinner than sour cream, this one is a bit thick upon coming out of the refrigerator and will thin out after a little time at room temperature. Feel free to serve it whichever way you prefer, thick or thin. —CS

MAKES 2 CUPS (480 G)

1 cup (120 g) raw cashew pieces, soaked in water overnight in the refrigerator

1 cup (235 ml) canned full-fat coconut milk

4 tsp (20 ml) distilled vinegar, divided

2 tsp (10 ml) lime juice

¾ tsp coarse kosher salt, plus extra to taste

¼ cup (60 ml) unsweetened plain cashew milk

Drain and briefly rinse the soaked cashews. Place the cashews, coconut milk, 2 teaspoons (10 ml) of the vinegar, lime juice and salt in a blender. Blend until thoroughly smooth, stopping the blender to scrape the sides as needed. Cover and store in the refrigerator for 24 hours.

(continued)

In a small bowl, combine the cashew milk with the remaining 2 teaspoons (10 ml) vinegar, and let it stand for 2 minutes to curdle and create buttermilk. Add an extra pinch of salt to the refrigerated mixture, and whisk the "buttermilk" into it until thoroughly smooth. Let it stand at room temperature for 2 hours. Whisk and store in the refrigerator for another 12 hours. This will help further develop the flavors.

Store leftovers in an airtight container in the refrigerator for up to 3 days.

Cashew COCONUT BASE

+GF +SF

Unsweetened, plain vegan yogurt isn't always easy to locate where I live. Fear not if you have the same issue: this cashew-based coconut mixture is a great stand-in for it in dressings and sauces, such as Creamy Harissa Sauce (page 412). —CS

MAKES 1½ CUPS (360 G)

1 cup (120 g) raw cashew pieces, soaked in water overnight in the refrigerator

1 cup (235 ml) canned full-fat coconut milk

Juice of ½ medium lemon (about 2 tbsp [30 ml])

¾ tsp coarse kosher salt

Drain and gently rinse the cashews. Combine all the ingredients in a high-speed blender or food processor. Blend or process until perfectly smooth, stopping to scrape the sides with a rubber spatula. Transfer to a medium bowl, cover tightly and let stand at room temperature for 4 hours. Transfer to the refrigerator for up to 1 week.

Creamy HARISSA SAUCE

+GFO +SF

A must-have for dipping with your Harissa Croquettes (page 175)! It would also be perfect to serve with crudités such as carrot sticks, celery, broccoli florets and more. —CS

MAKES ½ CUP (130 G) SAUCE

½ cup (120 g) Cashew Coconut Base (page 412)

1 tbsp (15 ml) grapeseed oil or olive oil

1 tsp harissa paste (use gluten-free)

1 tsp lemon juice

½ tsp coarse kosher salt

Place all the ingredients in a small bowl, stirring well to combine. Let it stand for 30 minutes before serving. Cover leftovers tightly and refrigerate for up to 3 days.

GOCHUJANG **Paste**

Better than sriracha sauce? You be the judge. I put this not-entirely-authentic Korean paste-slash-sauce on pretty much everything. The most authentic version takes more time to prepare and to ferment, while this one yields great flavor as well and is a cinch to make. —CS

MAKES 1 CUP, PLUS 1 TBSP (340 G) PASTE

½ cup (144 g) white miso

½ cup (160 g) agave nectar

⅔ cup (160 ml) water

5 tbsp (40 g) gochugaru (Korean red chile powder)

1 tsp onion powder

½ tsp garlic powder

¼ tsp coarse kosher salt

1 tsp brown rice vinegar

1 tsp toasted sesame oil

In a medium saucepan, whisk to combine the miso, agave, water, gochugaru, onion powder and garlic powder. Heat the mixture over medium heat until it starts to bubble slightly. Lower the heat to a simmer and cook until it reaches the consistency of tomato paste, about 15 to 20 minutes. Be sure to stir frequently throughout the cooking process! Turn off the heat.

Whisk occasionally until the paste reaches room temperature, about 15 minutes to 1 hour depending on the season. Whisk the salt, vinegar and oil into the paste. Transfer to an airtight container and store in the refrigerator until ready to use, up to 3 weeks.

ENCHILADA **Sauce**

Put this gorgeous red sauce to work in Enchilada Roja (page 91), or really any enchilada recipe of your choice.

To make a slightly cheesy sauce, feel free to add up to ½ cup (125 g) of Cashew Queso (page 415) to the sauce during the last two minutes of cooking. —CS

MAKES 1⅔ CUPS (395 ML)

1½ tbsp (23 ml) grapeseed oil or olive oil

1 shallot, minced

1½ tbsp (12 g) light spelt flour

3 tbsp (23 g) mild to moderate chile powder mix

2 tsp (6 g) Emergency Broth Powder (page 223)

1 tsp dried porcini powder

½ tsp ground cumin

½ tsp onion powder

½ tsp smoked sea salt, to taste

2 cups (470 ml) water

1 tbsp (15 g) adobo sauce from a can of chipotle peppers

½ tsp agave nectar

Heat the oil in a medium saucepan over medium-high heat. Add the shallot and sauté until translucent, about 4 minutes, stirring occasionally and adjusting the heat as needed. Sprinkle the flour onto the shallot and cook until lightly browned, stirring constantly, about 3 minutes. Add the chile powder, broth powder, porcini powder, cumin, onion powder and salt. Toast for 1 minute. Slowly add the water, whisking constantly. Add the adobo sauce and nectar, and bring to a low boil. Cook until slightly thickened, about 10 minutes. Whisk frequently. Use immediately or store in an airtight container in the refrigerator for up to 4 days.

SAUCES, DRESSINGS, PASTES & SPICES

PONZU **Sauce**

This is a great sauce for dipping into with your Tare Tofu (page 183), spring rolls and pretty much anything Asian-inspired! I find that it is a wee bit reminiscent of yeast extract spread (such as Marmite) when using yuzu kosho, a Japanese fermented paste made of yuzu fruit, chiles and salt. Yuzu kosho can be a little hard to locate, so feel free to use lime juice if unavailable. It won't be quite the same, but it will be great too. —CS

MAKES 1 CUP (235 ML)

½ cup (120 ml) tamari

3 tbsp (45 ml) mirin

3" x 2" (8 x 5-cm) piece of kombu, briefly rinsed

2 large dried shiitake mushrooms

¼ cup (60 ml) freshly squeezed orange juice (about ½ large juicy orange)

1 tsp (5 g) red yuzu kosho or 2 tbsp (30 ml) lime juice

Place the tamari, mirin, kombu and shiitake in a small saucepan. Bring to a quick boil, turn off the heat and soak for 20 minutes. Drain in a fine-mesh sieve lined with cheesecloth to catch any impurities. Briefly rinse the shiitake, if desired, and reserve for other recipes. Discard the kombu.

Add the orange juice and yuzu (or lime juice), and whisk to combine. Store it in an airtight container in the refrigerator for at least 24 hours before using to allow the flavors to meld. The sauce will keep for about a month if stored properly.

Yogurt AVOCADO DRESSING

+SFO +QP

This rather thick and tangy dressing-slash-spread can be added to taco recipes such as Citrus Chile Jackfruit Tacos (page 177) or served with tortilla chips and salsa for dipping. If you'd like to keep it slightly chunky to use as a spread, go for it: just blend all the ingredients except the pitted avocados, and then add the chopped avocados and pulse until the desired consistency is obtained. —CS

MAKES 1 CUP (240 G)

½ cup (120 g) plain unsweetened coconut yogurt (use soy-free)

2 tiny avocados, pitted, peeled and coarsely chopped

1 handful fresh cilantro

2 cloves garlic, peeled

1 tbsp (15 ml) lemon juice (add a few grates of the zest before cutting the lemon)

½ tsp coarse kosher salt

Place all the ingredients in a small blender. Process until perfectly smooth, stopping to scrape the sides as needed. Use preferably on the same day of preparation. Store covered in the refrigerator until ready to serve.

Peanut Butter MISO SAUCE

Serve this creamy sauce with Tsire Tempeh Bites (page 176) or with roasted vegetables of choice. It can do no wrong. —CS

MAKES 1 CUP (235 ML)

⅓ cup (60 g) natural peanut butter or other nut butter

1 tbsp (18 g) white miso

Juice of 1 lemon (2–4 tbsp [30–60 ml] to taste)

2 tsp (10 ml) toasted sesame oil

2 tsp (13 g) agave nectar

1 clove garlic, minced

1 tbsp (15 ml) brown rice vinegar or seasoned rice vinegar

⅓ cup (80 ml) water, more if needed

Place all of the ingredients in a blender. Blend until perfectly smooth. Add more water if needed in order to get a thick yet pourable dressing. If not using within the next hour, store it in the refrigerator in an airtight container until ready to use. The sauce might thicken a bit once refrigerated, so think ahead and bring it back to room temperature before use.

Cashew QUESO

+GF +SF +QP

I eat this cashew- and sweet potato–based queso by the spoonful straight out of the blender jar, right upon making it. It's that incredibly good. Use it as you would any queso, and for a spiced version, see the alternative in Mexican Baked Mac and Queso (page 90). Or you know, grab a spoon and just dive in. —CS

MAKES 3 CUPS (750 G)

1 cup (120 g) raw cashew pieces, soaked in water overnight in the refrigerator, drained and rinsed

1 cup (235 ml) water

¾ cup (180 ml) canned coconut milk

1 tbsp (15 ml) lemon juice

1 medium sweet potato (about 9½ oz [270 g]), baked, peeled and chopped

¼ cup (20 g) nutritional yeast

1 tsp coarse kosher salt or ½ tsp smoked sea salt

1 tsp Emergency Broth Powder (page 223)

1 tsp (5 g) maca powder

Place all the ingredients in a blender. Blend until smooth and thoroughly combined. Use as you would any queso.

Blackberry
BALSAMIC REDUCTION

+SF +GF

This one has a lot of zing and depth of flavor, with a side of blackberry-sweetness! Add this vinegar reduction to Rosemary Balsamic Roasted Potatoes (page 180), to sandwiches (spread some on one side, add mayo to the other, and vegan lunch meat in the middle), to summer-time strawberries—or anywhere balsamic reduction is called for. —CS

MAKES ½ CUP (120 ML)

1 cup (235 ml) balsamic vinegar

⅓ cup (106 g) seedless blackberry jelly or jam

⅛ tsp coarse kosher salt

Place all of the ingredients in a small saucepan. Whisk to combine. Bring to a low boil, and then lower the heat to a simmer. You want to see the mixture bubble slightly, but it shouldn't boil noisily. Cook down to about half the original amount, until thickened to a molasses-like consistency. This will take between 30 and 45 minutes. Be sure to stir frequently and adjust the heat as needed. Don't go wandering off too far either; it's best to keep an eye on things. Once cooled, transfer to an airtight container and store in the refrigerator for up to 2 weeks.

Tunisian BAHARAT

With the tongue-tingling power of peppercorn, the slight sweetness and warmth of cinnamon and the flowery flavor of rose leaves, this spice mix is a great addition to Fudgy Tahini Cookies (page 297), but also to your morning oatmeal, Middle Eastern dishes and more. —CS

MAKES 1½ TSP (6 G)

1 tsp whole rainbow peppercorns

1 tiny cinnamon stick, broken into smaller pieces

1 tsp culinary rose leaves

Place all the ingredients in a spice grinder and grind into a fine powder. Store in an airtight container at room temperature for up to 1 month.

TSIRE **Spice**

I'm always on the hunt for interesting, new-to-me spice mixes. This one doesn't disappoint: tsire is a warm peanut-based North African blend. It's a delight in Tsire Tempeh Bites (page 176) and Tsire-Spiced Hummus (page 179). —CS

MAKES 1 CUP (105 G)

¾ cup (90 g) unsalted roasted peanuts

1–2 tsp (2–4 g) chipotle powder or other chile powder, to taste

½ tsp ground ginger

½ tsp ground cinnamon

½ tsp ground cloves

½ tsp freshly grated nutmeg

¼ tsp fine sea salt

Place all of the ingredients in a food processor. Pulse until the peanuts are ground somewhat finely. Do not overprocess; you don't want the peanuts to turn into butter. Store in an airtight container at room temperature or in the refrigerator for up to 2 weeks.

Vegan RICOTTA

+GF

You don't need to spend a fortune on store-bought ricotta when you can make this easy recipe. Our ricotta tastes and feels like the real deal, and it also cooks like it. We put it in lasagna, on pasta dishes, in sandwiches and on top of salads. There's no wrong way to eat this. —LM + AM

MAKES ABOUT 3 CUPS (374 G)

16 oz (454 g) firm tofu

⅓ cup (83 g) vegan Greek-style yogurt (do not use coconut yogurt)

¼ tsp fine sea salt, or to taste

1 tbsp (15 ml) lemon juice

¼ tsp garlic powder (optional)

½ tsp extra-virgin olive oil

Put the tofu between several sheets of paper towel and put something heavy on top of it to press out the excess water. Press for about 20 minutes.

Put the tofu and the rest of the ingredients in a blender or food processor and blend until just combined. It should look curdled.

If you want a drier ricotta, line a colander with cheesecloth, pour the ricotta on top of the cheesecloth and let the excess water drain until it reaches the desired consistency.

Store in an airtight container in the refrigerator for up to 5 days.

Six-Ingredient Vegan
CHEDDAR CHEESE SAUCE

+GF

When you're craving a creamy cheese sauce, this is your go-to recipe. We worked on this recipe over and over, until we felt it was as close to the real thing as we could possibly get. Put it in a baked potato with cooked broccoli and coconut bacon bits, or pour it over macaroni to make mac and cheese. The possibilities are endless. —LM + AM

MAKES ABOUT 2 CUPS (465 G)

1 cup (112 g) raw cashews, covered in boiling water and soaked for 1–4 hours depending on the type of blender you have (If you have a high-powered blender such as a Blendtec or Vitamix, 1 hour is sufficient. Otherwise, soak for 3 to 4 hours until they look bloated and are slightly soft to the touch.)

1 sweet potato

1 tsp dry mustard

2 tsp (10 ml) apple cider vinegar

2 tbsp (10 g) nutritional yeast (see Note)

1½ tsp (7 g) fine sea salt (you can adjust the amount of salt according to your dietary needs, but it will alter the taste)

½ tsp onion powder

½–¾ cup (120–180 ml) water (adjust the water to make it as thick or as thin as desired)

Soak the cashews, then drain and rinse well.

Preheat the oven to 375°F (190°C).

Peel the sweet potato and wrap it in foil. Bake for an hour or until fork tender. When it's cool enough to handle, measure out 1 cup (210 g) of the potato. You can also peel it and cut it into cubes and microwave it, about 15 minutes.

Put the cashews, potato, mustard, vinegar, nutritional yeast, salt, onion powder and water in the blender, and blend on high speed until the sauce is thick and creamy. You shouldn't be able to see or feel any pieces of the cashews.

Note: We use Bragg's nutritional yeast. The flavor of nutritional yeast varies from brand to brand, which can alter the taste of the cheese sauce.

*SEE PHOTO INSERT

Four-Ingredient
HOMEMADE PIZZA SAUCE

+GF +SF

There's no need to buy jarred sauce that's full of ingredients you don't want to eat when you can make this fresh and easy sauce. We call it a four-ingredient sauce because you only need an onion, garlic, tomatoes and Italian seasoning to make it. We added a bit of olive oil, sugar and salt and pepper, but since they're kitchen staples, we really don't count them in the ingredients list. Make this the next time you bake your own pizza. You'll love it! —LM + AM

MAKES ABOUT 3 CUPS (746 G)

1 tsp extra-virgin olive oil or 2 tbsp (30 ml) water for oil-free

1 small red onion, finely chopped

2 cloves garlic, minced

24 oz (680 g) strained tomatoes (I use Pomi brand)

1 tbsp (2 g) dried Italian seasoning

½ tsp sugar

Fine sea salt and black pepper, to taste

In a medium saucepan, heat the oil or water over medium heat. Add the onions and stir to distribute evenly in the pan. Cook for about 15 minutes, stirring frequently, until the onions begin to caramelize. Add the garlic and stir. Cook for 2 minutes. Add the strained tomatoes, Italian seasoning, sugar, salt and pepper, and stir to combine. Bring it to a boil. Reduce the heat to a low simmer and cook for 15 minutes. Stir frequently so the sauce doesn't scorch.

Store in an airtight container in the refrigerator for up to a week or freeze for up to a month.

Classic Vegan
WALNUT PESTO

+GF +SF

In the Meyer household, pesto is a staple food. It probably ranks like this: almond milk, hot sauce, pesto. . . with the rest of the kitchen following way behind. However, after batches and batches of pesto, you learn to mix it up sometimes. Enter our classic vegan walnut pesto. Substituting pine nuts with walnuts adds some extra nutrients to this delicious dip. —LM + AM

MAKES 1 CUP (248 G)

⅓ cup (39 g) raw walnuts, toasted
2 cloves garlic, peeled
3 cups (180 g) chopped basil
1 tbsp (5 g) nutritional yeast
1 tsp fine sea salt
Black pepper, to taste
4 tbsp (60 ml) olive oil

Preheat the oven to 375°F (190°C).

Place the walnuts on a dry baking sheet and bake for about 4 to 5 minutes, or until they're lightly browned. Shake the baking sheet every minute and keep a close eye to make sure the walnuts do not burn. Remove the walnuts from the oven and allow them to cool for 5 minutes.

Bring a small pot of water to a boil. Take the peeled garlic cloves and place them in the water. Turn off the heat and let the garlic sit in the water for 2 minutes. Transfer the garlic from the water to the food processor with a slotted spoon.

Add the basil, walnuts, nutritional yeast, salt, pepper and olive oil to the food processor and pulse until the mixture is smooth, thick and uniform, about 1 to 2 minutes.

Healthy SINGLE-SERVING OIL-FREE PESTO

+GF +SF

Did we mention we love pesto? Here's our second take on this famous dip/sauce. While typical pesto is filled to the brim with oil, ours has a lighter taste. Take out that oil and insert an avocado. You retain the creamy texture of original pesto, but cut the caloric and fat intake! —LM + AM

MAKES 1 SERVING

¼ avocado
1 clove garlic, peeled
1 tbsp (5 g) nutritional yeast
1 cup (60 g) chopped basil
3 tbsp (45 ml) water
Salt and pepper, to taste

Put the avocado, garlic, nutritional yeast and basil in a food processor or blender and blend. Add the water 1 tablespoon (15 ml) at a time until you get the desired consistency. Add salt and pepper if you like.

SAUCES, DRESSINGS, PASTES & SPICES

Roasted TOMATO SPAGHETTI SAUCE

+GF +SF

Envision yourself sitting at a candlelit Italian restaurant. You're sipping on a huge glass of chianti with the whirl of the other patrons behind you. The scent of sweet tomatoes, olive oil and perfectly prepared pasta fill the air. But wait! You're at home, sitting on your couch, watching Netflix. How did this happen? The decadence of our roasted tomato spaghetti sauce will easily transport you to your favorite Italian restaurant in seconds. Plus, what's better than eating a restaurant-quality meal in your pajamas? —LM + AM

MAKES 4 CUPS (940 ML)

12 Roma tomatoes

1 tbsp (15 ml) and 1 tsp extra-virgin olive oil, divided

1 medium onion

3 cloves garlic

½ cup (118 ml) red wine

2 tsp (2 g) dried Italian seasoning

Salt and pepper, to taste

Preheat the oven to 400°F (204°C).

Prep the tomatoes by removing their cores, cutting them in half and laying them flat-side down on a rimmed baking sheet. Drizzle the tomatoes with 1 tablespoon (15 ml) of the olive oil and rub the olive oil evenly over the tomatoes. Place the tomatoes in the oven and roast them for about 25 to 30 minutes, or until the skins are blistered and black.

While the tomatoes are roasting, dice the onion and mince the garlic. Heat the remaining 1 teaspoon olive oil in a large saucepan over medium heat. Cook the onion until it becomes soft and translucent, about 15 minutes. At this point, add the garlic

and sauté for 2 minutes. Turn the heat to the lowest setting and stir frequently.

Remove the tomatoes from the oven and allow them to cool until you can safely remove the blackened skins. Remove the skins and put the tomatoes and the juice that remains on the baking sheet into the saucepan with the onions and garlic. Add the red wine and seasonings. Allow the sauce to simmer for 30 minutes over low heat, stirring occasionally. If you like a smoother sauce, blend with an immersion blender or a countertop blender.

CASHEW **Cheese**

+QP +SF +GF

Cashew cheese is a brilliant replacement for dairy cheese when living a vegan lifestyle. When soaked, cashews soften and when blended with a slew of spices, they carefully craft a cheese-like alternative. It is creamy, it is decadent, and with the use of nutritional yeast and apple cider vinegar, it actually mimics the tang of a traditional dairy cheese. Enjoy this vegan spread. —MR

SERVES 6 TO 8

1 cup (110 g) raw and unsalted cashews

⅓ cup (80 ml) water

2 tbsp (30 ml) apple cider vinegar or lemon juice

2 cloves garlic

2 tbsp (10 g) nutritional yeast

Salt, to taste

Soak the cashews in a bowl of water for at least 4 hours—this helps to soften the nut—drain and rinse the cashews. Pour them into a high-speed blender or food processor along with the rest of the ingredients. Blend until it turns into a creamy, silky "cheese." Store in an airtight container in the fridge.

CASHEW-COCONUT
Butter

+QP +SF +GF

Addictive. This is the only word that aptly describes the taste of this creamy, sweet, delectable nut butter—a nut butter that puts all the rest to shame.

Cashew butter is rich on its own, but when coconut is added to the lineup, tropical notes perfume the entire spread, satisfying a desire you didn't even know existed. Enjoy it spread onto toast, stuffed into dates, on top of fruit, in smoothies or all on its own. —MR

SERVES 6 TO 8

2 cups (220 g) unsalted cashews, roasted

2 tsp (7 g) pure vanilla powder

½ cup (38 g) unsweetened coconut shreds or desiccated coconut

Pinch of sea salt

Simply place the roasted nuts, vanilla and coconut into a food processor with a sprinkle of sea salt and blend until a thick and creamy nut butter forms. This should take about 15 to 20 minutes.

If you have raw nuts, you can toast them in the oven at 350°F (177°C) for 10 minutes. Set them aside until they are cool and ready for grinding.

Store the nut butter in an airtight container in the refrigerator and enjoy!

Peanut Butter
CARAMEL SAUCE

+SF +GFO

Not a fan of peanut butter? Roasted almond or cashew butters are also great in this caramel sauce. If the nut butter you use isn't salted, add a pinch of coarse kosher salt at the same time that you add the Sucanat to make sure it gets dissolved. —CS

MAKES 1 HEAPING CUP (305 G)

¾ cup (180 ml) full-fat canned coconut milk

¾ cup (144 g) Sucanat

3 tbsp (34 g) natural creamy peanut butter

1 tsp pure vanilla extract (use gluten-free)

In a saucepan, bring the coconut milk and Sucanat to a boil over medium-high heat, stirring to dissolve the sugar crystals. Continue to cook over medium heat, using a heat-resistant pastry brush to brush sugar crystals from the sides of the saucepan. Adjust the temperature as needed to keep the mixture from boiling over. Cook until the bubbling mixture reaches 230°F (110°C) on a candy thermometer, about 8 minutes.

Turn off the heat, and whisk the peanut butter and vanilla into the mixture. Let it cool completely, then refrigerate in a well-sealed mason jar for at least 1 hour or overnight, and keep for up to 2 weeks. The caramel will thicken as it cools.

Silky CARAMEL SAUCE

+GF +SF +QP

Five minutes, three ingredients and one pot is all that's needed to create a luscious caramel sauce. Serve it over ice cream, freshly baked pies, slathered onto toast or completely on its own—spoonful to mouth. —MR

SERVES 3 TO 4

¼ cup (55 g) coconut oil

¼ cup (60 ml) maple syrup

2 tbsp (23 g) unsalted cashew butter or almond butter

Pinch of sea salt

In a small saucepan, warm the coconut oil until melted. Remove it from the heat and add the remaining ingredients. Mix until a thick, luscious caramel sauce has formed. Store in the fridge for up to a week. Enjoy over ice cream, pies and dessert . . . or by itself!

Salted CARAMEL SAUCE

+SF +GFO

Give me all the caramel or toffee desserts. I mean it, I'll take caramel over chocolate stuff just about any time even though I'm a big chocolate fan. This sauce is the most important addition to the Salted Caramel Panna Cotta (page 298). It's a cinch to prepare and a delight to dive into, spoon first. —CS

MAKES ABOUT 1 CUP (265 G) SAUCE

1 cup (192 g) Sucanat

1 cup (235 ml) full-fat canned coconut milk

½ tsp Maldon sea salt

2 tsp (10 ml) pure vanilla extract (use gluten-free)

In a saucepan, bring the sugar, milk and salt to a boil over medium-high heat, stirring to dissolve the sugar crystals. Continue to cook over medium heat, using a heat-resistant pastry brush to wipe sugar crystals from the sides of the saucepan. Do not stir at this point to prevent crystallization, but gently swirl the saucepan instead. Cook until the bubbling mixture reaches 230°F (110°C) on a candy thermometer, about 10 minutes. Adjust the heat as needed and do not overcook or burn the caramel.

Turn off the heat and whisk the vanilla into the mixture. Let it cool completely, and then refrigerate in a well-sealed mason jar for at least 1 hour or overnight: the caramel will thicken as it cools. Will keep well for about 2 weeks.

Whipped
COCONUT CREAM

+SF +GFO

This fluffy, light dessert topping is going to become a staple in your refrigerator, if it isn't already. Add a dollop to Miso Sweet Potato Galette (page 299), Kesar Mango Cake (page 301), Peanut Butter French Toast (page 382) and anything that strikes your fancy. —CS

SERVES 8

1 (14-oz [414-ml]) can full-fat coconut milk or coconut cream

2 tbsp (16 g) organic powdered sugar

2 pinches of fresh or dried orange zest (optional)

1 tsp pure vanilla extract (use gluten-free)

Refrigerate the can of coconut milk for 24 hours before whipping the cream. Place the sugar and the optional zest and extract in a medium bowl. Scoop out the solid white cream from the coconut milk can (reserve the liquid to cook rice or curries), and place in a bowl. Using a handheld mixer with a whisk attachment, whip the cream for 5 minutes, or until stiff enough to stick to the whisk. Refrigerate until ready to use, or up to 3 days.

Raspberry CHIA JAM

+QP +GF

Gone are the days when canning was the sole expression of a handcrafted jam. This is a modern-day jam recipe that comes together in minutes. Just three ingredients are your key to homemade jam euphoria: Fruit, chia seeds and maple create a delightful jam every single time. Chia seeds create the gelatinous feel of jam. This ingredient is crucial to having thick jam. —MR

SERVES 4 TO 6

1 cup (150 g) fresh strawberries, or frozen and thawed

2 cups (300 g) fresh raspberries, or frozen and thawed

3 tbsp (45 ml) maple syrup

2½ tbsp (25 g) chia seeds

Start by cutting the fresh strawberries in half (green tops removed). Add the strawberries, raspberries and maple syrup to a small saucepan and simmer for 10 minutes over medium-low heat (keep the lid ajar). Mash the fruit as it simmers, but leave a few pieces whole for texture in the jam. Allow the mixture to thicken and reduce down. After 10 minutes, add the chia seeds, mix well and simmer for another 5 to 10 minutes.

Once the jam has thickened to your liking, remove and seal in an airtight container. Enjoy this jam on a piece of toast with almond butter for a very delicious and quick snack!

SAUCES, DRESSINGS, PASTES & SPICES

ABOUT
THE AUTHORS

EMILY VON EUW is the creator of the award-winning recipe blog, This Rawsome Vegan Life, as well as the bestselling author of three cookbooks: *Rawsome Vegan Baking; 100 Best Juices, Smoothies and Healthy Snacks*; and *The Rawsome Vegan Cookbook*. Em's passion in life comes from friendships, food, forests, mountains, meadows and music. They have presented at veg expos and festivals across Canada and the US and live in the lower mainland of British Columbia, Canada, on the traditional and unceded territories of the Musqueam, Squamish and Tsleil-Waututh First Nations. Emily is a nonbinary, genderqueer person and uses they/them pronouns.

KATHY HESTER is passionate about making healthy eating easy and delicious. You can find her recipes on her sites HealthySlowCooking.com and PlantBasedInstantPot.com, and on her private Facebook group, Vegan Recipes: Cooking with Kathy Hester. Her recipes are full of flavor and the meat eaters in your family will love them too. Her dishes have been featured in the *Washington Post, The Oregonian* and Yoga Journal Online, just to name a few. She is also the author of the bestselling cookbooks *The Vegan Slow Cooker* and *The Ultimate Vegan Cookbook for Your Instant Pot.*

LINDA AND ALEX MEYER are the mother-daughter duo and authors of *Great Vegan BBQ Without a Grill*, and the founders of the vegan blog Veganosity. They started their vegan journey five years ago after Alex chose to go vegan because of the health, environmental and ethical impacts of eating animal products. Linda was so inspired by Alex's new life-style that she soon chose to live a vegan lifestyle as well. Soon after, they created Veganosity so they could share their recipes with their friends and family. Alex has a master's in counseling psychology with a concentration in health psychology. They are both marathon runners. Veganosity has been featured in the *Washington Post, Vegan Food & Living* magazine, CountryLiving.com, Shape.com, Fitness Magazine.com, PETA.org and more.

MARIE REGINATO is a food photographer, writer and recipe developer, and has been cooking and blogging about her most popular recipes on her blog and Instagram account 8th and Lake, named one of The Best Healthy Food Accounts by MindBodyGreen. She is the author of *Alternative Vegan* and lives in Los Angeles, California.

CELINE STEEN is the creator of the blog Have Cake Will Travel, the author of *Bold Flavored Vegan Cooking* and the coauthor of several vegan cookbooks, including *The Complete Guide to Vegan Food Substitutions*, *The Complete Guide to Even More Vegan Food Substitutions* and *Vegan Sandwiches Save the Day!* She lives in Bakersfield, California, with her husband Chaz and cat Willow.

AMBER ST. PETER is the founder of the popular vegan blog Good Saint and the author of *Homestyle Vegan*. Her recipes have been featured on PETA, AOL, BuzzFeed, the Huffington Post and the *New York Times*. She lives in Fullerton, California, with her husband Alex and her dog Maddie.

INDEX

air fryer
    Air-Fried Green Tomato Po' Boys, 119
    Air-Fried Tempeh Skewers, 116
    Air-Fried Tofu Rancheros, 112-113
    Air-Fried Vegan Beignets, 108
    Air-Fried Vegetable Pakora with
        Tamarind Dipping Sauce, 117
    Air Fryer Cheater Samosas Using
        Spring Roll Wrappers, 118
Aloo Gobi, as Spicy Aloo Gobi, 122
appetizers
    Asian Tofu Vegetable Steamed
        Dumplings, 163
    Baked Jalapeño Poppers with
        Cilantro Lime Mayo, 147-148
    Cannellini Bean Dip, 167
    Easy Vegan Black-Eyed Pea Pecan
        Pâté, 158
    Four Layer Dip, 152
    Peanut Sriracha Glazed Tofu Satay,
        167
    Polenta Squares with Sun-Dried
        Tomato Pesto and Roasted
        Eggplant, 171
    Potato Stuffing Balls with a
        Cranberry Center, 43
    Roasted Corn Pique Salsa, 184
    Savory Pumpkin Pasties, 164
    Savory Stuffed Mushrooms, 150-151
    Spicy Chickpea Stuffers, 182
    Tsire Tempeh Bites, 176
    Vegan Potstickers, 170
    Vegan Pretzel Bites, 169

baharat, as Tunisian Baharat, 416
banh mi, as Tofu Banh Mi with
        Lemongrass, 52
bars
    7-Layer Bars, 284
    Almond Butter and Chia Jam Bars
        with Chocolate, 317
    Apricot and Coconut Bars, 153
    Avocado Mint Cream Bars with
        Chocolate, Two Ways, 334
    Blueberry Hazelnut Oat Bars,
        324-325
    Choc-Oat-Nut Granola Balls, 199
    Chocolate-Chip Cookie Protein Bars,
        364-365
    Chocolate-Gingersnap Fall Bars, 358
    Chocolate Mint Slice, 327
    Coconut Cookie Butter Bars, 255
    Coconut Twix Bars, 321-322
    Extra Chewy Chocolate Steelcut Oat
        Bars, 200-201

Fudgy Chocolate Peanut Butter Slice,
        329
    Pecan Pie Bars, 263-264
    Pecan Praline Bars with Salted
        Chocolate, 326-327
    Purple Sweet Potato Pie Bars, 265
    Raspberry Lemon Cheesecake Bars,
        294-295
    Strawberry-Rose Morning Bars,
        365-366
    Superfood Fudgy Mint Slice, 328
BBQ
    BBQ Jackfruit Stuffed Whole Wheat
        Potato Rolls, 161-162
    Blueberry Whiskey BBQ Salad
        with Tempeh and Roasted
        Potatoes, 240
    Slow Cooker Shredded Veggies and
        Jackfruit BBQ, 116
beignets, as Air-Fried Vegan Beignets,
        108
biscotti, as Cranberry Pistachio
        Biscotti, 288
biscuits
    Autumn Cinnamon Apple Biscuits,
        367-368
    Drop Biscuit Root Vegetable Pot Pie,
        78-79
blintzes, as Vegan Chocolate Blintzes
        Stuffed with Vanilla Nut
        Cream, 280-281
bourguignon, as Vegan Mushroom
        Bourguignon, 66-67
bowls
    Autumn Quinoa Bowls with Roasted
        Veggies, 49
    Cherry Berry Quinoa Breakfast Bowl,
        376
    Chocolate Pudding Bowls with
        Coconut Cream and Cherries,
        303
    Huge Rainbow Salad Bowl, 234
    Japanese Tempeh and Sushi Rice
        Bowls, 95
    Morning Greens Bowl, 366
    Peanut Butter and Berry Acai Bowl,
        349
    Spicy Noodle Bowl with Beet, Carrot,
        Zucchini and Sweet Tamarind
        Sauce, 143
    Sushi Bowl with Ginger Soy Dressing,
        62
    Udon Noodle Bowl with Miso Ginger
        Sauce, Edamame and Green
        Onions, 105

Vegan Poke Bowls, 76-77
    Warming Winter Grain Bowl,
        235-236
breads
    Autumn Cinnamon Apple Biscuits,
        367-368
    BBQ Jackfruit Stuffed Whole Wheat
        Potato Rolls, 161-162
    Crunchy Toast with Peanut Butter
        and Quick Berry Jam,
        389-390
    Gluten-Free Vegan Teff Oat Rolls,
        159-160
    Healthier Whole Wheat Strawberry
        Muffins, 371-372
    Honee Dough Twists, 172-173
    Lemon Chia Seed Loaf with Lemon
        Glaze, 347-348
    Mini Chocolate Chunk Scones,
        348-349
    Peanut Butter Chocolate Chip
        Banana Bread, 350
    Rosemary Focaccia Bread, 173
    Spiced Pumpkin Bread with Maple
        Vanilla Icing, 352
    Summer Rolls with Garden Veggies,
        Basil and Tahini Chili Sauce,
        188
    Vanilla-Glazed Matcha Scones,
        354-355
    Vegan Cornbread, 155
    Vegan Garlic and Cashew Cheese
        Pull-Apart Bread, 172
    Whole Wheat Cinnamon Sugar Pull-
        Apart Loaf, 268-269
    Yeast-Free Garlic Flatbread, 174
brownies
    Decadent and Dangerous Peanut
        Butter Blondie Brownies,
        295-296
    Fudgy Spelt Brownies, 302
    Gooey Brownies with Almond Butter
        Frosting, 329-330
    Raw Dark-Chocolate Brownies,
        273-274
    Salted Sweet Potato Brownies, 269
    Spicy Black Bean Brownies, 290
bruschetta
    Edamame Bruschetta, 157
    Green Bruschetta, 151
burgers
    Baked Black Bean Burgers, 124
    Edamame Rice Burgers, 54-55
    Marinated Portobello Cashew
        Cheeseburgers with Herbs
        and Tomatoes, 98-99

Mediterranean Hummus Burgers, 137

burritos
"California Burrito" Tacos, 27
Crispy Corn and Bean Burritos, 82–83
Easy Chickpeasy Breakfast Burritos, 346
Quinoa and Greens Burrito with a Cheesy Spread, 128–129
Umami Fusion Burritos, 85–86

cakes
Blueberry Strawberry Banana Ice Cream Cake, 332–333
Carrot Cake with Cashew Cream Cheese Frosting, Pistachios and Walnuts, 333
Chocolate Lava Cake, 291–292
Chocolate Molten Lava Cakes with Goji Berries, 332
Coffee Cream Cake with Choco Crust and Date Syrup, 307–308
Deep-Dish Apple Cinnamon Skillet Cake with Maple Vanilla Glaze, 256–257
Jicama Onion Cakes with Cumin, Coriander, Dill and Lemon, 99
Kesar Mango Cake, 301
Strawberry Cashew Cream Cake with Carob Drizzle, 306
Strawberry Shortcake, 285
Sweet Cherry Coffee Cake, 354
Vegan Baked Orange Carrot Cake Oatmeal, 368
Vegan Blueberry Buckle—No Oil Added!, 283–284
Vegan Pear and Cranberry Instant Pot Cake, 115

candies
Dates Dipped in Chocolate, 276
Easy Raw Snicker Slabs, 270–271
Five-Ingredient Peanut Butter Cups, 277–278
Homemade Galaxy Dark Chocolate with Raspberries, 277
Salted Chocolate Truffles, 322
Sexy Caramel Slice, 326
Vanilla Cashew Butter Cups, 267
Vegan Easter Creme Eggs, 258–259

caramel
Almond Cacao Cookies with Salted Maca Caramel, 316–317
Blueberry Coconut Smoothie with Baobab Caramel, 394
C3 Bonbons (Chocolate, Caramel and Cereal), 300
Caramel Chocolate Ganache Tart with Superfood Drizzle, 309–310
Cinnamon-Apple Galette with Caramel Sauce, 279–280

Coconut Twix Bars, 321–322
Deep-Dish Caramel Apple Pie, 309
Easy Raw Snicker Slabs, 270–271
Fierce Salted Caramel Cheesecake, 312–313
Jewel Fruit Tart with Caramel Almond Filling, 335
Peanut Butter Caramel Sauce, 421
Pumpkin Pie with Coconut Whipped Cream, 336–337
Salted Caramel Panna Cotta, 298–299
Salted Caramel Sauce, 422
Sexy Caramel Slice, 326
Silky Caramel Sauce, 422
Vanilla Coconut Shake with Peanut Butter Caramel, 406
casserole, as Penne Pasta Casserole, 73
chana masala, as Chana Masala: Quick Chickpea Curry with Rice, 124

cheesecake
Chai Cheesecakes with Chocolate Drizzle, 310–311
Fierce Salted Caramel Cheesecake, 312–313
Frozen Hot Chocolate Cheesecake, 293
Lemon Berry Cashew Cheesecake Bites, 285–286
Magical Superfood Cheesecake, 311–312
Mango and Passion Fruit Cheesecake, 278–279
Mini Key Lime Cheesecakes, 262–263
Mini Lemon and Blueberry Jam Cheesecakes, 314
Nut-Free Creamy Coconut Cheesecake, 331
Orange Chocolate Cheesecake, 261–262
Raspberry Lemon Cheesecake Bars, 294–295
Raw Blackberry Cheesecake, 274–275
Strawberry Cheesecake Smoothie, 390

chili
Roasted Sweet Potato Chili, 217
Vegan Instant Pot White Bean Soy Curl Chili, 114–115
clafoutis, as Cranberry Orange Clafoutis, 345
compote, as Old-Fashioned Fluffy Pancakes with Apple Spice Compote, 370

cookies
Almond Cacao Cookies with Salted Maca Caramel, 316–317
Almond Cookies with Spiced Apple Slices, 319
Amber's Famous Peanut Butter Cookies, 270

Banana Bread Cookies with Coconut Cream and Chocolate Sauce, 320
Banana Oatmeal Cookies, 251–252
Chocolate-Chip Cookie Protein Bars, 364–365
Chocolate Chip Skillet Cookie, 286–287
Chocolate Rosemary Cookies, 296–297
Chocolate S'mores Cookies, 254
Coconut Cookie Butter Bars, 255
Coconut Twix Bars, 321–322
Cranberry Pistachio Biscotti, 288
Dark Chocolate Rosemary Cookies, 256
Double Chocolate Peppermint Cookies, 257–258
Fudgy Tahini Cookies, 297–298
Gingersnap Buttercream Cookie Sandwiches, 259–260
Lemon Knot Cookies, 287
Maple Oatmeal Raisin Cookies, 321
Molasses Spice Cookies, 298
No-Bake Almond Butter Cookies, 273
Oreo-ish Tarts: Vanilla Whipped Coco Cream with Chocolate Cookie Crust, 308
Peppermint Oreos Dipped in Dark Chocolate, 318–319
Pumpkin Chocolate Chip Cookies, 264
Quick 'N' Easy Chocolate Macaroons, 322–323
Soft Pumpkin Spice Cookies, 289–290
Two-Bean Chocolate Chunk Cookies, 251
Vanilla Gluten-Free Vegan Pizzelles Made with Teff Flour, 281–282
White Chocolate Macadamia Nut Cookies, 268
crema, as Cashew Crema, 411–412
crepes, as Shiitake Chickpea Crepes, 92–93
crispies, as Dark Chocolate Crispies, 275
croquettes, as Harissa Croquettes, 175–176

crumbles
Nectarine and Pear Crumble, 271–272
Strawberry Rhubarb Crumble, 266
Strawberry Rhubarb Crumble with Almond Granola, 330–331

cupcakes
Carrot Cupcakes with Orange Vanilla Cream Frosting, 252
Double Chocolate Cupcakes with Buttercream Frosting, 305
Lemon Acai Cupcakes, 294

curry
  Chana Masala: Quick Chickpea
    Curry with Rice, 124
  Homemade Thai-Style Green Curry,
    37
  Homemade Yellow Curry Potato
    Soup, 215
  Lemon Curry Hummus, 166
  Pickled Mango Curry Wraps, 90
  Pumpkin Curry with Coconut Brown
    Rice, 36–37
  Thai Red Curry Vegetables with
    Sweet Potato Rice, 160
  Warming Coconut Curry and Lentil
    Soup, 226

dips
  Baked Sun-Dried Falafel with Tzatziki
    Dip, 132
  Cannellini Bean Dip, 167
  Edamame Guacamole, 196
  Four Layer Dip, 152
  Sweet Potato Fries with Lemon
    Cashew Chipotle Dip, 189
  World's Best Guacamole, 194–195
doughnuts
  Apple Cider Doughnuts, 356
  Baked Lemon and Thyme
    Doughnuts, 374
  Baked Pumpkin Cinnamon Sugar
    Doughnuts, 341
  Baked Pumpkin Spice Doughnuts
    with Chocolate Cinnamon
    Icing, 373–374
  Blood Orange Glazed Doughnuts,
    342–343
  Blueberry Breakfast Doughnuts,
    363–364
  Chocolate Coconut Doughnuts, 324
  Choco Nice Cream with Peanut
    Butter Oats, Chocolate
    Chunks and Doughnut Holes,
    389
dumplings
  Asian Tofu Vegetable Steamed
    Dumplings, 163
  Chik'n and Dumplings, 74–75

enchiladas
  Enchilada Roja, 91–92
  Enchilada Sauce, 413
  Texas BBQ Tempeh Enchiladas, 50
  Vegan Black Bean and Mushroom
    Enchiladas, 64–65

fajitas, as Mushroom Fajitas, 134
falafels
  Baked Sun-Dried Falafel with Tzatziki
    Dip, 132
  Sweet Potato and Turmeric Falafels,
    131
farina, as Kesar Mango Farina, 301–302

French toast
  Banana Cinnamon French Toast, 342
  Overnight French Toast, 355
  Peanut Butter French Toast, 382–383
fries
  Loaded Vegan Nacho Fries, 193
  Sweet Potato Fries with Lemon
    Cashew Chipotle Dip, 189
frittatas, as Vegan Veggie and Herb
    Frittata, 377
fudge
  Freezer Fudge Bites, 303
  Three-Ingredient Vegan Fudge, 325

galettes
  Cinnamon-Apple Galette with
    Caramel Sauce, 279–280
  Galette Crust, 97–98
  Miso Sweet Potato Galette, 299–300
  Savory Mushroom Galette, 94
  Sweet Pear Galette, 272
granola
  Cinnamon-Raisin Granola, 360
  Citrus and Tahini Granola, 360–361
  Healthy Homemade Granola,
    346–347
  Matcha Coconut Granola, 382
  Peanut Butter and Berry Acai Bowl,
    349
  Strawberry Rhubarb Crumble with
    Almond Granola, 330–331
guacamole
  Edamame Guacamole, 196
  World's Best Guacamole, 194–195

horchata, as Vegan Warm Cinnamon
    Horchata with Whole Grains
    and Almonds, 404
hot chocolate
  The Best Hot Chocolate, 399
  Frozen Hot Chocolate Cheesecake,
    293
  Peppermint Hot Chocolate, 398–399
  Vegan Hot Chocolate and
    Marshmallows, 407
  Vegan Hot White Chocolate,
    403–404
hummus
  Buffalo Sriracha Hummus, 195
  Caramelized Kimchi Hummus,
    178–179
  Garlicky White Bean Hummus, 195
  Kalamata Hummus, 155
  Lemon Curry Hummus, 166
  Mediterranean Hummus Burgers,
    137
  Paprika Hummus, 197
  Picante Black Bean Hummus, 196
  Tsire-Spiced Hummus, 179

ice cream
  Blueberry Blackberry Sorbet with
    Chia Pudding and Tahini, 315

Choco Nice Cream with Peanut
    Butter Oats, Chocolate
    Chunks and Doughnut Holes,
    389
  Homemade Strawberry Ice Cream,
    260
  Mango Rosemary Sorbet, 261
  Mint Chocolate Chunk Ice Cream,
    316
  Vanilla Cherry Nice Cream, 315
instant pot
  Instant Pot Cranberry Sauce with
    a Touch of Apple Brandy,
    113–114
  Instant Pot Rainbow Panzanella
    Salad, 107
  Instant Pot Vegan Black-Eyed Pea
    Jambalaya, 112
  Rosemary Alfredo Pasta, 47
  Vegan Instant Pot Teff Vegetable
    Soup, 110
  Vegan Instant Pot White Bean Soy
    Curl Chili, 114–115
  Vegan Pear and Cranberry Instant
    Pot Cake, 115
  Vegan Rarebit over Toast, 51

kimchi
  Caramelized Kimchi Hummus,
    178–179
  Caramelized Kimchi Tahini Toast, 187
  Forbidden Broth, 221
  Good Morning Miso Rice, 383
  Kimchi Mac and Sprouts, 80–81
  Kimchi Tofu Scramble, 384–385
  Spicy Kimchi Pizza, 81
  Umami Fusion Burritos, 85–86
  Wakame Ginger Kimchi, 181

lasagna
  Marinated Zucchini and Tomato
    Lasagna with Cashew Herb
    Cheese, 100
  Pumpkin Thyme-Ricotta Lasagna, 77
latkes, as Spiralized Vegan Latkes with
    Red Cabbage and Apple, 39
lemonade
  Cherry Chia Lemonade, 400
  Sparkling Mint Lemonade, 400
loaves
  Lemon Chia Seed Loaf with Lemon
    Glaze, 347–348
  Roasted Pecan Raisin Loaf, 386–387
  Roasted Veggie Lentil Loaf, 63
  Whole Wheat Cinnamon Sugar Pull-
    Apart Loaf, 268–269
lo mein, as Butternut Squash and Kale
    Lo Mein with Crispy Tofu, 42

mac 'n' cheese
  Baked Fresh Herb Vegan Mac 'n'
    Cheese, 72

Creamy Vegan Mac and Cheese with Other Good Stuff, 102
Mexican Baked Mac and Queso, 90–91
Vegan Mac 'n' Cheeze, 136–137
meatballs, as Spaghetti and Black Bean Meatballs, 67–68
meatloaf, as Smoky Southern-Style Meatless Meatloaf, 59
milk
Glorious Dairy-Free Chocolate Milk, 405
Golden Milk, Hot or Iced, 398
Turmeric Milk, 401
muesli, as Simple Overnight Oats/Bircher Muesli, 362
muffins
Blueberry Streusel Muffins, 343
Chunky Monkey Chocolate Banana Muffins, 372–373
Healthier Whole Wheat Strawberry Muffins, 371–372
Turmeric Blueberry Muffins, 380
Vegan Pumpkin Gingerbread with No Added Oil, 283

nachos
Loaded Vegan Nacho Fries, 193
Party-Size Jackfruit Nachos, 192–193
noodles
Chickpea Noodle Soup, 208
Noochy Fried Noodles, 82–83
Saucy and Sassy Cashew Noodles, 140
Spicy Noodle Bowl with Beet, Carrot, Zucchini and Sweet Tamarind Sauce, 143
Super Easy Sesame Cucumber Noodles, 38
Sweet Potato Noodle Salad with Sriracha Lime Peanut Sauce, 248
Udon Noodle Bowl with Miso Ginger Sauce, Edamame and Green Onions, 105
Veggie-Miso and Soba Noodle Soup, 227
Zucchini Noodle Pasta with Veggies, 127–128

oats
Baked Apple and Spice Overnight Oats, 381
Baked Jammy Overnight Oatmeal, 379–380
Baked Peach and Blueberry Oatmeal, 359
Banana Oatmeal Cookies, 251–252
Blueberry Hazelnut Oat Bars, 324–325
Choc-Oat-Nut Granola Balls, 199

Choco Nice Cream with Peanut Butter Oats, Chocolate Chunks and Doughnut Holes, 389
Cinnamon-Raisin Granola, 360
Citrus and Tahini Granola, 360–361
Fabulous Oatmeal with Berries and Seeds, 388–389
Gluten-Free Vegan Teff Oat Rolls, 159–160
Good Oats with Almonds, Coconut Sugar and Vanilla, 388–389
Healthy Homemade Granola, 346–347
Maple Oatmeal Raisin Cookies, 321
Savory Vegan Mediterranean Oatmeal, 376–377
Simple Overnight Oats/Bircher Muesli, 362
Vegan Baked Orange Carrot Cake Oatmeal, 368
oil, as Scallion-Infused Oil, 409

pad thai, as Raw Super Sprouts Pad Thai with Spicy Peanut Sauce, 63
paella, as Veggie Rainbow Paella, 133
pakora, as Air-Fried Vegetable Pakora with Tamarind Dipping Sauce, 117
pancakes
Christmas Morning Cranberry Orange Pancakes, 371
Coconut Bacon and Chocolate Chip Pancakes, 344
Lemon and Poppy Seed Pancakes, 358–359
Old-Fashioned Fluffy Pancakes with Apple Spice Compote, 370
Perfect Pancakes, 350–351
paninis
Lean Green Portobello, Pesto and Artichoke Panini, 136
Spanish Paprika Tofu Sandwiches, 93
Spinach and Sweet Potato Paninis, 55–56
panna cotta, as Salted Caramel Panna Cotta, 298–299
parfaits
Chia Pudding Parfait with a Dreamy Strawberry Smoothie, 357
Stewed Cinnamon Apples in a Yogurt Parfait, 357
pasta
Asian-Style Miso and Eggplant Pasta, 127
Baked Fresh Herb Vegan Mac 'n' Cheese, 72
Beet Ravioli with Almond Thyme Pâté and Basil, 104–105
Butternut Squash and Kale Lo Mein with Crispy Tofu, 42

Creamy Avocado Pesto Pasta, 125
Creamy Fettuccini Alfredo, 74
Creamy Vegan Mac and Cheese with Other Good Stuff, 102
Easy Stuffed Ravioli (Using Wonton Wrappers), 47–48
Full of Veggies Baked Ziti, 48–49
Kimchi Mac and Sprouts, 80–81
Mexican Baked Mac and Queso, 90–91
Minestrone Soup with Arugula, 211–212
One-Pot Pasta Arrabiata, 126
Penne Pasta Casserole, 73
Pumpkin Thyme-Ricotta Lasagna, 77
Rosemary Alfredo Pasta, 47
Spaghetti and Black Bean Meatballs, 67–68
Spring Vegetable Pasta, 34–35
Three-Ingredient Butternut Squash Pasta, 156
Vegan Mac 'n' Cheeze, 136–137
Vegan Mushroom Bourguignon, 66–67
Wild Mushroom and Ricotta Ravioli, 79–80
Zucchini Noodle Pasta with Pesto, 129
Zucchini Noodle Pasta with Veggies, 127–128
Zucchini Spaghetti with Sun-Dried Tomatoes and Basil, 141–142
pesto
Arugula Pesto and Zucchini on Rye Toast, 134–135
Classic Vegan Walnut Pesto, 419
Creamy Avocado Pesto Pasta, 125
Foolproof Creamy Pesto and Roasted Veggies, 34–35
Healthy Single-Serving Oil-Free Pesto, 419
Lean Green Portobello, Pesto and Artichoke Panini
Pesto Socca Pizza, 128
Polenta Squares with Sun-Dried Tomato Pesto and Roasted Eggplant, 171
Vegan Pesto and Portobello Flatbread Pizza, 57–58
Zucchini Noodle Pasta with Pesto, 129
pies
Deep-Dish Caramel Apple Pie, 309
Drop Biscuit Root Vegetable Pot Pie, 78–79
Gluten-Free Vegan Pumpkin Pie with a Teff Flour Pecan Crust, 282–283
Indian-Spiced Chana Dal Shepherd Pie, 86–87
Maple Pecan Pie, 336

Mashed Potato–Crusted Butternut
    Squash, Brussels Sprouts and
    Tofu Pie, 40
Mom's Lemon Meringue Pie,
    292–293
Pecan Pie Bars, 263–264
Pumpkin Pie with Coconut Whipped
    Cream, 336–337
Purple Sweet Potato Pie Bars,
    265–266
Taco Pie, 126
Vegetable Pot Pie, 30
pizza
    Four-Ingredient Homemade Pizza
        Sauce, 418–419
    Garlic and Herb Pizza Dough, 98
    Moroccan Pizza, 96–97
    Pesto Socca Pizza, 128
    Pizza Grilled Cheese, 139
    Spicy Kimchi Pizza, 81
    Tofu Ricotta White Pizza, 46
    Vegan Pesto and Portobello
        Flatbread Pizza, 57–58
    Yogurt Drizzle for Moroccan Pizza,
        97
popcorn, as Homemade "Cheesy"
    Popcorn, 197
popsicles
    Frozen Mango Lassi Pops, 337
    Orange Creamsicles, 339
    Superfood Double Chocolate
        Popsicles, 338–339
    Vegan Lavender London Fog Pops,
        338
porridge
    Colorful Coconut Porridge, 362
    Macadamia Milk Porridge with
        Blueberry-Lemon Jam, 361
pot pies
    Drop Biscuit Root Vegetable Pot Pie,
        78–79
    Vegetable Pot Pie, 30
potstickers, as Vegan Potstickers, 170
pretzels, as Vegan Pretzel Bites, 169
pudding
    Blueberry Blackberry Sorbet with
        Chia Pudding and Tahini, 315
    Chia Pudding Parfait with a Dreamy
        Strawberry Smoothie, 357
    Chocolate (Avocado) Mousse
        Pudding, 278
    Chocolate Pudding Bowls with
        Coconut Cream and Cherries,
        303
    Golden Milk Chia Pudding, 148

queso
    Cashew Queso, 415
    Mexican Baked Mac and Queso,
        90–91

ravioli
    Beet Ravioli with Almond Thyme
        Pâté and Basil, 104–105
    Easy Stuffed Ravioli, 47–48
    Wild Mushroom and Ricotta Ravioli,
        79–80
rolls
    BBQ Jackfruit Stuffed Whole Wheat
        Potato Rolls, 161–162
    Fresh Spring Rolls, 194
    Gluten-Free Vegan Teff Oat Rolls,
        159–160
    Slow Cooker Whole Wheat Spelt
        Potato Rolls, 111
    Vegan Cinnamon Rolls, 375

salads
    Blueberry Whiskey BBQ Salad
        with Tempeh and Roasted
        Potatoes, 240–241
    Bowl o' Salad Goodness, 249
    Chickpea Salad Sandwiches, 140–141
    Chik'n Caesar Salad Wraps, 138
    Chik'n Salad, 241
    Chile-Infused Chickpea Salad,
        233–234
    Crunchy Brussels Sprouts Slaw with
        Asian Pear, 122–123
    Easy Meatless Monday Taco Salad,
        70–71
    Farro Salad with Basil and Tomatoes,
        239
    Fresh Orange and Fennel Salad, 235
    Golden Beet Salad with Balsamic and
        Cashew Ricotta, 229
    Grilled Fig and Peach Salad, 238
    Herbed Lemon Tahini Potato Salad,
        230
    Huge Rainbow Salad Bowl, 234
    Instant Pot Rainbow Panzanella
        Salad, 107
    Jackfruit Tuna-Less Salad, 246
    Mediterranean Salad Wraps with
        Tahini Dressing, 246–247
    Niçoise Salad, 237–238
    Perfect Summer Salad, 236
    Pickled Cucumber Salad with Peas
        and Fresh Dill, 230–231
    Protein Superfood Bean Salad, 242
    Simple Grilled Zucchini Salad with
        Walnuts, 239
    Simple Tabbouleh, 121
    Simple Winter Salad, 237
    Smoky Potato Salad, 233
    Southwestern Roasted Corn and
        Black Bean Salad, 247–248
    Spicy Peanut Couscous Salad, 244
    Sweet Potato Noodle Salad with
        Sriracha Lime Peanut Sauce,
        248
    Tangy Purple Cabbage Slaw with
        Dijon and Horseradish, 231

Vegan BLT Salad with Smoky Spicy
    Mayo, 245
Vegan Caesar Salad with Homemade
    Dill Croutons, 232–233
Warm Acorn Squash, Lentil and
    Quinoa Salad with Sage
    Dressing, 243
Warming Winter Grain Bowl,
    235–236
Winter Citrus and Arugula Salad
    with Cranberry Orange
    Dressing, 244–245
salsa
    Beer-Battered "Fish" Tacos with
        Mango Salsa, 71
    Mint and Cilantro Salsa, 33
    Pan Con Salsa Y Aguacate, 386
    Roasted Corn Pique Salsa, 184
    Sweet Potato Tacos with Mint-
        Cilantro Salsa, 33
    Tacos with Tomato Corn Salsa and
        Spicy Nut Meat, 100–101
samosas, as Air Fryer Cheater Samosas
    Using Spring Roll Wrappers,
    118
sandwiches
    Air-Fried Green Tomato Po' Boys, 119
    Baked Black Bean Burgers, 124
    BBQ Pulled Jackfruit Sandwich with
        Slaw and Caramelized Onions,
        26
    Chickpea Salad Sandwiches, 140–141
    Edamame Rice Burgers, 54–55
    Gingersnap Buttercream Cookie
        Sandwiches 259–260
    Gochujang BBQ Sauce Sandwiches,
        84
    Japanese-Inspired Sandwiches, 89
    Lean Green Portobello, Pesto and
        Artichoke Panini, 136
    Marinated Portobello Cashew
        Cheeseburgers with Herbs
        and Tomatoes, 98–99
    Mediterranean Hummus Burgers,
        137
    Pizza Grilled Cheese, 139
    Sloppy Giuseppe, 84–85
    Spanish Paprika Tofu Sandwiches, 93
    Spinach and Sweet Potato Paninis,
        55–56
    Tempeh Reuben, 130
    Vegan Croque Monsieur, 56
    Vegan Sloppy Joe, 53
sauces
    Almond-Coconut Dipping Sauce, 194
    Basil and Tomato Chili Sauce, 142
    Caramel Sauce, 279–280
    Chipotle Almond Sauce, 101
    Chipotle Peanut Sauce, 142–143
    Creamy Harissa Sauce, 412
    Enchilada Sauce, 413
    Homemade Teriyaki Sauce, 48